TRANSPORTATION

TRANSPORTATION

John J. Coyle   Edward J. Bardi   Joseph L. Cavinato

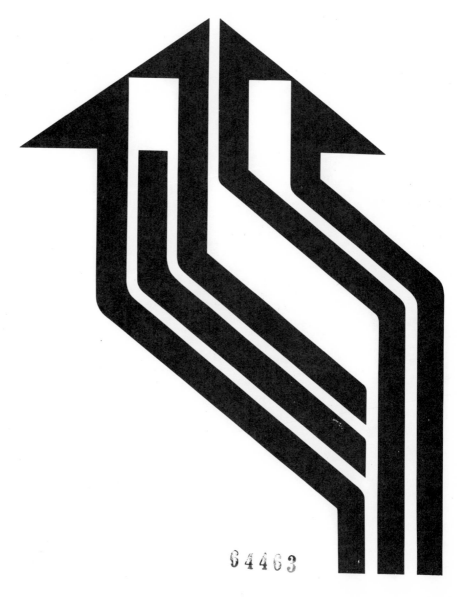

64463

WEST PUBLISHING COMPANY

St. Paul   New York   Los Angeles   San Francisco

Copy Editor: Sheryl Kyweriga
Cover: William A. DiMeo, art director/designer
Composition: Graph-Tronics

Copyright © 1982 by WEST PUBLISHING CO.
· 50 West Kellogg Boulevard
P.O. Box 3526
St. Paul, Minnesota 55165

Library of Congress Cataloging in Publication Data
Coyle, John Joseph, 1935—
    Transportation.
    Includes index.
    1. Transportation.   I. Bardi, Edward J.,
1943—   II. Cavinato, Joseph L.   III. Title.
HE151.C88   380.5   81-19875
ISBN 0-314-63158-5   AACR2

1st Reprint—1983

Dedicated to
Barbara
Carol
Mary

Contents

Contents

**CASE
Intercity Rate
Conference   278**

**14
Traffic
Management
280**

**CASE
Hi-Kite
Products   292**

Part VI — MANAGERIAL ISSUES: SUPPLIERS AND USERS 387

PREFACE

The transportation system in the United States will probably undergo as much change during the 1980s and 1990s as it did during the last two decades of the 19th century and the two decades following the close of World War II. The impetus for this change is related to a number of economic and noneconomic variables.

Many people would probably argue that the forces of deregulation will be responsible for bringing about the dramatic changes suggested above. In fact, one can find ample evidence in various periodicals and elsewhere of the dramatic changes and adjustment problems that carriers have experienced during the relatively short period of time since deregulation was initiated. Deregulation, however, is not the only factor causing changes in transportation.

The increasing cost of energy is also a major factor helping to reshape the transportation system and spur technological changes along with faster adaptation to new technology. For many years, the low cost of energy and the protective regulatory environment administered by the Interstate Commerce Commission covered up for some managerial and other types of inefficiencies in our transportation system. The combination of deregulation and higher cost of fuel have forced some carriers out of business and others to change significantly their methods of operations and marketing.

To mention only deregulation and higher fuel costs, however, would still not be the full explanation of all the changes that we have seen and will see during the 1980s and 1990s. Another major factor is and has been a concern with the environment. We have many new controls to provide better protection, which have impacted on transportation in a variety of ways. Other factors, such as safety concerns, high capital costs, inflation, low productivity, and lower economic growth will also cause change and help shape the transportation system during the last two decades of the 20th century.

But even all of the above factors do not tell the whole story and fully explain the changes. The last factor is the developing sophistication of the shippers who no longer look at transportation as an isolated purchase. Instead, they view transportation purchases in terms of their impact upon other cost areas, such as inventory, warehousing, and packaging. These more sophisticated shippers will also help bring about changes in transportation.

In light of all that is happening and will happen, we felt a need to write this basic transportation text to help bridge the gap for students of transportation between our current situation and what is coming in the future. *Transportation* does present topics and concepts traditionally covered in basic transport texts such as regulation. However, we have minimized the historical coverage of both the regulation and the development of the transportation system.

This text adds some new topics not usually found in basic transportation texts, and many of these topics fall under the area of management. In addition, such topics as urban transportation (freight and passenger), international transportation, and transportation equipment, receive attention. Because of all the changes suggested above, the current student of transportation should be given a broader exposure to transportation than typically given in the more traditional transportation text, which emphasize regulation, public policy, and transportation history.

We are grateful for the guidance and intellectual stimulation provided by our reviewers. Their suggestions after reading the first draft led to substantive improvements in the final copy of the text. We sincerely appreciate the efforts of the following individuals: E. Garland Keesling, Memphis State University; Kevin Horn, University of North Florida; Richard Poist, University of Maryland; Edwin P. Patton, University of Tennessee at Knoxville; and David Vellenga, Iowa State University.

The authors are indebted to a number of individuals for their help with the text. Special mention should be made of Dennis Gawlik and Harry Lengsfield for their contributions. In addition the authors would like to express appreciation to Kevin Boberg, Gary Kogon, Linda Nigh, Marva Hillard, Fred Babin, Lykes Steamship Co., Bob Berardis, Sea-Land Co., Lloyd Good, Canada Steamship Lines, John Kreitner, General Electric Co., Joe Parry, Marsh Engineering, Ltd., Ken Patrick, General Electric Co., Jim Wallingford, Valley Transfer Co., Martin Garelick, Amtrak, Kenneth Kirkpatrick, and Mike McInerney, Bowater Sales Co.

TRANSPORTATION

Part I

The Role and Importance of Transportation

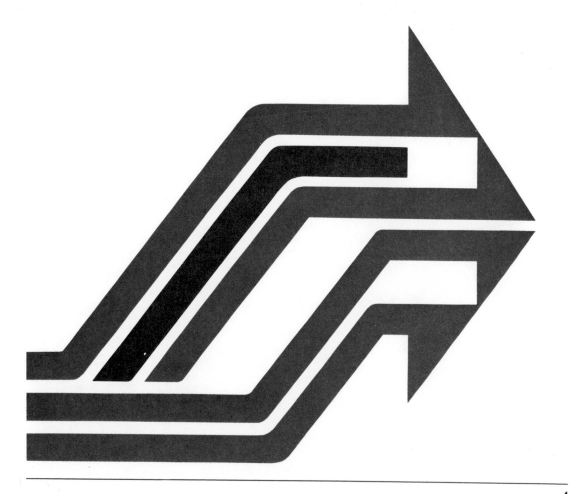

1   Transportation and the Economy

After reading this chapter you should:

1   Appreciate the historical significance of transportation.
2   Understand the economic role of transportation.
3   Be able to discuss the environmental significance of transportation.
4   Understand transportation's importance to politics.

Transportation is one of the tools required by civilized man to bring order out of chaos. It reaches into every phase and facet of our existence. Viewed from every standpoint, economic, political and military, it is unquestionably the most important industry in the world. You can no more operate a grocery store or a brewery than you can win a war without transportation. The more complex life becomes, the more indispensable are the things that make up our transportation systems.[1]

■ subtle nature

Transportation systems are so well developed that most citizens rarely stop to think about their benefits. Americans, though, use transportation every day in one form or another. It provides the thoroughfare for the nation's products, it provides a means for traveling to and from work, and it supports our communication networks. Seldom do individuals stop and wonder how restricted their life-styles would be if the U.S. Post Office lost its right to use any of the common modes of transportation.

■ chapter overview

In order to introduce the reader to the effects of a well-designed transportation system, this chapter will investigate the system's historical, economic, environmental, social, and political roles.

Historical Significance

The importance of transportation becomes more apparent when one develops an understanding of its history-making role. The growth of civilizations are directly associated with the development of transportation systems. The strength of ancient Egypt demonstrated the way in which one form of transportation, water, would become the foundation for a great society. The Nile River held Egypt together. It provided a means to transport Egyptian goods, a way to communicate, and a way in which Egyptian soldiers could move to defend the country. The

■ Nile River

Nile River, like all transportation systems, also affected the society's political and cultural development.

Transportation systems are capable of bringing people together. The

■ unification

centralization of ideas which accompanies the use and development of a system causes societies to develop common traits. Political opinions, cultural ideals, and educational methods are unified through the sharing of both good and bad experiences while traveling or living within the bounds of particular transportation networks.

■ separation

Yet, methods of transportation have also worked to break societies apart when those outside the common systems are alienated from them. For example, America's secession from Great Britain can be partly attributed to the localized systems developing in the thirteen colonies. Transportation to and from Great Britain was slow and inefficient, and Americans found that they could economically lead more efficient lives trading among themselves without having to pay dues to the government of King George III. As the colonies grew into a separate economic nation, political and cultural attitudes that were unique to America took hold.

■ growth examples

The United States continued to grow in tandem with its transportation network. Few families thought to expand west without first knowing that explorers had blazed trails or found rivers suitable for travel. The Erie Canal, steamboats, early turnpikes, and the rail system developed to enhance the economic and social needs of the growing nation. See Table 1.1 for an overview of transport developments in the United States.

■ present role

Today, our transportation system enhances our life-styles and protects us from outsiders. The strong U.S. transportation networks play a vital role in our national defense. The ability to transport troops acts as both a weapon and a deterrent in this age of energy shortages and global conflicts. The recent incidences in the region of the Persian Gulf place even greater emphasis on the importance of logistics in protecting our distant vital interests.

Table 1.1 U.S. Transport Developments

Year	Development	Year	Development
1774	Lancaster Turnpike — first toll road — Pennsylvania	1887	Federal regulation of transportation begins
1804	Fulton's steamboat — Hudson River — New York	1903	First successful air- plan flight — Wright Brothers
1825	Erie Canal — first canal — New York State	1904	Panama Canal opens
1830	B & O Railroad — Maryland	1916	Rail track mileage reaches peak
1838	Steamship service — Atlantic Ocean	1919	Transcontinental airmail service by U.S. Post Office begins
1865	First successful oil pipeline — Pennsylvania	1925	Kelly Act — airmail contract to private companies
1866	Bicycles are introduced — United States	1927	Lindbergh solo flight — New York to Paris
1869	Completion of transcontinental rail link	1956	Congress passes bill inaugurating Interstate System of Highways
1887	First daily rail service coast to coast	1961	Manned space flights begin

Economic Significance

■ example

Transportation systems have great economic significance. Their efficient operation is highly valued. A simple model will serve to illustrate this point. Consider a certain commodity which is desired in one location, provided it is offered below a certain price. In Figure 1.1, this commodity is produced at point A and costs OC at the point of production. The community desiring the commodity, located at point B, is the distance AB from A. The maximum price that people will pay for the commodity is shown on the vertical axis as OE, at community B.

If the original, inefficient transport system is utilized, it will cost a certain amount, CH, to ship the commodity from A to B. The CD portion of the cost line is known as the fixed cost, whereas the DH portion of the line is the cost per mile or slope. With this inefficient system, the total cost at B is OH, a price greater than the maximum cost limit in the community B or OE.

Now assume the transport system is improved. The cost per mile or slope is reduced and the transportation variable cost line becomes DJ. The cost at the community now becomes OJ, well below the maximum cost of OE. The market for the commodity would be expanded to community B, while production continues at A.

■ place utility

The reduction in transportation costs between points A and B gives the commodity "place utility." In the less efficient system, the goods would have no value because they would not be sold at the market. The more efficient method of transportation creates utility; the goods now have value at point B.

Figure 1.1 Landed Cost with Old and New Transport Systems

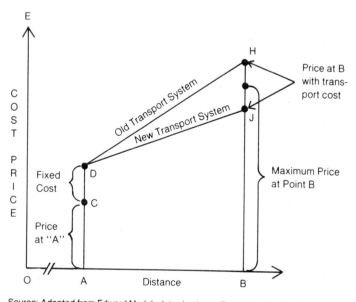

Source: Adapted from Edward Morlok, *Introduction to Transportation, Engineering and Planning* (New York: McGraw-Hill, 1978) p. 33.

■ time utility

The concept of "time utility" is closely aligned to that of place utility. The demand for a particular commodity may only exist during certain periods of time. If a product is at a market in a time when there is no demand for it, then it possesses no value. The demand for Halloween costumes only exists during specific times of the year. After Halloween passes, these goods have little value to the holder. Efficient transportation creates time utility by ensuring that products are at the proper locations when needed. For example, raw materials for production, fruits, and Christmas toys all need to arrive at certain locations during specific times or their value will be limited.

In addition, transportation gives goods utility through assurance that the goods will arrive without damage. The form of the product may be altered, however, to assure safe transportation. Mechanical products, glassware, and food all need special protection if they are to have any value at the time of arrival.

Transportation adds more utility to the economic value of goods. Efficient highway systems and modern modes of transportation mean geographic specialization, large scale production, increased competition, and increased land values. Geographic specialization entails the production of goods in the most efficient area. It is assumed that each nation, state, or city produces products and services that it is best suited for in terms of capital, labor, and raw materials. The concept of geographic specialization assumes that any one area can't produce all needed goods, hence, transportation is needed to send goods which may be most efficiently produced at A to point B in return for different goods efficiently produced at point B. The concept is closely aligned to the principle of comparative advantage. This principle assumes that an area will specialize in the production of goods for which it has the greatest advantage, or the least comparative disadvantage. Gain from specialization and trade will be mutually advantageous when the cost ratios of producing two commodities are different in different areas. Hence, Pennsylvania can concentrate on the production of steel, California on citrus fruits, and the Greek Islands on olives.

■ geographic
specialization

■ large–scale
production

Geographic specialization is complemented by large-scale production, but without the use of effective and efficient transportation networks, the advantages of scale economies, production efficiencies, and cheaper manufacturing facilities would be destroyed. The sources of production—raw materials and parts—need to be transported to the manufacturing facility, and the finished products must be transported out of an area at reasonable costs. Geographic specialization assumes that the large-scale production of the efficiently produced good is demanded at distances far from the production site. Obviously, one area cannot rely upon its comparative advantage and large-scale production without the use of systems to transport the goods efficiently to the distant areas requiring them.

Efficient transportation also provides the consumer with the benefit of increased competition. Without transportation, local entrepreneurs are capable of producing inefficient goods and charging high prices for

■ market area

their consumption. Transportation increases the market area for a product; thus, goods must be produced in the most efficient fashion or distant competitors will enter the market and legitimately capture its attention.

Transportation improvements are also credited with enhancing an area's economy by increasing the value of land that is adjacent to or served by the improvements. The land becomes more accessible and more useful. Today, the suburban centers provide excellent examples of

■ land values

land areas that have increased in value due to the accessibility that results from efficient transportation systems. Suburbanites can take advantage of nearby city life for work and pleasure and then retire to rural areas via public transportation networks to avoid crowded conditions. Commuters from Greenwich, Connecticut to New York City and from Cherry Hill, New Jersey to Philadelphia, Pennsylvania all reap both city and suburban benefits as the result of reliable train systems. Hence, the value of the land in these areas has increased to reflect the advantageous life-styles accompanying the growth of the new or improved transportation systems.

However, transportation does not always have a positive effect on land values. Noise and air pollution accompanying some networks decreases adjacent land values. The homeowners who have to bear this pollution suffer from overaccessibility.

■ major role

In an aggregate sense, transportation plays a major role in the overall economy of the United States (see Figure 1.2). In recent years, transporta-

Figure 1.2 GNP and Transportation

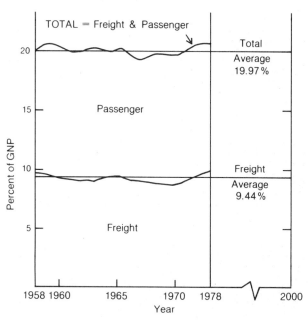

Source: Transportation Association of America, *Transportation Facts and Trends*, 16th ed. (Washington, D.C., 1980).

■ passenger
transportation

tion has accounted for over 20 percent of this nation's gross national product (GNP).[2] The major components of this expenditure stem from energy costs and the related costs for private autos.

Table 1.2 demonstrates the growing impact that passenger transportation has had on the economy. In 1978, the combined totals of for-hire and private transportation grew to over 12 percent of the GNP; 87 percent of this total came from expenditures in the private transportation sector. We should also note that expenditures have more than doubled in the 1970-1978 era for many of the categories. For example, excessive growth occurred in the following areas: new and used cars, tires and tubes, accessories, gasoline and oil, insurance, repair, small trucks, aircraft, bus and public transit, school buses, air, and rail. Inflation accounted for a portion of this growth, yet the growth in these areas was rampant.

■ freight
transportation

Table 1.3 shows the impact that freight transportation has had on the economy. Although the growth of the total freight bill as a percentage of the GNP has not been overwhelming, it does account for 9.05 percent of the GNP. Of the $192 billion spent for the transportation of freight in 1978, 79 percent went to highway carriers, 11 percent to railroads, 6 percent to water carriers, 1.6 percent to oil pipelines, 1.3 percent to airlines, and 1 percent to other miscellaneous carriers.

In terms of freight carried per ton-mile, railroads accounted for 36 percent of the 2,536 billion ton-miles of freight moved in 1978. Highway carriers moved an additional 24 percent of this total, pipelines followed with 23 percent, water carriers with 16 percent, and airlines with .2 percent. Although railroads are the leader in this category, their growth since 1947 has not been favorable. In 1947, railroads accounted for 67 percent of the ton-miles of freight carried.

Table 1.2 U.S. Estimated Passenger Expenditures (In Millions of Dollars)

Source/Year	1960	1965	1970	1975	1976	1977	1978
Private transportation							
Auto							
New & used cars	20,237	30,373	32,668	48,023	62,910	74,201	82,220
Gasoline & oil	14,414	19,595	29,329	52,679	57,227	62,251	67,877
Other related exp.	15,317	20,046	30,273	47,972	54,744	62,776	70,158
Total auto expenditures	49,968	70,017	92,270	148,674	174,881	199,228	220,255
Small trucks	327	1,097	2,420	6,129	6,987	7,767	8,609
Air							
Aircraft	202	343	354	966	1,188	1,515	1,726
Operating costs	693	1,027	2,275	3,767	3,983	3,730	3,917
Total private air	895	1,327	2,629	4,733	5,171	5,245	5,643
Total private expenditures	51,190	72,481	97,319	159,486	187,039	212,240	234,507
For-hire transportation							
Local (bus, taxi, rail, school)	2,803	3,159	4,643	9,103	9,074	10,237	11,356
Intercity							
Air	2,062	3,315	6,605	11,242	12,598	14,851	17,098
Bus	559	629	799	1,016	1,053	1,124	1,189
Rail	637	462	264	641	854	1,197	1,294
Water	14	12	12	16	7	17	21
Total intercity	3,272	4,418	7,680	12,915	14,872	17,189	19,602
International							
Air	598	997	1,925	3,448	3,742	4,204	4,399
Water	267	333	275	278	270	269	281
Total international	865	1,330	2,200	3,726	4,012	4,473	4,680
Grand total	58,130	81,388	111,842	185,230	214,997	244,138	270,145
Percentage of GNP	10.99	11.32	10.91	11.63	12.17	12.40	12.27

Source: Transportation Association of America, *Transportation Facts and Trends*, 16th ed. (Washington, D.C., 1980), pp. 10-11.

Table 1.3 U.S. Estimated Freight Expenditures (In Millions of Dollars)

Source/Year	1960	1965	1970	1975	1976	1977	1978
Highway transportation							
Truck - Intercity							
Regulated	7,214	10,068	14,585	22,000	26,000	31,000	36,500
Non-regulated	10,744	13,560	18,968	25,400	30,245	36,365	43,069
Truck - local	13,498	20,120	28,819	47,790	54,246	60,739	67,630
Bus	42	70	122	156	180	179	205
Total highway	31,498	43,818	62,494	95,346	110,671	128,774	147,404
Rail transportation	9,028	9,923	11,869	16,509	19,196	20,463	21,896
Water transportation							
International	1,765	2,081	3,187	4,928	5,441	6,686	7,303
Coastal-intercoastal	747	692	834	1,136	1,296	1,471	2,421
Inland waterways	312	381	473	950	1,139	1,125	1,300
Great lakes	227	213	239	348	390	326	521
Locks, channels, etc	287	391	376	526	594	680	834
Total water	3,338	3,758	5,109	7,888	8,860	10,288	12,379
Oil pipelines							
Regulated	770	904	1,188	1,874	2,137	2,792	4,907
Non-regulated	125	147	208	346	395	417	545
Total pipelines	895	1,051	1,396	2,220	2,532	3,209	5,452
Air transportation							
Domestic	220	478	720	1,073	1,247	1,484	1,729
International	134	280	451	765	805	873	925
Total air	354	708	1,171	1,838	7,052	2,357	2,654
Other	1,714	1,869	1,791	2,208	2,468	2,636	2,768
Grand total	46,827	61,127	83,830	126,069	145,779	167,227	192,553
Percentage of GNP	9.30	8.88	8.53	8.24	8.56	8.80	9.05

Source: Transportation Association of America, *Transportation Facts and Trends*, 16th ed. (Washington, D.C., 1980).

Thus, we can see that transportation plays several very important roles in the economy. See Figure 1.3 for another dimension of transportation. Good transportation spurs economic development by giving mobility to production factors, which permits scale economies and increased efficiency. Good transportation enlarges the area that consumers and industry can draw upon for resources and products. Good transportation expands the area to which a given plant may distribute its products eco-

Figure 1.3 Typical National Transportation Expenditure Percentages

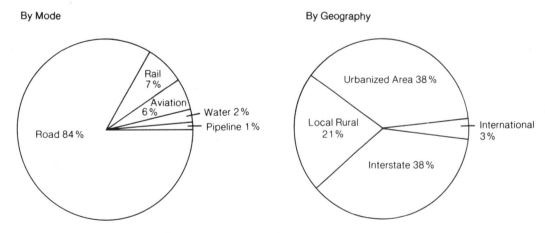

By Mode

Rail 7%
Aviation 6%
Water 2%
Pipeline 1%
Road 84%

By Geography

Urbanized Area 38%
Local Rural 21%
International 3%
Interstate 38%

Source: Transportation Association of America, *Transportation Facts and Trends*, 16th ed. (Washington, D.C., 1980).

nomically, and the resulting specialization and scale economies provide a wider choice for consumers at a lower cost. New transportation investments constitute a substantial part of all new investments in the United States and help to sustain and induce national economic growth.

Environmental Significance

■ environmental concerns

Although transportation provides the economy with numerous benefits, these positive aspects are not without associated costs. Transportation affects the environment negatively in terms of pollution and natural resource exploitation, although most citizens feel that the benefits provided by transportation far exceed these costs. The environmental problem of the future shall be to assess the relationship between industrial benefits and their external societal costs accurately.

■ pollution

Pollution is an external side effect of transportation with which no industry wants to be associated. The most serious form of pollution is the contamination of the air by various particles and gases. All forms of transportation are associated with this contamination to some extent, but combustion engines on vehicles seem to emit the greatest amount of pollutants. Overall, transportation accounts for 16.7 percent of the total air-polluting emissions in the United States (see Table 1.4). Three-quarters of this total comes from motor vehicles, particularly from gasoline. The polluting effects of aircrafts, railroads, and water vessels are minimal.

■ noise

Noise pollution is another harmful side effect of transportation. In the vicinity of superhighways and airports, noise pollution is a significant problem. Noise-sensitive environments, such as hospitals, schools, and

Table 1.4 Sources of Air-Polluting Emissions in the United States in 1969 (in Percentages)

Source	Particulates	Sulfur oxides (SO)	Nitrogen oxides (NO)	Carbon monoxide (CO)	Hydrocarbon (HC)	Total
Transportation						
Motor vehicles						
Gasoline	0.4	0.2	5.0	2.6	3.2	11.4
Diesel	0.1	0.1	0.5	0.0	0.3	1.0
Total motor vehicles	0.5	0.3	5.5	2.6	3.5	12.4
Aircraft	0.1	0.1	0.2	0.1	0.2	0.7
Railroads	0.1	0.2	0.1	0.0	0.0	0.4
Vessels	0.2	0.2	0.1	0.1	0.1	0.7
Nonhighway use of motor fuel	0.1	0.2	1.2	0.2	0.8	2.5
Total transportation	1.0	1.0	7.1	3.0	4.6	16.7
Stationary power sources	10.4	20.2	3.8	0.1	1.1	35.6
Industrial process	20.9	6.2	0.1	0.3	0.1	27.6
Solid waste disposal	2.0	0.1	0.3	0.2	0.2	2.8
Miscellaneous	16.4	0.2	0.1	0.5	0.1	17.3
Grand total	50.7	27.7	11.4	4.1	6.1	100.0

Source: U.S. Dept. of Transportation (1972, p. 68).

■ other pollution

residences, are forced to relocate in attempts to avoid this harmful side effect.

Water and land pollution are also of concern to transportation officials. The unnecessary destruction of land and wildlife threatens the expansion of transportation systems through various regions. Fortunately, new regulations, fines, and requirements to pay damages for marine life lost and shores spoiled will force greater concern for safety and will mean fewer accidents.

■ resources

Transportation is a major consumer of our scarce natural resources. Approximately 53 percent of America's refined petroleum is used in the transportation of passengers or goods. Highway travel alone accounts for 45 percent, air travel accounts for 5 percent, and the combined total of rail and water accounts for 2 percent of the total amount of petroleum consumed in the United States.

■ safety

In terms of safety, one of the most disturbing by-products of transportation is injury and loss of life. In 1970, over 58,000 persons lost their lives in the United States while engaged in transport. Approximately 91 percent of those fatalities occurred in highway vehicles. Table 1.5, though, points out that compared to 1947, the number of deaths in 1972 divided by the number of miles traveled in that mode measured in units of 100 million passenger-miles has declined. This positive statistic is the result of increased licensing regulations and more reliable vehicle designs. Unfortunately, trends in the area of safety for freight transportation aren't as promising. Train accidents, oil spills, and the threat of gaseous explosions while in transit have increased. With the increasing variety of products being shipped and the increasing volume of transportation, these problems require greater attention. We can hope that safety in the freight transportation area will soon parallel the progress made in the passenger area; however, much work remains to be done.

The nation's increasing demand for transportation services has imposed additional costs on society in addition to the monetary costs previously discussed. Over the past twenty-five years, great strides have been made, particularly at the national level, in mitigating those social costs, such as the negative impacts from transportation. Overall, the benefits far outweigh the costs to society, but vigilance is necessary. Table 1.6 indicates some of the actions taken to constrain the negative costs associated with transportation.

Social Significance

■ employment

Transportation works to the advantage of people by providing employment and enhancing travel. As an employer, transportation utilizes 11.1 percent of the work force (see Table 1.7). The percentage has declined since the 1950s, which indicates the increasing capital intensity of the industry. However, while employment has declined in the service aspects of the industry, the equipment-utilizing sectors have shown a relatively strong increase in employment.

In terms of human movements since World War II, the average number of miles of domestic intercity travel per person has increased sub-

Table 1.5 PASSENGER FATALITIES IN TRANSPORT VEHICLES*

Year	DOMESTIC SCHEDULED AIR CARRIERS # Number	Rate@	CLASS I INTERCITY BUS Number	Rate@	RAIL Number	Rate@	LOCAL TRANSIT Rate@ 1/	AUTO Number	Rate@	MOTORCYCLE Number	Rate@	WATER TRANSPORT Number 2/	GENERAL AVIATION Number	Rate 3/
1947	199	3.15			75	.16	n/a	15,300	2.60	n/a	n/a	1,244	1,352	90.00
1948	83	1.32			52	.13	n/a	15,200	2.50	n/a	n/a	1,364	1,384	94.17
1949	93	1.31			29	.08	n/a	17,700	2.70	n/a	n/a	1,484	896	79.36
1950	96	1.14			184	.58	n/a	20,200	2.90	n/a	n/a	1,502	871	82.05
1951	142	1.29			150	.43	.07	22,200	3.00	n/a	n/a	1,639	750	76.88
1952	46	.35			14	.04	.11	23,300	3.00	n/a	n/a	1,437	691	71.08
1953	86	.56			50	.16	.10	23,900	2.90	n/a	n/a	1,614	635	60.74
1954	16	.09			23	.08	.12	22,700	2.70	n/a	n/a	1,498	684	61.10
1955	156	.75	8	.05	19	.07	.13	25,100	2.70	n/a	n/a	1,452	619	50.90
1956	143	.61	16	.10	57	.20	.11	26,600	2.70	n/a	n/a	1,508	669	50.87
1957	31	.11	19	.12	17	.07	.11	25,600	2.60	n/a	n/a	1,574	800	56.08
1958	114	.43	20	.13	62	.27	.08	24,100	2.30	n/a	n/a	1,653	717	43.18
1959	209	.68			12	.05	.15	24,800	2.30	n/a	n/a	1,595	823	47.95
1960	297	.93	8	.05	33	.16	.02	24,800	2.20	731	n/a	1,478	787	44.49
1961	124	.38	14	.09	20	.10	.09	24,700	2.10	697	n/a	1,480	761	40.96
1962	121	.34	17	.10	28	.14	.04	26,800	2.20	759	n/a	1,445	857	43.62
1963	48	.12	38	.21	13	.07	.12	28,900	2.30	882	n/a	1,416	893	43.59
1964	65	.14	19	.10	9	.05	.09	31,500	2.40	1,118	n/a	1,464	1,056	48.42
1965	205	.38	44	.23	12	.07	.03	32,500	2.40	1,515	n/a	1,493	1,029	40.16
1966	59	.09	13	.07	27	.16	.07	34,800	2.50	2,043	n/a	1,630	1,151	34.50
1967	226	.29	23	.11	13	.09	.06	34,800	2.40	1,971	23.0	1,545	1,333	38.75
1968	258	.28	31	.16	13	.10	.10	36,200	2.40	1,900	23.0	1,625	1,399	37.81
1969	132	.13	8	.05	9	.07	.10	36,800	2.30	1,960	22.0	1,743	1,495	38.07
1970	0	.00	2	.01	10	.09	.13	34,800	2.10	2,330	23.0	1,651	1,310	40.85
1971	174	.16	15	.09	17	.24	.05	34,200	1.90	2,410	20.0	1,531	1,355	43.11
1972	160	.13	29	.17	48	.53	.16	35,200	1.90	2,700	17.0	1,568	1,426	41.94
1973	128	.10	29	.16	6	.07	.05	33,700	1.70	3,130	16.0	1,725	1,412	37.87
1974	158	.12	12	.06	7	.07	n/a	26,800	1.50	3,160	14.0	1,579	1,438	35.58
1975	113	.08	3	.02	8	.08	.07	27,200	1.40	2,800	11.0	1,570	1,345	31.73
1976	1r	.001	2	.01	5	.05	.09	27,650	1.34	3,000	16.0	1,371	1,320	29.49
1977	64	.04	6	.04	4	.04	.05	28,250	1.35	3,870	17.0	1,357r	1,436	30.00
1978	13	.01	2	.01	13	.13r	.05	28,450	1.30	4,530	20.0	1,321	1,459r	37.03r
1979	321	.12			7		.02						1,311	32.86

Source: Transportation Association of America, *Transportation Facts and Trends*, 16th ed. (Washington, D.C., 1980). p. 18.

\# Supplemental Air Carrier no longer shown. See 15th Edition for such data through 1978.

* Excludes crew members on public carriers, non-passengers killed by transport vehicles, and aircraft passenger deaths resulting from dynamite/sabotage accidents.

1/ Number of "local Transit" deaths not shown because source only publishes the rate.

2/ Includes passenger and crew deaths from all causes aboard vessels of all sizes, the majority of which occurred aboard small pleasure craft.

3/ Fatality rate per 100 million plane-miles. (See note in Source Data).

@ Fatality rate per 100 million Passenger Miles.

r Revised.

Table 1.6 Actions to Mitigate Negative Impacts of Transportation

Impact	Action
Noise	Vehicle and equipment standards; Noise R & D; Improved Aviation Operating Procedures; Environmental Impact Statements.
Air pollution	Emission Standards; Transportation Control Plans; Environmental Impact Statements.
Water pollution	Compulsory oil spill insurance; improved regulations concerning waste and hazardous materials handling; Environmental Impact Statement.
Marred visions	Billboard standards in interstate system.
Safety	55-MPH Speed Limit; increased safety regulation; safer design standards.
Petroleum dependence	55-MPH speed limit; auto fuel consumption standards; more realistic petroleum fuel costs.

Source: *National Transportation Trends and Choices*, 1977, p. 24.

■ human movement change

stantially (see Table 1.8). Changes in the technical nature of the transportation modes worked to enhance this growth in travel. Public air travel grew from 1.8 percent of person-miles in 1950 to 9.3 percent of person-miles in 1970. All the passenger carriers—except for the railroads—showed an increase during this period.

■ urban transportation

In urban areas, the amount of travel has substantially increased. This has been caused primarily by the spreading of a growing population and the increased land mass of urban areas. In terms of modal type of urban transportation used, a change can be identified. With the exception of the taxi cab, the absolute number and fraction moved via public transport has diminished.

Political Significance

■ overview

Transportation is treated differently from the rest of our economic activity because of its connection with the political life of a country. Transportation systems do not develop totally from decisions made in the private sector. Governmental intervention is needed to design feasible routes, to cover the expenses involved with building public highways, and to develop harbors and waterways. Since adequate transportation is needed in order to create national unity, the transportation network must be designed in such a manner that the leaders of government are in a position to travel rapidly to and communicate with the people they govern.

■ governmental responsibility

The government is responsible for aiding all passenger and freight transportation systems in which the costs cannot be covered reasonably by a central group of users. As a result of necessary governmental intervention, certain regulations exist which are designed to offer consumers the opportunity to transact in a competitive environment.

One outgrowth of regulation is the "common carrier." The common carrier has a duty to render service without discrimination based upon set rates for specific commodities.

The government's role as a regulator of transportation services does mean certain drawbacks for the public. For example, the concept of eminent domain involves forcing individuals to move and sell their land, even though they may not wish to do so. The government's power of em-

■ eminent domain

Table 1.7 U.S. EMPLOYMENT IN TRANSPORTATION AND RELATED INDUSTRIES
(Number of Persons Employed In Thousands)

	1950	1955	1960	1965	1970	1975	1978	1979
Transportation Services								
Air	86	128	191	229	351	362	396	423
Bus - Intercity & Rural	47	43	41	42	43	39	38	37
Local Transport	157	127	101	83	77	69	72	73
Railroads	1,391	1,205	885	735	627	538	535	546
Oil Pipe Line	29	27	23	20	18	17	19	19
Taxi	121	124	121	110	107	83	68	64
Trucking & Trucking Terminals	557	688	770	882	998	996	1,181	1,286
Water	237	237	232	230	215	190	207	225
Totals	2,625	2,579	2,364	2,331	2,436	2,294	2,516	2,673
Transportation Equipment Manufacturing								
Aircraft & Parts	283	761	646	624	669	514	529	605
Motor Vehicles & Equipment	926	1,010	829	945	914	892	1,103	983
Railroad Equipment	60	56	43	56	51	52	57	71
Ship & Boat Building & Repair	85	125	141	160	170	194	218	215
Other Transportation Equipment	25	37	33	- 57	111	115	157	157
Totals	1,379	1,989	1,692	1,842	1,915	1,767	2,064	2,031
Transportation-Related Industries								
Automotive & Accessory Retail Dealers	652	735	807	902	996	1,076	1,134	1,154
Automotive Wholesalers	176	196	215	255	320	367	419	436
Automotive Services & Garages	161	188	251	324	384	400	518	570
Gasoline Service Stations	343	387	461	522	614	616	644	586
Highway & Street Construction	210	242	294	324	331	297	279	280
Petroleum	282	330	311	292	333	380	448	491
Other Industries								
Truck Drivers & Deliverymen	1,131	1,275	1,418	1,387	1,356	1,325	1,307	1,300
Shipping & Receiving Clerks	260	253	240	300	359	419	455	466
Totals	3,215	3,606	3,997	4,306	4,693	4,880	5,204	5,283
Government Transportation Employees								
U.S. Department of Transportation*	18	16	38	45	66	75	74	74
Highway Employees — State & Local	380	475	532	571	607	604	583r	595e
Post Office	75	80	83	83	103	98	91	93
Other	18	17	18	16	12	13	13	
Totals	491	588	671	715	788	790	761r	775
TOTAL TRANSPORTATION EMPLOYMENT	7,710	8,762	8,724	9,194	9,832	9,731	10,545r	10,762
TOTAL EMPLOYED CIVILIAN LABOR FORCE	58,920	62,171	65,778	71,088	78,627	84,783	94,373	96,945
PERCENT TRANSPORTATION OF TOTAL	13.1%	14.1%	13.3%	12.9%	12.5%	11.5%	11.2%	11.1%

Source: Transportation Association of America, *Transportation Facts and Trends*, 16th ed. (Washington, D.C., 1980) p. 7.

* 1970 figures include all of DOT; prior years only, include FAA.

r Revised.

e Estimate.

Table 1.8 Intercity Domestic Travel Trends

	1950	1960	1970	1975
Gross National Product (billions)	714	986	1,438	1,594
Population (millions)	152	181	205	214
Intercity Travel				
Passenger Miles (billions)	505	784	1,185	1,311
Modal distribution (percent)				
Private auto	86.8	90.1	86.6	85.8
Private air	0.2	0.3	0.8	0.8
Public air	1.8	4.0	9.3	10.4
Public bus	4.5	2.5	2.1	1.9
Public rail	6.5	2.8	0.9	0.8
Public water	1.2	2.7	4.0	4.0
Urban Travel				
Total transit and taxi trips (millions)	n.a.	9,589	8,557	n.a.

Source: Transportation Association of America, *Transportation Facts and Trends*, 16th ed. (Washington, D.C., 1980).

inent domain gives it the right to acquire land for public use. Hence, many highways that are constructed cause the displacement of families because governmental intervention has opened the right-of-way for certain transportation routes. Although families may be displaced, the government's role is to act in the best interest of the public by designing routes that help the citizens of the nation efficiently carry on their business.

national defense

Closely connected with transportation's political role is its function as a provider of national defense. This function has long been recognized by governments. The Roman Empire built its great system of roads primarily for military reasons. Sir Winston Churchill once wrote: "Victory is the beautiful, bright-colored flower. Transport is the stem without which it could never have blossomed."[3] In the United States, the requirements of national defense have been advanced as a major reason for the construction of a system of nationwide, interconnected superhighways. Similarly, the large expenditures on air transport are based more on military and political considerations than on economic ones.

Although it is accurate to say that the American transportation system has been shaped by economic factors, political and military developments have also played important roles. Transportation policy incorporates more than economics—the expected benefits of the system extend beyond the economic realm.

Overview of Modern Transportation

The significance of our transportation system touches all aspects of life. For example, the location of transportation facilities has effects on the surrounding communities. Railroads and superhighways divide towns and neighborhoods; the location of highway interchanges can determine the location of manufacturing, retailing, and distribution operations. The character of a neighborhood or of a city is often determined by its ability to act as a transportation center. The port city of New Orleans, the rail city of Altoona, Pennsylvania, and St. Louis's role as the "Gateway to the West" are examples of towns that became known as the result of their ability to provide transportation services.

■ societal impact

In terms of the societal implications related to transportation, factors can be identified correlating network changes to changes in neighborhood characteristics. It should be mentioned, however, that transportation factors in connection with a whole series of other factors cause sociological change, rarely transportation factors alone. According to sociologists and urbanologists, the regional shopping centers, the higher-income commuter enclaves, and the resort, vacation, and amusement districts grow as the result of available transportation networks, as well as the relative expense of maintaining these areas.

■ decision areas

The consumer makes decisions based on transportation services, availability, cost, and adequacy. Product decisions (what products, or product, to produce or distribute) are closely related to the availability of transportation and the adequacy of the transporter to move the goods. Market area decisions are dominated by the ability of the transporter to get the product to market at a low cost. Purchasing decisions about parts, raw materials, supplies, or finished goods for resale must reflect transport costs in order to assess the logic of the transaction. Location decisions, too, are influenced by many transportation factors. The decisions about where plants, warehouses, offices, and stores should be located all take transportation requirements into consideration. And lastly, pricing decisions are strongly affected by the transportation operation. The logistics area of the firm is often considered a cost center; therefore, changes in the price of transportation will often have a serious effect on the prices of products in general.

■ transportation interaction

Overall, transportation interacts with three groups of our society: users, providers, and the government. Thus, transportation decisions are expected to consider all aspects of society in one form or another.

The role of the user is to make decisions that will maximize the relevant consumer-oriented goals. The power of the user lies in the ability to demand and pay (or not pay if the wrong service is offered) for certain forms of transportation.

The providers, both public and private, including agencies such as freight forwarders and brokers, must determine the demands of the system and the services to be offered. These decisions are made in light of total modal use, the importance of each mode to the economy, profits, and the way in which each company views itself in relationship to its competitors.

■ vital role

The government has decision-making power because transportation is vital to many aspects of American life, such as the gross working of the economy, employment, energy, the environment, national defense, and certain sociological concerns. The government attempts to act in the best interest of the public through various regulatory agencies. For example, the Interstate Commerce Commission (ICC), the Civil Aeronautics Board (CAB), and the Federal Maritime Commission (FMC) make critical decisions that directly affect the carriers that perform transportation services.

The decisions made by all three of these groups coalesce to form our transportation system. The character and the efficiency of the system are reflected by the manner in which the groups individually and collectively react to environmental changes.

Conclusion

This chapter has reviewed the role and significance of transportation in our society. We have determined that transportation affects us in the following areas: historical, economic, environmental, social, and political. Our advanced and complicated transportation network has affected us for the following reasons: historically, because the growth of nations relied upon transportation as the supporting foundation for communication, trading, and national defense; economically, because transportation plays a major role in widening markets and accounts for 20 percent of the GNP; environmentally, because transportation contributes to noise, air, and water pollution; socially, because transportation shapes the character of towns and employs over 12 percent of the population; and politically, because transportation is vital to national defense and to the workings of both our private and public lives.

Study Questions

1. What is meant by the time and place utility of transportation? What economic activity provides form utility?

2. Briefly explain the concept of comparative advantage. If a well-known lawyer can type his letters and briefs at the rate of 80 words per minute, and his secretary can only type at 40 words per minute, does this mean he should type his work? Why or why not?

3. What benefits are provided by having an efficient transportation network in an economy? What negative attributes are also related to transportation?

4. In passenger transportation: (a) What is the proportion of for-hire movement to the grand total of all passenger expenditures? (b) What are the three largest expenditure sectors in the auto area?

5. What proportion of the total gross national product is freight transportation? How is this total divided among the various forms of transportation?

6. What specific passenger and freight expenditures have climbed the most in percentage in 1970-1978?

7. What are the three largest sources of air pollution? What are the three largest kinds of air pollution?

8. In what areas has employment increased the decline in transportation since 1970?

9. According to statistics shown, how far does an average person travel in a year?

10. In the mid-1800s farmers in a group of counties in Central Illinois possessed a market outlet for agricultural goods by way of overland horse-drawn wagon and ferry to St. Louis. From there, the goods traveled down the Mississippi River to New Orleans (specific rates varied depending upon the water level and barge supply at one time). At New Orleans grain traders sold the products to markets in France and Belgium. Two east-west railroad mainlines were built through the counties that linked them with Chicago and New York with fast rail service. The railroad rates to New York were less than the St. Louis to New Orleans barge rates. New York opened a market to all of Europe. Trace the effects of this change upon the farmers, their land, the cities involved, and the commercial, social, and public institutions involved.

Notes

1. U.S. Senate, Committee on Interstate and Foreign Commerce, *National Transportation Policy*, December 1960, p. 29.

2. Donald Wood and James Johnson, *Contemporary Transportation* (Tulsa: Petroleum Publishing, 1980), p. 4.

3. Donald Harper, *Transportation in America* (Englewood Cliffs, N.J.: Prentice-Hall, 1978), p. 8.

Suggested Readings

Fair, Marvin L., and Williams, Ernest. *Economics of Transportation and Logistics.* Dallas: Business Publications, 1975, chap. 2.

Harper, Donald. *Transportation in America.* Englewood Cliffs, N.J.: Prentice-Hall, 1978, chap. 1.

Locklin, D. Philip. *Economics of Transportation.* 7th ed. Homewood, Ill.: Richard D. Irwin, 1972, chap. 1.

Morlok, Edward. *Introduction to Transportation, Engineering and Planning.* New York: McGraw-Hill, 1978, chap. 2.

Norton, Hugh S. *Modern Transportation Economics.* 2d ed. Columbus, Ohio: Charles E. Merrill, 1971, chap. 1.

Pegrum, Dudley. *Transportation: Economics and Public Policy.* 3rd ed. Homewood, Ill.: Richard D. Irwin, 1973, chap. 1.

Sampson, Roy, and Farris, Martin. *Domestic Transportation.* 4th ed. Boston: Houghton Mifflin, 1979, chap. 1.

Wood, Donald, and Johnson, James. *Contemporary Transportation.* Tulsa: Petroleum Publishing, 1980, chap. 1.

Case	## Highway Bypass Study

Earlyton is a growing community in the Midwest. It has one major rail-road mainline passing through it, and it is a crossroad for two U.S. federal highways that were developed in the 1930s. The east-west road was upgraded to four lanes in the 1960s. Both cross downtown at what is the town's major intersection. The town has a population of 100,000 and its downtown contains the major shopping area for it and the sur-rounding county.

County road planners are concerned with the overall traffic in the city. Much of the total traffic is through trucks and cars on the two highways. The railroad line often causes long backups on the high-ways and other streets. Downtown shipping traffic and parking is also a problem.

The county road planning commission is considering an "X"-shaped bypass to the north and east of the city to act as two routes around the town for the east-west and north-south highways. It will also overpass the railroad line.

What information should the commission collect in order to conduct a cost benefit analysis for this project? What other factors should the county consider?

2 Transportation and the User

After reading this chapter you should:

1 Be able to discuss the role and impact of transportation as it affects passengers.

2 Understand the effect of transportation on facility location and market areas.

3 Be able to discuss the interrelationship between transportation and pricing.

4 Understand the role of transportation in business logistics.

As noted in Chapter 1, transportation is an important and pervasive element in our society, and it impacts every person, either directly or indirectly. The goods we consume, our economic livelihood, our mobility, and our entertainment are in some way affected by transportation.

The growth of the U.S. economy, as well as the economy of most industrialized countries, is attributable, in part, to the benefits derived from mass production and division of labor. This specialization of labor and production results in an oversupply of goods at one location and an undersupply, or demand, for these goods at another place. Transportation bridges the supply and demand gap that is inherent in mass production.

The interrelationship between transportation and mass production points out the dependency of our society on transportation. As each of us specializes in the production of a particular good or service, we are relying upon someone else to produce the goods and services that we need to survive. Also, we are dependent upon transportation to move these goods and services to our location in an efficient and economical manner. Like the citizens of most industrialized societies, the U.S. citizens, as individuals, are not self-sufficient.

On a global scale, countries are beginning to recognize international dependencies. Many countries are dependent upon the United States to produce goods and services, and the United States is dependent upon countries for goods such as oil. Again, transportation plays a key role in this international dependency, or trade, by permitting the equalization of supply and demand on a global basis.

In this chapter our attention is directed toward the impact transportation has upon the users. The users of transportation include passengers, shippers, and receivers of freight. Emphasis is given to the impact of transportation on facility location, market areas, and the pricing decisions of freight transportation users. The business logistics approach that firms take when buying transportation is also discussed.

■ supply and demand gap

■ society dependence

■ chapter overview

Passenger Transportation

Transportation has a definite and identifiable effect upon the life-styles of Americans. An individual's decision as to where to work, live, and play is influenced by transportation. Cultural differences among geographic regions are lessened by the ability of residents to travel outside the confines of their region.

■ automobile

The automobile has been the form of transportation that most affects American life-styles. The convenience, flexibility, and relatively low cost of automobile travel has permitted individuals to live in a location that is different from the place in which they work. The growth of suburbs can be attributed to the automobile, since people can drive 10-50 miles, or more, one way to work. The automobile also enables people to seek medical, dental, and recreational services at varying locations throughout a region.

For long-distance travel, the automobile and the airplane have a major influence upon passengers. Without these methods of transportation, the recreational habits of many U.S. citizens would be drastically changed.

■ cultural impact

An outcome of all of this travel has been a broadening of thoughts and beliefs with respect to people of other regions and countries. Transportation can be viewed as the catalyst for a cultural melting pot process. As individuals travel, their thoughts, beliefs, and values are transferred to others, thereby minimizing the cultural differences among regions. Transportation has not been the sole factor contributing to the melting pot process, but it has enabled people to travel to different regions to view the culture of that area on a firsthand basis. Such knowledge of others helps us to understand each other and to promote peaceful relations.

A prime ingredient in increased passenger travel is economical transportation. Unfortunately, the rising cost of automobile and air travel, resulting from escalating energy costs, is beginning to cause a reduction in the amount of passenger travel and a subsequent change in life-styles. Instead of traveling long distances for a vacation, many people have stayed closer to home or have not traveled at all. Areas of the country that are highly dependent upon tourists have experienced serious economic downturns.

■ suburban living

The suburban flight has been somewhat stalled by the rising costs of automobile travel. The 50-100 mile round trip per day is becoming quite taxing for many families. Some recent developments indicate that families are returning to the cities to live where they can reduce the expense of travel to work. This trend is not overwhelming as of yet, but the next few years may see a stronger growth in the demand for city rather than suburban dwellings.

Facility Location

Transportation has been a major determinant in the location of industrial facilities since the industrial revolution. The cost of transporting raw materials into a facility and the cost of transporting finished goods to markets directly affect the profitability of the plant or warehouse. In addition, the time required to traverse the spatial gap between sources of supply, plants, warehouses, and markets affects other costs such as inventory and stockouts.

city location

Water transportation has played an important role in the location of many major cities. The early settlers to the United States relied upon water transportation to tie European markets and supply sources to the developing country. Thus, cities such as New York, Philadelphia, and Boston are port cities. As the American frontier was settled, the frontier was tied to these port cities that provided a source of supplies and markets for the western cities. Other cities—Pittsburgh, Cincinnati, St. Louis—developed along the internal waterways. As railroad transportation developed, however, cities and industrial facilities grew at locations that were not adjacent to waterways. Later, the automobile and truck enabled the development of cities and industrial facilities at virtually any location.

As the U.S. market grew, firms had to decide where new facilities should be located. Today, many firms are faced with the question of plant and warehouse location in light of changing markets, especially the exodus of people and many industries to the sun belt states, and changing raw material supply locations. As markets and supply locations change and transit times become longer, firms experience higher costs for transportation, inventory, and warehousing.

Overview of the Location Decision

Although transportation is a major factor in the facility location decision, it is not the only determinant. The cost of operating a facility at various locations and various community factors also have an effect upon the economic (cost and profit) advantage of one location over another. Figure 2.1 provides an overview of the locational determinants and their relative importance in the location decision process.

locational determinants

As indicated in Figure 2.1, transportation (logistics) is the first locational determinant considered. The distance to and from markets and raw material sources directly affects the cost of moving goods into and out of the proposed facility location. The transportation factor enables the decision maker to narrow down the possible sites. Once the number of possible sites is reduced, specific data are collected about the cost of operating the facility at various sites. The costs of fuel, labor, taxes, water, waste, and property are the major operating costs for a facility and will vary from location to location.

industry incentives

In addition to operating and transportation costs, community factors affect the location decision. Many communities offer incentives to firms —such as reduced taxes, reduced water and sewage rates, and building leases—if the firm will locate in the community. Such industry incentives reduce the overall operating costs and make a site more attractive.

employee conditions

Employee conditions have a direct bearing upon the quality of life in a community. Employee conditions include: population, climate, and recreational services. Employee conditions are part of the community factors affecting the location decision.

Figure 2.1 Overview of Locational Determinants

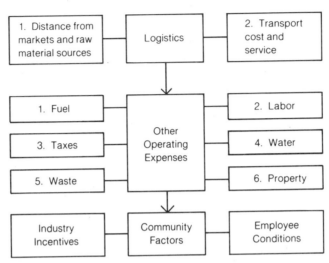

Source: John J. Coyle and Edward J. Bardi, *The Management of Business Logistics*, 2d ed. (St. Paul: West Publishing, 1980), p. 290.

Classical Theories of Location

The importance of transportation cost as a locational determinant can be seen through the examination of the facility location theories of von Thunen[1], Weber, and Hoover. Although others have made contributions to locational theory, these three theorists are generally considered to have provided the basis for today's least cost location decision process.

Johann Heinrich von Thunen was one of the first writers to theorize about the factors of production which affect the location of a facility. He was concerned with the location of agricultural production facilities. He wanted to minimize transportation cost and maximize profits for a given product.

■ agricultural production

To simplify the complexity of the problem, von Thunen assumed an isolated city-state surrounded by a plain of equal fertility. Any product could be grown with equal success at any location on the plain. The city produced all the manufactured goods required for farming, and the farms produced all the food required by the city (the market).

■ isolated city-state

Transportation cost was a constant rate per ton-mile for all commodities. For example, if the cost of transportation was $1 per ton-mile, total transportation charges would be $400 to transport 4 tons 100 miles, or $500 to transport 4 tons 125 miles. In addition, transportation was assumed to be equally accessible for all locations; that is, there were no transportation constraints.

■ transport cost

With complete mobility of production facilities, agricultural production would occur at the location where the farmer would maximize the difference between the market price and costs (production and transportation)—the profit maximizing point. With the market price fixed and production costs not varying by location, the transportation cost factor was the major locational determinant impacting profit-ability.

Von Thunen concluded that locations a greater distance from the market would incur a greater transportation cost. For products with low-value-to-weight ratios, locations at greater distances from the market would not be economical, since the high weight would mean high transportation costs which the low valued products could not sustain.

Consider the following example. Product A has a value of $5 per ton and Product B has a value of $50 per ton. If the transportation rate was $1 per ton per mile, Product A could not be produced more than 5 miles from the market, the point at which the transportation cost equals the selling price ($1/ton/mile x 1 ton x 5 miles). On the other hand, Product B could be profitably produced at a greater distance than five miles from the market because Product B has a greater value.

■ transit time

Von Thunen also considered the element of transit time important for determining the location of perishable products such as fresh fruits and vegetables. In other words, perishable products should be produced near the market to minimize the transit time, thereby assuring delivery of the products in good condition. The time required to make delivery determines whether or not the commodity can be sold at the market.

The outcome of von Thunen's work was the development of von Thunen's belts, a series of concentric rings around the city. Within each ring, the agricultural product that should be produced at that location was identified so that profitability could be maximized and the transportation cost and transit time minimized. Perishable products would be produced in the ring nearest the market; products with low-value-to-weight relationships would also be produced in the first ring. Products of high-value-to-weight ratios would be produced in the more distant rings.

■ industrial plants

Alfred Weber[2] was a German economist who developed a theory for the location of industrial plants. Weber's theory has more application to industrial facility location than that of von Thunen. Like von Thunen, Weber assumed that transportation would be equally accessible at a constant rate with respect to distance and weight. The rate was the same for both raw materials and finished goods.

Weber's theory is based upon total transportation cost minimization. The least cost location is one that minimizes the cost of moving raw materials to the plant and finished goods to the market.

■ raw material classification

From a transportation perspective, raw materials possess two distinct characteristics. First, raw materials may lose weight in processing, thereby influencing the total amount of weight to be moved and the total transportation cost. Second, the supply source of a raw material may be fixed to a specific location, thus affecting the distance that the raw material must be moved. Weber classified raw materials according to geographical availability and the weight lost in processing.

■ ubiquity vs. localized materials

The geographic availability characteristic states that a raw material is either ubiquitous or localized. An ubiquity is a raw material that is found at all locations—an example would be water. A localized raw material is found in certain locations only—an example would be coal. The localized raw material requires transportation from its specific supply source to the location of the plant (if the plant is not located at the supply source). However, an ubiquity does not require transportation, since it is found everywhere. Thus, a plant using an ubiquitous raw material (for example, the water used in soft drinks) would be located near the market.

In addition to the geographic availability characteristic, a raw material possesses a weight-lost-in-processing trait. A raw material that does not lose weight in processing is termed a pure, raw material, and one that does lose weight in processing is a weight-losing material. To minimize transportation costs, a plant using a localized weight-losing material would be located at the supply source. Pure raw materials, either ubiquitous or localized, will never bind production to their deposits. That is, the total transportation cost will be the same regardless of where the plant is located—at the supply source, the market, or in between on a straight line connecting the two. With pure raw materials, the total weight transported remains the same before and after processing.

■ pure vs. weight-losing

For a situation in which there is one market, one raw material source, Weber's location theory suggests that a plant be located near the raw material source if the raw material is a localized, weight-losing product. A market-oriented location is desirable when the raw material is an ubiquity. A localized, pure, raw material indicates that the plant location should be either at the source, at the market, or anywhere in between.

When more than one raw material source or market exists, however, Weber's theory does not provide a definitive answer to the plant location question. Through the use of the material index (center of mass concept), Weber attempts to solve the multiple source and market problem, but all too often, the material index approach suggests that the location should not be at the sources or the markets. A technique known as the grid technique[3] provides a definite location for a facility serving many markets and buying from many supply sources.

Edgar M. Hoover[4] is an American theorist who developed a least cost approach to facility location. Unlike von Thunen and Weber, Hoover considered demand factors such as the effect of transportation costs upon the price of the product, and the resultant demand for the product. However, his treatment of cost factors was expanded beyond that of the previous writers. He gave consideration to transportation costs, agglomerative forces, and industrial costs.

■ demand factors

In the transportation cost area, Hoover pointed out that transportation rates are not linear with regard to distance. Most transportation rates increase with distance, but not in direct relationship to distance. This nonlinearity of rates to distance is known as the tapering rate principle. (See Chapter 12 for a discussion of tapering rates.) For localized, pure, raw materials, the tapering rate principle makes the location of a plant at either the supply source or the market the optimum location (not anywhere in between as Weber's analysis suggested). The combination of rates for a location between the source and the market would be higher than the single rate from the source or to the market.

■ nonlinear rates

■ carrier availability

Hoover also noted that carrier availability is not homogeneous throughout the country. Some locations have greater numbers of carriers and therefore have the ability to meet more and varied shipper transportation requirements. A location that has few carriers available to provide service may charge higher transportation rates than areas that have many carriers who may lower the rate in order to attract shippers.

Finally, Hoover recognized the importance of transportation cost as it varies from company to company. For firms shipping in less-than-truckload (LTL) quantities, transportation costs may be more important than for firms shipping in truck load (TL) quantities. Also, the transportation characteristics of the firm's products have an impact upon the rates charged (for example, low density products, less than 10 pounds per foot, have higher rates) and upon the importance of the transportation cost factor as a locational determinant.

Transportation Rate Factors

In the above discussion of transportation cost in the location decision, the transportation rate was assumed to be linear with respect to distance and to be the same for all commodities. Here we will examine the realities of the transportation rate structure.

■ tapering rate effect

As Hoover noted, transportation rates are basically tapering in nature. That is, rates increase with distance but not in direct proportion, and the effect of the tapering rate is that the location of a facility will be near either the source or the market. For example, if the rate to move a product 200 miles is $3 per ton and $5 per ton to move 400 miles and the distance between the source of supply and the market is 400 miles, transportation costs will be minimized if the location is at either the source or the market where the $5 per ton rate will apply. If the location is at the midpoint, 200 miles, the applicable rate per ton is a total of $6: $3 into the facility and $3 out of the facility to the market.

In reality, transportation rates are different for raw materials than for finished goods. Rates on finished goods are usually higher than rates on raw materials. The impact of the rate differences is to pull the location toward the market. By locating at the market, the lower rated commodity (raw material) is transported rather than the higher rated finished good. A plant location near the market minimizes the distance that the high transportation cost commodity is moved. (This general statement must be tempered with the weight-losing raw material location implication, which pulls the location toward the supply source.)

■ blanket rates

Not all rates increase with distance. The blanket rate does not increase as the distance that the commodity is shipped increases. The blanket rate remains the same for all distances to or from the blanket area. Carriers publish blanket rates to ensure that the price of a product will remain competitive in a market area.

The implication of the blanket rate is that no one location within the blanket region has a transportation cost advantage or disadvantage. When blanket rates are present, the transportation cost factor is eliminated as a locational determinent. However, the blanket rate is found in only a few commodity movement markets.

A limited geographic area where blanket rates do exist is the commercial zone. The commercial zone is the area surrounding a city or town to which the rates quoted for the city or town also apply. The limit of the commercial zone is defined by the Interstate Commerce Commission (ICC) based upon the population of the city or town.

■ commercial zone

The commercial zone plays an important role in selecting the specific site for a facility. If the facility site is within the commercial zone, the rates quoted to and from the city or town will apply to the location selected, even though the site is not within the corporate limits of the city. Also, carriers with specific operating authority to serve a city, usually motor carriers, are legally permitted to provide service to a site outside the corporate limits of a city but within the commercial zone.

For example, consider the situation where an industrial park is built outside the commercial zone of a city. Of the approximately 100 motor carriers that could serve the city, only two motor carriers have interstate operating authority to serve the industrial park. A firm that located in the industrial park utilizes local cartage companies, at added costs, to haul freight into the trucking terminals in the city for dispatch to customer destinations. Because the lower commodity rates published by the two interstate carriers are not available at the industrial park, the occupants are forced to pay higher, class rates while negotiating with the carriers to publish commodity rates to and from the industrial park. To say the least, the industrial park described above will not develop until the commercial zone of the city is increased, through population and regulatory changes, to include the park site.

■ transit privilege

The transit privilege is another type of transportation rate structure that affects facility location. The transit privilege permits the shipper to stop the shipment in transit to perform a function that physically changes the commodity's characteristics. The shipper still pays the lower through rate from initial origin to final destination because the transit privilege assumes, for rate purposes, that the commodity does not stop in transit nor change physical characteristics. Transit privileges are not available for all commodities, only limited products and points have them. The transit privilege, like the blanket rate, eliminates geographic location advantages or disadvantages. For commodities that enjoy transit privileges, the transit points become definite location alternatives for the production facility.

Summary of Facility Location

The preceding discussion of the classical theories of location and the transportation rate implications points out the significance of transportation cost and service in the facility location decision. Transportation is usually the first factor to be considered in the location decision process. The elimination of high transport cost alternatives reduces the number of possible sites to be considered.

In the next section, the impact of transportation on the market area is considered.

Market Areas

Once a plant or warehouse is located, the transportation factor, cost and service, affects the market area that can be served from the facility. As the

■ cost and service

distance to the market (customer location) increases, the transportation cost becomes greater and transit time becomes higher. At some distance from a facility, the transportation cost, and consequently the price charged, becomes so great that the buyer will not purchase the product, or the buyer will purchase from a competitor. Likewise, as service levels drop and transit times increase, the buyer will eventually select a competitor to provide the product.

■ transit time

Transportation service levels, specifically transit times, affect the buyer's inventory level and inventory carrying costs. As the transit time increases, a buyer must increase the amount of inventory held, assuming lead time also increases. The increased inventory carrying cost (capital, warehousing, insurance, etc.) associated with longer transit times places a firm at a competitive disadvantage. Many firms utilize a three- to five-day transit time limit for the market area served by a plant or warehouse.

■ laid down cost

The significance of the transportation cost element in the determination of the market area is found in the laid down cost comparison of competing firms' products. The work of Fetter and Losch[5] suggests that the extent of the market area for two competing firms is the point where the laid down cost is equal to the products of the two firms. The laid down cost is defined as the production cost (production, marketing, and profit) plus the transportation cost from the plant or warehouse to the customer's location.

The market area for a seller will be the area where the seller has a laid down cost advantage over its competitor. The buyer will select the firm that offers the lowest price, lowest laid down cost. When the price for a product exceeds that of competitors, the firm is at a price disadvantage and will be unable to sell in that market.

Recognizing that transportation rates increase with distance and that rates are greater for smaller shipments, many firms have established distribution centers near market areas. Goods are transported to the distribution center from the plant in truckloads or carloads, which means lower transportation costs than if the goods were shipped in smaller quantities. This reduced transportation cost enables the firm to land the goods at a lower cost in the market than would be possible via small shipments direct to the customer. Note, however, that the savings in transportation costs may be offset by the increased cost of operating the distribution center.

To illustrate the impact of transportation cost upon the extent of a firm's market area, consider the example given in Figure 2.2. Two firms, U and T, are located 1,000 miles apart. Both produce the same quality product and incur the same production cost of $75,00 per unit. U has a

Figure 2.2 Extent of the Market Area

1,000 miles

U ————————————————————————————————— T

Production = $75.00/unit
Transportation = $1.20/unit/mile

Production = $75.00/unit
Transportation = $1.00/unit/mile

transportation cost of \$1.20 per unit per mile, while T incurs a transportation cost of \$1.00 per unit per mile. The extent of the market area between U and T is as follows:

$$\text{Laid down cost (U)} = \text{Laid down cost (T)}$$
$$\text{Production (U)} + \text{Transportation (U)} = \text{Production (T)}$$
$$+ \text{Transportation (T)}$$
$$\$75.00 + \$1.20 \, (x) = \$75.00 + \$1.00 \, (1000 - x),$$

where x = the distance from U's plant to the limit of the market area and $(1000 - x)$ is the distance from T to the market area limit.

Solving the equation for x shows that U has a market area of 454.5 miles from its facility and T has a market area of 545.5 miles from its facility. The firm with the lower transportation cost (T) has a greater market area than the firm with the higher transportation cost (U).

In an attempt to increase its market area, U establishes a distribution center (DC) at a point 300 miles from U's plant as indicated in Figure 2.3. The cost to land the freight at the distribution center and to operate the distribution center is \$200 per unit. The extent of the market area between the distribution center and T is as follows:

$$\text{Laid down cost (DC)} = \text{Laid down cost (T)}$$
$$\$75.00 + \$200.00 + \$1.20 \, (x) = \$75.00 + \$1.00 \, (700 - x)$$
$$x = 227.3 \text{ miles from the DC}$$

The extent of the market area for U is 527.3 miles (300 miles to the DC + 227.3 miles from the DC) and 472.7 miles for T. The extent of the market area is increased by a reduction in the cost of transporting the goods.

In summary, the cost of transportation and the level of transportation service provided has a direct impact upon the ability of a firm to competitively serve customers. As the distance to the market area increases, the cost to deliver goods increases and the time required to serve the market increases. At some geographic point, the transportation cost increases the price (laid down cost) beyond that offered by competitors, and the market area limit is reached. A limit to the market area is reached also when the transit time (transportation service level) is too high to be competitive.

Pricing Decisions

The price that a firm charges for its product is based upon a number of factors that affect demand and supply of the product. In addition, the price that is established is critical to the realization of the firm's goals—profit maximization, sales maximization, good customer relations, etc. A detailed discussion of the demand characteristics that must be considered in establishing a price is beyond our scope here. Our concern will be the impact of transportation on the pricing decision.

The transportation rate structure contains varying forms of quantity discounts, the carload or truckload rates offered to shippers who ship larger quantities at one time. Railroads offer carload rates for volumes of 30,000 to 40,000 pounds, and motor carriers offer three-, four-, or five-

■ rate discount quantities

Figure 2.3 Extent of the Market Area with a Distribution Center

	300 miles				700 miles	
U			DC			T
Prod. = $75.00/unit		Oper. = $200.00/unit		Prod. =	$75.00/unit	
Trans. = $1.20/unit/mile		Trans. = $1.20/unit/mile		Trans. =	$1.00/unit/mile	

volume rates at quantities ranging from 2,000 to 30,000 pounds. These lower rates are offered by the carrier who experiences lower costs and economies of operation when larger shipments are tendered at one time.

■ quantity discounts

For the user (seller), the volume of the transportation rate discount provides a basis for offering quantity discounts to its buyers. On larger shipments the user will realize a lower transportation cost per product unit and can pass this transportation cost savings on to the buyer. In addition, the user can utilize the transportation rate discount as a basis to justify to the government the price discount offered.

Although it may not be possible or desirable to establish a price discount at each transportation volume discount level, quantity discount schedules can be developed around these discount levels. A number of firms have their pricing schedules coincide with the rate discount volumes offered by the mode of transportation utilized; by doing so, they have a valid reason to offer the discount and a valid cost basis to justify the discount under Robinson-Patman Act requirements.

■ terms of sale

Another transportation impact on pricing is the FOB term of sale. (Originally, FOB meant "free on board" the ship; the seller incurred the transportation cost and responsibility for the shipment until it was placed on board the ship.) The FOB term of sale determines the transportation responsibility the buyer and seller will incur. Specifically, the FOB term indicates who is to incur the transportation charges for the shipment, who is to control the movement of the shipment, and where title to the goods passes to the buyer.

■ transport cost responsibility

Usually FOB has a named point associated with it. This named point is the point where the seller transfers transportation responsibility, the cost, and the title to the goods to the buyer. For example, FOB, Toledo indicates that the seller incurs transportation costs and responsibility up to Toledo; title to the goods passes to the buyer at Toledo. Two common FOB forms are: FOB, origin and FOB, delivered. Under the FOB, origin term of sale, the buyer incurs all transportation costs and responsibility for the shipment; title passes to the buyer at the time the carrier picks up the shipment. The exact opposite is true for the FOB, delivered, because in this case the seller incurs all transportation responsibility and cost.

■ title passage

The point at which the title is transferred is important in determining who bears the risk of loss or damage in transit. When the title passes to the buyer at origin, the buyer bears the risk of damage in transit and is responsibile for filing a damage claim with the common carrier. The seller may reduce its costs by transferring the title to the buyer at origin, thereby causing the buyer to incur all of the expense associated with

■ claim responsibility

■ zone pricing

■ built in subsidy

■ basing point pricing

claim filing and the possibility of nonrecovery of the damaged value. However, the buyer may look with a great deal of displeasure upon a seller who abdicated damage settlement to the buyer.

Some firms have developed a pricing strategy called a zone price that makes the price of the product the same at all geographic locations. To accomplish this, a seller must use a weighted average transportation cost, for the more distant buyers will incur a greater transportation cost than the buyers closer to the shipping point. Consider the example given in Figure 2.4 in which a firm located in Toledo has an equal price for customers located in Pittsburgh and New York. The cost to transport freight to Pittsburgh is $2.00 per unit and to New York it is $3.00 per unit. The firm has a production cost of $2.50 per unit and a price of $5.00 per unit. In order to offset the apparent loss of $.50 per unit in New York, the firm extracts a subsidy of $.50 per unit from the Pittsburgh buyer. If the volume of business increases in New York, the seller must increase the subsidy from Pittsburgh, increase the average transportation cost included in the price, or incur a loss (lower profit margin).

It should be noted that by utilizing a delivered price that is the same, for all buyers, the firm is capable of increasing its market area. However, this is only possible as long as the Pittsburgh buyer is willing to pay $2.50 for transporting the freight (the average freight cost) when the transportation cost is $2.00. The $2.50 per unit rate that the seller charges may be lower than the rate the buyer would pay if the buyer arranged for the transportation and paid the charge directly. This possibility exists if the seller consolidates orders and ships in large volumes and with low rates.

Some firms have adopted a basing point system of pricing. That is, the transportation charges included in the price are based on a particular point in a zone or region. Such a pricing policy is legal as long as the buyer has the option of buying FOB, origin and the sellers do not get together and collude about the base price. The basing point pricing system utilizes the concepts discussed above with regard to the built-in subsidy that is necessary in a zone price. Again, the weight average of the transportation cost is subject to change as the volume of freight changes among the customer locations in the zone.

In conclusion, transportation cost is a factor included in determining the price to be charged customers, the quantity discount schedule, and the extent of the market area. In the next section our attention is directed toward the business logistics approach utilized to control transportation.

Figure 2.4 Zone Pricing

Toledo	Pittsburgh	New York
Prod. = $2.50	Trans. = $2.00	Trans. = $3.00
	Price = $5.00	Price = $5.00

Business Logistics

■ evolution

Beginning in the early 1960s the business community began to take a more comprehensive approach to the management of the transportation function. More specifically, management recognized that transportation decisions had a cost impact on the operation of other functions in the firm and on the profit of the firm as a whole. As firms developed maturity in the functional areas of production, marketing, and finance, attention was turned to the logistics area—movement and storage—where possibilities for improvements in cost and service definitely existed.

About this time businesses experienced a proliferation of product lines to meet the increased demands and discriminating tastes of buyers. As new products were added, transportation, warehousing, and inventory costs increased. The increased costs of logistics forced firms to take an integrated approach to the move-store function so as to remain competitive and profitable. In addition, manipulation of the movement and storage functions produced varying degrees of customer service which could be used by marketing as a sales tool to differentiate the product in the market place and increase sales.

Definition of Business Logistics

■ movement and storage

■ definition of logistics

The essential elements of business logistics are movement and storage. The manipulation of these two broad functional areas in a cohesive manner is the essence of business logistics. A more specific definition of business logistics is as follows:

the physical movement of goods from supply points to final sale to customers and the associated transfer and holding of such goods at various intermediate storage points, accomplished in such a manner as to contribute to the explicit goals of the organization.[6]

As the above definition indicates, a firm's goods (raw materials and finished goods) are transported between raw material sources, plants, warehouses, and customer locations. The products must be made available in the quantity and at the location desired by the user. Logistics coordinates the movement and storage element so that the total logistics costs are minimized (a common logistics goal).

The movement function involves the selection and use of transportation companies. Selecting a carrier involves choosing a mode (rail, truck, etc.) and either a for-hire carrier (common, contract, etc.) or private carriage.

The quality of the transportation service provided affects the storage activity costs. The storage function incorporates the number, size, and location of storage facilities, and the control of inventory. In addition, the short distance movement of inventory within the warehouse, the order processing function, and the package decision are included in the storage function.

■ move-store relationship

The relationship between transportation and storage is direct. As noted above, the level of transportation service affects the cost of the storage function. For example, the use of a low transportation cost carrier that provides long transit times will require higher inventory levels and, consequently, higher inventory carrying costs. Conversely, the requirement that all customer orders be delivered within two days may necessitate the use of truck and air transportation which are higher cost modes than rail.

■ physical supply and physical distribution

It is quite common to find the business logistics function broken down into two areas: physical supply and physical distribution. Physical supply is concerned with the movement and storage of raw materials from supply sources to the plants. Physical distribution concentrates upon the movement and storage of the finished good from the plant to the warehouse and to the customer.

■ links and nodes

Finally, the business logistics function can be viewed as a series of links and nodes. The nodes are the fixed points in the system where the goods come to rest (raw material source, warehouses, plants, customer locations), and the link is the transportation used to connect the nodes. By viewing the logistics system as a series of links and nodes, the logistics manager can simplify a complex system into the basic logistics elements—movement and storage.

The use of the link-node concept is shown in Figure 2.5. In this example, a firm utilizes a warehouse to collect raw materials (RM) from three sources and ships the finished goods directly to the customer. The raw materials are shipped via truck at LTL rates to the warehouse where the supplies are consolidated into carload quantities and shipped to the plant via rail at carload (CL) rates. Customer orders are sent direct from the plant by truck at LTL rates.

A review of the link-node system shown in Figure 2.5 suggests that service improvements to the customer may be possible with the establishment of a warehouse between the plant and the market, permitting customer orders to be shipped a shorter distance. In addition, the plant shipments to the proposed market warehouse could be made in larger quantities at lower rates, resulting in transportation cost savings. However, the addition of the market warehouse would increase the cost of inventory, warehousing, etc. Consideration of system changes and the analysis of the costs and benefits of proposed changes is made easier with the use of the link-node approach.

Figure 2.5 Basic Transportation Flow of Product from Raw Material to Final Customer

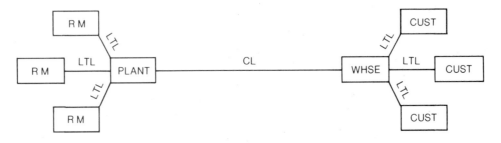

Total Cost Analysis

An inherent characteristic of the business logistics approach is the total cost analysis. The interrelationship between transportation, warehousing, inventory, and customer service, suggests that a decision made in one area of logistics has a definite impact upon other areas of the firm. No one area of logistics operates independently. The decisions made in the transportation area, for example, have an impact upon the cost of warehousing and inventory, product marketability and the cost of lost sales or productivity.

In the absence of a total cost approach to the transportation decision, a company may utilize a mode of transportation that has a low transportation rate. The use of a low transportation cost method of movement may minimize transportation costs, but it does not guarantee the minimization of total movement and storage costs. Low cost transportation usually is associated with slow service, which means higher warehousing and inventory costs and lower customer service.

■ cost trade-offs

The total cost analysis requires the decision maker to consider cost trade-offs within the system. A decision to use air rather than truck transportation would trade the higher costs of transportation for possible savings in warehousing, inventory, and increased sales. Cost trade-offs may result in lower overall logistical costs or higher total costs. The significance of the cost trade-off, and the total cost analysis, is the recognition of the interrelationship of the logistics variables.

Without a business logistics approach within a company, the total cost approach may pose some difficulties in implementation. For example, total costs may be lowered by the switch to higher-cost air transportation, since the higher transportation costs are traded for lower costs of warehousing and inventory. From the viewpoint of the total firm, such a decision would be desirable. However, from the traffic manager's viewpoint (performance is measured upon transportation costs incurred), the decision to use air carriage is not desirable. In the absence of an integrated, business logistics approach, the switch to air carriers probably would not be made.

■ relation to other departments

The total cost approach of business logistics emphasizes the interrelationship of logistics to other areas of the firm. The two functions most directly affected by logistics are marketing and production. Physical distribution activities are sometimes considered part of the marketing function, since the movement of the finished goods to the customer completes the sales transaction. The quality of the logistics service provided to the customer may be used as a marketing tool to enhance sales, or, if the service is unacceptable, logistics service may cause a loss in sales. Firms that are capable of offering logistics service levels that reduce a buyer's cost will have a competitive edge in the marketplace.

This logistics impact upon sales is considered in a total cost context by examining decisions in terms of cost of lost sales (profits). The level of inventory, the number and location of warehouses, and the carrier used to deliver goods determine the level of service provided and the resultant impact upon sales and profits. When changes are considered in any of these areas, the total cost of the proposed change must reflect the benefit of increased profits as well as the added cost of lost profits due to the service level changes.

The relationship between production and logistics stems from the physical supply activities which support the production process. More specifically, the production department is the customer for the raw materials required for manufacturing. The movement and storage functions establish a quality of service that will impact the cost of production. If goods are late or not available for use, the production line may be forced to stop. Most firms recognize that the cost of stopping the production line is extremely high, and that the potential total cost associated with low supply levels is also very high. Accordingly, the logistics decisions are made in such a manner as to assure high service levels and virtually no shortages.

Another total cost impact of logistics and production deals with the length of the production run and the amount of inventory generated. Cost trade-offs exist between long production runs that result in low production costs and the corresponding high inventory and inventory carrying costs. The length of the production run is determined by examining the total cost of the average production costs and the inventory holding costs at various levels of production.

The total cost concept of logistics provides an analytical framework for considering the impact of logistics decisions. Decisions in an area of logistics such as transportation have a cost trade-off effect with other areas of logistics and of the firm. The minimization of total logistics costs is the objective of logistics.

Conclusion

Transportation is an important and pervasive element in our society. As individuals living in an industrial society, we are highly dependent upon transportation to move goods from production points to consumption points. Transportation affects everyone's life-style, from where we work, live, and play to the people with whom we come in contact and the goods we consume. Transportation directly influences the location of industrial facilities, the extent of the market area served from a facility, and the pricing strategy utilized by firms. This chapter addressed the impact of transportation upon the users—passengers and shippers of freight. The business logistics approach to the management of the transportation function was also considered.

Study Questions

1. What are the major factors considered by firms today when evaluating new plant sites? Would the basis for decision be any different for a steel plant versus a computer assembly operation?

2. What present day tools of application for plant location analysis were provided by von Thunen, Weber and Hoover?

3. Soda bottling plants and bread bakeries have what in common. How is their location analysis different?

4. How might the elimination of: (a) blanket rates, and (b) in-transit rates change the location of some industries?

5. How does break-bulk distribution help extend a firm's market sphere?

6. Why is it important for a traffic manager in a manufacturing firm to be closely coordinated with the company's sales and pricing managers?

7. Distinguish between: (a) FOB origin, (b) FOB destination, (c) zone pricing, and (d) uniform price for all buyers.

8. What role has transportation played in business logistics?

9. Why would a logistics manager knowingly select a form of transportation that is higher in cost than one currently being used by his firm?

Notes

1. C.M. Warnerburg, trans., and Peter Hall, ed., *Von Thunen's Isolated State* (Oxford: Pergamon Press, 1966), p. 37.

2. Carl J. Friedrich, trans., *Alfred Weber's Theory of the Location of Industries* (Chicago: University of Chicago Press, 1929), p. 54.

3. John J. Coyle and Edward J. Bardi, *The Management of Business Logistics*, 2d ed. (St. Paul: West Publishing, 1980), pp. 294-99.

4. Edgar M. Hoover, *The Location of Economic Activity* (New York: McGraw-Hill, 1948), pp. 51-53.

5. See Robert B. Fetter and Winston C. Dalleck, *Decision Models for Inventory Management* (Homewood, Illinois: Richard D. Irwin, 1961), and August Losch, *Die Raumliche Ordnungder Wirtschaft* (Jena: Gustav Fischerverlag, 1940).

6. Coyle and Bardi, *Management of Business Logistics*, p. 6.

Suggested Readings

Coyle, John J., and Bardi, Edward J. *The Management of Business Logistics.* 2d ed. St. Paul: West Publishing Company, 1980, chap. 1.

Fair, Marvin L., and Williams, Jr., Ernest W. *Transportation and Logistics.* 3rd ed. rev. Plano, Texas: Business Publications, 1981, chaps. 2, 3, 4 and 5.

Friedrich, Carl J. *Alfred Weber's Theory of the Location of Industries.* Chicago: University of Chicago Press, 1929.

Greenhut, Melvin L. *Plant Location in Theory and Practice.* Chapel Hill, N.C.: University of North Carolina Press, 1956, pts. 1 and 2.

Hazard, John L. *Transportation: Management, Economics, Policy.* Cambridge, Md.: Cornell Maritime Press, 1977, chap. 2.

Heskett, James L.; Glaskowsky, Jr., Nicolas A.; and Ivie, Robert M. *Business Logistics: Physical Distribution and Materials Management.* 2d ed. New York: Ronald Press Company, 1973, chaps. 1 and 2.

Hoover, Edward M. *The Location of Economic Activity.* New York: McGraw-Hill Book Company, 1948.

Sampson, Roy J., and Farris, Martin T. *Domestic Transportation.* 4th ed. Boston: Houghton Mifflin Company, 1979, chaps. 3, 14 and 15.

Taff, Charles A. *Management of Physical Distribution and Transportation.* 6th ed. Homewood, Ill.: Richard D. Irwin, 1978, chaps. 1, 2 and 8.

Warnerburg, C.M. trans., and Hall, Peter, ed. *Von Thunen's Isolated State.* Oxford: Permagon Press, 1966.

Case   ### Sure-Fine Foods

Les Ford is a traffic analyst for Sure-Fine Foods, a vegetable canning firm with plants in Kansas City and Denver. His firm ships products "FOB the customer" which means Sure-Fine pays freight charges on all outbound shipments. Customers in nearby states pay the same amount for the goods that the customers pay in far away states. Sure-Fine's top management has felt that this uniform pricing scheme is one of the primary reasons the firm has remained competitive over the years.

Problems arose from time to time as customers wished to pick up their own purchases in their own trucks that were returning from hauls empty. Sure-Fine could not offer these firms discounts or freight allowances, because the Robinson-Patman Act prohibited special allowances to any one customer. Since this was the case, the customers were hauling their own freight but were paying for the freight charges anyway. In 1980, Congress passed the Federal Motor Carrier Act which for the first time permitted shippers to provide allowances to customers who pick up food products in their own vehicles when such goods are sold on a delivered price basis. Section 10732 of the Revised Interstate Commerce Act now reads as follows:

(a) Notwithstanding any other provisions of law, it shall not be unlawful for a seller of food and grocery products using a uniform zone delivered pricing system to compensate a customer who picks up purchased food and grocery products at the shipping point of the seller if such compensation is available to all customers of the seller on a nondiscriminatory basis and does not exceed the actual cost to the seller of delivery to such customer.

Les's problem deals with two customers who have notified his office that they wish to routinely take advantage of the new allowance. One firm is located about fifty miles away from the Kansas City plant, the point from which all of its products are shipped. The other customer is in Boston. Sure-Fine's sale price per case of food in question is $11.00. Of that, the transportation factor for national distribution is $3.00, and the sales and profit price is $8.00. The customer near the Kansas City plant is using private carriage; Les calculates the customer cost at $.50 per case. The Boston customer wishes an allowance of $4.75 which is the normal transportation charge from Kansas City to Boston.

Les's boss is expecting an analysis of this new law from him, as well as suggestions as to how to treat these two customer requests. What should he suggest?

Part II

Basic Modes of Transportation

3   Rail Carriers

After reading this chapter you should:

1   Understand the role of rail carriers in the total U.S. transportation system.
2   Be able to discuss the economic and operating characteristics of rail carriers.
3   Understand the important rail carrier service characteristics relevant to the users.
4   Be able to discuss the railroad system and its financial and managerial problems.

Throughout its history, the United States has viewed transportation as vital to the well-being of commerce, and for nearly a century railroads commanded the dominant position in the U.S. transport system. Rail transportation played a significant role in the economic development of the nation. The establishment of a transcontinental railway link in 1869 contributed to the population migration to the land west of the Mississippi, because expansion was no longer dependent on U. S. inland waterways.

■ historic role

Since the turn of the century, however, the railroad industry has declined. This decline has been well documented and can be attributed to the following events: the rise of alternate transport modes, primarily motor carriers and pipelines, and a resurgence of water transportation. In 1979, railroads transported only 37 percent of the total ton-miles transported by all modes, approximately 38 percent less than in 1929.[1] Railroads have also experienced a steady drop in their rate of return on investment (ROI), from 5.3 percent in 1929 to 2.7 percent in 1979.[2]

■ relative position in total system

In this chapter, the declining role of railroad transportation, the strengths and problems of the industry, and its overall condition, railroad revenues and costs, and the industry's service characteristics will be discussed in detail.

■ chapter overview

Industry Overview

■ class I carriers

U. S. railroads are classified as privately owned common carriers (Conrail and Amtrak are major exceptions). As a common carrier, a railroad must serve the general public. The industry is also composed of several classes of railroads. The Class 1 railroads, as of 1978, are those carriers that have at least $50 million in operating revenues. In addition, in 1978 these railroads had $30 billion in net investment and they represented about 98 percent of the total amount of rail traffic carried and 94 percent of total rail mileage.[3]

The U. S. railroad industry was composed of approximately 150 terminal and switching companies, as of 1979, and 300 line-haul firms, of which 41 were classified as Class 1 reporting railroads. During the pe-

number of carriers

riod 1929-1979, the number of Class 1 railroads was reduced from 162 to 41 (see Table 3.1), a dramatic loss that indicates the considerable change in the railroad industry in the last fifty years. In addition to a reduction in the number of railroads in existence, a shrinkage in line mileage occurred during the same fifty-year period (see Table 3.1). Line mileage expanded rapidly during the initial construction period 1830-1910 and reached a peak at 254,251 miles in 1916.[4] By 1929, line mileage was down to 249,433, and in 1979 had been further reduced to 190,180. This reduction is traceable largely to the abandonment of the duplicate trackage that was built during the "boom" periods of the industry's developmental years.

Figure 3.1 is a map describing the present railroad system of the United States. At the beginning of 1979, there were 190,555 miles of railroad lines (the aggregate length of all line-haul railroads) and 310,000 miles of track, with the greatest concentration in the industrial Northeast as well as the agricultural Midwest.

freight tonnage

In 1979, as indicated, the railroads shipped less than 37 percent of all ton-miles moved by all transport modes in the United States. This percentage of total ton-miles has been declining since its peak of 75 percent in 1929. However, actual ton-miles moved by the railroads has been steadily increasing. In 1979, approximately 913 billion ton-miles of freight were moved—an industry record.[5] These figures highlight the fact that even though railroads continue to move a record amount of goods, they are capturing less of the total transportation market because the other modes are growing even faster.

Service Characteristics

The decline in use of railroad transportation can be traced partly to the problems associated with the service characteristics of the line-haul firms. These characteristics are important factors in determining the competitive posture of the railroad system in relation to other forms of transportation. Historically, the industry has been troubled with prob-

Table 3.1 The Number of Railroads and Line Mileage (1929-1979)

Year	Class 1 Reporting Railroads*[a]	Railroad Line Mileage[b]
1929	162	249,433
1939	132	235,064
1949	128	224,511
1959	108	217,565
1969	75	207,526
1973	68	201,585
1976	52	192,396
1979	41	190,180

[a]Association of American Railroads, *Railroad Transportation: A Statistical Record 1921-1959*, 1960; also by the same author, *Yearbook of Railroad Facts*, editions for 1969, 1973, 1976, 1979.
[b]Transportation Association of America, *Transportation Facts and Trends*, 16th ed. (Washington, D.C., 1980), p. 31.
*$50,000,000 in operating revenues as of January 1, 1978.

Figure 3.1 Railroad Network

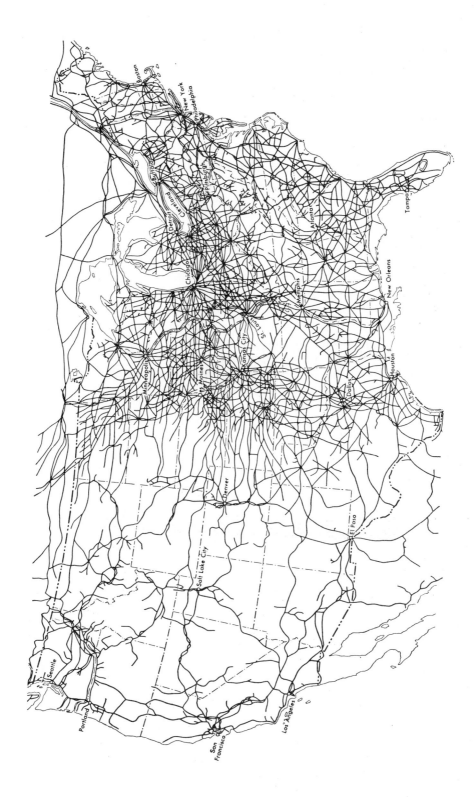

Source: Association of American Railroads, Washington, D.C.

lems of service and speed quality, a carry-over from the days when rail-roads possessed a virtual monopoly on inland transportation and were able to extract quasi-monopoly profits from the public while offering inferior levels of service.

■ service constraints

Railroads are constrained by fixed right-of-ways and therefore pro-vide differing degrees of service completeness. For example, if both the shipper and receiver possess railroad sidings, then door-to-door service can be provided. However, if no sidings are available, the movement of goods must be completed by some other mode. If line-haul mileage con-tinues to decline (as is indicated by current industrial trends), the indus-try will become less service complete and even more dependent upon other means of transport for the completion of many types of moves.

■ nationwide
network

The railroad system, unlike motor, air, or water transport, provides a truly nationwide network of service. Each railroad serves a specific geo-graphic region, and freight and equipment are automatically exchanged at interchange points. For example, a shipment between Philadelphia, Pennsylvania and Portland, Oregon might be handled by several different railroads depending upon the route chosen. Table 3.2 shows that 50 percent of railroad carloads were handled by two or more carriers in 1976. This through service is unique; however, multiple handlings can create rate division problems and delays in delivery.

■ recent improvement

Although on-time delivery performance and frequency of service have deteriorated in the past, recent years have shown some signs of im-provement. The current position of the industry has been restored to competitive levels on certain movements (particularly over long dis-tances). Railroads dominate the market for hauling 30,000 pounds or more over distances exceeding 300 miles. The industry hopes to expand its service to certain short-haul markets.[6]

■ carrying capacity

A large carrying capacity enables the railroads to handle large volume movements of low value commodities over long distances. Motor carri-ers, on the other hand, are constrained by volume and weight to the smaller truckload (TL) and less-than-truckload (LTL) markets. Furthermore, although pipelines compete directly with the railroads, they are restricted largely to the movements of liquid and gas (and then only in one direction).

■ equipment
flexibility

This kind of carload capacity, along with a variety of car types, permits the railroads to handle almost any type of commodity. For the most part, the industry is not constrained by weight and volume restrictions, and customer service is available throughout the United States. In addition,

Table 3.2 Multiple Car Handlings by Railroads in 1976

Number Of Cars	% Of Total Carloads
1	50
2	33
3	15
4 or more	2
Total	100

Source: Association of American Railroads, Washington, D.C.

railroads are able to utilize a variety of car types to provide a flexible service since the rolling stock consists of: boxcars, tankers, gondolas, hoppers, covered hoppers, flatcars, stockcars, and other special types of cars.

■ liability

Another important service characteristic is that the liability for loss and damage is completely assumed by the railroads. Railroads, however, have had a comparatively high percentage of goods damaged in transit (about 3 percent total tonnage shipped). Such damage occurs because rail freight often undergoes a rough trip due to vibrations and shocks (steel wheel on steel rail). In addition, the incidence of loss is usually higher than on other modes because of the high degree of multiple handlings. Excessive loss and damage claims have tended to erode shipper confidence in the railroad's ability to provide adequate service.

■ service innovations

In an attempt to attract more traffic, the railroad industry has been developing several service innovations, including TOFC and COFC movements (trailer-on-flatcar and container-on-flatcar), unit and run-through trains, and various rate schemes. Hopefully, such customer service programs will help revitalize the industry by allowing railroads to either expand into new markets or to recapture old ones.

Revenue

■ ROI

■ revenue position

Railroad ROI has been declining for many years as shown in Table 3.3. In 1979, the ROI was 2.7 percent—hardly a healthy figure in today's investment market. A summary of revenue measurements for Class I railroads for selected years 1929-1979 shows that revenue levels have also been unsatisfactory.

The total railroad operating revenue reached a record of $25.7 billion in 1979, up from $6.3 billion in 1929. This growth, however, is hardly satisfactory when the impact of inflation upon our economy is considered. If we use the implicit gross national product (GNP) price deflators of the U.S. Department of Commerce and convert past revenues to 1972

Table 3.3 Class 1 Railroad Revenue Trends (1929-1979)

Year	Operating Revenue (000,000)	Operating Ratio	Revenue Per Ton-Mile (Cents)	ROI (%)
1929	6,279.5	71.8	1.1	5.3
1939	3,995.0	73.0	1.0	2.6
1949	8,850.1	77.9	1.3	2.9
1959	9,825.1	78.4	1.4	2.7
1969	11,450.3	79.2	1.3	2.4
1973	14,795.8	78.1	1.6	2.3
1976	18,559.7	80.5	2.2	1.6
1979	25,714.1	95.3*	2.6	2.7

Source: Association of American Railroads, *Yearbook of Railroad Facts*, 1980 ed. (Washington, D.C., 1980), pp. 12, 15, 20, and 33.

* Expense data for the operation ratio in 1979 has been revised to include rents and taxes, other than income taxes as required under the new U.S.O.A., effective January 1, 1978.

constant dollars, we find that railroad revenues actually declined from an adjusted 1929 figure of $14.7 billion to $13 billion in 1976.[1]

The operating ratio for railroads has been increasing throughout the years (see Table 3.3). This percentage rise indicates that operating expenses have been rising faster than operating revenues and that the ratio itself is fast approaching that of other transport modes. The relative decline in the operating margin (the percentage difference between revenues and expenses) suggests that the railroad industry could find it difficult to meet some of its long-term financial obligations in the future.

■ revenue per ton-mile

Included in Table 3.3 are figures for the average revenue per ton-mile. These figures illustrate the changes in average freight charges for traffic handled in a particular year. In 1979, 2.6¢ were received for every ton-mile handled, up from 1.1¢ in 1929. The percentage increase in revenue per ton-mile for the period 1929-1979 was 136 percent, while inflation raised prices more than 400 percent during the same period. This suggests that even though the railroads carried a record amount of freight, the revenues generated by this increase in ton-mileage have been eroded by escalating prices and expenses.

■ ROI decline

ROI, a common yardstick used in choosing among different investment projects, has been declining since the turn of the century. In 1979, ROI was just 2.7 percent. ROI is also used to determine a company's, or an industry's, access to capital markets. The railroad industry has failed to exceed 5 percent ROI ever since World War II, whereas ROI for U. S. industries in general exceeds 10 percent. As a result, many railroads, but not all, have experienced capital shortages because of poor earning performance. If the trend continues, the railroad industry will face continued financial difficulties in the future.

Cost Structure

The railroad industry's cost structure in the short run (a period in which both plant and capacity remain constant) consists of a large proportion of indirect fixed costs rather than variable costs.[8] This situation exists because the railroads, along with the pipelines, are the only modes that own and maintain their own network and terminals. In addition, railroads, like the other modes, operate their own rolling stocks. In the past it had been estimated by some managers that up to two-thirds of the industry's costs did not vary with volume.[9] Today, it is believed that this figure is closer to 30 percent. This investment in long-lived assets has had a major impact on the cost characteristics of the industry. Cost structures will be discussed in more detail in a later chapter on costs and rates.

■ level of fixed costs

The major cost element borne by the railroad industry, and not found in the cost structure of other modes (excluding pipelines), is the operation, maintenance, and ownership of right-of-ways. Initially, a large capital investment is required and annual maintenance costs become a substantial drain on earnings. Capital expenditures in 1979 alone amounted to $3.3 billion.[10]

■ impact of right-of-ways

■ terminal facilities

Another major component of the railroad industry's high fixed costs are the extensive investments in private terminal facilities. These terminal facilities include freight yards, where trains are sorted and assembled, and terminal areas and sidings, where shippers and connecting railroads are serviced. Railroad passenger stations may also be included in this category if they are not subsidized by public authorities.

■ comparison
to other modes

Because of the large amount of fixed assets, the railroads as a group are not as responsive as other modes to the volume of traffic carried. Motor and water carriers, as well as the airline industry, are able to shift resources faster in response to changes in consumer demand because of their use of "free" right-of-ways. Motor carriers, for instance, pay for their costs through user charges, tolls, and various taxes (e.g., gasoline taxes). These charges are related and vary directly with the volume handled, thereby creating a variable rather than a fixed cost for the user. These circumstances place the railroads at a disadvantage.

■ equipment investment

The investment for equipment in rail transport, principally for locomotives and various types of rolling stock, has been enormous. In 1979, over $2.3 billion was spent on equipment. The Class 1 railroads operated 28,186 diesel electric locomotives and 1,217,079 freight cars.[11] In addition, other railroads, car companies, and shippers owned or leased about one-half million cars. The costs associated with equipment are both fixed and variable depending upon which costs are used and what time period is being considered.

It is apparent from our discussion that the railroads have a high proportion of expenses that are fixed and constant in the short run. However they also have costs that vary substantially with volume; these expenses will be discussed in the next section.

Cost Elements

■ variable cost

The cost elements of major concern to the railroad industry in the short run are the variable and semivariable costs of operation. Expenditures for fuel and labor are two examples of the many important variable costs that railway management must deal with. Furthermore, the expenses that are semivariable in nature are also very distinct. In 1979, semivariable costs, which included maintenance of way, structures, and equipment, accounted for 44.3 percent of total railroad outlays and amounted to $10.9 billion. These expenses increased by almost 15 percent over the previous year with $4.7 billion being used for the preservation of the way, while $6.2 billion was consumed in the upkeep of equipment.

■ maintenance
expense

These figures, however, are deceptive because they hide the fact that many railroads, because of their poor financial health, have allowed their physical plant and equipment to deteriorate at alarming rates. In fact, the Federal Railroad Administration estimated that over the past several years the industry has deferred more than $4 billion in maintenance expenses.[12] Railway management found it necessary to forgo maintenance in order to pay other pressing expenses, such as increased fuel and labor. If maintenance is not implemented on a regular basis, service could further deteriorate, and additional business would then be lost. If the railroads are to remain viable over the long run, they must not allow maintenance deferment.

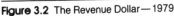
revenue proportion

Variable costs are one of the immediate concerns of railroad management, accounting for a large proportion of every revenue dollar spent by the railways. The division of the revenue dollar in 1979 is shown in Figure 3.2. The wage and tax category of labor dominates the distribution of operation revenues; fuel and power costs are the next largest group.

The total cost of labor was $12.7 billion or 55.8¢ of every revenue dollar in 1979. Average hourly gross earnings for all employees was $9.25, with an average annual earnings of $22,585.[13] Train and engine employees received average annual earnings of $26,982, while maintenance workers received approximately $19,900.[14]

wage expense

Together, these groups accounted for over 72 percent of the average wage dollar in 1979. It is also important to note that railroad employees receive, on the average, about 30 percent higher wages than their counterparts in the private sector.[15] Most managers believe that if railroads are to survive, major efforts to lower wage rates to the national average or changes in the work rules must be made.

fuel expense

Fuel and power costs have been steadily rising over the past ten years. In 1979, $2.4 billion was spent on fuel and power for locomotives—this represented 9.4 percent of the total operating revenue. As shown in Figure 3.2, fuel costs make up the second largest percentage of the revenue dollar. Fortunately, railroads have very efficient propulsion units, and productivity and fuel efficiency have increased dramatically since 1929. In the past fifty years, the railroads have more than doubled the revenue of ton-miles while reducing the locomotive units to less than one-half of 1929 levels. Thus, the industry has been able to partially offset the increase in fuel costs by making locomotives more efficient.

Overall, variable and semivariable costs are becoming more significant in rail transportation. The importance of these costs has some

Figure 3.2 The Revenue Dollar—1979

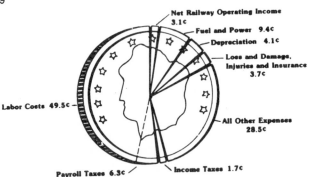

Source: Association of American Railroads, *Yearbook of Railroad Facts*, 1980 ed. (Washington, D.C.: 1980), p. 11.

implications for the number of carloadings handled and shipped by the carriers. These implications will be discussed in the next section.

Carloadings and Car Types

■ trend

■ increase in capacity

■ specialized nature

Railroad carloadings totaled 23.9 million in 1979.[16] The carload is the basic unit of measurement of freight handled by the railroads. A carload can vary in size and capacity depending on the type of car being utilized. Historically, the number of carloadings has declined since the turn of the century; there was almost a total of 53 million carloadings in 1929. This decline has primarily occurred because of the introduction of larger cars and the increase in productivity per car type.

The increases in average carrying capacity of railroad freight cars over the past fifty years have been dramatic. In 1979, the average carrying capacity per car stood at 78.8 tons, compared to 46.3 tons in 1929. Most of today's new cars have more than twice the capacity of the typical boxcar used fifty years ago. However, the carrying capacity of a new or rebuilt freight car could easily exceed 100 tons and the trend of increasing average capacity will continue in the near future. However, the 100-ton capacity probably represents the most efficient size with the present support facilities.

As mentioned earlier, the railroads own and maintain their own rolling stock. The characteristics of these cars have changed considerably to suit customer requirements, for example the conventional boxcar has been de-emphasized. Today's car fleet is highly specialized and is designed to meet the needs of the individual shipper.

Following is a list of eight generalized car types:

Boxcar (plain)	Standardized roofed freight car with sliding doors on the side used for general commodities.
Boxcar (equipped)	Specially modified boxcar used for specialized merchandise, such as automobile parts.
Hopper car	A freight car with the floor sloping to one or more hinged doors used for discharging bulk materials.
Covered Hopper Car	A hopper car with a roof designed for the transport of bulk commodities which need protection from the elements.
Flat Car	A freight car with no top or sides used primarily for TOFC service.
Refrigerator Car	A freight car to which refrigeration equipment has been added for controlled temperature.
Gondola Car	A freight car with no top, a flat bottom, and fixed sides used primarily for hauling heavy bulk commodities.
Tank Car	Specialized car used for the transport of liquids and gases.

■ fleet makeup

The total number and percentage of freight cars in service in 1979 is shown in Table 3.4. The plain boxcar has been surpassed by the hopper car and is followed closely in number by the covered hopper car. In addition, the largest increase in total new cars was covered hopper cars, up 38,870 from 1976. The composition of the railroad fleet has shifted from the accommodation of manufactured commodities to the movement of bulk goods. In 1979, over 60 percent of the total fleet was designed for the transport of bulk and raw materials.

Class 1 railroads own almost 72 percent of the rolling stock in use, while private companies hold title to 23 percent and the other classes of railroads make up the rest (see Table 3.4). Car companies and shippers are becoming increasingly more important in the ownership of railroad cars. In 1979, they owned almost all of the specially designed tank cars in use, and in the last three years they have purchased a substantial number of covered hopper cars, over 28,800 or 73 percent of all new cars of this type.

■ ownership

To remain competitive with the other modes, the railroads have increased their capacity to about 134 million tons—an industry record. The average freight train load also has increased; in 1979 over 2,000 tons were carried as compared to barely 800 tons in 1929.[17] This increase in capacity will be necessary if more bulk commodities are to be shipped longer distances in the future.

Commodities Shipped

■ trend overview

When the railroads were the primary source of transportation in the 19th century, they moved almost every available type of product or raw material. Today, the railroad system has evolved into a system that ships large quantities of heavy weight, low value commodities (bulk products). Motor carriers, on the other hand, concentrate on the handling of small

Table 3.4 Types and Number of Freight Cars in Service in 1979

Type	% Of Total	Total Number	Class 1 Railroad	Other Railroads	Car Companies And Shippers
Boxcars					
Plain	16.1	274,002	210,426	44,544	19,032
Equipped	10.5	179,217	109,220	9,771	226
Hopper cars	21.0	356,504	329,479	13,267	17,758
Covered hoppers	15.8	268,919	164,959	5,317	98,643
Flat cars	8.9	151,377	99,342	4,649	47,386
Refrigerator cars	4.8	81,266	64,924	3,392	12,950
Gondola cars	10.5	178,979	154,629	7,150	17,200
Tank cars	10.5	178,069	2,310	189	175,670
Other freight cars	1.9	31,977	25,790	3,248	2,939
Total	100	1,700,310	1,217,079	91,427	391,804

Source: Association of American Railroads, *Yearbook of Railroad Facts,* 1980 ed. (Washington, D.C., 1980), p. 50.

Table 3.5 Commodities With More Than One Million Carloadings In 1979

Commodity	Carloadings (000)	% of Total Carloadings	Cumulative % of Total
Coal	5,254	22.0	22.0
Metallic ores	1,765	7.4	29.4
Chemical and allied products	1,488	6.2	35.6
Grain	1,428	6.0	41.6
Motor vehicles and equipment	1,122	4.7	46.3
Pulp, paper, and allied products	1,097	4.6	50.9
Primary forest products	1,055	4.4	55.3

Source: Association of American Railroads, *Yearbook of Railroad Facts*, 1980 ed. (Washington, D.C., 1980), p. 26.

volume, high value finished goods, while water and pipelines carry the larger volumes of the lowest value types of bulk commodities. The railroads, therefore, find themselves engaged in intense competition with these other modes for the opportunity to ship many product categories.

■ variety

While railroads still handle a wide variety of commodities, more than 60 percent of total rail carloadings in 1979 involved the movement of bulk materials. Table 3.5 lists the products with more than 1 million carloadings carried by the railroads. Of the seven commodities shown in the table, only one, motor vehicles and equipment, is not a bulk commodity. Four other bulk commodity groups shipped by the railroads had just under one million carloadings.[18]

Bulk commodities are shipped most often by rail. Of the products moved, coal is the largest by far, followed by metallic ores and chemicals. Grain movements, ranking fourth, have increased at a significant rate in recent years, while the transport of motor vehicles has declined. In fact, only 9 of the 21 revenue groups increased from the 1978 levels.

■ coal tonnage

As mentioned above, railroads are the primary haulers of coal, accounting for approximately 75 percent of the total coal tonnage transported. In addition, coal constitutes almost one-third of the total tonnage handled by the railways. Its share of carloadings, which comprises more than one out of every five rail freight cars loaded in 1979, represents a marked change in transport. Table 3.5 indicates that 5.3 million carloadings took place, up by over 800 thousand from 1978 levels. Furthermore, rail coal traffic is concentrated in just a few railroads with four firms handling over 60 percent of the rail car tonnage.[19] This means that coal, because of its use as an alternative energy source, will continue to grow in importance and will probably remain the dominant commodity shipped by the railroads.

metallic ores

Metallic ores have also increased in total railroad carloadings. As a raw material input, metallic ores, used primarily in the production of steel (one of the leading indicators of the nation's industrial development), have increased in rail carloadings by 17 percent over 1976 levels. Table 3.5 shows that metallic ores comprise 7.4 percent of total rail carloadings. Domestic ores, which are produced from older mines, are generally of a lower grade, and they have to be supplemented by the increased transport of high quality iron ore imports. However, regardless of origin, iron ore distribution and movements should remain one of the key components of the railroad industry's commodity base.

chemicals

Chemicals and allied products, a great number of which are classified as "hazardous" by the U. S. Department of Transportation (DOT), are transported in specially designed tank cars. Most of this material is carried long distances (over 500 miles) in 180,000 privately owned tank cars. One hundred million tons of this highly rated traffic, or 1.5 million rail carloadings, traveled by rail in 1979. The railroads, in comparison with highway movements, safely transport chemicals, and this safety record has been steadily increasing for years. This type of long haul bulk material is ideally suited for rail movement.

grain

Grain and grain mill products, when considered together, constitute the second largest commodity group hauled by railroads. Total grain movement by rail amounted to 1.4 million carloadings in 1979, while grain mill products reached 900 thousand. The growth in domestic markets and the increase of exports to foreign consumers have been steady for many years. In fact, the exportation of grain and its related products accounted for over 55 percent of the total grain market in 1979. Because of this growth, distribution patterns might change, but the transportation of this high volume bulk material will keep grain an important rail commodity.

autos

Automobile rail carloadings, which are linked to the relative health of the domestic automotive industry, have decreased to 4.7 percent of total carloadings, down 0.6 percent in just three years. The total market share of automobile carriage has fallen sharply because of increased motor competition. However, completely redesigned rail cars, which protect against vandalism, pilferage, and the elements, will enable the railroads to recapture some of their lost market share.

Although the commodities shipped by the railroad industry have changed over the years, and the emphasis is now placed on the movement of low value, high volume bulk materials, the railroads are still the ideal mode of transport for many different types of goods, high value merchandise and raw materials alike. Figure 3.3 indicates projected traffic flows for 1990.

Economies of Scale

The railroad industry's cost structure, as previously indicated, contains a relatively high level of fixed costs along with substantial investments in plant and equipment. Economies of scale, or the long-term forces that lead to increased productivity when total cost of production decreases

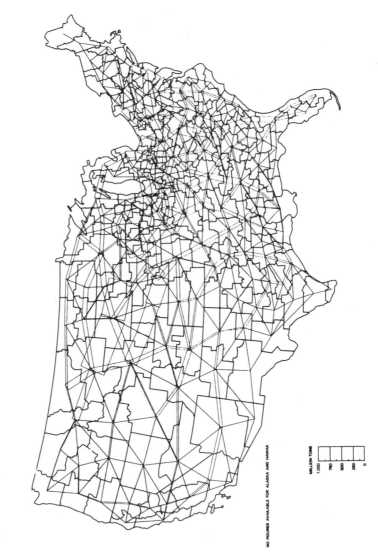

Figure 3.3 Projected Rail Traffic Flows for 1990

Source: U.S. Department of Transportation, *National Transportation Trends and Choices* (Washington, D.C.: Government Printing Office, 1977), p. 209.

■ rationale

on a per unit basis (as volume increases), are present in the railroad industry as evidenced by the emergence of a small number of larger railroads. Economies arise through equipment and managerial specialization as well as through the use of large, high volume vehicles. However, these large carriers need high and regular volumes of traffic to obtain the degree of efficiency needed to remain price and service competitive. Consequently, railroad management has developed a number of service innovations especially designed to take advantage of these economies.

■ TOFC and COFC

The concept of piggyback service was designed by railroad management to increase the service levels to intermodal customers. Piggyback traffic, which includes both TOFC (trailer on flat car) and COFC (container on flat car) service, accounted for 7.8 percent of total loadings in 1979, occupying 1.9 million rail cars and ranking second behind coal in total rail carloadings. When discussing piggyback service, consideration must be given to the individual concepts of TOFC and COFC movements.

■ explanation of TOFC services

TOFC service transports highway trailers on railroad flatcars. It combines the line-haul efficiencies of railroads with the flexibility of local motor pickup and delivery service. On-time deliveries, regularly scheduled departures, and fuel efficiency are the major reasons for the present growth and future potential of TOFC service. For example, a 100-car TOFC train (which places two truck trailers on each flat car) is more economical to run than 200 trucks over the road. Fuel is saved and railroad economies of scale are realized. Traffic congestion, road damage, and maintenance and repair costs are all reduced because of the reduction of the number of trucks out on the highways. Listed below are the seven standard TOFC plans, each providing coordinated intermodal transportation services; the trailers or tractors could be either rail, motor, shipper, or consignee owned.

1. Plan I—A railroad hauls the trailers of a motor common carrier while the motor carrier handles the ramp-to-door service at both ends.

2. Plan II—A railroad transports and provides door-to-door service for its own trailers.

3. Plan II¼—A railroad provides trailers, service, and either door-to-ramp or ramp-to-door motor service.

4. Plan II½—A railroad provides trailers, flatcars, and rail transportation while the shipper and consignee arrange motor pickup and delivery from the ramps.

5. Plan III—A railroad provides line-haul transportation and the shipper/consignee handles the ramp-to-door service of its own trailers.

6. Plan IV—A railroad provides line-haul transportation with the shipper providing door-to-door service of its own trailers.

7. Plan V—A railroad or common carrier provides the trailers, pickup, or delivery, with the railroad providing the line-haul transportation.[20]

Plan II½ is the most widely utilized, and it alone accounted for over one-half of all the trailers or containers shipped in 1977.[21]

■ COFC service

COFC is the international form of transportation of containers and is equivalent to domestic TOFC movements. A container does not have wheels and must therefore be placed on a flatbed truck for ramp-to-door delivery. The amount of handling is reduced as a container can be loaded and sealed at the origin and shipped directly to the consignee. Economies are realized because putting finished goods in containers means not only lower packaging and warehousing costs, but also faster transit times since time and effort are saved in the loading, unloading, and delivery of goods. In addition, the TOFC piggyback plans can apply to COFC shipments with the substitution of the container for the trailer in the movement. Furthermore, land-bridge traffic, which substitutes railroads for ocean vessels for part of the journey, has become more widely used in international commerce because it facilitates the handling of export/import commodities.

■ unit trains

The unit train, which evolved from the rent-a-train concept for the movement of goods, specializes in the transport of only one commodity, usually coal or grain, from origin to destination. Many times the shipper owns the cars, and the train is, in effect, rented to the particular shipper for a certain period of time. For example, a typical utility coal unit train move would involve the transportation of ten thousand tons of coal in 100 hopper or gondola cars, each with 100-ton capacities. The movement would be directly from the mine to an electric power-generating station with no stops in transit, and loading and unloading is accomplished while the train is moving. Because of the single commodity nature of the concept and the need to maintain regularly scheduled movements, empty back-hauls occur. However, this drawback is offset by the high revenue-producing capabilities of the unit train resulting from the improved overall car utilization.

■ other factors

The scale economies of the railroad industry have brought about the division and specialization of labor. Rail management has responded by increasing its use of computers and electric communications in order to help improve discipline and maintain control over rail operations. Elaborate information and communication systems have been developed so that a railroad's progress, status, and reliability can be monitored on an on-line basis. Car ordering and billing are simplified. Cars are traced and located, and orders are expedited at a faster rate. Computers are not a panacea, but they do help bring about increased efficiencies without any loss in service quality.

■ mergers

Historically, there have been many mergers in the railroad industry, and the size of the remaining carriers has correspondingly increased. Early rail mergers were formed to expand capacity in order to benefit from large volume traffic efficiencies and economies. Later, side-by-side combinations were made to strengthen the financial positions of many of the individual railroads. More recently though, end-to-end mergers were created to provide more effective inter and intramodal competition.[22] In fact, a presidential task force on railroad productivity stated that "the industry should be restructured into four or five continental systems that operate and compete . . . independently of other railroads and (they) would create effective intramodal competition in all the major regions of the country."[23] Customer service and reliability would be improved by these mergers, since the many types of operating costs, such as car switching, and clerical costs, such as record keeping, would be brought under control.

■ abandonment

Abandonment of significant portions of rail trackage was brought about by the lack of economies of density associated with overexpansion. Extensive amounts of excess trackage existed in many areas, and a contraction of the rail network was necessary for the railroads to remain competitive. Parallel and overlapping routes, therefore, have been eliminated wherever possible. As previously shown in Table 3.1, railroad line mileage has decreased by 24 percent since 1929. Table 3.6 shows the number and rate of railroad abandonment applications during the period 1929 to 1976. The percentage of approvals has been low until recently because of significant public opposition. The 4R Act to be discussed in Chapter 17 has had a profound effect on the number of abandonment applications and the adjudication process. The net result has been a sharply increased rate of approval. However, a report prepared for the U. S. DOT found that little economic hardship resulted from rail line abandonments because motor service was able to fill whatever vacuum the railroads left behind.[24]

Overall, economies of scale are present among railroads because of the large amount of fixed costs. These economies have important implications in determining the industry's competitive position.

Competition

The competitive position of the railroad industry has dramatically changed. The railroad was the dominant mode of transportation at the turn of the century; now the industry is faced with intense intra and intermodal competition. Consolidations within the industry have created a situation in which 98 percent of the traffic is handled by only forty-one Class 1 railroads. In addition, the railways compete with the other modes of transportation which have either evolved or matured since the 1920s. The industry's economic structure has developed into a fine example of a differentiated oligopoly.

■ oligopolistic nature of industry

Today, only a few railroads service a particular geographic location. Oligopoly occurs when there are a small number of interdependent large sellers, and the actions of one member are important enough to affect the decisions of the other carriers in the market. Barriers to entry exist because of the large capital outlays and fixed costs required and, consequently, pricing can be controlled by the existing firms. For this reason, economic regulations implemented by the ICC have brought the geographic coverage and rate-making procedures of the railroads under federal scrutiny and control so that intramodal competition might be promoted. Thus, because of the need to recover many of the high fixed

Table 3.6 Railroad Line Abandonments (1929-1976)

Year	Applications Filed	Applications Granted*	Percent Granted
1929-1969	65,363	41,907	64
1970	1,762	1,782	101
1971	3,142	1,287	41
1972	3,978	3,458	87
1973	4,436	2,428	99
1974	2,247	529	24
1975	3,309	708	21
1976	1,636	1,789	109
Cumulative	85,872	53,888	63

Source: Interstate Commerce Commission, *Annual Report of the Interstate Commerce Commission, Fiscal Year Ending June 30, 1976* (Washington, D.C.: U.S. Government Printing Office, 1976).

*Applies to applications granted in the fiscal period indicated, not necessarily filed in the same year. The application process was time-consuming because of the lengthy regulatory procedure involved.

costs while maintaining the market share, regulation has forced the railroads to set rates in a very competitive fashion.

■ market share

As noted earlier, the market share of railroad intercity tonnage has been steadily declining because of increased intermodal competition. Inroads into lucrative commodity markets have been facilitated by governmental expenditures that have primarily benefited competing modes. The government has provided an extensive local and national road system, including the interstate network, for motor carrier use. In addition, through improvements and maintenance of the inland waterway system by the U. S. Army Corps of Engineers, the government has also provided the right-of-way for water carriers. Thus, because of these governmental programs and the slow response of the railroad industry to change, railways now account for only 30 percent of total tonnage and 36 percent of total ton-miles shipped, figures totaling one-half the percentage of just 50 years ago.

Overall, the railroads have been very rate-competitive. Governmental influence, either in the form of economic regulation or expenditure programs aimed at benefiting other modes, together with intermodal competition, have forced the railways into making a determined effort to forestall industry decline by becoming more competitive and consumer-oriented in the areas of price and customer service.

Legislation

Several important transport legislations were enacted in the 1970s, and the railroad industry was one of the major targets of action. The Rail Passenger Service Act of 1970 created Amtrak, the government-sponsored railroad system responsible for the intercity movement of rail passengers. In 1979, Amtrak had an operating deficit of almost $600 million.

■ Amtrak

Only a few key "corridors" (the Northeast corridor, Boston, New York, and Washington, D.C.) are profitable enough to support regularly scheduled intercity passenger service. Cutbacks in route miles and scheduled service will probably occur even though Amtrak has reversed the long-term trend of declining intercity rail passenger ridership so that Amtrak's growing federal subsidy can be controlled.

■ 3-R Act

The Regional Rail Reorganization Act of 1973 (the 3R Act) authorized federal expenditures and loan guarantees for the creation of the USRA (United States Railroad Association) and Conrail (Consolidated Rail Corporation). Conrail was created by merging several bankrupt northeastern railroads, the most important of which was the Penn-Central, into a semipublic, "for profit," operating railroad. The USRA was the government agency responsible for the planning and financing of the restructuring. By 1980, over $3.3 billion in federal subsidies were granted to Conrail by the federal government to cover operating expenses. Although Conrail has projected it will break even by 1984, the current situation must improve dramatically if the projection is to be realized.[25]

■ 4-R Act

The Rail Revitalization and Regulatory Reform Act of 1976 (the 4R Act) was chiefly concerned with regulatory reform. It provided the initial funding for Conrail as well as financial assistance to all railroads in the form of government loans or loan guarantees. The 4R Act also contained provisions for the relaxation and reform of rate regulations in addition to changes in the regulation of railroad mergers and line abandonments.

■ Staggers Rail Act

The Staggers Rail Act of 1980, which brought the rail industry closer to free-market operations, was a major piece of railroad regulatory reform. It lessens the regulatory burden placed on the railroads by providing major changes in rail rate-making. The new rate provisions are intended to promote a competitive atmosphere by offering the railroads greater flexibility in the setting of individual rates and in the marketing of certain rail services. Hopefully, this act will enable the railroads to become more profitable and competitive in the years to come.

Labor

In 1979, labor constituted the largest expense for the railroad industry, accounting for 56¢ out of every revenue dollar or a total of $12.7 billion.[26] Labor employment over the last fifty years has declined by 60 percent to just 480,000 employees in 1979. Fewer employees have been needed because the railroads have developed several labor-saving devices such as railway maintenance machinery and innovations such as centralized traffic control.

■ unions

Railroad labor is represented by twenty-eight different unions, as opposed to the trucking industry where the vast majority of employees are members of one union, the Teamsters. There are three major classifications of labor unions: operating, nonoperating craft, and nonoperating industrial. Each represents a different category of employee. The large number of unions has created problems in labor relations for railroad management because each union jealously guards its rights and allows little room for compromise.

■ work rules

Railroad management believes that several of the work rules for the operating unions are either out-of-date or inefficient. The railroad industry wants to reduce the size of the standard train crew wherever possible. Many positions such as firemen are no longer needed. In addition, the dual basis for pay for a full day's work (either eight hours or 100 miles traveled) is inefficient and excessive. Furthermore, "seniority districts," or the establishing of artificial boundaries beyond which an employee is not authorized to work, must be relaxed so that operating efficiency can be realized.

Many railroad managers feel that major changes in updating work rules for rail employees must be implemented in the near future if the industry is to survive in its present form. Impediments between labor and management which restrict productivity gains, labor-saving methods, and technological advances should be broken down and replaced by mutual trust and cooperation.

Energy

■ energy comparisons

The energy shortages of the 1970s have made the United States increasingly more aware of the need to conserve natural resources. The U.S. government has decided to reduce the quantity of fuels and petroleum products that are imported into the country. Americans also want to preserve and, wherever possible, clean up the environment. The railroads then are in a favorable position, especially when compared to motor carriers, because they are an efficient energy consumer. For instance, a train locomotive uses less fuel than a truck tractor in pulling the same amount of weight. In fact, a study supported by the National Science Foundation indicates that railroads are more energy-efficient than any other freight mode, except pipelines (see Table 3.7). Railroads are also more energy-efficient in British Thermal Units (BTUs) per ton-mile than most of the other modes because they use only 670 BTUs per ton-mile.[27] Another study by the U.S. DOT concluded that railroads are more energy-efficient than the motor carriers even when measured in terms of consumption per ton-mile.[28] Furthermore, in addition to being a superior consumer of fuel, railroads cause less damage to the environment than do trucks. In 1980, railroad emissions, 0.9 grams per net ton-mile, were 75 percent less than truck emissions.[29] Railroads, therefore, in comparison

Table 3.7 Relative Fuel Efficiency of Transportation Modes

Mode	Actual BTUs Per Ton-Mile*	Price (Cents Per Ton-Mile)	Haul Length (Miles)	Speed MPH
Pipeline	490	0.27	300	5
Railroad	670	1.40	500	20
Waterway	680	0.30	1,000	—
Truck	2,800	7.50	300	40
Airplane	42,000	21.90	1,000	400

Source: Association of American Railroads, *More Miles to the Gallon . . . The Railroads* (Washington, D.C., 1974), p. 4.

*BTUs are British Thermal Units.

■ role in moving
energy products

to trucks—a major competitor—are able to move large amounts of freight with less energy and less harm to the environment.

The railroads economically shipped 5.5 million carloads of energy-yielding products in 1979; 94 percent of these loadings were coal movements. Because coal, which can be converted into electricity, is an abundant substitute for oil, electric utility companies are trying to convert their present processes to coal whenever possible. Since the railroads already transport approximately three-quarters of all the coal moved, they will be able to increase service to the utilities and capture more of the market by utilizing high volume unit coal trains. Hence, the railroads will be an important factor in the development of the nation's energy policy.

Conclusion

A general overview of the industry shows that the railroads, while still the dominant intercity transport mode, have been in a state of decline for the past fifty years. The industry structure, which has achieved large economies of scale, has been contracting, and there are only a small number of large firms remaining in the market. The long-term cost structure of these carriers includes large numbers of fixed investments, while the day-to-day operations are dominated by labor costs. The future of the railroads could be very promising. The potential exists for efficient long-distance transportation at reasonable cost and acceptable service levels, however, the problems discussed in this chapter, such as deferred maintenance, must be overcome if the industry is to live up to its potential.

Study Questions

1. Are railroads currently in a period of growth, maturity, or decline?

2. How has the volume of railroad freight traffic changed over the years with respect to: (a) model share, and (b) absolute tonnage?

3. What service characteristics are presented by railroads in comparison to other modes?

4. What is the "operating ratio"?

5. What various factors account for the railroad revenue per ton-mile of 2.6¢ as compared to the motor carrier 7.5¢?

6. If return on assets is profit divided by assets employed in the business, how might the railroads improve return on investment?

7. What "fixed costs" are inherent to railroads? Why are they so high in relation to total costs?

8. Why are labor costs in the rail industry not highly variable? In what other ways do labor costs represent problems for the industry?

9. What are the main "commodity markets" for today's railroads? What characteristics do these markets have versus those carried by other modes?

10. What is meant by "economy of scale"? How might it be present in this industry?

Notes

1. Association of American Railroads, *Yearbook of Railroad Facts,* 1980 ed. (Washington, D.C., 1980), p. 36.

2. Ibid., p. 20.

3. Ibid., p. 2.

4. U. S. Department of Commerce, Bureau of the Census, *Historical Statistics of the United States: Colonial Times to 1957* (Washington, D.C.: U. S. Government Printing Office, 1960), p. 429.

5. Association of American Railroads, *Yearbook,* p. 29.

6. Ronald D. Roth, *An Approach to Measurement of Modal Advantage* (Washington, D.C.: American Trucking Association, 1977), p. 11.

7. Reebie Associates, *The Railroad Situation: A Perspective on the Present, Past, and Future of the Railroad Industry* (Washington, D.C.: U.S. Department of Transportation, March 1979), p. 68.

8. Fixed costs remain the same over a period of time or a range of output (e.g., overhead expense). Variable costs change as the volume of output or activity changes (e.g., labor costs). Finally, semivariable costs contain some fixed and variable elements (e.g., setup costs on a production line).

9. R. J. Sampson and M. I. Farris, *Domestic Transportation: Practice, Theory, and Policy,* 4th ed. (Boston: Houghton Mifflin, 1979), p. 59.

10. Association of American Railroads, *Yearbook,* p. 4.

11. Ibid., pp. 49-50.

12. U. S. Department of Transportation, *A Prospectus for Change in the Freight Railroad Industry* (Washington, D.C.: U. S. Government Printing Office, 1978), p. 65.

13. Association of American Railroads, *Yearbook,* p. 57.

14. Ibid., p. 58.

15. The National Commission on Productivity and the Council of Economic Advisors, *Improving Railroad Productivity* (Washington, D.C.: U. S. Government Printing Office, November 1978), p. 211.

16. Association of American Railroads, *Yearbook,* p. 25.

17. Ibid., p. 40.

18. The commodity groups included here are: metals and products, food and kindred products; stone, clay and glass products; and grain mill products.

19. Reebie Associates, *Railroad Situation,* p. 268.

20. Missouri Pacific System, *Mo-Pac Guide to Intermodal Services TOFC/COFC* (St. Louis: Missouri Pacific Railroad, 1980), p. 3.

21. Association of American Railroads' press release (Washington, D.C., 1979), p. 342.

22. Reebie Associates, *Railroad Situation,* p. 342.

23. The National Commission on Productivity, *Railroad Production,* p. 161.

24. James Sloss et al., *An Analysis and Evaluation of Past Experience in Rationalizing Railroad Networks* (Washington, D.C.: U. S. Government Printing Office, 1974).

25. Consolidated Rail Corporation, *Summary of Business Plan* (Philadelphia, 1979), p. 5.

26. Association of American Railroads, *Yearbook*, p. 11.

27. Association of American Railroads, *More Miles to the Gallon . . . The Railroads* (Washington, D.C., 1974), p. 4.

28. U. S. Department of Transportation, *The Environmental Impact Statement* on "The Transportation Improvement Act of 1973" (Washington, D.C.: U.S. Department of Transportation, 1974), p. 25.

29. Association of American Railroads, *Yearbook*, p. 7.

Suggested Readings

Beier, Frederick J. "Cost of Locating On-Rail: Perceptions of Shippers and Practices of Carriers." *Transportation Journal*, Fall, 1977, pp. 22-32.

Harriss, R. G. "Economics of Traffic Density in the Rail Freight Industry." *The Bell Journal of Economics*, Autumn, 1977, pp. 556-64.

McElhiney, Paul T. *Transportation for Marketing and Business Students*. Totowa, N.J.: Littlefield, Adams, 1975, chap. 5.

Reebie Associates. *The Railroad Situation: A Perspective on the Present, Past, and Future of the Railroad Industry*. U.S. Department of Transportation, 1979.

Sampson, R. J., and Farris, M. I. *Domestic Transportation*. 4th ed. Boston: Houghton Mifflin, 1979, chap. 4.

Taff, Charles A. *Management of Physical Distribution and Transportation*. 6th ed. Homewood, Ill.: Richard D. Irwin, 1978, chap. 5.

U.S. Department of Transportation. *A Prospectus for Change in the Freight Railroad Industry*. Washington, D.C., 1978.

Wood, D. F., and Johnson, J. C. *Contemporary Transportation*. Tulsa: Petroleum Publishing Company, 1980, chap. 5.

Wyckoff, D. Daryl. *Railroad Management*. Lexington: Lexington Books, 1976.

| Case | Coal Mountain Railroad Company |

Coal Mountain Railroad Company

In 1970, the Coal Mountain Railroad Company replaced its fleet of six locomotives and 100 hopper cars and upgraded its track for a fifteen-year, single-unit train move. The equipment originally cost $3,000,000, and is being depreciated over a fifteen-year life. A profit and loss statement for the little railroad and its unit train are summarized as follows:

	1980
Revenue	$1,700,000
Operating expenses	$1,000,000
Depreciation	200,000
Net before taxes	$500,000
Taxes	200,000
Net after taxes	$300,000

The net income figure has held fairly constant due to wage and fuel escalation clauses in the unit train contract. The contract runs from 1970 to 1990.

Ignoring the investment in the land and track, what was the return on assets for the train in 1971?

What is the return in 1980, and what will it be for its last year of useful life in 1984?

What are your thoughts on the fact that in 1985 a new train will have to be purchased which will probably cost $11 million?

4   Pipelines

After reading this chapter you should:

1   Understand the role of pipeline transportation in the total U.S. transportation system.

2   Be able to discuss the economic and operating characteristics of pipeline carriers.

3   Understand the important pipeline service characteristics relevant to the users.

4   Be able to discuss the pipeline system and its financial and managerial problems.

■ unique nature

Transportation by pipelines is unique in many respects. Pipelines are an underground form of transportation and are largely unnoticed by the general public. They have been referred to as the "hidden giants" of the transportation industry. Pipelines are quite important in terms of total ton-miles accounting for approximately 25 percent of the freight ton-miles moved in the United States in 1980.[1] This volume of tonnage is especially significant since pipelines are very specialized in terms of the type of commodities they handle. Oil and a small number of other commodities mainly account for this large percentage of interstate traffic.

■ historical perspective

The pipeline industry is also unique in terms of its history. Pipelines have been with us for over one hundred years. The first successful oil pipeline was put into operation in 1865 in Pennsylvania near Titusville shortly after oil was first discovered in 1859. In spite of this one hundred year history, it was not until after World War I, with the discovery of oil in the southwestern part of the United States and the rise of the automobile in our society, that long-distance pipelines developed and became an important part of the transportation industry.

The first pipe that was laid in western Pennsylvania was a 2-inch pipeline approximately 5 miles in length. The cost advantage of pipeline transportation compared to movements by the teamsters was soon demonstrated. In spite of opposition and destructive tactics by the teamsters (a group that used teams of horses to pull barges up the canal), a series of pipelines were built in western Pennsylvania.

■ government entry

The federal government entered into the pipeline business briefly during World War II to construct two pipelines to help connect the Southwest Oil Fields with major refineries along the east coast. The two government pipelines that were built were commonly referred to as the "Little Inch" and the "Big Inch." The Big Inch extended from the Southwest (Longview, Texas) to the New York-Philadelphia refinery area. The "Little Inch" was a much shorter pipeline and only connected Corpus Christi to Houston, Texas. After the war, the "Big Inch" was sold to a private company and converted from a crude oil pipeline into a natural gas pipeline.

With this brief historical note as background, let us turn to a discussion of the pipeline industry. We will begin with an overview of the industry, followed by a discussion of the service and operating characteristics of pipelines, including other general factors such as cost structure and competition.

Industry Overview

The pipeline industry is unique in a number of important respects, including type of commodity hauled, ownership, and visibility. It is characterized by being relatively unknown to the general public. Pipelines are limited in the markets they can serve and in the commodities they can haul. Further, they are the only mode with no backhaul.

Tonnage, Revenues, and Network

Pipelines have played an important role in the transportation industry in the post-World War II era. Originally, pipelines were used to feed other modes of transportation such as railroads or water carriers. That has clearly changed in recent years.

As seen in Table 4.1, pipelines account for almost 25 percent of the total intercity ton-miles in the United States. Their relative position on a tonnage basis is comparable to that of the motor carrier industry. Their important position is in sharp contrast to the public visibility of the industry. Few people in the United States would guess that pipelines match trucking companies in traffic relevance.

The tonnage comparison is in sharp contrast to the revenue picture, as indicated in Table 4.2. Here the low rates of the pipeline, which are discussed later in the chapter, are reflected in the very small percentage of total revenue. The pipelines account for approximately 2 percent of the total transportation revenues, compared to motor carriers which garner over 50 percent of the total revenue for approximately the same share of intercity traffic.

■ revenue

■ network

The pipeline network, as reflected in Table 4.3, has grown steadily and in keeping with the growth in tonnage. However, Table 4.3 does not adequately reflect the increase in total capacity, since it does not show diameter of pipelines. As we will discuss later, pipeline diameters have increased in recent years, and the larger diameters have increased overall capacity.

Table 4.1 Pipeline Share of Intercity Traffic

Year	Ton-Miles Shipped (Billions)	Percentage of Total Transportation Intercity Ton-Miles
1945	129	12.4%
1950	129	12.1
1955	203	15.9
1960	229	17.4
1965	306	18.7
1970	431	22.3
1975	507	24.5
1979	605	23.4

Source: Transportation Association of America, *Transportation Facts and Trends*, 16th ed. (Washington, D.C., 1980), p. 8.

Table 4.2 Revenue Position of Pipelines

Year	Revenue (Millions of Dollars)	Percentage of Total Intercity Freight Revenue
1960	895	2.0%
1965	1,396	1.7
1970	2,220	1.7
1975	2,532	1.8

Source: Transportation Association of America, *Transportation Facts and Trends*, 16th ed. (Washington, D.C., July 1980), p. 7.

Types of Carriers

■ classification

There are a number of different ways of classifying pipelines. First, they are frequently classified as gathering lines or trunk lines, particularly in reference to the movement of oil. The trunk lines are further classified or subdivided into two types: crude and product lines. The gathering lines are used to bring the oil from the fields to storage areas before the oil is processed into refined products or transmitted as crude oil over the trunk lines to distant refineries (see Figures 4.1 and 4.2).

Early in the history of the oil industry, the refineries were located primarily in the eastern part of the United States, and thus the long-distance movement of oil was basically the movement of crude oil. The state of the technology in the industry also made it much easier to control leakage with crude oil than with refined oil products such as gasoline or kerosene. After World War II, however, refineries were developed at other locations, especially in the Southwest, and better technology made long-distance movement of oil products easier to accomplish.

■ trunk lines

Trunk lines are used for the long-distance movement of either crude oil or other products, such as jet fuel, kerosene, chemicals, or coal.

■ gathering lines

When comparing gathering lines and trunk lines there are several important differences to note. First, gathering lines are smaller in diameter, usually not exceeding 8 inches, whereas trunk lines are usually 30 to 50 inches in diameter. Gathering lines are frequently laid on the surface of the ground to ensure ease of relocation when a well or field runs dry. Trunk lines, on the other hand, are usually seen as permanent and are laid underground.

Table 4.3 Pipeline Network

Year	Miles of Pipeline
1945	137,545
1950	158,472
1955	188,540
1965	190,944
1970	213,764
1975	218,671
1979	224,811

Source: Transportation Association of America, *National Transportation Facts and Trends*, 16th ed. (Washington, D.C., 1980), p. 31.

Figure 4.1 Crude Oil Pipeline Network

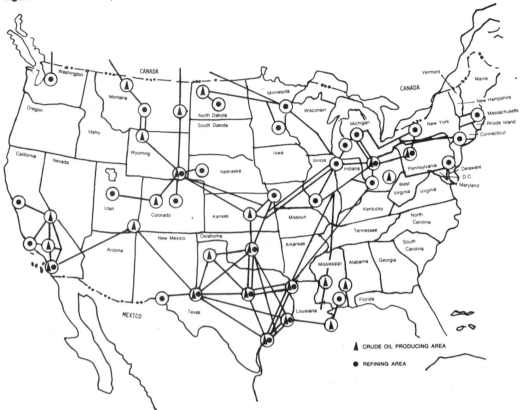

Source: Amoco Oil Company, 1976.

The term "trunk line" is often used in conjunction with oil movements and can refer to crude oil trunk lines which are used to move oil from tank farms to refineries in distant locations, or oil product lines which move the gasoline, jet fuel, and home heating oil from refineries to market areas. Technically, however, any long-distance movement via a large diameter, permanent pipeline implies a trunk line movement. Therefore, when coal, natural gas, or chemicals move via pipelines, such movement is classified as trunk line movement.

Table 4.4 Types of Intercity Pipelines and Mileage

Type of Pipeline	Intercity Mileage
Natural Gas	265,405
Crude Oil	103,127
Petroleum Products	67,764
Coal Slurry	273
Chemicals	4,050

Source: U.S. Department of Transportation, *National Transportation Trends and Choices*, (Washington, D.C.: Government Printing Office, 1977), p. 290.

Figure 4.2 Product Pipeline Network

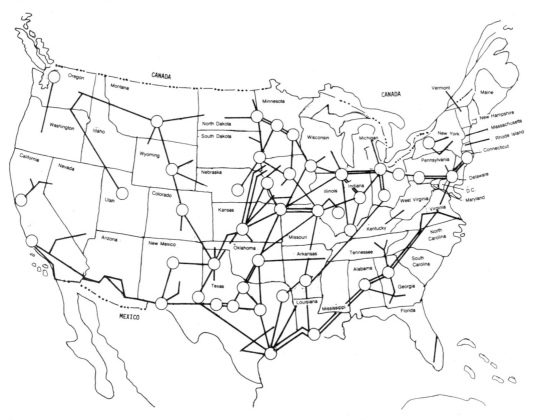

Source: Amoco Oil Company, 1976.

■ natural gas

Natural gas pipelines are an important part of our total pipeline network. They are regulated by a different agency than oil pipelines, the Federal Energy Regulatory Commission, and they account for the largest number of intercity pipeline miles—265,405 miles (see Table 4.4). The natural gas pipeline companies produce about 10 percent of the gas they transport. The remaining 90 percent is produced by independent companies.[2]

■ coal

Coal pipelines are frequently called slurry lines (see Figure 4.7) because the coal is moved in a pulverized form in water (one-to-one ratio by weight). Once the destination is reached, the water is removed and the coal is ready for use. Coal pipelines are used primarily for transporting coal to utility companies for generating electricity.[3] Coal pipelines use enormous quantities of water, which causes concern in several western states where they have been proposed.

■ chemicals

Chemical lines are another type of product line, although there are only a limited number of chemicals carried by pipelines. The three major chemicals are: anhydrous ammonia which is used in fertilizer, propyl-

Figure 4.3 Crude Oil Transfers

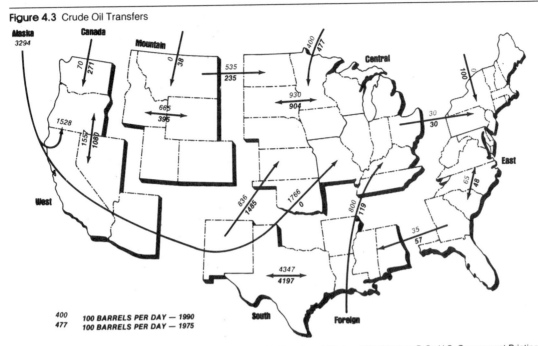

Source: U.S. Department of Transportation, *National Transportation Trends and Choices* (Washington, D.C.: U.S. Government Printing Office, 1977), p. 296.

Figure 4.4 Petroleum Product Transfers

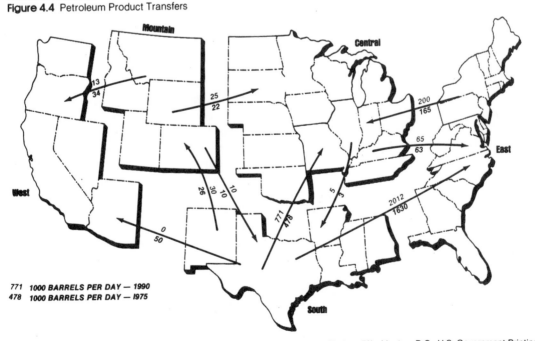

Source: U.S. Department of Transportation, *National Transportation Trends and Choices* (Washington, D.C.: U.S. Government Printing Office, 1977), p. 298.

Figure 4.5 Coal Transfers

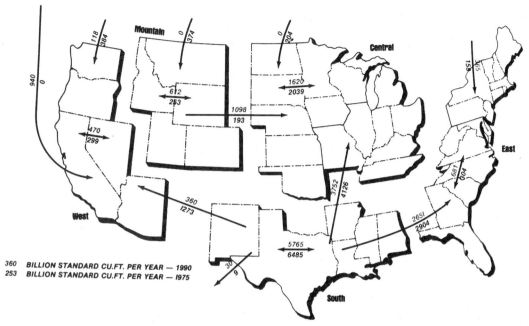

360 *BILLION STANDARD CU.FT. PER YEAR — 1990*
253 *BILLION STANDARD CU.FT. PER YEAR — 1975*

Source: U.S. Department of Transportation, *National Transportation Trends and Choices* (Washington, D.C.: U.S. Government Printing Office, 1977), p. 300.

ene which is used for manufacturing detergents, and ethylene which is used for making antifreeze.

Another way of looking at the pipeline industry is to divide it into for-hire or private carriers. In the pipeline industry, as in the railroad industry, the for-hire carriers are all common carriers and there are a limited number of private carrier operations. This is in sharp contrast to historical convention. When the pipelines first developed after the initial efforts of the Pennsylvania Railroad, the Standard Oil Company established the precedent of the pipelines being owned by the oil companies themselves. The pipelines were largely operated as subsidiaries and often used as a method of controlling the industry. However, the regulatory climate which developed after World War II, in particular a decision which was rendered by the Supreme Court known as the Champlin Oil Case, required pipelines to be operated as common carriers. Hence, although some private carriers exist, the industry is dominated by the for-hire common carriers.

■ for-hire vs. private

Number of Carriers

■ number and size .

The pipeline industry is similar to the railroad industry in terms of the small number of very large carriers. In 1980 there were approximately 108 carriers of oil and oil products offering for-hire service; these carriers accounted for approximately 85 percent of the ton-miles carried. The remaining 15 percent was carried by approximately twelve private carrier operations. The oligopolistic nature of the industry is demonstrated by the fact that twenty major integrated oil companies control about two-thirds of the crude oil pipeline mileage.

■ rationale

There are a number of reasons for the limited number of pipeline companies. First, there are high start-up costs (capital costs) to enter the industry. Second, like railroads and public utilities, the economies of scale are such that duplication or parallel competing lines would be wasteful. Large size operations are most economical, since capacity rises more than proportionately to increases in diameter, while investment per mile decreases as do operating costs per barrel.[4] For example, a 12-inch pipeline operating at capacity can transport three times as much oil as an 8-inch pipeline.

The regulatory climate of the Interstate Commerce Commission (ICC) also contributes to the limited number of companies because of the procedural requirements for entry and the associated legal costs. An additional factor is the industry itself which has been dominated by the large oil companies who joined together in the post-World War II era to develop pipelines from major fields of entry ports.

Pipeline Operations

■ investment

The pipeline industry is obviously an important segment of our total transportation system, as indicated by the tonnage figures previously cited. The U.S. Department of Transportation estimates that total pipeline investment is in excess of $21 billion based on historical costs. Also, the department estimates that it would cost about $20 billion to replace the system at today's costs.

Figure 4.6 Natural and Synthetic Gas Transfers

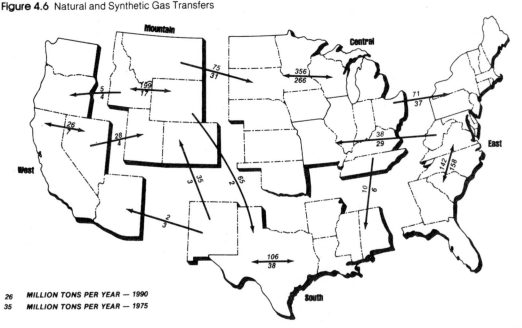

26   *MILLION TONS PER YEAR — 1990*
35   *MILLION TONS PER YEAR — 1975*

Source: U.S. Department of Transportation, *National Transportation Trends and Choices* (Washington, D.C.: U.S. Government Printing Office, 1977), p. 294.

Figure 4.7 Existing and Planned Coal Slurry Pipelines

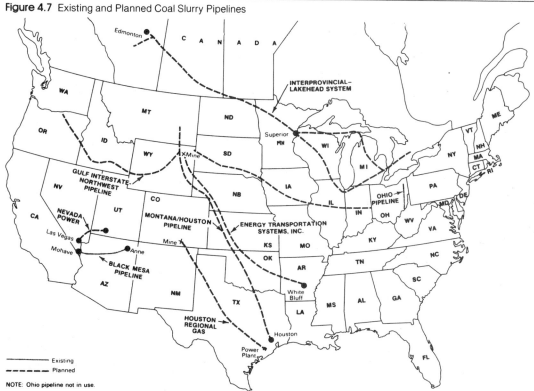

Source: U.S. Department of Transportation, *National Transportation Trends and Choices* (Washington, D.C.: U.S. Government Printing Office, 1977), p. 127.

■ initial movement

Gathering lines bring the oil, for example, from the fields to a gathering station where the oil is stored in sufficient quantity to ship by trunk line to a refinery. After refining the oil, the various products are stored at a tank farm before shipping via a product line to another tank farm with a market-oriented location. The last segment of the system, from the market-oriented tank farm to the customer, is most frequently accomplished by motor carrier movement.

Trunk lines, the major segments of the pipeline system, are usually over 30 inches in diameter. Stations to provide the power to push commodities through the pipeline are interspersed along the trunk line.

■ line movement

For oil movements, pumps are located at the stations, which vary in distance from 30 to 100 miles, depending upon the viscosity of the oil and the terrain. These pumping stations for large diameter pipelines can provide 3,000—6,000 horse power.[5] Compressors are used for the movement of natural gas, while pumps are used for the other liquid items that move through the pipelines.

■ loss and damage

Today's pipelines have a limited loss and damage record which stems from the industry's sophisticated approach to operations. The pipes are constructed of special high-quality alloy steel with a life expectancy of fifty years or more. The pipes are laid in long sections with a limited number of seams. High-quality electric welding of the seams prevents leakage.

maintenance

A preventive maintenance approach and sophisticated monitoring of the pipeline system are also key factors in limiting loss and damage and protecting the environment. The pipeline is coated with protective paints and resins, and special techniques are used to control corrosion after the pipeline is in the ground. Electric current is used to neutralize the corroding electrical forces that come naturally from the ground to the pipeline. Also, chemicals are used to deter corrosion on the inside of the pipeline.[6]

computers

Computers at the pumping stations continually monitor the flow and pressure of oil in the system. Any change indicating a leak is easily detected. Visual checks and searches by airplane are sometimes used to provide routine checks to locate leaks. Great care is rendered because of the potential losses, not only of the oil or other commodities themselves, but also because of the lawsuits that could ensue as a result of damage to property and the environment.

complexity

In the oil segment of the pipeline industry, sophisticated operating and monitoring techniques are used because of the different petroleum products moving through the product lines and the different grades of crude moving through the crude oil lines. There are fifteen grades of crude oil and a range of products including jet fuel, different types of gasoline (regular, unleaded, and premium), diesel fuel, heating oil, kerosene, and aviation fuel. When two or more grades of crude oil or two or more products move through a system at one time, the "batches" may need to be separated by a rubber ball called a batching pig. However, this is not always necessary because of the different specific gravities of the products which help to keep them separated.[7] Any mixing which does occur is of minor importance, since the higher grade items will be considered part of the lower grade items with which they are mixed. Usually products are scheduled one month in advance with kerosene moving first, then high grade gasoline, then medium grade, then the various other products, with home heating oil last. Before the cycle starts again, the pipeline is usually scoured to prevent mixing problems.[8]

Ownership

historical perspective

With some minor exceptions, oil companies have been the owners of the oil pipelines. In the 1870s, the Pennsylvania Railroad was involved in developing pipelines as feeders to the railroads, particularly in the Pennsylvania Oil Fields. However, the Standard Oil Company bought them out and started to develop pipelines more extensively in order to control the industry and to enhance their market dominance. As noted, the federal government entered into the pipeline business for a brief period during World War II.

ownership

As discussed previously, most of the pipelines are operated as common carriers on a for-hire basis, even though most oil pipelines are owned by the oil industry. Some are joint ventures because of the capital investment necessary for large diameter pipelines. Individual, vertically integrated oil companies control about 46 percent of the pipeline revenues with an additional 27 percent controlled by jointly owned pipelines. The remaining percentage is controlled by railroads, independent oil companies, and other industrial companies.[9]

Service Characteristics

■ rates

■ user costs

■ warehouse function

■ speed

■ dependability

■ completeness

■ types of products

A major advantage offered by the pipeline is low rates. Pipeline transportation can be extremely efficient, with large diameter pipelines operating near capacity. Average revenues for pipelines are below one-half of a cent per ton-mile, which is indicative of the low cost service of pipelines.

The low rates are complemented by two additional user cost-related factors. First, pipelines have a very good loss and damage record. Part of this is attributable to the products transported, but it is also related to the nature of the pipeline service, which provides underground and completely encased movement.

The second important cost-related factor is that pipelines can provide a warehousing function since their service is slow. In other words, if the product is not needed immediately, the slow pipeline service can be regarded as a form of free warehousing or storage.

On the other hand, slow speeds can be a service disadvantage in some instances and can contribute to higher inventory holding costs. (Products move through pipelines at an average of 3-5 miles per hour.) Because of the long lead times required for delivery, substantial amounts of oil and other products may have to be stored to meet demand.

Another positive service advantage of pipelines is their dependability. They are virtually unaffected by weather conditions, and they very rarely have mechanical failures. Although the service time is slow, scheduled deliveries can be forecast very accurately, diminishing the need for safety stock. In addition, the carriers assume liability for full loss with no extra charges. The nature of their liability is comparable to that of railroads.

Another aspect of interest to the transportation user is completeness of service. Here pipelines are somewhat at a disadvantage because they offer a relatively fixed route service which cannot be easily extended to a complete door-to-door service. That is, they have limited geographic flexibility. (However, since the source location for pipelines is known and refinery locations are also known and fixed for long periods, the fixed route service factor is not a critical problem.) Frequently, pipelines depend upon railroads and motor carriers to complete delivery, which adds to the user costs.

An additional service characteristic is the pipeline's capability to handle different types of commodities. The use of pipelines is limited to a rather select number of products: crude oil, oil products, natural gas, coal, and a limited number of chemicals. There is interest in using pipelines for other products, but the technology for such use has not yet been developed. Capsule and pneumatic pipelines offer a potential approach to diversify the products they carry.

Frequency of service, the number of times a mode can pick up and deliver during a particular period, is a characteristic of interest to some users. On one hand, the large tenders (shipment size requirements) and slow speed of the pipelines reduce frequency. On the other hand, service is offered twenty-four hours a day, seven days a week.

A factor related to the items already discussed is service flexibility. Pipelines are generally regarded as somewhat inflexible because they serve limited geographic areas and limited points within an area. Also, they carry limited numbers of commodities and only offer one-way service. Finally, the operations technology virtually precludes small shipment sizes.

In summary, pipelines offer a good set of services for particular types of products, but they have some serious limitations.

Operating Characteristics

In keeping with previous chapters, operating characteristics are primarily defined as commodities hauled, length of haul, and average load. As indicated above, pipelines transport a very select number of products, in fact, they are a very specialized carrier. The bulk of the movements by pipeline is crude oil and oil products. In 1979 this accounted for approximately 60 percent of total pipeline movements (see Table 4.2). Water carriers were next with about 35 percent of the total.

■ length of haul and shipment size

The length of haul in the pipeline industry is moderate. Crude oil movements average about 300 miles per shipment, and product lines average about 345 miles per movement. The average shipment size is very large because of the economic characteristics previously cited. The pipeline industry, in fact, used large minimum tenders as a means of controlling the oil industry at one time in their history.

Cost Structure

■ similar to rail

The pipeline segment of the transportation industry is similar to the railroad industry in terms of cost structure as it has a high proportion of fixed cost with low capital turnover. The pipelines, like the railroads, have to provide their own right-of-way by purchasing or leasing land and constructing the pipeline and pumping stations along the right-of-way. The property taxes, amortization or depreciation, the return to investors, and preventive maintenance programs all contribute to the high ratio of fixed to variable expenses.

■ right-of-way

In addition to the right-of-way costs, the terminal facilities of pipelines contribute to the high level of fixed costs. The same type of expenses associated with the right-of-way are evident with respect to the pipeline terminals, for example, depreciation and property taxes.

■ labor

Labor costs are very low in the pipeline industry because of the high level of automation. For example, the Trans-Alaska Pipeline System, built at a cost of $9.2 billion, is operated by 450 employees.[10] Another example of variable costs is the energy or fuel cost to power the system. Overall, many experts estimate that variable costs are only 30-40 percent of total costs in the pipeline industry and may be 25 percent or less in some pipeline systems.

As stated previously, the pipeline industry has significant economies of scale. The high fixed cost and the economies of scale help to explain the common pattern of joint ownership and investment in large diameter pipelines.

■ unique nature

Pipelines do not operate vehicles like other modes of transportation, since the carrying capacity is actually the pipe itself which is best regarded as part of the right-of-way. This is another unique element of the pipeline operation and helps to explain the lower element of variable costs, since vehicles are frequently a major source of variable expense.

Competition

Intramodal competition in the pipeline industry is limited by a number of factors. First, there are a small number of companies—slightly more than 100. The industry, therefore, is oligopolistic in market structure, which generally leads to limited price competition. Second, the economies of scale and high fixed costs previously discussed have led to joint ownership of larger diameter pipelines, as the construction of smaller parallel lines is not very efficient. Finally, the high capital costs preclude duplication of facilities to a large extent.

■ small numbers

■ intermodal

The most serious area of competition for pipelines is intermodal in nature. Technically, pipelines compete with railroads, water carriers, and motor carriers for traffic. However, even with these forms of transportation the amount of competition is limited. The most serious competition is water, or tanker, operations. The only mode of transportation that can come close to pipeline costs for transportation is water carriers. However, the limited coverage of water carrier service limits its effective competition.

Trucks have increased the number of products they carry that can also be carried by pipeline. However, this is complementary to the pipeline, since trucks perform a distribution function for pipelines.

Once a pipeline has been constructed between two points, it is difficult for other modes to compete. Pipeline costs are extremely low, their dependability is quite high, and there is a limited risk of damage. The major exception is probably coal slurry pipelines because of the water requirements which can make the costs comparable to rail movements. Water carriers come the closest to matching pipeline costs.

■ pricing

Pricing in the pipeline industry is unique compared to the major modal competitors. First of all, pipelines do not use a freight classification system, a system which underlies the class rates of railroads and motor carriers. The limited number and specialization of commodities make such a practice unnecessary. A crude oil pipeline or natural gas pipeline has little need for an elaborate classification system.

Even though pipelines have high fixed costs, the differential pricing practices so common in the railroad industry are virtually nonexistent among pipelines. The nature of the operation, one-way movement, limited geographic coverage of points, limited products, etc., provide little opportunity for differential pricing practices.

Pipelines quote rates on a per barrel basis; one barrel equals 42 gallons. Quotes are typically point-to-point or zone-to-zone. Also, minimum shipment sizes, usually called tenders, are required—these range from 500 barrels to thousands of barrels.

Pipeline rates are very low, which is reflected in the fact that they carry approximately 25 percent of the total intercity ton-miles and get only about 2 percent of the total revenues. Water carrier costs come closest to pipeline costs, and in fact, international super tankers have lower costs than most pipelines. However, these super tankers do not really compete with domestic pipelines. When considering pipelines with diameters of 30 inches or more, even ocean carriers have difficulty matching pipeline costs.[11]

Conclusion

Pipelines are a relatively old form of transportation, regulated since 1906. However, their importance was not really felt until after World War I. In the post-World War II era, they have gained increased importance with our dependence upon oil for energy. While still a very inconspicuous part of the transportation system to many individuals, the pipeline industry is as important as motor carriers in terms of intercity tonnage.

Study Questions

1. How do you explain the pipeline modal share of 24.5 percent of the total ton-miles, when its revenue share of the total freight market is only 1.8 percent?

2. What types of pipelines are in existence?

3. What cost, social, and industrial issues do coal slurry pipelines present?

4. Are economies of scale present in the pipeline industry?

5. What are the pipeline industry's service characteristics?

6. How does the pipeline industry's cost structure make it unique among the transportation modes?

7. Does the pipeline industry operate in a competitive market? Is the market different when speaking about short run and long run?

Notes

1. Transportation Association of America, *Transportation Facts and Trends*, 16th ed. (Washington, D.C., 1980), p. 5.

2. Donald Wood and James Johnson, *Contemporary Transportation* (Tulsa: Petroleum Publishing, 1975), p. 224.

3. Ibid., p. 226.

4. Arthur M. Johnson, *The Development of American Petroleum Products* (Ithaca, N.Y.: Cornell University Press, 1956), p. 3.

5. Wood and Johnson, *Contemporary Transportation*, p. 214.

6. Ibid.

7. Ibid., p. 215.

8. Ibid., p. 212.

9. U.S. Department of Transportation, *National Transportation Report* (Washington, D.C.: U.S. Government Printing Office, July 1975), p. 340.

10. Wood and Johnson, *Contemporary Transportation*, p. 231.

11. Donald Harper, *Transportation in America* (Englewood Cliffs, N.J.: Prentice-Hall, 1978), p. 275.

Suggested Readings

Campbell, Thomas D. "Eminent Domain: Its Origin, Meaning, and Relevance to Coal Slurry Pipelines." *Transportation Journal,* Fall, 1977, pp. 5-31.

Farris, Martin T., and Shrock, David. "The Economics of Coal-Slurry Pipelining: Transportation and Non-Transportation Factors." *Transportation Journal,* Fall, 1978.

Locklin, D. Philip. *Economics of Transportation.* 7th ed. Homewood, Ill.: Richard D. Irwin, 1972, chap. 26.

Norton, Hugh S. *Modern Transportation Economics.* 2nd ed. Columbus, Ohio: Charles E. Merrill, 1971, chap. 3.

Pegrum, Dudley F. *Transportation: Economics and Public Policy.* 3rd ed. Homewood, Ill.: Richard D. Irwin, 1973, chap. 2.

Rohleder, Gilbert V. "Pipelines—The Challenge of Regulation in a Free Economy." *Annual Proceedings of the American Society of Traffic and Transportation,* 1978, pp. 111-15.

Steingraber, Fred S. "Pipeline Transportation of Petroleum and Its Products." in *Transportation: Principles and Perspectives* by Stanley S. Hille and Richard F. Poist. Danville, Ill.: Interstate Printers and Publishers, 1974.

U.S. Department of Transportation. *Transportation Trends and Choices to the Year 2000.* Washington, D.C.: U.S. Government Printing Office, 1977, chap. 10.

Case   **Southern Cross Transport**

In the spring of 1981 the Southern Cross Steamship Company formed a subsidiary company that was to branch out into other lines of transportation. The managers of the new firm set about to investigate the feasibility of moving semirefined petroleum products from Galveston, Texas to the Northeast by pipeline. Such movement now is made on Southern Cross Company steamships which operate on a triangular route. The route begins in Maracaibo, Venezuela with crude oil to Galveston; the semirefined products are then moved to Charleston, South Carolina, New York, New York, and Boston, Massachusetts; the ships return laden with ballast to Venezuela. The pipeline would connect Galveston with Charleston, New York, and Boston. The ships would then be shifted to a Venezuela-Galveston round trip route.

To determine the feasibility of the pipeline, Southern Cross Transport managers need information on the present cost of semirefined movement. Several methods of costing have been suggested:

1. *Out-of-Pocket Method.* The additional expenses actually incurred by the movement of semirefined products from Galveston to Charleston, New York, and Boston.
2. *Marginal Cost Method.* The additional costs of operating the triangular route over a Venezuela-Galveston-Venezuela route.
3. *Average Cost Method.* The Galveston-Charleston-New York-Boston mileage times the average operating costs per mile, plus any accessorial charges incurred.
4. *Allocated Joint Cost Method.* Actual Galveston-Charleston-New York-Boston costs plus a share of the empty haul costs (these costs apportioned to the loaded hauls according to the value of the product).
5. *Full Round Trip Cost Method.* The costs which would be incurred to move semirefined products from Galveston to Boston (with intermediate stops), with an empty return to Galveston.

For purposes of computation, the following data may be assumed:

Mileage:	Boston-Venezuela direct	2,200 miles	
	Venezuela-Galveston direct	2,000 miles	
	Galveston-Charleston-		
	New York-Boston	1,800 miles	
Operating Costs per Ship-Mile:		$15 loaded	
		$13 in ballast	
Port Fees:	$500 for entry into each port		
Product Value per Shipload:	Crude Oil		$ 800,000
	Semirefined products		1,200,000
Loading or Unloading Times: 1 day each			
Port Time Cost per Ship-Day $3,000			

Compute the cost by each of the five methods. Which cost figure should be used for comparison with the pipeline cost, and why?

5 Domestic Water Carriers

After reading this chapter you should:

1 Understand the role of domestic water carriers in the total U.S. transportation system.

2 Be able to discuss the economic characteristics of domestic water carriers.

3 Understand the important domestic water carrier service characteristics relevant to users.

4 Be able to discuss the waterway system and its funding.

Ever since mankind discovered the buoyancy of water, the waterways have provided a vital transportation source for moving goods and people. Waterways are highways that are provided by nature; nature even provides the power—currents—to propel water vehicles. This natural highway and motive power has been improved upon by technological advancements in construction and engines; however, water transportation is still thought of as a form of transportation provided by nature.

■ role in U.S. development

Water transportation has played an important role in the development of the United States. For our early settlers, water transportation provided the vital link to markets in England and Europe. In addition, many of our major cities developed around water ports along the coasts. As the internal portions of the country developed, water transportation linked the settlements in the wilderness with the coastal cities. This natural highway, or waterway, was the only viable form of transportation available and was a prime determinant of population, as well as industrial and commercial, concentration at port cities.

Today, water transportation remains a viable mode of transportation for the movement of basic raw materials. Domestic water transportation competes rigorously with railroads for the movement of bulk commodities (e.g., grains, coal, ores, and chemicals) and with pipelines for the movement of bulk petroleum and petroleum products.

In 1979, domestic water carriers transported 431 billion ton-miles of intercity freight, or 16.7 percent of the total freight transported. The addition of domestic deep-sea service to the above intercity freight tonnage shows that in 1978, water carriers transported 28.5 percent of the total domestic ton-miles of freight (825 billion out of a total 2,886 billion) at a cost of $5.976 billion to shippers.[1] To perform this level of service, water carriers employed 225,000 people at an average 1978 annual compensation of $21,712.[2]

■ chapter overview

In this chapter, attention is directed toward the basic economic and operating characteristics of domestic water transportation. An overview of the industry is given first, followed by a consideration of water carrier costs, competition, terminals, and waterways.

Industry Overview
■ domestic carriers only

This chapter is restricted to domestic water transportation which consists of all water movements where the origin and destination of the shipment is the United States. Shipments that have a foreign country as either the origin or destination are classified as international shipping and are not included in this discussion.

Types of Carriers
■ for-hire vs. private carriers

An overview of the domestic water carrier industry is given in Figure 5.1. Like motor carriers, the first major classification of the domestic water transportation industry is between for-hire and private carriers. The private carrier cannot be hired and only transports freight for the company that owns or leases the vessels. Private water carriers are permitted to transport, for a fee, exempt commodities and, when they are hauling such exempt goods, they are technically exempt for-hire carriers. Bona fide private water carriers (transporting company-owned freight and exempt commodities) are excluded from federal economic regulation.

■ exempt carriers

The for-hire water carriers consist of regulated and exempt carriers that charge a fee for their services. Exempt carriers are excluded from the federal economic regulations administered by the Interstate Commerce Commission (ICC). Water carriers are exempt from economic regulation when transporting bulk commodities, both dry and liquid. Since the majority of freight transported by domestic water carriers consists of bulk commodities, exempt carriers dominate the for-hire segment of the industry.

■ common and contract carriers

Regulated water carriers are classified as either common or contract carriers. Economic regulation, similar to that controlling motor carriers (operating certificates, rates, etc.), is administered by the ICC. (The Federal Maritime Commission administers federal economic controls over international water carriers.) Though the major water traffic is exempt from regulation, a small number of common and contract carriers exist. In 1980, the ICC exercised controls over 182 water carriers.

■ internal water carriers

The domestic water carrier industry is most commonly classified by the type of waterway used. Carriers that operate over the internal navigable waterways are classified as internal water carriers. Internal water carriers utilize barges and towboats and operate over the principal U.S. rivers—Mississippi, Ohio, Missouri, Tennessee, Columbia, and Hudson, plus smaller arteries. Internal water carriers dominate the north-south traffic through the central portion of the United States via the Mississippi, Missouri, and Ohio rivers.

■ great lakes carriers

The Great Lakes carriers operate along the northeastern portion of the United States and provide service between ports on the five Great Lakes that border the states of New York, Pennsylvania, Ohio, Michigan, Indiana, Illinois, Wisconsin, and Minnesota. The lakeships normally remain on the lakes, but access to Atlantic and gulf ports is possible via the St. Lawrence Seaway. This Great Lakes to Atlantic traffic is classified as a coastal operation.

Coastal carriers operate along the coasts serving ports on the Atlantic

coastal and inter-
coastal carriers

or Pacific Oceans or the Gulf of Mexico. Intercoastal carriers transport freight between east coast and west coast ports, usually via the Panama Canal. Coastal and intercoastal carriers utilize ocean going vessels, but there are some operations that utilize ocean going barges (18,000-ton capacity). Currently, large quantities of petroleum, crude and refined, are moved between points on the Atlantic and the Gulf of Mexico. Likewise, oil from Alaska moves via coastal carriers to refineries along the Pacific coast.

Number of Carriers

few small firms

The regulated domestic water carrier industry consists of a limited number of small firms. In 1980, 182 water carriers were subject to ICC regulations. Out of this total, 100 (55 percent) earned less than $100,000 in annual gross operating revenues.

In a 1978 ICC report on the operation of 135 inland (internal) and coastal water carriers, 67 carriers earned more than $100,000 per year and had an average 1978 gross operating revenue of $8,110,000 from regulated freight.[3] For the 68 carriers that earned less than $100,000 per year, the average 1978 gross operating revenue was $78,700 from regulated freight. The conclusion is that the regulated water carriers reporting to the ICC are small businesses.

regulated vs. exempt
carriers

In addition, the regulated segment of the water carrier industry is quite small. In 1978, regulated carriers transported only 4.1 percent of the 827.3 billion ton-miles of waterborne traffic, while exempt carriers transported 66.6 percent, and private carriers handled 29.3 percent.[4]

Figure 5.1 Overview of Domestic Water Carrier Industry

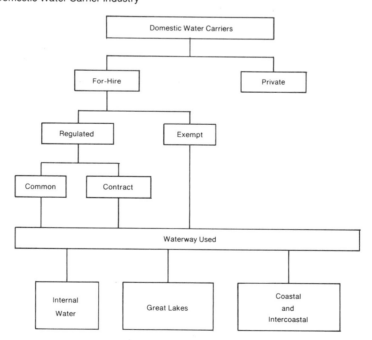

The number of carriers operating on the Great Lakes and the Mississippi River is given in Table 5.1. Only 6.7 percent of the Great Lakes carriers and 3.5 percent of the Mississippi River carriers are regulated (common or contract carrires) by the ICC. The majority of the carriers are exempt—64.2 percent of the Great Lakes carriers and 70.7 percent of the Mississippi River carriers. Private water carriers account for approximately one-fourth of the total carriers.

The percentage of carriers that are regulated, exempt, and private closely parallels the percentage of ton-miles handled by each type of carrier as indicated above. Thus, exempt carriers dominate the domestic inland water carrier industry.

Service Characteristics

■ low cost service

The major advantage of water transportation is low cost service. Water transportation is generally the lowest transportation cost mode for the shipment of nonliquid products. For liquid petroleum products, the pipeline is the lowest transportation cost mode. In 1978, barge revenues per ton-mile were .62¢ compared to 2.37¢ for rail, 11.5¢ for truck and 37.1¢ for air. Oil pipeline revenues per ton-mile in 1977 were .4¢ compared to .56¢ for barge.[5]

■ slow speed

This low transportation cost advantage for nonliquid products is associated with slow speeds. Transit time via water transportation is the longest (slowest speed) of the four modes that move nonliquids. The typical transit time under ideal conditions by barge is given in Table 5.2. For example, the transit time upstream from New Orleans to Pittsburgh is 338 hours or 14 days and 2 hours. The average speed over this route is 5.5 miles per hour (1,852 miles ÷ 338 hours). The downstream time for the Pittsburgh-New Orleans route is 210 hours, or 8 days and 18 hours. The average speed on this downstream route is 8.8 miles per hour (1,852 miles ÷ 210 hours).

In addition to long transit times, water carrier service is subject to disruption during winter months. Ice conditions from late December to

---

Table 5.1 Number of Water Carriers

	Number	Percent
Great Lakes		
Regulated	9	6.7%
Exempt	86	64.2%
Private	39	29.1%
Total	134	100.0%
Mississippi River and Gulf intracoastal (1975)		
Regulated	33	3.5%
Exempt	662	70.7%
Private	241	25.8%
Total	936	100.0%

Source: U.S. Army Corps of Engineers, *Transportation Lines on the Great Lakes System, 1976* and *Transportation Lines on the Mississippi River System and Gulf Intracoastal Waterway, 1975* (Washington D.C.: U.S. Government Printing Office, 1978).

Table 5.2 Typical Transit Times via Barge

Route	Miles	Upstream Transit Time (Hours)	Downstream Transit Time (Hours)
Pittsburgh - New Orleans	1,852	338	210
St. Louis - New Orleans	1,053	211	105
Pittsburgh - Houston	2,257	405	260
Kansas City - New Orleans	1,731	324	190
Chicago - New Orleans	1,418	272	152

Source: The American Waterways Operators, Inc., *The Big Load Afloat* (Washington, D.C., 1955), p. 15.

■ service disruption

early March preclude water transportation on the upper Mississippi River system and the Great Lakes. Low water level has also curtailed normal operations on segments of the lower Mississippi River system at times.

■ cost of disruption

Such disruption in service for two or three months increases the inventory costs of water transportation users. In anticipation of the water transportation stoppage, users will increase inventories prior to the winter months to ensure adequate supplies for operations during the stoppage. This added inventory cost is the reason that primarily low value commodities are transported by water.

■ poor accessibility

Poor accessibility is another characteristic of water transportation. In order to utilize water carriers, the shipper and receiver must have access to the waterway. Most volume users of water transportation have facilities located adjacent to a waterway. If the shipper or receiver is not located on the waterway, truck or rail transportation is required to bridge the accessibility gap.

■ packaging

Finally, the ride and freight handling characteristics of water transportation are more demanding than those in other modes. The freight is subject to weather, rough waters, and numerous handlings which all necessitate stringent, high cost packaging for protection. For example, a wooden crate is used to ship electronic equipment by water transportation, whereas a plastic covering has sufficed for air transportation. However, given that the majority of commodities transported by water is bulk commodities that require little, if any, packaging, the packaging factor is not a serious concern to most water carrier shippers.

In summary, water carriers offer low cost service that is slow and subject to disruptions during winter, that has limited accessibility, and that requires stringent packaging.

Operating Characteristics

The water carrier operating characteristics to be discussed include the commodities hauled, the average length of haul, and the load size. As discussed earlier, water carriers primarily transport bulk commodities. As indicated in Table 5.3, petroleum and petroleum products (bulk liq-

Table 5.3 Commodities Hauled by Domestic Water Carriers

Commodity	Tons (Millions)	Percent
Petroleum and its products	501.7	46.8
Coal and coke	146.9	13.7
Sand, gravel, and stone	101.8	9.5
Iron ore, iron, and steel	90.1	8.4
Chemicals	55.7	5.2
Grains	38.6	3.6
Logs and lumber	23.6	2.2
Seashells	10.7	1.0
All other	102.9	9.6
Total	1,072	100.00

Source: U.S. Army Corps of Engineers, *Waterborne Commerce of the United States, 1978*, pt. 5, National Summaries (Washington, D.C.: U.S. Government Printing Office) .

■ bulk liquids

■ dry bulk commodities

■ other commodities

■ length of haul

uids) accounted for 46.8 percent (501.7 million tons) of the total tonnage transported in 1978 domestic water commerce. Chemicals accounted for 5.2 percent of total tonnage (some chemicals are nonliquid).

The dry bulk commodities transported by water carriers are basic raw materials: coal and coke (146.9 million tons); sand, gravel, and stone (101.8 million tons); iron ore, iron and steel (90.1 million tons); grains (38.6 million tons); logs and lumber (23.6 million tons); and seashells (10.7 million tons). These dry bulk, basic raw materials account for 38.4 percent of the total tonnage transported by water carriers.

The other commodities, 102.9 million tons, transported in 1978 include such items as: waste and scrap (18.7 million tons), water (2.8 million tons), pulp and paper products (3.4 million tons), and motor vehicles (1.4 million tons). High value, manufactured products such as electrical equipment and photographic instruments account for a small portion of the total tonnage transported by water carriers. The conclusion that can be drawn from Table 5.3 is that water carriers transport primarily basic raw materials in bulk form (liquid and dry).

The average length of haul via water carriage varies by type of carrier. In 1978, the average length of haul was 392 miles for internal carriers, 535 miles for Great Lakes carriers, and 1,770 miles for coastal and intercoastal carriers.[6] The coastal and intercoastal distances are greater than those for all other modes. The railroad length of haul is greater than that of internal and Great Lakes carriers, but the water carrier shipping distance is greater than pipeline and truck.

As noted in Table 5.2, shipping distances are quite long over internal waterway routes, 1,400-2,200 miles. For example, a shipment of grain from Kansas City or Minneapolis is transported to New Orleans, a major exporting port for grain. The mileage to New Orleans from Kansas City is 1,434 miles, from Minneapolis, 1,731 miles. Petroleum and petroleum products are the majority of products that move from New Orleans to northern cities.

The cargo carrying capacity of water carrier vehicles is large. Barges are capable of handling 3,000 tons, with normal carrying capacities of

■ carrying capacity

1,000-1,500 tons. Great Lakes carriers have ships that average approximately 20,000 tons of carrying capacity. The carrying capacity of a 1,500-ton barge is equivalent to about fifteen rail cars and sixty trucks.

Cost Structure

■ low fixed, high variable costs

The basic cost structure of water carriers consists of high variable costs and low fixed costs. Like the motor carriers and air carriers, water carriers do not provide their own highways. The waterways are provided by nature, but maintained, improved, and controlled by the government. The carriers pay user charges—lock fees, dock charges, fuel taxes—for the use of the government-provided facilities. These user charges are directly related to the volume of business and, therefore, add to the variable costs.

The 1978 operating costs for water carriers reporting to the ICC are given in Table 5.4. The data in Table 5.4 indicate that 13.48 percent of the total costs is fixed and 86.52 percent is variable. Fixed costs include depreciation and amortization and general expenses. General expenses exceed depreciation and amortization by 2-1.

■ fixed costs

■ variable costs

The major variable expenses listed in Table 5.4 are line operating costs, operating rents, and maintenance. Line operating costs, 50.89 percent of total costs, include labor, fuel, user charges, and other direct operating costs. Operating rents, 13.05 percent of total costs, are those expenses associated with renting operating equipment and facilities. Maintenance expenses amounted to 9.04 percent of total costs.

■ insurance

Casualty and insurance costs are incurred by water carriers to hedge against the risk of loss and damage resulting from the forces of nature. The carriers take out insurance to subrogate losses, or they directly incur the cost of accidents as self-insurers.

Table 5.4 Domestic Water Carrier* 1978 Operating Costs

Functional Expense	Amount ($ Millions)	Percent of Total Cost
FIXED		
Depreciation & amortization	32.76	4.66%
General expenses	61.98	8.82
Total fixed	$ 94.74	13.48
VARIABLE		
Line operating	257.82	50.89
Terminal	32.44	4.61
Traffic	10.63	1.51
Casualties and insurance	38.16	5.43
Operating rents	91.77	13.05
Maintenance	63.59	9.04
Taxes	13.95	1.98
Total variable	$608.36	86.52
Total Cost	$703.10	100.00

Source: Interstate Commerce Commission, *Transport Statistics in the United States, 1978: Part 5, Carriers by Water* (Washington, D.C.: U.S. Government Printing Office), pp. 8-9.

*Great Lakes and internal carriers with revenues of $500,000 or more.

Labor

■ not labor intensive

Water transportation is not labor intensive. In 1978, 4.58 ton-miles of freight were transported for each water carrier employee. This compares to 1.62 ton-miles for each rail employee, .509 ton-miles for each motor carrier employee, and 8.62 ton-miles for each oil pipeline employee.[7]

The 1978 ICC *Statistical Report for Water Carriers*[8] indicates that labor compensation paid by one intercoastal carrier amounted to $173.5 million or 19.6 percent of the total operating costs. The average annual compensation paid by this intercoastal carrier was $21,354.

■ terminal handling

Labor is required at the terminal to load and unload general commodities. This labor is necessary to move freight from the dock onto the ship and into the appropriate hold for the voyage (and vice versa for unloading). In addition, labor is required to handle the loading and unloading of freight from connecting modes, such as truck and rail, and the storage of freight waiting to be loaded onto the ship or connection carriers.

Domestic water carriers, however, do not require much labor at the terminal, since the carriers primarily transport bulk commodities which lend themselves to mechanical loading. Great Lakes carriers have developed ships that are equipped with automatic unloading devices that reduce the amount of labor required to unload such ships.

Fuel

■ fuel mileage

Compared to the other modes, ships consume more fuel per mile. In 1978, three intercoastal carriers consumed 15.2 million barrels of fuel, or 638.4 million gallons, and operated 8.16 million miles. The mileage in 1978 was .0128 miles per gallon, which means that the vessels consumed 78.2 gallons of fuel per mile.

■ fuel efficient

In 1978, water carriers, international and domestic, consumed 230.8 billion barrels of fuel or 6.43 percent of the total fuel consumed by all modes.[9] This total fuel consumption by water carriers was less than that used by trucks, rail, and air, although the water carriers transported more ton-miles of freight than the other modes. Thus, it might be fair to conclude that water transportation is a more fuel efficient mode in terms of fuel consumed per ton-mile.

Economies of Scale

■ limited economies of scale

Like the motor carrier, the water carrier does not have significant economies of scale. The large portion of variable costs (approximately 90 percent), the small size of the carriers in the industry, and the ability to add small increments of capacity (one barge, for example) suggest that the economies of large scale operations are not great.

■ operating ratio

The operating ratio for ICC regulated carriers was 91.4 in 1978. The ratio is quite comparable to motor carriers and air carriers where economies of scale are not significant. The operating ratio for railroads, where economies of scale are significant, is in the 70s.

■ economies of operation

In the short run, however, the water carrier is capable of achieving economies of operation (productivity). A good example is the movement of twenty-five to forty barges in one tow with one towboat. On the lower portion of the Mississippi, a forty-barge tow, hauling 40,000-60,000 tons, is quite common. As the tow moves upstream, the channel width prohibits such operations, and the tow is reduced to five to twenty barges hauling 5,000-20,000 tons. The incremental cost of additional fuel, labor, and maintenance, to push a forty-barge tow is relatively small compared to a five-barge tow. But the improvements in the economies of operation cause an increase from 5,000-20,000 tons hauled to 40,000-60,000 tons, or an increase in output of 200-1200 percent.

Public Aids

■ cabotage

The water carriers have received various forms of aid from the federal government. U.S. cabotage laws require that coastal and intercoastal traffic be carried on in ships built and registered in the United States. The cabotage laws do not provide a direct subsidy to domestic carriers, but they do provide a monopoly for U.S. coastal and intercoastal carriers. This monopoly results from a complete prohibition against foreign-registered or foreign-built ships hauling domestic coastal and intercoastal traffic.

■ waterway construction

For domestic water carriers, the major public aid is the construction and maintenance of waterways. The construction of canals with public funds opens new markets and sources of revenue for water carriers. The construction of locks and dams on rivers makes the waterways navigable for domestic water carriers. The dredging of the Mississippi River, for example, is performed by the Army Corps of Engineers to maintain channel depth and width. Port facilities are maintained by federal and local monies.

■ user fees

To a limited extent, the water carriers do repay the governmental agencies for the various aids received. Lock fees on the St. Lawrence Seaway (but not on inland waterways) are paid to traverse locks, and port fees are paid to utilize the port facilities. Barge carriers are assessed a fuel tax of 4¢ per gallon comparable to the motor carrier fuel tax per gallon.

Summary of Cost Structure

In summary, the cost structure of the water carrier industry is characterized by high variable and low fixed costs. Water transportation is not labor intensive, and labor costs are approximately 20 percent of total costs. Further, the possibility for economies of scale is not significant in the water carrier industry.

Competition

■ limited number of carriers

Water carriers vigorously compete for traffic with other modes and to a limited degree with other water carriers. The rather small number of water carriers (see Table 5.1) elicits a limited degree of competition among water carriers. Since the number of carriers available on a given waterway is limited, there is little incentive for the water carriers to compete with one another as long as the total traffic volume is sufficient for all who are capable of transporting a particular cargo.

■ intermodal competition

The major water carrier competition is with other modes, basically rail and pipelines. Water carriers compete with railroads for the movement of dry, bulk commodities such as grain, coal, and ores. The movement of grain from the Midwest to New Orleans (export traffic) is possible by rail as well as by water carrier. The water carriers can utilize the Mississippi and Missouri river systems to connect the plain states with New Orleans. Both modes move sizable amounts of grain along this traffic corridor.

Rail and water carriers compete heavily to move coal out of the coal-producing states of Pennsylvania, West Virginia, and Kentucky. The water carriers are capable of transporting coal via the Ohio and Mississippi rivers to southern domestic consuming points (utilities) as well as to export markets.

On the Great Lakes, water carriers compete with railroads for the movement of coal, ores, and grain. Iron ore and grains originating in Minnesota, Wisconsin, and Michigan are moved across the Great Lakes to other Great Lake ports, or out of the Great Lakes region, via the St. Lawrence Seaway, to Atlantic and gulf ports or to export markets.

■ water and rail coordination

The Port of Toledo has become an interchange point between rail and water carriers for the transportation of coal. Railroads haul coal out of the coal-producing states to Toledo where the coal is loaded onto laker ships for movement to northern Great Lakes ports. In essence, the railroads overcome the water carrier accessibility problem by moving the coal from the mines to Toledo, which suggests that the modes are partners rather than competitors. Because the total cost of the water-rail combination is lower than the all-rail route, shippers continue to request the combined water-rail service.

■ rail major competition

Water carriers and pipelines are vigorous competitors for the movement of bulk liquids (petroleum and petroleum products). As indicated in Table 5.3, bulk liquids account for approximately 50 percent of the total tonnage transported by domestic water carriers. Bulk liquids are important commodities to both modes, and rigorous competition exists for moving bulk liquids along the Gulf, Atlantic, and Pacific coasts as well as the Mississippi River system.

To a very limited degree, water carriers compete with trucks. In most cases, trucks are utilized to overcome the accessibility constraints of water carriers, since trucks tie inland areas to the waterways.

Terminals

■ publicly financed ports

As indicated earlier, water carrier terminals are provided by the public. Most ports are operated by local government agencies, and many ports have publicly operated storage facilities. It has been recognized for a long time that water transportation is a catalyst to economic activity in a community, and this belief has been used as the reason for public investment in and operation of ports.

■ user investment

Private investment in and operation of port facilities is undertaken by many volume users of water transportation. The building of docks, terminals, and commodity handling facilities by individual shippers is common for firms that handle such commodities as grain, coal, and oil. The private facilities are designed to meet the unique needs of the individual firm.

■ mechanized handling systems

Over the past few decades, major port improvements have centered on the mechanization of materials handling systems, especially for internal waterway ports. Efficient handling of large volumes of bulk commodities has been a prerequisite for ports that desire to remain economically competitive with other ports along the waterway and for water carriers that seek to be competitive with other modes.

The port facilitates ship loading and unloading, which means that the port must be equipped with cranes, fork lifts, etc. Certain commodities like oil, grain, and coal require more technically advanced loading equipment such as pneumatic loaders and rail car dumping equipment. Such materials handling equipment reduces unproductive port delays and enables water carriers and ports to remain economically viable.

■ intermodal transfer

The port also facilitates the transfer of freight from one mode to another. To accomplish this intermodal transfer, the port is usually served by railroads and motor carriers. Terminals at the port will have railroad sidings to handle inbound and outbound rail freight as well as parking lots for motor carrier equipment.

Since water carrier vehicles carry larger loads than rail or motor carrier vehicles, storage facilities are necessary at the port. The storage areas receive cargo from many trucks and rail cars. This freight is held until sufficient volume is obtained to be handled effectively barge or ship. Conversely, when a loaded vessel arrives at port, the freight is unloaded, stored, and then dispatched in hundreds of railcars or trucks at some later date.

Conclusion

The domestic water carrier industry plays an important role in the movement of basic raw materials. Water carriers provide low cost, large volume transportation service that is relatively slow, subject to disruptions, and only accessible to shippers located near waterways. Water carriers have a high variable cost structure and limited economies of scale. The majority of domestic water carriers are exempt or private carriers.

Study Questions

1. Describe the significance of domestic water transportation to the United States.

2. Compare and contrast the different types of water carriers.

3. Discuss the service characteristics of water carriers.

4. What types of commodities are transported by water? Why?

5. Compare the cargo-carrying capacity of water carrier vehicles to that of the other modes.

6. Discuss the cost structure of water carriers and the reasons for this structure.

7. Do economies of scale exist in the water carrier industry? Why?

8. Comment on the types of public aids given to water carrier competition.

9. Describe the nature and extent of water carrier competition.

10. What functions are performed at the port?

Notes

1. Transportation Association of America, *Transportation Facts and Trends*, 16th ed. (Washington, D.C., 1980), pp. 4, 8.
2. Ibid., pp. 23-24.
3. Interstate Commerce Commission, *Transport Statistics in the United States: Carriers by Water* (Washington, D.C.: U.S. Government Printing Office, 1978), pt. 5.
4. Department of the Army, Corps of Engineers, *Waterborne Commerce of the United States* (Washington, D.C.: U.S. Government Printing Office, 1978), pt. 5, p. 11.
5. Transportation Association of America, *Transportation Facts and Trends*, p. 7.
6. Ibid., p. 14.
7. Ibid., pp. 8, 23.
8. Interstate Commerce Commission, *Statistical Report for Water Carriers* (Washington, D.C.: U.S. Government Printing Office, 1978).
9. Transportation Association of America, *Transportation Facts and Trends*, p. 33.

Suggested Readings

American Waterways Operators, Inc. *Big Load Afloat*. Washington, D.C., 1973.

Dibner, Brent, and Wise, Randall E. "A User-Oriented Approach to Inland Waterway Traffic Forecasting." *Annual Proceedings of the Transportation Research Forum*, 1978, pp. 488-498.

Harper, Donald V. *Transportation in America*. Englewood Cliffs, N.J.: Prentice-Hall, 1978, chap. 12.

Howe, Charles W. et al. *Inland Waterway Transportation: Studies in Public and Private Management and Investment Decisions*. Baltimore: The Johns Hopkins Press, 1969.

Jantscher, Gerald R. *Bread Upon the Waters: Federal Aids to the Maritime Industries*. Washington, D.C.: The Brookings Institution, 1975.

Johnson, James C., and Berger, Donald L. "Waterway User-Charges: An Economic and Political Dilemma." *Transportation Journal*, Summer, 1977, pp. 20-29.

Kendall, Lane C. *The Business of Shipping*. 3rd ed. Centerville, Md.: Cornell Maritime Press, 1979.

Lawrence, Samuel A. *United States Merchant Shipping Policy and Politics*. Washington, D.C.: Brookings Institute, 1966.

Lieb, Robert C. *Transportation: The Domestic System*. Reston, Va.: Reston Publishing Co., 1981, chap. 5.

U.S. Department of Commerce, Maritime Administration. *An Adequate and Well Balanced Merchant Fleet*. Washington, D.C.: U.S. Government Printing Office, 1978.

Wood, Donald F., and Johnson, James C. *Contemporary Transportation*. Tulsa: Petroleum Publishing Co., 1980, chap. 8.

Case	**Blythe Coal Company**

The Blythe Coal Company has been a leader in the open-pit coal mining industry ever since it developed a new and cheaper process than its competitors to mine the coal. This innovation has given Blythe a competitive advantage in the industry and has made its product highly demanded. One of Blythe's new customers, a large power plant, is located on the Mississippi River approximately 700 miles north of Blythe's mines. For months, the staffs of both the power plant and the coal mine have been trying to arrive at the most feasible and least total cost method of transporting the coal northward to the power plant. Two methods are the most obvious for consideration: rail and motor carriers, and water and motor carriers. The coal mine has a rail siding for loading the coal, but it must be transported by motor carrier to the power plant from the rail destination some twenty miles from the plant. This method allows for quick and reliable transit times but is more expensive than alternative methods.

The water-motor carrier method requires the coal to be hauled to the river port by motor carrier and then loaded onto barges. Since the power plant is located on the river, no extra transportation is required from the barge destination to the plant. Although this method of transportation is slower and less reliable than the rail-motor carrier alternative, it results in less total logistics cost.

Although the manager of a traffic department is directed to minimize total logistics costs, this cannot be his only criteria for evaluation. He must evaluate the nature of the commodity, its service requirements, its customers, its degree of price elasticity, and the percentage of its price that is made up by transportation costs.

1. If you were the traffic manager of the power plant, how would you want the coal to be transported?

2. If you were the traffic manager of the coal mine, how would you want the coal to be transported?

3. Would some trade-off exist between these two views if each manager had a different method?

4. What other criteria could you use to evaluate the situation?

6 Motor Carriers

After reading this chapter you should:

1 Understand the role of motor carriers in the total U.S. transportation system.
2 Be able to discuss the economic and operating characteristics of motor carriers.
3 Understand the important motor carrier service characteristics relevant to users.
4 Be able to discuss the highway system and its financing.

"If you got it, a truck brought it." This familiar trucking slogan emphasizes the very essence of the motor carrier segment of the U.S. transportation industry. Motor carrier transportation pervades almost every industry. Some industries and firms are dependent upon trucks to haul all inbound and outbound freight, and many cities and towns are served only by trucks. This reliance upon trucks is attributable, in part, to the efficient U.S. highway system which has made truck transportation accessible to virtually all shipping and receiving points.

In 1978, the United States paid $147.4 billion for highway transportation, approximately 78 percent of the total 1978 U.S. freight transportation bill.[1] Trucks transported 628 billion ton-miles of freight in 1979 or 24.3 percent of the total 1979 ton-miles transported by all modes.[2] Approximately 1,286,000 people were employed in trucking during 1979, with an average annual compensation of $19,081.[3]

■ chapter overview

This chapter examines the fundamentals of motor carrier transportation. Attention is given to the service, operating, and economic characteristics of trucking. In addition, the highway system and method of payment are considered. Initially, our attention is directed toward the overall industry characteristics of motor carriers.

Industry Overview

The importance of the motor carrier to the U.S. economy can be demonstrated in a number of important ways. However, the statistics presented do not really show the comprehensive scope and complexity of the motor carriers. Some additional information is necessary and appropriate.

Types of Carriers

The motor carrier industry is a grouping of heterogeneous carriers having different legal, service, and commodity characteristics. Figure 6.1 provides an overview of the interstate motor carrier industry with regard to its legal, service, and commodity characteristics.

■ private vs. for-hire carriers

The first major division of motor carriers is between for-hire and private. The for-hire carrier provides service to the public and charges a fee. The private carrier provides service to the firm which owns or leases the

Figure 6.1 Overview of Interstate Motor Carrier Industry

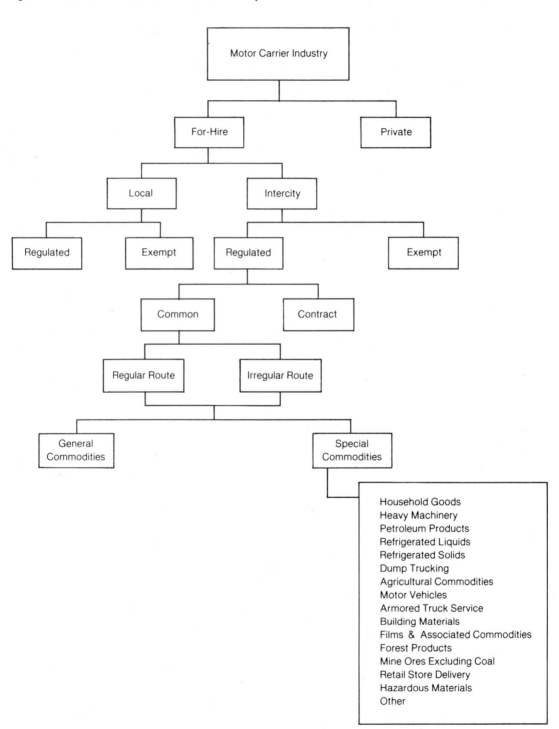

vehicles and, thus, does not charge a fee. The Motor Carrier Act of 1980 permitted private carriers to charge a fee for trucking services provided to a subsidiary that is 100 percent owned. Private carriers may transport exempt commodities, for-hire, but when operating in such a capacity, the private carrier is really an exempt for-hire carrier.

■ local vs. intercity carriers

For-hire carriers are either local or intercity operators. The local carriers pick up and deliver interstate freight within the commercial zone of a city. The intercity carriers operate between and among commercial zones which are defined by the Interstate Commerce Commission (ICC) to include the corporate limits of a municipality plus adjacent areas beyond the corporate limits determined by the municipal population.

■ exempt carriers

For-hire, exempt carriers are specifically exempt from economic regulation by the ICC. The exempt carrier gains this status (free of economic regulatory control) by the type of commodity hauled or by the nature of its operation (incidental to air transportation). In the absence of economic regulation, the laws of the market place determine the rates charged, the services provided, and the number of vehicles supplied.

■ common vs. contract carriers

The regulated for-hire carriers are either common or contract carriers. The common carriers are required to serve the general public upon demand, at reasonable rates, and without discrimination. The contract carriers serve specific shippers with whom the carriers have a continuing contract, thus, the contract carrier is not available for general public use.

■ regular vs. irregular route carriers

Common carriers are further defined as having a regular route or irregular route operating authority. Common carriers with regular route authority are authorized by the ICC to provide service over designated routes, for example, Toledo to Chicago via Interstate 75, Interstate 70, and Interstate 69. Irregular route authority permits the carrier to utilize any route to serve two points.

■ type of commodity hauled

Lastly, interstate common carriers, either regular or irregular route, are classified by the type of commodity that they are authorized to haul. Carriers may have the authority to transport general commodities, or all commodities not listed as special commodities in Figure 6.1, or the authority to transport specialized commodities only. A common carrier having special commodity authority only, for example, armored truck service, is not permitted to transport motor vehicles, general commodities, or the like. Thus, the availability of the common carrier is restricted by the commodity authorization of the ICC. In 1978, 59 percent of regulated carrier revenues went to general commodities carriers and 41 percent to special commodities carriers.[4]

Number of Carriers

■ many small carriers

The motor carrier industry consists of a large number of small carriers. As Table 6.1 indicates, there were approximately 59,000 for-hire carriers and 103,000 private carriers in 1979—a total of approximately 162,000 motor carriers. Of the 17,083 regulated carriers, 13,337 or 78.1 percent had annual operating revenues of less than $500,000. For 1980, the total number of regulated carriers had increased to 17,721, with 82 percent having annual operating revenues of less than $1 million.

Table 6.1 Number of Motor Carriers

Type of Carrier	1979	1980
For-Hire:		
Regulated		
Class I[a]	992	947
Class II	2,754	2,164
Class III	13,337	14,610
Total regulated	17,083	17,721
Exempt[b]	42,033	—[c]
Total for-hire	59,116	
Private:[b]	103,334	—[c]
Industry total	162,460	

[a]Classification by annual operating revenue: Class I = $3 million or more/year; Class II = $3 million to 500,000/year: Class III = less than $500,000/year. As of January 1980, the classification was changed to: Class I = >$5 million; Class II = $1 million to $5 million; and Class III = <$1 million.
[b]Charles A. Taff, *Commercial Motor Transportation*, 6th ed. (Centreville, Md.: Cornell Maritime Press, 1980), pp. 120 and 128.
[c]Not available

■ growth

A further look at the regulated carriers shows that the growth in number of carriers has been in the smaller, Class III size carriers. Table 6.2 indicates that 103 percent of the growth in regulated carriers from 1974 to 1980 was in the Class III category. The redefinition of revenue classifications explains part of the change from Class II to Class III.

■ entry constraints

A further explanation for the large number of small carriers is the limited capital constraint upon entry into the industry. Disregarding the regulatory constraint to common or contract operating authority, a trucking company may be formed with as little as $5,000 to $10,000 equity and the balance financed with the vehicle serving as collateral for the loan. However, most Class I carriers have terminals which increase the capital requirements and, thus, add a constraint to entry.

Finally, the Motor Carrier Act of 1980 eased the entry requirements for common carrier authority. The growth of new entrants is the result of small firms entering the industry.

Service Characteristics

The growth and widespread use of motor carrier transportation can be traced to the inherent service characteristics of the mode. In particular,

Table 6.2 Growth in Regulated Motor Carrier Segment

Year	Class I	Class II	Class III	Total
1980	947	2,164	14,610	17,721
1974	842	2,348	11,910	15,100
Change				
Number	105	-184	2,700	2,621
Percent of class change	12%	-8%	23%	20%
Percent of total change	4%	-7%	103%	100%

■ accessibility

the motor carrier possesses a distinct advantage over other modes in the area of accessibility. Technically, the motor carrier can provide service to virtually any location, although operating authority places restrictions on the areas and commodities served.

Motor carriers are not constrained by waterways, rail tracks, or airport locations. The U.S. system of highways is so pervasive that virtually every shipping and receiving location is accessible via highways. Therefore, motor carriers have potential access to almost every origin and destination.

■ freight pickup and delivery

The accessibility advantage of motor carriers is evident in the pickup or delivery of freight in an urban area. It is very rare to find urban areas served by a pickup/delivery network of waterways (excepting possibly Venice, Italy), railways (excepting possibly downtown Chicago), or runways (excepting possibly some town in Alaska). In fact, trucks provide the bridge between the pickup and delivery point and the facilities of other modes.

■ speed

Another service advantage of the motor carrier is speed. For shipments under 500 miles, the truck can usually deliver the goods in less time than other modes. Although airplanes travel at a higher speed, the accessibility problem of getting the freight to and from the airport via truck adds to the air carrier total transit time. In fact, the limited, fixed schedules of the air carriers may make trucks the faster mode.

For example, a truckload shipment being taken to a destination 400 miles away may take 8 hours to be delivered (400 miles ÷ 50 mph). Although the flying time between airports is 1½ hours, 3 hours may be needed for pickup and 3 hours for delivery, plus time for moving the freight from one mode to another. If the airline scheduled only one flight per day, the shipment could wait for up to 24 hours before being dispatched. The truck, however, proceeds directly from the shipper's door to the consignee's door.

■ small carrying capacity

When compared to the rail car and barge, the smaller cargo carrying capacity of the truck enables the shipper to utilize the truckload (TL) rate, or volume discount, with a lower volume. Many TL minimum weights are established at 25,000 to 30,000 pounds. Rail carload minimum weights are set at 40,000 to 60,000 pounds, and barge minimums are set in terms of hundreds of tons. The smaller shipping size characteristic of the motor carrier brings a discount which benefits the buyer and seller in terms of lower inventory levels and inventory carrying costs.

■ cargo safety

Another positive service characteristic is smoothness of transport. Given the suspension systems and the pneumatic tires used on trucks, the motor carrier ride is smoother than rail and water transport and less likely to result in damage to the cargo (although there is some cargo damage with truck transportation). This relatively damage-free service reduces the package requirements and, thus, packaging costs.

Lastly, the for-hire segment of the motor carrier industry has been quite customer (marketing) oriented. The small size of most carriers has enabled (forced) the carriers to respond to customer equipment and service needs.

In summary, the motor carrier industry enjoys service advantages in the areas of accessibility, speed, carrying capacity, and customer service.

Operating Characteristics

When discussing the motor carrier industry, consideration must be given to the commodities hauled, average load size and length of haul.

Trucks, for-hire and private, primarily transport manufactured, high-valued products. As Table 6.3 indicates, in 1972, trucks carried more than 50 percent of the tons shipped in the commodity categories listed. The list includes both food products and manufactured products, consumer goods, and industrial goods. In addition, trucks transport approximately 100 percent of the sheep, lambs, cattle, calves, and hogs moving to stockyards.[5]

■ commodities transported

Trucks transport less than 50 percent of the tons moved of commodities such as grain, primary nonferrous metal products, motor vehicles and equipment, and paper and allied products. Such commodities generally move long distances and in large volumes, and so, rail and water carriers have a cost advantage.

In 1977, Class I intercity common carriers had an average load of 13.52 tons and an average length of haul of 457 miles.[6] However, such statistics conceal the competitiveness of motor carriers for the 20 to 25 ton-size loads hauled 500 to 1500 miles or more.

■ shipment size and distance

Trucks dominate the market for hauling 10,000 pounds or less and 100 miles or less to 1500 miles or more.[7] For 30,000 to 60,000 pound shipments, trucks dominate the market for hauls of 300 miles or less. On shipments of 90,000 pounds or more, moving more than 100 miles, railroads are the dominant mode. In between these ranges, both modes compete vigorously.

The effects of shipment size, length of haul, and other operating characteristics of operating costs are discussed in the following section.

Table 6.3 Percent of Intercity Tons Hauled by Trucks in 1972

Commodity	Truck Portion		
	For-Hire	Private	Total
Meat & dairy products	41.7	39.1	80.8
Candy, beverages, & tobacco	25.7	58.5	84.2
Textile mill & leather	61.4	27.7	89.1
Apparel & related products	69.4	15.6	85.0
Rubber & plastic products	59.2	15.2	74.4
Stone, clay, & glass products	47.2	23.7	70.9
Fabricated metal products	55.3	25.1	80.4
Industrial machinery, except electrical	59.5	18.9	78.4
Communication products & parts	64.6	12.4	77.0
Transportation equipment, except motor vehicles	23.9	54.8	78.7
Electrical products & supplies	49.5	14.1	63.6
Instruments, photo equipment, watches, & clocks	63.8	10.9	74.7

Source: Transportation Association of America, *Transportation Facts and Trends*, 16th ed. (Washington, D.C., 1980), p. 13.

Table 6.4 Cost of Operating a Tractor-Trailer, July 1980

Cost Item	¢/Mile		Percent	
Fixed Cost				
Interest on vehicle	6.4		6.6	
Depreciation & interest on other items	1.2		1.2	
Management & overhead	5.4		5.6	
Total fixed		13.0		13.4
Variable Costs				
Vehicle depreciation	10.1		10.4	
Insurance	3.3		3.4	
Drivers	28.4		29.2	
Fuel	25.5		26.2	
Maintenance	9.1		9.4	
Tires	2.8		2.9	
Miscellaneous	3.9		4.0	
Total variable		84.1		86.6
Total cost		97.1		100.0

Basis: A ten tractor-trailer fleet, each truck operating one-way trips of 2,500 miles, returning loaded 75 percent of trips, and 131,000 miles per year.

Source: U.S. Department of Agriculture, *Fruit and Vegetable Truck Cost Report*, (Washington, D.C., July 31, 1980).

Cost Structure

■ low fixed high variable

The cost structure of the motor carrier industry consists of high variable costs and low fixed costs. Approximately 90 percent of the costs is variable, and 10 percent is fixed. The public investment in the highway system is a major factor contributing to this low fixed cost structure. In addition, the motor carrier is able to increase or decrease the number of vehicles used in short periods of time and in small increments of capacity. Lastly, the carriers, as a group, do not require expensive terminals, and this small investment in terminals contributes to the low fixed costs. The bulk of the motor carrier's cost, then, is associated with the daily operating costs of the carrier—the variable costs of fuel, wages, and maintenance.

■ example

This discussion of motor carrier cost will begin with the vehicle operating costs of fleets transporting fresh fruits and vegetables in tractor-trailers. These vehicles travel 131,000 miles per year. These data can be compared only to similar operations—that is, comparisons cannot be made to local trucking (pickup and delivery). Table 6.4 indicates that in July 1980, the total cost to operate a tractor-trailer was 97.1¢ per vehicle mile.

As indicated in Table 6.4, approximately 87 percent of the cost to operate an intercity tractor-trailer is variable. The remaining 13 percent is associated with the fixed costs of vehicle interest: depreciation and interest on terminals, garages, offices, management, and overhead (utilities, for example). For carriers handling less-than-truckload (LTL) freight, the fixed cost is higher. That is, additional terminals, management, and overhead expenses are required to handle the small size shipments.

Labor

The cost of drivers accounts for 29.2 percent of total costs per vehicle mile, as shown in Table 6.4. Labor costs, wages plus fringe benefits, usually absorb about 50 percent of a carrier's revenue dollar.[8] That is, 50¢ of every dollar in revenue goes for labor. In 1978, the average hourly gross earnings of nonsupervisory motor carrier employees was $7.79.[9] The average annual earnings in 1978 was $16,195, while average total annual compensation was $19,081[10] for trucking and warehousing employees.

■ wage level

The over-the-road (intercity) driver is typically paid on a mileage basis, for example, 22.5¢ per mile. The local drivers are paid by the hour. Most labor contracts require that the over-the-road driver be paid an hourly rate for operating delays resulting from loading/unloading, accidents, bad weather, and the like.

■ wage basis

Driver utilization in interstate commerce is regulated by the Department of Transportation, which enforces maximum hours of service regulations. Drivers are permitted to drive a maximum of ten hours after being off-duty for eight consecutive hours. A driver is permitted to be on-duty a maximum of fifteen hours after eight consecutive hours off-duty. In addition, no driver may drive after accumulating sixty hours on-duty in seven consecutive days, or seventy hours in eight consecutive days.

■ driving time regulations

Fuel

Fuel cost accounts for 26.2 percent of the total vehicle operating costs given in Table 6.4. The rapidly escalating price of fuel has resulted in a sharp rise in the relative proportion of fuel cost to total cost. For example, in 1976, the fuel cost per mile (comparable to that in Table 6.4) was 11.6¢ per mile or 19.8 percent of the total cost per mile. Carriers have experienced a 100 percent increase in diesel fuel prices from 1976 to 1980—from approximately 53¢ per gallon in 1976 to about $1.12 per gallon in 1980.

■ rising cost

Included in the price of fuel is a highway user tax imposed by both the federal and state government (4¢ per gallon, federal and 6.5-14¢ per gallon, state). The fuel tax plus other taxes for highway use are payments made by the carrier to the government for the construction, maintenance, and control of the highways. In 1979, the motor carrier industry paid $9.7 billion dollars in federal and state highway user taxes.[11]

■ user taxes

Operating Ratio

A measure of operating efficiency used by motor carriers is the operating ratio. The operating ratio measures the portion of operating revenues that goes to operating expenses:

$$\text{Operating Ratio} = \frac{\text{Operating Expenses}}{\text{Operating Revenues}} \times 100$$

Operating expenses are those expenses directly associated with the transportation of freight, but exclude nontransportation expenses and interest costs. Operating revenues are the total operating revenues generated from freight transportation services; nontransportation revenues are excluded. The operating ratio is often used by motor carriers to support rate increase requests before the ICC.

■ definition

An operating ratio of 94 indicates that 94¢ of every operating revenue dollar is consumed by operating expenses, leaving 6¢ of every operating

■ implication

dollar to cover interest costs and a return to the owners. Motor carrier operating ratios usually range between 93 and 96.

Economies of Scale

■ limited scale economies

There does not appear to be major economies to large scale trucking operations. Economies of scale come about through more extensive use of large size plants or indivisible inputs. However, the extensive use of indivisible inputs is not characteristic of all motor carrier operations. In addition, the large number of small firms—about 82 percent of the regulated carriers have annual operating revenues of less than $1,000,000—suggests that small size operations are competitive.

■ short-run utilization economies

In the short run, certain economies exist in the greater utilization of indivisible inputs such as terminals, management specialists, and information systems. The average cost of such inputs will decrease as output (greater utilization) increases. Such economies of utilization justify the rather large size firms that operate transcontinentally. Carriers that operate over wide geographic areas require more terminals, elaborate information systems, and more management specialists than those carriers that operate over narrow geographic areas.

■ limited investment

For truckload operations, very limited investment is required for terminals or information systems. The bulk of the truckload carriers' inputs (vehicle, labor, fuel) can be increased in response to rather small increases in demand, basically one truck at a time.

■ large size operations

Operational cost trade-offs exist between large and small carriers. Large scale operation does afford savings in terms of purchase economies of equipment and such inputs as money (interest), fuel, and parts. The small carrier may enjoy some of these purchase economies available from larger retailers of truck supplies, for example, truck stops. On the other hand, large trucking companies tend to be unionized; thus they pay higher labor rates.

Overall, long-term economies of scale do not appear to be significant in motor carrier transportation. This lack of scale economies has some implication for competition and the market's ability to control such competition.

Competition

■ number of carriers

Motor carriers do compete vigorously with one another for freight. With over 17,000 regulated trucking companies, rivalry among firms is intense. In addition, regulated carriers compete to a limited extent with the approximately 40,000 exempt carriers. However, the most severe competition for for-hire carriers comes from the private carrier who has shown dramatic growth.

■ ease of entry

As indicated earlier, the motor carrier industry cost structure is characterized by low fixed cost and high variable cost. This low fixed cost structure suggests that there is no capital constraint to industry entry. With a relatively small investment, an individual can start a trucking business and compete with an existing carrier. Thus, freedom of entry, discounting any regulatory constraints, appears to dominate the industry and suggests that "competition" among trucking firms can control the industry. Such a conclusion has been the basis for greater reliance on the market place and less reliance upon regulation.

capital requirement

It should be noted that certain segments of trucking have higher capital requirements than others and therefore have some degree of capital constraint to entry. The major segment which has extensive capital requirements for entry is the LTL carrier. The LTL carrier must invest in terminals and freight handling equipment that is simply not needed by the TL carrier. Special equipment carriers—carriers of liquified gases or frozen products—may have larger investments in equipment and terminals than those involved with general freight.

market orientation

On the whole, motor carriers have been market-oriented. Meeting customer requirements has been a common trait of motor carriers. The small size of the majority of the for-hire carriers permits individualized attention to be given to customers. As carriers have grown, this close carrier-customer relationship has been strained. However, the responsiveness to customer demands for service still dominates all trucking organizations, and shippers expect carriers to respond to their needs.

Equipment

Many of the motor carrier service advantages emanate from the technical characteristics of the truck. The high degree of flexibility, the relatively smooth ride, and the smaller carrying capacity of the truck are the unique characteristics that result in the greater accessibility, capability, cargo safety, and lower transit time of truck transportation.

flexibility

Flexibility refers to the ability of the truck to be operated free of a fixed highway. That is, each cargo unit (trailer) is pulled by a separate power unit (truck), thus eliminating the need to collect a number of cargo units to form a train that will be pulled by a power unit. The ability to operate a cargo unit separately reduces transit time delays resulting from the large cargo unit collection process.

The other dimension of motor carrier equipment flexibility is the lack of highway constraint. Unlike the railroad and water carrier, the motor carrier is not constrained to providing service over a fixed railway or waterway. The truck can travel over the highway, and there is a highway, paved or unpaved, serving virtually every conceivable consignee in the United States.[12]

The smooth ride afforded cargo shipped by trucks is a result of the use of pneumatic tires and improved suspension systems. The pneumatic tires provide a shock absorbing quality and, coupled with advanced suspension systems, provide a protection from highway roughness. The railroad ride is not as smooth, since rail cars use steel wheels against steel rails and the car's suspension system is rather stiff.

line-haul trucks

Motor carrier vehicles are either line-haul vehicles or city equipment. Line-haul vehicles are used to haul freight long distances between cities. City trucks are utilized within the city to provide pickup and delivery service. On occasion, line-haul vehicles will also operate within the city, but the line-haul vehicle normally is not very efficient when operated in this way.

The line-haul vehicle is usually a tractor-trailer combination of three or more axles (see Figure 6.2). The cargo carrying capacity of these vehicles is dependent upon the size (length) and the state maximum weight limits. A tractor-trailer combination with five axles (tandem-axle tractor and trailer) is permitted in most states to haul a maximum of 80,000 pounds gross weight. If the empty vehicle weighs 30,000 pounds, the maximum net payload is 50,000 pounds, or 25 tons.

■ net carrying capacity

The net carrying capacity of line-haul vehicles is also affected by the density of the freight. A $40' \times 8' \times 8'$ trailer has 2,560 cubic feet of space. If the commodity has a density of 10 pounds per cubic foot, then the maximum payload for the vehicle is 25,600 pounds (2,560 ft.^{3} $\times$ 10 lb./ft.^{3}). Shippers of low density freight (below 16 lb./ft.^{3}) are advocates of increased trailer cubic size in order to permit increased payload capacity of trucks.

■ density and capacity

City vehicles are normally smaller than line-haul vehicles and are single units (see Figure 6.2). The city truck has the cargo and power unit combined in one vehicle. The typical city truck is approximately 20 to 25 feet long with a cargo unit 15-20 feet long. However, there is a growing use of small trailers (20 to 27 feet) to pick up and deliver freight.

■ city trucks

In addition to the line-haul and city vehicle classifications, there are a number of special vehicles. These special vehicles are designed to meet special shipper needs. Consider the following:

Dry van - Standard trailer or straight truck with all sides enclosed.

Open top - Trailer top is open to permit loading of odd size freight through the top.

■ special equipment

Flat bed - Trailer has no top or sides—used extensively to haul steel.

Tank trailer - Used to haul liquids such as petroleum products.

Refrigerated vehicles - Cargo unit that has controlled temperature.

High cube - Cargo unit that has drop frame design or is higher than normal in order to increase cubic capacity.

Special - Vehicle has a unique design to haul a special commodity such as liquified gases or automobiles.

Figure 6.2 Line-Haul and City Vehicles

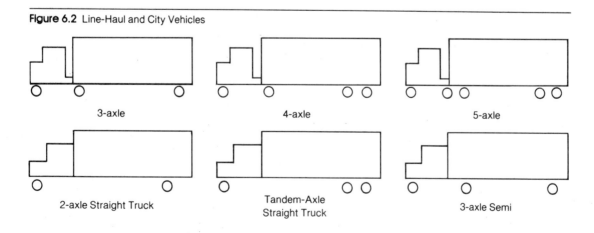

3-axle

4-axle

5-axle

2-axle Straight Truck

Tandem-Axle
Straight Truck

3-axle Semi

■ safety regulations

The federal government has established many rules and regulations governing the safety specifications of trucks. These regulations cover such areas as the number of lights on the vehicle, the types of brakes used, tire specifications, and other operating parts.[13] The overall length and height of the vehicle are prescribed by the various states.[14]

Terminals

Some motor carrier operations, namely TL operations, may not require terminals. The carrier uses the shipper's plant for loading and the consignee's plant for unloading. However, the LTL freight operations do require terminals. The terminals utilized by motor carriers can be classified as pickup and delivery, break-bulk, and relay. A discussion of functions performed at each type of terminal follows.

Pickup and Delivery Terminals

■ consolidation

At the pickup and delivery terminal, freight is collected from shippers and brought to the terminal where it is consolidated with other loads going in the same direction or to the same destination. The consolidated shipments are loaded onto a line-haul vehicle for movement to destination.

Upon arrival at destination, the terminal facilitates the delivery of the shipment. The line-haul vehicle is emptied, and the combined shipments are separated and reloaded onto city trucks. The city trucks complete the delivery to the ultimate consignee.

■ clerical functions

At the pickup and delivery terminal, other carrier functions are performed. The sales effort, billing, and claim handling for the shippers are at the terminal's location. Some carriers have limited vehicle maintenance performed at such terminals.

■ freight interline

Lastly, carriers will utilize the pickup and delivery terminal to facilitate the interline of freight from one carrier to another. A carrier may not have operating authority to transport the shipment to destination, but will cooperate with one or more carriers to complete the movement. When the shipment reaches the end of one carrier's line, it is transferred, via the terminal, to another carrier. Usually this transfer entails the unloading of the shipment onto the terminal floor, then reloading it into the subsequent carrier's vehicle.

Figure 6.3 Break-Bulk Terminal

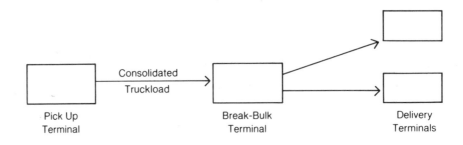

Pick Up Terminal   Consolidated Truckload   Break-Bulk Terminal   Delivery Terminals

Figure 6.4 Relay Terminal

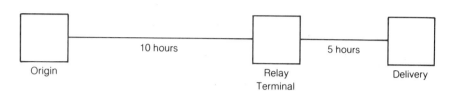

As can be seen, the pickup and delivery terminal serves many purposes. The break-bulk and relay terminals serve a much more limited function.

Break-Bulk Terminals

■ separate consolidated loads

■ location

The basic function performed at the break-bulk terminal is separation of combined shipments. As shown in Figure 6.3, a consolidated shipment from a pickup and delivery terminal moves, as a unit, the majority of the distance toward the respective shipment destinations. Such consolidated moves permit the carrier to realize economies of operation.

Consolidated truckloads arrive from many pickup terminals. Freight is unloaded, sorted by destination, and reloaded for dispatch to destination. For greater efficiency, break-bulk terminals are usually centrally located within the carrier's operating scope and at the juncture of major east-west and north-south highways. For example, a major motor carrier has a break-bulk terminal located at Toledo, Ohio. Toledo is at the juncture of Interstate 80 (east-west) and Interstate 75 (north-south).

Relay Terminals

■ driving time constraints

The relay terminal is necessitated by the maximum hours of service regulation that are imposed upon drivers. As indicated previously, drivers are permitted to drive a maximum of ten hours after eight consecutive hours off-duty. The relay terminal facilitates the substitution of one driver for another who has accumulated the maximum hours of service. (The term "slip-seat" has also been used to describe the relay terminal operation.)

As indicated in Figure 6.4, the location of a relay terminal is a maximum driving time of ten hours from an origin. If the relay terminal is located five hours from an origin, the driver can drive to the relay terminal and return within the maximum ten hours.

Using the example given in Figure 6.4, assume that the driving time is fifteen hours between origin and destination. Without the relay terminal, the transit time would be twenty-three hours. After ten hours of driving, the driver must go off-duty for eight consecutive hours. Upon resuming duty, the driver would drive five hours to destination. The total elapsed time is twenty-three hours (10 + 8 + 5).

With the relay terminal, the driver drives ten hours to the relay terminal, where another driver is substituted, and the vehicle driven to destination. The relay terminal, in this instance, reduces the transit time by eight hours, the mandated driver off-duty time.

■ team driving

An alternative to the relay terminal is the use of a sleeper team—two drivers. While one driver accumulates the off-duty time in the sleeper berth of the tractor, the other driver is driving. The sleeper team has been most successful where trips are long and have many destinations.

Highways

■ public financing

■ types of highways

Since the founding of the United States, the federal government has felt that government has the responsibility to provide highways to meet national defense and commerce needs. At first, the federal government was the sole financier of highways, but over the years the state and local governments have assumed a greater role. Today, the state and local governments assume the responsibility for maintaining and policing highways, with the federal government participating in the funding of highway construction.

The highway system consists of interstate, primary, secondary, urban, and Appalachian highways. The National System of Interstate and Defense Highways, approximately 42,000 miles in length, was designed to connect the major cities of the United States with four-lane limited access roads. (It has been 96 percent completed.) The primary highways connect lesser populated cities with major cities. Secondary highways are primarily in rural areas. Urban highways are streets and roads in urban areas. The Appalachian Development Highway System[15] is a 3,000 mile network of highways throughout the Appalachian states. (Approximately 50 percent of the network is complete.) Highway access is possible to virtually every shipper.

■ highway user taxes

The highway users—trucks and automobile operators—pay for the construction, maintenance, and policing of highways through highway user taxes. The total amount of taxes paid is dependent upon the use made of the highway. The motor carrier incurs a cost for use of the highway that is related to the amount of use. This situation contributes to the high variable cost structure of the motor carrier.

■ federal highway trust fund

The highway user taxes are assessed by federal and state governments. The federal highway user taxes are paid into a highway trust fund. From the highway trust fund, the federal government pays 90 percent of the construction cost for the interstate system and 50 percent of the construction costs for all other federal-aid roads. Table 6.5 indicates items taxed and the rate assessed by the Federal Highway Trust Fund.

■ state user taxes

The states also assess highway user taxes to defray the cost of construction, maintenance, and policing of highways. The state taxes include: fuel tax (6.5¢-14¢ per gallon), vehicle registration fees, ton-mile taxes, and special use permits. Recent fuel conservation by the U.S. population has caused considerable fiscal problems for many state highway departments; the reduced consumption of automobile and truck fuels has reduced the state fuel tax income, although the cost of construction, maintenance, and policing has increased.

■ user tax philosophy

Implied in the highway user tax concept is the philosophy that the highway predominantly confers benefits upon specific groups and individuals. Although the general public benefits from increased mobil-

Table 6.5 Highway Trust Fund Tax Rates

Fuel	4¢/gallon
New trucks, buses, & truck trailers	10% of manufacturer's sales price
Truck & bus parts & accessories	8% of manufacturer's sales price
New tires & tubes	10¢/pound
Retread rubber	5¢/pound
Lubricating oils	6¢/gallon
Federal use tax (26,000 lb. or more GVW*)	$3.00/1,000 pounds

American Trucking Association, *History and Philosophy of Highway Taxes and Cost Allocation Studies* (Washington, D.C., 1978), p. 1.

*Gross vehicle weight

ity and availability of a wider variety of goods and services, the motor vehicle user is presumed to be the major benefactor and is therefore expected to pay a larger share of the costs. Property owners pay property taxes that include assessments for streets (access to the property).

■ fair share

Much debate exists as to whether the various parties are paying a fair share; that is, do the trucks pay a fair share of the total costs of highways? In 1978, all motor vehicles paid $299 billion, of which trucks paid $109 billion or 36.6 percent.[16] As the debate continues, the central issue is whether the trucks should pay for the added construction and maintenance costs caused by heavier vehicles.

■ record keeping

Since each state must pay for the maintenance, policing, and construction of highways in their respective state, the states attempt to assure receipt of taxes for using a state's highways. For motor carriers operating over many states, this means buying vehicle registrations in many states, and maintaining records of miles driven in a particular state so that the state will receive a fuel tax or ton-mile tax. Such record keeping adds a cost to the carrier's operation.

■ state safety laws not uniform

Since the states have the right to protect the health and welfare of their citizens (police powers) and must pay for the maintenance of their highways, the states establish vehicle safety regulations governing truck weight, length, width, and speed. These regulations are not uniform and, thus, cause motor carriers problems when operating in different states.

■ operating problems

For example, the contiguous states of Iowa and Illinois have different maximum weight laws for five-axle combinations: Illinois permits a maximum weight of 73,280 pounds and Iowa, 80,000 pounds. This means a truck loaded to the legal limit of 80,000 pounds in Iowa would be illegal in Illinois. The motor carrier's productivity is thereby adversely affected by the state weight limits. Attempts are underway by the federal government to establish an 80,000 pound maximum weight for a five-axle combination in each of the states.

Conclusion

In this chapter, an overview of the organization of the motor carrier industry, plus its economic and service characteristics, was given. The motor carrier industry consists of a large number of for-hire and private carriers. The for-hire carriers are made up of common, contract, and exempt carriers. Trucks have a distinct accessibility over the other modes due to the pervasive highway system in the United States, and the ability to operate each vehicle separately. The motor carriers have high variable and low fixed costs, and economies of scale are limited. The highway system is financed by the public, but the motor carrier pays user fees which contribute to the high variable cost structure. Motor carriers primarily transport manufactured goods.

Study Questions

1. Define and compare the following types of motor carriers:
   a. common
   b. contract
   c. exempt
   d. private
   e. regular route
   f. irregular route

2. Explain why the majority of the regulated motor carriers are small (Class III).

3. What are the major service characteristics of motor carriers?

4. Describe the motor carrier operating characteristics relating to commodities hauled, shipment size, and distance.

5. Describe the cost structure of motor carriers and explain why it operates the way it does.

6. Comment on the significance of labor and fuel cost to total cost.

7. What is an operating ratio? What does it mean?

8. Do economies of scale exist for motor carriers?

9. Describe the competitive environment of motor carriers.

10. Define the characteristics of the different types of equipment used.

11. Define and compare the following terminals:
    a. pick-up and delivery
    b. break-bulk
    c. relay

12. Describe the methods utilized to finance highway construction and maintenance.

13. Discuss the nature and uses of the operating ratio. Why do so-called "normal" operating ratios differ between the different modes of transport? What implications do these differences pose for intermodal rate competition? (AST&T, Fall 1977, Exam #1)

14. It is often stated that an inherent advantage of the motor carrier is in the movement of freight short distances. Yet, many of the largest motor carriers are profitable coast-to-coast and border-to-border operations. Explain this apparent paradox. (AST&T, Spring 1979, Exam #1)

15. Compare and contrast the cost structure of the motor carrier industry and the railroad industry. Point out the reasons for any differences. (AST&T, Spring 1979, Exam #1)

Notes

1. Transportation Association of America, *Transportation Facts and Trends*, 16th ed. (Washington, D.C., 1980), p. 4.
2. Ibid., p. 8.
3. Ibid., pp. 23-24.
4. American Trucking Associations, Inc., *American Trucking Trends, 1977-78* (Washington, D.C., 1978), p. 7.
5. Ibid., p. 27.
6. Ibid., p. 29.
7. Ronald D. Roth, *An Approach to Measurement of Modal Advantage* (Washington, D.C.: American Trucking Associations, 1977), pp. 1-10.
8. American Trucking Associations, Inc., *American Trucking Trends, 1977-1978*, p. 15.
9. Ibid., p. 13.
10. Transportation Association of America, *Transportation Facts and Trends*, p. 24.
11. American Trucking Associations, Inc., *Truck Taxes by States*, 28th ed. (Washington, D.C., 1980), p. 3.
12. There are notable exceptions to this ability to serve. Shippers located on an island are served by water or air transportation. Other unique examples exist where the truck is physically unable to provide service.
13. For a complete listing of federal equipment specifications, see U.S. Department of Transportation, Federal Highway Administration, Bureau of Motor Carrier Safety, *Federal Motor Carrier Safety Regulations* (Washington, D.C.: U.S. Government Printing Office, 1980), pt. 2.
14. Through the police powers contained in the U.S. Constitution, the states have the right to establish regulations to protect the health and welfare of its citizens. Vehicle length and height laws are within these state police powers, as are vehicle speed and weight laws.
15. The Appalachian Highway System was designed to spur the depressed economy of that region.
16. American Trucking Association, Inc., *Truck Taxes by States*, 28th ed. (Washington, D.C., 1980), p. 3.

Suggested Readings

Breen, Denis A. "The Changing Motor Carrier Share of Intercity Manufacturers Traffic: Alternative Explanations." *Transportation Journal*, Fall, 1978, pp. 19-27.

Davis, Grant M.; Farris, Martin T.; and Holder, Jack J. *Management of Transportation Carriers*. New York: Praeger Publishers, 1975.

Germane, Gayton E.; Glaskowsky, Jr., Nicholas A.; and Heskett, J.L. *Highway Transportation Management*. New York: McGraw-Hill Book Co., 1963.

Hill, Donald M., and Morice, William D. *Motor Carriers: an Industry Profile*. Washington, D.C.: Peat, Marwick, Mitchell & Co., 1979.

Lieb, Robert C. *Transportation: The Domestic System.* 2d ed. Reston, Va.: Reston Publishing Co., 1981, chap. 4.

MacAvoy, Paul W., and Snow, John W., eds. *Regulation of Entry and Pricing in Truck Transportation.* Washington, D.C.: American Enterprise Institute, 1977.

Shrock, David L. "Economics of Scale and Motor Carrier Operations: Review, Evaluation, and Perspective." *ICC Practitioners' Journal,* September/October, 1978, pp. 721-45.

Taff, Charles A. *Commercial Motor Transportation.* 6th ed. Centreville, Md.: Cornell Maritime Press, 1980, chap. 2.

Throckmorton, John F.; Mueller, Paul M.; and Kolins, Roger W. *Motor Carrier Marketing Management.* Washington, D.C.: American Trucking Associations, 1980.

Wyckoff, D. Daryl, and Maister, David H. *The Motor Carrier Industry.* Lexington, Mass.: Lexington Books, 1978.

Wyckoff, D. Daryl, and Maister, David H. *The Owner-Operator: Independent Trucker.* Lexington, Mass.: D.C. Heath and Co., 1975.

Case   **Cheapway Trucking Company**

John Corio is the pricing manager for Cheapway Trucking, a medium size carrier in the South. The company has extensive terminals through which it handles TL and LTL traffic throughout a fourteen-state region. John's company had been an active participant in national and regional rate bureaus since the firm was founded prior to World War II. Recent passage of the Motor Carrier Act of 1980 and deregulatory shifts by the ICC are bringing about diminished use of rate bureau pricing.

Cheapway's main service competitor is Highway Trucking. It is a na-tional carrier with very efficient operations. In fact, its operating ratio is consistently at about 89%. Highway recently published a tariff that in effect provides for a 6% rate discount on LTL traffic whenever an entire shipper firm increases its total LTL gross revenues with High-way by 10% or more from one quarter to the next. The tariff is due to go into effect on July 1 (a few weeks away), with discounts going to those who qualify beginning in August. The base quarter for volume computations purposes is the April-June quarter of the current year.

John is seriously concerned with this for several reasons. One, there has never been discounting in the industry prior to this period. Two, the industry has been in a recession, so the base quarters will qualify nearly all shippers when business picks up. And, three, his president says that they can't match the rate discount, because Cheapway's operating ratio is about 95%. A discount of 6% will cause a deficit.

What can John do or suggest?

7   Air Carriers

After reading this chapter you should:

1   Understand the role of air carriers in the total U.S. transportation system.

2   Be able to discuss the economic and operating characteristics of air carriers.

3   Understand the important air carrier service characteristics relevant to users.

Since mankind's first successful attempt to fly about 80 years ago, the airplane has advanced to the stage where the most distant point on earth is a matter of hours away. Airplane travel is a common form of transportation for long-distance travel, and the only reasonable alternative when time is of the essence. The tremendous speed of the airplane is the prime reason for the growth of air transportation.

The major source of airline revenues comes from the movement of passengers. In 1978, for-hire air carriers had total revenues of $24.151 billion, of which $21.497 billion (89 percent) came from moving people.[1] In 1978, air carriers transported 5.2 billion ton-miles of freight, or .20 percent of the total ton miles, and received $2.65 billion, or 1.38 percent of the nation's freight bill.[2] Employment in the air carrier industry totaled 423,000 people in 1979 with an average annual compensation of $26,630 for persons employed by common carriers.[3]

■ chapter overview

In this chapter, the fundamentals of air transportation are examined. The economic, service, and operating characteristics are analyzed as well as the general nature of the air transportation industry.

Industry Overview

The airline industry is very much dependent upon passenger revenues to maintain its financial viability. However, to characterize airlines as simply movers of people presents too simplistic a view of their role in our transportation system. The airlines are a unique and important group of carriers that meet some particular needs in our society.

Types of Carriers

The air transportation industry is a grouping of heterogeneous carriers with different legal services and operating characteristics. Figure 7.1 provides an overview of the types of air carriers. The industry is not as complex as the motor carrier industry which has many more types of carriers (see Figure 6.1 for a comparison). Basically, the air carriers are either private or for-hire; the for-hire carriers are economically regulated (certificated) or exempt (noncertificated). In addition, for-hire, regulated carriers are either scheduled or nonscheduled.

Figure 7.1 Overview of Air Carrier Industry

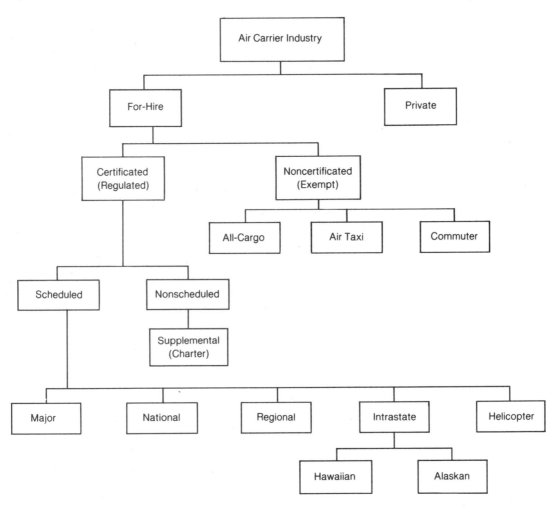

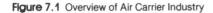

■ private carriers

Private air transportation is defined as a firm that transports company personnel or freight in planes that it owns or leases. The preponderance of private air transportation is utilized to transport company personnel, though emergency freight is sometimes carried on private airplanes as well. Rarely, however, is a private air carrier established to routinely carry freight.

Private air carriers are exempt from the Civil Aeronautics Board's (CAB) economic controls. Being exempt, the private carrier does not need a certificate to operate or to publish rates. However, the private air carrier is subject to the federal safety regulations administered by the Federal Aviation Administration (FAA) of the U.S. Department of Transportation.

■ noncertificated carriers

The for-hire carriers are classified into certificated and noncertificated carriers, as mentioned above. The noncertificated carriers are exempt from CAB economic regulations. No controls are exercised over the rates charged and routes served. There are three types of noncertificated air carriers: all-cargo, air taxi, and commuter.

■ all-cargo

The all-cargo carrier, as the name implies, transports cargo only, and was freed from economic regulation in 1977 when federal control over air freight transportation was eliminated. The all-cargo carrier is now controlled by the dictates of the market place and is free to set rates, serve routes, and use any size plane. At the present time there are four all-cargo lines: Air Lift International, Flying Tiger, Federal Express, and Alaska International.

■ air taxi

The air taxi is a carrier that will fly anywhere on demand. To be an air taxi operator, the carrier's plane is limited to a maximum payload of 7,500 pounds (18,000 pounds for all-cargo carriers) and sixty passengers. The air taxi does not maintain or publish a timetable.

The air taxi group has experienced rapid growth recently. This growth can be attributed to the decline in air service to smaller communities by the certificated carriers that are eliminating routes as permitted under recent air deregulation laws. Most new helicopter services begin as air taxis.

■ commuter

The commuter air carrier is technically a special type of air taxi. The commuter publishes timetables on specific routes that connect lesser populated areas with major cities. As certificated carriers abandon routes, usually low density ones, the commuter enters into a working relationship with the certificated carrier to continue service to the community. The commuter, then, connects small communities that have reduced or no air service with larger communities that have better scheduled service. The commuter's schedule is closely aligned with connecting flight schedules at a larger airport.

■ certificated carriers

The certificated carriers are subject to economic controls by the CAB. Such controls govern fares, schedules, routes, and service levels. The nonscheduled or supplemental (charter) carriers are subject to less stringent controls in these areas. These controls are changing and the CAB is scheduled to be abolished in 1985.

■ charter carriers

The charter or supplemental carriers utilize large planes to transport people or freight. The supplemental carrier has no time schedule nor designated route. The carrier charters the entire plane to transport a group of people or cargo between specified origins and destinations. Many travel tour groups are serviced by charter carriers. However, a big customer for charter carriers is the Department of Defense; it contracts with charter carriers to transport personnel and supplies. (For example, the Viet Nam conflict relied upon charters.) The rates charged and schedules followed are negotiated in the contract. Some examples of charter carriers include: Summit Airways and Zantop International.

■ scheduled carriers

The bulk of the air passenger travel is via scheduled air carriers. Scheduled carriers consist of U.S. major, U.S. national, regional, Hawaiian, Alaskan, and helicopter carriers. These carriers must receive a certificate to operate, and the CAB regulates fares, schedules, and routes.

■ major carriers

U.S. major carriers have $1 billion or more annual revenues and provide service between major population areas within the United States such as New York, Chicago, and Detroit. The routes served by these carriers are usually high density corridors, and the carriers utilize large capacity planes. The U.S. majors also service medium-size population centers such as Toledo, Ohio. Examples of U.S. major carriers are: United, Delta, American, and Eastern.

■ national carriers

U.S. national carriers have annual revenues of $75 million to $1 billion and operate between less populated areas and major populated areas and major population centers. These carriers operate scheduled service over relatively short routes with smaller planes. They "feed" passengers from outlying areas into airports served by the U.S. majors. Today, many of the U.S. national carriers operate over relatively large, regional areas and are stiff competitors for the U.S. majors on many routes. Examples of U.S. nationals include: Frontier, Piedmont, and PSA.

■ international carriers

Many U.S. major and national carriers are also international carriers and operate between the continental United States and foreign countries and between the United States and its territories (e.g., Puerto Rico). Since the countries served by international carriers has an effect on U.S. international trade and relations, the president of the United States is involved in awarding international routes.

■ regional carriers

Regional carriers have annual revenues of less than $75 million and have operations similar to the nationals. The carriers operate within a particular region of the country, such as New England or the Midwest, and connect lesser populated areas with larger population centers. Included in the regional carrier category are the following: Air New England, Air Wisconsin, Midway, Aspen, and Sun West.

■ intrastate carriers

The intrastate carriers consist of the Hawaiian and Alaskan lines. The Hawaiian carriers link the different Hawaiian islands, providing an alternative to water transportation to the residents and tourists of this state. The Alaskan carriers connect the outlying areas of Alaska with the major Alaskan cities. Both groups utilize small planes and operate over short routes.

■ helicopters

The final classification of air carriers, helicopters, consists of certified scheduled carriers utilizing helicopters. As of 1979, only one helicopter line was operating. The high cost of operating a helicopter and the limited carrying capacity (6 to 10 passengers) and range (approximately 300 miles) have made scheduled helicopter services noncompetitive with other air and surface carriers. The majority of new helicopter carriers are operating as air taxis.

In summary, as Figure 7.1 indicates, the air carrier industry consists of for-hire and private carriers, the for-hire carriers encompass scheduled, nonscheduled, and exempt carriers. The bulk of the revenue passengers are carried by U.S. major and national carriers.

Number of Carriers

The for-hire segment of the air carrier industry consists of a small number of large firms. In comparison to the motor carrier industry with over

59,000 for-hire carriers (regulated and exempt), the air carrier industry is made up of about 4,100 for-hire carriers.

Air carrier revenues are concentrated in the scheduled carriers. Approximately 93 percent of the 1978 industry revenue[4] was received by the scheduled carriers that represent less than 20 percent of the industry. The remaining 7 percent of the 1978 industry revenue was distributed among the 4,000 (approximately) air taxi, commuter, and charter carriers.

In reality there are more than four all-cargo carriers. The four all-cargo carriers have been joined by many certificated and noncertificated carriers in the air cargo segment as a result of the 1977 air cargo deregulation law. The law eliminated entry controls into the air cargo field thus enabling additional carriers to enter.

Lastly, private air transportation has been estimated to include approximately 40,000 company-owned planes, with about 500 of the major U.S. corporations operating a private air fleet.[5] In addition, there are thousands of planes used for personal, recreational, and instructional purposes.

Service Characteristics

■ speed

Undoubtedly, the major service characteristic (advantage) of air transportation is speed. The terminal-to-terminal time for a given trip is lower via air transportation than via any of the other modes. Commercial jets are capable of routinely flying at speeds of 500 to 600 miles per hour, thus making a New York to California trip, approximately 3,000 miles, a mere six-hour journey.

■ flight frequency

This advantage of high terminal-to-terminal speed has been dampened somewhat by reduced frequency of flights and congestion at airports. As a result of deregulation, the air traffic controllers' strike of 1981, and lower carrier demand, the number of flights offered to and from low density communities has been reduced in order to increase the utilization of a given plane. As noted in the previous section, commuter air lines have been substituted on some routes where major and national lines find the traffic volume to be too low to justify using large planes.

■ transfers

The use of commuters requires transfer and rehandling of freight since commuter service does not cover long distances.

■ congestion

Recently, air carriers have been concentrating their service on the high density routes, New York to Chicago, for example. In addition, many carriers have adopted the hub terminal approach in which most flights go through a hub terminal, Atlanta and Chicago are examples. These two factors have aggravated the air traffic congestion and ground congestion at major airports and increased the overall transit time.

■ benefits of speed

The shippers who use air carriers to transport freight are primarily interested in the speed of the service and its resultant benefits such as reduced inventory levels and inventory carrying costs. Acceptable or improved service levels can be achieved by using air carriers to deliver orders in short time periods. Stockouts can be controlled, reduced, or eliminated by responding to shortages via air carriers.

In addition, the packaging required for freight shipped by air transportation is usually less than for other modes. It is not uncommon in air transportation to find a palletized shipment wrapped with a piece of plastic. The relatively smooth ride through the air and the automated ground handling systems contribute to lower damage and, thus, reduced packaging need.

The cargo carrying capacity of most planes is small in comparison to the vehicles used in the other modes. The all-cargo carrying capacity of a wide body, four-engine jet is about 90 to 100 tons, whereas a regular body four-engine jet has a capacity of 35 to 40 tons. However, the same planes used for both passenger and cargo have cargo capacities of about 50 and 20 tons, respectively.

Normally, small shipments, less than 500 pounds, are moved by air carriers. Rates have been established for weights as low as 10 pounds, and rate discounts are available for shipments weighing a few hundred pounds. Adding freight to the baggage compartment on passenger flights necessitates rather small size shipments and thus supports rate-making practices for those shipments.

With the exception of absolutely impossible weather conditions such as zero ceiling or blizzards, air carriers are capable of providing reliable service. The carriers may not always be on time to the exact minute, but the variations in transit time are small. Sophisticated navigational instrumentation permits operation during most weather conditions.

Accessibility is one service characteristic that represents another disadvantage for air carriers. Passengers and freight must be transported to an airport for air service to be rendered. This accessibility problem is reduced when smaller planes and helicopters are utilized that are capable of taking off and landing in relatively short distances. Trucks are used to transport freight to and from airports, and most passengers use private automobiles. Limited accessibility adds time and cost to the air service provided.

Even given the above accessibility problems, air transportation remains a fast method of movement and the only logical mode when distance is great and the time is restricted. The cost of this fast freight service is high, about three times greater than truck and ten times greater than rail. The high speed and high cost suggest why air carriage is considered a premium mode of transportation.

As indicated earlier, the major revenue source for air carriers is passenger transportation. In 1979, approximately 89 percent of total operating revenues was derived from passenger transport. This revenue was generated from about 3.7 million passenger enplanements in 1979.[6] Air transportation dominates the for-hire, long-distance passenger transportation market.

In 1979, approximately 11 percent of total operating revenues was generated from freight transportation. The majority of the freight using air service are high value and/or emergency shipments. The high cost of air transportation is prohibitive for shipping low-value, routine commodities.

■ emergency shipments

For emergency shipments, the cost of air transportation is virtually inconsequential compared to the cost of delaying the goods. For example, an urgently needed part for an assembly line machine may have a $20 value, but if the air freighted parts arrive in time to prevent the assembly line from stopping, the value of that part may become worth hundreds of thousands of dollars. Thus, the $20 part may have an emergency value of $200,000, and the air freight cost is a small portion of this emergency value.

Examples of commodities that move via air carriers include: mail, clothing, communication products and parts, photography equipment, and industrial machinery.[7] Normally, one does not find basic raw materials such as coal, lumber, iron ore, or steel being moved by air carriage. In addition, certain high-valued, perishable commodities are moved by air carriers. Flowers, newspapers, and food delicacies are commonly moved intercity via airplanes.

■ length of haul

Air carriers transport freight long distances. In 1978, the average length of domestic haul was 1,115 miles.[8] This long distance can be compared to an average of about 600 miles for rail and 300 miles for truck. The high speed of the airplane makes a 1,000 mile or more trip a matter of hours versus days for the other modes.

For passenger travel, air carriers dominate the long-distance moves. In 1979, the average length of haul for passenger travel was 714 miles for air carriers.[9] This distance was approximately six times greater than that for intercity bus and nineteen times that of rail.

■ carrying capacity

The capacity of airplanes is dependent upon the type of vehicle. As noted above, some planes (four-engine, wide body) have a seating capacity of about 375 people and an all-cargo carring capacity of 90 to 100 tons. There are many medium-sized planes in use today with a seating capacity of 100 to 150 people and an all-cargo capacity of 35 to 40 tons. A 6 to 20 passenger capacity is common for the commuter plane.

In summary, the air carrier industry consists of regulated (certificated) and nonregulated (private and noncertificated) carriers that realize the bulk of their revenues from transporting passengers. The primary service advantage of air transportation is high speed. Typically, high-valued, emergency, or perishable freight is moved by air carriers.

Cost Structure

■ low fixed and high variable

Like the motor carriers, the air carriers' cost structure consists of high variable and low fixed costs. Approximately 80 percent of total operating costs is variable and 20 percent is fixed. The relatively low fixed cost structure is attributable to governmental (state and local) investments and operation of airports and airways. The carriers pay for the use of these facilities through landing fees, which are variable in nature.

As indicated in Table 7.1, fixed costs—including interest, administration, and depreciation—accounted for 20.1 percent of total operating

Table 7.1 1979 Airline Operating Costs-Percentage Distribution

Cost	Percentage
Fixed	
Interest	2.6
Administration, rentals, depreciation, etc.	17.5
Total fixed	20.1
Variable	
Labor	37.4
Fuel	28.8
Maintenance materials	2.2
Commissions	5.0
Passenger food	3.2
Landing fees	1.7
Advertising & promotion	1.6
Total variable	79.9
	100%

Source: *Air Transport, 1980* (Washington, D.C., 1980, pp. 3, 12, 13, 21.

costs for scheduled airlines in 1979. Variable costs—including labor, fuel, and commissions—amounted to 79.9 percent of total costs in 1979.

■ labor and fuel

Labor and fuel (37.4 and 28.8 percent, respectively) account for 66.2 percent of total operating costs. For 1979, labor costs amounted to $10.11 billion and fuel costs were $7.79 billion (see Table 7.2 for total costs).

■ agent commissions

Another variable cost is commissions, the fees paid to travel agents who book flights for passengers. The travel agents receive a percentage of the air fare for tickets issued on behalf of the carrier. This commission, usually 7%, is deducted from the air fare that the carrier realized. The passenger does not pay a higher fare for tickets purchased from a travel agent, and the passenger does not receive a discount if the ticket is purchased directly from the carrier.

■ other variables

In 1979, passenger food expense was 3.2 percent of total cost, approximately $865 million. Maintenance materials cost the airlines $595 million, 2.2 percent of total costs. Landing fees, advertising, and promotional expenditures were approximately $460 million and $430 million, respectively.

Table 7.2 U.S. Scheduled Airlines Operating Costs (in billions of dollars)

Expense:	1978	1979
Flying operations	7.02	9.93
Maintenance	2.65	3.02
General services & administration		
Passenger services	2.14	2.65
Aircraft & traffic servicing	3.89	4.62
Promotion and sales	2.66	3.46
administrative	.97	1.07
depreciation	1.55	1.68
Total Operating Cost*	21.52	27.04

Source: *Air Transport, 1980* (Washington, D.C., 1980), p. 21.
*Total operating costs include additional expenses not itemized.

In Table 7.2 the operating costs for U.S. scheduled carriers are presented by function for 1978 and 1979. Flying operations (crew, fuel, etc.) amounted to $9.93 billion or 66.2 percent of total costs. Maintenance was $3.02 billion or 11.2 percent. General service and administrative costs totaled $11.8 billion or 43.6 percent. Depreciation cost was $1.68 billion or 6.2 percent. (The total cost indicated in Table 7.2 includes other items not listed.)

Labor

As indicated in Table 7.1, labor costs represent 37.4 percent of total operating expenses. In 1979, major and national carriers employed 330,393 people at an average annual compensation of $30,003.[10] Average compensation includes wages and fringe benefits.

Airlines employ people with a variety of different skills. To operate the planes, the carrier must employ pilots, copilots, and navigators. The plane crew also includes the flight attendants who serve the passengers. Communications personnel are required to tie together the geographically spread operations. Mechanics and ground crews for aircraft and traffic service provide the necessary maintenance and servicing of the planes. The final component of airline employment consists of the office personnel and management.

■ skill requirements

■ safety regulations

Strict safety regulations are administered by the Federal Aviation Administration (FAA). Acceptable flight operations, as well as hours of service, are specified for pilots. Both mechanics and pilots are subject to examinations about safety regulations and prescribed operations. FAA regulations also dictate appropriate procedures for flight attendants to follow during takeoff and landing.

The wages paid to pilots vary according to the pilots' plane rating. That is, a pilot who is technically capable (he has passed a flight examination for a given type of aircraft) of flying a jumbo jet will receive a higher compensation than one who flies a single engine, six-passenger plane.

Fuel

■ rising cost

Rapidly escalating fuel costs have caused serious problems for the airlines in recent years. The average price per gallon of fuel for domestic operations was about 88¢ in October 1980, compared to 57¢ in 1979 and 39¢ in 1978. For international operations, the average price per gallon reached 112¢ in October 1980.

■ fuel consumption

The impact such fuel cost increases have had can be shown by analyzing fuel consumption for certain aircraft that are commonly used today. For example, a CAB report shows that the number of gallons of fuel consumed per hour for the following planes is as follows[11]:

747	3238 gallons/hour
DC-10	2261 gallons/hour
727	1287 gallons/hour
737/DC-9	868 gallons/hour

In October 1980, with fuel at 88¢ per gallon, the fuel cost per hour was

$2,849 for a 747, $1,989 for a DC-10, $1,132 for a 727, and $764 for a 737/DC-9.

As fuel costs have risen, carriers are scrutinizing planes utilized in the fleet as well as routes served. More fuel-efficient planes are being developed and will be added to carrier fleets in the future. In the short run, carriers are substituting smaller planes on low density (low demand) routes and eliminating service completely on other routes. Commuter lines have provided substitute service on the routes abandoned by major and national carriers.

■ plane size and route density

Equipment

■ operating costs and plane size

As mentioned above, the cost of operating airplanes varies. Larger planes are more costly to operate per hour than smaller planes, but the cost per seat mile is lower for larger planes. That is, the larger plane has the ability to carry more passengers; thus, the higher cost is spread over a larger number of output units. Table 7.3 provides 1979 hourly operating costs for four aircrafts used by major carriers.

An examination of Table 7.3 shows that the cost per block hour was $3,707 for the 378-seat 747 and $1,145 for the 95-seat 737/DC-9. However, the cost per seat mile was $0.022 for the 747 and $0.0399 for the 737/DC-9. This reduced operating cost per seat mile for larger planes indicates that economies of scale exist in air equipment.

Table 7.3 1979 Aircraft Operating Cost of Major Carriers ($Per block hour)

Operating Expense	747[a]	DC-10[b]	727[c]	737/DC-9[d]
Flying Operations				
Crew	$ 545.4	$ 506.7	$ 354.9	$ 329.0
Fuel & oil	1,918.4	1.308.8	746.0	493.5
Insurance	16.9	16.2	5.5	2.8
Other	.3	.8	.2	.1
Total	$2,481.1	$1,832.5	$1,106.6	$ 826.2
Maintenance — flight equipment				
Airframe — direct	202.1	177.2	68.0	73.7
Engine — direct	241.1	216.5	55.4	50.7
Overhead	292.5	257.0	103.6	106.4
Total	$ 735.7	$ 650.8	$ 227.0	$ 230.9
Depreciation, rentals, and amortization of capital Leases				
Depreciation — airframe	$ 223.3	$ 301.3	$ 93.7	$ 47.8
Depreciation — engine	75.1	77.1	21.4	10.1
Obsolescence	10.1	12.7	2.3	6.0
Rentals & amortization	181.8	60.0	22.0	24.4
Total	$ 490.3	$ 490.1	$ 139.4	$ 88.3
Total operating expenses	$3,707.1	$2,943.5	$1,473.0	$1,145.4
Total cost/seat mile	$0.0220	$0.0270	$0.0334	$0.0339

Source: Civil Aeronautics Board, *Aircraft Operating Cost and Performance Report* Washington, D.C.: U.S. Government Printing Office, July, 1980).

[a]Seat capacity = 378
[b]Seat capacity = 267
[c]Seat capacity = 122
[d]Seat capacity = 95

An important measure of operating efficiency used by air carriers is the operating ratio. The operating ratio measures the portion of operating income that goes to operating expenses:

$$\frac{\text{operating expenses}}{\text{operating income}} \times 100$$

Only income and expenses generated from passenger and freight transportation are considered.

Like the motor carrier industry, the air carrier industry's operating ratio is in the high 90s. Between 1975 and 1979, the air carrier industry had an operating ratio ranging from 94.0 to 99.2. The overall profit margin is small.

Another widely used measure of operating efficiency is the load factor. The load factor measures the percentage utilized of a plane's capacity:

$$\text{load factor} = \frac{\text{number of passengers}}{\text{total number of seats}} \times 100$$

Airlines have raised plane load factors to the low to mid 60s or to 62-65 percent. The particular route and type of plane (capacity) directly affect the load factor as does price, service level, and competition.

Again, referring to Table 7.3, the relationship among load factor, cost, plane size, and profitability can be seen. Assume that a route requires one hour to traverse and has a load factor of 65 percent; the average operating cost per passenger for a 747 is $15.13 ($3,707 per hour ÷ 378 [capacity] x .65 [load factor]). If the load factor dropped to 60 percent, or 227 passengers, the average hourly cost per passenger would increase to $16.33, a 7.9 percent increase in cost.

If the demand dropped to 85 passengers on the route, the load factor for the 747 would be 22.5 percent (85/378) and the hourly operating cost per passenger would be $43.62. At this level of demand, the carrier would substitute a smaller capacity plane, a 727 or 737/DC-9. With 85 passengers, the load factor for the 737/DC-9 would be 89.5 percent (85/95) and the average operating cost per passenger would be $13.47 ($1,145 ÷ 85). The small aircraft would be more economical to operate over this lower density (demand) route, and the carrier would substitute this more efficient plane (737/DC-9) on this hypothetical route.

Equipment substitution, however, may not be possible. If it is possible, substitution may result in excess capacity. The large, jumbo planes have large carrying capacities that may not be utilized in low demand routes. Thus, large capacity planes are used on heavy demand routes such as New York-Chicago and New York-Los Angeles and smaller capacity planes are used on low demand routes such as Toledo-Chicago and Pittsburgh-Memphis.

Economies of Scale

There do appear to be some economies of scale in large scale air carrier operations. Economies of scale result from more extensive use of large size planes or indivisible units. The small number of major and national carriers, approximately 30, that transport over 90 percent of the passengers suggest that large scale operations exist.

The information contained in Table 7.3 suggests the existence of economies of scale with large size planes. The cost per seat-mile for four

■ plane size and utilization

planes is depicted in Figure 7.2. Although not a complete picture, the graph does indicate lower costs per seat-mile as larger size planes, indivisible inputs, are used. Market condition (sufficient demand) must exist to permit the efficient utilization of larger size planes.

Another factor suggesting large scale operations for air carriers is the integrated communication network required for factors such as

■ communication network

operating controls and passenger reservations. Small local or regional carriers find the investment required for such a communication system rather staggering; but without the communication system, the emerging carrier cannot effectively operate (provide connecting service with other carriers and through ticketing to passengers). Such carriers have purchased passenger reservation systems from large carriers in order to be competitive.

The air carrier industry, overall, has a cost structure that closely resem-

Figure 7.2 Operating Cost Per Seat-Mile by Size of Plane

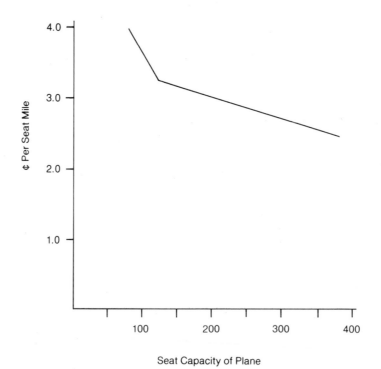

Seat Capacity of Plane

bles that of motor carriers. Long-run economies of scale, as compared to short-run economies of plane size and utilization, are not significant in the air carrier industry.

Federal Subsidy

■ purpose

Over the years the federal government has provided direct operating subsidies—that is, public service revenues, to air carriers. The subsidies have been provided to assure air carrier service over particular routes where operating expenses exceed operating incomes. The subsidies enable regional carriers to provide service to lesser populated areas that would probably not have air service, otherwise.

In fiscal year 1978, the federal government paid $76.2 million in subsidies to twelve regional carriers. This compares to $78.1 million paid in fiscal year 1977. Such subsidies are administered by the CAB which reviews the operating efficiency of the carrier as well as the public interest. Since 1968, the subsidies have totaled less than $100 million per year.

Competition

Competition among the air carriers is very intense, both in terms of rates and service, even though the number of carriers is small. As air carrier regulation was reduced in 1978, new carriers entered given routes (markets), thereby increasing the amount of competition.

■ excess capacity

As the competition has increased, fare wars have developed on high density routes in recent years, even though operating costs have increased. The fare reductions emanated from the existence of excess capacity (too many flights and seat miles on a route) and from carrier management attempting to attract passengers, via low fares, to fill the empty seats.

■ deregulation

As new carriers started to serve a route, fares fell (while costs continued to increase) as did profits. The end result has been a reduction in the number of carriers and flights on many routes, in particular, low traffic routes. After the passage of the Airline Deregulation Act in 1978, many communities experienced an influx of new carriers, many of whom exited within 12 to 18 months. Now these same communities (lesser populated areas) have fewer flights than before the deregulation act.

■ service competition

Competition in service takes many forms, but the primary service competition is the frequency and timing of flights on a route. Carriers attempt to provide flights at the time of day when passengers want to fly, usually 7:00 A.M. to 8:00 P.M. A heavy concentration of flights (departures) is found in the early morning (7:00 A.M. to 10:00 A.M.) and late afternoon (4:00 P.M. to 6:00 P.M.).

In addition to frequency and timing of flights, air carriers attempt to differentiate their service through advertising and passenger amenities. The promotion of such things as on-time arrival and friendly employees attempts to convince the passenger that a particular carrier has the desired quality of service. Gourmet meals and on-board movies are some of the passenger amenities that a carrier utilizes to entice passengers to use and reuse its service.

For cargo service, competition has been intense also. The complete deregulation of air cargo has resulted in competitive rates being pub-

■ cargo competition

lished by the air carriers, but these rates are still higher than those available via surface carriers. Freight shipping schedules have been marketed that emphasize low transit times between given points. To overcome accessibility problems, some carriers provide door-to-door service through contracts with trucking companies.

Although the number of major and national carriers is small, approximately 30, the competition among the carriers is great. This competition will become even greater as the carriers attempt to eliminate excess capacity resulting from currently reduced travel patterns.

Terminals

■ user fees

■ public financing and operation

■ airport services

■ hub concept

As indicated in the previous section on operating costs, air carriers have the terminal (airport) financed by the government. The carriers pay for the use of the airport through landing fees, rent and lease payments for space, taxes on fuel, and aircraft registration taxes. In addition, users pay a tax on airline tickets and air freight charges.

The growth and development of air transportation is dependent upon adequate airport facilities. So, to assure the viability of air transportation, the federal government took the responsibility of financially assisting the states in the construction of airport facilities. The various states and local governments assume the responsibility for operating and maintaining the airports.

In addition, the FAA operates and controls the airways. The FAA monitors the takeoff, landing, and flight of an aircraft. A good deal of the control is computerized, but the human element is still a vital link in the safe operation of the airways.

At the airport, the carriers perform passenger, cargo, and aircraft servicing. Passengers are ticketed, loaded and unloaded, and their luggage is collected and dispersed. Cargo is routed to specific planes for shipment to the destination airport or to waiting delivery trucks. Aircraft servicing includes refueling, loading of passengers, cargo, luggage, supplies (food), and maintenance. Major aircraft maintenance is performed at specified airports.

As carrier operations grow more complex, certain airports in the carrier's scope of operation become a hub. A hub airport serves as a focal point for the origin and termination of flights. Flights from outlying, lesser populated areas are fed into the hub airport where connecting flights are available to other areas of the region or country.

For example, Chicago is a hub airport for United Airlines. Flights from cities such as Toledo and Kansas City fly into Chicago where connecting flights are available to New York, Los Angeles, and Dallas. Delta Airlines utilizes the Atlanta airport in the same way. By utilizing the hub airport approach, the carriers are able to assign smaller aircraft to feed passengers into the hub over small density routes and to assign larger planes to the heavier density routes between the hub and an airport serving a major metropolitan area. In essence, the hub airport is similar to the motor carrier's break-bulk terminal.

Conclusion

The air carrier industry is primarily a transporter of passengers. Although air carriers transport freight, approximately 90 percent of the for-hire carrier revenues is derived from passengers. The majority of the air carrier revenues are concentrated in the major, national, charter, and air cargo carriers. The air carrier cost structure is characterized by high variable and low fixed costs, with fuel and labor accounting for 65 percent of total costs. The primary service characteristic of air transportation is its high speed, which makes air transportation advantageous for long-distance moves and emergency shipments. Since the cost of air transportation is high, typical air shipments are high-valued goods.

Study Questions

1. Compare and contrast the different types of air carriers.
2. Why are commuter lines growing so rapidly?
3. Discuss the service characteristics of air transportation.
4. Compare and contrast the service and cost characteristics of air transportation with those of rail and truck.
5. Discuss the cost structure of air carriers, pointing out the major reasons for this structure.
6. What is a load factor? How is it utilized by air carriers?
7. Comment upon the existence of economies of scale in air transportation.
8. What purpose does the operating subsidy to air carriers serve?
9. Describe the nature and extent of air carrier competition.
10. Discuss the functions performed at the airport.
11. During the past few years, air freight charter activity has become more popular to a variety of shippers. While scheduled air freight service will often meet the needs of the traffic manager, there are a number of conditions under which air charters make economic sense. Please identify and discuss three such conditions. (AST&T, Fall 1977, Exam #2).
12. The CAB recently authorized 25 percent discounts on fares for trips over 750 miles, even though most air carriers are not making a profit. What economic justification can be given for such an action? (AST&T, Spring 1975, Exam #1).

Notes

1. Transportation Association of America, *Transportation Facts and Trends*, 16th ed. (Washington, D.C., 1980), p. 5.
2. Ibid., pp. 4, 8.
3. Ibid., pp. 23-24.
4. Air Transportation Association of America, *Air Transport* (Washington, D.C., 1980), p. 1.

5. Robert M. Kane and Alan D. Vose, *Air Transportation*, 7th ed. (Dubuque, Iowa: Kendall/Hunt Publishing Co., 1979), p. 1-14.

6. Air Transportation Association of America, *Air Transport*.

7. For additional listings, see Airport Activity Statistics of Certified Air Carriers, Civil Aeronautics Board/Federal Aviation Administration (Washington, D.C.: U.S. Government Printing Office, 1980).

8. Transportation Association of America, *Transportation Facts and Trends*, p. 14.

9. Ibid., p. 15.

10. Air Transportation Association of America, *Air Transport*, p. 12.

11. Civil Aeronautics Board, *Aircraft Operating Cost and Performance Report*, (Washington, D.C.: U.S. Government Printing Office, July 1980).

Suggested Readings

Douglas, George W., and Miller, James C. *Economic Regulation of Domestic Air Transport: Theory and Policy*. Washington, D.C.: Brookings Institute, 1974.

Ellis, Raymond H. "Intercity Airline Schedules: Productivity vs. Level-of-Service Trade-offs." *Annual Proceedings of the Transportation Research Forum*, 1978, pp. 423-425.

Harper, Donald V. *Transportation in America*. Englewood Cliffs, N.J.: Prentice-Hall, 1978, Chap. 14.

Kane, Robert M., and Vose, Alan D. *Air Transportation*. 7th ed. Dubuque, Iowa: Kendall/Hunt Publishing Co., 1979.

Lieb, Robert C. *Transportation: The Domestic System*. 2d ed. Reston, Va.: Reston Publishing Co., 1981, Chap 6.

Sampson, Ray J., and Farris, Martin T. *Domestic Transportation*. 4th ed. Boston: Houghton Mifflin Co., 1979, Chaps. 2, 5, and 22.

Strasheim, Mahlon R. *The International Airline Industry*. Washington, D.C.: Brookings Institute, 1969.

Taneja, Kawal K. *The Air-Freight Industry*. Lexington, Mass.: D. C. Heath and Company, 1979.

Taneja, Kawal K. *The Commercial Airline Industry*. Lexington, Mass.: D. C. Heath and Company, 1977.

Wood, Donald F., and Johnson, James C. *Contemporary Transportation*. Tulsa: Petroleum Publishing Co., 1980, Chap. 7.

Wyckoff, D. Daryl, and Maister, David H. *The Domestic Airline Industry*. Lexington, Mass.: D. C. Heath and Company, 1977.

Case   Southeast Air

Southeast Air is an air taxi operation that was formed in 1972. It is privately owned by a group of former Air Force personnel who reside in Pateville. The company serves as a connector to trunk airlines in Metro and some local traffic is experienced. Its two lines extend from Metro: one goes east to Grandrun and one goes west to Pateville.

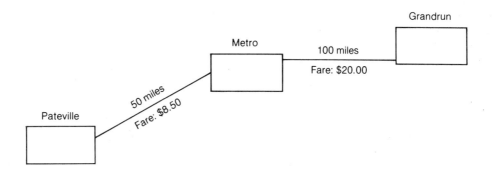

The operations of the firm are such that two planes are used in continuous schedules from 6:00 A.M. to 11:30 P.M. The planes have seats for twenty passengers. Four roundtrips are made between Grandrun and Metro each day (eight runs), and two of these continue on to Pateville (four runs each day). All business originates or terminates at Metro.

Grandrun is a town that has become built up since World War II with plants that have relocated from the north. Most of the business handled by Southeast is from executives and other professionals who use the line to Metro because there is no adequate bus or train service, or even any good highways between there and Metro. The line charges a $20 fare, and the planes consistently have a 95 percent load factor at that rate. Any lower fare does not attract additional passengers.

Pateville is a city with a much lower level of economic development and activity. The incomes of its citizens are lower and most of the industry is of the low labor cost type so often found in the region. It is not classified as a good "air city." Because there is good bus service and a good highway between Pateville and Metro, Southeast Air faces strong competition.

The line experimented with various fares over the past year, and the results of each rate are as follows:

Fare	No. passengers/day
$ 6.00	60
7.00	58
7.50	56
8.00	54
8.50	52
9.00	45
10.00	40
11.00	35
12.00	30

The competing bus company charges $4, and total transit time from downtown Pateville to downtown Metro by bus is only about forty-five minutes longer than the plane alternative.

The management of the firm is now faced with two external attacks that it must address in the next few weeks. One, is from the Redhound Bus Company who argues that the fare from Pateville to Metro is too low, and for that reason the air rate should be raised. They are naturally fighting for business that the airline took away when it initiated service to Pateville. Redhound's main argument stems from the fact that Southeast Air is operating the Pateville line below costs and that this constitutes destructive competition (an action that should be stopped by raising fares to a full cost level). Redhound is basing its argument on the annual report data that Southeast Air must file with the state regulatory agency each year (see Table 7.4).

Table 7.4 Financial Report of Southeast Air for the Latest Year

Revenues:		
Grandrun Line:	Fare: $20.00 Load factor: 95% Runs/day: 8 (four round trips)	20¢ per mile
Pateville Line:	Fare: $8.50 Load factor: 65% Runs/day: 4 (two round trips)	17¢ per mile
Costs:		
Flight costs and landing fees:	$1.40 per mile on both lines	
Overhead Costs:	Grandrun line:	Grandrun station fixed costs: $200/day Metro station fixed costs: $400/day Company airplane depreciation, repair and maintenance: $600/day Company management costs: $300/day
	Pateville line:	Pateville station fixed costs: $100/day

The second attack comes from the Grandrun Chamber of Commerce. Consisting of the various industries and professional groups in Grandrun, it has presented a complaint against Southeast Air to the state Public Utility Commission. Their argument is that the Grandrun line is being burdened to pay for the Pateville run. That is, losses on the Pateville line are made up by excessive profits on the 95 percent factor. The four runs to Pateville should pay their share of the costs.

These arguments are now of concern to the Southeast's vice president of finance. He is taking a fresh look at the Pateville run with an eye toward abandoning it. If the company does abandon the run it will retain the two planes and still have to pay the full rent it now pays at Metro.

1. Is Redhound's allegation correct? Is the company operating below costs on the Pateville run? Should they raise their rates, and if so, to what level?

2. Is Grandrun's Chamber of Commerce on firm grounds saying that it is subsidizing the Pateville passengers? If so, what arguments can be made for this practice?

3. Assuming you are the vice president of finance, would it be a sound decision to discontinue the two round trips per day to Pateville?

4. Suppose Redhound dropped their fare to $3.50 which would force the airline to drop its rate to $6.00; what should the firm's decision be then?

Part III

Special Carriers and Services

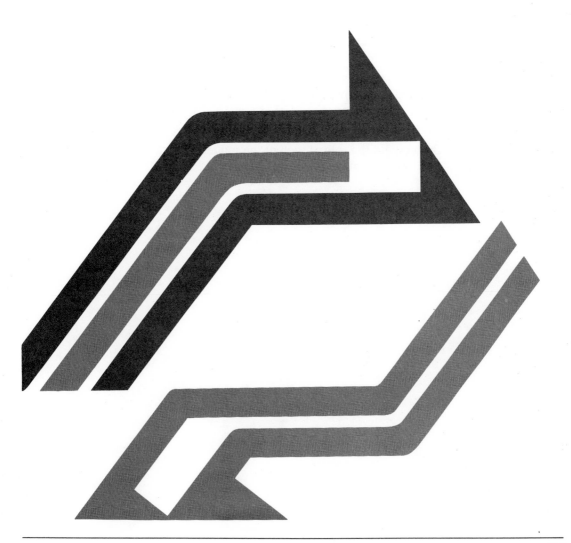

8 Transportation Equipment and Service

After reading this chapter you should:

1 Understand a market share overview of each of the modes of transportation.

2 Be able to discuss the types of equipment available from each of the modes of transportation.

3 Understand the services available to passengers via the various modes of transportation.

4 Understand the role of each of the modes of transportation in the total transportation system.

It is often difficult for students to visualize transportation, which is a service and not a physical, tangible product. It is helpful here to ask, What is the transportation product? It is a service to the user. It has basic characteristics that make obtaining this service similar to buying goods.

■ movement service

One aspect of transportation service consists of the *movement service*. This includes the speed, whether it is door-to-door or terminal-to-terminal, and the frequency of transportation. Another factor is the *equipment* used, which is a major consideration in both passenger and freight service. The equipment relates to passenger comfort, whereas in freight service it is a major factor in shipment preparation, size, and loading and unloading costs. The third factor is *price* or, in transportation, *rate*. This includes the primary charge made by the main carrier as well as any other peripheral costs borne by the user for that service. These additional costs include service accessment, packaging requirements, detention, demurrage, claims, and loss.

■ chapter overview

This chapter presents an overview of most of the available forms of freight and passenger services. Included in this discussion is an analysis of modal split which shows the macro-market share of the freight and passenger modes as well as modal selection factors which determine how shippers and passengers choose their transportation.

Freight Transportation

■ freight split

Approximately 9 percent of the U.S. gross national product (GNP) is spent in the form of freight movement.[1] On a for-hire intercity basis, this transportation activity takes place in the following ton-mile proportions, or modal split: railroads 36.6 percent, trucks 24.2 percent, Great Lakes shipments 3.9 percent, rivers and canals 11.9 percent, oil pipelines 23.2 percent and air .2 percent for a total of 100 percent.[2] Through the past three decades, the rail share of the total has been declining, but the actual number of ton-miles hauled has increased. That is, though it has lost market share, actual rail volume has grown. Private transportation is not included in the above split figures. Few statistics are collected in the private carriage area. Various sources estimate that between 40 and 60 percent of all transportation in ton-miles is private carriage, the majority of which is motor carriage.

■ revenues split

Modal split takes on another dimension when it is shown in terms of the proportion of total revenues. In this context, in 1978 the motor mode was highest with about 76.5 percent of total intercity traffic revenues; railroads received 11.4 percent, water carriers of all types 6.4 percent, oil pipelines 2.8 percent, and air 1.4 percent made up the rest of the total revenue.[3]

Analysis of ton-miles and revenue splits shows that the water mode carries low-value-to-weight commodities such as coal, fertilizers, chemicals, and petroleum products. Railroads, likewise, predominantly haul relatively low-value bulk commodities. Motor carriers, on the other hand, characteristically move higher-valued goods which tend to be finished commodities and shipments that are high in cost to move. The high revenue for motor carriers per ton carried is evidence of these phenomena. Air freight typically consists of movements of very high-valued goods such as pharmaceuticals, and medical supplies. These products require fast service and are capable of withstanding the relatively high rates of this mode.

The modal split phenomenon can be viewed visually as a pyramid. Figure 8.1 shows the approximate ton-mile market shares in terms of size of the groupings and relative position. The other phenomenon pertinent to this analysis is the competitive relationships of the modes. Commodity value per pound is high on the top, dropping to lowest on the bottom. In keeping with this is the speed of service (high on the top) as well as the level of rates charged (same). Also illustrated in Figure 8.1 is the fact that the greatest modal competition that motor carriers experience is with air carriers for commodities seeking superior service on the one hand, and a large degree of competition with railroads on the other. Railroads compete for high-valued goods against motor carriers and against water carriers for low-valued commodity traffic. Water carriers experience competition with railroads where routes and commodities are in close proximity. Pipelines repre-

Figure 8.1 Modal Split Relationships

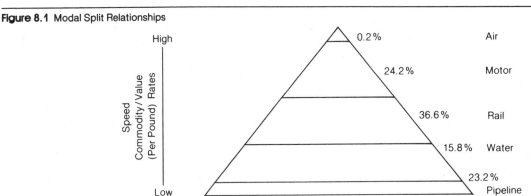

sent competition for both railroads and water carriers when large volumes of bulk liquid commodities can be hauled between two points on a long-term basis.

**Modal
Selection**

The above discussion provides some insights into the process of modal selection by freight shippers. Factors entering into the actual selection of a mode include transportation cost, transit time, transit time reliability, capability of the mode (size, weight, etc.), accessibility, and security. Modal selection is basically a long-term decision. It often comes into play when the firm is undergoing a major logistics system audit and analysis, or when new products or plants have been brought on-line. The use of one mode or another often involves major loading and unloading facility investment by shippers and receivers. Modal shifts, then, are generally not made easily. Firms will sometimes shift modes, though, when significant dissatisfaction arises.

Once the mode is selected, the firm must then select the specific carriers. Note that the entire set of key decision factors involved are presented in Chapter 14, Traffic Management.

**Supply of
Domestic Freight
Transportation**

Rail. The rail mode has many forms of equipment available for use. Rail cars have distinct movement characteristics for different commodities, shipments, or services.

Two broad categories of rail equipment exist: standard or specially equipped. Standard equipment consists of basic box, gondola, flat, and hopper cars which are provided for shipments on a nondiscriminatory basis. Special equipment consists of similar cars that have extra features which are more costly to provide and are usually more desirable for shippers to use. Specially equipped cars technically need not be made available for use by the entire shipping public. Because of their extraordinary investment costs, railroads often will not provide such equipment to particular shippers of specific low-rated commodities. Instead, the railroads will control these cars and offer them in a variety of ways. One is to treat them as "freerunners" which are controlled and made available for loading whenever compatible high-rated shipments are requested. Another control approach is to assign a group of specially equipped cars to a specific shipper for his exclusive use. These are often called "shipper pools." An example is rail cars for automobile parts—these cars have internal features usable only by one auto firm. A final major group of rail cars is shipper-supplied cars. These are cars which are either leased or purchased by shippers and are used only by them or other firms which sublease the cars. This is a practice employed by large shippers when they require a particular type of car and seek an assured supply of that type of rail equipment. Descriptions of specific forms of rail equipment are presented below.

1. Standard Box Cars. These are, in essence, enclosed boxes which provide sealed protection for shipments. These cars have no internal features other than a floor and walls into which nails can be driven

when bracing shipments. Standard box cars are used for packaged goods and some bulk commodities such as specialty ores and grain which require protection from the elements. Standard box cars typically are 40 feet long (4,000 cu. ft.) and 50 feet long (4,900 cu. ft.) and have payload capacities of 100,000 pounds or 50 tons. The smaller car is useful for commodities of 28 pounds per cubic foot or more, whereas the 50-foot car will fully "weigh out" at 100,000 pounds. The full visible capacity of the car will be loaded if the goods reach about 22 pounds per cubic foot. Some railroads have standard 60-foot box cars as well. The trend is for more 50-foot and 60-foot cars and fewer 40-foot cars.

2. Standard Flat Cars. These open platform-like cars are useful for moving large machinery such as construction and farm equipment. The flat car can be end, top, or side loaded in ways the box car will not permit.

3. Standard Hopper Cars. These are open top cars which also allow for unloading by bottom chutes. These are the primary bulk commodity mover for commodities that can withstand exposure to the elements. Coal, some ores, sand, gravel, and stone are moved in these cars. In periods of high grain movements when insufficient covered hopper cars are available, some railroads provide temporary plastic covers for these cars so that bulk grain can be shipped while being protected from the elements.

   Standard hopper cars come in two basic sizes: large and regular. The regular cars haul fairly dense goods such as coal; their cubic and weight capacities are designed for that traffic. Bulk wood chip movements are made by paper companies, but a full load of these are not economical in a regular plain hopper because wood chips are extremely light and bulky. In this situation several railroads have provided jumbo open top hoppers for this traffic.

4. Special Box Cars. Specially equipped box cars provide internal bulkheads and special cushioning devices which reduce shipper bracing expenses. These cars come in 40-foot, 50-foot, 60-foot, and 86-foot sizes. Some are insulated to protect ladings from heat and cold, and others have refrigeration equipment built into them. These cars, and all those following, are assigned to shipper pools, are owned or leased by shippers, or are distributed by railroads according to shipment profitability.

5. Covered Hopper Cars. These are basically hopper cars that have permanent tops with hatches that allow for top loading as well as sealed protection. These come in four basic cubic sizes, all of which typically hold 70 or 100 tons. The 1,900 cubic foot covered hopper is "ideal" for very dense commodities like lime in the 70 pounds per cubic foot range. The 3,200 to 3,500 cubic foot range car is good for fertilizers and flour having 50 to 60 pounds per cubic foot density. The 4,700 cubic foot covered hopper is cubed and weighted out on such goods as oats, corn, and wheat which are in the 42 to 45 pound per cubic foot range.

The 5,700 cubic foot jumbo covered hopper car is useful for light plastic pellets and some bulk free shipments. Covered hopper cars allow for bottom hatch or vacuum unloading.

6. Equipped Flat Cars. These cars are equipped with special tie-down equipment for securing trucks, autos, trailers, and frames. The auto flats come in two and three tier configurations. Some have bulkheads on the ends so that cut pulp wood or large packaged lumber can be moved. Some railroads have drop frame flat cars for moving extremely heavy goods such as utility boilers and turbines.

7. Equipped Gondolas. These are covered gondolas or cars equipped with troughs for coiled steel movement, or both. They eliminate much shipper bracing and cover protection.

8. Tank Cars. These haul bulk liquid or gas commodities such as chlorine, alcohol, corn syrup, or propane. Due to cleaning and contamination problems, the railroad industry has not provided this type of equipment. Instead, it has only been available by leasing from the shipper or purchasing from car builders.

9. Piggyback/Container Equipment. Piggyback shipments consist of highway trailers on special tie-down equipped flat cars. Container "boxes" are moved in this manner as well. These containers come in sizes of 8 feet by 8 feet, 12 feet, 20 feet, 35 feet, and 40 feet which are generally compatible for rail, highway, and container movement. Some containers are equipped with refrigeration, and others have enclosed tanks for bulk chemical, wine, or liquor movements.

Rail cars have generally evolved from the demands of special commodities. Many more unique cars exist; only the major categories are presented here. Though special cars exist or can be designed and constructed, the basic rail network (bridges, rail loads, etc.) of the United States has the capacity to accept cars weighing a total of 263,000 pounds. Since most cars weigh about 30 tons, the normal freight payload limit (unless the car is built for smaller loads) is 100 tons. Generally, if additional payloads are desired, the car weight itself will have to be reduced so that the 263,000 pound limit is not exceeded. Some research has been conducted into using lighter aluminum in car construction, but the extra material cost is generally regarded as not worth the small weight and revenue gain.

Some specially designed heavy payload flat cars can carry up to 200-ton, and in one instance, 400-ton loads. These cars, however, are limited to a few heavy capacity lines.

Motor-Hauled Highway Equipment. Highway equipment comes in five basic forms which are somewhat similar to the forms of rail equipment.

1. Van. This is a basic box having little interior bracing equipment, though it can be equipped with such. Vans come in all sizes from a single truck up to 45 feet to 55 feet long trailers. Some have open tops for overhead crane loading and can have canvas covers affixed for

weather protection. Other trailers are insulated and refrigerated.

2. Flat Trailer. These are designed for flexible loading and unloading from top, sides, and rear. Sometimes large construction equipment is seen on heavy capacity drop frame trailers. This is a form of equipment generally available through contract carriers or the special commodity divisions of common carriers.

3. Racks. These are special trailers that have racks affixed for carrying automobiles.

4. Bulk Trailer. These are special trailers designed for commodities such as dry chemicals, flour, cement, and fertilizers. The open top version of this trailer is often referred to as a dump truck.

5. Tanks. These are designed for bulk liquid movements.

The overall limitations of highway transportation are seen in federal and state size and weight restrictions. The highest federal interstate highway weight limitation is 80,000 pounds, which means about 40,000-42,000 pounds maximum can typically be hauled in the form of goods. Some states still adhere to a previous weight limit set at 73,280 pounds. Weight limitations are also present in the form of weight per axle. Length limitations are generally state imposed; 55 feet or 75 feet in overall length is allowed, with trailers being 45 feet and 55 feet respectively. Width limitations are typically 8 feet; generally this does not vary except in special permit situations. The motor carrier industry continually strives for increased length and weight limitations because this is one of the few readily available productivity gains the industry can seek. Some states allow a single tractor to haul two trailers and some allow three trailers, which brings labor cost savings in over-the-road operations and intermediate break-bulk handling.

Domestic Barge Capabilities. The domestic barge industry offers five basic barges for commodity movement.

1. Open Top Standard Barge. The current standard barge is 35 feet by 195 feet in overall dimensions and can carry up to 1,500 tons. Most carriers assess a minimum charge of 600 tons if the barge itself is not loaded with that weight. This standard size allows uniform tow make-up and traversing in combinations of six or nine barges in 600 foot long locks, or fifteen barges in 1,200 foot long locks.

2. Covered Hoppers. These are standard hoppers with removable hatches which protect lading from the weather. Lumber, some steel, and specialty coal are moved via this equipment. The barge firms sometimes are reluctant to invest in this extra feature because it is prone to handling damage.

3. Bulk Liquid Barge. Some barges are designed as tank barges which are used for gasoline, oil, and chemicals.

4. Integrated Tow Barge. This is a series of barges with a tow designed to operate together as one unit. In individual barge form they vary in de-

sign and shape. They are usually constructed for bulk chemical carriage.

5. LASH Barges. These are special covered barges found in the inland waterway system. They are loaded and towed to New Orleans where they are physically loaded onto a ship and carried overseas intact. Lykes Steamship Company is a major operator of several LASH ships between the Gulf of Mexico and Europe. The advantage of this system is that it avoids physical handling of the goods at the interfacing port.

Air Freight Movement. The air mode permits freight to be moved in three basic forms. Two primary services are also considered in this form of carriage. They are analyzed below.

1. Packaged Freight. This form of movement consists of hand loaded packages which are carried in the belly of aircraft. It is the least efficient form of loading and unloading since the airplane could otherwise be in flight during this dead time.

2. Igloos. These are pallets onto which packages or whole shipments are loaded and held in place by a net, cover, or blanket. This system makes for fast loading and unloading. The igloo shape of the shipment fits the internal wall contours of a narrow body airplane.

3. Containers. These are metal or fiberglass boxes into which freight is loaded for fast loading and unloading to and from the airplane. Containers come in all sizes and are usually designed with a specific airplane in mind. Containers are used for belly and main floor loading.

4. Wide Body Service. The movement of freight in any of the above forms is often sought on what is called "wide body service." This means movement on B747, DC-10, and L1011 aircraft. Shippers seek this service for particularly large payloads.

5. All-Freight Service. Many airlines offer all-freight plane service. The advantage of this is that palletized and large container shipments can be shipped on these flights. Otherwise, shipments would have to be broken up into sizes that would fit into the bellies of passenger aircraft.

Pipelines. This mode of service is only available for bulk carriage of liquid commodities or those commodities that can be made into liquid form by the addition of water in what is then called a "slurry." This mode of service is being considered for the movement of coal.

Passenger Transportation

The other 11 percent of the total 20 percent of the U.S. GNP consumed in transportation is incurred in passenger or people movement. The discussion that follows presents this activity in terms of travel market types, the passenger transportation " product," the available supply of passenger movement, and the role of the travel agent.

Types of Passenger Markets

This chapter presents what is referred to as intercity passenger transportation. Basic intercity passenger travel markets are of three types which are classified by the travel motive. Business travel is one form, and in the airline industry it is estimated to be the largest travel segment in such markets as New York to Washington and Chicago. The characteristics of this market can be described in many ways. For one, ultimate payment of the travel is borne by a party or firm other than the passenger. The demand for the service is not very price-sensitive which is indicated by the fact that the first class sections of airplanes are typically occupied by businessmen. Finally, business travel is very schedule-sensitive. That is, morning flights which arrive at a destination ahead of the bulk of the business day are in high demand, as are flights that originate after 4:00 P.M.

Vacation travel is another intercity passenger market. This market is generally not schedule-sensitive, and, in fact, flights and trips during the day are often sought. It is a price-sensitive market which can be evidenced by the strong airline promotion of fares. Another feature of vacation travel is that the travel itself is often part of the consumed activity. That is, the train ride, plane ride with movies and unique meals, and cruise ship tours become part of the vacation. Business and personal travel, on the other hand, represent travel demand that is secondary in nature.

Personal travel is a catchall term for travel that is not business or vacation oriented. It consists of trips to and from school or out-of-town jobs, or travel for medical or personal reasons such as funerals. This is a difficult travel segment to describe because travel motives are diverse. Carriers give their primary attention to business and vacation travel.

The Passenger Transportation Product

The passenger transportation product takes the form of equipment, facilities, price, and schedule.

The equipment and facilities consist of the conveyance and the comfort of the ride. The comfort can be smoothness on the one hand, or amenities such as meals, movies, and other diversions, on the other. Airlines place heavy reliance upon the width of the passenger seat as a selling item as well as convenience of luggage check-in and seat selection. Appearance of the equipment and facilities is closely evaluated by most travelers as well.

Price is another part of the passenger travel market. It is the "how-much-cost-to-travel" factor. Price includes the actual ticket fare plus access costs such as parking and enroute meals. In this setting, a transcontinental air trip can often be less than a lower fare bus ride, because the bus ride requires the passenger to purchase four days worth of meals.

The schedule is the other service item considered by consumers of passenger travel. It is the "when" of travel. This element makes auto travel preferable in most markets because of its flexibility. In business settings, however, the speed of transit is important. In particular, the time between origin point to destination point is the key factor. For example, train travel is highly desired in the Northeast Corridor between Washington and New York, even though it takes four hours, whereas the plane takes one hour to travel from airport to airport. The train, however, travels from downtown to downtown, and when travel to and from the airport and waiting time are considered, the train can be, and often is, fastest in this medium distance market.

An important factor in passenger travel is understanding the schedule and, in particular, the timetable. Many studies indicate that a majority of the public does not understand how to read a typical timetable. What follows here is a discussion of airline and rail timetables. Rail timetables resemble most bus and commuter timetables.

Air Timetables. Each airline publishes its own timetables in what is known as quick-reference form. Figure 8.2 shows the format of this timetable as it is published in the *Official Airline Guide (OAG)*, a publication that includes the schedules of nearly all the airlines in the world.

Suppose, for example, we wish to determine the details of a trip to Pittsburgh from New York. Figure 8.2 shows the *OAG* entry for this route.

The timetable shows 29 flights to Pittsburgh by AL (USAir), TW (TWA), and NW (Northwest), as indicated in the fifth column of the schedule. Examination of the main schedule body on pp.148-149 shows other data, too.

The fare structure is often different for each airline. The first class fare on TWA is $83.33 plus $6.67 tax for a total of $90.00. Round trip first class is $180.00. Round trip coach fare on the same plane is $150.00. Various other fares in excursion form are available ranging from $75.00 to $127.00.

The timetable is slightly more complicated to read when direct flights are not available between two points. For example, a trip from Spokane, Washington to Pittsburgh requires a change of planes enroute. These are available with changes of planes in ORD (the code for Chicago's O'Hare Airport), DEN (Denver), or MSP (Minneapolis-St. Paul). The trip originates in Spokane (airport code of GEG) and terminates in Pittsburgh (a code of PIT). Spokane is in the pacific standard time zone (PST) and Pittsburgh is in the eastern standard time zone (EST). Assume we have selected the 8:07 A.M. departure. The first 8:07 A.M. entry is our flight combination. This flight leaves Spokane at 8:07 and is Frontier Airline's flight 130, nonstop to Denver (Boeing 737), arriving there at 11:11 A.M. Denver time. A breakfast is served enroute. It is a two hour and four minute flight. We connect to TWA's flight 388, Boeing 707 (serving a snack) which leaves Denver at 2:20 P.M. This nonstop flight arrives in Pittsburgh at 7:03 P.M. The applicable fares are coach only on Frontier and first class or coach on TWA. The one way, coach-first class fare (designated as "A" in Col. 1) is $342.00, whereas the all coach fare labeled "G" is $223.00.

Other sections of the *OAG* show related information such as total itineraries for all flights, airplane information, and the location of airports in relation to local cities. The *OAG* is published in a North Ameri-

Figure 8.2 Example of Official Airline Guide Format

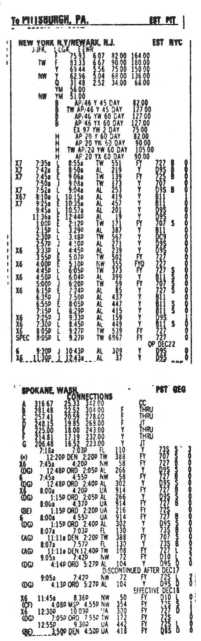

Column 1 indicates frequency:

X6 means not on Saturday
X7 means not on Sunday
SPEC shows TWA flight 6867 flies only on Dec. 22
"blank" means daily

Column 2 indicates time

Column 3 designates New York airports:

  E is Newark
  J is JFK Airport
  L is LaGuardia

Column 4 indicates arrival time in Pittsburgh:

  the nonstop flight takes about an hour and twenty minutes

Column 5 indicates airline name

Column 6 indicates flight number

Column 7 indicates classes of service and fare basis:

  F is first class
  Y is coach
  Q is special excursion fare

Column 8 indicates the type of equipment:

  707 is Boeing 707
  727 is Boeing 727
  D9S is a DC-9, stretch version
  B11 is a BAC-111

Column 9 indicates meals served enroute:

  B is breakfast
  S is snack
  L is lunch
  D is dinner

Column 10 indicates number of enroute stops:

  0 is nonstop
  1 is onestop

can version and a Worldwide version which includes air services in the rest of the world.

Railroad Timetables. Railroad and bus timetables (as well as commuter train timetables) are published in a format which typically shows the entire route of the train or bus. To illustrate, refer to Figure 8.3 which shows Amtrak's route between New York and New Orleans. Let's suppose we are interested in traveling from Atlanta to Baltimore. The timetable shows Train 19 going southbound, while our northbound Train 20 can be found by reading up the timetable. The train departs from Atlanta at 7:05 P.M. each day and stops at Gainsville, Georgia; Spartenburg, South Carolina; and other places and arrives in Baltimore, Maryland at 9:57 A.M. The train is called the Crescent and it has a dining car for all meals, a lounge car for beverages and snacks, coaches with reclining seats, as well as sleeping cars with private sleeping, toilet, and washing facilities. Baggage may also be checked between these two points.

**Intercity
Passenger
Travel Market**

The domestic passenger market can be shown in two contexts: first, for-hire, fare paying travel and second, for-hire with the automobile. Table 8.1 shows that airlines have the majority of all intercity for-hire passen-

Figure 8.3 Example of Amtrak Timetable Format

The Crescent

**New York
Washington
Charlotte
Atlanta
Birmingham
New Orleans**

READ DOWN						READ UP
19			Train Number			20
Daily			Frequency of Operation			Daily
Ⓑ ⊯ ✕ ☊			Type of Service			Ⓑ ⊯ ✕ ☊
	Km	Mi	*(Amtrak)*			
2 15 P	0	0	Dp **New York, NY** *(Penn Sta.) (ET)*		Ar	1 35 P
2 32 P	16	10	Newark, NJ			1 20 P
R 2 48 P	40	25	Metropark, NJ *(Iselin)*			
3 21 P	94	58	Trenton, NJ			12 28 P
4 01 P	145	90	Philadelphia, PA *(30th St.)*			11 50 A
4 28 P	188	116	Wilmington, DE			11 13 A
5 33 P	297	184	Baltimore, MD *(Penn. Sta.)*			9 57 A
♿ 6 10 P	346	215	Beltway Sta., MD *(Lanham)*			♿ 9 23 A
6 30 P	361	225	Ar **Washington, DC** *(ET)*		Dp	9 10 A
			(Southern)			
7 30 P	361	225	Dp **Washington, DC** *(ET)*		Ar	8 30 A
7 47 P	375	233	Alexandria, VA			7 50 A
F 8 18 P	414	257	Manassas, VA ●			F 7 14 A
F 8 52 P	470	292	Culpeper, VA ●			F 6 43 A
9 47 P	542	337	**Charlottesville, VA** *(Union Sta.)*			5 55 A
F 11 02 P	627	390	Monroe, VA ● *(Sweet Briar College)*			F 4 50 A
11 15 P	639	397	**Lynchburg, VA** *(Kemper St. Sta.)*			4 27 A
F 12 39 A	741	460	Danville, VA ⊕			F 3 17 A
1 40 A	818	508	**Greensboro, NC**			2 05 A
F 1 57 A	843	524	High Point, NC ●			F 1 40 A
2 44 A	899	558	Salisbury, NC			1 08 A
3 34 A	966	601	**Charlotte, NC**			12 20 A
F 4 03 A	1004	624	Gastonia, NC ⊕			F 11 47 P
5 03 A	1090	677	Spartanburg, SC ⊕			10 50 P
5 45 A	1140	709	Ar **Greenville, SC**		Dp	10 12 P
6 00 A	1140	709	Dp		Ar	9 57 P
F 6 35 A	1189	739	Clemson, SC ●			F 9 18 P
F 7 13 A	1242	772	Toccoa, GA ●			F 8 43 P
7 55 A	1302	809	Gainesville, GA			8 03 P
8 50 A	1381	858	Ar **Atlanta, GA** *(Peachtree Sta.) (ET)*		Dp	7 05 P
9 05 A	1381	858	Dp		Ar	6 50 P
10 25 A	1544	960	Anniston, AL *(CT)*			3 26 P
12 01 P	1647	1024	Ar **Birmingham, AL** *(Amtrak Sta.)*		Dp	1 55 P
12 15 P	1647	1024	Dp		Ar	1 40 P
1 31 P	1736	1079	Tuscaloosa, AL			12 07 P
F 2 05 P	1792	1114	Eutaw, AL ●			F 11 34 A
F 2 30 P	1834	1140	Livingston, AL ●			F 11 11 A
3 12 P	1892	1176	Ar **Meridian, MS**		Dp	10 38 A
3 27 P	1892	1176	Dp		Ar	10 23 A
F 4 28 P	1986	1234	Laurel, MS ⊕			F 9 31 A
F 5 05 P	2029	1261	Hattiesburg, MS ⊕			F 9 01 A
F 5 22 P	2055	1277	Purvis, MS ●			F 8 44 A
F 5 49 P	2093	1301	Poplarville, MS ●			F 8 21 A
F 6 34 P	2161	1343	Slidell, LA ⊕			F 7 39 A
8 00 P	2218	1378	Ar **New Orleans, LA** *(CT)*		Dp	6 45 A

ger travel. When the automobile is considered in this analysis, it has the majority share and the airline shrinks dramatically.

Supply of Available Intercity Passenger Travel

The supply of intercity passenger transportation services is perhaps best approached from the standpoint of two basic services: long haul and local conveyance.

Long Haul Passenger Travel. This includes the services of air and rail carriers as well as the automobile for moves beyond the sphere of a single city or locale.

1. For-hire Air Service. The United States has a very comprehensive air system. Long-distance passenger travel can be arranged on over twenty carriers. These carriers operate the larger jets such as the B747, L1011, and DC-10 and fly long haul routes. They also have shorter feeder routes served by B727 and DC-9 aircraft which complement the longer markets. These have been traditionally referred to as trunk carriers. Another group of air carriers were previously referred to as regional airlines. These carriers traditionally served short and medium length markets with smaller jets. The advent of air deregulation in 1978 allowed route expansion and mergers to take place to such a degree that these regionals are no longer confined to these markets alone. Southern Airlines now spans the entire United States as a result of mergers with North Central and Air West. Allegheny was previously confined to the Middle Atlantic states. By 1981 Allegheny, renamed USAir, will strongly serve the Southwest and Florida.

   Commuter airlines are a new class of air carriers that have evolved in recent years. They serve markets 75-150 miles in length, generally those markets that were abandoned by the former regional carriers when their jet equipment could no longer efficiently operate in such small markets. The commuter lines operate out of smaller cities; they have from six to thirty seats and serve as feeders to larger airlines. Some commuters even operate under the identity of larger carriers.

2. Private Air Carriage. Many corporations have developed their own private air services for the convenience and routing flexibility of company executives and employees. Though some of these operations would be difficult to justify on purely economic grounds, many firms have geographically dispersed plants which can rationally be

---

Table 8.1 Passenger Modal Split by Passenger-Miles

	For-Hire Only	For-Hire and Automobile
Airplane	79.5%	11.0%
Bus	13.1%	2.0%
Railroad	7.4%	.9%
Automobile	—	86.1%
	100.0%	100.0%

Source: *Transportation Facts and Trends*, 16th ed. (Washington, D.C., 1980), p. 4.

served by this form of carriage alone. This form of transportation is referred to as general aviation by the Civic Aeronautics Board and Federal Aviation Administration.

3. Railroad. Amtrak provides almost all intercity rail services in the United States. It is heavily used in the Northeast Corridor between Washington and Boston with branches to Harrisburg, Pennsylvania and Springfield, Massachusetts. It is used mostly by business travelers in corridor markets and in other markets like Los Angeles-San Diego, Chicago-Milwaukee, St. Louis-Chicago, and Chicago-Detroit. The remaining routes are long-distance markets such as New York-Florida and Chicago-Seattle that are used by personally motivated and vacationing travelers.

4. Bus. This form of passenger travel blankets the United States with a very extensive network. Greyhound and Trailways comprise nearly three-quarters of the passenger-mile segment. This industry experienced declines in ridership throughout the 1960s and 70s as air travel became relatively less expensive and as some Amtrak routes expanded. The bus also suffered from a general personal income growth that led to a greater proportion of the population owning and using the auto. The energy shortage of 1979 caused a resurgence of bus demand which might very well continue if energy shortages and high prices continue. The bus charter market is a very strong one for tours.

5. Cruises. This form of passenger travel is primarily used for vacation purposes only. It was a traditional transoceanic form of carriage until the 1950s, but it virtually disappeared as a traditional means of carriage once the jet permitted low cost travel. Today, cruises operate to warm water locations out of New York, Florida, and the West Coast. The freighter is another form of ship travel that provides interesting travel in limited accommodations on special schedules as freight service demands.

6. Private automobile. This is the predominant form of intercity travel. As noted in Chapter 11, Urban and Metropolitan Transportation, automobiles are generally regarded by most owners as being less costly to use than they really are. Typically, the owner compares the cost of tolls and a total cost of gasoline for point to point trip costs. This grossly underestimates the true cost of driving a car which includes oil, upkeep, tires, and insurance. Estimates by the U.S. Department of Transportation indicate that a 1980 medium-size auto costs 28¢ per mile to operate. This means a 500-mile trip (1,000 miles round trip) will cost in the long run $280. Approximate air fare for the same distance is approximately $175 at the end of 1980. Of course, the automobile is less expensive when three, four, or more people are in it. But, even then, the airline can sometimes be used less expensively on a transcontinental move for a family when total auto, meals, and lodging costs are considered. The most critical point in the analysis of the auto, however, is that the user carefully acknowledges its total true

costs and does not merely compute the cost of tolls and gasoline.

7. Rented Automobile. This is perhaps the highest noticeable cost per mile form of passenger transportation with the exception of the taxi. Rented cars serve a valuable short-term, flexible need at the destination point of many business and some vacation trips. The alternatives are often driving to the destination point, relying totally upon taxi service, or having no means of visiting remote locations.

Long-term leasing is becoming popular as an alternative to car ownership. This is an option used by many salesmen who find leasing to be relatively advantageous, especially when new car acquisition occurs every one or two years.

Local Conveyance. Long-distance passenger transportation typically interfaces with local, short haul transportation to and from the ultimate origins and destinations from the long haul terminal points. Four primary local conveyance for-hire means are currently available and a fifth is emerging in many areas.

1. Limousine. These are available at most airports. They range from vans to large buses and typically operate over a fixed route with set fares. Though they are easy to locate at an airport for trips away from the airport, they tend to be difficult to find at the outlying areas for trips to the airport. Typical limousine routes include stops at major hotels in a city and metropolitan area.

2. Bus. Bus services are available to and from most rail and air terminals by local transit organizations. These are usually slower, local services, but their fares are usually lower and they often serve more individual points than the limousine. A problem exists here too, though, with the lack of information available to the incoming passenger. Unless a person is already familiar with an area and will tolerate a possible interfacing wait, a long-distance passenger will generally utilize another means of local conveyance.

3. Taxi. This is a commonly used transportation interface to and from long haul terminal points. The economics of this form of movement are discussed in Chapter 11, Urban and Metropolitan Transportation.

4. Auto. This, too, is a common flexible means of local conveyance. The major choices are private auto and car rental. Parking facilities at long haul terminal locations are usually high in cost or limited in supply, or both. Many airport authorities rent parking services as concessions to private firms that will manage them. The bid awards are often made on the basis of the chosen operator projecting the highest return to the agency in terms of rent or a percentage of parking fees. Due to this process, there is an upward incentive built into the cost structure of these services.

5. Rail. Subway services are currently available to the Cleveland and Washington National Airports. A promoted rail-bus link is available

at New York's JFK and Chicago's O'Hare Airports. Current subway construction is taking place to link downtown areas with O'Hare and Atlanta's Hartsfield Airport. These direct links provide fast, low fare access to downtown areas without dependence upon the auto.

Another type of rail-air terminal link exists at Newark, New Jersey where the Amtrak station is linked by bus with the Newark Airport. There is also a rail-airport link at Baltimore-Washington International Airport. These services provide links between long-distance air and short- and medium-distance rails which serve many points not served by air.

A major problem exists in the interface among most for-hire long haul services as well as between them and many forms of local conveyances. Other than providing for car rental arrangements, airlines, railroads, and steamship firms rarely coordinate their services with other forms of transportation. Even with current airport interfaces, passengers have difficulty in learning about local services. This situation serves as a constraint to efficient through movement.

Role of the Travel Agent

The travel agent is a valuable but often overlooked and misunderstood facilitator of passenger travel. Though not providing movement service in and of themselves, travel agents provide a wide range of informational and arrangement services.

The travel agent is a link between the passenger, on the one hand, and carriers and hotels on the other. Their services include explaining the lowest cost and most direct transportation services as well as making reservations for and issuing tickets to the passenger. Agents also arrange for car rental, hotels, and complete tour services. The cost of using a travel agent is minimal to the passenger. The cost of a ticket purchased directly from an airline, Amtrak, or steamship company, for example, is the same as that arranged and purchased through a travel agent. The travel agent is compensated through a commission paid by the carrier. The passenger has the advantage of learning and possibly using all carriers' services through this one facilitator. The alternative would be to make arrangements and purchase tickets individually for each segment of a trip. The carriers would have to have offices in each town served, or passengers would have to make an additional trip to the terminal to make trip arrangements and purchase tickets. Travel agents, however, often have computer terminals with direct links to airline reservation systems that allow for fast travel arrangements.

Conclusion

The transportation user must be aware of the basic processes, procedures, and primary forms of transportation supply as well as the underlying economic principles governing them. While there were relatively few transportation options available to users after World War II, today the range of services, rate forms, and types of equipment present combinations of options that number in the hundreds. Modern transportation managers and users must know the basic forms of equipment available because this factor shapes the cost, price, and service configuration selected by shippers/consignees.

Study Questions	1. What factors comprise the "transportation product?"

1. What factors comprise the "transportation product?"

2. What is the modal split and how does it appear for the different modes in the United States?

3. Why are there some small, light weight capacity box and covered hopper cars while there also exist some larger, heavier capacity cars? Further, why are there some very large cars that have relatively light load carrying capacities?

4. What are the basic intercity passenger markets?

5. What is included in the "passenger transportation product"?

6. A complaint often heard is that there is insufficient coordination of passenger service between major airports and the surrounding metropolitan areas. Is this a justified complaint? Why or why not?

7. What is the role of a travel agent? Can airlines, for example, do without them?

8. Assume that you are the traffic manager of a large manufacturer of household appliances. What information would you want to know before making your carrier selection decision? (AST&T, Spring 1980, Exam #2.)

Notes

1. Transportation Association of America, *Transportation Facts and Trends* (Washington, D.C., 1977), p. 2.

2. Association of American Railroads, *Yearbook of Railroad Facts* (Washington, D.C., 1980), p. 36.

3. Transportation Association of America, *Transportation Facts and Trends*, 16th ed. (Washington, D.C.), p. 4. p. 22.

Suggested Readings

Chow, Garland. "The Status of Scale In Regulated Trucking: A Review of the Evidence and Future Directions." *Annual Proceedings of the Transportation Research Forum*, 1978, pp. 365-73.

Fair, Marvin L., and Williams, Jr., Ernest W. *Economics of Transportation*. Dallas: Business Publications, 1975, chaps. 7 and 8.

Harper, Donald V. *Transportation in America: Users, Carriers, Government.* Englewood Cliffs, N.J.: Prentice-Hall, 1978. chap. 1.

Kneafsey, James T. *The Economics of the Transportation Firm: Market Structure and Industrial Performance.* Lexington, Mass.: Lexington Books, 1974.

Pegrum, Dudley F. *Transportation: Economics and Public Policy.* Homewood, Ill.: Richard D. Irwin, 1973, chap. 5.

Sampson, Roy J., and Farris, Martin T. *Domestic Transportation: Practice, Theory, and Policy.* 4th ed. Boston: Houghton Mifflin Company, 1979, chap. 28.

Wood, Donald F., and Johnson, James C. *Contemporary Transportation*. Tulsa: Petroleum Publishing Co., 1980, chap. 13.

Case	Scandia Company

John Brill is the General Manager of the Scandia Company of St. Paul, Minnesota. Scandia is one of the United States' leading producers of wheat. Unlike most American wheat producers, Scandia exports 100% of their production to the Soviet Union.

Since 1973, prior to shipping to the Russians, Brill has arranged to use a transit privilege to allow the wheat to be ground to flour by the ABC Milling Company of Utica, New York. The wheat is shipped by rail from St. Paul to Utica for processing and again by rail to New York City for overseas transport via a Russian freighter.

The wheat is transported from St. Paul to Utica in bushels weighing approximately 42 pounds each. After the milling process, the flour is packaged in 200-pound cardboard drums for the two subsequent movements. Since 1973, Scandia has averaged annual shipments of wheat to Utica of 500,000 bushels and annual flour shipments from Utica of 105,000 drums. Presently, Brill is paying the through rate of flour from St. Paul to New York City at 32¢ per hundredweight.

The revenue which Scandia received from the Russians for a drum of flour is $1.35 above the price of a bushel of *wheat* in the Chicago market. The expense which Scandia incurs for milling in Utica is 7¢ per hundred pounds of wheat.

Brill has been analyzing the revenues and expenses associated with Scandia's dealings with the Russians. He is prepared for negotiations with Alex Volkoff next month regarding the future contract with them. Although the present contract is not being ruled out for renewal, John is considering two alternatives.

The first involves shipping the bushels of wheat to New York City via rail. Scandia will incur the freight charge of 38¢ per hundredweight. The bushels command a higher rate than the drums since handling costs are higher. The milling will be taken care of by the Russians and the purchase price will be 85¢ above the Chicago market price for a bushel of wheat.

The second alternative would also involve the Russians arranging for the milling. The Russians would be purchasing bushels of wheat at a price of 42¢ above the market price in Chicago (FOB St. Paul).

John has asked you to assist him in determining the best alternative from Scandia's point of view. Which do you feel is best? Why? Do you think Volkoff will accept this proposal? Which alternative do you think exemplifies the "happy medium" and stands the most likelihood of being accepted by both sides? Back up your conclusions with data. Are there any political considerations from Scandia? Explain.

9 Special Carriers

After reading this chapter you should:

1   Be able to discuss and understand the transportation services available to users, as well as the basic modal types of transportation.

2   Be able to discuss the special role of the household goods movers in the United States.

3   Understand how the special carriers relate to the basic modes of transportation.

4   Understand how regulations affect special carriers.

■ chapter overview

There are several forms of carriage in the United States in addition to the basic rail, motor, water, air, and pipe modes. Further, there are various special services provided by the above carriers that are also pertinent to the understanding of transportation activities. This chapter presents these special transportation features in three sections: special carriers, household goods services, and lumpers.

Special Carrier Forms

There are several special types of carrier services that represent a significant segment of the transportation services purchased by shippers. These forms of transportation often utilize the longhaul services of the five basic transportation modes.

Surface Forwarders

These carriers are regarded legally as common carriers and are subject to various entry/exit, price, service, and financial regulations of the Interstate Commerce Commission (ICC). Forwarders act as a carrier to the shipper and consignee, but they utilize railroads and sometimes motor carriers for the longhaul portion of the move.

■ description

Forwarders traditionally pick up and consolidate many small shipments (less-than-carload, LCL, or less-than-truckload lots, LTL), for long hauls. They earn a profit from the rate spread between what they charge shippers and what railroads charge them for longhaul services. In fact, they have a pricing advantage because they specifically know their longhaul costs of carriage. Previously, they acted to consolidate LCL lots into full box car loads, but in recent years their primary emphasis has been in the consolidation of piggyback loads. In piggyback services they will often accept a full trailer car dispatch (two trailers comprise a full rail car) thereby saving the shipper a cost penalty for half a car movement or avoiding a delay while the shipper loads another trailer to the same destination. In a small shipment consolidation, it is not uncommon for as many as two hundred separate shipments to be in a single trailer load.

The specific operational function of a surface forwarder is easily explained. A shipment originating in, for example, Atlanta will be picked up by Western Carloading's city pickup and delivery truck which operates within the commercial zone of that city. The shipper will receive a Western Carloading bill of lading and pay a freight charge from its tariff. The shipment will then be sorted and consolidated with others at Western's local terminal. This forwarder will then tender two full trailer loads to a railroad which will load them onto a piggyback car for longhaul movement to Los Angeles. At destination, Western will break down each trailer and distribute each shipment in its own city vehicles. If shipments originate or terminate outside the commercial zones of the forwarder's terminal cities, it will arrange for motor common carrier pickup and delivery.

■ operations

The forwarder is the common carrier to the shipper and consignee. It is responsible for claims, and it is the carrier through which shipment tracing is handled. It becomes another shipper in its legal relationship with the longhaul railroad. The forwarder, then, consists of a network of local city terminals that are linked by longhaul services obtained from railroads.

■ common carrier role

Forwarders have been declining in recent years in both absolute tonnage and relative market share. Air freight and motor common carrier aggressiveness in the LTL areas is partially responsible for this trend. Several forwarders, however, continue to operate profitably. The primary competition facing them is air freight on the one hand and motor carriers devoted to the LTL market segment on the other. To some extent, shippers' agents and shippers' associations have led to a declining market share for the forwarder.

■ market position

Forwarders present several advantages and disadvantages to the shipping public. On the positive side, in some markets they move small shipments with faster dispatch than other surface carriers. In many instances the rates they charge are below the alternate fast small shipment services. Further, a shipment moving via forwarder, even though it is handled by several firms, provides the shipper with only one carrier to arrange, ship, trace, pay, and with which to file a claim. On the negative side, the service and rates that forwarders offer to shippers might be the same as those offered by other carriers. But, here as in any other shipping area, the shipper should continually monitor its available transportation services from all sources and select those best in any given situation.

■ advantages and disadvantages

The future is generally bright for this form of carriage. Forwarders stand to gain from several changes in the field. Changed regulations and policies will no doubt enable forwarders to secure favorable contract rates with railroads; in the past, they could only use rates which were made available to any shipper. Forwarder movement volume should open the way for lower longhaul costs, and forwarders might gain back some transcontinental traffic as longhaul motor carriers experience higher fuel costs. Implementation of forwarder-like services by the motor carriers themselves, or a shift by motor carriers to moving their longhaul trailers by rail, might represent a competitory problem. Such

■ future

implementation would, in effect, cause the services of the two forms of transportation to converge. If that happens, the motor carrier size, strength, and structure of operations no doubt will provide them with a competitive advantage.

Air Freight Forwarders

■ description

These firms act in much the same way as surface forwarders. They are common carriers that consolidate small shipments for longhaul and eventual distribution. They primarily utilize the services of major passenger and freight airlines for longhaul service. The air freight forwarder serves the shipping public with similar pickup, single bill of lading and freight bill, one firm tracing, and delivery service as does the surface forwarder. The air freight forwarder, though, is generally used by shippers of goods having high-product-dollar value or time-sensitivity value, or both, because of high time value characteristics of the goods.

■ market position

The trend of air freight forwarders has been one of growth over the past two decades. As the air industry grew, so did acceptance of this generally high cost form of transportation for emergency and high cost per time value moves. A reason often stated, too, for air forwarder growth has been that these firms have concentrated upon offering door-to-door service from shipper to consignee. This service relieves a significant traffic arrangement burden from shippers and consignees. It also fills a void since most airlines tend to emphasize terminal-to-terminal services and have been involved only to a limited degree in surface pickup and delivery services. One adverse trend has occurred in this industry over the past several years in the form of limited passenger airline carrying capacity. Initially, freight being moved by air forwarders experienced delays from the trunk carrier's ability to handle all demanded traffic. Recent regulatory changes enabled several of these firms to provide necessary longhaul movement in planes owned or leased by the forwarder.

■ advantages and disadvantages

The air freight forwarder industry presents some major transportation service benefits to the shipping community. For one, speed of service is vital for many movements such as spare parts, emergency replenishment goods, medical components, and business documents. Further, this industry represents a single carrier, full door-to-door service. Its main disadvantage lies in its high rates, but these are usually considered by shippers in light of the service benefit received.

■ future

The future of the air freight forwarding industry is not stable for several reasons. On the positive side, air freight movements are unrestricted with regard to surface pickup and delivery movements. In 1980, this segment became exempt from all economic regulation; thus new origin and destination points far from terminal cities stand to present expanded opportunities for these firms. However, deregulation of air freight has brought about price and service instability. A possible shakeout of marginal carriers poses a survival problem for many. Energy costs are also a future cloud on the horizon for this industry. The fuel intensity of the airplane will probably shift much routine air freight traffic back to motor carriers, even though use of that mode would possibly incur higher inventory costs for the shipping public. The ultimate long-term picture of this industry might not be known until the middle 1980s.

Freight Brokers

■ description

The term "freight brokers" applies to persons or firms that negotiate for and link up shippers and truckers. Brokers find carriage for shippers and act as solicitors and bookers of freight for truckers. Currently, brokers are mostly found in the exempt agricultural commodities market. A hallmark of this market is that crop availability and carriage supply are constantly shifting. The broker acts as a clearinghouse for both shipper and carrier in an area where there are few fixed carrier facilities or year-round traffic demands.

■ roles

The nature of broker services and functions requires comparison of their roles to those of shippers and truckers. Surveys indicate that individual brokers serve anywhere from a few to several hundred shippers. These shippers tend to be grocery chain stores, packers, growers, wholesalers, food processors, and farm cooperatives. Basic shipper services include the arrangement for service, the verification of the trucker's reputation and references (as well as verification of equipment condition), a vehicle safety inspection, and the negotiation of a freight charge. Major broker services for truckers include, in addition to soliciting traffic, advising drivers of state weight limitations, using the broker's state operating authority, assisting in state fuel tax matters, and obtaining or providing cargo insurance or personal liability insurance. A broker will deal with anywhere from a few to 500 individual truckers during the course of a year. For the most part, these truckers are owner-operators. The broker typically charges the shipper for the freight movement, deducts a brokerage fee of between 7 to 10 percent, then remits the net amount to the trucker. Almost all brokers advance direct operating expense monies to the trucker prior to the haul. Some brokers actually engage in motor carrier operations. Many of these are refrigerator trailer moves.

■ rates

In most instances the rates for carriage in this market vary according to the relative demand and supply of shipments and trucks. A weekly sample of truck charges for agricultural movements is published by the U.S. Department of Agriculture for major origin-destination traffic areas by basic commodity groups. Table 9.1 is a sample of that report.

■ size

Broker firms tend to be small in nature. The Department of Agriculture has determined that the typical firm, about half of which are sole proprietorships, has up to eight full-time office personnel. Their methods of solicitation tend to be based upon personal contacts and phone calls. Brokers use both local and agricultural trade magazine advertising. Brokers are minimally regulated by the ICC through licensing, liability requirements, and record inspection regulations.

The trend in this transport sector has been a gradual increase in traffic in the past two decades. Increased food production and consumption have contributed to this increase, as well as the declining rail share of ag-

Table 9.1 Fruit and Vegetable Truck Rate Report

Region	New York	Atlanta	Chicago	Dallas	Denver	Los Angeles
Northeast						
Eastern NY—adequate						
(Apples)	$500 (0)	$1000 (+11)	$—	$—	$—	$—
Weekly range	500-550	900-1000	—	—	—	—
(Onions)	280 (0)	800 (0)	—	—	—	—
Weekly range	280-320	800-880	—	—	—	—
Western & Central NY—adequate						
(Vegetables)	600-1000	800-1020 (0)	—	—	—	—
Weekly range	600-1000	800-1020	—	—	—	—
Long Island, NY—slight shortage						
(Potatoes)	315 (0)	832-900	—	—	—	—
Weekly range	292-315	786-900	—	—	—	—
Mid-Atlantic						
New Jersey—S. Jersey area—adequate						
(Vegetables)	400-450 (0)	800-900 (0)	900-1000 (0)	—	—	—
Weekly range	400-450	750-900	900-1000	—	—	—
Appalachian District—Martinsburg, WVA—Winchester, VA—adequate						
(Apples)	—	720 (0)	—	—	—	—
Weekly range	600	680-720	—	—	—	—
Eastern NC—adequate						
(Sweet potatoes)	800	520-600	880	—	—	—
Weekly range	800	520-600	880	—	—	—
Western NC—adequate						
(Apples)	1140-1250 (0)	495-650 (0)	1092-1200 (0)	—	—	—
Weekly range	1140-1250	495-650	1092-1200	—	—	—

Table 9.1 *continued*

Region	New York	Atlanta	Chicago	Dallas	Denver	Los Angeles
Southeast						
S.W. Georgia—adequate						
(Peanuts)	880 (0)	—	704 (0)	—	—	—
Weekly range	880	—	704	—	—	—
Midwest						
West Central & Central Mich.—adequate						
(Apples)	—	—	495-540 (0)	—	—	—
Weekly range	—	—	495-540	—	—	—
(Celery—Last report)	—	—	525 (0)	—	—	—
Weekly range	—	—	525	—	—	—
(Onions)	—	760-800 (0)	440-480 (0)	—	—	—
Weekly range	—	760-800	440-480	—	—	—
(Potatoes)	—	810-900 (0)	495 (0)	—	—	—
Weekly range	—	810-900	495	—	—	—
Central Wisconsin—adequate						
(Potatoes)	—	1084 (0)	425 (0)	—	—	—
Weekly range	—	1084	425	—	—	—
Southeastern Wisconsin—adequate						
(Cabbage)	—	938-1000 (0)	375-400 0	—	—	—
Weekly range	—	938-1000	320-400	—	—	—
Minnesota-N. Dakota—Red River Valley—Grand Forks—adequate						
(Potatoes)	—	—	840 (0)	—	—	—
Weekly range	—	—	798-840	—	—	—
Southwest						
New Mexico—Las Cruces—Hatch District—adequate						
(Lettuce)	2750 (0)	2000 (0)	1900 (-5)	1000	1000 (0)	—
Weekly range	2500-3000	1750-2000	1900-2000	1000-1250	1000-1250	—

Table 9.1 *continued*

Region	New York	Atlanta	Chicago	Dallas	Denver	Los Angeles
Mountain						
Colorado—San Luis Valley—slight shortage to most areas						
(Potatoes)	—	—	1100-1200 (−7)	700-800 (−6)	280-300	—
Weekly range	—	—	1100-1200	700-800	280-300	—
Northern & Eastern—adequate						
(Onions)	—	—	—	675-700 (0)	—	—
Weekly range	—	—	—	675-700	—	—
Western Idaho—Malheur, Oregon—slight shortage, especially to Texas & Southeast						
(Onions)	—	1800	1280-1360 (+2)	1280-1400 (+2)	—	810-900 (0)
Weekly range	—	NA	NA	NA	—	NA
Eastern Idaho—slight shortage to Texas & Southeast; adequate—Midwest						
(Potatoes)	—	1900	1400-1500 (0)	1300-1400 (0)	—	—
Weekly range	—	NA	NA	NA	—	—
Western						
California—Southern—adequate						
(Citrus & Vegetables)	2700-2800 (−5)	2000-2200 (0)	1900-2000 (0)	1500-1700 (0)	1000-1200 (+5)	—
Weekly range	2600-3000	2000-2200	1600-2100	1500-1700	1000-1200	
Salinas—Watsonville—adequate						
(Vegetables)	2800-2900 (0)	2200-2500 (+2)	2000-2200 (0)	1800-2000 (0)	1200-1400 (0)	710R (0)
Weekly range	2800-3000	2200-2700	2000-2300	1700-2100	1200-1400	710R

Table 9.1 *continued*

Region	New York	Atlanta	Chicago	Dallas	Denver	Los Angeles
Central San Joaquin Valley—surplus						
(Grapes)	2800-3000 (+2)	2500-2600 (+6)	2000-2100 (+5)	—	—	494R (0)
Weekly range	2800-3000	2400-2700	2000-2100	—	—	494R
Karn District—adequate						
(Fruit & Vegetable)	2900 (+4)	2400 (+14)	2000 (+3)	1700 (0)	1200 (0)	NA
Weekly range	2800-2900	2300-2400	1900-2000	1600-1700	1200	NA
Lake County—slight surplus						
(Pears)	2800-2900 (-3)	2000	2000 (-7)	1750 (-8)	—	972R (0)
Weekly range	2800-3000	2000	2000-2200	1750-2000	—	972R
Northern California—South Oregon—Klamath Basin—slight shortage to Los Angeles						
(Potatoes)	—	—	—	—	—	765 (0)
Weekly range	—	—	—	—	—	765-810
Western Oregon—Salem—slight shortage to Los Angeles						
(Onions)	—	—	—	—	—	900
Weekly range	—	—	—	—	—	NA
Eastern Arizona						
(Lettuce)	NA	NA	NA	NA	NA	NA
Weekly range	NA	NA	NA	NA	NA	NA
Washington—Central—adequate						
(Apples & pears)	2876-2967 (0)	2374-2465 (-2)	1826-1917 (-5)	1917-2100 (-7)	1300 (+4)	1300 (-4)
Weekly range	2876-2967	2283-2465	1826-2054	1917-2100	1300-1400	1300-1400
(Onions & potatoes)	—	—	—	—	—	920-1150 (-9)
Weekly range	—	—	—	—	—	920-1150

Source: U.S. Department of Agriculture, *Fruit and Vegetable Truck Rate Report*, (Washington, D.C, October 14, 1980).

NA — Rate not available

— — No shipments or too few shipments to report.

R — Regulated

Truckload (40 ft.) — In areas where rates are based on per package rate, per load rates were derived by multiplying the package rate by the number of packages in the most usual load in a 40-foot trailer. First price mostly for Tuesday, October 14; second price range for week, Wednesday-Tuesday; percentage of change from same day last week shown in ( ).

ricultural movements until 1978. Deregulation of some rail agricultural movements might alter this trend in the long run.

This transportation sector finds and arranges for transportation in a key market in which service availability and prices fluctuate. Thus, brokers relieve shippers of a major traffic function burden. Client truckers utilize brokers to relieve them of a major fixed cost burden and communication expense. Some brokers, however, will maintain close ties with a local shipper to the detriment of the trucker.

■ future

The future of truck brokerage of agricultural products is mixed. In one sense, regulated carriers are becoming more active in directly soliciting low rate back-haul movements to their regulated commodity front-hauls. If this becomes a long-term trend, it will directly affect brokers. Fuel and general motor truck economic changes also pose a future problem for brokers. The trucker owner-operators have been affected negatively by fuel costs and the 55 mile per hour speed limit. The vitality of these truckers directly affects the supply of carriage that brokers can utilize. Deregulation of fresh fruits and vegetables moving via railroad might cause traffic diversion to that mode and cause it to move away from brokers and their client truckers.

On the other hand, the deregulatory initiatives by Congress in 1980 and by the ICC throughout the current period may lead to service and price exemptions in what has traditionally been stable regulated commodity markets. If other major product groups become unregulated, rate and carriage supply may require use of the broker. The growth of passenger brokers after the CAB removed restrictions in plane chartering, ticketing, and bulk booking processes is evidence of such use.

Shippers' Associations

These transportation entities are nonprofit cooperative consolidators or distributors of shipments owned or shipped by member firms. Their prime purpose is to group together members' shipments for line-haul in much the same way as for-hire, for-profit freight forwarders. These associations benefit members through better service and lower total transportation cost.

■ description

Shippers' associations primarily act as outbound consolidators of many small shipments. Within major metropolitan areas they often operate a freight handling terminal as well as pickup and delivery vehicles that collect (and sometimes deliver) freight for consolidation into piggyback trailers. The trailers are then shipped via common rail carriage at regular tariff or favorable rail contract rates. The association usually arranges for delivery via pool car or local cartage distributor truck firms in the destination city. The association is liable to the individual member shipper. Because it is a nonprofit association, it ideally redistributes any "profit" surplus to shipping members at the end of specified periods. In this way a shipper can reduce his regular total freight charge by up to 15 percent or more. Though most shippers' associations are organized and operated for outbound movements, some function as inbound transportation consolidators.

A shippers' association is chartered as a nonprofit body to serve only

■ organization

member firms. Once formed by two or more manufacturing or distributing firms, other firms usually can also join. All members usually pay a charter or entry fee which may or may not be refunded upon withdrawal from the association. The organization then hires a manager or management and employees; sometimes it acquires a terminal site. The association can, as does DRUMTOP Shippers' Association in Atlanta, operate pickup trucks in the area commercial zone. It pays regular outbound rates for rail longhaul services while charging members an association tariff rate for each movement. The profit is apportioned back to the shippers at specified intervals. This surplus is divided according to a pro rata share of shipped hundredweight, tons, or whole piggyback loads.

The overall trend of shippers' associations is positive. They have grown over the years to a point where they exceed freight forwarders in tonnage shipped. In fact, the rate of growth for this transportation medium exceeds the growth rate for total shipped tonnage in the economy.

■ legal perspective

Shippers' associations are in a unique legal situation for some of the following reasons. First, they are exempt from ICC regulation. Second, they must utilize for-hire carriers for long haul. Third, they are the only form of transportation that is not permitted to solicit traffic from the general public. They may only serve member firms; they may not solicit membership. They can, however, answer any inquiries on the part of a potential member firm. Finally, the rates charged, liabilities assumed, and other service features are not otherwise regulated.

■ advantages and disadvantages

A shipper enjoys several advantages by belonging to and utilizing a shippers' association. The associations can save the shipper transportation cost, and acquire better, faster service. Divisions or subdivisions of a conglomerate can enjoy the advantages of pooled transportation buying power in an association, while maintaining separate corporate identities. The major drawback to these organizations is that if not managed well, they might not be worth the membership cost and effort. Surplus allocation can also be a problem. If the shipment rate is based upon weight, a light, bulky product shipper might be at a disadvantage compared to a less frequent, but heavy product shipper. These factors, however, are two of the key areas that a prospective member should investigate before joining.

■ future

The future for shipper associations is relatively bright. They perform a function that acts to consolidate shipments in ways that are economical for long haul movement. In this manner it is a shared form of distribution that provides savings to its member users rather than a profit to a for-hire entity as is the case with forwarders.

Shippers' Agents

■ description

These transportation service entities act primarily to consolidate single traffic piggyback loads, so that lower cost twin trailer piggyback loads can be shipped and consolidation savings can be passed back to the shipper. Shippers' agents are also referred to as marriage brokers, consolidators, or agents. They are facilitators or arrangers of transportation only.

There is little or no legal obligation assumed by them, the legal shipping arrangement is between the shipper and longhaul carrier and not with the agent. Freight charge payment usually is made to the agent who, in turn, pays the longhaul carrier.

■ organization

Shippers' agents maintain simple management structures. They are primarily locally based and rely upon personal solicitation and local advertising. Because the basic transportation arrangement is between the shipper and longhaul carrier, the agent is beyond the realm of the economic regulations presiding over freight forwarders and implicitly existing in shippers' associations.

■ future

The trend of this shipping sector is generally positive. Agents play a cost savings role for both the shipper and the longhaul piggyback carrier, although very little specific industry-wide knowledge exists as to the number, size, and particular services performed by them.

■ advantages and disadvantages

Shippers often find that these firms can save transportation costs for them even after their fee is paid. By matching loads to specific destinations, agents improve shipment dispatch so that the single trailer is not held by the carrier until another one is sent to the same destination. Rail equipment utilization is enhanced when trailers are matched and shipped with full loads, and these agents act to solicit freight for the carriers.

A disadvantage associated with agents is in the area of liability. The shipper usually pays the freight agent who, in turn, pays the rail carrier. Ultimate freight payment liability, however, still rests with the shipper. There is the possibility, and it has occurred occasionally, that the agent will retain the freight charges and cease operations, leaving the shippers with, in effect, a second freight bill. The reputation and stature of an individual agent's operations are a couple of the investigative points a prospective shipper will want to analyze.

The future is also relatively bright for shipper's agents, especially in light of greater deregulation of the rail sector. Agents represent the pooled buying power of shippers. Opportunities may exist in the future for these firms to negotiate lower than normal general tariff rates or rail contract rates.

Farm or Agricultural Cooperatives

■ description

These are nonprofit organizations that move, or arrange for the movement of both exempt agricultural products and regulated goods of member farmers or agricultural organizations. Some perform over-the-road, longhaul movements with owned or leased equipment, some utilize owner-operators, and others act through brokers or act in a manner similar to shippers' agents. Their prime service to users is to find and arrange for transportation with generally favorable rates.

■ legal perspective

Their operations are technically exempted from regulation under Section 10526 of the Revised Interstate Commerce Act.[1] Cooperatives basically handle any regulated or exempt commodity for member agricultural firms. The legislation permits the cooperative to handle up to 50 percent of its total interstate tonnage for nonmember firms, as long as this sector is "incidental" to the primary member traffic. That is, nonmember tonnage is limited to the filling of empty back-haul movements. The co-op may move up to one-half of that portion (or 25 percent of the total tonnage) in the form of normally regulated commodities for non-member firms. The co-op is free to negotiate single shipment rates to and from any points and is not required to file tariffs, nor hold to an operating right, certificate, or permit.

These organizations are nonprofit and are governed by a charter. They operate in much the same way as a shippers' association. Over time there has been a great deal of political support from agricultural groups for allowing these organizations to exist. The Motor Carrier Act of 1980, for example, expanded nonmember regulated commodity limitation from 15 percent to 25 percent.

■ advantages and disadvantages

Advantages to the members accrue mainly from cost savings, arrangement of moves, and the reduction of empty back-haul costs. Disadvantages stem from poor management, for example, the co-op may not seek efficient services for its members. The future of farm co-ops includes greater expansion into the area of contracting for agricultural movements which are exempt in the rail sector.

Express and Courier Services

■ description

This carrier group offers fast service, usually door-to-door, for small, high-valued goods and documents. Often referred to as package express services, these firms usually limit service to 50-pound shipments. They often utilize air movements, but a major group, United Parcel Service (UPS), is predominantly a surface carrier that also provides a premium air service. These services are useful for shipments with a high dollar value density such as repair parts, medical supplies, and documents. In addition to the express firms such as UPS and Federal Express, there is also the parcel package service of the U.S. Postal Service.

■ operations

Express firms operate with large networks of terminals, pickup and delivery vehicles, and linehaul service. UPS is most notable in this regard. It began as a retail store delivery system, but it currently serves every point in the forty-eight states by utilizing 1,100 terminals, 55,000 vehicles, and 120,000 employees. It regularly serves 520,000 scheduled shipper pickup points and firms, though the general public may also ship from most of their terminals. In 1980 it handled 1.4 billion shipments on a reliable for-profit basis. The U.S. Postal Service, in comparison, handled 1.2 billion shipments and required a federal subsidy. The U.S. Postal Service does not contribute to highway license fees with its local vehicles, nor does it pay income taxes.

■ special services

Two express services deserve special attention; they are the package express services of the regular route bus firms and the Amtrak express service. These are terminal-to-terminal services which require shipper/consignee pickup and delivery. Their advantage is that the consignee knows when arrival will take place by referring to passenger timetables. Thus, same day arrival can take place within a working day, up to 400 miles distance in some instances.

The trend for these systems has been positive. Deregulation of the air freight industry in 1977 as well as that of 100-pound shipments or less

■ market position

service firms in the Motor Carrier Act of 1980 cleared the way for more operational efficiency by reducing many of the former restrictive routings, limited certificates, and hinderances to intermodal operations. The shipper experiences fast service when using these firms, but it is at a high rate cost.

■ future

The future is good for this sector because expansion and service innovations can take place without the impediment of the high legal costs incurred when confronting regulatory bodies.

Household Goods Industry

■ description

This industry sector consists of a group of motor carriers that are specifically organized to move the household goods of people and businesses. These firms, often called van lines, are geared to serve the market with specialized vehicles, local agencies with warehouses for storage, and pickup and delivery equipment as well as central dispatching operations. In all areas, however, the overall corporate name, or franchise, will appear on vehicles, local agencies, and in national advertising.

The specific segments of this industry fall into four groups. The first is the central franchise firms whose corporate name and operating certificate are used by the agencies and over-the-road vehicles. The franchise firms also provide a central dispatch function to coordinate the most efficient possible flow of vehicles between all points. The second group is the local agencies, each of which consists of a terminal and storage warehouse. The terminal is the local contact point for customer contact and shipment initiation. It generally supplies the packing and the pickup vehicle loading labor as well as delivery and unpacking man-

■ industry segments

power. In the event that household goods owners wish to move goods when vehicles are not available, or they wish to store goods temporarily, local agencies provide storage facilities. The third segment of this industry is the over-the-road vehicle owned by the local agency. Many local agents own their own tractor and trailer and hire employees who will perform outbound and inbound moves dispatched by the central firm. A fourth entity in this industry is the owner-operator who displays the corporate identity on the vehicle and who loads, hauls, and unloads shipments that are dispatched by the central franchise firm and are coordinated by local agents. This four-party system is not apparent to individual shippers who typically think that they are dealing with one corporate entity that has direct supervisory control over drivers and vehicles as well as all agencies. Instead, the household goods industry is a loose alliance of entities that share a single franchised identity and a communication system.

The household goods shipment process reveals the makeup of the functional relationships in this transport sector. Initially, the individual agent joins the franchise by paying an entry fee and adhering to certain centrally established standards. An individual owner-operator who generally performs longhaul services, acquires a vehicle and moving firm identity in much the same way. The actual shipment process is as follows. First, a home or apartment dweller contacts the local agent who generally visits the pickup point and determines an estimate of the shipment weight and evaluates the need for any special move tasks. The agent, in turn, calculates a total move cost estimate for the shipper. The shipper-carrier relationship is initiated when the shipper signs an "order for service" document which is transmitted to the central firm dispatch office for over-the-road vehicle assignment and scheduling. Generally, if an individual shipment is 7,500 pounds or more, a new run will be created based on that shipment. Smaller shipments are tacked onto existing runs. The home owner is then informed of the estimated arrival date. If packing is to be part of the hired service, local agency personnel perform this task a few days prior to pickup. The over-the-road vehicle then arrives, after having determined the total vehicle weight prior to loading. The driver will inspect the possessions, label them, and log them onto an inventory tally sheet along with notations about the condition of each item. The goods are then loaded, and the shipper is given a receipt (bill of lading). The pickup goods are usually loaded into a vehicle with other shipments which are often dropped off enroute (and others might be picked up) prior to the specific shipment delivery. The vehicle is then reweighed to determine the total shipment weight.

■ operations

The actual charges are based upon that weight as well as special charges which might be added for such things as weekend work; movement of large, heavy, special, or fragile items; or the need to climb stairs or use an elevator. Agency packing, too, is included in these charges, all of which can boost the total shipment cost by 30-50 percent.

■ charges

The shipment then moves to the delivery point. The driver can, and usually does, demand payment of freight charges in cash or by certified check unless certain credit arrangements are made in advance. Then, the shipment is unloaded. The new local agency then unpacks the boxes, if packing and unpacking was a part of the hired service. Any loss and damage claims are then filed through the new local agency.

Revenue distribution is usually made upon the following basis: 10 percent to the corporate franchise, 50 percent to the vehicle owner (agency or owner-operator), 25 percent to the pickup agency, and 15 percent to the destination agency. Packing service charges are distributed in various ways between the two local agencies.

■ revenue distribution

Many problems exist in this industry. First, people's individual possessions are being handled and moved—a major event for the shipper and family. Second, moving causes the shipper and his family a significant degree of stress, and problems in the actual move may aggravate the entire process. Third, the industry is made up of three or four separate parties (franchise, pickup, vehicle, and destination agencies). Very little direct control has traditionally existed by any one of these agencies over the other. The Household Goods Transportation Act of 1980 now binds actions by any agent or vehicle to the parent franchise holder.[2] Further, long-distance communications are necessary between all of them. Fourth, unless the shipper is being transferred by the military or a major national firm, the individual has little influence over the movers.

■ problems

■ market position

Trends in this industry are mixed. The market basically consists of about 17 percent military moves; the remaining is divided equally between individual shipper moves and moves booked under supervision of large employing firms. It is a very seasonal business. Typically 70 percent of all moves take place in the five-month period between May to September (representing only 42 percent of the year). This peak situation creates a great demand during a short period, and manpower and equipment investment utilization is low for the remaining part of the year. Further, some household goods moving firms have withdrawn completely from the field, while a few have discontinued shipping household goods in favor of moving fragile electronic items such as computers and copying equipment. This traffic requires the special equipment and handling expertise of the moving firms, but it is less seasonal in nature. Other firms divested from the household goods operations altogether in the 1970s when the military and corporations reduced the number of transfers in what appeared to be a long-term trend away from moving.

■ future

The future of household goods movement is tied to regulatory change and the innovative attitudes of the movers. Long-term fuel availability and other economic factors are having detrimental impacts upon the long-distance, over-the-road moving van and its owner. Household goods movement requires high capital investment in the tractor and van, and it requires much labor and energy. There is little improvement potential for the long-distance van in these three factors in the next decade. Many industry observers have noted that household goods customer service, productivity, and profitability improvement will have to come about through major changes in equipment and processes. Rail-hauled containers, moving boxes on flat beds, or the use of forwarders have been some of the suggestions made in this regard. These would diminish the role of the long-distance van. Whether the industry will shift in these directions remains to be seen.

Lumpers

■ description

"Lumpers" is a term that applies to individuals or loosely affiliated union groups that are employed in food warehouse loading and unloading motor carriage docks, terminals, and ports. They became a part of the industry through the supermarket chain and the terminal firms' reluctance to employ large loading and unloading teams, or to invest in highly mechanized forms of equipment to perform the work. The lumper, then, is a person who an independent truck driver would technically hire at curb side to assist in the unloading of goods inside the warehouse or terminal grounds. Typically, the driver would pay this person anywhere from $25 to $100 (the 1979 average was $50). Some independent drivers are reimbursed for this expense but many are not. The practice often borders upon extreme coercion and extortion. Even when the driver does not need such assistance, he is sometimes forced to pay for it just the same. The alternative has, in some instances, resulted in physical violence and vehicle damage. The practice is widespread, even though truckload rated shipments must be loaded by the shipper and unloaded by the consignee.

A description of this problem was published in an ICC press release in 1979.

An independent owner-operator transports a load of boxed meat, on pallets from a meatpacking plant in the Midwest to a receiving facility on the East Coast. The rate the carrier charges the shipper for transportation requires only that the driver back the trailer up to the receiver's docks and ready the meat for unloading. The cost of loading and unloading services is to be paid by the shipper. The trucker arrives at the receiving facility and immediately gets in line. When the truck reaches the front of the line, a lumper approaches and asks if the owner-operator wants help in unloading. The trucker—who knows that the shipper is supposed to pay for unloading and that the shipment of boxed meat can be unloaded fairly easily without the use of lumpers—declines the offer.

The trucker's refusal may mean that the lumper will not let him enter the area of the unloading dock, and it could take several days to get the shipment unloaded. If the owner-operator is allowed on the dock, the equipment needed to unload the shipment may not be furnished. Any help received from lumpers under these circumstances will be given grudgingly, and the truck will probably be the last one unloaded. In extreme cases, drivers have been forced into using lumpers through threats of physical violence. Some drivers have actually suffered beatings by lumpers.

Because of the high cost of waiting for several hours or days to unload and the possibility of physical danger, most owner-operators pay the lumper fees even when they do not want or need the help. In many cases, they are not reimbursed by the party legally responsible for paying the loading or unloading costs. Even if the carrier is paid, the owner-operator will usually receive only a percentage of the full amount, depending on the terms of the lease agreement with the carrier.

■ legal perspective

The Motor Carrier Act of 1980 was the first legislation to directly address this problem.[3] Section 15 of this act states that whenever a shipper or receiver requires an owner-operator of a motor vehicle in interstate commerce to be assisted in the loading or unloading, the shipper/receiver shall be responsible for providing the assistance, or shall compensate the owner or operator for all costs in obtaining the assistance. The act further makes it an unlawful act to coerce the hiring of such assistance, and provides for violation fines. Whether this law is sufficiently strong for this practice to be significantly reduced remains to be seen.

Conclusion

The transportation user is not confined to firms and services of the basic rail, motor, water, and air modes. Carriers that appear as hybrids of these modes, as well as special forms within each, are also available forms of transportation service. Recent regulatory changes in the rail, motor, air, and household goods sectors will no doubt cause other forms to evolve or some of the present ones to grow or diminish in importance. A complete study of transportation must include attention to these special forms as well as the basic ones.

Study Questions

1. How is a forwarder the same as, or different from, the main carriers they employ for line-haul services?

2. In the past few years several air freight forwarders have been forced to fly their own airplanes. Why has this happened? What advantages and disadvantages could arise as a result of this?

3. How is a broker different from a forwarder or carrier?

4. Shippers' associations are increasing in use and popularity. Why is this so?

5. How is a shippers' agent different from a forwarder? Will their role increase or decrease in the coming years?

6. What are the primary components of the household goods movement industry?

7. Why have there been problems with service reliability in this industry?

8. What are "lumpers" and what role have they played in trucking and warehousing? What suggestions would you have to alleviate problems associated with lumpers?

Notes

1. *Revised Interstate Commerce Act*, U.S. Code, vol. 49, sec. 10526.
2. *Household Goods Transportation Act of 1980, L. 196-454.*
3. *Revised Interstate Commerce Act*, U.S. Code, vol. 49, sec. 11109.

Suggested Readings

Brown, Terrence A. "Forwarder-Motor Contract Rates." *Transportation Journal,* Summer, 1974, pp. 19-24.

Guandolo, John. *Transportation Law.* 2d ed. Dubuque, Iowa: Wm. C. Brown, 1973, chap. 33.

Interstate Commerce Commission. *The Independent Trucker.* Washington, D.C.: Government Printing Office, 1977.

Lieb, Robert C. *Transportation: The Domestic System.* 2d ed. Reston, Va.: Reston Publishing Co., 1981.

Norton, Hugh S. *Modern Transportation Economics.* 2d ed. Columbus, Ohio: Charles E. Merrill, 1971, chap. 3.

Pegrum, Dudley F. *Transportation: Economics and Public Policy.* 3rd ed. Homewood, Ill.: Richard D. Irwin, 1973, chaps. 5 and 22.

Sampson, Roy J., and Farris, Martin T. *Domestic Transportation: Practice Theory and Policy.* 4th ed. Boston: Houghton Mifflin Co., 1980, chap. 5.

Stephenson, Frederick J. "Deregulation—The Air Freight Forwarder Experience." *ICC Practitioners Journal,* November/December 1975, pp. 39-55.

Taff, Charles A. *Management of Physical Distribution and Transportation.* 6th ed. Homewood, Ill.: Richard D. Irwin, 1978, chap. 18.

Case	Blue Lines Trucking

Blue Lines Trucking

John Langley is branch manager for Blue Lines, a national motor carrier at the Johnson City, Tennessee terminal. His freight is moved nightly to a hub terminal in Knoxville, Tennessee for sorting and direct line-haul movement to destination cities. His volume averages 4,000 cubic feet per night. Since a 45-foot trailer holds 2,640 cubic feet, normal volume between Johnson City and Knoxville consists typically of two runs per night, one full and one half full to Knoxville. They return early in the morning with the same payloads. The return trips bring in inbound freight that is further sorted and delivered that morning around Johnson City.

Blue Lines developed a reputation for reliable service throughout the years. Top management often felt that consistently operated partial load runs were a form of capital investment (though experienced as costs) that eventually built profitable traffic for the firm.

A recent recession and severe deregulation impact caused the company to experience a financial setback. Top management informed each branch manager that beginning on the first of next month their terminal performance will be largely based upon: (1) minimization of truck run mileage, and (2) load utilization of each run.

What would you suggest for Mr. Langley?

10 International Transportation

After reading this chapter you should:

1 Have an overview of international transportation companies and services.
2 Understand international transportation rate-making.
3 Be able to discuss major international transportation problems, issues, and policies.
4 Understand the agencies that control international transportation.

International transportation is an integral part of the study of transportation. Foreign trade is growing in tonnage and value for the United States as well as for most other nations of the world. Further, it is a purchase or sales activity engaged in by more and more firms, even medium and small firms and carriers. Although the primary economics and techniques of carrier management efficiencies are similar in international settings to those existing in domestic settings, the processes, the supply of transportation, and the public policy require separate treatment in this area.

■ chapter overview

This chapter examines foreign trade and presents the basic forms of transportation found in this realm. Rate-making systems are examined for both air and ocean trades. Several major areas of policy concern are covered that bear on the carriers, the United States, and relations with foreign nations. Finally, often overlooked in many texts, but a crucial part of international transportation, is the role of port planning and magnitude.

Extent and Magnitude of Trade

The United States is a large trading partner in the world. Although it does not engage in foreign trade to the extent that this economic sector plays in relation to the gross national product of some other nations, the magnitude of tonnage and value shipped as well as the extent of worldwide coverage makes U.S. trade processes a significant area of study. The United States trades with nearly all of the over 150 nations of the world. At the time of this writing only three or four nations are excluded due to political reasons.

The United States' largest trading partner is Canada with its many highway, rail, and water crossing points. Mexico has grown in trading significance as it has begun to develop in recent years. Trade with Canada and Mexico are relatively simple processes in that truck and rail can be used in a similar manner as that used for domestic moves. Documentation and custom processes still exist here, but this form of trade transportation need not be differentiated too much from the subjects discussed in other chapters of this book. The majority of this chapter will address ship and air transport as it relates to carriers and firms engaged in import and export activities by ocean and air.

U.S. Ocean-borne Trade

■ extent of U.S. ocean trade

The United States shipped or received over 775 million tons of ocean-borne cargo in 1977 which had a total value of over $171 billion. By the year 2000 this tonnage is expected to increase by 130 percent marking evidence of the future importance of this sector of transportation. Factors contributing to this growth are currency relationships, reduced trade barriers, growth of multinational firms, and a growing recognition by industry of commodity savings and product sales opportunities. This trade moves via air or ocean in several basic forms which include containers, break-bulk, liquid nitrogen gas or LNG, and tanker ships. The types of ships moving this trade are liners (container and break-bulk ships) with 5 percent of the tonnage, nonliner ships (bulk bottoms) with 38 percent of the tonnage, and tankers (with LNG) with 57 percent of the total tonnage. On a dollar value basis, the liner segment is much greater with the bulk haulers and tankers moving lesser shares.[1]

The U.S. trading partners are shown in Table 10.1 by type of service. Not surprisingly, with much tonnage being in tankers and bulk ships, the U.S. trading partners heavily weight the statistics with nations supplying oil and other basic bulk commodities. Liners and container ships, on the other hand, show heavy trading with industrialized nations; this trade is largely consumer products, food, chemicals, machinery, paper, wood, coffee, alcoholic beverages, autos, trucks, and grain.

Further insight into ocean-borne trade can be gained by examining the trade routes involved. The U.S. Maritime Administration has identified over forty major U.S. trade routes which link U.S. coastal areas with those in other continents. Table 10.2 shows that the largest trade route in terms of tonnage is between the U.S. gulf ports and the Caribbean, Central America, and the north coast of South America. This route

Table 10.1 Top U.S. Trading Partner Nations by Type of Ship (1977)

Liner[a]	Liner, Bulk, and Tanker[b]
1. Japan	1. Netherlands Antilles
2. Netherlands	2. Japan
3. W. Germany	3. Venezuela
4. United Kingdom	4. Canada
5. Taiwan	5. Nigeria
6. Belgium	6. Saudi Arabia
7. Italy	7. Bahamas
8. Hong Kong	8. Libya
9. Brazil	9. Netherlands
10. S. Korea	10. Indonesia

Source: U.S. Maritime Administration, *United States Oceanborne Foreign Trade Routes* (Washington, D.C.: U.S. Government Printing Office, 1979), app. H.

[a]Top 10 represents 54% of all U.S. liner trade.

[b]Top 10 represents 48% of all U.S. liner, bulk and tanker trade.

Table 10.2 Top Ten Trade Routes for U.S. (1977) (all ship services)

Route Number	Trade Route — Area	Tons(000)	% of total	Percentage for each route % export	% import
19	U.S. Gulf/Caribbean Basin	117,266	15.1%	7.7%	92.3%
4	U.S. Atlantic/Caribbean	103,483	13.3	2.5	97.5
13	U.S. Atlantic & Gulf/Mediterranean	63,195	8.2	33.2	66.8
21	U.S. Gulf/Europe (except Mediterranean)	45,088	5.8	79.8	20.2
29	U.S. Pacific/Far East	42,578	5.5	79.3	20.7
10	U.S. North Atlantic/Mediterranean	36,385	4.7	36.2	63.8
18	U.S. Atlantic & Gulf/India, Persian Gulf, and Red Sea	30,134	3.9	21.3	78.7
17	All U.S./Indonesia, Malasia & Singapore	29,269	3.8	6.5	93.5
22	U.S. Gulf/Far East	29,143	3.6	83.2	16.8
5,7,8, & 9	U.S. North Atlantic/United Kingdom & Continental Europe	24,510	3.2	55.8	44.2
All others	—	254,281	32.9	24.8	75.2
Total	—	775,332	100.0%	29.0%	71.0%

Source: U.S. Maritime Administration, *United States Oceanborne Foreign Trade Routes* (Washington, D.C.: U.S. Government Printing Office, 1979), app. F.

■ major U.S. ports

is largely an import one consisting of oil, bauxite, and coffee; it represents nearly 15 percent of the total U.S. ocean trade. In fact, the gulf ports ranging from Tampa, Florida to Galveston, Texas handle 44 percent of all U.S. ocean trade. In terms of specific ports, Table 10.3 shows the major U.S. entry and exit points according to liner and all-service ships. New York dominates in both groupings, although in recent years it has primarily been a break-bulk, liner port. For this reason it is often a preferred port for exporters. In the coming years, Norfolk, Baltimore, Philadelphia, and possibly New York will grow further as ports if U.S. coal exports increase as expected. Industrial and utility shifts from oil to coal energy in Europe and Asia are causing U.S. coal exports to move through these ports. Primary constraints in this trade are the adequacy of railroad yard, ship terminals, and harbor capacity to and in these four ports.

Table 10.3 Top Ranking Ports in U.S. (1977 in tons)

All Services (descending order)[a]:	Liner Services Only (descending order)[b]:
New York, NY	New York, NY
Gramercy, LA	New Orleans, LA
Houston, TX	Houston, TX
New Orleans, LA	Los Angeles, CA
Baton Rouge, LA	Baltimore, MD
Philadelphia, PA	Long Beach, CA
Norfolk, VA	Oakland, CA
Corpus Christi, TX	Seattle, WA
Baltimore, MD	Norfolk, VA
Long Beach, CA	Savannah, GA

Source: U.S. Maritime Administration, *United States Oceanborne For eign Trade Routes* (Washington, D.C.: U.S. Government Printing Office, 1977), app. G.

[a]Top Ten = 47.2% all port tonnage
[b]Top Ten = 69.7% of all liner port tonnage.

The specific types of ship services that carry U.S. ocean-borne trade are liners, tramps, and private vessels. Each type provides specific service features.

1. Liner. Liners are ships that ply fixed routes on published schedules. They typically charge according to published tariffs which are either unique to the ship line or according to conference tariffs made by several lines in a particular trade route. Liner services are of container or break-bulk, packaged types.

■ liners: break-bulk

Freight must be moved to the liner company's terminal at the port after the shipper has arranged for the freight booking or reservation. This freight is hand- or crane-loaded and stowed in accordance with ship weight and balance requirements. The quantity of various liner departures from New York and Oakland has caused these ports to be highly preferred by many shippers. Both of these ports are major terminuses for Sea-Land, a large container company.

■ liners: containers

advantage

Container movement is gaining over the traditional break-bulk method of ocean carriage. Where goods have to be heavily crated and packaged for break-bulk movement, a container often provides much of that needed protection. Further, where a break-bulk ship would often require many days to unload and load its cargo by small crane and manpower, an entire container ship can enter, unload, load and clear a port in less than twelve hours. Such speed has brought about labor savings to both the shipper and the liner company as well as increased ship (and capital) utilization. Since a ship is only earning revenue at sea, it is easy to see why containers have become a dominant form of packaged goods shipping.

disadvantage

Container service, while saving port and ship time, has brought about different operating and management concerns for the ship company. For one, this service requires a large investment in containers, because while some are at sea, many others are being delivered inland or are being loaded there for movement to port. So, while a ship might carry a thousand containers, an investment of 1,500 to 2,500 containers is necessary to support that ship. Another concern is control over the containers. Previous shipping line managements were port-to-port oriented. With inland movement of containers, control over this land movement becomes a necessity. The container itself is a large investment and represents an attractive holding or theft opportunity in areas of warehouse or housing shortages.

■ liners: LASH

The lighter-aboard ship (LASH) is a liner that carries barges that were loaded at an inland river point and moved to the ocean port via water tow. A specially designed ocean ship carries the payload and barge intact to a foreign port to be dropped off in the harbor. This system avoids port handling and enables fast ship turnaround and attendant high utilitization.

The economics of the LASH ship are similar to that of the container ship in that the ocean ship is high in capital cost, and the presence of barges or containers acts to decrease high stowage density. These two factors are generally traded off against the fast port turnaround provided by these systems.

Another type of ship found in liner services is a roll-on-roll-off ship, often referred to as a RORO ship. These ships are designed to handle trucks, trailers, and construction equipment which is carried much like a multi-level ferry boat. When in service with trailers, a RORO ship is like a container ship except that it has the wheel chases attached to the trailer body enroute. RORO ships are especially useful in carrying heavy construction equipment, because they are able to maintain an even keel while the equipment is being loaded and unloaded. This stability allows loading and unloading without the use of dock-side cranes that may not even be available.

■ liners: RORO ship

2. Tramp. The tramp ship is one that is hired like a taxi or leased auto. That is, it is a term for a bulk or tank ship that is hired on a voyage or time basis. On a voyage basis, a U.S. exporter of grain will seek a tramp ship that will become empty at a desired U.S. port. It will then be hired for one-way movement to a foreign port. Port fees, a daily operating rate and demurrage, will be part of the charter contract. Daily rates in the beginning of 1981 range from $6,500 to $13,000 per day for various ships. Time charters are usually longer term charters in which the shipper will make or arrange for more than a one-way move. Such charters are made with or without crews being provided by the ship owner.

■ tramp ships

3. Private Vessels. This term applies to ships that are owned or leased on a long-term basis by the firm moving the goods. Many oil ships fit this category as do automotive and lumber vessels. The economics of this form of ship movement are similar to those of private motor trucks.

■ private ships

Projections for the year 2000 show how the world fleet of ships is changing in composition. Table 10.4 shows the present and the year 2000 composition in terms of ships serving the needs of the United States. According to the projection, the largest growth will take place in partial container ships as well as in bulk and in LNG carriers. The use of tankers

Table 10.4 World Fleet Serving U.S. Trade

Type of Ship	Percentage of Ship	
	1975	2000
General Cargo	17%	11%
Partial Container	3	24
Full Container	2	2
Barge Container	1	1
Bulk	23	27
Combination	13	10
LNG	4	12
Tankers	37	13
Total all vessel types	100%	100%

Source: Temple, Barker, and Sloan, *World Fleet Forecast* (Washington, D.C.: U.S. Government Printing Office, 1979), pt. 1.

will decrease because of the expected number of super tankers, each replacing several present ones.

Ship size will shift upward thereby obsoleting smaller ships. The average tanker constructed during the 1970s carried 40,000 tons while the 1980 generation will move 120,000 tons. With crew sizes and the navigation equipment investment being approximately the same on each, the larger ship will be more economical.

Another element of interest in international shipping is that of ship registry. Although a ship might be owned by an American and plies a route between the United States and the Persian Gulf, it might be registered in and fly the flag of Liberia or Panama. These nations represent what are called "flags of convenience." That is, the owners derive certain benefits of taxes, manning, and some relaxed safety requirements by being registered in those countries rather than in the United States, Canada, or wherever. However, some activity has taken place recently with regard to labor rules in these countries which might serve to diminish the advantage of registering there.

■ "flags of convenience"

Ancillary Services

There are other service firms available in international shipping that are of concern to the student and to the users of the industry.

1. Air Forwarder. Several air forwarding firms operate in this realm in ways similar to domestic air forwarding companies. These firms represent a convenience to the shipper especially when more than one airline must be used in an interline setting, or when ground transportation is necessary at one or both ends of the air move.

2. International Freight Forwarder. These firms serve a useful purpose in arranging for through movement for the shipper. They do not necessarily act as consolidators nor earn their revenues in that manner like domestic forwarders. International freight forwarders act as agents for shippers by applying familiarity and expertise with ocean shipping to facilitate through movement. They represent the shipper in arranging such things as inland transportation, packaging, documentation, booking, and legal fees. They charge a fee in terms of a percent of the costs incurred for arranging these services. They play an invaluable role for shippers who are not familiar with the intricacies of shipping or those who do not have the scale nor volume to warrant having in-house expertise in this area.

■ forwarders

3. Nonvessel Owning Common Carrier (NVOCC). These firms act as consolidators and dispersion parties of containers that originate at or are inbound to inland points. The need for these firms arose from inbound containers being unloaded at inland points with little outbound turnaround traffic opportunity to be moved or loaded back to the port. Interior rail and truck firms often charge the same rate to move the containers whether or not the containers are unloaded or loaded. The NVOCC acts as a dispersion point for many inbound containers. It will seek outbound shipments in the same containers

■ NVOCCs

through solicitation efforts. It will then consolidate many containers for multiple piggyback car or whole train movement back to the port for export. The steamship line gains from broadened territorial traffic opportunities, as well as from the NVOCC solicitation services and control over the containers. Shippers and receivers gain from the shipping expertise and processes at the NVOCC as well as from expanded and simplified import and export opportunities.

4. Ship Broker. These firms act as middlemen between the tramp ship owner and a chartering shipper or receiver. The brokers' extensive exposure, contacts, and knowledge of the overall ship market makes them valuable parties in these arrangements. They are compensated on the basis of a percentage of the chartering fees.

5. Ship Agent. Ship agents act on behalf of a liner company or tramp ship operator (either owner or charterer) to represent their interests in facilitating ship arrival, clearance, loading, unloading, and fee payment while at a specific port. Liner firms will use agents when the frequency of sailings are so sparse that it is not economical for them to invest in their own terminals nor to have management personnel on site.

6. Land, Mini-, and Micro-Bridges. These three services have become significant parts of international shipping over the past decade. Their reasons for development are largely due to the carrier efficiencies gained from them that also bring benefits to the shippers.

■ "bridges"

Land bridge. This system consists of containers moving between Japan and Europe by rail and ship. That is, originally containers were moved entirely by ship between Asia and Europe across the Pacific and Atlantic oceans and through the Panama Canal. Ship fuel and capital costs as well as Panama Canal talks caused there to be economies in moving the containers by water to a U.S. Pacific Coast port, thence by entire trainload across the United States to another ship for transatlantic crossing to Europe. This system reduces transit time and liner company ship investment.

Mini-bridge is a similar system that is used for movements between, say, Japan and New York, Philadelphia, Baltimore, Charleston, New Orleans, or Houston. Rather than move all-water routes from Asia to these cities through the Panama Canal, mini-bridge consists of transpacific water movement to Seattle, Oakland, or Long Beach, California, then by rail to the destination east coast or gulf coast city. Mini-bridge services likewise operate from Europe to west coast cities and New Orleans and Houston, with water-rail transfer taking place at New York or Charleston, South Carolina.

Mini-bridge saves transit time and ship line separating costs and investment, but another benefit accrues to the shipper/receiver in loading and unloading cost savings by avoiding what is called a "50 mile rule." Here is an example. When containers replaced break-bulk shipping, many stevedores lost work and incomes. As part of a labor settlement, it was arranged that any container must be loaded or unloaded by stevedores if it was loaded at a shipper's facility or unloaded at a consignee's facility within 50 miles of the container point of embarkation or debarkation. This system often requires handling at times inconvenient for the shipper/receiver or at a cost much higher than what would be incurred by the shipper's own labor. An all-water movement from a San Jose, California shipper to a consignee in Europe through ship loading at Oakland, California, would require such stevedore container packing. A mini-bridge move by container train from California for containership movement from New York to Europe causes San Jose to be beyond the 50-mile radius of the New York containership loading point. Thus, the San Jose shipper avoids stevedoring loading and enjoys faster transit time to Europe.

Micro-bridge is an adaptation of mini-bridge, only it applies to interior nonport cities such as St. Louis. Micro-bridge operates in a way similar to the NVOCC system. Here, too, a container is loaded at the interior point for transference to the ship at the port. This avoids truck movement to the port for actual loading into the container at the port terminal.

Rate-Making in Foreign Transportation

Rate-making in this realm is presented from the standpoint of three major transportation supply sources available to shippers: air, liners, and chartered tramp ships.

International Air

The economies of international air freight carriage are largely similar to domestic movement. The differences lie primarily in institutional factors relating to national agreements and the International Air Transport Association (IATA). This is an international air carrier rate bureau for both passenger and freight movement. IATA has long served as a collective rate-making body composed of the U.S. overseas airlines in various route trades. Prices for both passenger and freight traditionally tended to be set at sufficient levels so as to cover most costs of many of the higher cost or lower load factor carriers. This system enhanced a supply of service as well as brought a stability to the rate structure. U.S. government policy shifts in the late 1970s tended to encourage rate flexibility and greater route expansion; these factors are initially seen as decreasing the effectiveness of IATA-made prices. This situation is discussed further in the chapter along with other policies.

Liner Rate-Making

Costs. Liner operation, as with most ships, is largely fixed and common in nature. It has been estimated that roughly 10 to 20 percent of the total costs of ship operation are variable and these are in fuel, loading, and unloading costs.[2] Liner companies tend to have large overhead costs in the form of managements which are necessary for solicitation purposes.

The liner ship is usually specifically constructed for a particular trade route. That is, such things as ship dimension, hatches, size and type, cargo space and loading crane configuration, and engine type are designed around the ports to be visited, cargoes to be moved, and even the wave patterns experienced in a particular trade. These factors cause a ship that is designed for, say, Asian traffic to be less economical for United States to European trades.

A majority of the total costs of operating a ship are fixed in nature. Since cargo loading, unloading, and fuel are the only primary variable costs, the ship's operation cost is roughly the same regardless of the commodity hauled. The problem of determining a cost per pound entails a difficult fixed cost allocation process, which can be arbitrary at best. Ship operators will often determine unit costs in terms of cost per cubic foot of ship space so as to better evaluate and price for the range of commodities handled.

Since the cost of owning and operating the ship manifests itself as a relatively fixed cost per day regardless of the commodity hauled, ship operators attempt to solicit and charge rates that will maximize the overall total revenue of the entire ship. This condition brings about the tendency of pricing according to the principles of value of service pricing. That is, a floor of variable costs must be covered as a minimum, then, the blend of high and low value-per-pound commodities, as well as the host of traffic elasticities, leads to pricing according to what the traffic will bear in such a way that revenue will be maximized.

The Conference of Rate-Making. Liner firms have long banded together into collective rate-making bodies called steamship conferences. These serve a similar purpose as that provided by domestic rail and motor rate bureaus. Conferences date back to the last century when several liner firms banded together in the United Kingdom to calculate Calcutta trade. Since then they have developed into a current state in which several characteristics can be noted.

Conferences are made up of member liner firms only. The organization is international in scope since liner firms of many nations will belong to one. They are also territorial in scope. For example, the Pacific Westbound Conference includes U.S. and foreign carriers originating freight at Pacific Coast ports between California, Alaska, and Canada for destinations in Japan, Korea, Taiwan, and Hong Kong. Another conference made up of some of the same countries, as well as others, will cover eastbound traffic between the same points. A range of firms belong to conferences. Some operate on sparse schedules while others might offer weekly service. American carriers with new ships costing to $15,000 per day will be in the trade along with foreign carriers, some of which might cost only $6,000 to $7,000 per day to operate.

The actual rate system in conferences reflects the ship and liner firm economics previously discussed. Since ship operators experience a relatively fixed cost per day, and weight is not necessarily a variable cost expense, rates are constructed to also accommodate density of freight. Many rates are assessed on a weight basis, either on a 2000-pound short ton or a 2,240-pound long ton. Products that might occupy more of a proportionate share of space relative to their weight are often charged on a "weight or measure" basis (WM). That is, the carrier would charge a dol-

■ liner costs

■ conferences

■ weight or cubic tons

lar rate per ton based upon shipment weight or "cubic tons" which are computed at every 40 cubic feet. A shipment assessed at $60 W/M that weighs 5 weight tons but occupies 280 cubic feet would be charged $420 (7 cubic tons at $60). This system somewhat enables the carrier to recoup a minimum cost per cubic foot of space of ship capacity. Figure 10.1 is a copy of a liner tariff by Lykes Steamship on its Atlantic and Gulf to China route.

Another feature of conference rate-making deals with what are called "contract" rates and "noncontract rates." Noncontract rates are the base rates. Contract rates are those that are charged to shippers who have signed "exclusive patronage agreements" with the conference. This means that the shipper will be charged rates approximately 10-15 percent lower than the noncontract rates in exchange for using only member liner firms of the conference. The exclusive patronage agreement evolved from a deferred rebate system, but that was replaced by the agreement in U.S. trade as a result of American regulatory policy. The two rate levels are the reason this system is referred to as a dual-rate system. A shipper not having signed an agreement must pay the noncontract rate. Contract shippers unable to book space on a conference ship may use a nonconference liner without jeopardizing the discount. Further, a contract shipper may use tramp ships for bulk cargoes without conflicting with the agreement. Figure 10.1 shows a tariff that has a single rate for all shippers and consignees. Competitive pressures in the late 1970s caused a few steamship lines to eliminate the contract/noncontract system and replace it with a single rate system.

One problem facing conferences and shippers in recent times is fluctuating international currency levels. That is, a Japanese steamship firm receiving revenues in dollars might find that rate and revenue to be unprofitable due to an upward relationship of the yen against the dollar. This does not necessarily harm the American flag carrier that pays the ship mortgage and wages in dollars, but the Japanese ship experiences a negative impact in that its obligations must be paid in yen terms. The conferences developed a currency adjustment factor (CAF) which is a surcharge on the rates used to recover any such related losses. These surcharges also fluctuate with currency relationship shifts. Problems have occurred with different conferences charging different CAFs as well as land portions of mini-bridges also being subject to the charge. In essence, the CAFs tend to harm U.S. exports in ways that are contrary to the devalued dollar and highly-valued currency of a foreign country. This is a continuing subject of debate and policy consideration by the Federal Maritime Commission.

Another problem area relating to ocean export and import movements is the competitiveness, location, and rail network relationships of various U.S. ports. Some ports are in direct lines between producing and consuming areas of the nation and major ocean routes, but others require longer land moves or experience less frequent ship sailings. As a result, railroads traditionally serving the less competitive ports often charged a rate for inland moves on export and import shipments that caused a

Figure 10.1 Sample of Liner Tariff

LYKES BROS. STEAMSHIP CO., INC.				FMC NO. 119	ORIG/REV 37th	PAGE 46
					CANCELS 36th	PAGE 46
ATLANTIC & GULF/CHINA WESTBOUND LOCAL FREIGHT TARIFF NO. 119					EFFECTIVE DATE	
FROM: U. S. ATLANTIC AND GULF PORTS AS SPECIFIED IN RULE 1		TO: PORTS IN THE PEOPLES REPUBLIC OF CHINA, AS SPECIFIED IN RULE 1			May 7, 1981 EAN	
					CORR NO	187

SECTION 1 · COMMODITY RATES

EXCEPT AS OTHERWISE PROVIDED HEREIN, RATES AND CHARGES ARE IN U.S. DOLLARS AND CENTS AND APPLY PER TON OF 2204.62 LBS. (W) OR 35,314 CUBIC FEET (M), WHICHEVER PRODUCES THE GREATER REVENUE. (FOR APPLICATION OF RATES, SEE RULE 2)

COMM CODE	COMMODITY DESCRIPTION AND PACKAGING	RATE BASIS	RATES COLUMN 1	RATES RESERVED	ITEM
	HOUSEHOLD-GOODS AND PERSONAL EFFECTS	W/M	148.00		350
	HYDRAULIC TESTING MACHINERY To Hsinkang Only	W/M	142.00		400
	INSTRUMENTS (Except Industrial Process) N.O.S. for Controlling, Indicating, Measuring, Recording, Testing or Transmitting, Non-Electrical Quantities, Electric or Electronic To Shanghai Only	W/M	137.00		500
	INSTRUMENTS, Measuring, Controlling and Scientific: N.O.S., To Shanghai Only Spectroscopy, To Hsingkang	W/M W/M	137.00 142.00		520
(R)	IRON AND STEEL, VIZ: Stainless Steel Rods To Shanghai Only KEENE GOLD DREDGE, Expires with June 7, 1981 KRAFT LINER BOARD, IN ROLLS	W/M W/M W	154.00 157.00 132.00		550 553 555
	LABORATORY APPLIANCES or APPARATUS, N.O.S.	W/M	164.00		570
	MACHINERY, N.O.S.	W/M	170.00		572
(R)	MACHINERY, for Liquid Crystal Display MEMBRANE OXYENATOR, Adult	W/M W/M	154.00 132.00		573 573.5
	NORMAL BUTYL ALCOHOL, TO: Whampoa, Expires with June 6, 1981 (N) Effective June 7, 1981	W/M W/M	147.00 155.00		574

FOR EXPLANATION OF ABBREVIATIONS, REFERENCE MARKS AND SYMBOLS, SEE PAGE 2. DGE/0321 ITS(202)347-8770

through move to be the same rate as that over a direct port route. This was traditionally encouraged by the Interstate Commerce Commission (ICC) in an effort to equalize port relationships. However, ICC policy shifts and railroad financial postures in the late 1970s are such that many observers feel port equalization might not be a favored policy in the future and that normal cost and market relationships should evolve.

The conference type system has withstood a great amount of pressure and criticism as well as support over the years. Adverse pressure has come from two main sectors. One is overtonnage of shipping capacity in the late 1970s. That is, the amount of ship carrying space plying the oceans is greater than the freight being moved. This situation leads to price cutting in any cartel-like relationship and ship conferences experienced the pressure when some liner firms withdrew from the conference. Another pressure problem area has been with price cuttings by ship firms owned and operated by the U.S.S.R. in U.S. to Japan and U.S. to European markets. The Atlantic and Pacific Ocean arms of the Russian steamship organizations entered into these markets in the 1970s with significant rate-cutting that severely affected the traditional firms. In many instances, this practice was seen by many as unfair, because the Russian firms appeared to be operating at below variable cost. However, labor and capital costs of these ships were paid in Russian currency, and profit was not necessarily the motive. Market entry and obtaining hard Western currencies was no doubt the objective. That is, the motive for operating was different than the other lines' long run profit objective. The situation came to a head in 1980 when U.S. stevedores refused to service these ships as a result of the Russian invasion of Afghanistan. By early 1981, these organizations no longer operate to or from the United States.

The conference system has often been criticized from several vantage points. These criticisms are similar to those against domestic rate bureaus, because rates are higher than they would be under free-market competition. Inefficient liner firms are protected, and rate innovations are not encouraged. Further, the practice of restricted conference membership by liner firms might leave poor quality service to some areas.

Rate conferences do provide some benefits which contribute to their long-term existence. They provide a somewhat stable rate structure which fosters uniformity of rates and procedures. Further, individual shipper discrimination is reduced in that any economic discrimination that is taking place is done so uniformly.

Tramp Ship Cost Rate Factors

Costs. Tramp ships are generally not controlled by a specific route with a single commodity. Large oil tankers that are built for time charters for specific origin-destination markets are the exception. The basic tramp vessel might haul coal, grain, fertilizers, and lumber in the same year. Adaptability is necessary so as to minimize lost revenue possibilities that will arise. These vessels might not always be of low cost, optimal design for any of the movements, but that is a basic trade-off to being flexible. This general construction means general internal features and hatches as well as the capability to enter into most ports of the worlds.[3]

The economies of ship construction are critical to the tramp vessel, especially the tanker. The nontanker vessel is generally built to hold between 5,000 and 8,000 tons of cargo. This is a good range for a majority of cargo lot sizes shipped by firms. The tanker, on the other hand, is usually designed for crude oil movements, and here the larger tankers can competitively move oil at costs much lower than smaller vessels. This is due to economies of scale in both construction and operation, the larger ships being less costly to operate. In fact, many 200,000 deadweight ton (DWT) tankers have the same number of crew members as those carrying only 40,000 DWT. Labor economies exist on new ships through the technological advances in navigation and operating systems. Where boiler rooms previously required a large number of personnel, many now function through computerized and automated control direct from the bridge. Navigational safety and optimum route planning is even enhanced with direct satellite links that can pinpoint ships' locations within a few hundred yards.

A major consideration of tramp owners is the nation in which the ship is registered. The nation of registry requires the shipowner to comply with specific manning, safety, and tax provisions. Liberia, Greece, and Panama are nations imposing relatively loose requirements in such areas. For this reason many of the world ships are registered in these countries.

Tramp Ship Rate-Making. A tramp ship owner experiences costs, like those of the liner, that are largely fixed in nature. Ownership costs present themselves in depreciation and interest costs. Fuel is not as greatly variable with the commodity weight load as is ship speed or at-sea versus port time. The key is that the shipowner minimizes empty nonrevenue miles and days.

Three primary forms of ship rental or chartering systems are in use. These are the voyage, time, and bareboat or demise charter. Each one is distinct. The voyage charter is one in which the shipowner mans, operates, and charters the vessel, similar to a taxicab. Shippers seek voyage charters for primarily one-way and sometimes two-way trips. The owner is constantly seeking charters subsequent to present charters in order to minimize empty moves to the next charter.

The time charter is one in which the shipowner rents the vessel and crew to a shipper for use over a period of time which will often include shipper use of it for several shipments. The owner has his ship productively tied up for a longer period of time than in the voyage charter and the shipper might judiciously arrange his moves in such a way that is less costly than through several voyage charters.

The bareboat or demise charter is one in which the owner usually rents the vessel for a long period of time while the chartering party supplies the crew and performs the physical operation of the vessel. In this setting, the owner is seeking to recoup capital and interest costs and to be assured that the ship will be safely operated. Ship brokers in New York and London handle most ship chartering in this area.

The market for ship chartering is a fluid supply and demand situation.

The charter rate situation at any one time can be one of feast-or famine for ship owners. This market can fluctuate over both short- and long-term time spans. In the short run, the demand for a ship and charter rates at a single port area will depend upon shipper movement needs and available ship supply within a time span as short as a month. In another way the market can be considered glutted or tight depending upon the number of ships or ships of a certain type that are available in the world during a span of a year.

Long run conditions have affected the world charter market in several ways. In one context, the growth in world oil consumption dropped after the 1973 energy crisis. Much ship tonnage was still being constructed at the time that was expected to be profitably used throughout the 1970s. So the growth rate of new ship capacity coming on-line continued to exceed the lowered growth rate of oil demand. Another market depressing factor was the reopening of the Suez Canal in the mid-1970s. For several years ships carrying oil from the Persian Gulf to Europe and North America had to travel around Africa. Once the Suez Canal reopened, a medium-size ship could make a roundtrip in much less time. With the same number of ships in the market suddenly capable of making more trips per year, the world capacity of ship carriage effectively increased which caused supply to exceed demand from this cause as well. A major U.S. grain sale to Russia or China has the effect of boosting charter markets in both existing grain-carrying ships and tankers which can be converted for such cargoes. This market was not very continuous during the 1970s, and, in fact, the 1980 U.S. grain embargo to Russia tended to harm this market until other nation sales took up some of the supply. All these factors point to the high capital commitment and risk situation in this area for ship owners.

International transportation managers face economic considerations that are broadly covered above, although this form of transportation is not subject to the complete set of domestic regulations imposed by the ICC and CAB. In the international area, matters of international policy strongly affect transportation management and planning.

International Transportation Problems, Issues, and Policies

Two major policy areas are of concern in this area. One relates to the Federal Maritime Commission (FMC) and to foreign policy in regulation of international waterborne rates and practices to and from the United States. Another revolves around international air transportation. A third area relates to promotion of the United States merchant marine fleet, but the basics of this issue are covered in Chapter 19, Financing Private and Public Transportation Systems.

Federal Maritime Commission Regulation of U.S. Ocean Rates

The FMC is perhaps the weakest of the three U.S. transportation regulatory agencies which also include the CAB and ICC. The FMC's primary jurisdiction is over U.S. ocean-borne foreign trade as well as ocean movements between the U.S. mainland and Puerto Rico, Hawaii, and other U.S. possessions.

Primary regulatory powers held by the FMC relate to overcharges, discriminatory practices, rebates, conference procedures, or foreign freight forwarder misdeeds. The agency does not have rate powers similar to those traditionally held by the CAB and ICC which relate to fixing of rate maximums, minimums, exact rate prescriptions, or general rate increases. These powers only exist over domestic carriers plying domestic trades. The agency has attempted to gain congressionally mandated powers through the years over the rates of foreign carriers in U.S. ocean-borne trades, but these attempts have not been successful. Lack of White House and State Department support for these moves are felt by many to be a reason for these failures. Ocean maritime trade matter is often seen as a minor factor in the total diplomacy picture. Further, foreign carriers and their governments are such that the FMC would face opposition in obtaining key cost information necessary in rate cases. As a result, the FMC has been of little help to U.S. importers and exporters who feel harmed by specific rates and rate levels in ocean trades. The agency has been active, however, in port, conference, and carrier practices dealing with personal discrimination.

One example of recent rate concern, in which the U.S. exporter interests have seemingly been harmed, is in the apparent disparity of outbound versus inbound rates. Specifically, in the late 1970s rates on many export commodities were higher than the same import commodities over some of the same lines. One study showed some of these rate disparities to be as high as 79 percent with an average disparity of 32.2 percent.[4] This means that a U.S. exporter is, in a sense, penalized when exporting in comparison to a shipper of the same commodity who is moving it into the United States. A Department of Transportation study set forth several reasons for this phenomenon which included higher outbound loads and excess capacity on inbound moves, the need to promote inbound moves more than outbound moves, as well as some other cost-related reasons. Be that as it may, the issue started in the 1950s, and since this time the FMC has had less power, other than to collect general information relating to the problem.

The future of the FMC is not very closely tied to the deregulatory shifts within the CAB and ICC. Although it is a weak agency, it does play a role in protecting firms and shippers from many discriminatory practices that would no doubt prevail without its existence.

United Nations Conference on Trade and Development (UNCTAD) and Foreign Trade Allocations

■ 40-40-20 proposal

The United Nations (UN) has long been concerned with problems of ocean shipping industry development in third world nations. This concern relates to the inability of many nations to develop home flag shipping industries, because of the presence of flag of convenience shipping lines and their low costs of operation. The UNCTAD meetings during the past few years have evolved toward the UN imposing a worldwide requirement that trade by ship between nations be allocated according to a percentage formula. The formula, called the 40-40-20 division, would permit a nation to use its own flag ship in trade with a second nation for up to 40 percent of the volume shipped. The second trading nation partner can use its flag ships for up to 40 percent of the bilateral trade also. Ships of third nations can handle only up to 20 percent of the remaining trade between the two nations.

Though this system would no doubt tend to develop shipping industries in nations that do not currently have such industries, or having only weak ones, it is being resisted by the United States and many other nations due to the inherent inefficiencies it would bring about. World trade routes would tend toward hub and spoke patterns from each nation, and little cross trading would exist. Where there are traffic imbalances between two nations, much empty hauling would exist. In all, it would represent an artificial restraint of trade in the form of transportation.

Air International Regulation

Matters of concern in the international air carriage area relate to air safety and economic regulation. There is no single international regulatory body covering rate and route matters in the international air area. Instead, the pattern of route and rate establishment evolves from: national policy, use of the bilateral system of operating rights as negotiated after World War II by many nations of the world, the new U.S. policy of open competition encouragement, and the International Air Transport Association (IATA), a long standing international rate bureau.

ICAO. The International Civil Aeronautics Organization is basically a navigation and safety body concerned with worldwide consistency in air traffic control, airport design, and air safety features. The organization attempts to cause commonality in terms, practices, equipment, and facilities which would otherwise be very confusing if each nation developed and used different navigational systems.

National Air Policy. The root of economic regulation and its analysis stems from national, political and economic choice and the international air area is, perhaps, where such regulation is most usable. The development of the airplane and air service after World War II corresponded with the growth of most nations in the world. Most nations today, no matter how small, have a national flag carrier for reasons similar to the reason national interest exists with home steamship lines. One reason is that a national flag carrier provides representation abroad. Another reason is that the presence of the home carrier in a route can sometimes serve to prevent undesirable discrimination against traffic flows to and from the country. Still another reason is that the flag carrier can be operated by the country as an inducement for trade and tourism in that nation. Many carriers are owned and operated by their national governments at losses so that favorable balance of payments, hard currency inflows, and local economic gains can be enhanced. Finally, some nations operate airlines as a form of security link for diplomats and other national citizens. These reasons are often overriding the profit motive in the decision to develop and operate national flag carriers abroad. These carriers, for the most part, operate at losses, the deficits of which must be made up by the national government. A difficulty exists for the privately owned, for-profit U.S. carriers such as Pan Am and TWA which must compete against those other carriers on many routes that cannot profitably support two or more carriers. Be that as it may, it is crucial to understand that not all international carriers are in existence on a for-profit basis, and that various home national policies often dictate their behavior.

The Post-World War II Bilateral Rights System. Several rounds of international negotiations took place after World War II in order to provide a rational system for air development in the world. As these negotiations progressed, many nations accepted what became known as bilateral agreements for airlines between their lands and others. As practiced, it meant that Nation A could designate one of its carriers to fly between its main city and that of Nation B. Nation B could also certify its carrier over the same route. In this way, Air France and TWA have been the traditional Paris-New York carriers. Since New York has been such a high volume traffic center, many foreign lines can be seen there with routes linking it to their home nations. Pan Am and TWA historically have been represented on those same routes as well with the American flag.

Third flag nation carriers have typically been allowed to enter into many markets. For example, Carrier C flying under bilaterally established rights between Nation C and Nation B is often permitted to fly beyond B to A with traffic between those two points. This can be evidenced by the over twenty different national airlines that fly between Paris, London, and New York. Lufthansa, the German flag airline, flies passengers between New York and Lima, Peru on this basis.

U.S. Open Policy. The deregulatory shift in the U.S. rail and motor modes has spilled over into a more liberal international air policy on the part of the U.S. government. Many U.S. cities, other than New York, Miami, Los Angeles, and San Francisco, are originating or developing sufficient traffic volumes to warrant direct overseas air service. The CAB and White House policy during the late 1970s and early 1980s encouraged the opening up of more U.S. cities to direct service. This coincides with a shifted national policy of seeking more competition among the airlines. As a result, the U.S. has awarded international routes to both U.S. and foreign carriers at cities such as Atlanta, Boston, Dallas, Denver, Minneapolis, and St. Louis. The open policy has brought direct service which is a convenience over having to change airlines at gateway cities such as New York. Whether or not true price reductions come about will remain to be seen as carriers experience post-introduction route traffic patterns. Many foreign nations are slow to accept the new open policy because the policy is expected to open up other foreign, major cities in exchange for gaining access to other U.S. cities. Again, the price benefit to the traveler is as yet unknown; the future role of IATA being a major factor in this area.

IATA. The International Air Transport Association is a collective rate-making body of international air carriers. The IATA is based in Montreal and has traditionally functioned in ways similar to a domestic rate bureau.

Collective fare and rate-making in international air carriage under IATA has fostered a relatively stable pricing system over the past few decades. New York to London fares have usually been the same regardless of the carrier. "Competition" under this type of system is generally limited to schedule positionings and in-flight amenities. This system also serves to protect the higher cost carrier while providing possibly higher than normal economic profits to the low-cost carrier.

■ IATA air conference

IATA has been the subject of official government criticism under the recent deregulatory thrusts in the United States. The more liberal route award actions by the CAB and White House administration have tended to weaken the strength of IATA, since these awards are often predicted upon the applicant airliners' promotional fare plans.

The future picture of international air policy is unclear. On the one hand, nearly every nation of the world has a home airline operating on routes emanating from it as well as leading to prime third-flag routes. The opportunity for monopoly profits and strong one-nation influence upon a route (something more common in the past) is perhaps a diminishing phenomenon. The influence of the United States and major Western European nations in international air markets is not as great as it once was since modern equipment can be acquired by almost any airline in the world. Finally, many major nation governments are finding difficulty or displaying reluctance in continuing to subsidize the home nation airline deficits. These lines will then be seeking strategies for profit or positive cash flow opportunities in ways heretofore not used in their management approaches. This trend might cause the foreign governments to protect the home carrier thereby enabling it to earn a profit. Such moves might include, but are not limited to, a strengthening of IATA-like fare setting, and schedule and flight limitations by competing flag carriers. As the 1980s evolve, this situation might become more clear.

Port and airport development represents large capital outlays and planning activities that are often beyond the normal capabilities of individual carriers. For these reasons, nations, states, and cities throughout the world are deeply involved in port and airport development. The vitality of a region's economic activity is closely linked with that of the capacity and efficiency of the airports and ports it uses to interface with other regions and nations.

Role of Port Authorities in International Transportation

The term port authority applies to a state or local government that owns, operates or otherwise provides wharf, dock and other terminal investments at ports. In many instances, these include the major city airport as well. The primary reasons for the existence of these organizations are: to allow for comprehensive planning, to provide the large physical investment base, and to provide for certain political needs within the area.

Port authorities are organized along various lines. One is local to the port or terminal. This body seeks to maximize benefits to one particular port site. An example is Oakland, California which actively competes against and, in fact, has diverted significant amounts of traffic away from the Port of San Francisco which is in the same bay area. Another authority organization is statewide. Maryland, Virginia, Georgia, and Louisiana are examples. Here, one agency oversees all the ports within the state. This body seeks to manage various ports within the state area. The general taxing authority of the state backs up the financing efforts of these bodies. The third major authority organizational structure is bistate in nature. This body is concerned with a port area across state lines. The Port of New York and New Jersey covers the water area and airports in New York City and the Delaware River Ports Authority spans Philadelphia, Pennsylvania and Camden, New Jersey.

Port authorities serve various roles which include the following. Some own all waterfront rights and rent waterside access rights to shipping companies and terminal firms. This is the case under Louisiana law which evolved from French legal precedent in which the state controls access to the water. Some others actually develop waterways and pier terminal facilities and rent them to users (on short- and long-term bases) who do not have the scale of operations to support or perhaps do not wish to actually own such assets. This capital financing role is perhaps the major benefit provided by these port authorities. In the container boom of the 1960s and 1970s, ports acquired container loading facilities so as to develop such traffic through them. These assets, in many cases, would not exist nor would the traffic be found there today were it not for these public investments. Port authorities also serve to promote overall trade through their port areas. This includes industrial development efforts, the offering of favorable financing, representation before regulatory bodies, and the encouragement of adequate transportation facilities on land.

Future of International Transportation

International transportation will grow in importance as more manufacturing and merchandising firms become involved in overseas sourcing and marketing. Long standing domestic firms in many industries face competition against foreign-based manufacturers that can produce and load goods at customer docks as cheaply as the goods can be produced locally. This phenomenon is fostered by reduced trade barriers, relative currency fluctuations, and the competitiveness of ocean carriers. This exporting and importing used to be confined to the large firm; it is now a basic activity in many medium and small U.S. firms.

The cloud on the international trade horizon is nationalism. This ranges from tariff protection to political constraints and home flag carrier protection. Such nationalism tends to appear whenever a home industry is threatened by foreign competition or forces. The Jones Act in the United States is one such example, though not a significant one on the world scene.[5] Be that as it may, pressures in supply-short or economically sluggish nations can tend to cause constraints which hinder international trade and transportation.

A final point on this topic relates to individual traffic and distribution managers. Most firms are becoming involved in international purchasing and marketing. The process requires different procedures than those for domestic trade. It is a discipline that is different in many ways from related domestic activities. The supply of transportation, rate-making, and public policy concerns are somewhat different than counterpart domestic areas.

Conclusion

International transportation is governed by the same set of underlying economic principles as other forms of carriage, but ownership patterns, processes, procedures, and government policies cause it to appear different than those in the domestic area. The economy of the United States is becoming more dependent upon international trade. Students and managers can no longer remain isolated within the domestic sphere alone. Changes in operational features and international policies require a firm to maintain a constant monitor on this area so that products may flow as efficiently as possible.

Study Questions

1. Distinguish between (a) liner, (b) bulk, and (c) tanker trades.
2. What economies and costs arise with LASH services?
3. What types of ships will gain in use between now and the year 2000?
4. Distinguish between the different types of "bridges" (e.g., mini-, micro- and land). Why are they popular today?
5. How is international air and ocean rate-making different than the processes employed in the domestic trades of rail and truck?
6. Why do many carriers charge "weight or measure" rates?
7. How do international currency fluctuations complicate the rate-making and charge system?
8. What are the pros and cons of conference rate-making?
9. Why is the nation in which a ship is registered such a major factor for carriers?
10. Ocean rate regulation by the Federal Maritime Commission has been criticized as weak. Comment.
11. What are port authorities? What arguments can be made for this form of port planning and investment?
12. In recent months, dramatic reductions have been made in air fares on some domestic routes and on services between the United States and Britain. What economic justifications or objections can be offered in relation to these reductions? (AST&T, Fall 1977, Exam #1)

Notes

1. U.S. Maritime Administration, *United States Oceanborne Foreign Trade Routes* (Washington, D.C.: U.S. Government Printing Office, 1979), pt. 1.
2. Roy Nersesian, *Ships and Shipping* (Tulsa: Penn Well Publishing, 1981), chap. 9.
3. U.S. Maritime Administration, *Relative Costs of Shipbuilding* (Washington, D.C.: U.S. Government Priting Office, 1979), chap. 2.
4. U.S. Maritime Administration, *The Impact of Bilateral Shipping Agreements in the U.S. Liner Trades* (Washington, D.C.: U.S. Government Printing Office, May 1979), chap. 5.
5. *Merchant Marine Act of 1920*, sec. 27.

Suggested Readings

Amundsen, Paul A. *Current Trends in Port Pricing.* Washington: Maritime Administration, 1978.

Bess, David. *Marine Transportation.* Danville, Ill.: Interstate Printers, 1967.

Dowd, Lawrence P. *Introduction to Export Management.* Burlingame, Calif.: Eljay Press, 1977.

Gamble, John K. et al. *Marine Policy. A Comparative Approach.* Lexington, Mass.: Lexington Books, 1977.

Jansson, Jan Owen, "Intra-Tariff Cross-Subsidization in Liner Shipping." *Journal of Transport Economics and Policy*, September 1974, pp. 294-311.

Kendall, Lane C. *The Business of Shipping.* Centreville, Md.: Cornell Maritime Press, 1979.

Murr, Alfred. *Export/Import Traffic Management and Forwarding.* Centreville, Md.: Cornell Maritime Press, 1979.

St. Joer, C.E., "Geography—The Last Barrier to International Trade," *Annual Proceedings of the National Council of Physical Distribution Management*, 1977, pp. 435-440.

Wood, Donald F., and Johnson, James C. *Contemporary Transportation.* Tulsa: Petroleum Publishing Co., 1980, Chap. 9.

Case   ## American Consumer Products, Inc.

Andy Flaggman is vice president of distribution for American Consumer Products, Inc., a large food, clothing, and appliance conglomerate in the United States. He is working with his staff on the forthcoming year's transportation and distribution budget. Under examination are the steamship charges for company export movements through Oakland, California to Japan and import shipments in the reverse direction. Company traffic is almost exclusively in containers. The lines used up to now have charged consistent rates, since they all belong to the Pacific Westbound Conference and the counterpart eastbound conference into the United States. A westbound container of canned meat, for example, is charged $1,100 to Kobe, Japan. Eastbound shipments of handbags are charged $950. The transportation department, like all others, is under pressure to reduce costs. This has been difficult in export/import trades, because of the high fuel surcharges and currency adjustment factors that have caused Andy's Pacific basin shipping costs to rise faster than most line item costs in the firm since 1975.

Agents for the Far East Steamship Company (FESCO) approached Andy's department and proposed a westbound rate of $925 and an eastbound rate of $700. This appeared to be a welcome alternative to the conference lines' rates.

Andy had some background knowledge of FESCO. The company started in the U.S.-Japan trade on a small scale in the late 1960s. It recently became a major line, due to its rate cutting which averages about 20 percent from those of the conference ships. It is owned and operated by the shipping arm of the U.S.S.R. It demands freight payment in U.S. dollars or Japanese yen only. Because its ships are built in Russia, crews are exclusively Russian. The only western purchases made by the line are for fuel (cheapest in the United States), food, and payment for port fees. Steamship interests throughout the world acknowledge that FESCO mainly serves to obtain western currencies for Russia. The line operates marginally, but the primary gain is the hard currencies. The rate cutting, however, is now endangering other steamship lines, several of which said they will be forced to cease operations if FESCO continued to divert traffic away from them.

Andy's conflict is now between FESCO's low rates and the higher rates of the U.S., Japanese, and German lines that are in the westbound and eastbound trade and in competition with FESCO.

What should Andy do?

11 Urban and Metropolitan Transportation

After reading this chapter you should:

1 Understand the importance of transportation in relation to the viability of metropolitan areas.

2 Be able to discuss the major problems in urban transportation.

3 Be able to discuss the major transportation alternatives in metropolitan areas.

4 Understand the special needs of urban freight movements.

■ chapter overview

Transportation is vital to the health and vitality of cities and surrounding metropolitan areas. Most of the discussion up to this point in the text has dealt with intercity freight and passenger transportation which link geographic areas. This chapter presents the essential factors relating to passenger and freight transportation within and around metropolitan areas.

Transportation and the Vitality of a Metropolitan Area

■ spoke effect on highways

A transportation network is a direct link between the city and the metropolitan area it serves. In one context, the growth pattern of cities and their surrounding economic spheres was largely shaped by the transportation systems available for local passenger and freight movements. An historical examination of city population growth patterns in the late 1800s and the early part of this century would reveal population density near the spoke-like patterns of the street, local railway, subway, and trolley systems that were in place. Even in the 1960s, many interstate highways and beltways that were built through lightly populated surrounding areas soon grew with retail store, service, and residential development. The growth around Washington, D.C., can be seen in this way. Rockville, Wheaton, and Columbia, Maryland, as well as Springfield, Fairfax, and McLean, Virginia, experienced growth largely due to the construction of Interstates 495, 695, 95, and 270 surrounding and emanating from the core city.

■ catalytic effect

In another way, city growth and transportation can be viewed as having a catalytic effect upon each other. That is, the existence of population or economic activity will tend to attract transportation, and the existence of good transportation will generally cause economic development to take place. Many of the urban highway projects of the 1950s and 1960s, and those remaining to be built today, parallel heavily trafficked routes between the urban center and an outlying area. Urban planners design subways and major bus routes along the lines of existing population and traffic patterns. On the other hand, when a highway or subway route is constructed, major investment and growth can soon be seen around the exits or stations. In addition, real estate values will rise as a result of the presence of good transportation. They will also rise when new transportation services are available that reduce travel time to the major work and shopping areas.

Transportation is a part of a city's infrastructure. That is, its existence and operation are not final consumable services in the economy; rather, urban passenger and freight movement enables other economic and recreational activities—the demanded consumables—to take place. The existence of transportation permits work, education, shopping, recreation, and health activities to occur. Without transportation, these functions would be inefficient or would not take place at all. In this way, transportation is a vital part of the region's health and strength. When transportation is slow, unreliable, and costly, it will cause the main economic activities of the area to be likewise. The efficient passenger and freight movement in and around a city, then, is a key to the economic and social costs of the area.

■ infrastructure

Urban Transportation Trends

Several changes have taken place over the past few decades that dramatically affect urban transportation networks and the metropolitan areas they serve. Again, many of these changes are interrelated in such a way that discussion of trends about the transportation network itself cannot be separated from events in the urban area.

Since 1945, the economic sphere of most cities has spread beyond the actual city limits into what is now seen as a central business district (CBD), suburbia, secondary quasi-business district locales, and exurbia. Many metropolitan areas have actually begun to touch what is called regional sprawl. This can be seen in the Baltimore-Washington, Philadelphia-New York, New York-Hartford, Chicago-Milwaukee, Pittsburgh-Cleveland, Dallas-Ft. Worth, Los Angeles-San Diego, and Orlando-Tampa areas.

■ urban spread

The city spread can be linked largely to both increased population and the growth of the automobile and truck. After World War II, there was a significant shift toward home and auto ownership and away from urban apartment life-styles. This movement was followed by highway growth which further fostered the trend. In many cities the shift by middle class families out of the cities was accompanied by a physical and economic deterioration of the urban core. At the same time, many industries shifted to the outskirts of cities in quest of larger facilities that were not confined by streets, utilities, and other physical, center city constraints. In some cities, clerical and white collar industries also shifted to the suburbs for reasons of either greater flexibility, lower cost, or better working environment.

The cost structure of a city and metropolitan area can be determined by reviewing pertinent service cost along with personal living expenses. Service costs include the costs of fire and police protection, water, electricity, sewage, refuse, schools, and administration as they all translate into taxes paid by the public. Personal costs primarily include commuting costs. These two cost elements, personal and service,

■ urban cost structure

can be combined to present a cost structure for a city and surrounding region as shown in Figure 11.1.

Figure 11.1 shows that as a city spreads in size, total service and personal costs tend to increase either through direct personal outlays or through taxes. These costs are due mainly to the larger investment required to reach persons in outlying areas. For example, digging for a water line that will serve fifty families costs roughly the same as a line that will serve several hundred. Further, in-place investment in the city is underutilized, whereas new service placement must be created in the suburban area.

■ urban transportation system trends

City spread and its cost directly affect urban transportation systems. The population spread primarily leads to longer routes that are less densely utilized than routes serving a thickly populated urban area. Decreased utilization and longer routes have caused several problems which eventually led to the demise of privately owned urban passenger systems in the 1960s and 1970s.

Following World War II, ridership declines were experienced on most transit systems in the country. This often led to deficit financial performance which caused these systems either to disappear, to be subsidized by public agencies, or to be taken over by the public agencies.

Some Causes of the Urban Passenger Transportation Problem

The automobile has often been referred to as the "fifth freedom" held by Americans. It has pervaded life-styles to the extent that it is often used even in the face of alternative lower total cost transportation options. The personal convenience and privacy of the auto has, in many cases, created an intolerance of the waiting, walking, and crowding often associated with public forms of transportation. The convenience and privacy

Figure 11.1 Approximate Cost Structure For a City and Surrounding Area for a Given Population

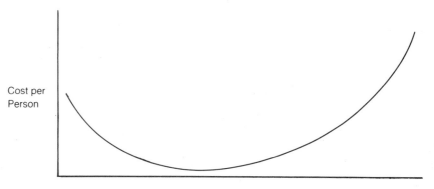

Cost per Person

Geographic Square Miles

■ the auto

factors, accompanied by relatively inexpensive availability of gas and oil for several decades, created a dramatic diversion to the auto and away from public transport. This diversion was felt mostly in shopping and recreational intracity trips and to a lesser extent in commuting trips.

■ land use shifts

Urban sprawl has been accompanied by the growth of suburban shopping centers. This has caused a large shift in such things as retail purchasing, theaters, and restaurants, to suburban locations and away from downtown stores. Thus, shopping trips to downtown areas during the day or in the evening via public transit systems tended to disappear.

The drop in shopping and recreational use of public transit systems meant negative utilization impacts for these systems. Formerly, they were intensively utilized by commuters in the morning, shoppers during the day, commuters in the evening, and people attending theater, cultural events, and restaurants in the evening. Transit equipment often

■ peak and valley problem

only experienced twelve to fifteen hours per day utilization, while employees often physically operated public transit for full-shift periods.

When only commuting demand remains, a transit system experiences travel demands similar to that shown in Figure 11.2.

The peak situation calls for greater demand than before, but the demand is largely concentrated in two two-hour periods per day for only five days per week—roughly only 6 percent of the week is represented by full utilization. It is not uncommon for a city like Washington, D.C., to require 2,000 buses in service during rush hours, only to have half of them in service during the day, a quarter of them in the evening, and only 5 percent during the night and early morning. This peak/valley demand problem means that capital investments are largely underutilized and many operating employees who are paid full eight-hour shifts are only required to work runs which take half to three quarters of that time.

Figure 11.2 Transit System Peak and Valley Problem

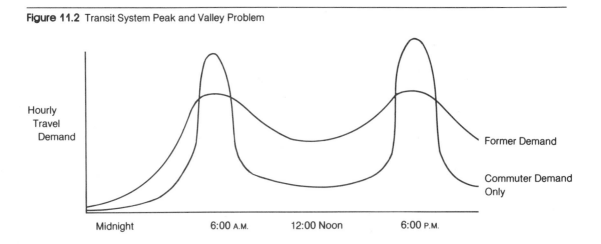

In many cities some bus drivers and train crews are paid for a full day for one trip into the city in the morning and one trip at night.

Transit industry wages climbed in ways that have hampered productivity gains. In the 1960s, larger buses permitted more passengers to be handled per run, which also meant more were handled per operating employee. More passengers per run and higher fare levels caused a 14 percent increase in revenues per mile on an industry average. In spite of this gain, wages per mile increased during the same period by 29 percent.[1] In the New York City subway system the current 50¢ fare does not even cover labor costs much less energy, overhead, and investment costs.

■ wage increases

Statistics by the American Transit Association indicate that overall productivity measures for all U.S. industries rose from a base of 100 to an index level of 143 from 1955 to 1967. In the same period the transit industry's productivity dropped from 100 to 92. In this time span, employment alone in the transit industry rose by 35 percent.

■ productivity decline

Many observers state that technological advances basically ceased in the bus, trolley, and rail industries after World War II. This cessation brought few cost savings or other efficiency advances to the field (which is partly reflected in the declining ridership and profitability of the industry). So, firms were left with few sources of cost savings and riders with few incentives to shift back to or remain with the industry as it aged.

Declining ridership, less utilization, more employees, higher wages, and little innovation combine to increase the per-passenger cost of service. These factors create a spiral which causes more passengers to shift away from the system, leaving the smaller number of remaining transit passengers to bear the existing costs by another increase in unit costs and fares.

Gradually over a two-decade period, the industry found it could not survive under private ownership. Whereas public urban transportation was viewed in the late 1960s and early 1970s as a *desirable* service for cities to retain, many public agencies began to subsidize urban transportation operations, to invest in them, or to purchase them outright for public agency operation. Since the beginning of the emerging energy crunch in the 1970s, urban transportation services are now viewed as a necessary component to the viable function of cities and their environments.

Toward Solutions to Urban Transit Problems

A comprehensive analysis of the passenger movement problem includes a review of primary trip market needs, examination of the available modal split, and a review of the entire range of actual service solutions, as well as the assistance funding programs.

Urban-related trip demands fall into three broad categories which provide insights into origin-destination density patterns. The first is the work or school trip. The need for this type of trip is the most consistent and repetitive because it has one origin and one destination. The work

■ primary trip markets

point is often a concentrated employment stop (office, factory, etc.). The second major trip need in a household unit is the trip to shop for food and other necessities. This, too, can be repetitive in pattern. The third type of trip, miscellaneous, includes recreational and medical trips. Miscellaneous trips are the least repetitive and are not always conducive to transit service attraction.

■ modal split

The modal split for urban passenger needs covers the range from the pedestrian to the private auto, taxi, van, bus, light rail systems or street cars, subway, railroad, and, in some instances, water. The percentage break down of each varies by city, and even comparisons of cities of similar size often show consistency on this basis. The split is dependent upon the quality of each form and the habits of the population. Los Angeles, for example, is widely dispersed. The auto is seen on the highways with a very low average number of riders. San Francisco, on the other hand, has a subway system and highly defined routes due to the city having bays and a few bridges; its commuting pattern is different. Washington, D.C. is a city in which car pooling has long been encouraged by government agencies. The average number of passengers per car in Washington is higher than in most cities.

Range of Alternative Passenger Movement Systems

The list of passenger movement alternatives is large since some new forms have evolved over the years. These movement alternatives roughly fall into three groups which are often classified as hardware options, quasi-hardware solutions, and policy options.

Hardware Options. Hardware options are those forms of urban passenger movement that can be described as equipment or investment.

1. Automobiles are the most common and flexible form of urban passenger transportation available. One outstanding feature of the private auto is its cost of operation. The per-trip cost of the private auto is not readily noted by the user. Many people perceive the major costs of the auto in terms of gasoline cost and miles per gallon. On the whole, the total costs of the automobile operation are relatively high, and, in a majority of cases, it is more expensive than most other options. The U.S. Department of Transportation (DOT) recently determined that a 1980 economy mileage, middle-size sedan costs 28¢ per mile when all costs of oil, tires, insurance, depreciation, and general upkeep are calculated together. However, private individuals generally do not rationally evaluate all these monetary costs and, if they do, often the trade-off for convenience is a dominating decision factor.

2. Car pooling is a concentrated use of the auto which is encouraged by many firms and public agencies. Car pools can go far in reducing highway, parking, and energy demands.

3. Highways and streets represent the public agency investment into auto and truck use. They are financed by user taxes and other appropriations. As discussed in Chapter 19, future highway expansion will only come about with some difficulty. The physical conditions

of existing roads require more state and local resources to be put into maintenance and repair, and little is often left over for new construction. New highway development is also hindered by environmental land opposition as well as the view that the long-term energy outlook will discourage future growth rates in highway demands.

4. Parking facilities must be linked with highways and streets. Parking facilities are often provided by public agencies as a revenue source, and new facility construction can be encouraged or discouraged through planning and zoning decisions.

5. Taxis serve as relatively short-distance substitutes to the private auto. They are, however, primarily useful for random movements. Efforts to apply this system to pooled commuting has met with mixed success. The cost of auto ownership and operation is reflected directly in the taxi cost structure. The energy cost problem has made many taxi firms abandon the practice of cruising streets. Instead, many must be called from a central point for each origin-destination move. This increases the stem time, which serves to increase unit trip costs further.

6. Demand-response systems are designed around the concept of variable travel patterns for individual traveler needs. That is, buses, vans, and, in one project in Morgantown, W. Virginia, a rail vehicle respond to an individual call for service. People calling in at about the same time are then matched for a route that is "created" for the origin demands and drop-off points desired. These systems have been usually implemented as part of an experimental demonstration project sponsored by the federal government. Public acceptance of them tends to be quite high. But, once the assistance agencies allowed these demonstration project monies to terminate, many local community agencies allowed the services to drop. There are, however, a few systems operating successfully and at a profit. Westport, Connecticut has one that functions as a commuter line to and from a railroad station in the mornings and evenings; it links residential areas with shopping and medical centers, using a loosely defined schedule and route on an on-call response basis during the day. The system is available as a demand-response taxi system at all other times. Westport is a densely populated community where many citizens are without autos. In this one situation, the operation is a success.

7. Van pools are encouraged by many states and the DOT. A discussion of the one van pool in the San Francisco area illustrates how they work. The state purchased a fleet of vans capable of holding 12 to 15 people. There is a central phone number which receives calls from people interested in forming a van pool. Once a group of persons is assembled in, say, Walnut Creek, which is a commuting suburb about thirty miles east of the city, a legal entity is created which leases the van at reasonable cost from the state. Such an arrangement avoids a large capital layout by the commuters. Three drivers volun-

teer from the group to drive the van on a schedule and route according to the needs of all involved. The gas, oil, and insurance costs are shared by the group. In many cities, free downtown parking is provided for the van. In the Bay Area, filled vans cross the bridges toll-free. Public acceptance of this concept is fairly high. Every filled van basically has the effective capacity of twelve to fifteen autos and reduces downtown parking needs and the attendant air pollution.

8. Minibuses have been implemented by many cities on routes in downtown areas to improve mobility among shoppers and others taking short trips in the area. By providing frequent, low fare buses along a fixed route, the long walks necessary in many downtown areas are greatly reduced. These systems are basically a competitive response by downtown agencies and businesses to the convenience of shopping centers.

9. Buses are a primary form of urban passenger transportation. They largely replaced the former trolley system. They have the advantage of route flexibility and one-person operation. Efficiency gains have been made with bus systems in two primary ways. One is with the "exact fare" system which requires the passenger to board the bus with the specific fare and not expect the driver to make change. This reduces robbery exposure, but the main benefit comes from relieving the driver of the burden of handling money. It was estimated in one city that drivers spent between 7 and 10 percent of their time making change, which was cutting into driving and transit time. Another innovation has been the "articulated" bus. This is a regular bus that has a half bus hitched onto the back with an enclosed connection between the two units. This expands a normal sixty-passenger bus into one holding ninety passengers. This conceptually reduces the need for additional buses and drivers. Each bus, power unit, and driver are performing fifty percent more productively in terms of payload.

10. Pooled buses have been acquired by some companies and apartment complexes for use by employees or tenants. These operate between outlying areas and a major employment center. Apartments operate the buses on either a profit or a nonprofit basis and companies, usually on a nonprofit basis. Many firms encourage their formation by employee cooperative groups. Institutional problems have arisen in many company systems. One is that some state transportation statutes do not allow the companies to operate these buses on a fare charging basis, another is that the Internal Revenue Service regulations are such that an employee tax liability might exist on free or subsidized service. These problems will no doubt be resolved as public policy recognizes the energy and resource efficiency of this system. One lessened constraint is that the Revised Interstate Commerce Act now exempts these moves in vehicles with fifteen passengers or less.[2]

11. Electric buses which are powered electrically from overhead wires, operate in a few cities. These buses are very quiet and release no downtown pollution, though in another sense, they shift the vehicle exhaust pollution in the downtown area to the outlying area surrounding the generating plant.

12. "Light rail systems" is a modern term for what was traditionally known as the trolley. They are called light rail systems because a lighter load is experienced and a smaller rail can be used in comparison to traditional subway or railroad systems. The light rail system largely died out in the United States between 1920 and 1955. During the 1960s and 1970s the only systems remaining were in Boston, Newark, Philadelphia, Pittsburgh, Cleveland, New Orleans, and San Francisco (which has both regular trolley and cable car systems).

13. Subways are fixed route, tunnel/above ground/surface systems usually capable of fast, high payload services. Subways have long existed in Boston, New York, Philadelphia, and Chicago. Since 1970 new subways have opened in San Francisco, Washington, and Atlanta. Baltimore will probably open the next subway system in the 1980s and several other cities are also planning them. The advantage of the subway is that it is capable of fast transit with up to one thousand passengers per train. A subway does, however, require a very large planning effort and investment.

    One problem exists in the new subway systems—a problem that stems from the technology. The last system was constructed in the 1920s, and no new systems were built until San Francisco designed and built one (called BART for Bay Area Rapid Transit) in the 1960s and 1970s. BART was built with new equipment and control systems that represented a quantum leap in technological advancement spanning fifty years. Many components of that system had never before been used or tried. As a result, "learning curve" problems are being experienced on the BART system that can and are being avoided by subsequent systems. Many of these problems have been reduced or avoided on the Washington and Atlanta systems and on other systems in present design stages. Be that as it may, the BART system, while not providing the total service level originally planned for, does provide an efficient, excellent service that a large segment of the population depends upon.

14. Rail systems include regular railroad passenger operations such as those seen in Boston, New York, Philadephia, Baltimore, Washington, D.C., Detroit, Chicago, and San Francisco. Often called commuter lines, these train systems operate over regular rail lines to points beyond the normal subway routes. In most cities these operations are run by regular railroad companies that are under operating contracts or service subsidies from public agencies. Though few new routes are being considered at this time, most existing ones are still operational and are being upgraded as a result of public agency subsidy or investment. For example, in New Jersey a major electrifica-

tion project is underway and the state of Maryland has acquired new equipment for routes between Baltimore and Washington.

15. Water, another passenger movement alternative, includes ferry and boat operations, which survive to this day in New York between Staten Island and Manhattan, and in San Francisco to the city from Larkspur and Sausalito. Several more operate in the Seattle area. These serve points that generally cannot be served with volume in any other manner, such as long distances and alternative routes that are impractical to serve by bus or rail. Ferry and boat operations are not expected to grow significantly as movers of urban populations.

16. Systems for handicapped people have been developed, based on federal government administrative regulations. These regulations have required cities to reduce mobility constraints in transit operations for handicapped people. Some are complying by altering existing facilities, while others are experimenting with separate van and auto systems. Evidence of these mobility-reduction efforts can be seen in the form of elevators in new subway systems and lift platforms on some new buses.

The various transportation alternatives currently found in operation offer different cost and service capacity configurations. Of prime planning importance is that an agency estimate the future travel demands, then attempt to implement the most desirable and cost effective system to satisfy those needs. Table 11.1 presents some typical route capacities for various alternatives.

No one system excludes the use of another. For example, when the subway opened in Washington, some traditional bus routes were scheduled less frequently, and the released equipment was deployed to new routes that act as feeders to new outlying subway stations.

Quasi-Hardware Alternatives. Many transit planning and operating op-

Table 11.1 Transit Systems Capacities

Method	Capacities	
	Vehicles/hour	Passengers/hour
Auto (1.2 passengers)		
City street	600–800	720–960
Freeway	1,500–2,000	1,800–2,400
Van (12 passengers)		
City street	500–750	6,000–9,000
Freeway	1,250–1,766	15,000–21,000
Transit bus (50 passengers)		
City street	60	3,000
Exclusive busway	600	30,000
Subway (10 car train)	30	30,000–60,000

Source: A. Scheffer Lang and Richard M. Sobernan, *Urban Rail Transit* (Boston: MIT Press, 1964), chap. 2.

tions include altering the present use of existing hardware systems through inducements or penalties and restrictions.

1. Bus lanes. This system is working with a great degree of success in many cities. In the I-95 commuter route into Washington, D.C., for example, an exclusive bus lane was built in the middle of the highway. Where a car might take an hour to enter the city in congested traffic, a bus on the separate lane often arrives downtown in one-half or one-third of the time.

2. Tolls. Many cities charge fewer or no tolls at all for van pools or autos with four or more passengers in them. This encourages the use of combined movement in autos. In another context, it has often been suggested that key bridge tolls should be raised to very high levels, for example, $5.00, during rush hour periods in order to smooth out the peak/valley travel problem.

3. Fares according to time. Many bus and subway systems offer lower fares in off-rush hour periods in order to smooth out travel demands. Some offer senior citizen fares during the midday to spur greater demand during this period and to possibly discourage some people from traveling during the rush hours.

4. Parking fees and facilities. Another possible transportation device is parking fees. Some cities assess special taxes in order to provide revenues for other transportation activities or to discourage use of parking altogether. Many cities have attempted to discourage or limit auto use by restricting new parking growth through planning and zoning.

Policy Options. Many transportation solutions can be planned with various policies that do not necessarily call for investment.

1. City planning. This activity includes describing current traffic demands, estimating future flows, and projecting various ways in which investments and policies can be shaped to meet those demands. During the 1960s a large amount of this activity took place with federal funding. In these grants, studies were conducted for the years 1990 and 2000 to determine the shape and demands of the next several decades. Suggestions were made for specific types of future transportation networks.

2. Architectural design and zoning. Some cities, Minneapolis for example, have sought to separate people, and automobile, and truck moves by restructuring the downtown areas. In Minneapolis many downtown blocks have the main shopping areas on second floor levels which are interconnected by enclosed pedestrian walkways above the street.

3. Staggered work hours. Washington, D.C. has employed this system by having entire agencies adopt work days that vary from 7:00 to 4:00 to 8:30 to 5:30 in half-hour increments. In this way the peak travel demands on the city's streets and highways are spread out.

4. Restricted downtown traffic. Some cities have experimented with the

idea of restricting downtown vehicle traffic completely during the main workday. This creates an entire pedestrian mall out of the core of the central business district. Chicago has one main street that is a mall on which only buses can travel. This reduces congestion in the main area to some degree. Singapore only allows automobiles that have a high fee sticker affixed to them to travel into the downtown area between 7:00 A.M. and 5:00 P.M. This reduces auto congestion and encourages the use of more fuel-efficient buses.

5. Freight control. Another traffic control policy device that has received much attention but has not been attempted in the United States on a permanent basis is the restriction of downtown truck traffic during rush and midday hours. This device complicates retail store deliveries and pickups, but it reduces traffic flow problems for buses and cars.

Research and Development

Research in the urban passenger realm has been conducted in the above three areas of hardware, quasi-hardware, and policy. A majority of this research has stemmed from federally supported research studies and experiments. Urban rail vehicle hardware is tested at the DOT's rail test facility at Pueblo, Colorado. As stated before, many projects and policies are a result of the comprehensive area studies and plans that were conducted for nearly all metropolitan areas.

Many research and development plans consist of federally funded experiments. These fall into the category of demonstration projects, and they are designed to determine whether or not different approaches to urban transportation tend to achieve desired results such as increased ridership or altered transportation habits by the public. Examples of such projects have been demand-response systems, transit marketing experiments in such areas as bus and trolley painting, timetable publishing and wide distribution to the public, advertising, telephone information services, transit stop identification and shelter improvement, and fare/schedule alteration.

Funding

■ UMTA funding

The primary source of funding in the urban transportation area has been the Urban Mass Transportation Administration (UMTA) of the DOT. UMTA funding falls into four broad categories. The first includes planning studies to determine the extent and scope of transportation needs in an area. This funding activity was strong in the late 1960s; many transportation economic consulting firms were involved in conducting these studies. A second major funding category is capital assistance, in which UMTA provides a capital grant of 80 percent of the purchase of a bus and related capital goods. Such assistance means that a city could receive a fleet of $80,000 buses for only $16,000 each. In addition, assistance is available for financing the remaining 20 percent of the purchase price. More recently, some assistance has been available for operating expenses, however, this may pose some difficulty. For example, if a transit district knows it can readily receive funding for operating losses, it might become lax in operating discipline and labor management. In the past few years some funding for operating expenses has taken place, but only on special grant appropriation bases.

A third funding category is the Highway Trust Fund. Originally, this fund was designed to finance 90 percent of the Interstate Highway System, much of it being used for urban highway projects. The fund still re-

■ highway trust fund

ceives 4¢ per gallon fuel tax, but many of the projects have been completed or shelved. The fund has been the source for some non-Interstate Highway System Projects, but in these cases, the funds are still applied primarily to auto/highway areas. Attempts continue to apply some of these funds to rail-oriented projects. Highway interests oppose such moves on the grounds that these other projects might dominate to the exclusion of necessary highway work.

A final major funding category consists of transit bodies or district commissions. Examples are the Washington Metropolitan Area Trans-

■ miscellaneous sources

portation District, the Southeastern Pennsylvania Transportation Authority, and the Tri-State Commission in the New York, New Jersey, and Connecticut areas. These bodies are formed to study or administer transportation in multiple-community regions. The Washington Commission covers three state areas and many counties and towns. The Tri-State Commission spans almost 1,500 separate community governmental bodies. The combined commissions can study the comprehensive needs and problems of an entire area and can pool the resources of the larger area to provide transportation services that no single area could perform without great difficulty.

Issues and Problems in Urban Passenger Transportation

■ energy

Energy is the key factor that has shaped, and will continue to do so, urban passenger movement. The auto is perhaps one of the least fuel efficient forms of transportation on a per passenger basis. Many urban transportation hardware and policy actions are designed to implicitly discourage this type of movement. Car pooling, van pooling, and other forms of transportation operating on the principle of passenger consolidation are more energy efficient.

■ environment

Two additional factors are the environmental and fiscal hindrances to further highway development and use. Cities and states are under federal mandates to reduce air and noise pollution. A major means of reducing pollution is auto restriction. Environmental concerns have also limited further highway growth in many urban areas because of real and perceived land use and social impacts. In addition, state and city fiscal problems have served to limit the growth and encouragement of auto/highway development. As noted in the chapter on financing transportation systems, many states are having difficulty maintaining and repairing the streets and highways, without building more of them.

■ auto flexibility

Overall decreases in auto use, however, come slowly even in the face of greatly improved, available alternative services. The convenience of the auto and its wrongly perceived low cost of operation (typically seen only as gas costs in the short run) tend to perpetuate auto use until the automobile that is used for commuting must be replaced. The opening of a new subway line, then, often requires several years of operation before desirable levels of traffic are attained, largely due to the perpetuation of automobile use. The passenger shift will generally not take place at the opening of a new service, but will occur at the decision point of purchasing a replacement automobile.

The peak and valley problem pervades the entire urban passenger transportation area. Its existence spells high investment with low capital and employment utilization. Until the peak can be spread out or the valley built up, chronic fiscal underperformance will be experienced in all areas.

Finally, urban passenger transportation is generally regarded as a social service and no longer as a for-profit activity. Public agencies have generally subsidized or acquired public transportation so that what are deemed essential public services can be continued. Even where cash surpluses exist, the typical practice is to apply them, often as cross-subsidies, to other areas. This is the case with the ferry operations in the San Francisco Bay area which are subsidized by bridge revenues from the Golden Gate Bridge.

Urban Freight Movement

■ types of movement

Little attention has been paid to urban freight movement, though it is a major and vital activity. It generally consists of four primary types of movements which have somewhat distinct characteristics. These are inbound (for consumption), outbound (city-export to other areas), within city moves, and through movements or the transfer of goods from one mode to another (rail-truck, truck-ship, truck-air, etc.). Primary attention is typically paid to local pickup and delivery operations because this tends to be where high cost productivity problems exist.

The truck is responsible for nearly 90 percent of all tonnage moved in this realm. In 1972 urban freight moves cost $57 billion, which indicates the magnitude of this segment. The specific characteristics of these movements can be noted in Table 11.2.

Urban Goods Flow Problems

■ peak and valley

■ vehicle productivity

Problems associated with urban freight movements are somewhat similar to those encountered in urban passenger settings. First, a peak and valley of sorts exists since drop-off operations are performed in the mornings, whereas pickups take place toward the end of the working day. Since most businesses are only open during the daytime hours, often these two stops must be performed by two different vehicles.

Another inherent problem with urban freight movements is the relatively low productivity of the vehicles and drivers involved in congested downtown operations. The revenue received, related to the cost per vehicle and man-hours of operation often translates into a deficit for many truck firms. Two of the many individual firms that have overcome this problem are United Parcel Service (UPS) and APA Trucking in North Bergen, New Jersey. These two firms diligently offer a disciplined operation that, although often above prevailing competitive service prices, offers high quality services. Firms such as these, though, tend to be the exception and not the rule.

Finally, freight operations are often viewed by city planners as a congestion factor that hinders efficient passenger movements. However, freight operations and passenger movements tend to constrain each other, and the priority of either tends to evolve from the particular point of view.

Toward Solutions to Urban Freight Movement Problems

Several possible actions can be taken to reduce the high cost, low productivity problem of urban goods movement. One is that the carrier can act only as a terminal to long haul carrier services. This means that the long haul carrier does not provide city pickup and delivery services. Instead, shippers and receivers tender or pickup the freight from the carrier at its terminal. This avoids a major low productivity activity for the carrier. Though sound in principle, long haul carriers fear this approach will cause a loss of firm identity and advertising in the downtown area.

■ terminal concept

Another solution to this problem borders upon logistics management in that it calls for the movement of larger lot sizes. By moving larger shipment sizes, the carrier experiences an increased revenue or lower unit cost per shipment. This is not always practical for the small retail store that cannot accommodate larger shipments nor invest in such quantities, but it would result in fewer carrier trips, fewer stops, and an increased desirability to serve the larger shipment market segment.

■ shipment size

Another solution is to restrict freight operation hours by shifting to before the morning rush hour and after the evening rush hour. Freight restriction could be accomplished by prohibiting trucks in certain areas

Table 11.2 Intracity Goods Transportation*

Local Distribution	Tons (millions)	Percent	Annual Number of Stops (millions)	Percent	Vehicle Miles of Travel (millions)	Percent
Services	244	11.7	14,218	79.8	7,270	31.1
Food	111	5.3	1,333	79.8	7,270	31.1
Paper	58	2.7	1,316	7.4	2,397	10.2
Energy	292	14.0	166	1.0	1,435	6.2
Durable Consumer Products	33	1.6	111	0.6	1,239	5.3
Building Products	4	0.2	235	1.3	1,194	3.8
Building Products	538	17.1	40	0.2	878	3.8
Beverages	50	2.4	302	1.6	816	3.5
Before/After Intercity Line-Haul						
For-Hire	657	31.5	91	0.5	1,545	6.6
Private (over-the-road)	282	13.5	34	0.2	93	0.4
Total Pickup and Delivery	2,089	100.0%	17,846	100.0%	23,374	100.0%

Source: Kearney: Management Consultants, *A Primer on Urban Goods Movement* (Chicago: A. T. Kearney, 1976), p. 9.
*248 Urbanized Areas

■ timed deliveries

during the working day. It would not harm the carriers to any great degree; in fact, it would allow for use of the vehicles throughout the day, and congestion would be reduced. Resistance to this approach, however, has come from retailers who generally do not wish to remain open for longer hours.

■ pooling

A further approach to solving some of the urban goods movement productivity problems consists of cooperative pickup and delivery systems. In ideal form, a cooperative arrangement would consist of all shippers or receivers in a given area pooling their inbound deliveries or outbound pickups, using one vehicle that would serve various firms' terminals at the city outskirts, thus consolidating pickups and deliveries.

■ taxation

A final recommendation that has been set forth relates to architectural incentives for business facilities in urban areas. Specifically, these incentives pertain to real estate tax incentives for constructing pooled off-street loading and unloading docks similar to docks that now serve many stores in enclosed shopping centers.

The future of urban goods movement will largely be shaped by energy and the capital considerations of the carriers involved. Energy has an effect upon the per-hour cost of operating. Escalating energy and capital costs will either cause carriers to increase rates in a pass-along cost manner, to attempt to alter pickup and delivery methods, or to withdraw from the market segment altogether. The problem rests with the private carriers and their customers. It is unlikely that solutions will come from the public sector. Instead, the various public agencies might be the cause of further negative impacts due to traffic flow restrictions. Clearly, the current trends and courses of action cannot be expected to continue. Some of the solutions discussed here will no doubt be forced into use in the future.

Conclusion

Urban and metropolitan passenger and freight transportation forms are subject to the same basic laws and principles of transportation economics as long haul, privately owned forms. This sector of the field appears unique in several ways. The factors that contribute to this observation are diverse. The urban passenger systems are predominantly publicly owned, operated, or subsidized since profit is difficult to attain. Service is often the social goal to seek rather than financial return. Solutions to service and/or financial problems range from physical investments to public policies. The urban freight area is also a sector facing cost and service problems. Congestion and other factors that cause low vehicle and employee productivity lead to high unit freight movement costs. Solutions in this area appear to be slower forthcoming than those in the passenger realm.

Study Questions

1. Why must urban transportation analysis be made in terms of a metropolitan area rather than the central city itself?

2. In what way does transportation play a role in the economic health of an area?

3. What trends have taken place since 1945 that have caused problems in urban transportation?

4. Why is a spread-out city more costly than one that is concentrated?

5. How would you describe the overall trends of the urban passenger industry from 1950 to 1970?

6. What are the relative merits of van pools?

7. Cite why the automobile with a few passengers in it is a problem from a transportation efficiency standpoint?

8. Is there one hardware solution for all cities? If not, why not?

9. Why must the study of urban passenger transportation be made from many areas instead of simply in light of the hardware (vehicles) itself?

10. Why will solutions to the urban freight problem come from the private sector and not the public sector?

Notes

1. American Public Transit Association, *Transit Fact Book* (Washington, D.C.).
2. *Revised Interstate Commerce Act*, U.S. Code, Sec. 10923.

Suggested Readings

American Public Transit Association. *Transit Fact Book.* 1978-1979 ed. Washington, D.C.: The American Public Transit Association, 1979.

Anderson, J. Edward. *Transit Systems Analysis and Design.* Lexington, Mass.: Lexington Books, 1978.

Farris, Martin T., and Harding, Forrest E. *Passenger Transportation.* Englewood Cliffs, N.J.: Prentice-Hall, 1976, chap. 2.

Hazard, John L. *Transportation: Management, Economics Policy.* Cambridge, Md.: Cornell Maritime Press, 1977.

Highway Research Board. *Urban Commodity Flow.* Washington, D.C.: National Academy of Sciences, 1971.

Hille, Stanley J., and Poist, Richard F. "Urban Transportation Problems." *Transportation: Principles and Perspectives.* Danville, Ill.: Interstate Printers and Publishers, 1974.

Lieb, Robert C. *Transportation: The Domestic System.* Reston, Va.: Reston Publishing Co., 1981, chaps. 21, 22.

Owen, Wilfred. *The Metropolitan Transportation Problem.* rev. ed. Washington, D.C.: Brookings Institute, 1966.

Pikarsky, Milton and Christensen, Daphne. *Urban Transportation Policy and Management.* Lexington, Mass.: Lexington Books, 1976.

Wood, Donald F., and Johnson, James D. *Contemporary Transportation.* Tulsa: Petroleum Publishing Co., chaps 4, 14.

| Case | Central Transportation Authority |

The general council of the Central Transportation Authority (CTA) of Central County is currently seeking ways to finance the purchase of a new bus and van. Federal, state, and local funding have been cut back, and these cuts have caused the CTA to obtain its share of the purchase prices from other means. Eighty percent of the initial bus cost of $100,000 will still be borne by the federal government, but the state share of 10 percent has disappeared. No federal funding is currently available for the $28,000 van, but the state will pay for one-half of it. Additional funds are also needed for higher than expected operating costs.

The CTA has responsibility over buses, taxis, one authority-owned downtown parking garage (multi-story), regulation over privately owned parking garages in the city, and it has a heavy influence over the county road system within the operating sphere of the bus routes.

The CTA's agenda at the coming meeting includes the financing of the new bus which would be used on a new route that connects a major senior citizen complex with downtown. The van financing is also being considered; it will be specifically designed to handle handicapped persons who cannot utilize the existing buses or taxis. Both the van and bus will be proposed, along with a 25¢ a visit parking tax applicable at the three garages, and an increase in on-street parking meter fees. Downtown parking and street congestion are also subjects on the agenda as is a warning notice from the state environmental protection body about excessive automobile pollutants in the town's air over the past few months.

Is the council sound in its approach of a 25¢ parking fee? What else might it do?

Part IV

Theory
and Practice
of Rates

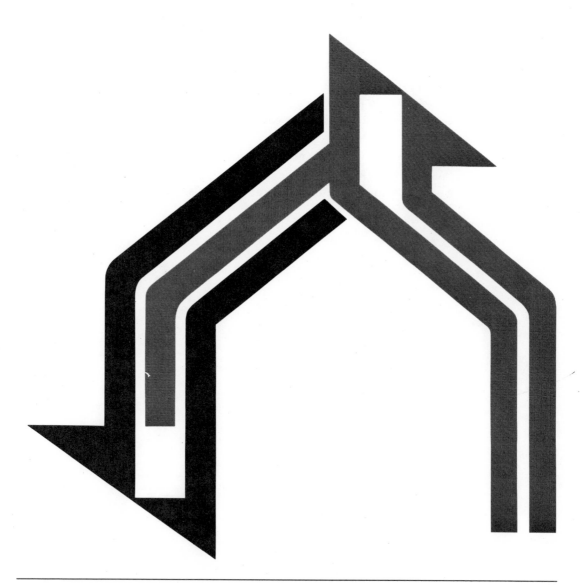

12 Cost and Pricing in Transportation

After reading this chapter you should:

1 Appreciate the complexity of the transportation markets for pricing purposes.

2 Understand the different cost concepts that can be used in pricing.

3 Be able to discuss the general cost structure of the different modes of transport.

4 Understand value-of-service and cost-of-service pricing.

The regulation of business on a comprehensive basis by federal statute was initiated in the United States in 1887 when the Original Act to Regulate Commerce was passed by Congress. This initiating legislation primarily established a framework of control over interstate rail transportation. To a large extent, the underlying rationale for the regulatory package was based upon the railroads' discriminatory rate practices. Control of rates became the central issue in setting up the regulatory framework.

Since the beginning efforts in 1887, Congress has significantly increased the scope and magnitude of business regulation, not only in transportation but in other industries as well. Much experience has been gained with regulation during the last "90 plus" years, but rate regulation is still a controversial issue. In fact, the deregulation efforts which have swept through various segments of the transportation industry in recent years have focused on issues associated with rate control.

Individuals studying transportation should have a thorough exposure to the theoretical underpinnings of the rates or prices of transportation agencies. While the transportation industry is not completely unique compared to other industries, there are enough differences to justify a thorough discussion of transportation pricing. The first part of this chapter on transport rates will explore the market structure of the transportation industry. The section on market structure will be followed by an analysis of carrier cost structures with an emphasis upon how costs affect rates of carriers. A discussion of value-of-service pricing will follow in the next section. The final part of the chapter will treat cost-of-service pricing and compare it to value-of-service pricing.

■ chapter overview

Market Considerations

Before discussing the characteristics of the transportation market, a brief review of basic market structure models is appropriate. Such a discussion will provide some insights into the unique nature of the transportation market situations.

■ pure competition

It would be best to begin by describing pure competition. The necessary conditions for pure competition are generally stated as follows: there are a large number of sellers; all sellers and buyers are of such a small size that no one can influence prices or supply; there is a homogeneous product or service; and there must be unrestricted entry. The demand curve facing the individual firm is one of perfect elasticity, which means the producer can sell all output at the one market price, but none above that price. While pure competition is not a predominant market structure, it is frequently used as a standard to judge optimal allocation of resources.

■ monopoly

If pure competition is one type of market structure, the other extreme is a perfectly monopolistic market with only one seller of a product or service for which there is no close competitor or substitute. In such a situation, the single seller is able to set the price for the service offered and should adjust the price to its advantage, given the demand curve. In order to remain in this situation, it is necessary that the single seller be able to restrict entry. The single seller maximizes profits by equating marginal cost and marginal revenue and may make excess profit in the economic sense.

■ oligopoly

A third type of market structure is oligopoly. As described previously, oligopoly may be defined as competition among a "few" large sellers of a relatively homogeneous product that has enough cross elasticity of demand (substitutability) so that each seller must, in pricing decisions, take into account competitors' reactions. In other words, it is characterized by mutual interdependence among the various sellers. The individual seller is aware that in changing price, output, sales promotion activities, or quality of the product that the reactions of competitors must be taken into account.

■ monopolistic competition

The fourth type of market structure is monopolistic competition. This type of market structure can be defined as a situation where there are many small sellers, but there is some differentiation of products. The number of sellers is great enough and the largest seller small enough that no one controls a significant portion of the market. No recognized interdependence of the related sellers' prices or price policies is usually present. Therefore, any seller may lower price to increase sales volume without necessarily eliciting a retaliatory reaction from competitors.

This brief description of the four basic market models is by no means complete. The interested student can obtain additional perspectives from any standard microeconomics text. For our purposes, the above discussion provides enough background to focus more closely upon transportation markets.

A general statement classifying the market structure of the entire transportation industry cannot be made because it is necessary to view structures in particular market areas. In the railroad industry, for example, there exists a variety of different services, involving the transportation of thousands of different commodities between tens of thousands of different stations or geographic points, via a multiplicity of different routes, and under various conditions of carriage.[1] The market structure in transportation must describe the situation at any one point, and even then the situation will differ between commodities. Therefore, for purposes of pricing in transportation, we must describe the situation between two points for one commodity.[2] In other words, the relevant market area for establishing prices is one commodity moving between two points.

■ relevant market area

For example, a particular railroad that provides service between Pittsburgh and Cincinnati may find that the movement of ordinary steel approximates what we have described as monopolistic competition. There are likely to be a large number of other carriers, especially common and contract motor carriers, that provide essentially the same service.

■ examples

However, for the movement of a very large, sophisticated generator, the railroad may face an oligopolistic market on the move between Pittsburgh and Cincinnati, since none of the motor carriers may be able to haul such a large piece of equipment, and the railroad may be competing with only a few water carriers. It is possible that we could find some commodity where the railroad would be operating in a monopolistic position because of restrictions on operating authorities. Finally, there may even be a product where the situation approaches pure competition. In fact, this may be true for certain steel products, given the availability of rail, motor, water, and private carrier. In summary, the relevant market situation for transportation consists of one commodity moving between two points, and perhaps, even in one direction.

We could describe, of course, the market structure for a particular mode of transportation in one market in more detail. This is especially true with respect to the railroad industry, the water carrier industry, and the pipeline industry. We could describe a typical situation in *each* of these industries and make it fit one of the economic models described previously. For example, we could say that between two particular cities the water carriers are faced with oligopolistic conditions. From this, we could discuss the general pricing behavior of the industry.[3] However, there is intermodal competition present in transportation, and it is necessary to take this fact into consideration in order to adequately describe the market situations. Also, as we have stated, the situation varies by commodity.

■ modal market

The complexity of the situation does not eliminate the validity of the economic models described above. It only means that in order to make use of these models we must have knowledge of the situation which exists in the particular market. Although this may seem to be too much to expect at first, it can be accomplished. The elaborate classification system for rates (discussed in the next chapter) distorts the situation somewhat, but in our economy it is commodity rates which are the most important in terms of total intercity ton-miles. Commodity rates are competitive rates on commodities between specific points. In setting these rates, it is necessary for a carrier to have knowledge of the relevant market area. With this knowledge, it is possible to use one of the economic models which have been described. Although there will be instances when carriers may find it expedient to generalize more in adjusting rates, a much narrower focus is customary in the day-to-day negotiation and analysis of these rates.

The important point about our analysis is that while transportation competition has indeed become more intense in the last three or four decades, the intensity is uneven. Therefore, all four types of markets can be found in transportation markets. This makes pricing very challenging. In addition, the derived nature of transportation demand further complicates the pricing situation.

Cost Concepts

■ accounting cost

The simplest concept or measure of cost is what has sometimes been labeled as accounting cost, or even more simply as money cost. These are the so-called bookkeeping costs of a company and include all cash outlays of the firm. This particular concept of cost is not difficult to grasp. The most difficult problem with accounting costs is their allocation among the various products or services of a company.

If the owner of a trucking company, for example, was interested in determining the cost associated with moving a particular truckload of traffic, we could quickly arrive at the cost of gasoline, oil, and the driver's salary associated with the movement. It might also be possible to determine how much wear and tear on the vehicle was associated with the truck trip. However, we must also consider how much of the president's salary, the terminal expenses, and the advertising expense should be included in the rate or price. These costs should be included in part, but how much should be included is frequently a perplexing question. Our computation becomes even more complex when a small shipment is combined with other small shipments in one truckload. Some allocation would then be necessary for the gasoline expense and the driver's wages.

■ economic cost

A second concept of cost is economic cost, which is different from accounting cost. The economic definition of cost is associated with the alternative cost doctrine or the opportunity cost doctrine. Costs of production, as defined by economists, are futuristic in nature and are the values of the foregone alternative products which could have been produced with the resources used in production. Therefore, the costs of resources are their values in their best alternative uses. To secure the service or use of resources, such as labor or capital, a company must pay an amount at least equal to what the resource could obtain in its best alternative use. Implicit in this definition of cost is the principle that if a resource has no alternative use, then its cost in economic terms is zero.

■ sunk cost

The futuristic aspect of economic costs has special relevance in transportation because once investment has been made, one should not be concerned with recovering what is sometimes referred to as "sunk costs."[4] Resources in some industries are so durable that they can virtually be regarded as everlasting. Therefore, if no replacement is anticipated, and there is no alternative use, then the use of the resource is costless in an economic sense. This is of special importance in the railroad industry.

■ rail example

Railroads have long been regarded as having durable and, therefore, costless resources. That is, some of the resources of railroads, such as cement ties, some signaling equipment, and even some rolling stock, are so durable and so highly specialized that they have no alternative production or use potential. So, the use of such resources, apart from maintenance, is costless in an economic sense. Consequently, in a competitive pricing situation, such resources could be excluded from the calculation of fixed costs. Also, such specialized resources can be eliminated in comparing cost structures.[5]

While the economic logic of the above argument on the use of durable, specialized resources is impeccable, it is frequently disregarded by rate-makers and regulators. In a sense, the elimination of such costs from pricing calculations defies common sense. Also, from the money or accounting cost perspective, these costs should usually be included.

■ cost differences

The conclusion which must be drawn is that economic costs differ from money or accounting costs. Money costs are by their very nature a measure of past costs. This does not mean that money costs do not have any relevance in the economic sense. Past costs do perform a very important function because they provide a guide to future cost estimates. However, complete reliance should not be put upon historical costs for pricing in the transportation industry.

■ social cost

There is a third category of costs—social costs—which may also be considered. Some businesses may not concern themselves with social costs unless required to do so by law. These costs take into consideration the cost to society of some particular operation and may, in fact, outweigh money cost. For example, what is the cost to society when a company releases its waste materials into a stream? Today there are many regulations and controls administered by various regulatory agencies to protect society from such costs. These agencies make the business organization responsible for social costs. (For example, strip-mining operators are customarily required to back fill and plant.) In spite of such controls, however, there are still instances when chemicals or other hazardous materials are discharged or leak out and society has to bear the cost of the cleanup operations as well as the health hazards.

We are not trying to castigate business organizations, nor suggest that all investment decisions result in negative social costs, because in fact, there can be social benefits to society from business investments. However, to ensure that our discussion is complete, social costs must be considered.

Analysis of Cost Structures

■ separable and common cost

There are two general approaches to an analysis of a particular cost structure. Under one approach, costs may be classified as those which are directly assignable to particular segments of the business (such as products or services) and those which are incurred for the business as a whole. These two types of cost are generally designated as separable and common costs, respectively. Usually, common costs are further classified as joint common costs and nonjoint common costs. The former concept refers to a situation where products are necessarily produced in fixed proportions. The classic example is that of hides and beef. Stated simply, the production or generation of one product or service necessarily entails the production or generation of another product.

It is a generally accepted fact that large transportation companies, especially railroads, have a significant element of common costs since they have roadbed, terminals, freight yards, and so on, the cost of which is common to all traffic. However, the only evidence of true jointness appears to be the back-haul.[6] Nonjoint common costs are those which do not require the production of fixed proportions of products or services. The latter type of common costs are more customary in transportation. For example, on a typical train journey on which hundreds of items are carried, the expenses of the crew and fuel are common costs incurred for all the items hauled.

■ fixed versus variable cost

Under the other basic approach to analyzing a particular cost structure, costs are divided into those that do not fluctuate with the volume of business in the short run and those that do. The time period here is assumed to be that in which the plant or physical capacity of the business remains unchanged. The two types of costs described are usually referred to as fixed and variable costs, respectively.

■ cost variations

It is important to note that in the first approach described (common and separable), the distinction is made with the possibility in mind that costs will be traced to specific accounts or products of the business. In the latter approach (fixed and variable), the distinction is made in order to study variations in business as a whole over a period of time, and the effect of these variations upon expenses. In other words, with fixed and variable costs we are interested in the fact that some costs increase and decrease with expansion and contraction of business volume, whereas other costs do not vary as business levels change.

■ overlap

Since there are two different approaches to studying costs, it is possible that a certain cost might be classified as common on the one hand and variable on the other, or common under one approach and fixed under the other, and so on for all the possible combinations. Therefore, the only costs directly traceable or separable are the variable costs which are also separable. For example, fuel expense is generally regarded as a variable cost, but it would be a common cost with a vehicle loaded with less-than-truckload (LTL) traffic.

■ fixed cost

The second approach of cost analysis, namely, fixed and variable costs is important and should be discussed further. As indicated previously, fixed costs are constant in nature irrespective of the enterprise's volume of business. These fixed costs may include maintenance expenses on equipment or right-of-way (track) caused by time and weather (not use), property taxes, certain management salaries, interest on bonds, and payments on long-term losses.

A business has a commitment to its fixed costs even with a zero level of output. It is important to note that fixed costs may, in certain instances, be delayed, or to use the more common term—deferred. The railroads frequently delay or defer costs. For example, maintenance of railroad right-of-way should probably be done each spring or summer, particularly in the northern states. Freezing and thawing, along with spring rains, wash away gravel and stone (ballast) and may do other damage. However, although this maintenance can be postponed, just as house painting, for example, may be postponed for a year to two, sooner or later it has to be done if the business wants to continue to operate. There is a fixed commitment or necessity which requires the corrective action and associated expense.[7] The important point is that the fixed expenses occur independently of the business volume experienced by the organization.

■ variable cost

Variable costs, on the other hand, are closely related to the volume of business. In other words, firms do not experience any variable costs unless they are operating. The fuel expense for trains or trucks is an excellent example of a variable cost. If a locomotive or vehicle does not make a run or trip, there is no fuel cost. Additional examples of variable costs include the wear and tear that is associated with automobile use, as well as the cost for spark plugs and other engine parts.

Another related point that should be noted is that railroads and pipelines, like many public utility companies, are frequently labeled as decreasing cost organizations. We will discuss the relevance of this phenomenon to pricing later in this chapter, but it deserves some explanation now.

■ decreasing cost industries

Railroads and pipelines experience a high proportion of fixed costs in their cost structures. There is some debate about the percentage, but the estimates range from 20 to 50 percent. Contrast this with motor carriers where the average is 10 percent. As railroads produce more units, the proportion of fixed costs on each item will be lower. More importantly, this decline will occur over a long range of output because of the large scale capacity of most railroads.

An example of the above situation is useful here. Let us assume that a particular railroad incurs $5 million of fixed costs on an annual basis. In addition, let us assume that the railroad is analyzing costs for rate-making purposes between Bellefonte, Pennsylvania and Chicago, Illinois. In its examination of cost, the railroad determines that the variable cost on a carload is $250 between Bellefonte and Chicago.

While it may be unrealistic, let us assume that the railroad only moves ten cars per year. The cost would be as follows:

Fixed cost	$5,000,000
Variable cost	2,500 (10 cars × $250)
Total cost	$5,002,500
Average cost per car	$ 500,250

If it moves 1,000 cars, the cost would be:

Fixed cost	$5,000,000
Variable cost	250,000 (1,000 cars × $250)
Total cost	$5,250,000
Average cost per car	$ 5,250

If it moves 100,000 cars per year, the cost would be:

Fixed cost	$ 5,000,000
Variable cost	25,000,000 (100,000 × $250)
Total cost	$30,000,000
Average cost per car	300

The relationship is easy to see. If we continued adding cars to our example, the average cost (AC) would continue to decline. Theoretically, average cost would have to level out and eventually increase due to decreasing returns, but the important point is that the high proportion of fixed costs and the large capacity cause the declining average cost over a great range of output (see Figure 12.1).

The significance of the declining cost phenomenon to a railroad is that volume is a very important determinant of cost and efficiency. Furthermore, pricing the service to attract traffic is a critical factor in determining profitability, particularly where there is competition from alternate modes of transportation.

Another cost concept which is of major importance in our analysis is marginal cost because of its key role in understanding pricing decisions. Marginal cost may be defined as the change in total cost resulting from a

Figure 12.1 Average Cost and Output

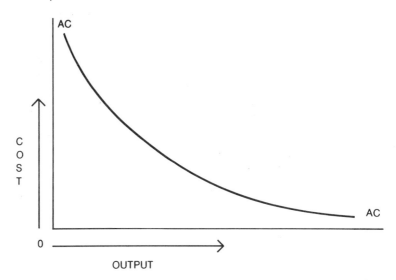

■ marginal cost

one-unit change in output, or as additions to aggregate cost for given additions to output. This latter definition probably makes more sense in transportation because of the difficulties of defining the output unit. Marginal cost can also be defined as the change in total variable cost resulting from a one-unit change in output, since a change in output changes total variable cost and total cost by exactly the same amounts. Marginal cost is sometimes referred to as incremental cost, especially in the transportation industry.

■ out-of-pocket cost

There is one other type of cost which should be mentioned because of its importance in rate decisions—out-of-pocket costs. Out-of-pocket costs are usually defined as those costs which are directly assignable to a particular unit of traffic and would not have been incurred if the service or movement had not been performed. Within the framework of this definition, out-of-pocket costs could also be either separable costs or variable costs. Although the above definition states that out-of-pocket costs are specifically assignable to a certain movement, which implies separable costs, they can definitely be considered as variable costs since they would not occur unless a particular shipment was moved. The definition also encompasses marginal cost since it can be associated with a unit increase in cost.

The vagueness of the out-of-pocket costs definition has left the door open to the types of cost included as a part of their calculation. The difficulty lies in the fact that from a narrow viewpoint, out-of-pocket costs could be classified as only those expenses incurred because a particular unit was moved. For example, the loading and unloading expense attributable to moving a particular shipment, plus the extra fuel and wear and tear on equipment (relatively low for railroads) could be classified as out-of-pocket costs. On the other hand, a broad approach might be used in defining out-of-pocket costs in regard to a particular shipment, thereby including a share of all the common variable expenses attributable to a particular movement between two points.

The confusion surrounding the concept of out-of-pocket costs would seem to indicate a justification for eliminating its use. However, the continued use of the term would be acceptable if its definition were made synonymous with the definition of one of the particular economic costs which its definition implies—marginal costs—since this term is important in price and output decisions and evaluations of pricing in economics.

While attention is devoted to cost structure in the separate chapters dealing with each of the modes of transportation, some consideration will be given in this section to an analysis of modal cost structures. Such discussion is useful and actually necessary background to the analysis of the approaches to rate-making which follow the discussion of cost structures.

Rail Cost Structure

One of the characteristics of railroads, as previously noted, is the level of fixed costs present in their cost structures. It is a commonly accepted fact that a relatively large proportion of railway costs are fixed in the short

■ high fixed cost

run. At one time, it was believed that over one-half of rail costs were fixed, and some individuals estimated that these costs ran as high as 70 percent of total cost. The exact proportion of fixed expenses is subject to some debate; however, it is generally accepted that fixed expenses constitute a significant portion of railroad total costs ranging from 20 to 50 percent. The high proportion of fixed cost can be explained by railroad investment (in such things as track, terminals, and freight yards) which is much larger than the investment of motor carriers, for example. For this reason, railroads are generally regarded as having increasing returns, or decreasing costs per unit of output.[8]

As has been indicated, a significant amount of railroad costs are also common expenses, since replacement costs of a stretch of track are shared by all traffic moving over it. This is also true with respect to other items of cost, including officers' salaries. Some of these common costs are also fixed costs, while others are variable costs.

Motor Carrier Cost Structure

■ high variable cost

The motor carrier industry is exemplified by a high proportion of variable costs. It has been estimated that variable costs in the motor carrier industry are 90 percent or more of total costs.[9] This high degree of variability is explained to a large extent by the fact that motor carriers do not have to provide their own right-of-way since roads are publicly provided. It is true that motor carriers do pay gasoline taxes and other taxes to defray the cost of providing the highways, but these expenses are variable since they are dependent upon the use made of the highway.

It should also be pointed out that the economic concept of the "long run" is a shorter period in the motor carrier industry than in the railroad industry. The operating unit, the truck, has a shorter life span than the rail operating unit. It is smaller and, therefore, more adaptable to fluctuating business conditions. The capital investment required is smaller, too, and plants can be expanded and contracted easier.

The motor carrier situation varies greatly with respect to common costs. Companies that specialize in LTL traffic will have a significant proportion of common cost, whereas contract carriers with only two or three customers who move only truckload (TL) traffic will have a high proportion of separable costs. Other companies will be in the middle of the two extremes since they will carry a mixture of TL and LTL traffic.

Other Carriers' Cost Structures

■ water carrier

Information on water carrier cost structures is less prevalent because many companies are privately owned or exempt from economic regulation. The cost structure is probably very similar to that of motor carriers since their right-of-way is also publicly provided. There are some differences, however, since the investment per unit of output is greater, and a large volume of traffic is necessary to realize mass movement potentialities.[10]

■ pipelines

The pipeline companies have a cost structure similar to that of railroads. The fact that they have to provide their own right-of-way and the fact that their terminal facilities are very specialized means that they have a large element of fixed and usually sunk costs. They also usually have significant common costs since they move a variety of oil products through the pipeline.

■ airlines

The airline companies have a cost structure similar to that of water carriers and motor carriers because of the public provision of their right-of-way. Also, terminal facilities are publicly provided to a large extent, and the airlines pay landing fees based upon use. Airlines tend to have a significant element of common cost because of small freight shipments and the individual nature of passenger movements; for example, airlines very seldom sell a planeload to one customer.

Value-of-Service Pricing

Value-of-service pricing is a frequently mentioned and often criticized approach to rate-making that has generally been associated with the railroad industry. Part of the problem associated with value-of-service pricing is that there are a number of different definitions of it offered by various sources. Therefore, we will first develop a workable definition of the term.

■ definition

One rather common definition of value-of-service pricing in transportation is pricing according to the value of the product, for example, high-valued products are accorded high rates for their movement, and low-valued commodities are accorded low rates. Evidence can be found to substantiate this definition by examining the class rate structure of railroads.

■ cost approach

Several points are in order here. First, even if we took a cost based approach to setting rates, high-valued commodities would usually be charged higher rates because they are typically more expensive to transport. There is generally more risk involved in moving high-valued commodities, and more expensive equipment is necessary. Second, the value of the commodity is a legitimate indicator of elasticity of demand, for example, high-valued commodities can usually bear a higher rate since transportation cost is such a small percentage of the final selling price.

■ value of commodity

In a situation where a carrier has a complete monopoly, to consider value-of-service pricing only in terms of the value of the commodity would not lead to serious traffic losses. It would be analogous to the idea behind progressive income taxes, that is, setting rates upon the ability or willingness to pay.[11] But where alternatives are present at a lower price, shippers are not willing to pay a higher price based upon the value of the product alone. This is one of the reasons why the motor carriers were able to make serious inroads in rail traffic during their early development. They undercut the rates on high-valued commodities where the railroads were the most susceptible to competition. In essence, we are saying that the value of the commodity gives some indication of demand or ability to bear a charge, but competition will also obviously affect the demand for the service.

■ third degree price discrimination

Value-of-service pricing has also been defined as third-degree price discrimination or a situation where a seller sets two or more different market prices for two or more separate groups of buyers of essentially the same commodity or service.[12] There are two necessary conditions before a seller can practice third-degree price discrimination. First, the seller must be able to separate buyers into groups or submarkets according to their different elasticities of demand; this separation enables the seller to charge different prices in the various markets. The second condition is that the seller must be able to prevent transfer of sales between the submarkets. That is, the buyer must not buy in the lower-priced market and sell in the higher-priced markets.

These conditions for third-degree price discrimination can be fulfilled in the transportation industry as well as in other regulated industries such as the telephone industry. For example, in transportation, shippers are separated according to commodities transported and between points of movement. Our previous discussion of the relevant market area in transportation implied that there were different or separable customer-related markets, for example, one commodity between each pair of shipping points, each with a separate elasticity.

■ separation of customers

Another point that is relevant to our discussion is the nature of "essentially-the-same-commodity-or-service."[13] Actually, we need only recognize that many transportation companies sell multiple or heterogeneous services that are technically similar. For example, the rail movement of a unit train of coal and a trailer-on-flatcar (TOFC) movement of television sets or glassware are very different in terms of time, equipment, terminal facilities, and so on.

■ multiple services

If we think back to a point that was made earlier about railroad costs, that is, the high level of fixed costs and the need to attract traffic, value-of-service or differential pricing makes sense from the perspective of the railroad. Remember that railroads will experience declining average costs with increases in volume. If shipments are priced properly, this could mean increased revenues from higher volumes with more profit.

■ rail situation

The key to success lies in being able to determine the appropriate costs and to estimate demand elasticity in the various markets. This essentially means determining what the shipper is willing to pay for the service, given the competition in the market from other carriers, the demand for the product itself, and any other factors affecting demand.

Let us assume that a particular railroad is establishing prices on three different commodities.[14] One of the commodities is large computer systems which have very high value and for which there is limited substitutability. The second commodity is color television sets which are of medium value and have some substitutes. The third commodity is coal which is low in value and has substitutes.

■ example

Let us assume further that the value of a particular computer system is $200,000 and that it weighs a ton. If the rate charged for movement was $1,000 per ton, it would still only be 1/2 percent (.005) of the value of the product. The color televisions may have a value of $10,000 per ton. Therefore, a rate of $1,000 between the same points would represent 10 percent of the value. Finally, the coal may be worth $50 a ton. A rate of $1,000 would represent 2,000 percent of its value. Therefore, charging a common price will discourage some shipments, particularly of the low value coal variety.

Figure 12.2 Coal Example

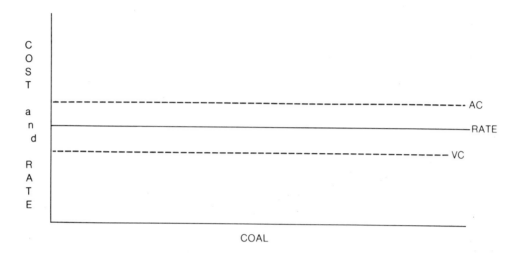

The railroad's concern is the price that each of these items should be charged in order to attract the traffic and maximize the revenue of the railroad. In the case of coal, let's assume that $3 per ton will attract a large volume of coal, that the variable cost (VC) is $2 per ton, and that the average (AC) or fully allocated cost is more than $5 per ton (see Figure 12.2).

As for the color television sets, let us assume that a rate of $500 per ton is reasonable to shippers in light of competition and other factors, and that this amount is equal to the average cost of moving a ton of television sets. Finally, assume that we decide to charge $1,000 per ton on the computers, which is higher than the average cost. The last two examples are depicted in Figures 12.3 and 12.4

Figure 12.3 Television Example

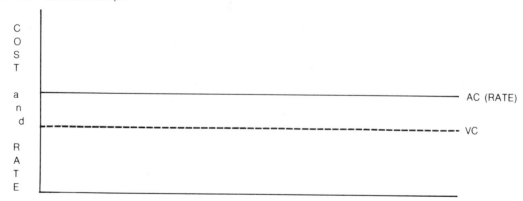

Figure 12.4 Computer Example

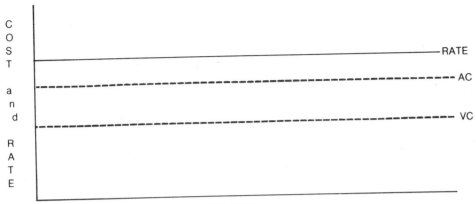

COMPUTERS

Our example is obviously simplified. However, it does point out some of the underlying logic behind value-of-service or differential pricing. In all three instances, each particular commodity is paying more than its variable cost and making a contribution to what we have labeled average cost, which might also be a concept of fully allocated cost.

Someone might argue that the coal shippers are not paying their full share and the computer shippers are paying too much. However, another argument that is frequently advanced in such instances is that if the coal did not move (remember it is paying more than the associated variable cost), then the other traffic (computers and televisions) would have to pay an even higher rate to help cover the costs of running the railroad. The same analogy applies to the super saver fares charged by the airlines. Full-fare passengers complain sometimes that they are subsidizing discount-fare passengers. Actually, full fares could be higher if the special fares were not offered.

■ analysis of example

Several points need to be emphasized before we take up a consideration of cost-of-service pricing. First, the example we used is simplified. The determination of cost is a difficult task. Second, most railroads and many other carriers would be considering more than three commodities between two points. Third, the examples used applied to railroads, since it is more attractive in situations with high fixed costs; yet other carriers, even motor carriers, may find differential pricing attractive. Fourth, some difference would exist in rates among commodities because of cost differences; for instance, it costs more to handle televisions than it coal. Finally, the elasticity of demand for a particular commodity may change with competition, or because of some other factors. Therefore, high rates on higher-valued commodities have to be continually evaluated.

Cost-of-Service Pricing[15]

As indicated previously, there are two separate concepts in cost-of-service pricing, namely, basing rates upon average cost or basing rates upon marginal cost. In order to give adequate treatment to both sides, let

■ assumptions

us make some simplifying assumptions and make use of diagrams. The assumptions are: the product or service is homogeneous, only one group of customers is involved, and this group of customers is responsible for all costs.

■ profit maximization

If the firm desired to maximize its profits (see Figure 12.5), it would produce quantity O-A and charge price O-R. The firm would be making excess profits in the economic sense, since the price is above average cost, and the firm is not producing at a point for optimal allocation of resources.

Based upon what may appear to be undesirable features, we might decide to impose regulation upon this firm. Now, if the "regulators" want to set a single price that would cover the firm's cost of production and at the same time sell all the output, then the price should be O-S and the output O-B. In this instance, we would be basing the price or rate upon average cost. There would not be any excess profit in the economic sense, and society would be receiving more output at a lower price.

■ average cost approach

■ marginal cost approach

It appears that the average cost approach is more socially desirable than the unregulated, profit maximizing approach. What are the attributes of the marginal cost approach? If price is set at marginal cost equal to demand, we have a higher price (O-T) and less output (O-C) than the average cost approach yields. The advocates of an absolute marginal cost approach argue that the output between O-C and O-B is such that the marginal cost of producing these additional units of output is greater than what buyers are willing to pay for the extra units supplied, since the marginal cost curve is above the demand curve over this range of output.[16]

Figure 12.5 Average Cost Example

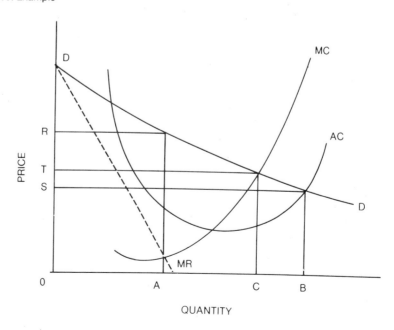

In Adam Smith's terminology, we are saying that the value in use is not as great as the cost of producing the additional output. Therefore, there are alternate uses in which the resources used to produce this additional output are valued more highly by consumers. When stated in this manner, the argument is based upon logic usually advanced under a label of "welfare economics."[17] It should be noted that under the marginal cost solution presented in Figure 12.5 there would be excess profits because price is above the average cost. However, this need not be a problem since the excess profits can be used to pay taxes.

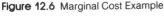

One of the arguments frequently raised against a strict marginal cost approach to rate-making is that under decreasing cost conditions, if the firm equates marginal cost with demand, then it will necessitate the firm's operating at a loss (see Figure 12.6). However, the advocates of a strict marginal cost approach would still present the argument that there are individuals willing to pay the marginal cost of the additional output between O-A and O-B and, therefore, it should be produced. There is one obvious solution,[18] and that is to allow the government to make up the deficit through a subsidy. These subsidies could be offset by the taxes collected in the previous example. There are also additional ways to offset governmental subsidies.

Thus far in our discussion, no attempt has been made to substantiate one approach or the other. We have merely presented the arguments advanced by advocates of each approach. Before any critique can be presented of these alternate approaches, we should examine the assumptions that were made at the outset.

In regard to the assumption that only one group of customers is served, this is not the typical situation, except in very special cases among regulated transportation companies. Likewise, costs are not usu-

Figure 12.6 Marginal Cost Example

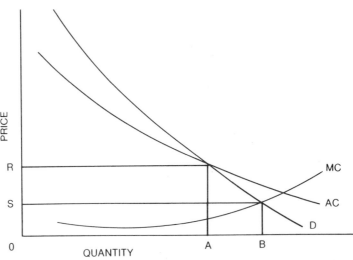

ally separable according to the classes of customers, but rather, common costs are quite typical, particularly with respect to railroads. We have already mentioned that output was not homogeneous in many instances; rather, what we have are heterogeneous or multiple services. Regulated industries are not peculiar in this respect since so many firms have common costs.

■ common cost

The presence of common costs raises some problems for cost-of-service pricing, particularly the average cost approach. If we are to base rates upon average or fully-allocated costs, it becomes necessary to apportion these costs by some arbitrary means. Average cost pricing with fixed or common costs, or both, makes these costs price-determining when they should be price-determined. In other words, fixed costs per unit depend upon the volume of traffic, and the volume of traffic depends upon the rate charged. To some extent, then, cost is a function of the rates, not the rates a function of the cost.[19] In fact, it could be argued that not only do costs determine rates but that rates determine cost, in other words the situation is analogous to the chicken and egg argument.

■ marginal cost approach

The presence of common costs does not raise the same theoretical problem for marginal cost pricing, since no arbitrary allocation of these costs is technically necessary. However, we may encounter problems since marginal cost may only be determinable with large blocks of output such as a trainload or even a truckload. The output unit we want to price can be much smaller with less-than-carload (LCL) and less-than-truckload (LTL) size shipments. There are some additional problems of a more practical nature with respect to strict marginal cost pricing. For example, in transportation, marginal costs could fluctuate quite widely depending upon the volume of traffic offered. The requirement of published rates would necessitate the averaging of these marginal costs to stabilize them, which would make them unequal with theoretical marginal costs.

We have raised some problems of a theoretical and practical nature with respect to cost-of-service pricing. An obvious question is whether cost-of-service pricing has any relevance for establishing rates in regulated industries.

■ role of rates

Rates charged by transportation companies are actually one of the criteria that guide intelligent shippers in selecting the mode of transportation or carrier that is most appropriate for their shipment. When the modal choice or carrier decision is made properly, the shipper will balance the carrier's rate against the carrier's service characteristics such as transit time, reliability, and loss and damage record.

In order for the transportation decision to be properly made, it can be argued that the rate charged should reflect the cost of providing the service in order to ensure carrier and economic system efficiency. The rate(s) of carriers should be related to cost, but not to some arbitrary allocation of cost.

■ indivisable costs problem

Railroads and pipelines require large, indivisable capital inputs because of their rights-of-way, terminals, and so on. The associated high fixed costs which are common costs to most of the traffic will, if averaged over the units of traffic, have to be allocated on an arbitrary basis, which will in turn lead to unwise and uneconomical pricing decisions. Adherence to an average cost or fully-allocated cost approach does not make any sense in such situations.

Cost-oriented rates should be related to what we have defined as marginal cost or variable cost. Such costs, measured as precisely as possible, should serve as the floor for individual rates. Some traffic will move if rates are above marginal or variable cost, whereas other traffic will move at rates close to marginal cost, particularly under competitive circumstances. In other words, differential pricing seems to make sense in most instances, but our rationale needs further explanation.

■ decreasing cost
industries

In the presentation of cost-of-service pricing, mention was made of decreasing cost industries. Some regulated firms fall into this category. If rates are based upon strict marginal cost, the firm experiences a loss. As was stated previously, a subsidy could be paid, but this is not likely to be done. Therefore, the firm has to recover its fixed costs. To accomplish this on the basis of an average cost approach is not acceptable. However, it can be accomplished by using marginal cost as a floor for rates and using the value-of-service, or, if you will, demand to establish how far above this minimum the rate or price should be set.

■ charging what the
traffic will bear

In our previous discussion of the definitions of value-of-service pricing, an intentional omission was made, and that is that value-of-service pricing is sometimes defined as charging what the traffic will bear. In actuality, this phrase can assume two meanings. First, it may be used to mean that prices are set so that on each unit the maximum revenue is obtained regardless of the particular costs involved. That is, no service should be charged a lower price when it would bear a higher price. The second meaning, which can be more conveniently expressed in a negative form and which is germane to our discussion, is that no service should be charged a price which it will not bear when, at a lower price, the service could be purchased. This lower price will always cover the marginal cost incurred by the company in providing the service.

■ elasticity of demand

As implied previously, the differences in the elasticities of demand for the different services will determine the actual level of the rates. It should be remembered that the presence of indivisibilities in the cost structure necessitate the dissimilar pricing. Therefore, the greater the amount of the indivisibilities in the cost structure, the greater the need for dissimilar pricing and its consequent practice of segregating services according to demand elasticity.

■ dissimilar pricing

There is one final point that should be treated, and that is the desirability of dissimilar pricing. Dissimilar pricing allows common and fixed costs to be spread out over large volumes of traffic. In other words, dissimilar pricing may render economical benefits, since prices may be lower than they otherwise would be. It is not unusual to hear statements in the railroad industry that the rates on high-valued commodities subsidize coal traffic. However, coal will not move unless the rates are relatively low. It could be argued that as long as the coal rates cover more than the marginal cost of the movement, they allow the railroad to charge lower rates on other traffic.

In conclusion, we can say that dissimilar pricing is the logical approach for rate-making in regulated industries. Cost indivisibilities necessitate the practice of discriminatory pricing, but we have approached this within what we might call a cost framework. Marginal cost sets the minimum basis for rates, while fixed or common costs are, in effect, allocated on the basis of demand elasticity.

Conclusion

Pricing of carrier services is frequently a difficult task because of the complexities which exist in the transportation marketplace. Competition has increased among transportation companies as noted in the chapter, but the intensity of the competition is uneven. Therefore, all four basic economic market situations can be found which makes pricing a challenging process.

The cost structure of carriers also makes pricing and rate-making more complex. For example, the presence of common costs, particularly among railroads, means that such costs cannot be assigned to specific units of traffic. The problem of common costs is more significant among some carriers than others, but all modes of transportation must deal with such costs to some extent.

The increased competition has led some individuals to advocate complete reliance upon what might be called a cost-of-service approach to rate-making. However, the common costs experienced by carriers raises some problems with completely relying on cost-of-service pricing. Consideration must be given to demand characteristics of various products in establishing rates because of the cost indivisibilities associated with common costs. In other words, cost and demand have a role to play in setting transportation rates.

Study Questions

1. Describe and analyze the basic forms of markets in an economical sense.

2. How can carriers have almost all market forms along certain routes?

3. Distinguish between accounting cost and economic cost.

4. What is a social cost?

5. How do joint and common costs differ, appear the same, and each complicate the task of determining the costs of transportation service?

6. How do fixed costs appear to provide economies for volume operation for railroads?

7. What are marginal costs?

8. How do railroad and motor carrier cost structures differ?

9. What is value-of-service pricing and why has it been popular in railroad rate-making?

10. What is cost-of-service pricing?

11. What is meant by one commodity "subsidizing" another? Is this justified in carrier pricing?

12. If the present price of gasoline was $1.50 per gallon and an added tax of 10¢ per gallon reduced gasoline consumption by 10 percent, what would this indicate with respect to the elasticity of demand for gasoline? Indicate the factors that primarily determine the elasticity of demand for a product or service? (AST&T, Spring 1975, Exam #1)

13. Many individuals think that the price of transportation service should, as a matter of principle, reflect the cost of providing such service. If so, why have there been so many arguments concerning the application of this approach in the rate-making decision process? What do you believe is the best solution to this problem? Why? (AST&T, Fall 1977, Exam #1)

14. Differentiate between the following theories or methods upon which to base transport pricing? Discuss each fully: (a) variable cost; (b) fully distributed cost; and (c) marginal cost.

Notes

1. Winthrop M. Daniels, *The Price of Transportation Service* (New York: Harper and Brothers, 1942), p. 1.

2. John R. Meyer et. al., *The Economics of Competition in the Transportation Industries* (Cambridge, Mass.: Harvard University Press, 1959), p. 205.

3. For an excellent analysis of industry pricing behavior see Meyer, *Economics of Competition*, pp. 203-11.

4. William J. Baumol et al., "The Role of Cost in the Minimum Pricing of Railroad Services," *Journal of Business* 35 (October 1962): 5-6. This article succinctly presents the essence of sunk versus prospective costs.

5. A. M. Milne, *The Economics of Inland Transport* (London: Pitman and Sons, 1955), p. 146.

6. This problem was argued in the economic journals at an early date by two notable economists. See F. W. Taussig, "Railway Rates and Joint Cost Once More," *Quarterly Journal of Economics* 27 (May 1913): 378; F. W. Taussig and A. C. Pigou, "Railway Rates and Joint Costs," *Quarterly Journal of Economics* 27 (August 1913): 535 and 687; A. C. Pigou, *The Economics of Welfare*, 4th ed. (London: Macmillan and Co., 1950), chaps. 17 and 18. An excellent discussion of this debate is contained in the following: D. P. Locklin, "A Review of the Literature on Railway Rate Theory," *Quarterly Journal of Economics* 47 (1933): 174.

7. For an excellent discussion see George W. Wilson and George M. Smerk, "Rate Theory" in *Physical Distribution Management* (Bloomington, Ind.: Indiana University, 1963), pp. 2-4.

8. George W. Wilson, *Essays On Some Unsettled Questions In the Economics of Transportation* (Bloomington, Ind.: Foundation for Economic and Business Studies, 1962), pp. 32-33.

9. Interstate Commerce Commission, Bureau of Accounts and Cost Finding, *Explanation of Rail Cost Finding Principles and Procedures* (Washington, D.C.: Government Printing Office, 1948), p. 88.

10. John Meyer et al., *The Economics of Competition In the Transportation Industries* (Cambridge, Mass.: Harvard University Press, 1960), pp. 112-113.

11. G. W. Wilson, "Freight Rates and Transportation Costs," *The Business Quarterly* (Summer 1960): 161-62.

12. John J. Coyle, "A Reconsideration of Value of Service Pricing," *Land Economics,* (Winter 1964): 193-99.

13. For an extended discussion see Coyle, "Reconsideration of Pricing," pp. 195-98.

14. This example is adapted from Wilson and Smerk, "Rate Theory," pp. 7-10.

15. This section is based upon the discussion in J. J. Coyle, "Cost-of-Service Pricing in Transportation," *Quarterly Review of Economics and Business* 57 (1964): 69-74.

16. Coyle, "Cost-of-Service Pricing," p. 27.

17. Harold Hotelling, "The General Welfare in Relation to Problems of Taxation and of Railway and Utility Rates," *Econometrics,* 6, No. 3 (July 1938): 242.

18. R. W. Harbeson, "The Cost Concept and Economic Control," *Harvard Business Review* 17 (1939): 257-63.

19. Ibid.

Suggested Readings

Baumel, William J., et al. "The Role of Costs in the Minimum Pricing of Railroad Services." *Journal of Business* 35 (October 1962): pp. 1-15.

Barrett, Colin. "The Theory and Practice of Carrier Rate Making." *Transportation and Distribution Management.* October, 1972.

Coyle, John J. "A Reconsideration of Value of Service Pricing." *Land Economics* 68 (Fall 1963): pp. 193-99.

Davis, Grant M., and Combs, Linda J. "Some Observations Concerning Value of Service Pricing in Transportation." *Transportation Journal,* Spring, 1975.

Harper, Donald V. *Transportation in America: Users, Carriers, Government.* Englewood Cliffs, N.J.: Prentice-Hall, 1978, chaps. 7, 8.

Kahn, Alfred E. *The Economics of Regulation: Principles and Institutions.* Vol. 1, pt. 3. New York: John Wiley and Sons, 1970.

Locklin, D. Philip. *Economics of Transportation.* 7th ed. Homewood, Ill.: Richard D. Irwin, 1972, chap. 7.

Nelson, James R., ed. *Criteria for Transport Pricing.* Cambridge, Md.: Cornell Maritime Press, 1973.

Pegrum, Dudley F. *Transportation: Economics and Public Policy.* Homewood, Ill.: Richard D. Irwin, 1973, chaps. 7, 8.

Roberts, Merrill J. "Transport Pricing Return." *Transportation Journal,* Spring, 1973, pp. 5-17.

Case   ## Transmountain Bus Lines

Transmountain Bus Lines operates eight basic routes throughout the
East connecting Boston, New York, Philadelphia, Washington, D.C.,
State College, Pennsylvania, and Cleveland. The company operated
profitably for the past several decades, but since 1978 cost increases
and declining passenger demand on many routes have caused the company to have some unprofitable periods.

Top management hired Harry Hatchet as senior cost analyst in the
Finance Department. His task is to determine which, if any, unprofitable operations can be discontinued. He is examining the individual
bus runs from State College to Washington, D.C. and return. His approach is to eliminate any runs that result in a loss for the company
when calculated on a fully allocated cost basis.

His costing personnel have audited the runs and have developed the
required information as follows:

Bus Run #	Lv. S.C.	Lv. Wash.	# Passgr's/ Round Trip	Total Round Trip Revenue*	Variable Costs Per Bus Run*
SCW104	6:00 A.M.	11:00 A.M.	40	$ 640	$ 500
SCW102	7:00 A.M.	noon	60	960	500
SCW100	8:00 A.M.	5:00 P.M.	90	1440	500
SCW101	4:00 P.M.	9:00 P.M.	70	1120	500
SCW103	5:00 P.M.	10:00 P.M.	50	800	500
				$4960	$2500

*All revenues and costs are per day.

The company overhead costs associated with the State College/
Washington route total $1,500 per day. This cost is for management,
terminal expenses and a group of costs allocated by the corporate headquarters. On the State College/Washington route this prorata cost is
$300 per bus round trip per day (the total $1,500 divided by the number of round trip bus runs in that route service).

Should any of the bus round trips be eliminated? What will occur
when a bus round trip is eliminated? Assume that passengers from an
eliminated run are lost from the company.

13   Rate-Making
In Practice

After reading this chapter you should:

1   Understand the nature and role of carrier tariffs.
2   Be able to determine general rates of carriers.
3   Understand some of the special rates of carriers.
4   Appreciate carrier rate bureaus and their role in rate-making.
5   Understand the impact of rate levels on the financial viability of carriers.

A complete understanding of carrier cost economics and behavior is a necessary prerequisite to effective management of carrier pricing. This chapter presents an in-depth overview of the general and specific forms of pricing that are employed by carriers of all types. The form of each rate is discussed and analyzed along with the primary inducements for the carrier and its users. This chapter presents general rate forms as well as a majority of special forms that are in common use. The role of rate bureaus is discussed, since a large part of the United States' rate system was established via these institutions. Further, rate negotiations are becoming a larger part of rate-making, and rate regulatory changes have brought about a closer contact between the shipper and carrier.

The overall carrier pricing function revolves around costing, rates, and tariffs. Most carriers employ costing personnel who are responsible for determining the overall cost and productivity of the carrier operations as well as the specific routes, customer services, or equipment needs. The work of cost analysts should serve as a pricing input to rate personnel who are responsible for establishing specific rates as well as

general rate levels for the carrier. Tariffs are the actual publications in which most rates are actually printed. Some firms print their own tariffs which are often referred to as individual tariffs, or use a rate bureau that is common to many carriers to establish and publish rates. These tariffs are referred to as agency tariffs.

Rates can be categorized into two broad groups with several subtypes within each group. One broad group is general rates, which includes class, exceptions, and commodity rates. The other broad group of rates is often referred to as specific rates which are comprised of those that relate to specific functions. Some groups are designed around the size or characteristics of the shipment; others relate to routes or general area applications. Some are tied to particular time services while others pertain to certain service factors. A last major specific group is contract rates which are found in most modes.

General Rates[1]

■ rate structures

These are the class, exception, and commodity rate structures in the United States. The class rate system provides a rate for any commodity between any two points. It is constructed from uniform distance and product systems. Exception rates are designed so that carriers in particular regions may depart from the product scale system for any one of many reasons which will be discussed later. Commodity rates, on the other hand, are employed for specific origin-destination shipping patterns of specific commodities. Each one of these three systems has a particular purpose.

It would be simple if all transportation services were sold on the basis of ton-miles, that is, we would have to pay X dollars to move one ton, one mile. But, in fact, transportation services are not sold in ton-miles, but rather they are sold for moving a specific commodity, such as pickles, between two specific points, Toledo, Ohio and New York, New York. This fact gives some insight into the enormous magnitude of the transportation pricing problem. There are over 33,000 important shipping and receiving points in the United States. Theoretically, the number of different possible routes would be all the permutations of the 33,000 points. The result is in the trillions of trillions. In addition, it is necessary to consider the thousands and thousands of different commodities and products which might be shipped over any of these routes. There are also the different modes to consider and different companies within each mode. It also may be necessary to give consideration to the specific supply-demand situation for each commodity over each route.

■ magnitude of pricing problem

Class Rates

■ base points

Since it is obviously impossible to quote trillions and trillions of rates, the transportation industry has taken two major steps toward simplification.

The first was to consolidate the 33,000 shipping points into groups. So, the nation was divided into geographic squares. The most important shipping point (based on tonnage) in each square serves as the rate base point for all other shipping points in the square. The purpose of this is to reduce the potential number of distance variations for rate-making purposes. The distance from each base point to each other base point was determined by the railroads and placed on file with the Interstate Commerce Commission (ICC) and published in the National Rate Basis Tariff. The distance between any two base points is referred to as the rate basis number. The first simplifying step reduced the number of possible origins and destinations for pricing purposes.

■ national scale of rates

The second step deals with the thousands and thousands of different items which might be shipped between any two base points. The railroads have established a national scale of rates which has been placed on file with the ICC and gives a rate in dollars per hundred weight (cwt), which is dollars per cwt for each rate basis number. These rate scales are the basis for a simplified product classification system.

Classification simply means grouping together products with similar

■ products classification

transportation characteristics so that one rating can be applied to the whole group. Items which are of high demand and high value might be placed in Class 100, which means they will be charged 100 percent of the first class rate. Items of low value such as coal, might be placed in Class 17½, which means they will be charged 17½ percent of the first class rate. This percentage number for the appropriate classification is called a class rating, and it is the group into which a commodity is placed for rate-making purposes.

■ pricing system

Now the number of possible pricing situations has been sufficiently reduced to allow the formation of a transportation pricing system. The price of moving a particular item between two particular points is determined as follows. First, look at the rate basis point for the origin and for the destination and then determine the rate basis number between the two base points. Next, determine the classification rating (class rating) for the particular product to be shipped. Finally, find the rate in the proper class rate tariff that corresponds to the appropriate rate base number and class rating. Multiply this rate, which is in cents per cwt, by the total shipment weight in cwt to determine the cost to move that specific product between those two points.

■ definition

The word *tariff* is commonly used to mean almost any publication put out by a carrier or a tariff publishing agency which concerns itself with the pricing or services performed by the carrier. All the information needed to determine the cost of a move is in one or more tariffs.

■ class rate charges

Let us give an example of the mechanics involved in determining the class rate charges for a motor carrier movement. Assume we are shipping wine in bulk from Baltimore to Philadelphia. What would be the correct class rate charges for shipping: (1) 40,000 pounds; (2) 15,000 pounds; and (3) 35,000 pounds?

1. A 40,000-pound shipment of wine in bulk.
   a. The rate basis number found in Middle Atlantic Conference (MAC) Tariff 41-A, page 182, is 66, at the intersection of rate groups Philadelphia and Baltimore in the vertical and horizontal portions of the tariff respectively (Table 13.1).
   b. The class ratings and minimum weight, found in the National Motor Freight Classification A-9, page 183, for wine in bulk, item #111510, are less than truckload LTL = 100, truckload (TL) = 50, and minimum weight = 40,000 lbs., 40.2. Since our shipment weighs 40,000 lbs. the TL rating of 50 is used—the lower, volume rating (Table 13.2).
   c. The applicable rate is given in MAC Tariff 41-A, page 184, and is determined by the intersection of the horizontal line of rate basis number 66, D30M, and the vertical line of class 50. This gives the class rate of 84¢ per cwt (Table 13.3).
   d. The transportation charge is found by multiplying the rate per cwt times the number of cwt's in the shipment, or:

$$40,000 \text{ lbs.} = 40,000/100 = 400 \text{ cwt}$$
$$400 \text{ cwt @ 84¢ per cwt} = \$336$$

Table 13.1 Table of Rate Basis Numbers

COMPOSITE PAGE

MAC TARIFF 41-A

TABLE OF RATE BASIS NUMBERS

AND RATE GROUPS (Note 5)	Aberdeen....Md.	Abingdon....Md.	Alexandria...Va.	Annapolis...Md.	Baltimore...Md.	Bel Air....Md.	Bradshaw...Md.	Cabin John..Md.	Carderock...Md.	Cedarhurst..Md.	Clarksville..Md.	College Park..Md.	Conowingo...Md.	Sykesville..Md.	Washington..D.C.	Woodstock....Md.
							BETWEEN RATE GROUPS (Note 5) — APPLY RATE BASIS NUMBERS (For Rates, see SECTION 1)									
Camden..............N.J.	58	58	73	79	66	70	58	80	86	70	70	70	59	58	70	70
Chester...............Pa.	50	53	68	74	62	66	53	78	83	66	66	68	54	66	68	66
Clementon...........N.J.	59	64	76	81	70	74	68	84	89	74	76	76	64	74	74	74
Hempstead..........N.Y.	92	93	103	114	100	103	93	113	118	106	102	103	93	102	103	102
Hicksville...........N.Y.	99	99	109	120	106	109	99	118	124	98	108	109	99	108	109	108
Hightstown..........N.J.	66	68	79	88	74	77	68	87	92	77	77	77	68	77	77	77
Hopewell............N.J.	64	66	79	88	74	77	66	87	92	77	76	77	68	77	77	77
Jamesburg..........N.J.	68	70	80	88	74	79	70	89	94	79	79	79	70	79	79	79
Jersey City.........N.J.	76	77	87	98	84	87	77	97	102	86	86	87	77	86	87	86
Lansdale............Pa.	61	64	76	83	70	74	64	86	91	73	74	76	64	74	76	74
Malvern.............Pa.	57	58	74	81	68	74	59	83	88	68	73	73	57	73	73	73
Manville............N.J.	68	70	80	89	76	79	70	90	95	79	99	80	70	79	80	79
Morristown......N.J. *C	86	87	97	108	94	97	87	107	112	96	96	97	87	96	97	96
¶D	77	79	90	99	86	87	79	100	105	87	87	90	76	87	90	87
Mount Holly.........N.J.	62	64	77	83	70	76	64	86	91	74	74	76	64	74	76	74
Mount Kisco....N.Y. #A	111	101	111	122	108	111	101	121	126	110	110	111	101	110	111	110
ØB	88	89	99	110	96	99	89	114	119	98	98	99	89	98	98	98
Newark.............Del.	41	44	64	68	56	61	44	72	77	59	59	62	47	59	62	59
Newark..............N.J.	76	77	87	98	84	87	77	97	102	86	86	87	77	86	87	86
New Brunswick......N.J.	68	70	80	89	76	79	70	90	95	79	79	80	70	79	79	79
New Castle..........Del.	46	50	66	73	61	66	50	76	81	66	64	66	53	64	66	64
New York(Note 1)....N.Y.	76	77	87	98	84	87	77	97	102	86	86	87	77	86	87	86
Norristown...........Pa.	58	61	74	81	68	73	61	83	88	70	73	73	59	73	73	73
Nyack..............N.Y.	84	86	96	105	90	92	86	102	107	90	92	92	84	92	92	92
Penns Grove.........N.J.	53	57	70	79	64	77	57	80	85	74	68	70	58	68	70	68
Perth Amboy.........N.J.	76	77	87	98	84	87	77	97	102	86	86	87	77	86	87	86
Philadelphia.........Pa.	56	58	73	79	66	70	58	80	85	70	70	70	59	70	70	70
Phoenixville.........Pa.	58	59	74	83	70	74	59	84	89	70	73	74	59	73	74	73
Piermont............N.Y.	84	86	96	105	90	92	86	102	107	87	92	92	84	92	92	92
Plainfield...........N.J.	70	73	83	91	77	80	73	93	98	80	80	83	73	80	83	80
Plymouth Meeting.....Pa.	58	62	76	83	70	74	62	84	89	73	73	74	61	73	74	73
Port Chester....N.Y. #A	88	90	99	110	96	99	90	109	114	98	98	99	90	98	99	98
ØB	86	90	98	107	92	96	90	106	111	96	96	96	90	96	96	96
Riverhead...........N.Y.	111	112	122	133	119	122	112	132	137	109	121	122	112	121	122	121
Riverside...........N.J.	59	66	76	83	70	74	64	84	89	74	74	74	64	74	74	74
Trenton.............N.J.	62	66	77	85	73	76	66	86	91	76	76	76	66	76	73	73
Westwood........N.J. *C	82	85	95	103	88	90	85	102	107	90	92	92	84	92	92	92
¶D	72	80	90	98	83	83	80	100	105	90	90	90	80	90	90	90
Wharton.........N.J. *C	86	87	97	108	94	97	87	107	112	96	96	97	87	96	97	96
¶D	76	79	90	98	84	86	79	97	102	83	86	90	76	87	87	87
White Plains....N.Y. #A	88	90	99	110	96	99	90	109	114	98	98	99	90	98	99	98
ØB	86	90	98	107	92	96	90	106	111	96	96	96	90	96	96	96
Wilmington..........Del.	44	50	66	72	59	64	50	74	79	64	64	64	51	64	64	64
Woodbury...........N.J.	59	64	76	81	70	74	64	84	89	74	74	74	64	74	74	74
Yonkers........N.Y. #A	88	90	99	110	96	98	90	109	114	98	98	99	90	98	99	96
ØB	86	90	98	107	92	96	90	106	111	92	96	96	90	96	96	96

Source: Middle Atlantic Conference Tariff 41-A, Washington, D.C.

Table 13.2 National Motor Freight Classification

COMPOSITE PAGE

111400-112420   NATIONAL MOTOR FREIGHT CLASSIFICATION A-9

Item	ARTICLES	CLASSES		
		LTL	TL	(w)
111400	**LIQUORS, BEVERAGE:**			
111420	**Beverages,** alcoholic, carbonated, containing not exceeding 6 percent of alcohol by volume, in glass containers or metal cans in boxes...	65	35	30.2
111450	**Liquors,** alcoholic, NOI, in glass or in metal cans in barrels or boxes, see Note, item 111452; in Package 1352; or in bulk in barrels; also TL, in tank trucks, see Rule 370.................	100	50	40.2
111452	Note—Wooden boxes must be nailed with cement-coated nails; or must be encircled by two or more continuous metal or wooden straps; or must be encircled by one wire or metal strap around the center or by one wire or metal strap around each end, securely fastened to prevent removal; or all side joints must be sealed with metal seals and ends nailed.			
111470	**Liquors, Malt: Ale, Beers, Beer Tonic, Porter, Stout** or non-intoxicating **Cereal Beverage,** in glass in bottle carriers with tops securely fastened, see Note, item 111473, in glass or metal cans in barrels or boxes, in metal dispensing containers less than 5 gallons capacity in carriers made of 500 pound test solid fibreboard, in boxes enclosed in crates, or in bulk in barrels; also TL, in open top carriers, or in metal cans in fibre boxes, not sealed, or in Packages 174, 186, 238, 788, 966, 1145, 1155, 1162, 1257, 1261, 1360 or 1376.................	65	35	50.2
111473	Note—Bottle carrier containers made of fibreboard need not meet the certificate requirements of Rule 220 and Rule 290 but must be equipped with partitions full shoulder height of the bottles loaded therein. Such partitions must touch all four sides of the carrier. Inner packaging must comply with Rule 290 or Package 174.			
111490	**Vermouth,** in containers in barrels or boxes, or in bulk in barrels...........................	100	50	40.2
111510	**Wine,** NOI:			
Sub 1	In glass in wicker baskets, covers sealed...	150	50	40.2
Sub 2	In containers in barrels or boxes, see Note, item 111452; in Package 1342; or in bulk in barrels; also TL, in tank trucks, see Rule 370...	100	50	40.2
114000	**MACHINERY GROUP:** Articles consist of Machinery or Machines, or Parts Named, see Notes, items 114012 to 114024, inclusive, as described in items subject to this grouping.			
114012	Note—LTL shipments of machinery or machines, loose or on skids, must have small detachable parts removed and shipped in barrels or boxes. Such barrels or boxes must be specified on shipping orders and bills of lading. Fragile parts not detached must be protected.			
114014	Note—Unless otherwise provided, parts or pieces weighing 50 pounds or over of KD machinery and machines may be accepted loose or on skids and classed as in packages when such parts or pieces are shipped with the articles of which they form a part and classes are provided for such KD machinery or machines in packages.			
114016	Note—The following fittings, power equipment or power transmission appliances for machinery or machines, will, if shipped in mixed TL with such machinery or machines, be taken at the TL class and at not less than the TL minimum weight applicable on such machinery or machines: air compressors; belts; boilers, including fire brick and fire clay for setting; boiler parts, boiler fronts and grate bars; clutches; cog, gear, pulley or sprocket wheels; electric generators; engines; exhaust fans or rotary blowers; feed water heaters; foundation anchors or rods; fuel economizers; motors; pipe or pipe fittings; power pumps; power control switchboards; shafts or shafting; shaft collars, couplings, hangers or pillow blocks; smoke flues, smoke stacks or turbine water wheels, in packages, loose or on skids, as provided in separate description of articles for TL quantities.			
114090	**Air Cleaners or Air Filtering Machines,** electrostatic or mechanical, without blowers or fans, LTL, in boxes, crates or if weighing each 500 pounds or more, on skids; also TL, loose or in packages..	85	55	24.2
114110	**Air Cleaners, Coolers** other than water evaporative type, **Dehumidifiers, Heaters** other than portable, **Humidifiers or Washers,** with blowers or fans, see Note, item 114112............	85	45	24.2
114112	Note—Also applies on accompanying wrought iron or steel pipe parts.			
114130	**Air Coolers,** water evaporative type, with blowers or fans, with or without heating action, in boxes or crates:			
Sub 1	Portable, without stands, see Note, item 114132...............................	85	45	24.2
Sub 2	NOI..	110	{ 70	14.2
			85	10.2
114132	Note—Applies only on coolers of the hand portable type, without wheels or casters, net weight not in excess of 50 pounds each.			
150600	**PAPER:**			
150620	**Absorbent Base for Impregnation and Making Laminated Plastics,** in packages...........	65	35	36.2
150640	**Artists' Board,** pulpboard or fibreboard, cloth covered, painted or coated, in packages......	70	45	24.2
150650	**Autographic Register, Cash Register, Computing Machine or Ticket Issuing Machine,** other than forms, cards, checks or tickets, see Note, item 150652, plain, or ruled, not otherwise printed, see Note, item 150654, in boxes..	55	35	36.2
150652	Note—Also applies when interleaved with carbon paper or backed with carbon.			
150654	Note—Also applies when the articles bear marginal lettering or numbering for identification purposes.			
151010	**Ground Wood Paper,** other than newsprint and unfinished blank wall paper, fibre content consisting of not less than 60 percent ground wood, including such papers as catalog, directory, drawing, manila, novel, poster, printing, tablet or writing paper (will not include paper which has been further processed after its original manufacture), see Note, item 151012, in packages:			
Sub 1	In rolls 16 inches or more in diameter, or in sheets measuring 336 square inches or more......	55	35	40.2
Sub 2	In rolls less than 16 inches in diameter, or in sheets measuring less than 336 square inches....	55	35	36.2
151012	Note—Bills of lading and shipping orders must contain notations reading: "Ground wood papers, other than newsprint and unfinished blank wall paper, fibre content consisting of not less than 60 percent ground wood."			
151192	Note—Applies on chemically treated paper such as used for manufacturing washers, gaskets or packing shapes.			
151210	**Paper,** dusting or polishing, in boxes...	70	40	36.2
151230	**Paper or Paperboard,** surface coated with flock, NOI, in packages.....................	100	50	30.2
151250	**Paper,** NOI, not printed, in packages...	70	40	36.2
151270	**Pari-mutuel Ticket Issuing Machine Paper,** printed, requiring further printing, in rolls in boxes..	70	35	36.2

Source: *National Motor Freight Classification A-9*, Washington, D.C.

Table 13.3 Class Tariff

COMPOSITE PAGE

MAC TARIFF 41-A

SECTION 1
TABLE OF CLASS RATES FOR CLASSES 100 AND LOWER

APPLICATION OF WEIGHT GROUPS:

    A – Applies on LTL or AQ shipments weighing each less than 2,000 pounds.
    B – Applies on LTL or AQ shipments weighing each 2,000 pounds or more but less than 6,000 pounds.
    C – Applies on LTL or AQ shipments weighing each 6,000 pounds or more.
    D – Applies on TL shipments (See Note A).
    D30M–Applies on TL shipments, minimum weight 30,000 pounds (See Note A).
    NOTE A: Where the charge under the rates in Line D30M is lower than the charge under the rates in Line D on the same shipment via the same route, such lower charge will apply.

CLASSES — RATES IN CENTS PER 100 POUNDS

RATE BASIS NUMBER	WEIGHT GROUP	100	92½	85	77½	70	65	60E	60	57	55	50	50K	47½	45	42½	40	37½	35	32½	30	27½
33	A	181	171	161	153	143	134	135	126	120	117	110										
	B	121	114	106	98	89	85	87	80	76	73	68										
	C	88	82	75	69	62	58	60	54	52	49	46										
	D	77	72	66	61	55	51	54	48	46	44	41	41	40	38	36	34	33	31	29	27	25
	D30M	75	70	64	59	53	49	52	46	44	42	39	37	37	35	33	31	29	28	26	24	22
65 66	A	277	261	244	229	213	200	196	186	177	173	160										
	B	216	202	187	172	157	148	145	138	131	127	116										
	C	180	167	153	140	127	118	115	109	103	100	91										
	D	168	156	143	131	119	111	108	102	97	94	86	86	86	81	77	73	69	64	60	56	51
	D30M	166	154	141	129	117	109	106	100	95	92	84	81	80	76	72	68	64	59	55	51	47
67 68	A	286	269	252	235	218	205	201	191	183	178	164										
	B	225	210	195	178	162	154	151	143	137	132	120										
	C	188	174	160	146	132	124	120	114	109	105	96										
	D	176	163	150	137	124	116	113	107	102	99	90	90	89	85	80	76	71	67	62	58	53
	D30M	174	161	148	135	122	114	111	105	100	97	88	84	84	79	75	71	67	62	58	54	49
69 70	A	289	272	255	239	221	207	203	194	185	180	167										
	B	228	213	198	182	166	156	153	145	139	133	123										
	C	191	177	163	149	135	126	123	116	111	106	98										
	D	179	166	153	140	127	118	115	109	104	100	92	91	91	86	82	77	73	68	63	59	54
	D30M	177	162	151	138	125	116	113	107	102	98	90	86	85	81	76	72	68	63	59	55	50
71 72 73	A	295	277	259	243	225	211	206	197	188	183	169										
	B	233	218	202	186	169	159	156	148	142	137	125										
	C	197	183	168	154	139	129	126	119	114	110	100										
	D	184	171	157	144	130	121	118	112	107	103	94	94	94	89	84	80	75	70	65	61	56
	D30M	182	169	155	142	128	119	116	110	105	101	92	88	88	83	79	74	70	65	61	56	52
74	A	299	281	262	246	228	214	209	199	190	185	171										
	B	238	221	205	189	172	162	158	151	144	139	127										
	C	201	186	171	157	142	132	128	121	116	112	102										
	D	188	174	160	147	133	124	120	114	109	105	96	96	95	90	86	81	76	71	66	62	57
	D30M	186	172	158	145	131	122	118	112	107	103	94	90	89	85	80	76	71	66	62	57	53
75 76	A	305	287	269	250	232	218	213	203	194	189	174										
	B	244	228	212	194	176	167	162	155	147	143	130										
	C	207	192	177	161	146	137	132	126	119	116	105										
	D	194	180	166	151	137	128	124	118	112	109	99	99	99	94	89	84	79	74	69	64	59
	D30M	192	178	164	149	135	126	122	116	110	107	97	93	92	88	83	78	73	69	64	59	54
77	A	309	290	271	254	234	219	215	205	196	190	176										
	B	247	231	214	197	178	168	164	157	149	144	132										
	C	211	196	180	164	148	138	134	128	121	117	108										
	D	197	183	168	154	139	129	126	120	114	110	101	101	100	95	90	85	80	75	70	65	60
	D30M	195	181	166	152	137	127	124	118	112	108	99	94	94	89	84	79	74	70	65	60	55
84	A	328	307	287	269	248	232	227	217	206	201	186										
	B	267	248	230	212	192	181	176	169	160	155	142										
	C	230	213	196	180	162	151	146	140	132	128	117										
	D	215	199	183	168	152	141	137	131	124	120	110	110	109	103	98	92	87	81	76	70	65
	D30M	213	197	181	166	150	139	135	129	122	118	108	103	102	97	92	86	83	76	71	65	60
87	A	336	316	295	275	254	238	231	221	212	205	190										
	B	275	257	238	218	198	186	181	173	166	159	146										
	C	239	221	203	186	168	156	151	144	138	132	121										
	D	223	207	190	174	157	146	141	135	129	124	114	113	113	107	101	96	90	84	78	73	67
	D30M	221	205	188	172	155	144	139	133	127	122	112	107	106	101	95	90	84	79	73	68	62
88 89 90	A	346	325	303	283	261	244	238	228	217	211	195										
	B	285	266	246	226	205	192	187	180	171	164	151										
	C	248	230	212	194	175	162	157	151	143	138	126										
	D	232	215	198	181	164	152	147	141	134	129	118	118	118	112	106	100	94	88	82	76	70
	D30M	230	213	196	179	162	150	145	139	132	127	116	111	110	105	99	93	88	82	76	70	65

Source: *Middle Atlantic Conference Tariff 41-A*, Washington, D.C.

2. A 15,000-pound shipment of wine in bulk.
   a. The rate basis number is again 66, but the rating used is 100 because the weight of the shipment is less than 40,000 lbs., the weight required to use class 50.
   b. From MAC Tariff 41-A, the rate for class 100 at the rate basis number 66, C, is $1.80 per cwt.
   c. The transportation charge is $270 and is determined as follows:

$$15{,}000 \text{ lbs.} = 150 \text{ cwt}$$
$$150 \text{ cwt @ } \$1.80 \text{ per cwt} = \$270$$

3. A 35,000-pound shipment of wine in bulk.
   a. The shipper has the option of shipping the shipment at TL or LTL when the weight of the shipment is less than the minimum weight specified in the tariff, but the shipper will be charged for at least the minimum weight specified to get the lower volume rate. The shipper has the option of utilizing the rate that results in the lowest charge.
   b. In this case the 35,000 lbs. is less than the 40,000 lbs. minimum, but it is cheaper to ship this as 40,000 lbs. (the basis of determining the transportation charge) at 84¢ per cwt than as the actual weight of 35,000 lbs. at $1.80 per cwt, or:

$$350 \text{ cwt @ } \$1.80 \text{ per cwt} = \$630 \text{ or}$$
$$400 \text{ cwt @ } 84¢ \text{ per cwt} = \$336$$

In this case the shipper would elect to ship the 35,000 lbs. as 40,000 lbs. and pay $336 rather than $630.

The latter example points out the need for the shipper to analyze at what volume it becomes profitable (lower cost) to ship an LTL size shipment as a TL shipment at the TL minimum weight and lower TL rate. This can be accomplished by determining the weight break—the volume at which the LTL charges equal the TL charges at the TL minimum weight. That is,

$$\text{LTL rate} \times (\text{WB}) = \text{TL rate} \times \text{minimum weight}$$
$$\text{where WB} = \text{the weight break volume}$$

Plugging in the numbers from part 3 of the above example we find the weight break to be:

$$\$180 \text{ (WB)} = 84¢ \text{ (400)}$$
$$\text{WB} = 187 \text{ cwt (rounded off)}$$

Next, a rather simple decision rule can be established for use by shipping clerks to determine when it is economical to ship an LTL shipment as a TL shipment. In this example the decision rules are as follows:

1. If the shipment weighs less than 187 cwt (WB), ship actual weight at LTL rate ($1.80 per cwt);

2. If the shipment weighs between 187 cwt (WB) and 400 cwt (minimum weight), ship as 400 cwt (minimum weight) at the TL rate (84¢ per cwt); and

3. If the shipment weighs more than 400 cwt, ship actual weight at TL rate (84¢ per cwt).

Exception Ratings

Although the classification and class rate system is the backbone of the transportation pricing system, in reality only about 10 percent of all volume, carload (CL) and truckload (TL), freight moves under this pricing system. The remaining 90 percent moves either under an exception rating (rate) or commodity rate.

■ exception ratings

Exception ratings are published when the transportation characteristics of an item in a particular area differ from those of the same article in other areas. For example, large volume movements or intensive competition in one area may require the publication of a lower exception rating; in this case, the exception rating applies rather than the classification rating. The same procedures described above apply to determining the exception rate, except now the exception rating (class) is used instead of the classification rating. An example of an exception tariff is the MAC Tariff 10 R (Table 13.4).

■ exception rate examples

Continuing with our earlier example of moving wine in bulk from Baltimore to Philadelphia, we find that item #9540, Liquors, Beverages: Wine, etc., makes an exception to the TL rating found in the National Motor Freight Classification A-9 (Table 13.2). The classification rating was 50, whereas the exception rating is 45. For a shipment of 40,000 pounds of wine in bulk and using the same procedure outlined for determining class rates, the intersection of the horizontal line of rate basis number 66, D30M and the vertical line of class 45 in MAC Tariff 41-A (Table 13.3), the exception rate is 76¢ per cwt. The transportation charges then become 400 cwt @ 76¢ per cwt—$304, a savings of $32 over the class rate charges.

Commodity Rates

A commodity rate can be constructed on a variety of bases, but the most common is a specific rate published on a specific commodity or group of related commodities between specific points and generally via specific routes. Commodity rates are complete in themselves and are not part of the classification system. If the commodity you are shipping is not specifically stated, or if the origin-destination is not specifically spelled out in the commodity rate, then the commodity rate for your particular movement is not applicable. When a commodity rate is published it takes precedence over the class rate or exception rate on the same article between the specific points.

■ definition

This type of rate is offered to those commodities that are moved regularly in large quantities. Such a pricing system, however, completely un-

Table 13.4 Exception Tariff

COMPOSITE PAGE

MAC TARIFF 10-R

SECTION 4
EXCEPTIONS TO NATIONAL MOTOR FREIGHT CLASSIFICATION
(See Item 380)

ITEM	ARTICLES	CLASSES (Ratings)		
		AQ	LTL	TL
9400	LAMPS OR LIGHTING GROUP: Lighting Fixtures, electric or gas, NOI, other than cast iron, with or with- out globes or shades; or Parts, NOI, other than cast iron or other than glass, in barrels, boxes or crates................................... APPLICABLE ONLY for local or joint hauls via Byrnes, L.I. Motor Cargo, Inc.	200	..	..
9420	LAMPS OR LIGHTING GROUP: Lighting Fixtures, fluorescent(Note A), with equipment of electrical apparatus, with or without equipment of lamps(Note B) or Parts, NOI, in boxes or crates.. NOTE A: Applies only on lighting devices designed for permanent wiring to walls, ceilings, floors or posts or other similar mountings. NOTE B: Accompanying equipment of iron or steel or plastic reflectors may be in packages. APPLICABLE ONLY for local or joint hauls via Rupp-Southern Tier Freight Lines, Inc. (File R-261)	200	..	..
9440	LEATHER OR LEATHERBOARD: (File R264) Leather, NOI, or Enameled or Patent Leather...............................	..	..	45
9460	LICORICE MASS, in packages..	..	..	37½
9480	LIQUORS, BEVERAGE: (Files R198;D5152) Liquors, alcoholic, NOI: In glass in cases or in bulk in barrels............................... In bulk in barrels in bond (Note A).................................. NOTE A: This item shall be understood to embrace goods on which the Internal Revenue Tax has not been paid but does NOT include goods moving under U.S. Customs Bond.	..	..	® 45 ® 70 ® 50 Ⓣ 40
9500	LIQUORS, BEVERAGE: Liquors, malt: Ale, Beer, Beer Tonic, Porter, Stout or non-intoxicating Cereal Beverages; In glass in bottle carriers with or without tops securely fastened or without tops; or in glass or metal cans in barrels or boxes; in boxes enclosed in crates; or in bulk in barrels, Min. Wt. 10,000 lbs............ APPLICABLE ONLY on traffic moving under rates shown in Tariff 8-R, MF-ICC A-1458 and Tariff NY-1-J, PSC-NY-MT A-120. (File R205) NOT APPLICABLE for local hauls via Apex Express, Inc., Eastern Freight Ways, Inc., Royal Motor Lines, Inc., nor Victor Lynn Lines, Inc., nor for joint hauls via these carriers and their connections.	..	..	32½
9540	LIQUORS, BEVERAGE: (Files R198;D5152) Wine, in containers in barrels or boxes, or in bulk in barrels............	..	..	45
9760	MACHINERY, APPLIANCES AND SUPPLIES, electrical: As enumerated in List No. 11, Section 2, in straight or mixed truckloads(except as otherwise provided)... As enumerated in List No. 12, Section 2, in straight or mixed truckloads(except as otherwise provided)...	..	.. ..	40 55
9780	MACHINERY GROUP: (Files D918;E6568) Air Coolers, Coolers, other than water evaporative type, Dehumidifiers, Heaters, other than portable, Humidifiers or Washers, with blowers or fans, with or without air filters (Note A): Weighing each less than 600 lbs., TL Min. Wt. 24,000 lbs.(Note B).......... Weighing each 600 lbs. or more, TL Min. Wt. 20,000 lbs............... NOTE A: Ratings also apply on Wrought Iron or Steel Pipe Parts. NOTE B: When from Buffalo, Dunkirk, New York and Syracuse, N.Y., or Avenel(Middlesex Cy.), Jersey City, Newark or Trenton, N.J., truckload minimum weight shall be 23,000 lbs.	..	.. ..	40 40

® - APPLICABLE ONLY for local hauls via Newburgh Transfer, Inc., or for joint hauls via this carrier in
    connection with The Davidson Transfer & Storage Co.
® - NOT APPLICABLE for local or joint hauls via Fleet Motor Lines, Inc., or carriers shown in Notes 11
    and 12, except Feuer Transportation, Inc., Long Transportation Company, or Perkins Trucking Co.,
    Inc.
Ⓣ - NOT APPLICABLE for local or joint hauls via Fleet Motor Lines, Inc., or carriers shown in Notes 11
    and 12.
Ⓝ - APPLICABLE ONLY for joint hauls via Newburgh Transfer, Inc., and its connections, except as noted.

Source: *Middle Atlantic Conference Tariff 10-R*, Washington, D.C.

dermines the attempts to simplify transportation pricing through the
class rate structure. It has caused transportation pricing to revert to the
publication of a multiplicity of rates and adds greatly to the complexity
of the pricing system.

■ commodity tariff
example

An example of a commodity tariff, MAC Tariff 41-A is given in Table 13.5. Again, continuing with our example of shipping 40,000 pounds of wine in bulk from Baltimore to Philadelphia, we find that item #28450 of MAC Tariff 41-A contains a commodity rate of 57¢ per cwt with a minimum weight of 23,000 pounds for this movement of wine. (This rate does not apply on the movement of wine in bulk from Philadelphia to Baltimore). Notes 2 and 3 refer to surrounding points to which the commodity rate also applies (remember the blanket area concept referred to earlier). For the movement of 40,000 pounds of wine using the commodity rate, the transportation charges are $228 (400 cwt @ 57¢ per cwt). The commodity rate results in the lowest charge of the three types of rates, which is what generally happens.

Shipment Characteristics

■ special rates

A myriad of special rate forms have evolved over the years either as a result of special cost factors or in order to induce certain shipment patterns. In their basic form these special rates appear as either class, exception, or commodity rates. Special terms, described below, apply to them which describe the special situations or purposes for which they are designed.

One set of special rates relates to size or character of shipment. Carriers generally experience certain fixed costs for each shipment. Many rate forms have been developed which take advantage of the fact that additional units or weight in each shipment do not incur additional amounts of these fixed costs.

LTL/TL or LCL/CL Rates

Less-than-truckload shipments (LTL) require several handlings as illustrated previously. Each one of these handlings requires manpower, materials handling equipment, terminal investment, and additional communications and tracking effort. A truckload shipment (TL), on the other hand, is generally loaded by the shipper and moved intact to the destination where the consignee unloads it. No intermediate handlings are required, nor does it have to be loaded or unloaded by carrier personnel. The direct movement also avoids intermediate terminals. As a result of these factors, larger TL shipments have lower rates than LTL shipments. The same specific principle applies in carload (CL) versus less-than-carload (LCL) movements by rail.

Multiple Car Rates

Railroads offer volume discounts for moves of more than one carload when they are shipped as a single string of cars from one point to another. The cost of moving several cars in a single shipment is proportionally less than the cost of each car moved singly. The multiple car movement of say, ten cars, can be handled by the same effort (empty car drop-off, pickup, intermediate and delivery efforts, and documentation) as a single car shipment. The only basic difference is the additional weight moved in the larger string of cars. Because of this economy of movement, railroads offer such rates in coal, grain, fertilizer, chemical and many other basic commodity moves.

Table 13.5 Commodity Rate Tariff

MAC TARIFF 41-A

SECTION 3
COMMODITY RATES IN CENTS PER 100 POUNDS UNLESS OTHERWISE SPECIFICALLY PROVIDED

ITEM 28350:   (File B4700)
LIQUORS, BEVERAGE:
  Liquors, Malt:
  Beer, in bottles or cans in boxes, or in bulk in barrels.

FROM	TO	TL RATE	MIN. WT.
New York(Note 1),N.Y.:			
Zone 1..................	Points named in Note A.....	60	28M
Zone 2..................	Points named in Note A.....	62	28M

NOTE A: Rates apply TO:
  Aberdeen......Md.   Chesapeake City..Md.   Elkton........Md.   Havre De Grace....Md.   Rising Sun......Md.
  Bel Air......Md.   Conowingo........Md.   Forest Hill...Md.   Perryman..........Md.
  NOT APPLICABLE for local or joint hauls via Service Trucking Co., Inc.

ITEM	COMMODITY	FROM	TO	TL RATE	MIN. WT.
28400	LIQUORS,BEVERAGE: Vermouth,in containers in barrels or boxes or in bulk in barrels. (File IR1698)	New York(Note 1),N.Y.:	Baltimore(Note 3)......Md.	79 70	23M 30M
		Zone 1.............	Washington(Note 4)....D.C.	81 73	23M 30M
		Zone 2.............	Baltimore(Note 3)......Md.	81 72	23M 30M
			Washington(Note 4)....D.C.	83 75	23M 30M
		Pennington........N.J.	Baltimore(Note 3)......Md.	67	23M
		Philadelphia.......Pa.	Washington(Note 4)....D.C.	69 57	23M 30M
28450	LIQUORS,BEVERAGE: Wine,NOI,in containers in barrels or boxes or in bulk. (Files P3583;A198)	Baltimore(Note 3)..Md.	Philadelphia(Note 2)...Pa.	57	23M
		Philadelphia(Note 2) ....Pa.	Washington(Note 4)....D.C.	69 57	23M 30M
28475	LIQUORS,BEVERAGE: Wine,NOI,actual value not exceeding $3.00 per gallon, in containers in barrels or boxes.	②⑤ Newark.........N.J. (File E3366)	Baltimore(Note 3)......Md.	80 71 Ⓛ⑪ 64	23M 30M 80M
			Washington(Note 4)....D.C.	82 74 Ⓛ⑪ 64	23M 30M 80M
28500	LIQUORS, BEVERAGE: Wine,NOI,in containers in barrels or boxes. (File E3366)	New York(Note 1),N.Y.: ②⑤ Zone 1.........	Baltimore(Note 3)......Md.	79 70 63	23M 30M (Note A)
			Washington(Note 4)....D.C.	81 73 63	23M 30M (Note A)
		②⑤ Zone 2........	Baltimore(Note 3)......Md.	81 72 65	23M 30M (Note A)
			Washington(Note 4)....D.C.	83 75 65	23M 30M (Note A)

(Concluded on next page)

Ⓛ - { Where the weight of a single shipment is in excess of the weight that can be transported in a single
vehicle (truck or trailer), the following provisions will govern:
  (1) The entire shipment must be available for receipt and movement by the carrier at one time and
      place on one bill of lading.
  (2) Rate will NOT apply on shipments requiring more than two vehicles. The excess over the quantity
      that can be loaded in two vehicles will be treated as a separate shipment.

Source: *Middle Atlantic Conference Tariff 41-A*, Washington, D.C.

Incentive Rates

The term "incentive rates" generally applies to a rate designed to induce the shipper to load existing movements and equipment more fully. These special rates usually apply only to weight or units loaded over and above the normally shipped quantities. For example, suppose an appliance manufacturer typically ships in carload quantities that only fill a car to 80 percent of its actual capacity. That is, the carload rate minimum is say, 40,000 pounds and the car is typically loaded to 48,000 pounds, but 60,000 pounds of appliances can physically be loaded into it. The carrier would prefer to have this car more fully loaded. In an incentive rate situation, the carrier would offer a rate lower than the carload rate that would only apply to the weight above the 48,000-pound norm in this example. It is more economical for the carrier to move more weight in existing moves than to make additional moves. By inducing the shipper to load each car more fully, fewer cars and moves would be required over the course of a year, and the same actual volume would be shipped.

Unit Train Rates

Unit trains are integrated movements between an origin and destination. These trains usually avoid terminals and so do not require intermediate switching or handling of individual cars. In many situations the shipper or consignee provides the car investment. The railroad experiences economies through high car utilization and reduced costs of movement, because the rates are low in comparison to individual moves. Again, it is more economical to handle larger single movements than many individual moves.

Per-car or Per-truckload Rates

Per-car or per-truckload rates are single charge rates for specific origin-destination moves regardless of shipment commodity or weight. These rates also apply to container movements where the carriers' costs of movement are dominated by moving the equipment and not specifically by the weight of the shipment.

Any Quantity Rates

Any Quantity (AQ) rates provide no discount or rate break for larger movements. That is, there exists an LTL rate but no TL rate for large shipments. The AQ rates apply to any weight in a shipment. They are usually found with large, bulky commodities such as boats, suitcases, and cages where there are no economies realized by the carrier for larger shipments.

Density Rates

Some rates are published according to density and shipment weight rather than by commodity or weight alone. These rates are common in air container shipments. Here, a rate is published as, say, $10 per cwt for shipments up to 10 pounds per cubic foot, $9 per cwt for 11 to 20 pounds per cubic foot, and $8 per cwt for 21 pounds per cubic foot and up. These are applied when the carrier assesses rates on the basis of weight but does not experience much lesser costs for lighter-weight containers. Here, in fact, the carrier would experience a loss of revenue (due to low weight) when moving a given amount of cubic footage.

Area, Location, or Route Rates

There are a number of rates that relate to areas, location, or routes. These special rates deserve consideration and discussion.

Local Rates

Local rates apply to any rate between two points served by the same carrier. These rates include full cost factors for pickup, documentation, rating, billing, and delivery.

Joint Rates

Joint rates are single rates published from a point on one carrier's route to another carrier's destination. They are usually lower in total charges than the combination of the local rates because of through movement economy.

Proportional Rates

Many carriers experience a competitive disadvantage when their line is part of a through line that competes with another, more direct line. If a combination of local rates was charged, the through movement cost might still be higher than the charges over the direct route. In this situation the carrier might publish a proportional rate (lower than the regular local rate) which applies only to through moves to certain destination points beyond its line.

Differential Rates

The term "differential rates" generally applies to a rate published by a carrier that faces a service time disadvantage compared to a faster carrier or mode. For example, water carriers often publish differential rates that are below those of railroads. In this way the lower rate somewhat overcomes the longer transit time disadvantage inherent to the water carriers. The term differential is also found in situations where an extra charge is assessed for high cost services such as branch lines.

Water-compelled Rates

The term "water-compelled rates" is used in the rail industry in the central part of the United States where railroads compete with barge carriers in basic commodity movements. The barge carriers enjoy lower operating costs which translate into lower rates. Railroads serving points along the Ohio, Mississippi, and Missouri rivers must then lower their rates in response to this competition.

Per-mile Rates

Some rail, motor, and air carriers provide rates which are based purely upon the mileage involved. This is a common practice in bulk chemical truck moves as well as air charter movements. Railroads also use these rates in special train movements (high, wide, and heavy). Similarly, special moves such as circus trains and some postal moves are based on these rates.

Terminal-to-Terminal Rates

Terminal-to-terminal rates, often referred to as ramp-to-ramp rates, apply between terminal points on the carrier's lines. These rates require the shipper and consignee to perform the traditional pickup and delivery function. Many air freight rates and some piggyback rates are found in this form.

**Blanket or
Group Rates**

Blanket or group rates apply to or from whole regions rather than points. For example, all shippers of lumber from an area in Oregon and Washington are generally treated as having the same origin. Destinations eastward are grouped into zones in which all receivers in an entire state might pay the same rates regardless of the special origin point in the Pacific Northwest. Blanket systems are found in food shipments from California and Florida. These rates equalize shippers and consignees, since specific plant location is not a factor in determining the rate charged.

**Time/Service
Rate Structures**

The Staggers Rail Act of 1980 specifically sanctioned rail contract rates, many of which can be classified as time/service rate structures. These rates are generally dependent upon the transit time performance of the railroad in a particular service. One such contract provides for a standard rate for a transit time service norm. The shipper pays a higher rate for faster service and a lower rate for longer service. Another contract calls for additional shipper payments to the carrier for fast return of empty back-haul shipper-leased cars. These rate forms either place incentives and penalities in areas where they tend to create desired results, or they reduce undesirable performance.

Contract Rates

Contract services are commonplace in motor carriage and in rail, as well as in water and in some air moves. These services are governed by contracts negotiated between the shipper and carrier, not by generally published tariffs. Some specific contract service features that are typically found are listed here.

■ volume rates

One basic contract calls for a reduced rate in exchange for a guarantee of a certain minimum tonnage to be shipped over a specified period. Another contract calls for a reduced rate in exchange for the shipper tendering a certain percentage of all tonnage over to the contracting carrier. In both these instances, a penalty is often enforced so that the shipper will pay up to what the regular rate should have been, if the minimum tonnage is not shipped.

■ rate by equipment
supplied

Another type of rail contract calls for the rate to be higher or lower depending upon the specific type of car supplied for loading and shipment. The higher rates apply on cars that avoid shipper bracing and blocking expenses. These are also the same cars which represent higher capital investment or daily per diem expense for the railroads.

■ car supply charges

A few contracts require the shipper to pay a monthly charge for the railroad which supplies certain special equipment for the shipper's exclusive use. This charge tends to increase the shipper's use of the cars; he no longer views them as free capital goods that can be used for temporary storage or loosely routed and controlled. Here, the shipper has the incentive to utilize these cars in a way that benefits himself as well as the carrier supplying them.

■ motor contract rates

Many different rate and service configurations are found in motor carriage. These contract services call for such things as scheduled service, special equipment movements, storage service in addition to movement, services beyond the vehicle such as retail store shelf stocking by the driver, small package pickup and movement, bulk commodity movement, or hauling of a shipper-owned trailer.

A great degree of flexibility surrounds the contract of both rail and motor carriage. Carriers and shippers are relatively free to specifically tailor contract services to particular movements, equipment, and time-related services. The key in any contract service is to identify the service and cost factors important to each party and to construct inducements and penalties for each.

Other Rate Structures

Several other rate forms are in use which serve particular cost or service purposes.

Corporate Volume Rates

A new rate form called the corporate volume rate came into existence in 1981. It is a discounted rate for each LTL shipment that is related to the total volume of LTL shipment that a firm ships via a specific carrier from all shipping points. Generally, the more volume a shipper tenders to a particular carrier, the greater the discount. One such rate, fostered by the General Electric Company with the many carriers it uses, provides for up to a 25 percent rate discount when volume by GE triples in any period over a base period.

Released Rates

Released rates are lower than the regular full value rates which provide for up to total value carrier compensation in the event of loss or damage. Instead, released rates only provide for carrier obligation up to certain limited dollar amounts per pound shipped. They are traditionally found in air freight, household goods, and a small number of motor and rail hauled commodities. During 1980, regulatory changes allowed flexible use of this rate form in most types of service and commodities.[2]

Empty Haul Rates

An empty haul rate is a charge for moving empty rail or motor equipment that is owned or leased by or assigned to a particular shipper. The existence of this type of rate tends to induce the shipper to fully load all miles of the equipment movements.

Two-way or Three-way Rates

The terms "two-way or three-way rates" apply to rates which are constructed and charged when back-haul or triangular moves can be made. The intent here is to tie a front-haul move with what would have been another firm's front-haul move. In this way, neither firm incurs the penalty for empty back-hauls. Some bulk chemical motor carriers offer these rates. They reduce total transportation charges for the shippers, and the carrier's equipment is more fully utilized than it would be otherwise.

■ new freedom

New regulatory standards legislated in 1980, as well as altered administrative ICC policies, have created a realm of flexibility and creativity in rate forms. Carriers are relatively free to develop rate systems to benefit them and shippers in ways that were not common in the past, nor even existent. The keys to any pricing system, however, are that it: induces the buyer to buy in ways beneficial to the seller, is simple to understand and apply, and maximizes the financial resources of the seller.

Rate Bureaus and Rate-Making

■ rate bureaus

Rate bureaus have traditionally played a major role in rate-making in the economy. These bureaus are organizations that act as collective rate-making forums and publishing agents for many member carriers. Nearly all railroads and a majority of the largest motor carriers belong to one or more of these organizations. Regulatory changes in the late 1970s and in the two regulatory acts of 1980 somewhat restructured the functions of these bodies, but they still serve useful, efficient purposes in rate-making and especially publishing.

■ power of attorney

The primary rate bureaus are the classification bureaus of the National Motor Freight Classification (NMFC) for motor carriers and the Uniform Freight Classification (UFC) for the railroads. These groups collectively establish the class ratings and uniform distance scales (rate base points and numbers) for these modes. Each member carrier provides the bureau with a power of attorney document which then enables the bureau to publish rates, ratings, or rules in its behalf. If a carrier wishes to withdraw from a bureau, it merely terminates the power of attorney.

There are several regional rate bureaus within each mode which publish class rate tables, exception rates, commodity rates, and rules for members within each group. Figures 13.1 to 13.11 show the geographic scope of these major groups.

■ rate bureau restrictions

Rate bureaus operate from the authority provided by the collective individual member carriers. Rate proposals are typically submitted to the bureaus for collective voting by the membership. Local railroad rates cannot be voted upon by the bureau, but such rates may be published in the bureau tariffs. The Staggers Rail Act of 1980 limits collective discussion and voting of joint rates to only those carriers that are direct connectors in such routings.[3] Motor carrier bureaus will likewise come under a similar restriction in 1984 when a provision of the Motor Carrier Act of 1980 takes effect. A further rate bureau limitation to be implemented by 1982 will be that rate bureaus will be restricted from voting upon general level increases. After that time, individual carriers will only be allowed to raise rates selectively on various commodities in response to overall cost increases.

■ advantages

Rate bureaus traditionally have had several pluses and minuses in their organization and functions. On the plus side, they provide a great degree of consistency or uniformity of rates and rules in a region. That is, changes come about after much analysis, discussion, and often public input. Since changes come about slowly, there is sufficient time for the public to react. Rate bureaus also enable the carriers to publish their rates with a great degree of printing economy. In a study conducted by Cavinato and Kogon in 1979, it was revealed that motor carrier tariff pages would possibly increase by a median factor of 2.49 times, with a possible high 1st/2nd quartile change of 6.47 times and a low 3rd/4th quartile change of 1.02 times.[4] A major increase in tariff pages would complicate the traffic management task.

Some drawbacks exist in rate bureaus, however. Rate bureaus have been criticized for tending to restrict rate innovations. They are also felt by some to protect low efficiency carriers and provide little incentive for efficient carriers to reduce rates. It must be noted, however, that any member carrier can exercise the right of independent action and publish a desired rate in the face of other member carrier opposition.

■ disadvantages

The lawful position of rate bureaus rests with the Reed-Bulwinkle Act of 1948 in which rate bureau collective rate-making activities are specifically exempted from antitrust laws. Through the years, many political efforts were made to repeal this exemption. As we enter the 1980s, rate bureaus still exist, though they are restricted by the above legislation and by policy actions of the middle 1970s which enhanced the protection of individual member independent actions.

■ antitrust immunity

Figure 13.1 Railroad Rate Territories

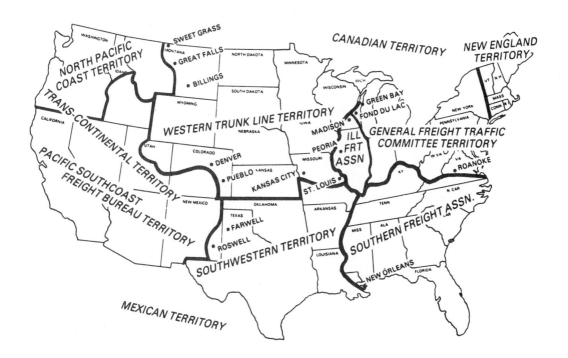

Figure 13.2   Middle Atlantic Conference

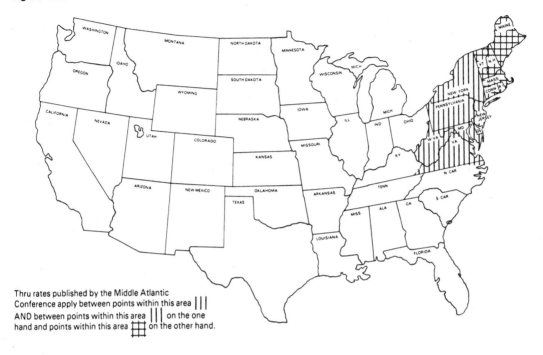

Thru rates published by the Middle Atlantic
Conference apply between points within this area | | |
AND between points within this area | | | on the one
hand and points within this area ⊞ on the other hand.

Figure 13.3   Rocky Mountain Motor Tariff Bureau

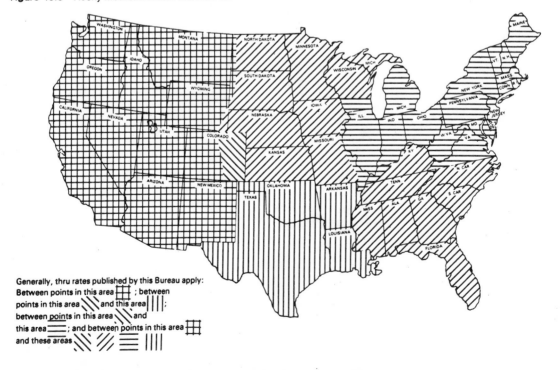

Generally, thru rates published by this Bureau apply:
Between points in this area ⊞ ; between
points in this area ╲╲╲ and this area | | | ;
between points in this area ╲╲ and
this area ≡ ; and between points in this area ⊞
and these areas ╲╲ ╱╱ ≡ | | |

Figure 13.4   Pacific Inland Tariff Bureau

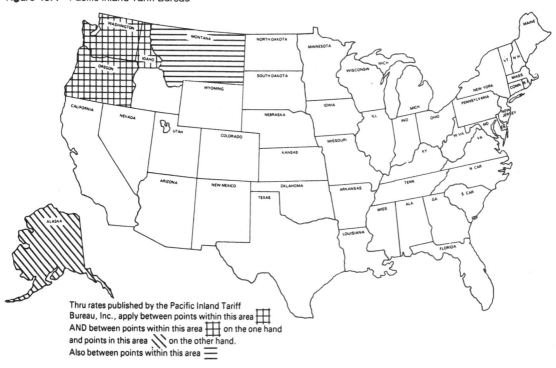

Thru rates published by the Pacific Inland Tariff
Bureau, Inc., apply between points within this area ⊞
AND between points within this area ⊞ on the one hand
and points in this area ⧅ on the other hand.
Also between points within this area ≡

Figure 13.5   Southern Motor Carriers Rate Conference

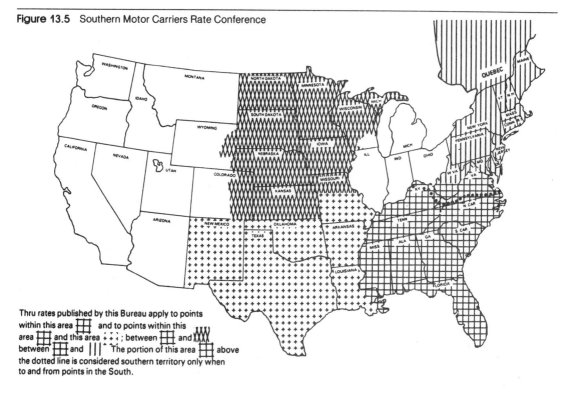

Thru rates published by this Bureau apply to points
within this area ⊞ and to points within this
area ⊞ and this area ⁺⁺⁺; between ⊞ and ⧓
between ⊞ and ‖‖‖ The portion of this area ⊞ above
the dotted line is considered southern territory only when
to and from points in the South.

Figure 13.6   The New England Motor Rate Bureau

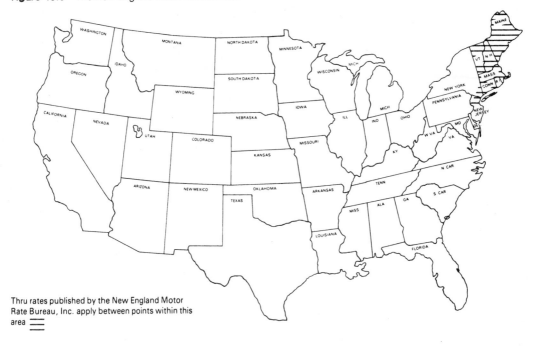

Thru rates published by the New England Motor
Rate Bureau, Inc. apply between points within this
area ═══

Figure 13.7   Central States Motor Freight Bureau

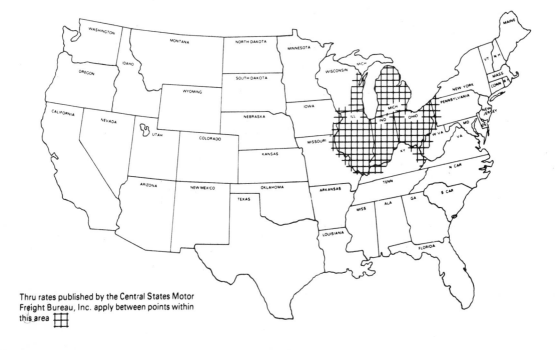

Thru rates published by the Central States Motor
Freight Bureau, Inc. apply between points within
this area ▦

Figure 13.8   Middlewest Motor Freight Bureau

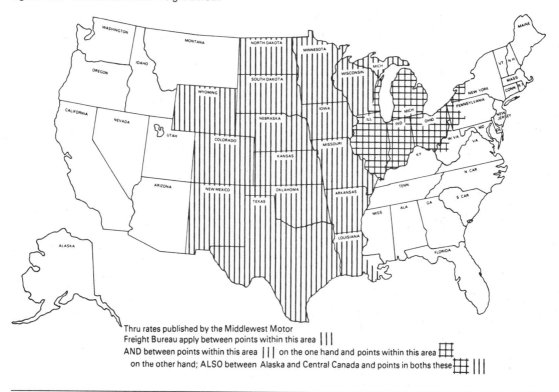

Thru rates published by the Middlewest Motor
Freight Bureau apply between points within this area ⦀
AND between points within this area ⦀ on the one hand and points within this area ⊞
on the other hand; ALSO between Alaska and Central Canada and points in boths these ⊞ ⦀

Figure 13.9   Central and Southern Motor Freight Tariff Association

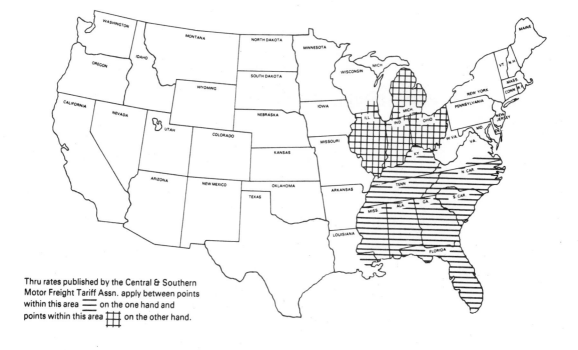

Thru rates published by the Central & Southern
Motor Freight Tariff Assn. apply between points
within this area ═ on the one hand and
points within this area ⊞ on the other hand.

Figure 13.10 Western Motor Tariff Bureau

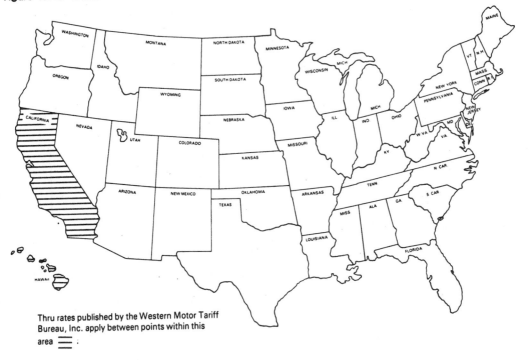

Thru rates published by the Western Motor Tariff
Bureau, Inc. apply between points within this
area ≡ .

Figure 13.11 The Eastern Central Motor Carriers Association

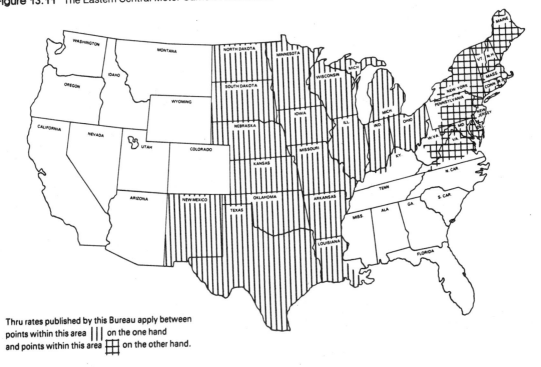

Thru rates published by this Bureau apply between
points within this area ||| on the one hand
and points within this area ⊞ on the other hand.

Rate Level Issues and Carrier Financial Health

The term "general rate levels" applies to the carrier and rate bureau practice of across the board rate increases. That is, all the carriers in a certain rate bureau might experience a common cost increase from, say, a new labor contract. In the past, the carriers would meet at the bureau and collectively establish how much the general level of rates on all traffic would have to rise to recover the cost impact and return the group of carriers to a target profitability level. Such an increase might compute to 4.7 percent, which would mean that the rates on all traffic (all commodities and routes by member carriers) in the region would be raised by this amount. General rate level making has also been called ex parte rate-making. It differs from the changes in specific rates which are called rate adjustments.

■ general rate levels

The 1980 regulatory and administrative policy changes have brought restrictions against this industry-wide form of general rate level making. It is said by many to be too aggregate in its approach because it ignores many of the value and cost-of-service principles that should be practiced in sound rate-making. Therefore, beginning in the early 1980s, general rate increases by rate bureaus of all member carriers will not be approved or allowed. Instead, each carrier will have to rely upon individual actions in the form of rate adjustments or independent general rate increases. The ICC intends rate increases to be accomplished by specific rate adjustments, rather than by across the board increases. Be that as it may, carrier pricing managers will have to be sharply in tune with their own firm's costs as well as the overall profit level that is reasonable or can be expected in order to translate these standards into proper rate adjustment actions.

■ restricted use

Motor Carrier Rate Levels

The traditional approach to motor carrier rate levels has been through the operating ratio which is the total operating expenses divided by total operating revenues. If a carrier has $1,500,000 in operating expenses and $1,600,000 in operating revenues, then its operating ratio would be .9375 or 93.75 percent. Or, stated another way, out of every revenue dollar, 93¾¢ goes to operating expenses with the remaining 6¼¢ for profit and debt charges.

■ operating ratios

The operating ratio was traditionally applied in motor carrier rate bureau actions. If the regulatory commission accepted 94.5 percent as an operating ratio norm, then general rate levels were adjusted by attaining that percentage after industry-wide cost increases. For example, if an agency allowed 94.5 percent and the carrier cost level increased to an expected yearly level of $1,600,000 (operating ratio of 100 percent), then the new revenue level that would bring it back down to 94.5 percent would be calculated as follows:

$$\text{Operating ratio} = \text{Operating expenses}/\text{Operating revenues}$$
$$.945 = \$1,600,000/\$?$$
$$\$? = \$1,600,000/.945$$
$$\$? = \$1,693,122$$

or an increase in rates to yield $93,122 more in total revenues.

Check: .945 = $1,600,000/$1,693,122

This would mean a general rate level increase of 5.82 percent.

■ shift in policy

The ICC shifted its stance on the acceptance of the operating ratio in 1978. It claimed that the ratio was not valid for several reasons, including the fact that financing sources and stockholders rarely looked at the operating ratio as a decision factor in lending funds or purchasing stock. The ICC stated that return on equity has greater validity as measuring a standard that the financial field uses in order to judge motor carrier industry health.

The return on equity (ROE) tool is used as follows:

$$ROE = \left(\frac{\text{Revenues—allowable expenses}}{\begin{array}{l}\text{Balance sheet value of preferred}\\\text{stock, common stock, paid in}\\\text{capital and retained earnings}\end{array}} \right)$$

In 1978, the ICC further stated that a sound return on equity for general commodity motor carriers is 14.6 percent. Using this standard, we can show how general rate level making would take place.

Revenues for carrier group ($000) $1,632,122
Allowable expenses reflecting new cost increases   1,700,000
Sum of carriers' preferred stock,   50,000
   retained eck, and paid in capital and   150,000
   retained earnings   500,000 $ 700,000

$$ROE = \frac{\$1,632,122 - 1,700,000}{\$700,000}$$

$$= -9.7\%$$

Since this would be below the target norm of 14.6 percent, the carrier group would use the same information in the following manner to determine the new rate level or total revenue requirement.

$$.146 = \frac{\text{Revenue} - \$1,700,000}{\$700,000}$$

Revenue = .146 ($700,000)+$1,700,000
Revenue = $102,200+$1,700,000
Revenue = $1,802,200

Revenue increase of $170,078 or about 10.4 percent.

That is, the traditional rate level system would cause the carrier to raise all rates by 10.4 percent to yield new revenues of $170,078 and a target return on equity of 14.6 percent.

Railroad Rate Levels

The basic general rate level approach to railroad pricing has been the return on asset (ROA) measure. Since railroads are capital intensive ven-

■ return on assets

tures with investments in track, equipment, terminals, and so on, the profitable utilization of invested asset dollars has evolved into an individual firm and industry measure.

The return on assets tool, in its basic form, is total profits divided by the book value of assets employed in the firm. The answer is a percentage that indicates how well that invested asset money is performing in the firm. It is a measure used by finance personnel to compare one railroad with another, or the industry as a whole with other capital intensive industries.

Specific calculation of the return on asset measure is performed as follows:

Purchase cost or value of asset	$60,000,000
– Accumulated depreciation	– 20,000,000
= Book value of assets	40,000,000
Revenues	$20,000,000
Expenses	17,600,000

$$\text{ROA} = \left(\frac{\text{Revenues} - \text{Expenses}}{\text{Book Value of Assets}} \right)$$

$$= \frac{20,000,000 - 17,600,000}{40,000,000}$$

$$= \frac{2,400,000}{40,000,000}$$

$$= .06 \text{ or } 6 \text{ percent}$$

In a general rate level situation, if the above railroad experienced a significant cost increase of $2,000,000 to a total of $19,600,000, then the new required revenue level is calculated as follows:

$$\left(\frac{\text{Revenue} - 19,600,000}{40,000,000} \right) = .06$$

$$\text{Revenue} - 19,600,000 = (.06)(40,000,000)$$

$$\text{Revenue} - 19,600,000 = 2,400,000$$

$$\text{Revenue} = \$22,000,000$$

The new revenue requirement is $22,000,000, or an increase of 10 percent from $20,000,000 to $22,000,000.

General Rate Level Summary

■ no full expense control

Regulatory and administrative policies have turned against industry wide rate level making because of several inherent problems with this overall pricing approach. Looked at in one way, this pricing approach does not fully lead to strict expense control. The industry as a whole could exercise loose cost control which would allow costs to climb. This would then give justification for higher rate levels and revenues in order to bring the profitability measure back in line with the desired norm. For this reason, the ICC and many state regulatory agencies could scrutinize accounting records to determine the validity or reasonableness of expenses. Some firms could practice excessive entertaining which would increase their overall expense level, and some expenses would not be allowed in the analysis (thus the term "allowable expenses" is often used in such cases).

■ pricing bias

Another criticism against rate bureau general rate level pricing is that when unprofitable and marginal carriers are aggregated to determine an industry-wide revenue requirement, the already profitable carriers stand to enjoy a greater profit from the rate increase. That is, the profitable carriers become more profitable and the marginal carriers are protected. There is, according to this argument, little incentive for rate-reducing competitive actions by the stronger carriers.

■ elasticities ignored

A final criticism of this system is that individual commodity or traffic segment elasticities tend to be ignored with this pricing approach. There has been some evidence of nearly whole commodity markets unexpectedly diverting away from railroads after new rate level increases have taken effect. This criticism has some foundation. It is the intent of regulatory policy-makers to induce individual rate adjustments through specific cost and market analysis of each form of traffic hauled. This change will no doubt call for greater employment and negotiation opportunities in carrier pricing as well as bring about a higher level of sophistication in this end of the business.

General rate level or ex parte pricing has long been an industry practice in rail and motor modes. Though the modes will be restricted from applying this concept to industry-wide rate changes in the future, individual carriers as well as investors and lenders will no doubt continue to use the operating ratio, return on equity, and return on asset measures to compare different carriers' profitability and to determine revenue requirements for target profit levels.

Rate Negotiations

■ negotiations common

Negotiations between shippers and carriers have long been a part of the transportation scene. With the new, flexible regulatory standards of the 1980s, rate negotiations will become more common than in the past. The traffic manager and carrier pricing manager are no longer constrained by collectively established rate bureau rates. Today, and in the future, carrier competition will require individual pricing managers to adopt entrepreneurial approaches to pricing. More direct contact is beginning to take place between carrier pricing managers and those responsible for shippers' routings.

■ negotiation objective

The objective of any good negotiation process is for both sides to experience, or at least to perceive, a gain. For the shipper, who is usually the party initiating the negotiation, it means lower per pound or per unit transportation costs which may or may not result in lower product sales prices. Other negotiation objectives are faster transit time service or more or improved forms of equipment supply. The carrier's objective

■ contribution margin

should be a higher contribution margin on the traffic involved. This contribution margin is measured as the surplus remaining from total revenues after direct variable expenses have been deducted. The contribution margin is a reliable, usually easily traceable, measure that is not complicated with the overhead allocations that can often mask the inherent profitability of the examined traffic segment. The key for both the carrier and shipper, however, is to carefully attempt to define the elasticity of the relationship between them and the other party.

From the carrier's standpoint, the essence of rate negotiation is the contribution margin. Assume, for example, that the carrier now charges $850 per load and this rate attracts 1,500 loads per year which cost $400 each in directly traceable variable costs. This present situation is summarized as follows:

Rate/charge: $850 × 1,500 loads	= $1,275,000
Variable costs: $400 × 1,500 loads	= (600,000)
Contribution margin	$ 675,000

Examples of an undesirable negotiation from the carrier's standpoint would be a lower rate not resulting in additional loads, or an insufficient number of additional loads (needed to increase the contribution margin). An illustration of this could be:

Rate/charge: $800 × 1,625 loads	= $1,300,000
Variable costs: $400 × 1,625	= (650,000)
Contribution margin	= $ 650,000

The carrier's contribution to overhead and profit actually decreased by $25,000, even though total revenues increased as did the number of loads. Only the shipper gains in this situation.

An example of a successful negotiation from both the shipper and carrier standpoints can be seen in the following diagram.

Rate/charges: $750 × 2,000 loads	= $1,500,000
Variable costs: $400 × 2,000	= (800,000)
Contribution margin	$ 700,000

In this situation the shipper's transportation costs are lower, and the additional loads moved at that rate bring a sufficient number of additional loads to increase the contribution of the carrier to $700,000.

■ competitive situations

While the key for the carrier is to gain a greater contribution margin, competitive situations between carriers often are such that the carrier is faced with reducing its rate or losing the traffic segment altogether. In this situation a lower contribution margin is a necessary alternative unless equipment and manpower can be more profitably utilized in other traffic.

Table 13.6 is a rough guide to rate negotiations. The pricing manager must know the variable costs of each traffic segment accurately as well as have a relatively good feel for the pro rata share of fixed costs and overhead costs apportioned to each segment. This latter cost is referred to as a fully allocated cost, determined as follows:

$$\text{Fully allocated cost} = (\text{Variable cost per unit}) + \left(\frac{\text{Total fixed costs}}{\text{\# of loads in system}} \right)$$

Situations that can and do exist in the relationship between the rate charged and the variable and fully allocated costs are analyzed in the table. At the very worst, traffic should not be carried below variable costs, and at the very best, equipment and resources should be applied to traffic yielding at least fully allocated costs or higher levels.

■ perspectives

Several perspectives must be considered in the rate negotiation process. First, a successful negotiation is one in which both parties gain from the event. Unless that is accomplished, the "nonwinning party" might possibly back away from commitments made in the process. Further, a party not gaining from a negotiation will view it as wasted effort with little or no positive return for that firm.

■ other outcomes

Another point is that a lower rate is not always a necessary outcome of

Table 13.6 Operating and Investing Guide in Pricing Situations

Price in Relation to Fully Allocated Cost	Operating and Investing Decisions
Rate below variable cost	Do not handle traffic unless it is filling in empty backhaul of traffic that is paying for entire round trip. Backhaul revenue must still exceed additional costs of backhaul costs incurred. If traffic is fronthaul, terminate it or raise rates to compensatory level.
Rate at variable cost	Same points as above. Attempt to shift equipment to other traffic segments.
Rate above variable cost but below full cost	Traffic results in positive contribution margin within life of the assets involved. Will not result in positive rate of return analysis upon end of useful life and replacement analysis of same assets.
Rate at fully allocated cost	Same as rate above variable cost but below full cost. In inflationary times, such a rate will still result in negative rate of return because of higher capital cost of replacement assets.
Rate above fully allocated cost	Best situation. Problem of only shifting assets to other segments with higher profit.

rate-related negotiations. Though rate personnel are usually involved in negotiations, other outcomes than a reduced rate level may occur. Carriers might offer better equipment which will eliminate many shipment preparation costs, or a better car supply altogether. Still other outcomes might be more reliable transit times or faster ones which reduce the shipper's total costs of transportation.

■ knowledge of own costs

A major key to sound rate negotiation is that the carrier know its own costs of carriage, including the costs of labor, fuel, equipment, capital, and movement. Having this information on hand is a plus, because without it the negotiator might consent to a rate below his firm's true costs of carriage.

■ knowledge of shipper

Another crucial rate negotiation factor for carrier personnel is to be as knowledgeable as possible about the shipper's transportation costs, network, and available transportation options including other modes or market choices. Carrier negotiators should also be knowledgeable about the overall market structure and situation of the commodity involved. Without this knowledge, the negotiators could be bluffed into concessions that are not necessary. In many situations, this blind spot has led many carriers to assume that the market in negotiations is highly elastic when it might in all actuality be relatively inelastic.

■ derived demand

A further point about negotiations is to keep in mind that transportation service faces a derived demand situation. The carrier should not reduce a rate unless the additional volume will yield a greater contribution margin. When speaking in terms of more actual loads, the shipper should guarantee that additional volume. In many markets, however, the transportation cost element of the shipper's total landed product cost is not sufficiently great for a rate reduction to cause more product sales. Again, this situation is different when the carrier faces the prospect of no future traffic at all unless the negotiation results in the shipper's wishes.

■ other actions

There are two corollary points which thread through these considerations. One is that shippers must be mindful of their market clout with carriers. There have been instances in which continued shipper demands for rate reductions have eventually caused a railroad to seek abandonment of the line, or a carrier to drop service to the shipper entirely. In this instance, the shipper's negotiating strength reached an extreme limit. There is a problem when the carrier does not know its own costs and thus becomes a "nonwinner" in negotiations. The second corollary point is that the carrier should know when to walk away from traffic under question. This is becoming easier as common carrier obligations are changing and carriers have greater freedom in traffic selection.

Conclusion

■ innovative rates

Rate negotiations in the 1980s will no doubt be termed innovative. Relaxed legislative and administrative regulatory standards now permit rate and service configurations that previously would have met legal obstacles. The fast paced advent of rail contract rates is evidence of this. Rates will continue to be the subject of future negotiations, but services, obligations, and equipment will probably play a greater role. The key to rate negotiation is that a rate or service configuration provide the proper economic incentives while reflecting the costing structure of the given situation.

The present and future rate scene calls for a greater costing and pricing expertise than in the past. No longer can carriers maintain a follow-the-leader stance, even when involved in rate bureaus. Specific costs are a key to carrier survival.

Finally, carrier pricing managers will become more entrepreneurial. In past decades many carrier pricing personnel could perform their daily duties with little face-to-face interaction with their shipper-client traffic managers. Today, and in the future, the job necessitates being closer to the carrier-shipper transaction and maintaining a flexible posture within the overall market place. Deregulation will call for closer ties between carrier pricing managers, sales forces, and company customers.

■ entrepreneurial posture

Study Questions

1. Distinguish between a tariff and a rate.

2. Define the following: a) class rating
   b) rate base number (RBN)
   c) rate table
   d) exceptions rating
   e) commodity rate

3. How are less-than-truckload shipments different than truckload shipments?

4. How are multiple car rates different than incentive rates? What is the justification for each?

5. What reasoning exists for charging according to the type of equipment supplied or charging less because the shipper provides the equipment for carriage?

6. Why are two-way and three-way rates economical for many shipments of bulk commodities?

7. What are the pro and con arguments for rate bureaus?

8. In the possible absence of rate bureaus, how will rate information be accessible?

9. How are operating ratio and return on equity rate level making different? Why did the ICC switch from using one to another?

10. What key elements are in a good rate negotiation?

11. Among many proposals for tariff simplification, it has been suggested that the classification or commodity rating should be in strict accordance with product density and no other factor. Identify and explain the merits or shortcomings of this suggestion. (AST&T, Spring 1975, Exam #1.)

12. Section 12 of the Motor Carrier Act of 1980 encourages the use of "released rates" (or released value rates). What is a released rate? What

effect will the use of released rates have on the firm's logistics costs? (AST&T, Fall 1980, Exam #2.)

13. Name three possible advantages and three disadvantages for shippers entering into rail contract rates. (AST&T, Fall 1980, Exam #2.)

Notes

1. This material is based upon: Coyle, John J., and Bardi, Edward J., *The Management of Business Logistics*, second edition (St. Paul: West, 1980), pp. 237-46.

2. Motor Carrier Act of 1980, sec. 12. Staggers Rail Act of 1980, Pub. L#. 96-448, sec. 211.

3. Staggers Rail Act of 1980, U.S. Code, vol. 49, sec. 10706.

4. Joseph L. Cavinato and Gary B. Kogon, "An Assessment of the Impacts From Full or Partial Repeal of Section 10706 (Antitrust Immunity) Upon the Motor Carrier Industry and its Users," *ICC Practitioners Journal* 47, pt. 4, 1980.

Suggested Readings

Colton, Richard S., et al. *Industrial Traffic Management*. 5th ed. Washington, D.C.: The Traffic Service Corporation, 1973, chap. 3.

Davis, Grant M., and Brown, Stephen W. *Logistics Management*. Lexington, Mass.: D. C. Heath and Co., 1974.

Fair, Marvin L., and Williams, Ernest W. *Economics of Transportation and Logistics*. Plano, Tex.: Business Publications, 1975, chap. 17.

Flood, Kenneth V. *Traffic Management*. 3rd ed. Dubuque, Iowa: William D. Brown Company Publishers, 1975, chaps. 4, 5.

Harper, Donald V. *Transportation in America: Users, Carriers, Government*. Englewood Cliffs, N.J.: Prentice-Hall, 1978, chap. 9.

Locklin, D. Philip. *Economics of Transportation*. 7th ed. Homewood, Ill.: Richard D. Irwin, 1972, chaps. 3, 8.

McElhiney, Paul T. *Transportation for Marketing and Business Students*. Totowa, N.J.: Littlefield, Adams, 1975, chap. 10.

Pegrum, Dudley F. *Transportation: Economics and Public Policy*. Homewood, Ill.: Richard D. Irwin, 1973, chaps. 9, 10.

Rakowski, James P. "Innovative Ratemaking and Railway Efficiency." *The Logistics and Transportation Review* 9 (1973).

Taff, Charles A. *Management of Physical Distribution and Transportation*. 6th ed. Homewood, Ill.: Richard D. Irwin, 1978, chaps. 14, 15, 16.

| Case | Intercity Rate Conference |

Intercity Rate Conference

Three motor carriers belong to a small rate bureau in the mid-Atlantic region. They each operate in the same general markets. In late 1977, the bureau filed a revised tariff for the group to reflect increased costs of operations. The increase was approved by the ICC which held that a group operating ratio of 94.3 percent is adequate. Key financial data for each carrier and the group as a whole is presented below as it appeared in the rate increase application.

			$000's	
Categories	Carrier 1	Carrier 2	Carrier 3	Group
Revenues	$1,000,000	$100,000	$500,000	$1,600,000
Operating expenses	(980,000)	(85,000)	(485,000)	(1,550,000)
Other revenues & costs	(20,000)	10,000	10,000	0
Net before taxes	0	25,000	25,000	50,000
Taxes	0	(10,000)	(12,000)	(22,000)
Net after taxes	$ 0	$ 15,000	$ 13,000	$ 28,000
Total assets	$ 210,000	$ 20,000	$ 95,000	$ 325,000
Current liabilities	$ 50,000	$ 2,000	$ 45,000	$ 97,000
Long term debt	100,000	9,000	0	109,000
Stock	50,000	3,000	40,000	93,000
Retained earnings	10,000	6,000	10,000	26,000

Analyze this situation. Specifically, what are each firm's and the total group's operating ratios, return on assets, return on equities, and any other key financial indicators? Was the increase justified for all three firms?

14 Traffic Management

After reading this chapter you should:

1 Understand the general nature of the traffic management function.

2 Be able to discuss the line responsibilities of a traffic manager.

3 Understand the staff responsibilities of a traffic manager.

4 Be able to discuss the future directions of traffic management.

Traffic management is the traditional term for the task of obtaining and controlling transportation services for shippers or consignees or both. It is a term applied to a position or an entire department in almost any extractive, raw material, manufacturing, assembling, or distribution firm. The study of transportation economics, including carriage supply and pricing, cannot be complete without an analysis of those activities employed to acquire, use, and pay for transportation freight services. While transportation represents approximately 20 percent of the gross national product (GNP), freight movement alone is about 45 percent of that, or 9 percent of the GNP. The traffic manager and his/her firms are *the* consumers of freight transportation services.

Traffic has traditionally held a low-status position in the firm. Since the 1950s, however, it has risen in corporate stature to a position that commands a large part of total corporate expenditures. In many firms it is the core of a physical distribution department. Transportation in the firm exists in close trade-off relationships with purchasing, warehousing, inventory control, packaging, production scheduling, and marketing. As such, traffic management requires close coordination with these other departments, both with counterpart departments in other firms as well as with carrier firms.

■ chapter overview

What Is Traffic Management?

Traffic management is a special form of procurement which entails both line and staff activities. It is a field that has grown in both importance and corporate recognition in the past few years. However, it is a field that is currently undergoing a tremendous degree of flux as a result of changes in the regulations applying to and affecting transportation.

Traffic Management as a Procurement Function
■ procurement and purchasing

Traffic management is very much a special form of procurement and purchasing. Procurement is a term that applies to a wide range of activities that basically consist of obtaining goods for the firm. Procurement includes analysis and activities in the areas of (1) quality, (2) pricing, (3) specifications, (4) supply source, (5) negotiations, (6) inspection and assurance of quality, (7) timing, (8) creative value analysis of alternative methods and sources, (9) capital analysis, (10) make or buy decisions, (11) legal and regulatory constraints, and (12) general management. All of these factors provide the firm with a system to obtain the physical goods and special services it requires.

The actual goal or mission of purchasing can be the optimization of one factor or a blend of several similar to the objective employed in many purchasing departments. Here, the purchasing personnel are guided by what is called the "balancing value" objective which is: optimum quality, lowest final cost to the firm, and assurance of long-term supply.

■ balanced value objectives

Traffic management performs all of these specific activities in its acquisition and control of transportation *services* for the firm. Traditionally, a minimum transportation goal was employed for this function. In most firms, this was replaced by a goal of minimum total distribution expense. Today, many first establish a customer service goal, then evaluate traffic and distribution in terms of minimized total distribution costs while attaining the service goal. This, in a way, is similar to the balanced value approach.

■ transport goals

Line and Staff Functions

■ line functions

Originally, traffic management was a clerical activity devoted to shipping or receiving the firm's goods. Today, it entails a range of line functions that are often specialized and require communications and data systems. Traffic managers must observe field trends, evaluate potential procedural and system changes, plan for the implementation of appropriate changes, and propose some of these changes to top management. The full range of general management activities is now found in traffic departments.

Growth of the Traffic Function

■ expansion of function

The traffic function has grown in several respects. First, the total cost of freight has come under close scrutiny as one of the firm's prime costs requiring major control efforts. That is, the magnitude of absolute freight expenditures by many firms rises to a point where it becomes desirable to pay close attention to it by management processes rather than by rote clerical procedures. Second, the range of transportation choices available to the firm makes it necessary to have personnel who can evaluate all choices and select the best one(s) in each particular situation. At the end of World War II, there were only about two dozen transportation service, equipment, and price options available (including rail, motor, and express); today there are almost one hundred available options. Further, firms recognize today that traffic is one of the keys to corporate marketing strategy and internal productivity. All these factors have contributed to the growth in the status and recognition of the traffic function within the firm.

Regulatory Change

■ changes in environment adaptation

Traffic is a field that has largely been guided by legislative and administrative regulations, and these constraints have required the traffic manager to have a highly technical background. The current state of regulations is changing so that many of these past rules are being altered, reduced, or eliminated. Traffic management will have to develop a flexible posture and stand ready to adapt to change as its environment shifts and new opportunities are presented. These changes will pervade every line and staff activity in traffic management, where in the past a large part of traffic consisted of *price* management by way of tariff analysis. In the future the traffic manager will be more involved with *cost* analysis and management.

Line Aspects of Traffic Management

The daily activities of traffic management are numerous. While observation of a traffic office might not reveal its "system," there is a line process at work. Figure 14.1 illustrates this process.

Shipment Planning

■ coordinated schedules

Traffic management continually monitors inbound and outbound shipping schedules which should be coordinated with purchasing and distribution or production. A key task here is to maintain a continuous flow of product by not hindering it with the unavailability of transportation, that is, no equipment or service. Further, physical loading and unloading must be planned according to the efficient use of docks and labor. Management must ensure that transportation is not scheduled too early or in excess of actual needs, because dock and track congestion and equipment detention and demurrage charges will result.

Carrier Selection

■ selection process

This task involves selecting the actual carrier that will move the shipment. In rail contexts, this might be largely confined to the carrier that has a siding into the plant. But even here, the traffic manager has wide latitude in enroute selection through use of intermediate or alternative route carriers. This is the case even if the plant-serving carrier also reaches the destination point. In motor carrier firms, traffic managers will initially often give shipment preference to the firm's own private carriage vehicles, or use a contract carrier before considering common

Figure 14.1 The Line Process of Traffic Management

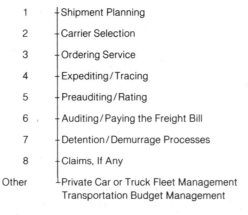

1	Shipment Planning
2	Carrier Selection
3	Ordering Service
4	Expediting / Tracing
5	Preauditing / Rating
6	Auditing / Paying the Freight Bill
7	Detention / Demurrage Processes
8	Claims, If Any
Other	Private Car or Truck Fleet Management Transportation Budget Management

carriers. Within both rail or motor selection, traffic managers evaluate a number of factors. The most commonly cited factors are listed here.

Length of Transit Time. Speed of origin to destination is often a key selection factor that favors direct single line over joint carrier movements and seeks to avoid major congested terminals. In some instances, slow transit time is sought when neither the shipper nor consignee wish to physically hold the goods in inventory. In this instance, the transportation vehicle is acting as a rolling warehouse in which the goods in transit are not incurring warehouse storage charges.

Consistency in Transit Time. Some movements require consistent delivery that both the shipper and consignee can predict and expect. This is a crucial factor for tightly scheduled assembly operations, or situations in which the consignee wishes to hold little inventory until actually needed in production. The consistency factor often causes some traffic managers to prefer either slower carriers, or more expensive ones that are highly reliable, rather than faster carriers that attain transit time with fewer percentages of shipments.

Rates. This is a major selection factor. Many firms, however, will select a carrier that does not offer the lowest possible rate, choosing to select a carrier on the basis of total logistics costs, including transportation.

Availability of Equipment. When transportation service or equipment is difficult to obtain, shippers often select carriers on the basis of their ability to supply equipment for shipment. With specialized rail equipment, a shipper often specifically routes shipments over each road in approximate proportion to the number of specialized cars that each carrier provides for that shipper's use.

Loss and Damage Factors. The relative incidence of loss and damage and the ensuing promptness and percentage of claim settlement often play a role in carrier selection. Loss and damage is a negative factor that represents lost cash opportunity and additional shipper costs. While low loss and damage experience with a carrier is rarely a major selection factor, poor experience with a particular carrier will often lead to its rejection in the future.

Reciprocity. Shippers will often use particular carriers because those transportation firms purchase the shipping firm's goods. This is often the case with equipment purchases and other capital goods.

Cooperation. This is an intangible and often psychological factor that can become the key selection factor when most or all of the above are roughly equal. Under the general heading of cooperation are such attributes as competence of the salesperson; ease of shipment tracing; availability of information about the carrier, its services. and equipment; and willingness to negotiate rates and service improvements.

Ordering Service

This task involves contacting a railroad car distributor who will arrange empty car delivery or making a call to a trucking firm's local dispatcher.

In both instances the carrier personnel will need to be informed of the shipper's name and pickup point, weight and sometimes cube measurement of the shipment, commodity, and destination. Upon vehicle arrival, steps to specifically load the equipment are initiated. These steps are often based upon plans established in the first step (shipment planning). They include crew assignment, loading arrangement, bracing, dunnage, documentation, and any other special needs.

Expediting/Tracing

These activities consist of keeping track of shipment progress and alerting the carrier of any enroute changes that might be necessary. Some shippers have direct computer links with carrier shipment systems. These provide daily position reports of all the shipper's rail cars or shipments. Expediting/Tracing is a valuable control tool for the shipper or consignee because they can plan production and assembly around shipment progress or problem.

Preauditing/Rating

Preauditing is the process of determining what the proper freight charges for a shipment should be. Often shippers preaudit shipments prior to billing by the carrier so that freight bill errors in the forms of overcharges and undercharges can be reduced or avoided.

Auditing/Paying the Freight Bill

Auditing entails checking the accuracy of the freight bill after it is presented by the carrier or after it has been paid. Some firms do this in-house, while others hire outside consultants to perform this job after the bill has actually been paid. The traffic department generally confirms the freight bill and passes it along to the office responsible for payment.

Detention/ Demurrage Processes

Detention is a charge assessed by a motor carrier against a shipper or consignee for keeping equipment for loading or unloading beyond a period specified. Demurrage is the same concept in the rail industry. The traffic manager is usually responsible for monitoring, managing, and paying for detention and demurrage obligations. He must trade-off the loading, unloading, and personnel costs against the cost of holding carrier equipment.

Claims

Loss and damage sometimes occur to shipments while in the possession of carriers. Shippers or consignees will then file claims to recoup part or all of these damaged amounts. Overcharges found on the freight bills are also taken care of by traffic managers.

Private Car and Truck Fleet Management

In some firms, the traffic manager is also responsible for private rail car and truck fleet management. This entails coordination and control tasks with the goal of minimizing fleet costs and providing quality service.

Transportation Budget Management

The transportation budget is the major overriding financial control mechanism in all these tasks. The traffic manager must keep track of current and future activities and expenditures and relate them to the original plan. Energy cost escalators have created major problems for most traffic managers who attempt to operate within planned budgets. Escalation will no doubt continue to be a complicating cost and budget problem in the future.

Staff and Administrative Aspects of Traffic Management	Traffic management has grown over the years to become more than a mere line activity. Many planning tasks or staff activities have developed as support functions. These other activities serve to increase the cost efficiency or customer service capability of the above line activities.
Mode Selection	The traffic manager selects the mode for specific classes of shipments or products, market areas, or for each plant or warehouse. Each mode offers specific inherent service and cost advantages. Usually, the selection process is made infrequently so that routing and carrier selection personnel can operate within the modal choice.
Service/Supply Assurance	The 1970s brought several periods of carrier supply disruption due to fuel cost and supply problems. As a reaction to those events, many firms have prepared for such future occurrences by planning for alternative and backup forms of transportation. This is a contingency type of management that heretofore was not necessary, nor was it employed until recent times.
Rate Negotiations	This activity is increasing in importance because of regulatory changes that came about in the late 1970s through the motor and rail legislation which allow greater price flexibility. Rate negotiations are a commonplace activity now that adherence to the published rate bureau tariff rate is not viewed as a fixed standard. Negotiations require a large degree of preparation and analysis and proper approach and conduct. A strong negotiation which attains a rate that the carrier eventually finds unremunerative and incapable of serving effectively is to be avoided. In this instance both the shipper and the carrier lose.
Service Negotiations	Rail and motor contract services are increasing in use, and many negotiations take place for specific services rather than lower rates. These include specific car supply or transit time performance. Here, too, a sound analysis and approach is necessary.
Regulatory Matters	Traffic managers and staffs are usually involved in routine regulatory processes before the Interstate Commerce Commission (ICC) and other federal and state agencies. These regulatory processes include rate protests, shipper support for permanent common or contract authority, rail abandonment petitions, or temporary authority applications. Many firms employ specialists in this area who are licensed to practice before the ICC, either lawyers or practitioners who have passed the qualifying examination administered by the ICC.

Policy Matters

Traffic managers will often become involved in presenting their firms' policy positions in proposed legislative or ICC administrative regulation proceedings. These policy areas relate to carrier credit regulations, rail rate regulation standards, exempt transportation, or any other proposed change in the field. When involved in these areas, the traffic manager will conduct analyses, prepare position statements, be active in industry associations representing the firm, and often submit testimony on the firm's behalf.

Planning Annual Transportation Requirements

Another staff-related task is interpretating the firm's purchasing, production, and marketing plans for future periods and translating the plans into specific shopping needs. These needs represent the specific type of equipment needed and the quantities and timing of its use. The automobile manufacturers must often work with railroads several years in advance so that rail cars exist when new automobile models of specific sizes and shapes roll off assembly lines. In shorter term contexts, this planning often entails leasing rail equipment, arranging for contract carriage, or merely determining whether the existing carriers will be capable of handling the forecasted shipments.

Budgeting

Traffic managers play the key role in establishing transportation budgets for future periods. The budget is usually constructed by integrating volumes, expected modal mixes, specific shipping patterns, and expected inflationary impacts.

Capital Budgeting

This activity is presented in detail in Chapter 19, Financing Private and Public Transportation Systems. Capital budgeting is the entire process of analyzing the technical and financial feasibility of proposed major asset acquisitions such as private fleets, rail cars, new docks, expanded rail sidings, computer systems, or warehouse and dock space. It is an engineering and cost-oriented activity that brings the traffic manager into contact with engineering and finance personnel as well as top management.

Information Systems

The astute traffic manager will always seek ways to capture and report information relating to the services attained and to individual manager performance. Many firms monitor and report cost and transit time performance for all movements, including the private fleet. Cost recoveries and claims progress is another information area of interest. In all, efficient performance evaluation and decision-making information systems are a prime necessity in the system. The traffic manager can make recommendations about the design of these systems.

Systems Analysis

The combinations of transportation services and rates offered by carriers number in the hundreds. There is, too, no one best way of always transporting a firm's goods. Where motor might be a proper choice in normal periods, air freight might be necessary occasionally. What is a good choice one day might be a poor one the next. Within traffic management, continuous analyses must take place in order to put together the best service and total cost configuration.

On a higher plane, traffic management must be integrated within the overall materials management and distribution scheme of the firm. In this context, traffic management is often forced to make suboptimized decisions in light of overriding system factors for the total cost and service pattern of the firm.

Management and Executive Development

Traffic and transportation are changing at a fast pace, in a manner not experienced in recent times. It is imperative that all personnel keep track of changes in the field, analyze them, and provide for positive action by the firm. They must also update their personal technical knowledge and management skills in light of future needs. Development of the self is accomplished by being widely read in all aspects of transportation and management, keeping in contact with others through professional associations, taking advantage of educational opportunities, as well as being able to gain overall perspectives on how a present task and position fit into an overall business strategy scheme.

Traffic Management Perspectives

The traffic management decision process requires two distinct systems views in daily as well as yearly planning activities. The first pertains to daily transportation selection decisions. This systems view entails weighing the lowest or most reasonable cost alternative carrier or service. The second view relates to examining the available manpower within the traffic department and assigning these resources in the most advantageous manner.

Total Cost of Transportation

Traffic managers need to know the lowest cost transportation alternative. Careful analysis indicates that the total cost of transportation is much more than the actual rate or freight charge. Selection of an alternative on the basis of rate alone might lead to an improper choice. A view of all costs of transportation is necessary.

Rate. The rate (total charges) is a major part of the total cost of transportation. This rate might be available only when using certain forms of equipment, over fast or slow routes, or via certain carriers.

Access. Another major cost is access or pickup and delivery. A rate might be applicable only on ramp-to-ramp or terminal-to-terminal bases. In another context, a shipper or consignee might only be able to use the rail transport mode by moving the goods by company truck to a car spotted on a public team track. This double handling requires many man and vehicle hours. Several piggyback movement plans require shipper or consignee pickup and delivery, the costs of which must be added to the rate for service.

Packaging. This cost factor relates to the type and cost of packaging. For example, a piece of machinery moving by rail and ocean carrier requires heavy wood crating, which means money spent for lumber and man-power. When moving by air, however, the same piece might only require a heavy pallet, a plastic sheet, and some banding.

Bracing/Dunnage. Another cost is that of protecting the goods from movement and damage within the transportation vehicle. This might require lumber, pallets, inflatable bulkheads, or special rail or truck equipment supplied with racks, bulkheads, and crossbars.

Insurance. This cost element is important with high-valued goods that the firm insures while in-transit. The insurance might be for total value, or only for a portion in excess of what is generally believed to be a maximum amount that carriers would pay in loss and damage situations. This is the case with released value rates which are lower than regular rates in that released rates obligate the carrier to pay less than the full value of the goods.

Loss and Damage Experience. The normal amount of loss and damage typically experienced in the use of one mode versus another is a critical factor. This information should be known in terms of actual dollar amounts, as well as in the context of percentage of loss in relation to the entire amount transported. Another point that must be considered here is the amount of loss and damage pay-back from each carrier. Though a carrier might experience less loss and damage, its pay-back settlements might be less, making it more costly in total terms over another carrier that damages more but fully settles its claims. Still another element to be considered here is the length of time each carrier takes to settle its claims. A carrier taking a long time to settle a claim in full is harming the claimant to the extent of the lost cash opportunity of the amount of settlement. If a firm's money is worth 10 percent a year, and a carrier takes six months to settle a $6,000 claim, this represents a lost cash cost of $300 to the claimant who may have already purchased a replacement item.

Speed. Total origin to destination transit time is another cost element that must be considered in this analysis. The longer a shipment takes to get to a destination, the longer it will generally take for the shipper to be paid by the consignee. This, too, is a lost cash opportunity cost. Similarly, the cost of production line downtime due to unavailability of a part might be so high as to make a chartered airplane cost of shipment appear low in relation to the downtime penalty.

All of these factors must be analyzed so that the traffic management function costs can be specifically known and managed properly. These costs provide the basic input to judicious management of the entire corporate distribution or procurement system. In many instances the traffic department will actively choose higher total traffic cost alternatives in order to satisfy overriding customer service goals, or to attain corporate-wide minimized total costs. In these situations, the traffic manager should know the department's costs so that requests for using the higher cost alternative can be properly evaluated in light of the budgetary benefits attained elsewhere in the firm.

Traffic Department Human Resources Management

Another major area of managerial analysis that traffic managers are concerned with is the utilization of manpower within the department. Typically, a key area of discretion for the traffic manager lies with the assignment of rate and analytical personnel to either preauditing and postauditing of freight bills, or to creative analytical projects that seek varied transportation and distribution methods. These decisions are being forced in many firms because many departments are required to show a profit or return to the company from employee wage dollars spent. In this regard, traffic managers must often determine whether manpower hours will return more for the firm if allocated to auditing freight bills or to new transportation process analysis. Since freight bills can be audited by outside auditing firms (the fees of which are based upon a percentage of the overcharges recovered), these manpower hours can often more productively be applied in the transportation analysis area.

Conclusion

Traffic management will continue to grow in importance in the firm. In many firms the costs of transportation climbed at a higher percentage than overall purchase or production costs since 1975. This causes a recognition of the need to find creative ways to supply adequate transportation at reasonable costs in the future. Much of this recognition is coming from top management, which has traditionally regarded transportation as a relatively minor cost and activity in the firm. Attention is now being paid to transportation as a significant cost and strategy factor in the overall corporate scheme.

This trend, along with regulatory changes, now places the traffic manager in a different light. Top management expectations are high for finding new ways of moving the firm's goods. Regulatory changes have shifted thinking from that of how to comply with traditional laws and administrative rules to that of either protecting the firm's transportation supply in the future, or of how to best take advantage of new service and price flexibilities.

Traffic management will continue to develop. New forms of carriage with different rate and service configurations are developing. The traffic manager will have to keep abreast of these developments and select the best ones for the firm. The job is complicated by the fact that there is no one best way of moving the firm's goods. Products can be transported via one method for several weeks, then situations change and another method becomes the most appropriate. One mode might be used for several days, then air freight might be used, which exceeds the normal budget allowance for one day. This varied managerial setting makes performance evaluation of traffic managers a difficult task. The traffic manager is continually making trade-off decisions within his function and on behalf of the entire firm.

Study Questions

1. How is traffic management like a special form of purchasing?

2. What is different between a traffic manager's job and that of a purchasing manager?

3. How would you distinguish the job of traffic management of many years ago with that of today?

4. Why is consistency of transit time often regarded as a more important carrier selection factor than length of transit time?

5. Traffic management is merely the job of shipping the firm's goods. Evaluate this statement.

6. Should the traffic manager seek to minimize his total costs of freight charges?

7. Will traffic management become more important in the firm in the future, or will it become a relatively minor function?

Suggested Readings

Arizzi, Vincent J. "The Role of a Corporate Staff Transportation Group." *Transportation Journal*, Winter, 1974, pp. 41-52.

Bardi, Edward J. "Carrier Selection from one Mode." *Transportation Journal*, Fall, 1973, pp. 23-29.

Bowersox, Donald J. *Logistic Management*. New York: Macmillan Publishing, 1974, chaps. 6, 8.

Coyle, John J., and Bardi, Edward J. *The Management of Business Logistics*. 2nd ed. St. Paul: West Publishing, 1980, chap. 9.

Flood, Kenneth U. *Traffic Management*. 3rd ed. Dubuque, Iowa: William C. Brown Co., 1975.

Heskett, J. L. et al. *Business Logistics*. 2nd ed. New York: Ronald Press, 1973, chap. 19.

Lee, Lamar and Dobler, Donald W. *Purchasing and Materials Management: Text and Cases*. New York: McGraw-Hill, 1977.

Sampson, Roy J., and Farris, Martin T. *Domestic Transportation: Practice, Theory, and Policy*. 4th ed. Boston: Houghton Mifflin Co., 1979, chaps. 16, 17, 18.

Taff, Charles A. *Management of Physical Distribution and Transportation*. 6th ed. Homewood, Ill.: Richard D. Irwin, 1978.

Wager, Charles H. et al. *Industrial Traffic Management*. 5th ed. Washington, D.C.: The Traffic Service Corporation, 1973, chap. 14.

Case   **Hi-Kite Products**

John Kaufman is traffic manager for Hi-Kite Products, a consumer products company with annual sales in 1980 of about $100 million. John is nearing retirement and must begin to arrange for his successor. He started with the company in 1945 as a tariff filer, a function that entailed filing supplements to tariffs. In the ensuing years, he moved through all the posts in the department. He has been the firm's head traffic manager since 1961.

He is currently reviewing the job description of his post which he helped to write in 1962 along with the company's personnel manager. He felt it has accurately described the traffic manager's job until recently. It is summarized as follows:

Traffic Manager — Corporate

-Responsible for maintaining tariff file encompassing established carriers in Hi-Kite areas.

-Supervise functions of expediting and tracing.

-Prepare rate protests and follow through on them before ICC and appropriate state agencies.

-Prepare and present shipper testimony in support of new carrier operating applications.

-Conduct rate analyses to determine most economical routings.

-Supervise rate/freight bill auditing functions.

-Manage private truck fleet.

In 1980, the department consisted of two tariff filers, six rate auditors, two expediters, a regulatory analyst, one rate analyst, and a private fleet dispatcher who supervised one clerk and seven drivers.

Should John Kaufman use the above description to guide him in selecting his replacement three years from now? Why or why not?

Part V

The Government's Role in Transportation

15 An Overview of the Regulatory System

After reading this chapter you should:

1 Understand the rationale for government regulation.
2 Be able to discuss the general nature of regulation.
3 Understand the institutional arrangements for regulation of transportation.
4 Be able to discuss the major legal forms of transportation.
5 Understand the major regulatory issues.

Transportation is an intermediate or linking function between various activities of society and sectors of the economy. In that sense, transportation is a means to the many ends sought by society. Ideally, it should be assessed in terms of its contributions to helping society meet those ends compared to the costs involved.

■ resource allocation

Resources in the United States are allocated to various ends through two main processes. The first is the political process wherein the public or its elected representatives vote with ballots. The second is the market process where the people vote with their dollars. In other words, people buy certain products or services and not others, and therefore, commit resources or inputs to the products or services purchased in the marketplace.

The United States has traditionally relied heavily on the market process to provide transportation. Since the early part of this century, however, Congress has created and funded a growing number of transportation programs. In recent years, federally controlled and allocated funds have accounted for almost 5 percent of the nation's total expenditures for transportation. State and local governmental expenditures have been at an even higher level. All three levels of government, however, have been reluctant to abandon the market process, particularly with respect to vehicle ownership and operation.[1]

■ government participation in allocation

Overall, the current allocation of resources to transportation reflects both a market allocation process and a political allocation process. Ideally, the political process should recognize the potential inadequacies of an unrestrained market that provides for each individual's basic necessities and that acts to prevent or mitigate market imperfections. Furthermore, the market process should operate within such constraints to efficiently provide the transportation the society wants and is willing and able to pay for. This blend of government and marketplace interac-

■ political and market blend

tion in the transportation area is important to understand. The government role is many-faceted including, as suggested above, loans and subsidies, direct control over rates, routes, service, and so on, and safety regulations to protect the citizenry. All facets of the government's role are of importance in this discussion. A convenient starting point for developing an understanding of this role would be to discuss the nature of regulation. Following the discussion of the nature of regulation, attention will be given to institutional arrangements and the legal classifications of carriers as they have been defined and developed under the U.S. regulatory system. The final section will discuss some of the basic regulatory issues.

Nature of Regulation

■ variable controls

In the United States the government influences the activities of business in many different ways. The amount of influence in business activity varies from providing the legal foundation and framework in which business operates to governmental ownership and control. There is a long history of governmental regulation and control, but even today there is still some opposition on the part of managers to the governmental activity which influences their operations.

The amount of governmental control and regulation has increased as the United States has grown and prospered. If one would compare the controls exercised by the government 150 years ago with those in existence today, the former would probably seem insignificant. The expansion of governmental influence, however, has been necessitated to some extent by the increase in the scope of activity, complexity, and the size of the individual firm.

■ economic theory

In the United States, we tend to view our economic activity as one of private enterprise. Competition is a necessary requirement to a free enterprise economy. The allocation of scarce resources can be decided in the competitive market. The case for free-market enterprise and competition has been developed by economists for over 150 years.

The definitions of pure competition and free market involve a number of conditions, as pointed out in an earlier chapter, which may not exist in reality. According to this school of economic theory, products are justified only by the willingness of people to buy them. A product should not be sold at a price below costs associated with the marginal cost of the last unit. The theory also assumes that people are able to assess whether a given economic act will make them better off—either as producers or consumers and that people will use personal resources to achieve a more positive life-style.

■ monopoly

Our belief that competition is most conducive to the betterment of all is joined by a feeling that monopoly or monopolistic practices are undesirable. The problem would be simple if our market structures took the form of either perfect competition or monopoly. Most individuals would not quarrel with governmental regulation of monopoly and a valid case would be made for little or no governmental interference in an economy characterized by perfect competition. However, the prevailing situation is not this simple. The market structures usually take some form between the extremes of perfect competition and monopoly.

The imperfections in the marketplace in a free enterprise economy provide the rationale for governmental control. The control exercised by the government can take one of several forms. One form is that of maintaining or enforcing competition, for example, the antitrust actions of the government. Second, the government can substitute regulation for competition as it does in transportation. Third, the government can assume ownership and direct control as it has done with the post office.

■ forms of control

The basic problem of regulation in our society is that of establishing or maintaining the conditions necessary for the economical utilization of resources under a system of private enterprise, that is, the blend situation mentioned in Chapter 12. Regulation must seek to maintain a competitive framework and rely on the competitive forces whenever possible.

The institutional framework for regulating transportation is provided by federal statute. A perspective on the overall legal basis for regulation is important to the student of transportation, and we will examine this topic in the next section.

Institutional Arrangements

The legal system of the United States is based upon common law and civil or statutory law. The former is a basic system to most English-speaking countries since it was developed in England. Common law relies upon judicial precedent, or principles of law developed from former court decisions. Therefore, if one wants to find out what the law is on a particular topic it is necessary to search out the court decisions to see what was originally decided about the topic. When a court decision establishes a rule for a situation then that rule becomes part of the law of the land. As conditions change, the law sometimes needs further interpretation. Therefore, an important feature of the common law system is that it changes and evolves as society changes. We have many examples of such change in interpretation in the area of federal and state control or responsibility for regulating transportation.[2] Common law involves a continuous process of court interpretation.

■ common law approach

The common law approach fits well with a free-market enterprise system, since the individual is the focus of attention and can engage in any business that is not prohibited. Each individual is essentially regarded as possessing equal power and responsibility before the law.[3] The early regulation of transportation developed under the common law. The obvious connection is with the concept of common carriage which has already been discussed and will be considered in more detail later in this chapter. Common law rules were developed for those common carriers, since they serve all shippers on a similar basis, at reasonable rates, and without discrimination. The foundation of later statutory regulation was actually developed under common law by the early 1800s.[4]

■ common law and free market

■ statutory law

■ common law and
statutes

       Statutory law or civil law is based upon the Roman legal system and is
characteristic of continental Europe and the parts of the world colonized
by these countries. Statutory law is enacted by legislative bodies, only it
is a specific enactment. It is in a sense a written law that is more apparent
and easier to check. A large part of the laws pertaining to business control in general and to transportation in particular are based upon statutory law. However, two things are important to know in this regard.
First, common law rules are still very important in the transportation
area since many statutes were in effect copied from common law principles. Second, statutes are usually general and need to be interpreted by
the courts. So, in the United States there is a very close relationship between common law and statutory law.

■ state regulation

       The regulation of transportation began at the state level under the
common law system when a number of important rules for regulation
were developed, as well as the basic issue of whether business could
even be regulated at all. In the latter regard, a concept of "business
affected with the public interest" was developed under the common law.
State regulation also included use of charters for some of the early turn-
pike companies and canal operations. The development of the railroad
necessitated a move to statutory regulation, which was in effect by 1870
with the passage of granger laws in various states. These granger laws
were the product of the granger movement which began about 1867 in
states such as Illinois, Iowa, Minnesota, and Wisconsin. Grangers were
organizations formed by farmers in various states and functioned as political action groups where farmers could discuss problems. The granger
movement was started by the farmers through their Grange organizations because of their dissatisfaction with railroad rates and service. The
development of state laws, and later federal laws, also gave rise to independent regulatory commissions which are considered in the next section.

Role of the
Commission

■ background

       The Interstate Commerce Commission (ICC) was the first independent
regulatory commission to be established in the United States at the
federal level. It was set up under the Act to Regulate Commerce in 1887.
Originally, the ICC had somewhat limited powers. However, over the
years it has evolved as the most comprehensive and powerful commission in the country. The independent regulatory commission is somewhat peculiar to the United States. It is a unique contribution of this
country to the scheme of regulating private industry.[5] Since the creation
of the ICC, independent regulatory commissions have been set up in
other spheres of federal control. For example, the Federal Trade Commission was established in 1914, the Federal Power Commission in 1930,
the Federal Communications Commission in 1934, and the Civil Aeronautics Board in 1938.

■ role

       Our federal government is set up under a system of checks and bal-
ances in three separate branches—the executive, judicial, and legislative. The independent regulatory commission is an administrative body

created by the legislative authority operating within the framework of the Constitution. The members of the ICC are appointed by the president and approved by the Senate for a fixed term of office.

■ powers

The ICC serves as an expert body providing a continuity to regulation that neither the courts nor the legislature can provide. The ICC exercises legislative, judicial, and executive powers. As a consequence, it has often been labeled as a quasi-legislative, quasi-executive, and quasi-judicial body. It may be regarded as a fourth branch of the government. When the ICC acts to enforce statutes, it serves in the executive capacity. When it rules upon the reasonableness of a rate, it serves in its judicial capacity. When it fills out legislation by promulgating rules or prescribes a rate for the future, it exercises its legislative powers.

■ relationships

As was implied in the previous section, our regulatory laws are very often stated in vague terms such as reasonable rates, inherent advantages and unjust discrimination. Therefore, in administering and interpreting the law the ICC exercises broad discretionary powers over the regulated transport firms. We must not, however, lose sight of the fact that the ICC is still limited by the regulatory laws. It can only carry out the law to the best of its ability. The ICC is also subject to the opinions of the courts, so let us turn next to the consideration of what role the courts play in the regulatory scheme.

Role of the Courts

Even though the ICC plays a powerful role in regulating transportation, it is still subject to judicial review. The courts are the sole judges of the law and only court decisions can serve as legal precedent under common law. The courts make the final ruling upon the constitutionality of regulatory statutes and the interpretation of the legislation. The review of the courts acts as a check upon arbitrary or capricious actions, actions which do not conform to statutory standards or authority, or actions which are not in accordance with fair procedure or substantial evidence. The parties involved in a commission decision have the right, therefore, to appeal the decision to the courts.

■ constraint

■ commission as experts

Over the years the courts have come to recognize the ICC as an expert body on policy and the authority on matters of fact. Therefore, the courts have limited their restrictions on ICC authority. The courts will not substitute their judgement for that of the ICC on such matters as what constitutes a reasonable rate or whether a discrimination is unjust, since such judgements would usurp the administrative function of the commission.

With this brief excursion through the maze of transportation regulation, let us now turn to a consideration of the basic legal classes of carriers. The next section provides a summary of the concepts developed by common law, statutory law, and the ICC.

Legal Classifications of Carriers[6]

Transportation firms that are engaged in interstate transportation of property are classified into four categories: (1) common, (2) contract, (3) exempt, and (4) private. The first three are for-hire carriers while the latter is not, that is, private transportation is provided by the firm desiring movement of its goods and the service of a private carrier is not made available (sold) to other shippers.

Common Carrier

■ service requirements

The common carrier is a for-hire carrier that serves the general public at reasonable charges and without discrimination. The common carrier is the most highly regulated (from the standpoint of economic matters) of all the legal types of carriers. The economic regulation imposed upon these carriers is directed toward protecting the shipping public and ensuring sufficient supply, within normal limits, of transport service. Thus, use of a common carrier in the logistics system requires the logistics manager to have knowledge of these regulations as they affect the type and quality of transport possible by common carriers. A thorough discussion of transportation regulation is not intended here, rather, the implications of these regulations upon the quality and cost of common carrier link service is of primary concern. The distinguishing facets of the common carrier are rooted in the level of economic regulation imposed upon the carriers.

■ background

The essence of this regulation is found in the legal service requirements imposed upon the common carrier. These requirements are: to serve, to deliver, to avoid discrimination, and to charge reasonable rates. Embedded within these service requirements is the underlying principle of public protection, because the common carrier is recognized as being a business enterprise which affects public interest. To guarantee the continued provision of the level and quality of transportation service that is required for the economy to function, the federal government has resorted to regulatory controls to achieve these objectives. These legal service requirements are not imposed upon the other types of carriage.

■ duty of service

The requirement that the common carrier serve the public entails the carrier's transporting all commodities offered to it. The common carrier cannot refuse to carry a particular commodity or to serve a particular point within the carrier's scope of operation. This suggests that the shipper is assured a supply of transport service since the common carrier cannot refuse to transport the firm's commodities, even if the movement is not the most profitable for the carrier. There are, however, two qualifications to this requirement: one, the carrier is required to provide service up to the limits of its physical capacity, where capacity is determined by the level of plant necessary to meet normal carrier demand, and second, the common carrier is required to serve those shippers within the carrier's shipping public. For example, a common motor carrier of household goods is not required to serve a shipper of bulk oils: the bulk oil shipper is not within the carrier's public.

Common carrier entry requirements are regulated by the ICC for rail, motor, and water and by the Civil Aeronautics Board (CAB) for air. A common carrier must prove to the regulatory agency that a public necessity exists for the proposed service and that the provision of the proposed service will be a public convenience. It may be argued that this regulatory constraint upon entry is a protective device for the sole benefit of the carrier, but in the long run, protection of the carrier is also protection of the public. Entry control protects the common carrier from excessive amounts of ruinous competition and thereby assures a continuous and stable supply of transportation to the public.

■ duty of sale, delivery

The delivery requirement refers to the common carrier's liability for the goods entrusted into the carrier's care. The common carrier is required to deliver the goods in the same condition that existed when they were tendered to the carrier at origin of the shipment, or more specifically, the common carrier is liable for all loss and damage or delay resulting to goods while in the care of the carrier. There are limited exceptions to this absolute level of liability; they are acts of God, acts of public enemy, acts of public authority, acts of the shipper, and the inherent defects of the goods. The shipper, then, is able to transfer the risk of cargo damage, or the bearing of this risk, to the carrier when the common carrier is used over the link. The ICC assures the shipping public that the common carrier is capable of paying such cargo liability claims by either controlling the financial stability of the carrier or by requiring the common carrier to purchase cargo liability insurance. It should be pointed out that the shipper indirectly pays for this transfer of cargo damage risk to the carrier through the carrier's building this factor into its pricing structure.

■ duty not to discriminate

Additional protection for the shipping public is found in the requirements that the common carrier not discriminate among shippers, commodities, or places. Discrimination occurs when the carriers charge different rates or provide different types of service for essentially similar movements of similar goods. It should be recognized, however, that there are forms of permissible discrimination. For example, charging lower rates for volume movements and higher rates for less-than-volume movements is discriminating in favor of the larger volume shipper. But, the volume rates must be the same for all shippers shipping a given commodity between two given points and vice versa for the less-than-volume rate. Cost difference also justifies quoting different rates for volume and less-than-volume movements.

■ duty to charge reasonable rates

Finally, the duty to charge reasonable rates constrains the carrier from charging excessively high rates which is entirely possible with limited entry into the marketplace. The regulatory bodies are responsible for protecting the shipping public from excessive rates that result in excessively high profits; profits that are above those considered reasonable for the industry. At the same time, the regulatory bodies are also responsible for assuring that the carrier rates are high enough to ensure the survival of the carrier and consequently the continued supply of service to the public. Therefore, requiring the carrier to charge reasonable rates has two protective dimensions: protection of the shipping public from rates that are too high and protection of the carrier from charging rates that are too low, with the latter ultimately resulting in the protection of the public through the assurance of the continued supply of transportation services.

An unusual pricing procedure exists in the common carrier sector, and that is the joint publication of rates by carriers. The carriers get together and publish rates through rate bureaus which result in the equality of rates charged by competing carriers in one mode. This form of collective pricing is permitted under the Reed-Bulwinkle Act of 1948. The ICC still oversees the reasonableness of the rates, and the carriers have the ability to take independent action—to charge a rate that is different from its competitors.

In summary, the common carrier might be considered the backbone of the transportation industry. The common carrier makes itself available to the public, without providing special treatment to any one party, and is regulated as to the rates charged, the liability assumed, and the service provided. The common carrier is used quite extensively by many shippers.

Contract Carrier

■ definition

The contract carrier is a for-hire carrier that does not serve the general public, but rather serves one or a limited number of shippers under specific contract. The contract carrier is also regulated with respect to economic matters, but there are no legal service obligations imposed upon the contract carrier. The terms of the contract contain provisions pertaining to such things as the rates to be charged, liability, type of service, and the equipment that is to be provided by the carrier. Usually the rates via contract carrier are lower than by common carriers. The regulatory bodies do control entry into this sector of transportation, but the requirement of proving public convenience and necessity is eliminated for securing contract carrier authority.

■ service

The contract carrier provides a specialized type of service to the shipper. The carrier does not serve the public in general and therefore can tailor its services to meet the needs of the specific shipper(s). Since the contract carrier does not serve the public and therefore does not have general purpose equipment, it is possible for the carrier to utilize special equipment and to arrange pickup and delivery to satisfy the few shippers with whom the carrier is contracted. In general it may be assumed that contract carriage is essentially similar to that possible with private transportation, at least in terms of the level of service provided.

■ scope of operations

One serious problem exists in the use of a contract carrier and that pertains to the carrier's availability. Unlike the common carrier that is required to be available to all, the contract carrier is available only to those shippers with whom the carrier has signed a contract and to those shippers for whom the contract carrier has secured a permit to serve from the ICC or CAB. Thus, the contract carrier is not as readily available as the common carrier, and the establishment of a contract carrier to serve a firm will entail the shipper's intervention and assistance so that the carrier can obtain a contract authority to operate as a contract carrier.

Exempt Carrier

The exempt carrier is a for-hire carrier that is not regulated with respect to economic matters, that is, this carrier is exempt from economic regulation. There are no regulations governing rates charged or services pro-

■ definition

vided by the exempt carrier. The laws of the marketplace determine the rates, services and supply of such carriers. The only controls to entry into this sector of the transport industry are those pertaining to capital requirements, which are not seriously restrictive for some modes.

■ service

An exempt carrier gains this status by the type of commodity hauled or by the nature of its operation. For example, a motor carrier is classified as an exempt carrier when transporting agricultural products, newspapers, livestock, and fish. With respect to the type of operation, examples would include motor carriers whose operations are primarily local, water carriers that transport bulk commodities such as coal, ore, and grain or water carriers that haul bulk liquids in tank vessels.

By reason of the limited number of exempt carriers, that is, the limited number of areas where exempt carriers are possible, the availability of such carriers is restrictive. But firms make significant use of these carriers for those commodity movements, such as agricultural products, for example, where exempt carriage is possible. The primary reason for using an exempt carrier is that of lower transport rates. For the movement of industrial commodities, however, the exempt carrier is not a viable means of transport service.

Private Carrier

■ definition

A private carrier is essentially a firm that provides its own transportation. The private carrier is not for-hire and not subject to federal economic regulations. More specifically, private carriage is any person who transports property of which such person is the owner, lessee, or bailee in interstate or foreign commerce when such transportation is for the purpose of sale, lease, rent or, bailment or in furtherance of any commercial enterprise. The crucial aspect of the legal distinction of a private carrier is that the transportation function must not be the primary business of the controlling firm, or stated differently, the primary business of the owner of the carrier must be some commercial endeavor other than transportation.

The most prevalent type of private transportation is the motor vehicle; the preponderance of private motor vehicle fleets has made private carrier synonymous with private motor carrier. One estimate on the importance of private trucking is that 75 percent of the trucks are involved in private transportation. The relative ease of capital requirement for entry into motor transport and the high degree of accessibility via motor vehicle has made this mode most advantageous to shippers who wish to provide their own transportation. It should be pointed out that private transportation by water does exist primarily for the movement of bulk raw materials. To a much lesser extent private rail carriers prevail in the movement of bulk products short distances, for example, within a plant, between plants, or from plants to rail sidings. Private aircraft has made substantial inroads in the movement of company personnel and to a lesser degree the movement of emergency shipments of property for a firm.

■ rationale

The basic reasons for a firm to enter into private transportation are cost and service. With the trend of for-hire carrier rates on the increase, some firms have found private transportation a means of controlling transportation costs. Basically, these costs can be reduced by private transportation if the private carrier operation is conducted as efficiently as for-hire operations. If this same degree of efficiency is possible, private transportation should be lower in cost, theoretically, since the for-hire carrier profit is eliminated. However, one major operational problem, the empty back-haul, has resulted in elevated costs.

The next section develops some of the important regulatory issues that have been raised thus far in our discussion.

Basic Transportation Regulatory Issues

The preceding discussion has alluded to many of the basic issues that are contained in the regulation area. As transportation laws have been passed, funding programs initiated, and rules developed to control service, the fundamental policy issues that have emerged are: private ownership, public investment, common carrier concept, unimodal focus and competition.

Private Ownership

■ reliance on private enterprise

■ market forces and resource allocation

■ quasi-government agencies

■ survival assurance

One of the basic underlying philosophies of transportation policy is the reliance upon private enterprise to provide transportation services. National transportation policy encourages private individuals and firms to own and operate transportation companies in the United States. Only in rare instances has the government provided transportation services— for example, the federal government operated the railroads during World War I, and it now operates the Alaskan Railroad.

The state and federal government recognized that private enterprise and the competitive environment are more likely to provide efficient and economical service than the federal government. Profit and survival motives are strong market forces demanding economical operation of transportation facilities. In the absence of the profit incentive, resources are not always allocated in the most efficient manner.

In recent years there has been a trend toward a greater federal role in the operation of the railroads. The establishment of Amtrak and Conrail as quasi-governmental entities has caused great concern throughout the transportation industry, as it has been viewed as the first step toward nationalization of the railroads.

Although Amtrak and Conrail are not federal agencies, the financial backing provided to them by the federal government assures survival, even at a continuous loss as has been the case since the inception of both. The continued operation of an inefficient and unprofitable company, however, places the other railroads at a competitive disadvantage and such operation channels resources (federal money, labor, and fuel) to an uneconomical enterprise. At the time of this writing the president was considering the introduction of a bill in Congress to sell the profitable lines to private railroads and abandon the nonprofitable routes.

Public Investment

The federal government has fostered public investment in transportation facilities that require huge amounts of capital or that must be acces-

■ highway system

sible to many people. The best example of public investment in transportation is the highway system. The federal government has paid 90 percent of the construction cost of the interstate highway system; the states have paid the remaining 10 percent. The users pay for the construction and maintenance of the highways through highway use taxes.

Public investment has also been quite extensive in the waterways and airways. The development of waterways and airways offers tremendous economic advantages to the surrounding communities. When a waterway is improved, a harbor deepened, or port facilities modernized, surrounding firms have access to low cost water transportation. Economic activity in the community is increased and jobs are created. Since these facilities make use of public money, the private transportation companies are given equal acess to the facilities, unless entry controls over routes (air carriers, for example) prohibit the carrier from servicing the facility.

■ waterway and airport development

■ operating subsidies

In order to promote the development of air carriers, the federal government makes direct operating subsidies to carriers that provide needed service to communities. In such cases, the operating subsidy offsets the operation deficit incurred by an air carrier and can be construed as a public investment in air transportation to lesser populated communities.

Public investment in highways, waterways, and airways assures equal access to private transportation companies and an unconstrained flow of goods and people throughout the country. If the highways were privately owned, a highway owner could conceivably establish an unreasonable charge for the movement of a commodity. Likewise, private ownership of waterways or airways could severely restrict transport flows. Public investment in these facilities is one way to ensure that the flow of goods over transportation routes will not be restricted by private investors seeking maximum profit.

■ public access

Common Carrier Concept

There has been a long held principle that transportation is an industry affected by public interest. The importance of transportation to the overall economic and social development of a country is ingrained in the common carrier concept. The regulatory controls exercised over the common carrier clearly indicate that transportation has certain responsibilities to the public, for example, responsibility to charge reasonable rates, as discussed earlier in this chapter.

■ service responsibilities

A closer look at these common carrier duties indicates that the carrier must be responsive to public demand. Common carriers must provide service to all without discrimination and at reasonable rates. In addition, the requirement to deliver ensures the carrier's legal responsibility for the commodities tendered for shipment. A common carrier is not permitted to refuse to transport a shipment because the potential for damage is too high, the profitability for the move is too low, or the shipper is disliked.

■ requirement to serve

In return for serving the public, the common carrier is given a controlled competitive market in which to operate. That is, entry into the

■ controlled entry

common carrier field is controlled. A new carrier, or existing common carrier desiring to extend its operations, is required to prove that the proposed service is for public convenience and necessity. Such entry controls could be viewed as a means of assuring a stable supply of transportation service to users as well as a means of "protecting" common carriers from excessive competition.

■ exemptions

The common carrier concept has been voided in certain modes since the development of regulation, including current regulatory change. Historically, the controls exercised over motor, air, and water transportation exempted certain types of operations from common carrier regulations. These exempt carriers were not required to provide service to the public and were free to enter or exit the exempted market at will. The forces of the marketplace were to assure an adequate and acceptable level of service to this exempt public. A greater reliance upon competition is the essence of the public policy ingrained in the recent regulatory changes governing common carrier entry controls as will be discussed in Chapter 17.

Unimodal Focus

■ one mode at a time

The national transportation policy that has emerged in the form of regulations, investment, and promotions, has not been multimodal in nature. Public policy is primarily unimodal, with apparently little attention to the crossover impact upon competing modes. Since the modes developed at different times, it is quite understandable that government policy toward transportation has emphasized a particular mode at a particular time.

■ modes development

During the early settlement state of the United States, emphasis was placed upon water transportation development. In the mid 1800s to the mid 1920s, the railroad industry was a prime catalyst for the development of the interior and western portions of our country. Around the mid 1920s, the automobile and truck began to emerge as a major transportation alternative linking outlying areas to rail and water facilities. Finally, in the 1940s, air transportation began to emerge as a quick and economical means of long-distance passenger travel. At each of these developmental states, the government was faced with either developing policies to promote a struggling new transportation industry or placing controls on a powerful, mature transportation industry.

The unimodal approach to national transportation policy has resulted in unequal treatment of the transportation modes. Regulatory exemptions for motor, air, and water transportation have placed railroads at an unfair competitive disadvantage. Public investment in highways, waterways, and airways has been greater than public investment in railroad transportation. In addition, operating subsidies for air carrier operations and urban transit operations have not been equally distributed to other modes.

■ modal advantages

However, the unimodal approach has recognized that each mode has distinct and inherent advantages that must be preserved and encouraged. The speed of air transportation would not be available if the unimodal policies promoting air transportation were not fostered. The same is true for the cost and service benefits realized from the water, rail, and highway transportation unimodal policies.

Currently, there is a growing need to develop a multimodal transportation policy that will enable each mode to realize its inherent cost and service benefits. A multimodal policy must give consideration to the current environmental, energy, and social conditions. Unequal regulatory and promotional treatment must be rectified so that modes can compete fairly. As federal resources are allocated to transportation, the total impact on all modes must be examined in light of public needs.

Competition

■ competition promotion

The promotion of an equitable competitive environment within which transportation companies operate has been a basic policy of the federal government. Various transportation regulations are directed at preserving the competitive environment or protecting a mode from unfair competitive practices. For example, the CAB has been charged with the responsibility to assure that air carriers do not utilize unfair competitive practices, and railroads are precluded from operating in a manner that would result in market dominance.[7] In each situation the regulatory goal is to promote competition or, conversely, to prevent monopoly.

■ exempt carrier example

The competitive policy issues are most evident in the exempt carrier concept. The exempt carrier is relieved from all economic regulations and is controlled by the marketplace (competition). A carrier is free to charge the price that users are willing to pay and is free to enter and exit the industry. Where existing carriers are making high profits, new carriers will enter the market or existing carriers will shift from hauling low profit commodities to transporting high profit goods.

■ intermodal competition

Intermodal competition has also been promoted at the federal level. Many regulatory decisions have encouraged water and rail competition by protecting the water carrier from the ruinous and destructive pricing practices of the railroads. The water carriers on the Great Lakes have complained about railroads establishing unit train rates from coal fields direct to upper Great Lakes destinations. Without a proportional rate to the lower lake ports, the joint rail-water rate would not be competitive with the all-rail unit train rate.

■ constraints to competition

Not all regulations and public policy practices have enhanced the competitive environment. Controls over entry into the common carrier segment of transportation did not increase competition. As noted earlier, control over entry was designed to protect the public from unstable supply conditions. Also, when recovery of public investment and operation of highways, airways, and waterways does not consider costs of capital and operation in setting user charges, the railroads are placed at an unfair competitive disadvantage. However, such noncompetitive policies have developed to meet a variety of national needs, and the competitive environment policy has taken a lower priority in these instances.

Conclusion

This chapter has provided a background for the discussion of the development of regulation which will follow in the next chapter. Although there are many other dimensions that could be covered in terms of the legal dimensions that are quite technical in nature, an attempt has been made to highlight the important points and issues of regulation.

Study Questions

1. How do the political and market processes interact to allocate resources?
2. Describe the forms of control that government can use to correct market imperfections. What are some of these imperfections?
3. What is the role of the Interstate Commerce Commission in regulation? The courts?
4. List and discuss the legal classifications of carriers.
5. Outline the basic duties of common carriers in the current transportation environment.
6. Why should a company consider entering private carriage when there are many carriers willing to serve it?
7. In what ways has the federal government fostered public investment in different types of transport facilities?
8. How is the common carrier concept affected by the common good of the country?
9. What is unimodal policy? How did it affect the development of the different modes?
10. How does economic regulation promote competition? How does it hinder it?

Notes

1. U.S. Department of Transportation, *National Transportation Trends and Choices* (Washington, D.C.: U.S. Government Printing Office, 1977), p. 5.
2. Dudley F. Pegrum, *Public Regulation of Business*, (Homewood, Ill.: Richard D. Irwin, 1959), pp. 21-24.
3. Ibid.
4. Ibid., pp. 543-45.
5. Ibid., p. 290.
6. This section is based upon: John J. Coyle and Edward J. Bardi, *Business Logistics Management*, 2d ed. (St. Paul: West Publishing Co., 1980), pp. 215-20.
7. Market dominance refers to the absence of effective competition from other carriers and modes for the traffic to which the rate applies. The Staggers Act of 1980 further defined market dominance as a revenue to variable cost ratio exceeding 160 percent.

Suggested Readings

Alexander, David, and Moses, Leon N. "Competition Under Uneven Regulation." *American Economic Review.* May, 1963, pp. 466-73.

Friedlander, Ann F. *The Dilemma of Freight Transport Regulation*, Washington, D.C.: Brookings Institute, 1969, chap. 2.

Friendly, Henry J. *The Federal Administrative Agencies.* Cambridge, Mass.: Harvard University Press, 1962.

Guandolo, John. *Transportation Law.* 2nd ed. Dubuque, Iowa: William C. Brown Co., 1973, chaps. 55-60.

Harper, Donald V. *Transportation in America: Users, Carriers, Government.* Englewood Cliffs, New Jersey: Prentice-Hall, 1978, chaps. 19, 20.

Kahn, Alfred E. *The Economics of Regulation: Principles and Institutions.* vol. 1. New York: John Wiley and Sons, 1970, chap. 1.

Locklin, Philip D. *Economics of Transportation.* 7th ed. Homewood, Ill.: Richard D. Irwin, 1972, chaps. 13, 14.

Moore, Thomas G. *Freight Transportation Regulation.* Washington, D.C.: American Enterprise Institute for Public Policy Research, 1972, chap. 1.

Pegrum, Dudley F. *Transportation Economics and Public Policy.* 3rd ed. Homewood, Ill.: Richard D. Irwin, 1973, chap. 11.

Phillips, Jr., Charles F. *The Economics of Regulation.* rev. ed. Homewood, Ill.: Richard D. Irwin, 1969.

| Case | Contract Carrier Decision |

A recent action taken by the ICC has allowed a carrier to hold both a common carrier operating certificate and a contract carrier permit (dual authority). Your firm (a large discount department store chain) has been using the services of a common carrier for the past few years and has enjoyed suitable service from this carrier. However, this carrier has recently acquired a contract permit and is offering you contract service from warehouse to warehouse. You are puzzled as to the possible benefits of using contract service, and you ask your traffic department to prepare a report describing your carrier's present method of operation and his new contract service. The report reads as follows:

"Said carrier's common authority operates on a relay system. It spots a trailer at our warehouse to load at our convenience. Once loaded, the carrier transports the trailer to its closest break-bulk terminal. There it is consolidated with other shipments that are to travel to the same area of the country. Once it is properly loaded, the trailer is hooked to a tractor, and the unit is sent to the next break-bulk terminal in the system where a fresh driver is assigned to the unit to be driven to the next break-bulk. This is done until the unit reaches the break-bulk that serves the destinations of the merchandise in the trailer. The merchandise is then broken down to be taken to the appropriate city terminal to be delivered to its proper destination (our city store). Using this type of operation requires approximately 120 hours to move freight across the country.

"The contract service would begin with a loaded trailer being picked up at our warehouse by a pair of the carrier's drivers. This trailer would be transported to one of the company's warehouses where it would be dropped, and then another loaded trailer would be picked up and would be transported to another of the company's warehouses.

This would be repeated until the carrier's drivers complete a cross country round trip. This type of operation would require 72 hours to move freight across country. However, the new operation will require the purchase of forty new sleeper tractors, sixty-five new trailers, and the addition of fifty-five new drivers. The added cost to the carrier of this new operation is going to be reflected in its contract rates for the first few years of operation."

Using the information given above, would you employ the carrier's contract service? Explain your answer and describe what criteria you used to evaluate your decision. What impact do you think this decision will have upon the transportation industry?

16 Development of Transport Regulation

After reading this chapter you should:

1 Understand the changes in the transport market which accompanied changes in regulation.

2 Be able to discuss the major regulatory changes which occurred from 1880 to 1975.

3 Understand the reasons why changes in regulation were necessary.

4 Appreciate the scope and nature of our regulatory process.

The preceding chapter discussed and analyzed the foundations of regulation under our legal system and the Constitution. This chapter will trace the development of regulation in the United States as it has evolved under the legal system. Since there is much detail connected with the legislative history of transportation in the United States, an effort will be made to summarize and simplify that development as much as possible. Even with the current trend toward deregulation, it is important to have an understanding of the development of regulation, since it played such an important role in shaping our transportation system.

■ chapter overview

The first section will discuss the early stages of regulatory development up to World War I, with a particular focus on railroads. The second section will analyze the era of positive regulation ushered in by the Transportation Act of 1920. The third section will discuss the development of intermodal regulation which commenced in 1935. The final part of the chapter will analyze some of the recent changes in regulation.

The Era of Development: 1850–1920

■ state origins

The regulation of transportation by statute, began at the state level in the 1870s and the federal level in 1887. However, transportation companies were regulated long before this time under the common law. Also, it is accurate to state that the more formalized statutory regulation was a response to railroad development. The discussion of transportation development and regulatory development in this section will start at a point in time prior to railroads.

Transportation System Development

The original settlements in the United States were typically along navigable bodies of water. These included the original thirteen colonies which were located contiguous to the Atlantic Ocean as well as later developments located along navigable rivers.

The industrial revolution, starting in the early part of the nineteenth century in the textile industry in New England and the iron industry in Pennsylvania, was stymied to some extent by the lack of a flexible means of efficient transportation. The access to new markets in the Midwest and to the supplies of raw materials was hindered by the lack of a good east-west transportation system.

■ Erie Canal

The first major breakthrough came in 1825 when the Erie Canal opened in the state of New York. The canal provided access from New York City to the Midwest by connecting the Hudson River with Buffalo on the edge of Lake Erie. The success of the Erie Canal led to a rash of canals being built in other states including Pennsylvania, New Jersey, Ohio, and Indiana. Most of the canals were built with state funds, which caused some problems for the railroads when they began to develop. That is, the states that provided funding for canals were reluctant to provide state funds for railroads which were a rival form of transportation. The major exception was the state of Maryland which could not build an east-west canal system to compete with the Erie Canal because mountains formed a geographic barrier to such a system. The period from 1825 to 1850 was the most successful for the canals, but the railroads soon ended their dominance. However, the Erie Canal continued to operate profitably long after 1850.

■ B & O Railroad

The first railroad of any significant length used for general freight and passenger service was the Baltimore and Ohio Railroad chartered in 1827 by Maryland. For all intents and purposes, the initiation of service by the B & O in 1830 marks the beginning of railroad transportation in the United States. The years from 1830 to 1850 were a period of slow growth for the railroads, but after 1850 railroads began to develop at a rapid rate. The decade from 1880 to 1890 was the period of greatest growth when over 70,000 miles of track were added to the railroad network, an increase of 75 percent. The peak year for total railroad mileage in operation in the United States was 1916.

■ rapid rail growth

The rapid development of railroads from 1850 to 1900 was due to many factors. One of the most important was the availability of private capital, some of which was furnished by foreign sources. The westward movement of population and the financial support of the federal, state, and local governments were also important factors accounting for the rapid growth. Another factor was the great growth in American industry during the same period and the need for new raw material sources and new markets.

■ rail problems

The railroads dominated the transportation scene from 1880 to 1920, and they were the first "big business" in the United States. Unfortunately, the "seeds of destruction" of the railroads were sown during this period of greatest growth and development. The size and scope of the railroad companies and the inherent tendency toward price discrimination led to railroad regulation. The railroad system became overexpanded. Railroads were built connecting villages and hamlets that could not possibly provide enough traffic to make the investment profitable. Also, too many competing lines were built among the major business centers. The overexpansion, in addition to the financial malpractices of the railroad promoters, left railroads with an inflated capitalization base. These two factors were responsible to a large extent for the difficulties in which the railroads found themselves at the time of World War I. Rising costs with inadequate increases in revenues also aggravated the situation.

Overexpansion, financial malpractice, rising costs, and inadequate revenues help explain the weakened financial structure of many of the railroads in the twentieth century, but this is not the entire story. The railroads in World War I were the mainstay of the transportation system. However, heavy wartime demand forced people to seek alternative

■ competition development

sources of service where possible. The motor carrier demonstrated its worth during this time. The truck, although it did not account for a large percentage of the wartime traffic, nevertheless, served as an "eye opener" to the shipping public. There were 158,500 private motor truck registrations in 1915; by 1920 there were 1,107,600. The rise in the number of automobiles was also phenomenal. In 1910 there were 458,377 registrations and by 1920 this figure had increased to over 8,000,000. This increase in automobile use had a telling effect on the railroad passenger market. Although the highway network did not really begin to develop rapidly until the initiation of federal aid in 1921, public demand had a positive effect on the development of local and state roads between 1910 and 1920.

In summary, it can be said that the weakened financial condition of the railroads was attributable to a large extent to poor planning and overcapitalization. In addition, by the 1920s, the "truck" and the private automobile began to seriously compete for the traffic formerly carried almost exclusively by the railroads.

Legislative Developments

The abuses practiced by the railroads before 1870 were substantial; however, the groups affected were such a small minority of all shippers that national attention was not, at first, focused upon them. High rates for lo-

■ granger laws

cations where there was no competition was one abuse that was particularly irritating to the shippers located at these points. Granger laws to regulate railroads were passed in some of the states to alleviate this situation. However, the laws were sometimes ineffectual because they were too harsh or attempted to legislate maximum rates. However, as noted in the last chapter, the granger laws and related court cases set the stage for federal regulation and were important to the overall learning process associated with regulation.

By 1870, national attention was finally drawn to the discriminatory practices of the railroads. In 1874, there was a report in the Senate by the

■ congressional efforts

Windom Committee which recommended both government construction of competing railroads and development of inland waterways as a solution to the problem. The recommendations of this committee, however, were not carried out.[1] Nevertheless, the matter still received attention in congressional discussions. These early discussions resulted in a bill being passed in the House in 1878 (the Regan Bill), but it was rejected in the Senate.[2]

In 1885, the Senate passed the Cullom Bill to regulate railroads as a substitute for the Regan Bill, but it was not passed by the House. A joint committee was appointed to settle the differences of the two branches of the legislature. The famous Cullom Report of 1886 was the result of this action. This report was very influential in shaping the Act to Regulate Commerce of 1887.

■ Cullom Report

Federal action was made almost mandatory by the decision of the Supreme Court in the Wabash Case of 1886 in which it was held by the court that a state could not control rates on interstate traffic.[3] As a consequence, the Act to Regulate Commerce was passed in 1887 to fill the vacuum created by this decision.

■ Wabash Case

The original act contained provisions that are important to this discussion. Section 1 required that rates must be "just and reasonable." These concepts were taken from common law, but there were no concise definitions provided. Personal discrimination was outlawed under Section 2. Personal discrimination consists of charging different shippers different prices for like and similar services. This particular form of discrimination was most offensive to shippers, although the railroads themselves were glad in some instances that personal discrimination was prohibited, since in some cases large shippers coerced the railroads to grant low rates or to provide special services.

■ provisions of original act

■ personal discrimination

Section 3 of the original act prohibited undue preference and prejudice in setting rates. In effect, discrimination between places, shippers, and commodities was banned by this particular section. It is worth noting that the mere existence of inequality of rates did not prove that the rates were unlawful. It was necessary to prove similarity of circumstances and conditions for the rates to be declared unlawful. Long and short haul discrimination, a special type of place discrimination, could have been prohibited under Section 3. However, the practice was quite prevalent in the era before the regulation of railroads, and the members of Congress thought that it should be specifically outlawed. Long and short haul discrimination was, therefore, prohibited by Section 4 of the act. This type of discrimination consists of charging more for a shorter haul than a longer haul over the same route, in the same direction, and for the same commodity. Pooling agreements whereby traffic or revenues were shared by railroads to prevent competition were outlawed by Section 5.

■ undue preference and prejudice

■ long and short haul clause

■ pooling

In addition to the important sections dealing with rate regulation and control, the Act to Regulate Commerce contained some additional provisions that we shall note. First, it established a five-member Interstate Commerce Commission (ICC) which was the first independent regulatory agency under our legal system. The act also required that rates be published in tariffs open to the public and on file with the ICC. This regulatory control probably did as much as anything else to help eliminate discriminatory pricing practices. Shippers now had access to information about the rates of their competitors and could protest to the ICC if necessary. The railroads were prohibited from charging more or less than the published tariff price.

■ publication of rates

The ICC was also allowed to inquire into the management of railroads, to require annual reports, and to require a uniform statement of accounts. The act also set up procedures for complaints against violations of the act by shippers, carriers, or others. Finally, the act authorized the ICC to determine its rules of practice and procedure. Overall, the act of 1887 was of major importance in establishing a framework for comprehensive economic regulation. However, it was a compromise in many respects because of the strong opposition to its passage which existed in Congress at that time from the railroads and certain large shippers.

The success of the federal laws regulating transportation was short-lived. The ICC undertook its duties with the serious determination of able men, but its limited power to effectively regulate the railroads soon became apparent.[4] The difficulty arose from two sources. First, there were inherent defects in the laws because of compromises, and second, the Supreme Court helped to render the regulation ineffectual in a series of cases.[5] Regulation remained in a state of what might be termed the doldrums until after the turn of the century.

At the turn of the century, the public demanded more effectual regulation primarily because of the consolidation movement in the railroad industry and the rise in freight rates which came about in the last decade of the nineteenth century.[6] The Expediting Act of 1903 and the Elkins Act of 1903 were the result of public clamor. The former sought to speed up court action on ICC orders, and the latter strengthened laws regarding personal discrimination.[7] Specifically, the Elkins Act provided criminal penalties for regulated common carriers, their officers, and their agents for willful failure to adhere strictly to their tariffs. In addition, there were provisions for criminal penalties for carriers and shippers which knowingly offered, gave, or solicited rebates and other special concessions. The fact that shippers could also be fined was a major deterrent to personal discriminatory practices.

Although the Elkins Act of 1903 was important in terms of controlling personal discrimination, it did not restore the power of the ICC which was lost by the Supreme Court cases, nor did it address any of the major weaknesses of the original act of 1887. A major step in this direction was made by Congress in 1906.

The Hepburn Act of 1906 was designed to strengthen prior regulations and to provide the ICC with positive powers to prohibit the abusive practices of the railroads. The act extended the ICC's jurisdiction and enlarged its size to ten members. The most important measure contained in the act gave the ICC power to prescribe rates for the future by establishing maximum rates. The act also increased the power of the ICC over through routes and joint rates, mandated thirty days notice for rate changes, extended the ICC's power over personal discrimination, and gave it power to make its orders binding upon the carriers.[8] The Hepburn Act contained the Commodities Clause which prohibited railroads from hauling almost all commodities which they produced, mined, owned, or had an interest in. In addition, this clause made the act applicable to pipelines, rail express, and sleeping car companies. The legality of these provisions was upheld in the courts.[9] Overall, the

■ problems

■ Elkins Act

■ provisions

■ Hepburn Act

Hepburn Act was a major piece of legislation that did much to restore the power of the ICC.

The Hepburn Act made the regulation of transportation much more effective than it had been prior to its enactment. It was evident shortly thereafter, however, that further changes were necessary to provide adequate protection to the shipping public. To remedy this situation, Congress passed further legislation in 1910. The Mann-Elkins Act of 1910 gave the ICC the power to suspend proposed changes in rates and also reworded the Long and Short Haul Clause to restore its effectiveness. In addition, a commerce court was established to speed up adjudication of ICC cases, and the ICC was authorized to institute hearings on its own motion, as well as to prescribe reasonable classifications.

- Mann-Elkins Act

Following the Mann-Elkins Act of 1910, a number of shorter and less comprehensive acts were passed, some of which will be noted here. In 1912, the Panama Canal Act was passed which made it unlawful for a railroad to own, control, or have any interest in any water common carrier with which the railroad may or did compete, unless approved by the ICC. In 1913, the Valuation Act was passed which directed the ICC to determine the fair value of railroad properties for rate-making purposes. The Commission Organization Act of 1917 broadened the procedural powers of the ICC so as to authorize it to act through various divisions having the powers and jurisdiction of the full commission.

- Panama Canal Act

This review of the legislation prior to 1920 illuminates its restrictive nature. Congress and the public were concerned with checking the abusive practices of the railroads, especially in the area of rates. The weakness of this type of regulation was pointed out by developments immediately before and during World War I when there was a progressive decline in railway earnings, and railroad credit suffered as a result.[10] The regulatory structure was partially to blame for this situation. The ICC had not devoted any attention to a comprehensive structure of rates. The outlawing of pools and the application of the antitrust laws based upon a belief in competition as an effective regulator of rates had encouraged low rates, wasteful hauls, and unduly elaborate service.[11] The federal government assumed control of the railroads during World War I. Rates had not been increased sufficiently to meet higher operating costs, and the equipment of many carriers was in a poor state of repair.

- overview of legislation

The Era of Positive Regulation: 1920-1935

- ownership issue

At the close of World War I, there were extensive congressional hearings and debates about the question of government ownership of the railroads. Given the precedent of government control during the war and the weakened financial condition of the rail system, Congress seriously considered buying out the private owners and having a public railroad system.

The question of ownership was a favorite topic of conversation throughout the country at this time and was a debate topic for colleges and high schools during one academic year. It was finally decided that railroads should be returned to their private owners, but Congress felt that some change in the nature of the regulation was necessary. Before examining the provisions of the Transportation Act of 1920, we will undertake a brief review of the changes in the transportation marketplace.

Transportation Developments

The motor carriers were just beginning to develop when World War I began. The priority system among shippers established by the government for rail movements during the war helped to spur motor carrier development, since shippers looked for alternative means of transportation. The railroads viewed the motor carrier as a means of accessorial service to their lines. Some railroads probably hoped that the motor carrier would serve a consolidation and distribution function for less-than-carload (LCL) traffic and help them solve the almost continual problem that they experienced with this type of traffic. It was clear by 1930, however, that motor carriers were developing into a very competitive alternative for certain types of traffic.

■ motor carriers

Statistical evidence as to tonnage is rather fragmentary for this period. However, it has been estimated that motor carriers were responsible for 4.2 percent of the total intercity ton-miles in 1929.[12] By 1932, truck traffic was accountable for 9.4 percent of total intercity ton-miles.[13] One should note, however, that because of the short haul nature of traffic, this figure seriously understates the importance of motor transportation. On a strict tonnage basis, this figure would be about 24 percent.[14] The number of motor truck registrations is also indicative of the growing importance of motor carriers during this period. As was previously stated, the 1920 truck registrations were just over 1,000,000, but by 1925 they had climbed to over 2,400,000. In 1930, there were over 3,500,000 registrations.

■ water carriers and pipelines

Water carriage was in a stage of revival during this period and was once again providing competition, especially for transcontinental traffic. The opening of the Panama Canal in 1914 was to a large degree responsible for the revival of water carriage. The pipelines were also providing increased competition, because of the growth in demand for gasoline which spurred increased crude oil movements.

The ICC had this to say about the changing conditions:

■ ICC summary

The problems confronting the railroads have changed very greatly in the past 15 or 20 years. In that period the country has been covered with thousands of miles of hard-surface highways, and over these millions of automotive vehicles now operate. In both the passenger and the freight fields they compete vigorously with the railroads for much traffic which was hitherto regarded as immune to competition. To a considerable extent these vehicles have made it possible for individual shippers to provide themselves with transportation. Competition with the water carriers has increased materially, owing to the opening of the Panama Canal routes, the improvement of many inland waterways, and the Government's expenditures on shipping. Pipeline competition has greatly increased not only in the transportation of crude oil but also in the carriage of refined oils and of natural gas, which substitute for coal carried by the railroads. Electric transmission lines are also operating as a substitute for coal carriage, and the construction of many more is in progress or in contemplation. Changed industrial methods and the relatively high level of rail rates have induced a tendency to the decentralization of industrial operations for the very purpose of lessening the transportation burden.[15]

This brief summary serves to point out the changes that took place in the transportation market in the early part of this century. The railroad industry, long considered to be the backbone of the transportation system of the country and immune to intermodal competition, felt the effects of increased competition by the other modes of transportation. Although the railroads still hauled well over half the total intercity ton-miles of freight, the inroads made by the other modes of transportation were indicative of the forthcoming changes.

Regulatory Developments

Extensive congressional hearings were held following World War I, not only to settle the government ownership issue, but also to thoroughly review the existing legislation. The resulting legislation under the Transportation Act of 1920 can be divided into three categories: (1) provisions for returning control of the railroads to the private sector; (2) provisions to make regulation more complete; and (3) provisions necessary to remedy existing defects in the regulatory system.[16] There was an underlying emphasis upon trying to ensure financial soundness in the rail system.

government aid

In the first category there were several provisions to ensure that the transition from government to private control would take place as smoothly as possible. The government guaranteed earnings for six months, established a loan fund for improvements, and allowed the railroads a ten-year period in which to pay for improvements made by the federal government. In the second category the ICC was given control over security issues, abandonments, and combinations.[17] The third category was the one that received the most attention, since it ushered in an era of what has been termed positive regulation.

minimum rate control

One of the more important measures under the third category was that the ICC was given the power to establish minimum rates. It will be remembered that the ICC was given the power to set maximum rates in 1906 to protect the shippers. It was believed that in some instances competition could drive rates too low, to the detriment of the carriers. Therefore, the ICC was given the power to set a "floor" below which rates would not be able to fall. The ICC was also given power to allow pooling agreements when they would be in the public interest and jurisdiction over new railroad construction. Finally, the rule of rate-making was the most important of the provisions designed to remedy defects in the regulatory structure.

■ rule of rate-making

■ recapture clause

The rule of rate-making was similar to the ICC's control over minimum rates in that it represented a new concept in rate-making. Heretofore, the primary concern of the ICC in rate matters was the protection of the shippers. The rule of rate-making directed the ICC's attention to the earnings of the railroads to ensure an adequate transportation system. In effect, the rule of rate-making stipulated that the railroads were entitled to a fair return upon the fair value of their property. The Recapture Clause was enacted as a part of the legislation. This clause provided that in the event that a railroad made more than the prescribed return, one-half of the excess was to be paid to the ICC. The ICC was to place the excess in a contingency fund, and from this fund it could make loans to the less profitable lines for capital expenditures or to refund maturing obligations. Loans from the fund were to bear an interest rate of 6 percent and had to be adequately secured. The carriers themselves had to place their share of the excess in a trust fund, and it was to be used only to pay interest, dividends, and rentals in the event that carriers did not earn the stipulated return in any one year.

In summary, the Transportation Act of 1920 enacted the rule of rate-making and the Recapture Clause. The ICC was vested with the power to prescribe minimum rates and correct intrastate rates which discriminated against interstate commerce. The ICC's power was codified or clarified respecting division of joint rates and the Long and Short Haul Clause.

■ additional provisions

In addition, the ICC was authorized to modify the prohibition against pooling as long as certain criteria were met to protect shippers and to require the common use of terminals. Also, the ICC was authorized to prepare a plan for the voluntary consolidation of railroads. Furthermore, the act of 1920 prohibited certain financial aspects unless approved by the ICC, including consolidation and unification, construction and abandonments, assurance of securities, and interlocking directorates. The act also established the Railway Labor Board for deciding disputes.

■ Hoch-Smith Resolution

The so-called "positive thrust" of the Transportation Act of 1920 was stymied with the passage of the Hoch-Smith Resolution of 1925. Although this was not a major piece of legislation, the Hoch-Smith Resolution was passed to appease several industries that were upset about the ICC rate level increases in the early 1920s. The resolution directed the ICC to consider, in adjusting freight rates, conditions in the several industries and to investigate the rate structure of the railroads. Also, it directed the ICC in light of the depression in agriculture, to establish the lowest possible rates (compatible with adequate service) for agricultural products.

The next several years were basically free of any modifications in legislation. The great depression which began late in 1929 caused problems for many industries, including railroads. It took Congress several years to respond, but economic conditions demanded some action. The result was the Emergency Transportation Act of 1933 which continued the trend of so-called positive regulation which was started in 1920.

The title of the act of 1933 is indicative of the nature of its provisions.

■ Act of 1933

The railroads were feeling the adverse conditions of the country, namely, declining traffic, reduced earnings, and financial distress. The act contained both temporary and permanent provisions which, it was hoped, would alleviate the situation of the railroads.

■ emergency provisions

Under the emergency provisions of the act, a federal coordinator of transportation was established. The federal coordinator had essentially two duties. He was to aid the railroads in bringing about operation economies through cooperative action among railroads, and he was to investigate and consider other means of improving transport conditions.

■ permanent changes

There were also several permanent legislative changes made by the act of 1933. First, the ICC was given expanded powers over rail consolidations and unifications in hopes that this would introduce some economies of operation and help solve problems. In addition, changes were made in the rule of rate-making, and the Recapture Clause was repealed, ending the grand scheme of Congress to stabilize rail earnings. However, the amended rule of rate-making was destined to become one of the most significant and controversial items of legislation in the next legislative period. The amended rule of rate-making read as follows:

In the exercise of its power to prescribe just and reasonable rates the Commission shall give due consideration, among other factors, to the effect of rates on the movement of traffic; to the need, in the public interest, of adequate and efficient railway transportation service at the lowest cost consistent with the furnishing of such service; and the need of revenues sufficient to enable the carriers, under honest, economical, and efficient management, to provide such service.

In summary, the era of 1920 to 1937 represents an important epoch in our legislative history because of the new thrust by Congress to consider what the regulated companies needed to provide adequate service—they needed reasonable revenue to maintain equipment and attract capital. The grand plan in the form of the rule of rate-making and the Recapture Clause was not successful as originally conceived, but nevertheless the important directional change was made. The amendment of the rate-making rule helped to set the stage for the next era of regulation, namely, the era of intermodal regulation.

The Era of Intermodal Regulation: 1935-1960

As indicated, transportation legislation prior to 1935 was for all intents and purposes designed to regulate a monopolistic industry. Very little attention had been directed toward the other modes which were developing, particularly in the period following World War I. The ICC was cognizant of these changes in the marketplace and called attention to them in their annual reports and various cases. Congress finally responded in the depth of the depression with the Motor Carrier Act of 1935 which precipitated a series of acts to extend legislative control to other modes of transportation. Before taking up a consideration of these legislative changes, let us turn to a brief discussion of the developments in the market which initiated these changes.

Transportation Developments

The ICC discussed the problem in the transportation markets in its 1938 annual report.[18] The ICC stated that the railroad industry was in serious trouble again. Railroads had experienced a mild recovery from 1932 to 1937 when the freight tonnage index reached a high of 99.2 compared to 49 in 1932.[19] However, the index fell again, reaching 53.7 in August of 1937.

■ rail decline

The ICC stated that the primary cause was the drop off in demand attributable to the depression coupled with the great increase in competitive forms of transportation. In addition to these two factors, there had been a growing tendency for decentralization of industrial operations; a substitution of natural gas, hydroelectricity, and fuel oil for coal; substitution of products requiring short hauls for products requiring long hauls; and the decline in tonnage of exports and imports. The large amount of indebtedness and past financial exploitation were also contributing factors.

■ increased competition

The increase in competition is of immediate importance here. The ICC termed it a "transportation revolution" which took place in a remarkably short period of time.[20] The motor vehicle was the most important factor in this revolution. In 1938, the motor vehicle was by far the most important means of transportation in the carriage of persons, and it had been growing in importance by "leaps and bounds" in the carriage of property as well. While this remarkable development had been taking place, there had been a growth in intercoastal water transportation via the Panama Canal and increased use of inland waterways made possible by government expenditures to improve them. In addition, pipelines were extended and put to new uses and air transportation was born, which in the words of the ICC, "grew like Jack's bean stalk."

This marked growth in transportation facilities was characterized by an appreciable growth of private transportation as opposed to for-hire transportation. This growth was not confined to passenger automobiles. There was also a remarkable growth in private trucks in the farming sector and commercial firms and a growth in private carriage by water and air.

The ICC made the following comments which serve to elucidate the problem:[21]

Private capital enterprise have been responsible only in part for this transportation revolution. The extraordinary development of highway transportation could not have been accomplished, save for the expenditures of billions of Federal and State funds in the construction and maintenance of a network of paved highways covering the entire country. Public funds have likewise been responsible for the building of the Panama Canal and for the construction or improvement of many inland waterways, harbors, and docks. Similar aid has been given to air transportation.

■ ICC comments

The vast increase in the supply of transportation facilities thus accomplished was made without any general plans, prevision of results, or attempt to shape or control them on the part of the Government. The railroads are not the only carriers that have suffered from the conditions so created. The bankruptcy of a large number of the railroad companies has attracted much attention, but the fact is that the same malady has afflicted motor carriers, particularly those engaged in the carriage of property, certainly to as great an extent. Their general financial condition has been most distressing, and this has been true of water carriers and air carriers in general. The one exception has been the pipelines, whose efficiency and low operating costs, together with favorable business affiliations, have made them prosperous.

■ freight tonnage

The first year for which reliable statistics are available concerning the distribution of intercity freight traffic is 1939 (see Table 16.1). In this year it has been estimated that railroads accounted for 62.4 percent of the total, motor trucks for 9.7 percent, oil pipelines for 10.2 percent, the water carriers on the Great Lakes for 14 percent, and the water carriers on rivers and canals for 3.7 percent. However, in 1940 the respective figures were 61.3 percent, 10 percent, 9.6 percent, 15.5 percent, and 3.6 percent. Each of the groups concerned experienced an absolute increase in traffic between 1939 and 1940, but their relative positions had changed remarkably in just one year.[22]

The changes that took place in the period from 1935 to 1960 in the transportation market are perhaps more significant than the changes in any other era (except possibly for the period from 1870 to 1900 when the rail network was being laid at a rapid rate). Competition among the various modes of transport increased to a greater degree. Billions of dollars of federal funds were spent on highways, waterways, and airways with a consequent increase in the number of operating units.

■ technological change

During this time, technological innovations occurred which have had a marked effect on the service of the carriers. Piggyback is a good example of an innovation which has had a strong impact on the service offered and has increased rail carloadings. Another example is the tri-level rail cars for hauling automobiles which enabled the railroads to substantially reduce their rates on this traffic. Similar innovations in technology occurred in all of the modes.

A significant trend in the post-World War II era has been the relative decline of the common carrier. The gross national product (GNP), adjusted for price change, increased 26 percent between 1946 and 1959. The

Table 16.1 Distribution of Intercity Freight 1939-1960*

Mode Year	Rail	Motor	Pipeline	Water	Air	Total
1939	62.4	9.7	10.2	17.7	.00	100
1940	61.3	10.0	9.6	19.1	.00	100
1960	44.1	21.8	17.4	16.7	.07	100

*Expressed as a percentage

■ common carrier decline

increase in intercity ton-miles during this same period was estimated at about 40 percent. In 1946, unregulated transportation accounted for only 21 percent of total intercity ton-miles, but by 1961 it was estimated that 33 percent moved by unregulated carriers.

As suggested, the changes which took place between 1935 and 1960 were phenomenal in many respects. They set the stage for some important changes in regulation in response to the changes in the transportation market.

Regulatory Developments

As stated in the introduction of this section, the first major step toward regulation on an intermodal basis at the federal level was the passage of the Motor Carrier Act of 1935. However, it should be noted again that the ICC had been given jurisdiction over oil pipelines in 1906 under the Hepburn Act. Also, the ICC had some limited control over water lines because of the Panama Canal Act. It is safe to say, however, that the Motor Carrier Act was the most significant addition to intermodal regulation.

Essentially the Motor Carrier Act of 1935 established for the motor for-hire carriers and brokers a comprehensive set of economic regulations substantially similar to that for the railroads. These regulations became Part II of the Interstate Commerce Act. Part I pertained to railroads and pipelines.

The act of 1935 began with a declaration of congressional policy which set forth certain objectives such as preservation of inherent advantages, foster sound conditions in the industry, promotion of adequate service at reasonable rates, and encouragement of coordination. The ICC was given responsibility for the administration of the regulation which included general jurisdiction over motor vehicle carriers engaged in transporting persons or property in interstate or foreign commerce. The jurisdiction included some exemptions such as agricultural products, horticultural products, and fish. The act recognized four types of carriers—common, contract, private, and brokers. (Some individuals would include exempt carriers.) The ICC was given the authority to prescribe certain safety regulations and also authority over the service of motor carriers. In the latter regard, the ICC required common carriers to obtain a certificate of public convenience and necessity and contract carriers had to obtain a permit. The primary purpose of these instruments was to control entry. The ICC was given extensive control over rates of common motor carriers similar to that which they exercise over the railroad. The ICC also had authority over accounts and reports, combinations, and securities.

■ motor carrier act

As noted, the most important concern of Congress and the common motor carriers was control of entry. The low capital requirements of the motor carrier made entry relatively easy. Therefore, potential carriers wishing to offer for-hire service had to apply for a certificate of public convenience and necessity to operate as a common carrier, or a permit to operate as a contract carrier. Carriers that had been in operation prior to the passage of the act were protected by a grandfather Clause as long as they could prove that they had been in lawful operation. Overall, the Motor Carrier Act provided an elaborate framework of regulation for a segment of the industry. This set the stage for additional regulation to cover other areas of transportation.

■ Civil Aeronautics Act of 1938

The Civil Aeronautics Act of 1938 established the system of federal regulation of air transportation. The act, as modified by an executive order in 1940, established the Civil Aeronautics Board (CAB) which was an independent regulatory authority within the Department of Commerce. The CAB took over some safety regulations formerly exercised by the Department of Commerce.

In addition to the transferred regulations, the CAB was empowered to establish the compensation to be paid to airlines for carrying the mail, and to administer the system of economic controls over airlines, including rate regulation and entry control. Also, the CAB had a unique responsibility for promotion and regulation.

In addition to the CAB, the Civil Aeronautics Administration (CAA) also was established within the Department of Commerce. The CAA had two primary functions. The first was to promote aviation by establishing and maintaining the airway and airport system. The second was to establish and enforce safety rules, examine air personnel, test aircraft, control air traffic, and investigate accidents. The promotional responsibility of the CAB and the CAA was an important difference to previous legislation.

The approach established for regulating airlines was unique in several respects. Congress felt that more control was necessary because of the infant industry status of the airlines as well as the airlines' importance for national defense.

■ Transportation Act of 1940

The next major piece of legislation was the Transportation Act of 1940. Part III of the act set up a system of economic regulation for the domestic water carrier industry which was substantially the same as Parts I and II of the Interstate Commerce Act. There were some important differences in the water carrier legislation as compared to the rail transportation legislation. In particular, the act of 1940 followed the precedent of the Motor Carrier Act and set forth certain exempt carriers. However, the exemptions applied to liquid or dry commodities in bulk and originally applied to three or less commodities in bulk in a single tow. The net effect of this exemption was that about 90 percent of the tonnage was exempt from regulation. Also, the act did not vest the ICC with the power to treat discriminatory rates or to award damages against carriers.

■ rule of rate-making

The rule of rate-making was also amended under the Transportation Act of 1940. This act represented the first attempt by Congress to deal comprehensively with transportation problems since the Transportation Act of 1920. The rule of rate-making was made applicable to the motor carrier in 1935, but it now carried an additional stipulation that the ICC should consider the inherent advantages of the motor carrier. These inherent advantages were not defined, but the terminology suggested that Congress felt that different cost and service characteristics were present in the motor carrier industry.[23]

The regulation of the additional modes of transportation complicated the regulatory structure. The act of 1940 sought to alleviate the situation by a statement of national policy which read as follows:

■ national policy

It is hereby declared to be the national transportation policy of the Congress to provide for fair and impartial regulation of all modes of transportation subject to the provisions of the Act, so administered as to *recognize and preserve* the *inherent advantages of each;* to promote safe, adequate, economical and efficient service and foster sound economic conditions in transportation and among the several carriers; to encourage the establishment and maintenance of reasonable charges for transportation services, without unjust discriminations, undue preferences or advantages, or *unfair or destructive competitive practices* to cooperate with the several States and the duly authorized officials thereof; and to encourage fair wages and equitable working conditions; all to the end of developing, coordinating, and preserving a national transportation system by water, highway, and rail, as well as other means, adequate to meet the needs of the commerce of the United States, of the Postal Service, and of the national defense. All of the provisions of this Act shall be administered and enforced with a view to carrying out the above declaration of policy.

A comprehensive analysis of this policy is not possible here since it could be the subject of an entire chapter. However, one can readily discern a protective air in the wording of the policy statement as indicated by the underscored sections above. Some of the above is a carry-over from the policy statement of the Motor Carrier Act of 1935 and indicates the concern of Congress with having the ICC regulate additional modes of transportation, that is, motor and water. Also, you should note some of the practical nature of the policy, for example, wages, and working conditions.

■ other provisions

In addition to the declaration of a national transportation policy and regulatory provisions for water carriers, the 1940 act made changes in legislation regarding consolidations and other forms of railroad unifications. The railroads were made responsible for the burden of proof for any change in rates. The Long and Short Haul Clause was also amended.

■ Freight Forwarder Act

In 1942, the Freight Forwarder Act was passed by Congress. This extended the same general plan of economic regulation to surface freight forwarders that is followed in the first three parts of the Interstate Commerce Act for rail, motor, and water carriers.

With the passage of the Freight Forwarder Act of 1942, Congress had successfully completed a legislative package that encompassed all of the basic modes of transportation. Most of the regulation was administered by the ICC. The major exception was air transportation which was administered by the CAB.

Following the close of World War II, the first piece of legislation of any significance was the Reed-Bulwinkle Act of 1948 which legalized joint rate-making by common carriers through their rate bureaus. The act extended antitrust immunity to carriers participating in a rate bureau and required the ICC to approve the agreement under which the individual bureaus operated.

After the Reed-Bulwinkle Act was passed, there were a series of minor acts passed which amended the Interstate Commerce Act by: (1) confirming the ICC's authority to regulate the use by motor carriers of motor vehicles not owned by them; (2) requiring motor contract carriers to file their actual rates or charges with the ICC; (3) revising the definition of motor contract carrier and also the standards of proof for the granting of new permits; (4) modifying the requirements for obtaining a freight forwarder permit; and (5) requiring all Section 22 (government contract rates) rate tenders to be filed with the ICC.

In 1958, Congress passed the Transportation Act of 1958 which was the first major piece of legislation in the post-World War II era. One of the most significant parts of the act was the modification made to the rule of rate-making which admonished the ICC and instructed them "not to hold up rates to a particular level to protect the traffic of another mode."

Evidence offered in the congressional hearings indicated that the ICC had adopted a protective policy in regulating competitive rates between modes of transportation. Rates in many instances were set on a differential basis to protect traffic of certain carriers, particularly those competing with rail carriers. The change in the rule of rate-making was made after extensive hearings in Congress. The amendment was not intended as a substantive change in the particular statute, but rather as an admonishment to the ICC to refrain from its protective approach to rate-making.

The act of 1958 was similar in some respects to the Emergency Transportation Act of 1933. One of the reasons for the act was the serious financial condition of the railroads. The situation was such that the railroads had difficulty maintaining their credit. In order to alleviate this situation and to rectify other problem areas, temporary and permanent provisions were encompassed in the act.[24] Under the temporary provisions of the act, a system of guaranteed loans was inaugurated to assist the railroads in acquiring the necessary funds for capital expenditures and for the maintenance of equipment and facilities. The government did not lend money directly to the railroads but only guaranteed loans when the carrier was unable to obtain funds at reasonable rates of interest without such a federal guarantee. The aggregate amount of guaranteed loans could not exceed 500 million dollars.[25]

In terms of longer-run changes, an important section of the 1958 act dealt with intrastate rates and service. Two decisions rendered by the Supreme Court in 1958 limited the effectiveness of the ICC in removing discrimination against interstate commerce.[26] This situation was remedied by the act of 1958 and the procedure for removing intrastate discrimination was made more expeditious. The ICC was also given au-

Reed-Bulwinkle Act

miscellaneous acts

Act of 1958

rule of rate-making

financial aid

intrastate rates

thority over the discontinuance of passenger train service.

Two other important amendments made by the Transportation Act of 1958 were directed toward the motor carrier industry. One of the amendments was concerned with limiting the expansion, by judicial interpretation, of the agricultural exemptions under the motor carrier provisions. The other amendment sought to prevent private carriers from hauling for-hire traffic. These two groups of carriers had posed a real problem for the ICC. In many instances, they were operating illegitimately and performing a common or contract service. These unregulated operations were labeled as the "grey area," and a report was issued by the ICC to study the problem.

■ motor carrier provisions

After the Transportation Act of 1958, there was a lengthy void in the passage of transportation legislation as the marketplace expanded for freight movement, and carriers expanded into different markets. A minor act was passed in 1966 entitled the Incentive Per Diem Act which authorized the ICC to fix per diem compensation for the use by one railroad of the cars of another. The purpose of the act was to allow the ICC to set incentive charges to encourage purchase of new equipment by the railroads; the old per diem rates were so low that they discouraged new equipment purchase.

Also in 1966, Congress passed the Department of Transportation Act which established a federal department of transportation (DOT) to which the activities and responsibilities of numerous government agencies, including the ICC's regulation of the safety operations of railroads and motor carriers, were transferred. The act also charged the new cabinet level secretary to exercise leadership in transportation matters and develop transportation policies. Further, the secretary was charged with additional responsibilities such as the gathering of data relevant to transportation decision making. The act was hailed as a major force for needed change and for focusing attention upon the crucial nature of transportation in the economy. Figure 16.1 shows the organization of the U.S. Department of Transportation along with the responsibilities of other federal agencies.

■ DOT established

The next act of this era was the Rail Passenger Service Act of 1970. This act established the National Railroad Passenger Corporation, usually referred to as Amtrak. Under the auspices of this act, Amtrak took over, on May 1, 1971, the operation of most of the nation's passenger rail service over a basic system established by the secretary of transportation. Amtrak utilized the right-of-way of existing railroads and paid for such use. The act was seen as a way to solve the long existing problem of losses or deficits which were associated with passenger operations, and at the same time as a way of salvaging some part of the interstate rail passenger system. It should be noted that Amtrak was incorporated as a "for-profit" organization.

■ Amtrak

The final act of this era was the Regional Rail Reorganization Act of 1973 (3-R Act) which was passed as a rescue measure for the seven major railroads operating in the northeast quadrant of the country who were seeking reorganization under Section 77 of the Bankruptcy Act.

■ 3-R Act

Figure 16.1 Transportation Organizations

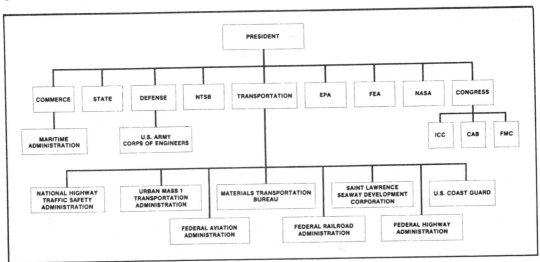

OFFICE OR AGENCY	RESPONSIBILITY
President	Rules on matters relating to international air transit by U.S. air carriers and foreign air carrier operations to the U.S. Appoints members of Federal agencies and appoints chairman of CAB and FMC.
Department of State	Develops policy recommendations and approves policy programs concerning international aviation and maritime transportation.
Maritime Administration	Promotes merchant marine; grants ship mortgage insurance; determines ship requirements, ocean services, routes and lines essential for development and maintenance of the foreign commerce of the United States, maintains the National Defense Reserve Fleet; develops ship designs, marine transportation systems, advanced propulsion concepts, and ship mechanization and management techniques. The Maritime Subsidy Board awards subsidies and determines the degree of services and specific routes of subsidized operators.
Corps of Engineers	Constructs and maintains river and harbor improvements. Administers laws for protecting navigable waterways.
Environmental Energy Administration (FEA)	National air and water pollution and noise control programs and regulations. Sets emission standards and noise standards.
Federal Energy Administration (FEA)	Energy conservation programs and regulations, contingency planning for allocation and rationing of energy.
National Aeronautics and Space Administration NASP)	Aeronautical and space research.
National Transportation Safety Board	Determines and reports causes, facts, and circumstances relating to transportation accidents; reviews on appeal the revocation, suspension, or denial of any certificate or license issued by the Department; and exercises all functions relating to aircraft accident investigations.
Interstate Commerce Commission	Regulates, in varying degrees by mode of transport, surface carrier operations, including rates, routes, operating rights, abandonment and mergers; conducts investigations and awards damages where applicable and administers railroad bankruptcy. Prescribes uniform systems of accounts and records, evaluates property owned or used by carriers subject to the Act; authorizes issuance of securities or assumption of obligations by carriers by railroad and certain common or contract carriers by motor vehicle. Develops preparedness programs covering rail, motor, and inland waterways utilization.
Civil Aeronautics Board	Regulates carrier operations, including rates, routes operating rights, and mergers; determines and grants subsidies. Assists in the development of international air transport and grants, subject to Presidential approval, foreign operating certificates to U.S. carriers and U.S. operating permits to foreign carriers.
Federal Maritime Commission	Regulates services, practices, and agreements of water common carriers in international trade. Regulates rates and practices of water common carriers operating in domestic trade to points beyond continental U.S.

■ Conrail

Following the extensive process prescribed by the act for the restructuring of the rail network in the northeast, the Consolidated Rail Corporation (Conrail) took over portions of the bankrupt lines and began operation on April 1, 1976.

The acts establishing Conrail and Amtrak marked, in some ways, a new epoch in transportation legislation. To some, it signaled the first step toward complete ownership of the railroads by the government or at least toward more government regulation. To others, it signaled the need for some major legislative overhaul, and these others point to the Rail Revitalization and Regulatory Reform Act of 1976 (4-R Act) as perhaps the most comprehensive piece of transportation legislation ever passed by Congress. Whatever one's view of the significance of the establishment of Conrail and Amtrak, there is no question that both were controversial but important measures taken to help solve problems in the railroad industry.

The two acts establishing Amtrak and Conrail signaled the end of one era and the beginning of another, namely, the end of the era of intermodal regulation and the start of an era of deregulation. However, while the 4-R Act set the stage for rail deregulation, it was in some ways an extension of the 3-R Act of 1973 since it provided the funds for the rehabilitation of Conrail.

The Birth of a New Era in Regulation

■ 4-R Act

The major purpose of this section of the chapter is to discuss the 4-R Act of 1976 and to set the stage for Chapter 17 which is concerned with the deregulation of transportation. The 4-R Act encompassed changes of major proportions and was in part a response, as indicated, to a series of rail bankruptcies in the 1960s and early 1970s. But, the act was also a response to changes in the transportation market. We will again examine those changes before detailing the parts of the 4-R Act.

Transportation Developments

The changes which took place in the three decades following World War II, 1945 to 1975, were very significant. Competition among modes increased to a great degree. Billions of dollars of federal funds were spent on highways, waterways, and airways, and technological innovations occurred which have had a marked effect on the service of the carriers.

■ common carrier decline

A significant trend in the post-World War II era has been the relative decline of the common carriers. The GNP, adjusted for price change, increased 26 percent between 1946 and 1959. The increase in intercity ton-miles during this same period was estimated at about 40 percent. In 1946, unregulated transportation accounted for 21 percent of the total, but in 1961 it accounted for 33 percent of this growing market. In 1975, unregulated transportation accounted for at least 50 percent of the total intercity ton-miles.

■ mergers

Another significant change in the transportation industry has been the merger movement, particularly in the railroad industry. Mergers combat declining profits and emphasize improved efficiency through elimination of duplicated services. Some mergers have sought improvement through market extension. This has been particularly true in the motor carrier industry.

Perhaps the most important change has been the shifts which occurred among modes of transportation. The railroad industry has been the big loser (relatively speaking), as pointed out in Table 16.2. The railroads carried approximately 67 percent of the traffic in the last year of the war (1945); trucks, for example, carried 6.5 percent. By 1975, the rail share had fallen to under 37 percent, whereas the motor carrier share had risen to over 21 percent. Pipelines had enjoyed a growth pattern similar to motor, whereas water carriers and airlines had remained relatively stable. It is important to note, however, that the actual ton-miles were increasing for all modes during this period due to the great growth in the economy.

■ freight distribution

With the transportation market changes mentioned above as background, a discussion of the 4-R Act can follow. As stated above, this piece of legislation provided some of the most significant changes in transportation legislation since the Transportation Act of 1920. It was probably the first major step toward deregulation, although deregulation was not its primary reason for coming into being. As the title suggests, the act was aimed at rescuing the railroad industry from what many people thought was financial collapse.

Railroad Revitalization and Regulatory Reform Act of 1976

The 4-R Act was very comprehensive in scope and attempted to redress a number of problems associated with transportation, particularly with regard to railroads. The most important regulatory changes probably had to do with railroad rate-making. The act contained new standards to be applied in determining whether rail rates were just and reasonable. The ICC could no longer declare that rates that were equal to or above variable cost were unjust or unreasonably low. This was particularly important in competitive situations where the railroads, as we have seen, have been maintaining for years that rates should be judged upon variable or out-of-pocket cost when determining reasonableness to meet competition.

■ 4-R Act and rate-making

■ rate standards

In addition, the new standards also stated that no rate was to be judged too high for purposes of the reasonableness test unless the ICC determined that the carrier had market dominance. The ICC was charged with determining the appropriate standards for market dominance.

Table 16.2 Intercity Share of Freight Ton/Miles*

Year/Mode	Rail	Motor	Water	Pipeline	Air
1945	67.2	6.5	13.9	12.4	0.01
1960	44.1	21.8	16.7	17.4	0.07
1975	36.8	21.3	17.1	22.3	0.19

Source: Transportation Association of America, *Transportation Facts and Trends* (Washington, D.C., 1976), p. 8.

*Expressed as a percentage.

■ protective rate-making prohibition

The act also reasserted that the ICC was not to engage in protective rate policies—or what has become known as umbrella rate-making. This change modified the rule of rate-making by stating that rates were not to be held up to a particular level to protect the traffic of any other carrier or mode unless the ICC found that the proposed rates would reduce the going concern value of the carrier proposing the rate change(s). As a further amplification of this test, the act stated that any rate equal to or exceeding variable cost could not be found to reduce the going concern value of the carrier proposing the rate change.

■ zone of reasonableness

The changes indicated above moved rate control an important step toward deregulation. There were important new freedoms for intermodal rate-making implied in the legislation. In addition, the act set up the concept of a zone of reasonableness which allowed carriers to change rates with some degree of freedom. Under the provisions of the act, in the two years following the passage of the act, the carriers were allowed to raise or lower rates by as much as 7 percent from the level of rates in effect at the beginning of the year. While the ICC retained the power to suspend rates for a period of up to seven months, the burden of proof in those rate cases was shifted to the complaining party, which had to prove that the rate could cause injury, and that it should be found unlawful as a result. This was an important change in the law for carriers seeking to change their rates.

■ other provisions

The act also added statutory procedures and time limits for cases involving division of joint rail rates. The ICC was given exclusive jurisdiction to determine whether changes in proposed interstate rates relate properly to the interstate rates for such traffic and whether the appropriate state commission has acted within 120 days after proposed rates were filed. These two changes were designed to correct associated problems with joint rate divisions and interstate rates.

The ICC was given several directives related to rate matters under the 4-R Act. First, it was directed to establish standards for rail rates based upon seasonal, regional, or peak period demand for service. Second, the ICC was directed to establish rules for expeditious publication of separate rates for distinct rail service.

■ abandonment

Another major section of the 4-R Act dealt with service matters of railroads, including mergers. Abandonment or service discontinuance of a rail line was forbidden unless a certificate was issued by the ICC which stated that present or future public convenience did not require the service. Abandonment of an interstate line required serving a copy of an application with the state involved, but railroads could appeal directly to the ICC if no action was taken in 120 days after applying to the state. Advance notice of intention to abandon was to be provided by carriers which could be fulfilled by publication of rail maps showing which line(s) were being considered for abandonment.

■ mergers

The act stated that first authority on mergers and requisitions of control remains with the ICC, but the act gave the secretary of transportation an expanded and important role in such cases. The act further stated that the secretary had the authority to prepare plans and proposals, including the comprehensive restructuring of the rail system. The results of informal hearings were to be reported to the ICC, but the ICC could not act on any application without first obtaining the opinions of the secretary of transportation and the attorney general. The act established time limits on ICC action on mergers by requiring that the ICC had twenty-four months to conclude evidentiary proceedings. After proceedings, the ICC was required to render a decision within 180 days unless Congress granted an extension.

Other service matters addressed by the 4-R Act included a direction to the ICC to revise car service rules; the act also amended the car service provisions, including incentive per diem rates and the distribution of cars for unit service. Finally, in the service area, the act reported the provisions relating to compulsory extension of rail lines.

The act also contained a substantial number of more general or miscellaneous provisions, some of which should be presented and discussed. The ICC was given the authority to grant exemptions from regulations when not required by the public interest. The act established the Office of Rail Public Council as a new independent office within the ICC. It also set up the Rail Services Planning Office within the ICC with specified duties. The act required the ICC to issue regulations prescribing a uniform cost and revenue accounting and reporting system for all rail common carriers.

The ICC was further directed to submit within two years a plan to modernize and revise the Interstate Commerce Act. Also, the act changed the ICC's power over issuance of rail securities (except equipment obligations) by making it no longer exclusive. In addition, the act prohibited discriminatory state tax treatment of transportation property.

■ funding

The final part of the act had to do with funding. As indicated previously, funding was necessary to implement the restructuring of the bankrupt railroads of the Northeast into Conrail under the final system plan approved by the U.S. Rail Administration (USRA) as set up under the 3-R Act. A sum of $2.1 billion was made available to Conrail. Funding was provided by granting the new organization power to issue bonds and stocks to the USRA. Also, a $600 million government loan program was established to finance railroad rehabilitation of plant and equipment. In addition, loan guarantees of up to $1 billion were provided to finance purchases of equipment and plant, and $1.75 billion was made available for improving rail passenger service in the Northeast.

While there are several other provisions that could be detailed, the above discussion provides exposure to the most important parts of the act. As stated earlier, the 4-R Act was very comprehensive in scope.

Conclusion

This chapter has attempted to analyze the development of transportation regulation that took place during a period of almost one hundred years. While we have moved into an era of deregulation, it is important for us to have some appreciation of the tremendous scope and complexity of the regulation which has occurred.

Our analysis of transportation regulation suggests that there were several major periods, and an attempt has been made to relate these developments to changes in the transportation markets. The eras presented in this chapter include: (1) the development of regulation, (2) the positive approach to regulation, and (3) intermodal regulation. Also, it has been suggested that the 4-R Act introduced a new era, namely, deregulation. This topic is so important that the next chapter will be devoted to its consideration.

Study Questions

1. It is often said that the problems railroads face today were created during the great growth period in the 1880s, yet during this period of growth, the railroads realized high profits. How can this be so?

2. Why was the Act to Regulate Commerce a major event in government policy?

3. The final version of the Act to Regulate Commerce was actually written and shaped by railroad interests. Why would this be so? Give some arguments as to why the industry would have done this.

4. What were the key points in that original act?

5. The Elkins Act dealt with certain forms of discrimination. Are the major elements of that law just as applicable today through the current deregulation of transportation as they were in 1903?

6. How would you describe the emphasis of regulation prior to 1920 as compared to that after 1920?

7. The ICC had a difficult time determining what a "just and reasonable" rate should be. The Rule of Rate-making, enacted in 1920, was designed to alleviate some uncertainties in the area as well. Why could not a simple per mile formula for all rates be enacted by Congress for carriers and the ICC to follow when making rates?

8. How would you describe the different phases of transportation regulation that have occurred in the United States?

Notes

1. Calvin Crumbaker, *Transportation and Politics* (Eugene, Ore.: University of Oregon Press, 1940), p. 6.

2. Ralph L. Dewey, *The Long and Short Haul Principle of Rate Regulation* (Columbus, Ohio: Ohio University Press, 1935), p. 59.

3. *Wabash, St. Louis and Pacific Railway Co. v. Illinois*, 118 U.S. 557 (1886).

4. Russel E. Westmeyer, *Economics of Transportation* (New York: Prentice-Hall, 1952), p. 113.

5. *Cincinnati, New Orleans, and Texas Pacific Ry. Co. v. Interstate Commerce Commission*, 162 U.S. 116 (1896); *Interstate Commerce Commission v. Alabama Midland Railway Company*, 168 U.S. 144 (1897); *Interstate Commerce Commission v.*

Cincinnati, New Orleans, and Texas Pacific Railway Company, 167 U.S. 479 (1897).

6. Marvin L. Fair and Ernest W. Williams, Jr., *Economics of Transportation* (New York: Harper and Brothers, 1959), p. 445.

7. D. Philip Locklin, *Economics of Transportation* (Homewood, Ill.: Richard D. Irwin, 1960), p. 255.

8. Ibid., pp. 215-217.

9. *United States v. Delaware and Hudson Railroad*, et al., 213 U.S. 257 (1909); *Interstate Commerce Commission v. Illinois Central Railroad Company*, 215 U.S. 452 (1910); *Interstate Commerce Commission v. Chicago, Rock Island and Pacific Railway Company*, 218 U.S. 89 (1910); *Interstate Commerce Commission v. Union Pacific Railroad Company*, 222 U.S. 541 (1912).

10. Ibid., p. 131.

11. Truman C. Bigham, *Transportation: Principles and Problems* (New York: McGraw-Hill, 1946), p. 171.

12. Coordination of Motor Transportation, 182 ICC 263 (1932).

13. U.S., Congress, House, *Report of the Federal Coordinator of Transportation, 1934*, 74th Congress, 1st sess., 1935 H.R. 89, p. 15.

14. Ibid. [The same page as preceding note.]

15. *Emergency Freight Charges, 1935*, 108 ICC 4 (1935).

16. Locklin, *Economics of Transportation*, p. 225.

17. Westmeyer, *Economics of Transportation*, pp. 140-143.

18. *Fifty-Second Annual Report at the Interstate Commerce Commission* (Washington, D.C.: U.S. Government Printing Office, 1938), p. 1.

19. Ibid., p. 2 (1923-25 as the base).

20. Ibid., p. 17.

21. Ibid., pp. 17-18.

22. Association of American Railroads, Bureau of Railway Economics, *Railroad Transportation: A Statistical Record* (Washington, D.C., 1960), p. 34.

23. Ernest W. Williams, Jr., *The Regulation of Rail-Motor Rate Competition* (New York: Harper and Brothers, 1958), p. 14.

24. Robert Harbeson, "The Transportation Act of 1958," *Land Economics Journal* 35 (May 1959): 156-157.

25. Locklin, *Economics of Transportation*, p. 255.

26. *Chicago, Milwaukee, St. Paul, and Pacific Railroad Company v. Illinois*, 335 U.S. 300 (1958) and *Public Service Commission of Utah v. United States*, 356 U.S. 421 (1958).

Suggested Readings

Fair, Marvin L., and Guandolo, John. *Transportation Regulation*. 8th ed. Dubuque, Iowa: William C. Brown Co., 1978.

Fulda, Carl H. *Competition of Regulated Industries: Transportation*. Boston: Little, Brown and Co., 1961, chap. 2.

Harbesen, Robert W. "Transportation Regulation: A Centennial Evaluation." *ICC Practitioners Journal*, July/August, 1972, pp. 628-33.

Lieb, Robert C. *Transportation: The Domestic System*. 2nd ed. Reston, Va.: Reston Publishing Co., 1981, chaps. 11-15.

Locklin, D. Philip. *Economics of Transportation.* 7th ed. Homewood, Ill.: Richard D. Irwin, 1972, chaps. 9-12, 29, 32, 34, 35.

MacIntyre, A. Everette. "Status of Regulatory Independence." *Federal Bar Journal,* Winter, 1969.

Moore, Thomas G. *Freight Transportation Regulation: Surface Freight and the Interstate Commerce Commission.* Washington, D.C.: American Enterprise Institute for Public Policy Research, 1972, chap. 3.

Pegrum, D. Dudley. *Economics of Transportation.* Homewood, Illinois: Richard D. Irwin, 1974, chaps. 12-15.

U.S. Interstate Commerce Commission. *The Regulatory Issues of Today.* Washington, D.C.: The Commission, 1975.

Williams, Jr., Ernest W. *The Regulation of Rail-Motor Rate Competition.* New York: Harper and Brothers, 1958.

Case   Phillip Jones Steel Corporation

The Phillip Jones Steel Corporation produces heavy bulk steel items such as construction girders, bridge structures, and highway supports. Its made-to-order production process permits the company to avoid any large-scale warehouse system, but it puts heavy emphasis on the transportation system. Previously, Phillip Jones was shipping its steel products by rail from its plant in Pittsburgh to points south and west. Because of the rail's relatively slow transit time and Phillip's lack of any rail siding, along with the nature of the industry being somewhat seasonal and highly price competitive, Phillip Jones has decided to switch to motor carrier. The company is hoping that this switch will alleviate problems associated with the lack of rail cars available during peak periods, accessibility of rail, speed, and adaptability of some rail equipment to some special steel products.

However, Phillip's choice of motor carrier does not end its problems. The corporation must now decide which type of motor carriers to use: common carrier (special hauling division), private motor carrier, or contract carrier. Although all three types are motor carriers, each would have its own advantages and disadvantages if used to haul the heavy bulk steel products manufactured by Phillip Jones.

If your job was to choose which type of motor carrier to use, what criteria would you use to evaluate each type's usefulness? What disadvantage would be inherent for each type of motor carrier in this case? How would the competitive nature of the steel industry affect your analysis and final decision? How would you justify your choice to top management? If the industry to be served was highly seasonal and price inelastic, would your final choice be altered? If so, how?

17 Changing Direction of Regulation

After reading this chapter you should:

1 Understand the nature and provisions of the Airline Deregulation Act of 1978.

2 Understand the nature and provisions of the Motor Carrier Act of 1980.

3 Understand the nature and provisions of the Staggers Rail Act of 1980.

4 Appreciate the impact of the changing direction of regulation.

The previous chapter set the stage for our discussion of deregulation. You will recall that the United States entered into a new era of regulation in 1975. The first major act passed in this new era was the 4-R Act of 1976. One of the major focuses of this particular piece of legislation was the financial rescue of the railroads, particularly in the northeastern part of the United States. Some sections of the act, however, were devoted to deregulation. Therefore, it is convenient to think of the 4-R Act as the start of an era of deregulation.

■ chapter overview

There have been three major pieces of legislation dealing with deregulation since the passage of the 4-R Act in 1976. These acts deal with individual modes of transportation. Because of their complexity and comprehensiveness, it would be best to discuss each of these acts separately and to analyze their major provisions. We will begin with a discussion of airlines followed by a discussion of motor carriers and railroads.

Airline Deregulation

■ Civil Aeronautics Act

As indicated previously, regulation of interstate air transportation began in the United States in 1938 when President Roosevelt signed into effect the Civil Aeronautics Act of 1938 which established the Civil Aeronautics Board (CAB) to protect airlines against economic problems. The act was quite comprehensive and was based in part on the regulation which had developed for other modes of transportation. It was hoped that the act would allow the airlines to enjoy the order and stability required for acquisition of capital and eventual long-term growth.

As was the case with regulation of the other modes of transportation, there were numerous critics of the regulations that were imposed on the airlines and of the policies emanating from the CAB. The critics were, perhaps, even more vociferous with respect to the airlines, because of the airlines' reliance upon passenger movements.

It could be argued that during the period from 1975 to 1978 the CAB began to move toward de facto deregulation and to place more reliance

■ de facto deregulation

on free-market forces. The CAB, under the chairmanship of Alfred Kahn who was appointed by President Carter with the objective of deregulating the airline industry, began extending operating authority to carriers who offered low fare proposals. That is, the CAB started using a lower fare proposal for applicants as an entry criterion. If a carrier did not submit a lower fare, the CAB would use its traditional criteria for entry, which of course were more restrictive.

■ mere competition

During this period the CAB also began to issue operating authority on a more permissive basis as a means of increasing price competition. The carriers were given the right to decide how much competitive service to offer. When the CAB initiated the more liberal entry policy, it was primarily concerned with not crowding the market. However, they became less concerned, eventually, about overcrowding and more concerned about having enough slots at airports in popular market areas.

■ critics

The CAB's action resulted in criticisms. Some people argued that traditional regulatory structure should be maintained. They contended that the objectives of increased rates and route competition could be adequately accomplished without the indiscriminate issue of permissive authority to all applicants. Carriers like U.S. Air, who operate on a more regional basis, were in favor of the newer policies. They complained that the entry policies of the prior forty years had placed the large trunk lines at a distinct advantage in terms of route service capabilities and equipment.

■ concerns of smaller carriers

Small carriers thought that the absence of entry controls would cause more carriers to enter markets than the markets could sustain, which would lead to losses for all competitors. The five largest carriers, United, Eastern, TWA, Delta, and American (the Big Five), already had about 75 percent of the domestic trunk line revenues, and the little air carriers were afraid that the big carriers would move in on some of the more lucrative small markets under the new policies. In addition, other carriers thought unlimited entry would lead to chaos in the airline industry.

The CAB, however, did not concede any of these arguments. Board members believed that Congress should pass legislation to protect their regulatory efforts from reversals. Congress responded and on October 24, 1978, President Carter signed the Airline Deregulation Act[1] into the law. The act dismantled regulations that had protected airlines from competitive market forces, and it indicated that the CAB would be abolished by 1985.

Airline Deregulation Act

The Airline Deregulation Act of 1978 amended the Federal Aviation Act. The new act dealt with a number of important issues, but the primary focus was rate-making.

■ zone of reasonableness

One of the major issues in rate-making was the so-called "zone of reasonableness." The act indicated that within a specifically defined zone, airlines would be free to set fares without having to worry about them being suspended, unless the rate was deemed too predatory. The zone ceiling allowed airlines to raise fares 5-10 percent above the established standards of the CAB; the floor was to be 50 percent below the standards. This zone meant that there was not much concern about rates being set too low. In fact the carriers were given much freedom to reduce rates.

■ market variations

Another area of concern with the Airline Deregulation Act was market-by-market variations in fares. The act indicated that an individual carrier would not have to charge equal fares for markets of equal distance. In addition, the fare for a market of a shorter distance could be higher than the fare for a market of a longer distance. This is called long and short haul discrimination. This change removed arbitrary standards of comparison based upon distance and allowed carriers much more freedom in establishing competitive rates for some of the lucrative markets. For example, the fares between Philadelphia and Miami during the winter months could be lower than the fares between Philadelphia and Toledo, even though the latter trip was a shorter distance.

■ discount fares

Another item that the act dealt with was discount fares. According to the new legislation, discount fares would no longer have to meet the profit impact test which had previously been used as proof that the proposed discount would in fact increase overall industry profits. (Increased profits were often difficult to prove and discouraged a number of discount proposals.) The new legislation gave carriers much more freedom in deciding whether to put discount fares into effect.

■ class versus coach fares

Another rate-related change in the new act affected the first class/coach class differential. The changed section stated that carriers would no longer have to maintain a fixed percentage relationship between the fare charged to these two different classes of customers. The fixed percentage relationship had long been a policy of the CAB. This change gave carriers more freedom to exercise their discretion in establishing an appropriate relationship between the two fares, even to the extent of different relationships between market areas.

■ route additions

Another provision of the act gave airlines the opportunity to file a notice which would automatically add one route per year between any one pair of points. In addition, each carrier was permitted to protect one of its routes from automatic entry once per year. This represented a dramatic change in entry control for the airline industry.

■ dormant routes

Another section of the act granted dormant routes to the first carrier that applied within thirty days after a route was declared dormant. A route was proclaimed dormant if a carrier failed to provide service five days a week for thirteen weeks out of a twenty-six week period. Small communities that were receiving air service when the act was passed were guaranteed service under a subsidy program described in the legislation. This was based upon a concept of "essential air service." Also, the act provided unemployment benefits for airline employees below management level who would lose their jobs as a result of deregulation. Some individuals feel that this latter provision established a dangerous precedent which could negate some of the gains from deregulation.

The CAB was authorized to evaluate the public convenience and necessity for new services until 1982. However, the burden of proof was shifted to the opponent of the proposed service, which represented a substantive change in the law. It should also be noted that the act did not change any of the standards concerning preference, prejudice, or discrimination. These criteria could be used for suspending a fare and for finding a new fare unlawful.

Highlights of Deregulation in the Airline Industry

■ dormant routes

The most immediate visible reaction to the passage of the new act was the number of carriers who applied to take advantage of the dormant route provision. Within a month after the passage of the act, the CAB had awarded various carriers the operating authority to serve 230 dormant routes.[2] For example, Braniff Airlines, which was one of the smaller trunk lines, expanded its route system by about one-third as a result of the dormant route provision of the new act. It added eighteen new cities to its routes during the first year and, in effect, initiated service in fifty-seven of the nation's top sixty markets. The initial result of the rapid entry of Braniff Airlines into these various markets was that Braniff sustained a substantial loss in profit.[3]

Other airlines adopted different strategies with respect to the newfound freedom. For example, United Airlines followed a strategy of participation in only the most profitable markets of the 1980s. They attempted to eliminate flights on route segments that had lost money or that had been only marginally profitable.

■ strategy of regional carriers

The nation's eight regional carriers that had traditionally connected smaller cities with the regional centers served by the major trunk lines changed their strategy also.[4] The deregulation freed the regionals to expand and compete with the large airlines. Airlines started to abandon their service to a number of small- and medium-size communities which were not big generators of traffic. As a consequence, commuter airline companies began filling many of the service gaps left by the so-called regional carriers. It is predicted that commuter service will continue to grow; some predict that it will increase by about 120 percent in terms of passenger enplanements in the 1980s.

■ impact upon airports

One of the major concerns with the passage of the Airline Deregulation Act was the impact upon airports. The carriers could now abandon routes as well as enter them. As a result, many communities have received less service since the passage of the deregulation act. For example, in the first year after the act was passed, 260 cities received a decrease in aircraft departures. Although commuters tried to fill these gaps, the service was not the same. At the other end of the spectrum, the larger cities experienced an expansion of service, creating a problem of not enough landing space.[5] Some type of allocation system was necessary to assign landing slots for new carriers. There have been a number of proposals, including one for an auction system allowing carriers to bid for slots. This problem of overcrowded airports and the possible abandonment of some airports will remain a critical problem during the 1980s.

It should be noted that the Airline Deregulation Act of 1978 reduced the authority of the CAB prior to its demise on or before January 1, 1985.

■ demise of
the CAB

At that time, the regulation of certification and rates will cease and other responsibilities of the CAB will be transferred to other federal agencies as follows: (1) the provision of compensation for air service to smaller communities and the authority of the CAB with respect to foreign air transportation will go to the Department of Transportation (DOT); (2) the determination of rates for carriage of mail in interstate and overseas transportation will go to the postal service; and (3) authority with respect to mergers and agreements will go to the Justice Department. The expiration of the CAB by January 1, 1985 at the latest will remove all industry protection from the antitrust laws (a protection that the industry had enjoyed during its period of regulation).

■ other restrictions
on CAB

It should also be noted that among the restrictions and limitations on the CAB's authority prior to its expiration date are: (1) exemption from regulating the routes and rates of commuter service for planes under a capacity of fifty-six passengers or for cargo service with a maximum payload of 9 tons; (2) exemption from regulating fares, rates, and services where planes have a capacity of less than thirty passengers; and (3) exemption from regulating other air services if the CAB finds it to be in the public interest.

■ other provisions

The act also directed that entry of new carriers and additional routes for existing carriers were to be encouraged and authorized. After public notice of an application for entry or extension, the CAB has only 150 days to issue a recommendation for a decision and 90 days thereafter to make its final decision. The act does not allow any agreement between airlines which limits capacity or sets rates or fares except for joint rates and charges. Interestingly, the CAB is given additional responsibility for determining subsidy needs of carriers serving smaller communities.

■ air cargo
deregulation

It should be noted that air cargo transportation was effectively deregulated by a 1977 enactment. Entry was no longer subject to the convenience and necessity criterion after the 1977 act; carriers only had to show that they were fit, willing, and able to carry out the service. The air cargo carriers were not allowed to restrict points to be served or the rates to be charged. The CAB was allowed to remove rate discrimination, but it had no additional authority over cargo rates in domestic air commerce. Consequently, we have seen a number of important changes in the air cargo industry, particularly with all-cargo carriers such as Tiger International which has expanded service and introduced new rates to compete more effectively with motor carriers.

With all of the above as background, let us turn our attention next to the 1980 deregulation of the motor carrier industry.

The Motor Carrier Act

■ background

On July 1, 1980, President Carter signed the Motor Carrier Act of 1980. This particular act was the result of more than eighteen months of continuous study. The proposal to deregulate the motor carrier industry was very controversial. To a large extent, it was opposed by the regulated members of the industry who thought that regulation meant stability and reasonable competition, which, in turn, provided the shipping public with good service at a reasonable cost. The proponents of deregulation stated a number of benefits to be gained, including the possibility of lower rates and better service because of the natural competitive environment that would develop in the industry.

■ industry overview

As noted previously, the regulated portion of the motor carrier industry includes both common and contract carriers. These carriers are listed in three classes based upon revenue and are subdivided into those who carry general freight, specialized goods, or household goods. The general freight carriers have two-thirds of the assets and equipment and employ about 80 percent of the personnel. They also earn about 70 percent of the net income.

■ new federal policy

The basic legislation establishes a new federal policy which was designed to promote a competitive and efficient motor carrier industry in order to accomplish certain goals, which include meeting the needs of shippers, receivers, and consumers while allowing price flexibility and encouraging greater efficiency of operation. In addition, one of the goals of the legislation is to provide adequate service to small communities.

■ opportunities for new carriers

The legislation offers increased opportunities for new carriers to get into the trucking business and for existing carriers to expand their service. This is accomplished in several ways. Section 5 of the act, which will be discussed below, modifies the traditional public convenience and necessity test to make it easier for motor common carriers of property to obtain operating certificates. This modification requires the Interstate Commerce Commission (ICC) to grant a certificate if it finds that an applicant meets the fitness test and that there is evidence of a useful public purpose for the service. Exceptions can be made only if persons protesting the application prove to the satisfaction of the ICC that the proposed service is inconsistent with public convenience and necessity. This is a reversal of previous policy in which the applicant had the burden of proof to demonstrate that the proposed service was consistent with public convenience and necessity. The public convenience and necessity test is eliminated altogether for some types of services such as transportation of food by independent owner operators and in the transportation of small shipments. In these cases, the ICC will only consider whether or not the applicant meets the fitness test. To avoid long and expensive proceedings, Section 5 of the act also limits which motor carriers can protest applications.

■ circuitous routes and gateways

Another section of the act, Section 6, allows carriers to expand their service and, at the same time, eliminate inefficient and fuel-wasteful restrictions on their operations. Specifically, the ICC is directed to eliminate, within six months, certain circuitous route restrictions and gateway restrictions that prohibit carriers from traveling the most direct routes. Furthermore, carriers are allowed to file applications for the removal of other restrictions such as those prohibiting them from carrying certain commodities or stopping at intermediate points along the routes.

The act also makes some significant changes in the area of rates. The motor carrier industry now collectively sets the rates it charges to the

■ limits on
collective rate-making

public through the rate bureaus. Section 14 limits the permissible scope of collective rate-making. Beginning in 1984, carriers may not collectively vote on or discuss single line rate proposals. However, carriers will be allowed to continue discussing and voting on general increases and decreases in some other matters, provided that any such discussion is limited to industry average carrier cost and does not include individual markets or particular single line rates. Carriers will also be prohibited from discussing or voting on rates which carriers proposed pursuant to this act's provisions in the zone of rate freedom area. In addition, Section 14 makes certain changes in the way rate bureaus operate, including opening rate bureau meetings to the public.

■ rate freedom

In the pricing reform area, the act allows motor carriers and freight forwarders greater freedom to set rates in response to market demands. In particular, Section 11 gives them the right to raise or lower their rates by 10 percent without ICC interference—that is, a zone of flexibility is established. That 10 percent can be widened by the ICC if it finds there is enough competition to regulate the rates.

■ price flexibility

Another section of the act addresses pricing flexibility. It allows a carrier and a shipper to negotiate reduced transportation rates in exchange for a limited liability on the property being transported. Further, the act contains quite a number of other important provisions which address many of the concerns expressed in the committee hearings, such as cost of transporting food and waste of energy. These important provisions are summarized below.[6]

Summary of Provisions of the Motor Carrier Act

The Motor Carrier Act of 1980 was so important that a detailed summary should be provided. No attempt will be made to evaluate the various sections. The scope and magnitude of the changes are obvious by examining the various sections.

National Transportation Policy. This provision promotes competitive and efficient transportation service in order to: (1) meet the needs of shippers, receivers, and consumers; (2) allow a variety of price and service options; (3) allow the most productive use of equipment and energy resources; (4) enable adequate profits and fair wages; (5) provide and maintain service to small communities and small shippers; (6) maintain a privately owned motor carrier system; (7) promote minority participation; and (8) promote intermodal transportation.

Entry. The entry provision authorizes issuance of certificates if the ICC finds the applicant fit, willing, and able and if the applicant shows additionally that the service proposed will serve a useful public purpose and is responsive to a public demand or need—unless the protestants show the service to be inconsistent with public convenience and necessity.

Restrictions on Operating Authority. The ICC, 180 days after enactment, must eliminate gateway and circuitous route limitations and implement procedures to process individual motor carrier applications in order to remove certificate operating restrictions. The latter procedure would be designed to: (1) allow the broadening of the categories of property authorized; (2) authorize service to intermediate points; (3) provide round trip authority in lieu of one-way authority; (4) eliminate narrow territorial limitations; and (5) eliminate other unreasonable restrictions that cause fuel to be wasted, are inefficient, or are contrary to the public interest. Fuel efficiency and small community service would be major factors in restriction removal cases. Additionally, a person holding both a common carrier certificate and a contract carrier permit could mix both types of traffic in the same vehicle.

Exemptions. This provision adds to the exempt agricultural commodities list: fish or shellfish by-products not intended for human consumption and livestock and poultry feed, agricultural seeds, and plants if transported to a site of agricultural production or to a business selling agricultural goods. All incidental-to-air motor freight operations are exempted and new exemptions are added for used pallets, shipping containers, and devices; natural crushed vesicular rock to be used for decorative purposes; and wood chips.

Food Transportation. This provision permits sellers of food and grocery products using a uniform zone-delivered pricing system to compensate customers who pick up purchased products, provided this compensation is available to all customers on a nondiscriminatory basis, and that the compensation does not exceed the actual delivery cost to the seller. The ICC is directed to monitor the extent to which any savings realized are passed on to the ultimate consumer and may require reports and other information for that purpose.

Private Carriage. Intercorporate hauling for compensation is permitted for wholly owned subsidiaries if the ICC is given notice and is given a list of participating subsidiaries and an affidavit of 100 percent ownership, if the notice is published in the Federal Register, and if a copy of the notice is carried in the cabs of vehicles providing the transportation.

Contract Carriers. Entry rules are modified by deleting the number of shippers as a consideration in granting a permit for property carriers. Protests are limited and master permit proceedings are prohibited. A provision enabling the master permitting of one-truck processed food haulers is included and is subject to the same requirements as those included for master certification. Permit restrictions are eased regarding particular industry or geographic area limitations and regarding existing limitations on holding both a permit and certificate to transport property of the same route or in the same area.

Zone of Rate Freedom. Creates a ± 10 percent zone of rate flexibility within which the ICC may not investigate, suspend, revise, or revoke any rate on the basis of reasonableness. This zone can be increased by 5 percent if the ICC finds sufficient competition and additional benefits from more flexibility. After two years, the zone will be adjusted to account for changes in the Producer Price Index. Actions within the zone must be individual. ICC authority against discriminatory practices or predatory pricing will remain applicable to changes within the zone of reasonableness.

Released Rate. This provision enables individual common carriers to offer released rate alternatives without ICC approval. The ICC may require carriers to keep regular rates in effect as an option. As to existing collectively made released rates, adjustments can be made until January 1, 1984, but no new collectively made released rates may be established (Section 14).

Rule of Rate-Making. This provision directs the ICC to adopt revenue standards which allow carriers to "achieve revenue levels that will provide a flow of net income, plus depreciation, adequate to support prudent capital outlays, assure the repayment of a reasonable level of debt, permit the raising of needed equity capital, attract and retain capital in amounts adequate to provide a sound motor carrier transportation system in the United States, and take into account reasonable estimated or foreseeable future costs."

Rate Bureaus. After January 1, 1981, only those carriers with authority to participate in the rate proposal may vote. After January 1, 1984, discussion of and voting upon single line rates will be prohibited, excepting that if the Motor Carrier Rate-making Study Commission does not submit a final report before January 1, 1983, the date will be postponed until July 1, 1984. The other changes required in rate bureau operations are: (1) rate bureaus cannot interfere with independent actions; (2) bureaus, upon request, must divulge the names of the proponent of a rule or rate and admit persons to proceedings; and (3) bureaus must have written authority on file from carriers being represented for voting purposes.

A Motor Carrier Rate-making Study Commission will be established to make a full and complete study of collective rate-making and of the need for continued antitrust immunity. The ten-member commission will be comprised of six Congressional members and four members appointed by the president. Of the latter, two must be motor carriers.

Lumping. This provision makes any coercion to load or unload vehicles unlawful and includes strong civil and criminal penalties. Language is also included requiring the parties involved to agree as to who is responsible for loading and unloading vehicles.

Written Contracts—Exempt For-hire Carriage. This provision authorizes the ICC in cooperation with the secretary of agriculture, to require the use of written contracts for exempt agricultural transportation and for brokerage services.

Motor Carrier Brokers. This provision adopts a general fit, willing, and able test for licensing of brokers—other than household goods brokers.

Finance Exemptions. This provision increases the thresholds for ICC jurisdiction over the carrier issuance of securities and assumptions of indebtedness. The present $1 million threshold is raised to $5 million for securities; the present $200,000 threshold is raised to $1 million for notes. The threshold is also raised for ICC jurisdiction over consolidations and mergers from the present $300,000 to $2 million (aggregate gross revenue).

Uniform State Regulation. This provision directs the DOT and ICC, in consultation with the states, to develop recommendations to provide a more efficient and equitable state regulatory system regarding licensing, registration, and filings. These recommendations are to be made within eighteen months after enactment.

Pooling. This adds a new provision to existing law providing for expedited consideration of pooling arrangements by the ICC. Carriers are to file the agreement not less than fifty days before its effective date. Prior to its effective date, the ICC is required to determine whether the agreement is of major transportation importance or will unduly restrain competition. If neither factor is found to exist, the agreement will be approved. If either factor exists, more formal consideration will be given.

Mixed Loads. This provision allows carriers to transport mixed loads of regulated and exempt commodities in the same vehicle. The provision also makes clear that such mixing does not affect the unregulated status of the exempt property nor the regulated status of the property being transported pursuant to a certificate or permit issued by the ICC.

Joint Rates and Through Routes. This provision authorizes the ICC to require the establishment of through routes and joint rates between motor carriers of property, and between those carriers and water carriers. The ICC cannot require carriers to include in a through route substantially less than the entire length of its route unless unreasonable circuity is involved. The new provision also ensures that the carriers will not be subjected to unfair or unreasonable demands to provide such service. Further, it requires all carriers participating in coordinated service to promptly pay divisions or make interline settlements with other carriers that are party to the service arrangement. Finally, if participating carriers become unduly delinquent in the settlement of such divisions or interline settlements, the coordinated service may be suspended or cancelled under rules prescribed by the ICC.

This provision also authorizes freight forwarders to enter into contracts with rail carriers or water common carriers for certain transportation movements. Currently, surface freight forwarders may contract only with motor common carriers.

Temporary Authority and Emergency Temporary Authority. This provision authorizes the ICC to grant temporary authority for up to 270 days and emergency temporary authority for up to 30 days. The ICC may extend the emergency temporary authority for an additional 90 days.

In addition, the new provision directs the ICC to take final action on applications for temporary authority within 90 days of their filing and on applications for emergency temporary authority within 15 days.

Cooperative Associations. This provision allows agricultural cooperative associations to haul up to 25 percent of their total interstate tonnage in nonfarm, nonmember goods in movements incidental and necessary to their primary business as cooperative associations. The previous percentage of such movements was 15 percent.

The ICC is also empowered to require cooperative associations transporting such nonfarm, nonmember goods to prepare and maintain records and file reports relating to such transportation in such a form as is required by the Commission. The purpose of the record keeping and reporting requirements is to ensure that the co-ops comply with the tonnage limitation and other requirements of the statute.

The new section authorizes the ICC to bring a civil action to enforce the record keeping and reporting requirements when violated by such associations. Civil and criminal penalties are included for violations.

Enforcement. This provision extends the current three-year deadline for formal investigations for rail carriers to all carriers. If the investigation is not concluded in three years, it is automatically dismissed.

This section also clarifies when a freight loss or damage claim is disallowed for purposes of filing court action. The new provision states that an offer of compromise will not constitute such a disallowance, unless the carrier specifically informs the claimant, in writing, that its claim is disallowed and gives reasons for the disallowance. Further, any communications received from a carrier's insurer will not constitute a disallowance, unless the insurer, in writing, informs the claimant that the claim is being disallowed, gives reasons, and informs the claimant that the insurer is acting on behalf of the carrier.

Merger Procedures. This provision establishes dealines for each step involved in the ICC merger proceedings. For example, evidentiary proceedings must be completed within 240 days, and a final decision must be reached by 180 days thereafter.

Small Community Service Study. This provision requires the ICC to conduct a study of service to small communities with an emphasis on communities having a population of 5,000 or less. The study is to include an analysis of the common carrier obligation to provide service to small communities, an assessment of whether the ICC is enforcing the obligation, and an evaluation of the effect of this legislation on service to small communities. Further, the ICC shall make specific recommendations regarding ways to ensure motor carrier service to small communities; the ICC's report is due September 1, 1982. The section also authorizes the appropriation of such sums as are necessary to conduct the study and to make the report.

Minimum Financial Responsibility for Motor Carriers. This provision transfers the authority to establish financial responsibility for bodily injury and property damage by motor carriers, from the ICC to the DOT.

The secretary is directed to establish minimum financial responsibility for for-hire carriers operating in interstate commerce. The minimum level is $750,000 per incident per vehicle. That minimum level can be reduced for a two-year period but to not less than $500,000 if such reduction will not adversely affect public safety and will not present a serious disruption of transportation service.

A separate provision covers public liability for carriers transporting hazardous substances, as defined by the secretary; oil or hazardous substances, as defined by the administrator of the Environmental Protection Agency (EPA); or hazardous wastes, as defined by the EPA. The provision applies to all carriers (private, exempt, and public) and, in this respect, it tracks the preemption aspects of the Hazardous Materials Transportation Act.

Coordinated Transportation Services. This provision permits motor carriers to deliver to or receive from a rail carrier a trailer moving in trailer-on-flat-car service at any point on the route of the rail carrier if the motor carrier is authorized to serve the origin and destination points of traffic.

Highlights of Motor Carrier Deregulation Activity[7]

■ number of applications

There have been a number of impacts since the passage of the Motor Carrier Act of 1980, and an overview of these changes is provided in this section. One of the important changes has been the number of applications being filed for motor carrier operating authorities—there has been an upward trend. This is true for both the common and contract segments of the industry and reflects a broadening of the territorial coverage of existing carriers and an influx of new carriers. It is also an indication of the growth in the degree of competition and the operational flexibility in the motor carrier industry.

■ rate activity

There has also been a dramatic increase in rate activity with an emphasis on reductions in motor carrier truckload rates through independent actions on the part of carriers. Less-than-truckload (LTL) rates have also been subject to some reductions; there has been a tendency toward cost-related discounting concepts. The low general level of business activity which created an excess capacity and the need for additional freight revenue during the early 1980s helped cause the reductions in rates. Another response to excess capacity was to move resources into new routes; this was made easier by the new entry standards. Presumably, the resulting increased competition has also lowered rate levels.

■ private carriage

Previous limitations on private carriage were relaxed to the extent that such transportation units may now transport for a fleet organization on a for-hire basis. Such service has grown at a rapid rate. The potential for growth was clearly indicated during the hearings which preceded the passage of the act—one of the criticisms then, especially since the energy crisis of the early 1970s, was the number of limitations placed on operating authorities by the ICC.[8]

■ contract carriers

The early results under the revised regulations indicate that the contract carrier segment of the industry has also expanded dramatically. In addition, dual operations, that is, combined common and contract carriage which used to be severely restricted, have become more plentiful. As competitive pressures increase, more flexibility will be required to meet the demands of shippers in various segments. It is anticipated that a number of private carriers will file for contract carrier rights of authority. The net effect of this will be an increase in competition for the truckload traffic, which will have a stabilizing or downward trend effect on rates.

The act added a number of new subject areas to the statutes regulating the industry. These included, for example, the removal of operating restrictions and conversion of contract carriers and common carriers. There is no question that the act significantly changed the structure of economic regulation of the motor carrier industry. There will be some people, no doubt, who will argue that the act did not really lessen regulation because it added a number of new responsibilities and studies to the existing law. With regard to the Motor Carrier Act of 1980, perhaps it's fair to use the phrase which has been bandied about much in the last decade, namely, reregulation. There is no question that there are new found freedoms contained in the act, but there is also a suggested list of additions which will make the act rather difficult to administer in the next several years.[9]

■ overview

Railroad Deregulation

On October 14, 1980, President Carter signed into law the Staggers Rail Act of 1980.[10] The statute was not the wholesale deregulation that was hoped for by some proponents of change in railroad regulation, but it did significantly ease the regulation on the railroad industry in a number of particular areas by making substantive changes in the rules governing rate-making, car control, and other major areas. In looking at the act, it would probably be most convenient to examine it by dividing it into three major sections, namely rate-making, management, and other provisions.[11]

Rate-Making

The most extensive changes in regulation provided by the act are in the provisions on railroad rate-making. Although protection for rail-dependent shippers was retained, Congress clearly intended that the disciplines of the competitive marketplace would control most rate-making. The new rate provisions curtail activities of rate bureaus and move to phase out general rate increases, but they also offer a new measure of flexibility in the setting of rates and in the marketing of rail services.

Maximum Rates. Nearly two-thirds of all railroad rates will be freed from maximum rate regulation under a provision that limits ICC jurisdiction to those rates where railroads exercise "market dominance" and charge a rate above a threshold level set initially at 160 percent of variable costs. This rate will rise 5 percentage points a year until 1984, when it will be dependent upon a "cost recovery percentage" to be determined by the ICC. The percentage associated with cost can vary from 170 to 180 percent of variable costs.

Zone of Rate Flexibility. A carrier can raise any rate by the percentage increase appearing in the railroad cost index which will be published quarterly by the ICC. For the first four years after enactment, rates can be raised to 6 percent a year above the cost recovery index with a cumulative maximum of 18 percent. After that, annual increases will be limited to 4 percent and will be restricted largely to carriers not earning adequate revenues.

Shippers can still bring a complaint case on the 6 percent and 4 percent increases after the rate has gone into effect. But the ICC cannot suspend those increases and can only investigate those that are more than 20 percentage points above the threshold, subject to a maximum of 190 percent of variable cost. In a shipper-initiated complaint, the burden of proof is on the shipper. In an ICC investigation, the burden of proof is on the carrier.

Minimum Rates. Railroads will be permitted to reduce rates more easily to meet motor and water carrier competition under a provision that any rate that contributes to the "going concern value" shall be considered reasonable. Going concern value has been defined as a rate that equals or exceeds variable cost.

General Rate Increases. General rate increases are limited to joint rates and are to be eliminated completely by January 1, 1984, unless the ICC finds that elimination is not feasible. The ICC cannot eliminate them before April 1, 1982, but until then, general rate increases are to be limited to recovery of inflation costs.

The ICC may institute an index system to supplant evidentiary requirements in a general rate increase. After elimination of general rate increases, the ICC could prescribe a percentage increase that individual carriers could accept or "flag-out."

The percentage prescribed by the ICC may be in a range broad enough to allow carriers to differentiate between commodities as necessary to recover inflationary cost increases.

Rate Bureaus. There can be no discussion of, or voting on, single line rates, and no discussion of, or voting on, joint line rates unless a carrier can "practicably participate in the movement." The definition of "practicably participate" will be left to ICC discretion.

No later than January 1, 1984, discussion of joint line rates will be limited to carriers forming part of a particular route. Transcripts or recordings of meetings and records of votes must be submitted to the ICC.

Protection will be granted from "parallel action" antitrust allegations in which a carrier has a single line rate and participates in a competing joint rate.

Surcharges and Cancellations. For the next three years, carriers may apply a surcharge to any joint rate that does not yield 110 percent of variable cost. Any surcharge must apply equally in dollar amounts to all routes between the points to which the surcharge applies in order to prevent predatory discrimination between routes.

Unless affected shippers and carriers consent, a carrier's revenues cannot exceed 110 percent of the railroad's variable costs as a result of a surcharge, except that carriers with inadequate revenues may apply a surcharge to cover all costs of service on lines carrying less than 3,000,000 gross ton-miles (1,000,000 gross ton-miles if an adequate revenue carrier). Carriers earning adequate revenues may not surcharge traffic on lines carrying over 3,000,000 gross ton-miles per year.

Carriers may cancel the application of a joint rate to any route not providing 110 percent of the railroad's variable costs. The ICC may reopen the route if shippers or carriers provide the cancelling carrier revenue that is equal to 110 percent of variable costs through a new rate, division, or surcharge.

Divisions. ICC proceedings will be expedited, with a nine-month limit for taking of evidence. Final action must be taken within 180 days after completion of a proceeding.

Contracts. Contract rate agreements are specifically legalized, and all contracts must be filed with the ICC. Grounds for shipper complaint against a contract are severely restricted.

Service under contract shall be separate and distinct from common carriage by rail. Once approved, the ICC cannot require a carrier to violate the contract. Contract enforcement is restricted to the courts.

Discrimination. Under the new law, the existing discrimination provision of the Interstate Commerce Act does not apply to contracts, surcharges or cancellations of routes, separate rates for distinct services, rail rates applicable to different routes, or business entertainment and solicitation expenses.

Investigation and Suspension of Rates. Time limits of proceedings are reduced from seven months to five. To get a suspension, a shipper must show likelihood that its protest will prevail on merits, that it will suffer substantial injury, and that a refund is inadequate protection. If a suspended rate is finally approved, the shipper will be required to pay any undercharges resulting from suspension, plus interest.

Notice. The notice period is reduced from thirty days to twenty days for rate increases and to ten days for rate decreases.

Recyclables. With the exception of iron and steel, rates for recyclables are to be limited to the average ratio of revenue to variable costs necessary for railroads to cover all costs and earn a reasonable return on investment.

Released Value Rates. A carrier may establish deductibles and limit liability to preestablished values.

Savings Provision. Any rate in effect on the date of enactment that is not challenged within 180 days of October 14, 1980, and not found to be unreasonable shall be deemed to be lawful and may not thereafter be challenged. A rate may not be challenged within the 180-day period unless the carrier has market dominance.

Management

Railroads have been restricted, far more than many other businesses, by regulations concerning business practices and day-to-day management of their companies. The Staggers Rail Act moved to alter some of these restrictions and return decision making to management.

Car Service. ICC car service orders will be restricted to emergencies having regional or national significance, but the ICC's authority to require joint use of terminals during emergencies will be expanded to include all facilities. Emergency services are to be performed by employees who would otherwise have performed the service if there had been no emergency.

Premium charges may be imposed for special services to improve car utilization.

Shippers are authorized to seek approval for agreements among themselves with respect to private car compensation. Approval having been received, they may negotiate with the railroads and, if they fail to agree, any party may petition the ICC to set compensation levels.

Incentive per diem is eliminated.

Cost Accounting. A new board with a three-year life will be created to establish new cost accounting principles which will be implemented by the ICC. Carriers can adopt their own accounting system as long as they meet the standards, but carrier systems must be certified by the ICC.

Business Entertainment. Railroads may entertain customers on the same basis as other businesses.

Other Provisions

The act also included a number of special provisions. Some of these provisions were attached to help insure passage of the act in Congress.

Abandonments. Abandonment standards remain unchanged, but proceedings will be speeded up with unprotested abandonments permitted 75 days after application. Protested but uninvestigated abandonments will be permitted 120 days after application. The final decision on protested and investigated applications must be made within 255 days of filing.

The maximum time limit to effective date of a permitted abandonment is set at 330 days. The act creates a mechanism that requires a railroad to sell a line that has been approved for abandonment to responsible persons offering either to subsidize or acquire the line. If parties fail to agree on an offer for subsidy or purchase of an abandoned line, the ICC can establish terms and conditions.

Mergers and Other Transactions. Carriers and shippers may jointly ask the ICC to provide alternative motor carrier service if a shipper is inadequately served.

A merger application of two Class I carriers is expedited without changing current substantive standards. However, the ICC must consider whether the transaction would have an adverse effect on competition among rail carriers in the region. Substantive standards for mergers not involving two Class I railroads are reduced.

Financial Assistance. The Redeemable Preference Share program is extended for two years and an additional $700 million is authorized, with $200 million earmarked for reducing Conrail's labor force. The 3-R Act electrification loan guarantee authorization for Conrail is extended to include all railroads.

Conrail Studies and Emergency Funding. USRA and Conrail must each submit a report to Congress covering the effect of different funding alternatives on the region. Each report shall include recommendations concerning projected funding requirements, Conrail structure, and necessary legislative action. Conrail is required to prepare special reports on alternatives to present labor agreements and on savings resulting from the Staggers Rail Act, potential transfers or abandonments, other potential cost savings, and potential revenue increases.

Rock Island and Milwaukee Amendment. The ICC is empowered to impose fair and equitable labor protective conditions if negotiations fail.

Issues about the constitutionality of the Rock Island and Milwaukee Acts are to be decided in the U.S. Court of Appeals for the Seventh Circuit. The act specifically provides for the availability of redress under the Tucker Act.

San Antonio Rate. Rail coal rates to San Antonio may not exceed 162 percent of variable costs before September 30, 1987. After that, the rate can be raised by an amount equal to no more than inflation plus 4 percent per year until the critical return point (CRP) is reached.

Entry. The standard for granting a permit for construction or operation of extensions or additions of railroad lines is eased. Once a permit is granted by the ICC, a railroad cannot refuse permission to another railroad to cross its line. The ICC may also order reciprocal switching agreements.

Feeder Railroad Development Program. For three years following enactment, any financially responsible person, excluding Class I and II carriers, can acquire a rail line with a density of less than 3 million gross ton-miles per year upon an ICC determination, after a hearing, that: (1) the carrier operating the line refuses to make reasonable efforts to provide adequate service; (2) transportation over the line is inadequate for a majority of shippers using the line; (3) sale of the line will not adversely affect the railroad operating the line—either financially or operationally; and (4) sale of the line will be likely to result in improved transportation for shippers using the line. Payment must not be less than net liquidation value or going concern value—whichever is greater.

After three years, the density criterion is removed, and any rail line can be acquired on the same basis. The ICC can also require the sale of lines proposed for abandonment. If a line is sold and the subsequent operator stops service, the selling carrier has the right to repurchase the line at the original selling price plus interest.

Highlights of Railroad Deregulation Activity

Like the Motor Carrier Deregulation Act, the Staggers Rail Act can be regarded as a mechanism for reregulation of the industry. The regulatory structure for railroads was developed over a period of more than 90 years and has not been completely eliminated. There have been changes which give the railroads more freedom and flexibility, but there have also been some additions made to the regulation as noted above.

With motor carriers and airlines, the most important areas of change had to do with entry and exit from service and rate-making. For the railroads, the rate-making area is and will be the most important since the entry and exit issue is so much more complex and long-term in nature. As we have seen in the summary of the Staggers Rail Act, the ICC cannot consider the effect of a freight charge on any other mode of transportation when it prescribes minimum rates. The ultimate test will be whether the rate(s) contributes to the going concern value of the proposer (which is defined as a rate which is above variable cost).

■ impact on rate-making

The fact that the burden of proof shifts in maximum rate situations to the shipper(s) or other parties should have an important impact upon rate regulation. Carriers will raise rates more frequently than in the past. Previously, judgments of market dominance also placed the burden of proof upon the carrier. Now, the carrier must only prove that a rate is below the ICC's jurisdictional threshold percentage of revenue-variable cost. Once the carrier has provided evidence of its variable costs, then it will be up to the shipper to show that the rate generates revenues in excess of the ICC's jurisdictional threshold.

■ burden of proof

The Staggers Rail Act provides the railroads with more opportunity to adjust rates to meet competition, but also with more opportunity to raise rates to meet rising costs. The latter is particularly important given the inflationary circumstances of recent years. Many individuals have felt that rail rates have lagged far behind other costs.

■ market adjustment

As indicated in our summary of the Staggers Rail Act, the new zone of reasonableness which took effect October 1, 1980, allows rates to be raised 6 percent per year above inflation. Also, any part of a 6 percent increase not implemented in a year in which it is authorized may be carried over to a succeeding year. However, no rail carrier may have an increase greater than 12 percent in any one year for the first four years, even within the zone of reasonableness.

■ zone of reasonableness

Rate bureaus face an uncertain future under the Staggers Rail Act. It would appear that the role of the rate bureaus will be limited to that of tariff publishers. There is no question that the role and importance of rate bureaus has been decreased.

■ rate bureaus

The Staggers Rail Act really opened the way for the railroads to start negotiating contract rates with large shippers. The railroads have shown interest in such rates for many years, but the ICC has precluded them from this area. There are some individuals who feel that one-half of the

■ contract rates

total volume of rail traffic may move under contract rates by 1990.

The contract rate area shows the most promise in the area of long-distance volume movements of high density, bulk freight. Railroads and shippers are becoming increasingly cost conscious in evaluating contract rates. The carriers are looking at the cost of each movement against the revenue gained to eliminate cross subsidization. Some carriers and shippers are putting penalties for delays and premiums for better service into the contracts. Long haul movements will have to involve two or more carriers and stipulated revenues and equipment sharing.

It should be noted that short to medium haul movements also have potential for contract rates. These contracts will take longer to develop, but will have potential for the railroads. Also, the railroads may find themselves involved in competitive bidding for contracts, for example, hauling sludge for municipalities.

As indicated previously, there is no question that the Staggers Rail Act ushered in a new era in rail regulation. The 4-R Act precipitated deregulation for railroads, but the Staggers Rail Act represented the first real step in this direction. The Staggers Rail Act will have the same historic importance as the Act to Regulate Commerce of 1887 and the Transportation Act of 1920. A resurgence or a demise in the rail industry in the 1980s lies more in the hands of rail managers now than at any time since 1887.

Conclusion

The era of deregulation which started in 1975 has dramatically increased in importance by the passage of major acts affecting airlines, motor carriers, and railroads. Some people will argue that we have reregulation as opposed to deregulation, since regulation was not eliminated. However, major changes were made in terms of entry restrictions and rate flexibility. There is already much evidence to indicate that the transportation industry will undergo significant change in the next ten years. The relative position of the various modes will depend on their response to the new competitiveness in the marketplace.

Study Questions

1. What arguments can be set forth allowing rate adjustment with a "zone of reasonableness" without fear of protest?

2. A certain airplane of one airline originates in Baltimore, stops in Pittsburgh, and flies nonstop to San Francisco. The round trip fare from Baltimore to San Francisco and return is actually less than the round trip fare from Pittsburgh to San Francisco and return. Why is this possible? Shouldn't regulation prevent this sort of practice?

3. What are the key features of airline deregulation as it has taken place since 1978?

4. The Motor Carrier Act of 1980 amended the National Transportation Policy section of the Interstate Commerce Act. What main philosophy

is contained within these additional regulatory changes by Congress?

5. How has the new Motor Carrier Act of 1980 changed who can enter the for-hire trucking business?

6. A "zone of rate flexibility" exists in the new motor carrier and railroad sections of the Interstate Commerce Act as a result of the new 1980 legislative additions. What arguments pro and con can be made for such freedom?

7. What changes have the new laws brought forth for rail and motor carrier rate bureaus?

8. What economic justification exists for railroad contract rates?

9. What is the overall thrust of the Staggers Rail Act of 1980 in comparison to the original Act to Regulate Commerce (1887)?

Notes

1. These provisions are adapted for the Statement of Darius W. Gaskins, Jr., Chairman of the Interstate Commerce Commission, before the Subcommittee on Surface Transportation, U.S., Congress, House, *The Airline Deregulation Act of 1978—Conference Report on S. 2493*, Pub. L. 95-504, 95th Cong., 2d. Sess., 1978, H.R. 1779.

2. "CAB Assigns Dormant Rights to Carriers," *Aviation Week and Space Technology*, Nov. 20, 1978, p. 40.

3. David Griffiths, "Reform Rekindles Carrier Optimism," *Aviation Week and Space Technology*, Oct. 23, 1978, p. 28.

4. "The Regionals Wider Reach," *Business Week*, Feb. 19, 1979, pp. 77-79.

5. Douglas R. Sease, "Terminal Illness," *The Wall Street Journal*, Oct. 23, 1978, p. 1.

6. U.S., Congress, Senate, *Examining Current Conditions in the Trucking Industry and the Possible Necessity for Change in the Manner and Scope of Its Regulations, Part 3*, 96th Cong., 2d Sess., 1980, H.R. 6418, pp. 1018-1156.

7. Office of Policy and Analysis, Interstate Commerce Commission, *Highlights of Motor Carrier Deregulation Activities*, (Washington, D.C., Dec. 4, 1980).

8. Donald Topper, "The Motor Carrier Act: An Examination," *The Private Carrier*, Nov. 1980, pp. 10-12.

9. Donald V. Harper, "The Federal Motor Carrier Act of 1980: Review and Analysis," *Transportation Journal*, Winter 1981, pp. 30-33.

10. U.S., Congress, House, *The Staggers Rail Act of 1980—Conference Report on S. 1946*, Pub. L. 96-448, 96th Cong., 2d Sess., 1980, H.R. 1430.

11. This summary is adapted from Association of American Railroads, *Basic Provisions of the Staggers Rail Act of 1980* (Washington, D.C., 1981).

Suggested Readings

Harper, Donald V. "The Federal Motor Carrier Act of 1980." *Transportation Journal*, Winter, 1981.

Lieb, Robert C. *Transportation: The Domestic System*. 2d ed. Reston, Va.: Reston Publishing Co., 1981, chap. 13.

Moskal, B. S. "Throwing out the Rules on Trucking." *Industry Week*, July 7, 1980.

Panzar, J. C. "Regulation, Deregulation, and Economic Efficiency: The Case of the CAB." *American Economic Review*, May, 1980, pp. 311-15.

Wagner, William B., and Dean, Michael C. "A Prospective View Toward Deregulation of Motor Common Carrier Entry." *ICC Practitioners Journal*, May/June, 1981, pp. 406-18.

Case   **On-Time Carrier**

On-Time Carrier, a Class III common motor carrier, has recently been experiencing a decline in revenue and an increase in customer complaints. The causes of these simultaneous conditions have been difficult to determine because of the complexity and expanse of On-Time's transportation network. In addition to these problems is the onset of winter weather with severe conditions resulting in certain sections of the country. Severe weather conditions have, in the past, resulted in less than efficient operation of On-Time's system.

Part of On-Time's problems has been the lack of an effective marketing program. This knowledge has been ascertained in part by customer complaints concerning lack of information on pickup times, delivery times, transit times, and total charges. Upon further investigation, On-Time was highly embarrassed to discover that it has yet to identify its market areas, its customers, and exactly what service it was attempting to sell. On-Time's previous success was based exclusively on "seat of the pants" management that was confronted by an industry made up of relatively few motor carriers. However, in a growing industry such as the motor carrier industry, On-Time discovered that to succeed it must have a future game plan to define its business and to set up a monitoring system to check its progress. Also, On-Time decided that it was necessary to be able to differentiate its service from the service of other motor carriers in order to offer the customer an advantage by using On-Time carriers.

If you were hired by On-Time as marketing consultant, how would you first attack its problems? What questions would you ask to gain information necessary to your analysis? How would you define On-Time's market area? Its customers? Its service? What type of future marketing plan could you construct for On-Time? What service level standards would you set to monitor this plan? How would you maintain or alter these service levels, for example, during the winter months?

18 National Transportation Policy

After reading this chapter you should:

1 Understand the need for a national transportation policy and who establishes it.

2 Be able to discuss the important aspects of public promotion of transportation by mode.

3 Understand the declared national transportation policy in the United States.

4 Have an overview of future national transportation issues.

■ no unified policy

The federal government has played an important role in molding the transportation system that exists in the United States today. The federal government's role has been defined through various laws, rules, and funding programs directed toward controlling and promoting the different modes of transportation. The federal government's policy toward transportation is made up of a composite of these federal laws, rules, funding programs, and regulatory agencies; however, there is no unified federal transportation policy statement or goal that guides the federal government's actions.

■ chapter overview

In addition to the Congress and the president, there are more than sixty federal agencies and thirty congressional committees involved in setting transportation policy. There are three independent regulatory agencies that interpret transport law, establish operating rules, and set policy. Lastly, the Justice Department interprets statutes involving transportation and reconciles differences between the carriers and the public. Each of these groups has made decisions that have affected the development of transportation.

The purpose of this chapter is to examine the national transportation policy, both explicit and implicit, that has molded the present U. S. transportation system. Although the national transportation policy is constantly evolving and changing, there are some major underpinnings upon which the basic policy is built. These basic policy issues will be examined as well as the declared statement of national transportation policy contained in the Transportation Act of 1940.

Why Do We Need a Transportation Policy?

A good starting point for examining the nature of our national transportation policy is the consideration of our need for such a policy. The answer to the question of need lies in the significance of transportation to the very life of the country. Transportation permeates every aspect of a community and touches the life of every member. The transportation system ties together the various communities of a country, making possible the movement of people, goods, and services. The physical connection that transportation gives to spatially separated communities permits a sense of unity to exist.

importance of transportation

In addition, transportation is fundamental to the economic activity of a country. Transportation furthers economic activity—the exchange of goods that are mass-produced in one location to locations deficient in these goods. The carry-over benefits of economic activity—jobs, improved goods and services and so on—would not be reaped by a country's citizens without a good transportation system.

economic benefits

An efficient transportation system is fundamental to national defense. In times of emergencies, people and materials must be deployed quickly to various trouble spots within the U. S. or throughout the world to protect American interests. Without an efficient transportation system, more resources would have to be dedicated to defense purposes in many more locations. Thus, an efficient transportation system reduces the amount of resources consumed for national defense.

national defense

Many of our transportation facilities could not be developed by private enterprise. For example, the capital required to build a transcontinental highway is very likely beyond the resources of the private sector. Efficient and economical rail and highway routes require governmental assistance in securing land from private owners; if the government did not assert its power of eminent domain, routes would be quite circuitous and inefficient. Furthermore, public ownership and operation of certain transportation facilities, such as highways or waterways is necessary to assure access to all who desire to use the facilities.

public investment

The purpose of transportation policy is to provide direction for determining the amount of national resources that will be dedicated to transportation and for determining the quality of service that is essential for economic activity and national defense. National policy provides guidelines to the many agencies that exercise transportation decision-making powers and to Congress, to the president and to the courts who make and interpret the laws affecting transportation. Thus, transportation policy provides the framework for the allocation of resources to the transportation modes.

resource allocation

decision guidelines

The federal government has been a major factor in the development of transportation facilities—highways, waterways, ports, and airports. It has also assumed the responsibility to:

federal responsibilities

ensure the safety of travelers

protect the public from the abuse of monopoly power

promote fair competition

develop or continue vital transport services

balance environmental, energy, and social requirements in transportation

plan and make decisions.[1]

This statement of the federal government's transportation responsibility indicates the diversity of public need that transportation policy must serve. The conflicts inherent in such a diverse set of responsibilities will be discussed in a following section.

Declaration of National Transportation Policy	The Transportation Act of 1940 included a statement of national transportation policy. This statement was made by Congress to provide direction to the Interstate Commerce Commission (ICC) in administering transportation regulation. This statement remained the sole formal declaration of national transportation policy from 1940 until 1980 when Congress made additions to the 1940 statement in the Motor Carrier Act of 1980.

■ 1940 Transportation Act

The 1940 declaration of national transportation policy is as follows:

■ 1940 policy statement

It is hereby declared to be the national transportation policy of the Congress to provide for fair and impartial regulation of all modes of transportation subject to the provisions of this Act, so administered as to recognize and preserve the inherent advantages of each; to promote safe, adequate, economical and efficient service and foster sound economic conditions in transportation and among the several carriers; to encourage the establishment and maintenance of reasonable charges for transportation services, without unjust discriminations, preferences or advantages, or unfair or destructive competitive practices; to cooperate with the several States and the duly authorized officials thereof; and to encourage fair wages and equitable working conditions;—all to the end of developing, coordinating and preserving a national transportation system by water, highway, and rail, as well as other means, adequate to meet the commerce of the United States, of the Postal Service, and of the national defense. All of the provisions of this Act shall be administered and enforced with a view of carrying out the above declaration of policy.

The Motor Carrier Act of 1980 amended the above policy statement with regard to motor carrier transportation of property:

■ 1980 Motor Carrier Act

■ 1980 policy statement

With respect to transportation of property by motor carrier, to promote competitive and efficient transportation services in order to (A) meet the needs of shippers, receivers, and consumers; (B) allow a variety of quality and price options to meet changing market demands and diverse requirements of the shipping public; (C) allow the most productive use of equipment and energy resources; (D) enable efficient and well-managed carriers to earn adequate profits, attract capital, and maintain fair wages and working conditions; (E) provide and maintain service to small communities and small shippers; (F) improve and maintain a sound, safe, and competitive privately-owned motor carrier system; (G) promote greater participation by minorities in the motor carrier system; and (H) promote intermodal transportation.

Although the declaration of national transportation policy is general and somewhat vague, the statement does provide a guide to the factors which should be considered in transportation decision making. However, the statement contains numerous conflicting provisions. This section analyzes the incompatibility of the various provisions.

First, the declaration is a statement of policy for those modes regulated by the ICC. Therefore, only railroads, oil pipelines, motor carriers, and water carriers are considered. Air transportation is excluded from consideration.

■ air carriage exclusion

The requirement of "fair and impartial regulation" also overlooks the exempt carriers in motor and water transportation. The exempt carriers are eliminated from the economic controls administered by the ICC and, therefore, are not included in the stated policy provisions.

■ exempt carriers
exclusion

Congress requested the ICC to administer the transportation regulation in such a manner as to recognize and preserve the inherent advantage of each mode. An inherent advantage is the innate superiority one mode possesses in the form of cost or service characteristics. Such modal characteristics change over time as technology and infrastructure change.

■ inherent advantage

It has been recognized that railroads have an inherent advantage of lower cost in transporting freight long distances and that motor carriers have the advantage for moving freight short distances, less than 300 miles. If the preservation of inherent advantage was the only concern, the ICC would not permit trucks to haul freight long distances, over 300 miles, nor railroads to haul freight short distances. However, the shippers demand long-distance moves from motor carriers and short-distance moves from railroads and the ICC permits these services to be provided.

■ safety/economy/
efficiency

Safe, adequate, economical, and efficient service is not totally attainable. An emphasis on safety may mean an uneconomical or inefficient service. Added safety features on equipment and added safety procedures for employees will increase total costs and cost per unit of output and may reduce the productivity of employees. However, safety has taken precedence over economical and efficient service when lives are involved.

■ adequate service

Providing adequate service has been constructed to mean meeting normal demand. If carriers were forced to have capacity that is sufficient to meet peak demand, considerable excess capacity would exist, resulting in uneconomical and inefficient operations. Fostering sound economic conditions among the carriers does not mean assuring an acceptable profit for all carriers. Nor does it imply that the ICC not guarantee the survival of all carriers. The ICC must consider the economic condition of carriers in rate rulings so as to foster stability of transportation supply.

The policy statement regarding reasonable charges, unjust discrimina-

- common carrier
obligations

tion, undue preference, and unfair competitive practices is merely a reiteration of the common carrier obligations. No attempt was made by Congress to define these concepts. The ICC was given the task of interpreting them as it heard and decided individual cases.

Following the passage of the 1940 Transportation Act, a number of laws provided some degree of definition for these common carrier policy statements. For example, the Staggers Rail Act of 1980 defined a reasonable rail rate as one that was not more than 160 percent of variable costs. The Motor Carrier Act of 1980 defined a zone of rate freedom where a rate change of ± 10 percent in one year is presumed to be reasonable. Both acts defined the normal business entertainment of shippers as acceptable practice and not an instance of undue preference.

- reasonable rate
definition

- federal/state
cooperation

The cooperative efforts between the federal and state governments have not always been smooth. The very foundation for federal regulation of transportation was the judicial decision that only the federal government could regulate interstate transportation. The states, through police powers, have the right to establish laws regarding transportation safety. Thus, states have enacted laws governing the height, length, weight, and speed of motor carrier trucks, for example. However, the federal government has attempted to standardize weight and speed laws on interstate highways. One approach they have taken has been the threat of withholding federal highway money from states that do not comply.

- fair wages
- equitable working
conditions

Finally, the ICC was charged with the responsibility of encouraging fair wages and working conditions. No attempt was made to interpret the terms "fair wage" and "equitable working conditions." A wage that is deemed fair by an employee may be unfair to an employer. An air-conditioned cab may be equitable working conditions to a driver, but it is merely an added cost to the employer. In addition, both of the above examples may conflict with the policy statement regarding the promotion of economical and efficient service.

- policy goals

The stated goal of the national transportation policy is to provide a system of transportation that meets the needs of commerce, the U.S. Postal Service, *and* national defense. It is possible that a system that meets the needs of commerce may be insufficient to meet the needs of national defense during an emergency situation. In addition, a system that has the capacity to meet national defense needs will have excess capacity for commerce and postal service needs during peace times and will be inefficient and uneconomical.

For example, the United States maintains a merchant marine fleet that can be called into service to haul defense material during a national defense emergency. However, this fleet may be twice the size of that needed for commerce. There are many government critics that claim a fleet with such excess capacity is a waste of resources. The defense advocates argue that national defense needs dictate that such a fleet be operated to preclude dependency on a foreign country for water transportation during defense emergencies. As the arguments rage on, one can see the conflict that exists in the stated national policy goals.

■ motor carrier emphasis

The additions that the Motor Carrier Act of 1980 made to the declaration of national transportation policy were quite general as well as vague and conflicting. The Motor Carrier Act policy amendment places an emphasis on motor carriers. Specific sections of the amendment single out specific problems unique to motor carriers and formally state basic transportation and social policies issues in light of these specific problems. For example, the statements regarding shipper, receiver, consumer needs, small community and small shipper requirements, and a competitive, privately owned motor carrier system emphasize the private ownership, common carrier service concept as well as issues of competition.

Who Establishes Policy?

National transportation policies are developed at various levels of government and by many different agencies. The specifics of a particular policy may reflect the persuasion of a group of individuals (for example, a consumer group) or of a single individual (for example, an elected official). The purpose of this section is to examine the basic institutional framework that aids in the development of national transportation policy.

■ president

Executive Branch.[2] There are many departments within the executive branch of government that influence (establish) transportation policy. At the top of the list is the office of the president. The president has authority over international air transportation and foreign air carriers operating into the United States. The president also appoints individuals to head the various agencies that influence transportation and to head the three regulatory agencies—the Interstate Commerce Commission (ICC), Civil Aeronautics Board (CAB), and Federal Maritime Commission (FMC).

■ state department

The Department of State is directly involved in developing policy regarding international transportation by air and water. The policies and programs designed to encourage foreign visitors to the United States are implemented by the U. S. Travel Service. The Maritime Administration is involved with ocean (international) transportation policy. It determines ship requirements, service, and routes essential to foreign commerce. In addition, international transportation policies and programs

■ military

are shaped by the Military Sealift Command, Military Airlift Command, and Military Traffic Management and Terminal Service—agencies responsible for the movement of military goods and personnel.

■ energy department

On the domestic level, the Department of Energy develops policies regarding energy availability and distribution (fuel and rationing). The U. S. Postal Service contracts for the transportation of the mail; such contracts have been used to promote air transportation as well as motor and rail transportation at other times. The Department of Housing and Urban Development (HUD) consults with the Department of Transportation (DOT) regarding the compatibility of urban transportation systems within the HUD-administered housing and community development programs. The Corps of Engineers is responsible for constructing and maintaining rivers and harbors and for protecting the navigable waterways.

■ DOT

The DOT, however, is the most pervasive policy influencer at the domestic level. The secretary of transportation is responsible for assisting the president in all transportation matters, including public investment, safety, and research. Within the DOT are the following agencies:

U. S. Coast Guard—enforces safety laws regarding navigation, ships, and ports

Federal Aviation Administration—enforces air safety regulations, develops and operates airways, and administers airport programs

■ DOT agencies

Federal Railroad Administration—administers railroad safety regulations, financial aid programs, and Alaskan Railroad (owned by United States)

Federal Highway Administration—administers highway trust fund, highway safety programs, and motor carrier safety regulations

Urban Mass Transportation Administration—coordinates urban mass transit system through funding programs, research, and design

National Highway Traffic Safety Administration—develops and implements motor vehicle safety standards

St. Lawrence Seaway Development Corporation—administers U. S. portion of St. Lawrence Seaway, and sets tolls charged

Maritime Administration—administers subsidies to U. S. flag ship firms.

Congressional Committees.[3] The laws that are formulated by Congress are the formal method by which Congress influences national transportation. The congressional committee structure is the forum in which Congress develops policy, programs, and funding for transportation. The congressional committees are quite significant in transportation.

■ Senate committees

Within the Senate, the two standing committees that bear on transportation policy are the Commerce, Science, and Transportation Committee and the Environment and Public Works Committee. The Commerce, Science, and Transportation Committee is concerned with the regulations of the modes, the promotion of air transportation (subsidies and construction funding), and the promotion of water transportation (Maritime Administration programs). The Environment and Public Works Committee is concerned with internal waterway and harbor projects, highway construction and maintenance projects, and air and water pollution regulations.

■ House of Representatives committees

The House of Representatives standing committees relating to transportation include the Interstate and Foreign Commerce Committee, Public Works and Transportation Committee, and Merchant Marine and Fisheries Committee. The Interstate and Foreign Commerce Committee has jurisdiction over railroads, the Railroad Labor Act, and air pollution. The Merchant Marine and Fisheries Committee is concerned with international water transportation and Maritime Administration programs. The Public Works and Transportation Committee is concerned with internal waterway and harbor projects, the regulation of all modes, and urban mass transportation.

In addition to the above standing committees directly related to transportation, there are numerous other congressional committees that have an impact on transportation. Federal funding may be decided in the Appropriations Committee, Senate Banking Committee, Housing and Urban Affairs Committee, House Ways and Means Committee, or Senate Finance Committee.

Regulatory Agencies. The ICC, CAB, and FMC are independent agencies charged with implementing the laws regulating transportation. The agencies have quasi-judicial and quasi-legislative powers, and when they decide on a case (for example, reasonableness of rates), the agencies are exercising quasi-judicial powers. The courts enforce agency decisions.

Judicial System. The courts have been called upon to interpret laws or reconcile conflicts. In doing so, the courts have an impact upon transportation policies. Carriers, shippers, and the general public may call upon the courts to change existing policy through interpretation of statutes. As the regulatory commissions exercise quasi-legislative and quasi-judicial powers, the affected parties seek recourse to the courts to determine legality of the decisions. The role of the courts is basically to interpret the meaning of policy as stated in laws, regulations, and executive orders.

■ role of courts

Industry Associations. One facet of national policy development that is often overlooked in the study of transportation is the role of industry associations in shaping national, state, and local promotion, regulation, and policy. These associations exist in most industries, and many of the transportation industry associations are based in Washington, D.C.

■ purposes served

Industry associations in transportation serve two basic purposes: establishment of industry standards and policy formulation and influence. The organizations are nonprofit entities that derive their powers and resources from individual member firms. They act on the charges given them by their members. In transportation, the railroads in the Association of American Railroads and the motor carriers in the American Trucking Associations often meet to resolve matters of equipment conformity and loss and damage prevention. On the policy side, these associations develop legislative and administrative ruling concepts that favor the collective membership, or they serve as a united front against proposals that are perceived to be harmful to the group.

■ carrier associations

The major industry associations in the transportation field have evolved from specific modes. The Association of American Railroads (AAR) represents the larger railroads in the United States; it was instrumental in the passage of the Staggers Rail Act of 1980. The American Trucking Associations (ATA) is divided into thirteen subconferences including regular common carriers, household goods carriers, local and short haul carriers, bulk tank firms, contract carriers, automobile transporters, and private carriers. The Air Transport Association of America (ATAA) represents the airline industry in the United States. The American Waterways Operators (AWO) consists of barge operators on the inland waterway system. The Freight Forwarders' Institute (FFI) serves member carriers in that mode. The National Motor Bus Operators Organization (NAMBO) represents common and charter bus firms. The Committee of American Steamship Lines (CASL) represents the subsidized U. S. flag steamship firms.

■ shipper associations

A major association exists for the interests of large shippers. The National Industrial Traffic League (NITL) represents shippers and receivers in transportation policy and regulation matters. It is active before congressional bodies as well as the regulatory agencies.

The Transportation Association of America (TAA) has the health and vitality of the entire U. S. transportation system as its concern. It becomes involved in policy issues that relate to two or more modes, or between modes and shippers as well as investors. The TAA was largely instrumental in the passage of the act that created the DOT, as well as the passage of the Uniform Time Standards Act which caused all areas of the United States electing to recognize daylight savings time to do so at the same time in April. Previously, each state did so on different dates which caused major confusion in railroad and airline scheduling systems and timetable publication. At one point, United Airlines had to publish 27 different timetables during the spring as various states recognized daylight savings time on different dates. Since it was enacted in 1967 the Uniform Time Standards Act has simplified these facets of transportation management.

There are other groups and associations involved in transportation policy, including nontransportation special interest groups such as the Grange and the labor unions. Various governmental agencies such as the Department of Agriculture and the Department of Defense actively function to influence existing and proposed legislation, rules, and policies on their behalf, or for the groups within them.

One of the most important governmental policy issues has been public promotion of transportation. All of the above groups and associations have been involved over the years in this important area. The topic is of such importance as a policy issue that it is considered in detail in the next section.

Public Promotion

This section presents an overview of the major transportation planning and promotion activities conducted in the United States public sector. Promotion connotes encouragement or provision of aid or assistance so transportation can grow or survive. Planning and promotion are general terms used to loosely refer to programs, policies, and actual planning. Programs involve actual public cash investments into or funding for transportation activities both privately and publicly owned. Agencies make policies to encourage beneficial actions or impacts for transportation. Planning determines future transportation needs, then establishes policies or programs to bring about certain goals through the public or private sector. All three activities promote transportation and cause it to grow or survive in instances where pure market forces would not have done so. The following discussion presents those forms of promotion found in the United States.

Air

■ air traffic control

The domestic air system received the benefits of several government programs. Foremost is the Federal Aviation Administration's (FAA) air traffic control system. It is the right-of-way system for the airlines. The navigation and traffic flow control system is used by every aircraft in flight. It is a necessary standardized safety system which is provided at little direct fee cost to the airlines. The FAA is a part of the U.S. DOT and is, in fact, its largest subagency in terms of employment and annual expenditures.

■ air subsidy

Another direct air system benefit is the subsidy system administered by the CAB. These subsidies generally apply to short and medium nonjet flights to cities that are unable to support high traffic volumes. The subsidy has been a significant support mechanism for regional airlines. In recent years, the growth of air commuter lines has enabled the regional airlines to discontinue service to small cities. The Air Deregulation Act of 1978 accelerated this trend which results in a lessened need for regional airline subsidies. This act might also cause increased political pressure for subsidies for commuter lines serving very small cities.

The U.S. Postal Service also provides substantial support to airlines. In the airline industry's early years, its prime earnings came from this subsidy system. In recent years mail income has not been as significant, but this subsidy still is a major revenue source for the industry.

■ terminal development

State and local agencies help promote the airline industry through air terminal development and construction. Terminals represent substantial capital investments which would be difficult for the industry to finance and construct. State and local bodies are able to raise the necessary large construction funds at reasonable municiple bond interest rates, often backed by the taxing power of the community. The airlines then rent terminal and hanger facilities as well as pay landing fees for each flight. This system avoids the problem of capital investment cost lumpiness for the airlines, since it is generally more economical for the agency to construct in large segments rather than to add on in small increments as volume increases.

■ safety rules

Many aircraft safety matters are handled by the federal government. The FAA provides aircraft construction and safety rules as well as pilot certification. This relieves the industry from many research, development, and information tasks related to safety of the system. In another capacity, the National Transportation Safety Board investigates accidents so that many can be avoided or reduced through aircraft specification or flight procedures.

Another indirect form of promotion to this industry comes from the military. Defense contracts for military airplane development often provide spillover benefits to commercial aviation in the form of mechanical or navigational aircraft improvements. Without military-related research and development activity, advancements in this area would no doubt occur at a slower pace.

A last form of airline promotion, which is not found in the United States system, is direct government ownership, operation, or subsidy of air service. This is common with foreign airlines that serve the United States and other routes. In these instances, African, Asian, many European, and the Latin American lines are subsidized so the countries can operate their airlines for purposes of national pride, have some degree of control over traffic to and from their nations, and gain balance of payment benefits and hard currencies through ticket sales and revenues.

flag airlines

A related form of such home flag airline promotion exists here in the United States and in most foreign nations. In the United States there is a requirement that only American flag carriers with domestically owned aircraft and domestic crews may originate and terminate domestic passengers and freight. Many foreign lines serve both New York and San Francisco, for example, with a flight originating abroad, but these flights are limited to international passengers. The only way in which a foreign line may originate and terminate a passenger in two U.S. cities is when that passenger is exercising stop over privileges as part of a tour or through movement. This home flag requirement serves to protect the domestic lines.

air user charges

Several forms of user charges exist which are essentially designed, in whole or part, to have the modes pay for many of the public benefits they receive. As mentioned before, landing fees are charged to repay investments or incur revenue for specific airports. A major user charge is levied against passenger movements through ticket taxes. As part of the Airport-Airways Development Act of 1970, the funds are collected in the form of an 8 percent passenger ticket tax. Until 1980, a 5 percent air freight tax was collected as well. An international $3 per head tax is also part of this user tax as are some aircraft registration fees. Many of these funds go into the Airport and Airway Trust Fund which is to be used for airport facility projects on a shared basis with local agencies.

Motor and Highway

With regard to public promotion, the highway system and motor carrier firms have a joint relationship. There is no direct promotion to motor carriers themselves, but indirect benefit comes to the industry through highway development.

highway construction and repair

The Federal Highway Administration branch of the DOT is responsible for federal highway construction and safety. A predecessor agency, the Bureau of Public Roads, carried out the mandate to build the Interstate Highway System which was paid for on a 90 percent-10 percent federal-state sharing basis. Today, the agency is largely devoted to highway research, development, and safety. It is also charged with certain repair projects on critical parts of the Federal and Interstate Highway System. The motor industry benefits from this system in the form of increased access, speed, and safety since without it they would have to travel more congested routes presenting safety hazards.

The National Highway Traffic Safety Administration is responsible for highway and auto safety. It also conducts major research into vehicle safety, accidents, and highway design related to safety. This agency provides administrative regulations for certain minimum automobile safety features.

The Bureau of Motor Carriers Safety is a noneconomic regulatory body whose main purpose is truck safety. Though this agency imposes strict standards on truck safety, the long-term benefit is increased safety for everyone on the highways.

Highway development also comes from states and various regional planning commissions. One example is the Appalachian Development Commission which is charged with improving the infrastructure and economy of that region. Many highway building and improvement projects are funded by this agency.

■ motor user charges

User charges are present in the highway systems in several forms. A major form is the gas and fuel tax. States look to this per gallon tax as a major revenue source for highway construction and upkeep. The federal government receives 4¢ per every gallon for the Highway Trust Fund which is the financing source of the Interstate Highway System. Many states are switching from a per-gallon to a percent-of-sales-price method of fuel-based taxation, since in recent years the number of gallons of fuel sold has decreased, thereby leaving state agencies with less revenue in times which demand greater highway maintenance. The percent-of-sales-price approach can avoid much of this decline. Another public revenue source is the federal excise tax on road tires. States also obtain revenues through vehicle registration fees. These are mostly assessed upon a vehicle weight basis so as to recoup, somewhat, a proportionate share of construction costs related to heavier versus light vehicles. Further, some states assess a ton-mile tax. Finally, tolls are a form of user taxes on many turnpikes and bridges.

■ highway trust fund

Two major controversies are currently taking place with regard to highway user charges. One is with the Federal Highway Trust Fund. The tax money that goes into this fund is collected primarily for interstate highway construction. Approximately 96 percent of the interstate system has been built, but doubt exists over whether the remaining portions, mostly very costly urban sections, will ever be built. Meanwhile, the fuel tax continues to be collected and accumulated in the fund. Many auto and trucking interests are seeking to have this money released for needed federal, interstate, and state highway repair and maintenance which is now technically the responsibility of the states. The issue is volatile in that some legislation has been passed and many policies are leaning toward using monies from that fund for nonhighway urban transportation projects.

A second problem with user taxes is on the state level. Most states collecting vehicle fees and fuel taxes only return a portion of them for highway purposes. Some states have earmarked some of these funds for education and other uses. In addition, industry groups continue to seek a greater share of these funds for highway development and improvement.

Rail

The railroads currently can avail themselves of direct assistance from the Regional Railroad Reorganization Act of 1973, the Railroad Revitalization and Regulatory Reform Act of 1976, and the Staggers Rail Act of 1980. Most of the assistance is in the form of track repair and motive power acquisition financing. These provisions are attempts to overcome the problem of poor equipment and facilities which lead to poorer service and blighted financial conditions, which usually perpetuate into a further downward spiral.

Another form of funding has been available as a subsidy to lines that are abandoned by railroads but that states and other groups continue to operate. This assistance was designed to make rail line abandonment easier by railroads while still allowing service to be continued.

■ Conrail

The Consolidated Rail Corporation has been the subject of special federal funding and promotion. It has received special appropriations for operations and capital improvements, mainly through provisions of the Regional Railroad Reorganization Act of 1973.

■ research and development

Research and development in this mode essentially disappeared in the late 1950s. Financial problems in most railroads caused cutbacks in the research and development area, thereby stagnating the technology. In response to this situation, the Federal Railroad Administration (FRA) was created as part of the DOT in 1966. The FRA has become a major source of gains in railroad technology as well as safety. An FRA test facility at Pueblo, Colorado is used to test improvements in existing power and rolling equipment as well as to develop advanced high speed rail technologies for the future.

■ Amtrak

Another form of help to the rail industry is Amtrak. In 1969, the industry's intercity passenger train deficit reached over $500 million. Because the ICC, DOT, and the public deemed many of these services as essential to the public need, the railroads could only discontinue them slowly after major procedural steps were taken. Amtrak was created to relieve this burden from the railroads while at the same time providing some of the needed services to the public. Thus, much of the passenger train deficit was shifted from the railroads and their shippers and stockholders to the federal taxpayer.

Domestic Waterway Operations

The inland barge industry receives two major forms of federal promotion. The first is from the Army Corps of Engineers which is responsible for river and port channel dredging and clearances as well as lock and dam construction. Operation and maintenance of these facilities rest with the corps as well. The second is provided by the coast guard which is responsible for navigation aids and systems on the inland waterway system.

■ dredging and construction aid

Until recently the barge industry paid no user charges except what could be interpreted as a very indirect form through general income taxes. A major controversy over a critical lock and dam on the upper Mississippi River at Alton, Illinois, brought the free use issue to a head. The competing railroad industry lobbied to prevent this lock from being improved and enlarged. The resulting legislation and appropriation provides for improvement of that lock and initiation of a 4¢ per gallon fuel tax user charge for that industry.

International Water Carriage

■ construction subsidy

The American flag overseas steamship industry receives major assistance from the federal government through the Maritime Administration (MARAD). The Merchant Marine Act of 1936 was designed to prevent economic decline of the U.S. steamship industry. One major facet of this act is construction differential subsidies (CDS). These are paid by the Maritime Administration to U.S. steamship yards that are constructing subsidized lines' ships. A ship that might only cost $20 million to build in Asia might cost $30 million in a U.S. yard. Without CDS, U.S. lines would build their ships abroad and American ship building capacity would cease to exist. Instead, the steamship line pays, say, $20 million and MARAD pays the other $10 million to construct the ship in the United States. The survival of the U.S. shipyard is also viewed as essential to U.S. military capability. The Merchant Marine Act of 1936 also provides for operating differential subsidies (ODS) which cover the higher-cost increment resulting from having higher-paid American crews on ships, rather than less costly foreign labor.

■ indirect promotion

Several indirect forms of promotion exist in this industry as well. First, the Merchant Marine Act of 1920 created what is generally referred to as cabotage laws, in the United States. These laws exist in most nations in order to protect home flag fleets. The U.S. law states that freight or passengers originating and terminating in two U.S. points may only be transported in ships constructed in the United States and owned and manned by U.S. citizens. The United States also has a cargo preference law which assists the U.S. fleet. Enacted in 1954, it stipulates that at least 50 percent of the gross tonnage of certain U.S. government owned and sponsored cargoes must be carried in U.S. flag ships. This law extends to Department of Defense military goods, foreign aid by the State Department, surplus food movements by the Department of Agriculture, and products whose financing is sponsored by the Export-Import Bank.

Several planning and facilitating promotional efforts also assist the American flag ocean fleet. MARAD continually studies and develops plans for port improvements and ways in which export-import movements can be made more efficient. The Department of Commerce has a subagency whose prime purpose is to stimulate export sales which also benefit the U.S. fleet.

■ MARAD control

Two points should be brought out here with regard to the major funding and support roles played by MARAD. One deals with the control MARAD has over the lines it subsidizes. The agency exercises decision powers over the design and construction of each ship. It also plays a major role in the routes taken by each one. In this manner, the agency makes certain decisions which are normally within the discretion of carrier managements. This form of control is unique to the transportation industry in the United States.

The other point relates to the rationale for such extensive assistance to this one industry. A strong home shipping fleet is a vital part of national

Nationalization

■ reasons for
nationalization

This is an extreme form of public promotion. It basically consists of public ownership, financing, and operation of a business entity. There are no true forms of nationalization in the U.S. transportation system except the Alaska Railroad which is owned by the DOT. Nationalization is a method of providing transportation service where either financing, ownership, or operation was not possible in a private manner. Foreign country railroads and airlines are examples of nationalization. Transportation service would probably not exist in a desirable form, or at all, without such government intervention in many lands. Advantages of nationalization that are often cited are that services can be provided which would not exist under private ownership, and capital can be attracted at favorable rates. But, nationalized organizations have been criticized as slow to innovate, unresponsive to the general public, subject to the same labor reduction as private enterprise, dependent on large management staffs, and subject to political influence.

While the public promotion issue is one of the more important policy issues confronting the United States today, there are still important policy issues that deserve consideration. In an attempt to provide a thorough overview, the final section of this chapter reviews the recommendations of the National Transportation Policy Study Commission.

Future National Transportation Policies

In 1976, the National Transportation Policy Study Commission (NTPSC) was established and was given the charge to undertake a full and complete investigation into U.S. transportation needs and into the resources, requirements, and policies of the United States to meet such expected needs. In 1979, the NTPSC presented its final report which contains major recommendations regarding national transportation policy.[4] The major policy recommendations are given below.

Government Organization

■ single regulatory agency

1. The ICC, CAB, and FMC should be abolished and a single federal transportation commission should be created to perform the residual regulatory duties of these bodies.

■ DOT as lead agency

2. The U.S. DOT should be restructured so that it becomes the lead agency in all nonregulatory federal actions directed primarily toward transport objectives. For example, transportation programs designed to foster regional economic development should be consolidated under the DOT.

■ congressional
committees consolidation

3. Congress should consider consolidating committee transportation jurisdiction so that it is not spread over thirty committees, as is currently the case.

These recommendations emphasize the need for the federal government to take a uniform approach to transportation.

Economic Regulation

■ rate freedom

1. Providers of passenger and freight services (carriers) should be allowed to raise and lower rates within a zone of reasonableness defined by Congress. The antitrust laws should apply to these firms.

2. Only those carriers that can actually provide service to particular customers should be permitted to participate with other carriers in rate bureau activities designed to establish a published, yet collectively arrived at, rate.

■ rate bureau

■ equal application of ease of entry regulations

3. Carriers should be allowed easier access to, and exit from, servicing particular markets.

4. Federal and state regulations should be applied equally to all carriers. For example, all modes in the freight market should be granted authority to enter into long-term supply contracts.

Many of the above economic regulatory policies were incorporated into the deregulations acts of 1978 (air) and 1980 (rail and motor). These policies rely upon the forces of the marketplace and permit greater pricing freedom by the carriers.

Noneconomic Regulation

■ productivity gains

■ cost-effective safety standards

1. The federal government should study the benefits of a uniform federal standard on the interstate highway system, although states should maintain their individual authority to establish length and weight standards for trucks.

2. Management and labor cooperation and flexibility should be encouraged to facilitate productivity gains.

3. The federal government should increase its efforts to promulgate equitable and cost-effective safety standards. Penalties for not enforcing or complying with these standards must be increased, and enforcement should be strict and vigorous.

These statements are directed toward efficient, economical, and safe transportation systems. Productivity improvements through labor-management cooperation are essential to improved efficiency and economy. Cost-effective safety standards must be enforced rigorously or the standards will be ineffective. Finally, the cooperation between the state and federal governments is given a mixed emphasis, but it might be concluded that the policy statement recommends a federally established standard speed limit on the interstate highway system, with the states establishing individual limits on truck size and weight.

Ownership and Operations

■ private ownership

1. Federal policies should encourage private ownership and operation of transportation by relying on the marketplace.

2. A federally assisted social service agency should consider the ability of local private sector carriers to provide needed transportation services before that agency directly provides the transportation itself.

3. Amtrak should be restructured to achieve more cost-effective operations.

4. Federal laws and regulations impeding ownership of more than one mode of transportation should be eliminated.

■ mergers

5. Transportation firms should be allowed to merge, subject to antitrust law enforcement.

These policy statements indicate the need to have an overall reduction in federal involvement in transportation and to rely more upon the marketplace. Private ownership and operation of transportation is more desirable than government ownership and operation of transportation companies.

Finance, Pricing, and Taxation

■ abandonment

1. Transportation companies should be allowed to divest themselves of capital assets that are unprofitable if neither public nor private bodies provide subsidies.

■ modal trust funds

2. Modal trust funds for highways, airports, and inland waterways should be retained.

■ user charges

3. Users of transportation facilities should be assessed charges that reflect the costs occasioned by their use, except where it is determined that federally assisted transportation facilities serve nontransportation social and economic objectives, as in the case of mass transit.

4. Effective economic analysis should be required of all existing and proposed major federal policies, programs, and regulations.

■ local autonomy

5. Federal financial assistance to state and local governments for transportation programs should be more flexible, giving the local officials more authority to transfer the funds from one program to another.

6. States should be actively encouraged to include bikeways and pedestrian walkways in the design of highway facilities receiving federal assistance.

7. Subsidies to the U.S. Merchant Marine industry should be continued, but only where the subsidies clearly benefit the national defense.

■ regulation minimization

8. Federal involvement in regulation of the transportation industry should be minimized to allow cooperative free market forces to operate, thereby improving the economic health of the industry.

Throughout these policy statements one sees an emphasis upon the free marketplace to control prices and the economic health of the carriers. Users and those who benefit from federal actions should pay for the benefits received. The economic effect of proposed federal actions should be calculated to determine if the benefits outweigh the costs of the programs.

Planning and Information

■ research and development
■ federal planning

1. More federal support should be available for research and development efforts in transportation.

2. State and local governments should be able to use any federal transportation assistance for transportation planning purposes.

3. Surplus world-wide ocean shipping freight capacity should be eliminated through international negotiations.

■ data

4. A national transportation data center should be created within the DOT, subject to adequate privacy protection.

■ local consideration

5. More consideration should be given to local conditions when national guidelines are formulated.

The NTPSC emphasized in these policy statements that federal involvement (including financial assistance) in transportation research and planning is essential to the future development of the U.S. transportation system.

Energy

■ oil price deregulation

1. Prices of domestic crude oil should be deregulated.

2. The federal government should encourage the development and use of energy-saving technologies such as improved engine design.

3. The federal government should foster the development of alternate fuels such as oil, shale, and gasified coal.

■ energy conservation

4. The federal government should continue to foster energy conservation efforts, such as the mandated fuel efficiency standards.

The thrust of these statements is to recognize that the importance of an adequate supply of fuel is essential to an efficient and economical transportation system.

Conclusion

In this chapter attention was directed toward the national transportation policy as it exists in formal statements, informal policy issues, and proposed formal statements. The nation's transportation policy is constantly changing, as is the transportation industry. Future transportation policy must recognize the future needs of society. Our transportation system must satisfy a constantly evolving and conflicting set of requirements.

Study Questions

1. Discuss the manner in which the federal government has impacted the development of the U.S. transportation system.

2. Why is there a need for a national transportation policy?

3. What has been the policy toward private ownership of transportation?

4. Discuss the relationship of public investment with the private ownership policy.

5. Why has a unimodal approach been taken in national policy?

6. What role has competition played in transportation policy?

7. Analyze the various provisions of the 1940 and 1980 statements of national transportation policy.

8. Describe the role played in the development of national policy by: the executive branch, judicial system, congressional committees, and regulatory agencies.

9. How have industry associations influenced national policy?

10. Analyze the major policy recommendations of the National Transportation Policy Study Commission.

11. In recent years, some individuals have proposed that a number of problems of the railways could be solved by nationalization of the rail right-of-way network. Give arguments for and against this proposal. (AST&T, Fall 1977, Exam #1).

Notes

1. U.S. Department of Transportation, *A Statement of National Transportation Policy* (Washington, D.C., 1975), p. 1.

2. The material in this section is adapted from Transportation Association of America, *Transportation Facts and Trends*, 16th ed. (Washington, D.C., 1980), pp. 34-36.

3. Ibid., p. 34.

4. National Transportation Policy Study Commission, *National Transportation Policies Through the Year 2000* (Washington, D.C.: U.S. Government Printing Office, 1979).

Suggested Readings

Fair, Marvin L. and Williams, Jr., Ernest W. *Transportation and Logistics.* Rev. ed. Plano, Texas: Business Publications, 1981, chap. 24.

Harper, Donald V. *Transportation in America.* Englewood Cliffs, N.J.: Prentice-Hall, 1978, pt. 3.

Hazzard, John L. *Transportation: Management, Economics, Policy.* Cambridge, Md.: Cornell Maritime Press, 1977, sec. 5.

Lieb, Robert C. *Transportation: The Domestic System.* 2d ed. Reston, Va.: Reston Publishing Co., 1981, pt. 5.

National Transportation Policy Study Commission. *National Transportation Policies Through the Year 2000.* Washington, D.C.: U.S. Government Printing Office, 1979.

Pegrum, Dudley F. *Transportation Economics and Public Policy.* 3rd ed. Homewood, Ill.: Richard D. Irwin, 1973, pt. 4.

Sampson, Roy J. and Farris, Martin T. *Domestic Transportation: Practice, Theory and Policy.* 4th ed. Boston: Houghton-Mifflin Co., 1979, pt. 7.

Secretary of Transportation. *A Statement of National Transportation Policy.* Washington, D.C.: U.S. Government Printing Office, 1975.

Transportation Association of America. *Transportation Facts and Trends.* 16th ed. Washington: Transportation Association of America, 1980, pp. 34-37.

Atlantic & Midland Railroad Company

Harold Harwood is vice president of governmental affairs for the Atlantic & Midland Railroad Company (A&MRR). His office is continu-
ously involved in policy, legislative, and ICC matters in Washington
that are for the good of the company and the industry as a whole. He
reports directly to the railroad's executive vice president. His problem,
at hand, relates to two legislative proposals made by the current administration in Washington. If enacted, they will create or increase
taxes on inland waterway barges and establish what will amount to a
toll on ships entering and leaving U.S. coastal ports. Both proposals
will be fought by powerful water interests.

The A&MRR extends from the Atlantic Coast inland to the Midwest.
It has enjoyed the recent export coal boom traffic from mines along its
lines to its coal facilities at Norfolk and Philadelphia. It competes with
another major railroad in the region as well as barge lines along the
Ohio River. The A&MRR also faces competition from Ohio River and
Mississippi River barge lines that carry freight to New Orleans for export to foreign ports. This traffic would otherwise travel over A&MRR
or its railroad competitor to Atlantic ports for export.

The tax proposals are in two parts. The deep water port proposal is
designed to recoup government costs of dredging, maintenance, and
navigation aids in coastal ports. It would assess a tax on each inbound
and outbound ship movement based upon the gross weight (ship and
freight). The tax would be uniform to all U.S. ports. It would be paid
directly by the ship or its agent. Naturally, coal movements through
A&MRR coal loading facilities at Norfolk and Philadelphia would be
affected by this tax.

The other proposal is for taxes that are for recouping all or part of
the inland waterway dredging, lock and dam, and navigation system
costs. Currently, only a small fuel tax is collected as a result of a late
1970s issue over reconstruction of Lock and Dam Number 26 at Alton,
Illinois. The new system would extend taxes to all inland waterways.
Borne by barge operators, the tax proposals call for any one or a combination of additional fuel taxes, ton-mile taxes, or lock toll charges.

Harold's specific problem is one of allocating his department's time
to where it would do the most good. Policy issues such as these involve
considerable amounts of such things as staff time, travel, and evidence
costs in Washington. He must weigh these proposals against the time
that would be spent in other policy issues dealing with other
agencies—the ICC, the Association of American Railroads, the Internal
Revenue Service, and the Department of Labor, for example.

Should Harold align the A&MRR to support either or both proposals?
Why or why not?

Part VI

Managerial Issues: Suppliers and Users

19 Financing Private and Public Transportation Systems

After reading this chapter you should:

1 Understand the uses and sources of capital in transportation.
2 Be able to discuss the capital needs and sources for private and public transportation companies.
3 Understand capital investment decision making.
4 Understand public planning and promotion of transportation.

Transportation systems, whether they are privately owned or publicly held, require capital financing for new or expanded construction. Most private transportation firms finance their projects, but some forms of transportation cannot exist on regular freight or passenger revenue, so they must rely upon public agency financial sources or assistance. In almost all modes, various forms of direct assistance, support, or encouragement are made by agencies of state and federal governments. All of these actions comprise the field of financing and promoting transportation systems.

This chapter presents an overview of capital and its application in transportation systems. It is a factor that has become increasingly costly in the past decade, and yet the transportation industry is in greater need of it today than at any time in the past. Firms and public agencies use a variety of analytical tools to evaluate the financial benefits of proposed capital investments. These tools are presented in this chapter, since they will be some of the most necessary ones for a transportation manager to have in the future.

■ chapter overview

Capital: Its Uses and Sources

■ definition

Capital is a term for the resources that are available for investing in assets that produce output. Whereas operating funds are typically the resources devoted to such things as raw materials purchases, labor, and energy, capital represents funds that are used for the purchase or acquisition of assets that will be used to produce actual output. These assets include such things as land, structures, terminals, transportation vehicles, and rights-of-way. When capital is applied to these producing assets, the task is often referred to as capital investment, capital expenditure, or reinvestment.

Transportation firms are heavy users of capital. Overall, between $2 and $3 worth of capital must be invested in the industry for it to produce $1 of annual revenues. Large outlays for locomotives, track, rail cars, airplanes, barges, trucks, pipelines, and terminals attest to the large need for capital. When a mode or firm is relatively stable, large investments are required yearly for mere reinvestment in replacement ventures. When a mode or firm is expanding, this need is much greater.

From the firm's point of view, capital is needed for growth and expansion of its capacity, replacement, improvements, and recently for compliance with antipollution requirements. Capital is also needed to combat times of inflation when the firm must cut back on its capital

■ capital intensive

purchases in order to pay for higher fuel or labor expenses which are not always covered by proportionate increases in revenue or productivity. Similarly, long-term company deficits will tend to lessen the available capital for reinvestment because the firm must tap its savings to pay for operating losses. This latter situation is debilitating because the losses restrict replacement and improvement which serve to reduce the product or service quality of the firm and lead to further losses. This downward spiral has been evident in the business history of many corporate and industry failures. Adequate capital, then, is a key to long-term survival and viability.

Capital is generally available from many sources. For one, a firm's own savings, or internally generated cash profits, often serve to build a reserve for investments. The bond market is another capital source

■ capital availability

through a debt obligation method. Mortgages through bank and insurance firms are another source, as are pension fund securities. Stock sales, called equity financing, represent yet another source. Still others include leasing, sale and lease-back, public aids, construction grants, and subsidies. All of these sources represent long-term capital or financing sources for asset investment purposes. But, while there is a range of capital financing available, it often can be difficult to obtain even for very promising investment projects.

The supply and demand situation for capital is now a highly competitive market. On the demand side, the need for capital in the United States is growing significantly. In the 1955-1964 period the U.S. economy required $760 billion in capital. In the next ten-year period, the nation required $1.6 trillion, and in the 1975-1984 period it will need $4.5 trillion. But, it is not just firms planning new investments that require capital. Residential construction, increases in inventories, and financing of federal, state, and local government deficits all require and compete for capital.

On the supply side, energy and other inflationary forces have lessened the flow of available capital. The 1970-1980 trend in the stock market has made it difficult for many investors to channel capital through this source. Demographic and other market forces have slowed the ability of pension funds to provide the capital market with funds. Even on an

■ capital shortage

individual basis, inflation, home heating, and social security deduction increases leave relatively less for people to save or invest. The future shows a continuing capital shortage in the U.S. economy. Projected federal government deficits must be financed by borrowing on the open capital market, thus funds are absorbed that otherwise could go to private capital needs. Similarly, federal deficit financing contributes to inflation which absorbs potential capital in a more pervasive manner.

All these trends have caused transportation managers and observers to pay greater attention to capital availability and application. Carriers are more attentive to the task of determining long-range capital needs and sources. Whereas entire rail car or truck fleets were purchased in the past with a cursory analysis of need and financing, the future will require sound analytical approaches in these areas. And, in industries which must depend upon public assistance, closer attention will no doubt be paid to the application of the taxpayers' dollar. Further, whether it is for private or public firms, public promotional policy will play a large role in the financing of transportation.

Capital and its Financing in Privately Owned Carriers

A flow of capital is required in all privately owned carriers. Replacement of older, less fuel-efficient power units, the need for improved vehicles, or the demand to expand capacity create the need for capital. Mere replacement of older units with similar new units places a demand on increased capital. Whereas a plain box car cost $10,000 in 1970, the same unit today costs approximately $25,000.

Though capital is of concern in the overall economy, it is a particular problem in transportation for several reasons. Transportation is an industry requiring huge outlays for its rights-of-way, power units, and carriage capacity. In 1980, a single long haul locomotive cost over $750,000, a medium-range passenger jet cost $20 million, a plain barge cost more

■ capital intensive transportation

than $300,000, and a stripped tractor-trailer unit cost $60,000. When considered in the context of the needs of entire firms and modes, it is easy to visualize the magnitude of capital demands in this one part of the economy. It is estimated that the privately owned transportation system in the United States has over $200 billion invested in it. If 10 percent of the system required a capital turnover (a conservative estimate), then approximately $20 billion is needed yearly.

A contributing problem for transportation is normal and inflationary increases in the cost of capital goods. Many presently available planes and other vehicles contain efficient features, but they are very costly. But even when considering improvement features, many observers cite an inflationary trend in transportation capital goods that exceeds the rise in the cost of living index felt by consumers.

Another capital problem is that many carriers must apply available capital to servicing debt bonds. Even when total debt is kept constant, many firms must pay off a past 4 percent interest debt obligation by

■ debt obligation service

floating a new one of the same principle amount bearing a 10 or 11 percent interest rate. This problem is compounded when the debt structure is sufficiently large so as to prevent either further debt financing or to cause equity financing to be too risky for the market.

Still another problem is the relative inability of transportation firms to attract capital at affordable interest rates. With the exception of several

■ high interest rates

very successful firms, the transportation industry as a whole has tended to produce lower profits than many other nontransportation industries. This translates into a lower attractiveness for outside investors.

The specific background of each transportation mode presents a clearer indication of the problems facing individual carriers. The following discussion presents each mode in terms of future capital needs, the application of capital, the magnitude of capital requirements, and insights into financing sources and problems.

The Air Industry

The present and future needs of the air industry include forecasted passenger demands estimating an average growth rate of about 5 percent per year for the next decade. This requires a growth in aircraft movements of about 2 percent per year, considering fuller use of existing planes as well as the phasing in of larger ones.

Capital equipment investment needs through 1990 are estimated to be approximately 70 percent for growth and 30 percent for replacement. Retirement of older aircraft is becoming a crucial point now that many existing planes are coming to the end of their useful economic lives of eighteen to twenty years. Maintenance costs climb on older equipment;

■ equipment needs

they are uneconomical from the standpoint of being engineered and built in a period of very low fuel costs. They are now too costly to operate profitably. Some have difficulty in meeting newly mandated noise requirements at many airports. Further, the introduction of new planes makes the older ones relatively obsolete from an operating efficiency standpoint. For both growth and replacement reasons, the industry must reequip itself with the new, improved aircraft available in the early 1980s.

The air commuter industry represents another sector of future capital demand. Air commuter firms are presently relatively small, typically operating with fleets ranging from one to twenty planes. Many of the former regional airlines are suspending or abandoning service to smaller cities because it is now more economical to serve them with aircraft seating from six to thirty passengers.

The magnitude of capital needs reflects some future problems of the industry. The industry had $18 billion invested in aircraft and $2.8 billion in ground equipment in 1977. In the 1980-1989 period, the industry will require an additional $61 billion in capital to finance its equipment growth and replacement needs. This figure includes $15 billion for pure growth, $16 billion for replacement, and $30 billion for inflation.

Available sources for this new capital will be a major problem. One traditional capital source is internally generated cash from profitable oper-

■ capital sources

ations. In the 1960s the industry could normally generate about 15 percent of its equipment purchases from this source. By the late 1970s, this had dropped to only 4 percent. Long-term debt is another capital source, but many airlines have reached limits on this source. Long-term debt was $3 billion for the industry in 1966; by 1975 it had climbed to $5.7 billion. Whereas the interest on this debt was $127 million in 1966, it had climbed to $402 million in 1975. Many carriers are at debt ceilings in terms of the amount of outstanding borrowings and the amount of cash required to pay yearly interest. Sales of equity securities is another financing source. These sales represented $1.1 billion in 1966, climbing to $2.5 billion in 1975. Here, too, many carriers are not currently able to sell more equity securities to use as a funding source.

The borrowing and stock selling ability of the industry can be seen clearly by its past profit experience. Problems such as three recessions in a decade and fuel cost escalations have resulted in a relatively poor profit history. The industry profit margin on sales has been only between 0 and 2 percent in the past decade. Annual net income has ranged from a deficit to a 1978 high of $1 billion. Return on investment has likewise ranged from 1 1/2 percent to a 1978 high of 13 percent with a decade average of 6 percent. It is projected that a return of 15 percent is required for the air industry to attract more debt and equity financing. This has caused many industry observers to note that there will be a serious gap between industry capital needs and sources in the 1980s.

■ depressed profits

The impact of deregulation, further fuel increases, and a sluggish economy in the beginning of the 1980s have also clouded the capital situation. In one sense, deregulation has harmed some carriers and markets by increasing competition; a few carriers have overextended their routes. On the other hand, deregulation has created a more flexible environment for matching specific equipment economies to particular route markets. In any event, a state of flux exists which has brought about an additional uncertainty factor in the industry, elevating the risk perceived by financial markets.

■ deregulation

Motor Carriers of Freight

■ short life term

Capital needs of the motor carrier industry are a short-term phenomenon of three to seven years compared to those of rail and air, which can typically be fifteen to twenty years in equipment life, depreciation, and financing. Information is lacking about capital invested in the entire industry because a significant portion of motor carriage exists in the form of private and other exempt sectors for which few statistics are collected. Complicating the situation further is the existence of owner-operators, the number of which is difficult to determine at any particular time.

■ change in financial makeup

In terms of capital trends in this industry, some changes have been taking place. It has traditionally been a high volume but low profit industry. Leasing has been a large capital source. The small firm nature of the industry, the relatively low collateral position of most carriers, and the traditional operating ratio, general rate-making standard that is employed have all fostered leasing as a major capital source. During the 1960s and 1970s, many large firms grew to financial positions in which equipment and terminals were purchased and long-term debt and publicly traded equity financing came into being. These publicly financed firms represent only a few hundred of the over 17,000 estimated for-hire carriers in operation.

Many sources of financing are available in this industry. The ones employed by each carrier will vary according to the needs and choices available. The various forms of financing found in this industry are listed below.

Conditional Sale. This is an equipment loan in which the lender holds title to the equipment. The carrier receives the title to the asset upon final payment of the loan. It is common for equipment manufacturers or leasing firms to offer this financing method.

Leasing. Many leasing arrangements are found in motor carriage. They vary according to length of terms, whether services for maintenance are provided, and whether the equipment is returned to the owner or passed on to the leasee at the end of the term.

Chattel Mortgage. This is a loan made to the carrier for the purchase of equipment or terminals. Title to the equipment is held by the carrier. A lien on the equipment exists in the event that the carrier defaults on the mortgage payments.

Revolving Credit. The industry typically experiences large outlays in the spring of the year due to vehicle license fee payments made to each state. Many carriers experience seasonal periods of low revenue as well. To assist the carrier through these periods, revolving credit arrangements are often used. These consist of a credit line made available to the firm from a bank. The carrier draws upon it as needed and pays it back upon a schedule or within a certain time period.

Sale and Lease-back. With this method of terminal financing, the carrier purchases land and constructs a terminal to its specifications. It will then sell the terminal but immediately lease it back for a long-term period. In this way the carrier receives its cash investment out of the asset so it can utilize that cash in other areas.

Bonds. This is a security that is sold for cash and is paid off in different time periods or at one future date. In the meantime, the carrier pays interest to the holders of the debt.

Stock. Some firms have sold stock to a limited number of private individuals, or on the stock market to the general public. Publicly traded motor carrier stocks appeared in greater numbers during the 1960s and 1970s as compared to earlier periods.

■ capital attraction problems

Problems of capital attraction in the motor carrier industry also vary by carrier, but some underlying factors are considered by all of the industry financing sources. One factor is that motor carriers represent a high financing risk. It is an industry in which all firms, small to large, are subject to sudden shifts in financial condition as a result of business swings, cost impacts, and economic conditions. Because of its low profit margin, high volume nature, it depends upon a high cash flow. High cash and security reserves are not a typical hallmark of firms in this industry. Sudden drops in business are a serious concern because the firm still must meet lease, labor, and other periodic obligations. Another major concern that financial sources have is the current deregulatory movement. The influx of many carriers and the state of uncertainty other deregulatory developments have caused, have altered the relative stability of the industry. In some settings, many marginal carriers have existed under the former system because of protected routes and collective rate bureau actions which tended to provide some insulation from full market forces. The changed situation increases the financing risk in all carriers, including the established ones.

Specific financing of small- and medium-size trucking firms is different when little or no track record of past nonlease financing exists. A lease provides lender security in an asset that can often be flexibly leased elsewhere. Many other forms of financing provide less security and are, therefore, of greater concern to the lender. In nonlease financing processes, the carrier must satisfy many of the financing source's concerns. Past and present financial position, profit, and cash flow as well as pro forma statements provide many tangible indicators of risk as well as ability to serve the debt and pay it off. Also, many lenders examine how the firm determines which business to seek and analyze the firm's resource performance. This is often done by evaluating the systems employed in determining costs and evaluating the terminals, traffic lanes, regions, and key middle manager spheres of responsibility. The greater the detail and the faster the reporting of these factors, the more assured the financing sources are that the firm can respond to needed change quickly. Further, the tenure of management personnel is often analyzed in several ways. A firm that employs many persons in their sixties will have many retirements and possible successions that might bring major shifts in strategies. This can often be viewed as a risk. A balance of age within management ranks presents a more comfortable financing posture. Similarly, planned executive development and exposure to various facets of the firm by career track managers help assure that a balanced management exists. And, finally, a statement as to how the firm weathered past hurdles such as recessions, major acquisitions, mergers, and fuel crises indicates how well the management team may handle future problems.

■ small- and medium-size firm financing

Railroads

Future capital needs in this industry are for replacement, upgrading, and growth. Normal equipment replacement must be done with rolling stock that costs many times the original item, unit for unit. Some fuel efficiency or capacity improvement factors are found in the new capital goods, but these are minor. Upgrading is a serious capital problem for many of the railroads that deferred maintenance on track and equipment in past years. This deferred maintenance policy has a spiraling negative effect. When the upgrading is finally performed, it is done at a much higher cost.

■ capital needs

Many railroads need capital for growth. Railroads are less energy-intensive than motor carriers. Motor-rail rate comparisons over long distances are shifting to favor the railroads. In the long run this mode will no doubt recapture some long- and medium-distance traffic from motor carriers. Further, the resurgence of coal is boosting the demand for rail to haul that commodity. Finally, railroads require large amounts of future capital just to refund old debts, or to "roll it over" by selling new issues in order to obtain funds to retire old ones.

■ growth

Total net investment in assets in the industry is about $30 billion. Aside from land and structures, railroads have approximately 1.7 million freight cars and 28,000 locomotives. Capital expenditures in 1978 were $2.78 billion, which is nearly $500 million more than in 1976. The need to make more investments in future years for replacement and growth will no doubt increase further. Increased utilization of existing equipment is one way in which railroads can theoretically reduce the need for additional assets. The miles moved by each freight car can be increased by faster movement, the cars can be loaded more heavily, and they can be turned around faster by shippers and consignees. On an overall national car fleet basis, these improvements have been made infrequently. Some carriers have made strides, however, by improving car distribution and movement control.

rail financing

Sources of rail financing include bond and stock sales as well as other popular means. Conditional sales agreements are used for a majority of locomotive purchases in which the security is held by a bank or other lending institution. Many roads obtain equipment through a quasi-leasing method in the form of per diem or mileage rentals. Most roads acquire automobile rack cars from rail car manufacturers on long-term bases through this mechanism. Each car has the road's name on it and is controlled by that road, but it is paid for by whichever road it is traveling over on any particular day. Another source of capital equipment has been nonrailroad firms which have speculated in the car supply business. In some instances the shippers or receivers of unit trains provide the cars. This is common in many coal movements. In other areas many shippers provide covered hopper cars with their names on them. Tank cars must be provided by shippers because railroads have not, traditionally, been willing to provide them. Finally, various government-backed loans and grants are available for track and other physical plant improvements.

rail financing problems

The industry as a whole has a spotty history of financing problems, though many successful firms are exceptions. The firms collectively have had a low overall return on investment since the 1950s. Carriers in the southern and western districts are relatively profitable, but the unprofitable roads affect the operations and financial concerns of the entire industry. Another problem is that the industry can only generate about one-fourth or one-third of its capital expenditure needs from retained funds. The $2.77 billion in capital expenditures in 1978 only contained $750 million in internally generated cash. Thus, this mode must seek large financing from outside sources and it does not, as a whole, present an extremely favorable risk position to the finance community. This can be seen by the fact that rail bond issues today cost one-half to three-quarters of a percentage point more than those of nonrail firms. The profit and debt-equity proportion position of the industry in the past decade has been such that new equity financing is difficult to obtain. One bright spot in this situation, however, is that some profitable railroads have energy and other resource incomes and profits. Capital is attracted to the entire firm at favorable quantities and rates in these situations. Further, the future fuel-related competition of railroads and motor carriers will no doubt improve traffic, revenues, and profits for rail-roads.

Domestic Water

The ownership of the inland barge industry is primarily held by individuals and firms. Very little stock is available to the general public. It is an industry with a large number of small firms. Capital financing predominantly comes from internal cash generation and chattel mortgage or conditional sales agreements.

Two major financial problems exist in this industry. One is the high inflation rate in the price of barges and tows. Examination of the 1970s will show this rate to be higher than the overall rate of the consumer price index. Another problem is that the investment into and replacement of dams and locks has slowed. This right-of-way structure system is the responsibility of the Army Corps of Engineers. Recent efforts of the corps to seek large additional federal appropriations for upgrading the existing water system have not resulted in amounts that are maintaining past system capacities. The impacts have been lock delays which slow transit time and cause the same asset base to move less freight in a year. Thus, equipment utilization stands to decrease in the future and this decrease will require more carrier investment.

■ right-of-way structure

This section has presented the needs, sources, and problems of capital financing in the major domestic modes. The approaches to financing are relatively the same in all modes. Equipment utilization is a key to total asset needs. All modes are experiencing severe capital acquisition cost inflation. In all instances, the approach for actually acquiring replacement or new assets is the same in principles, logic, and application.

Approach to Private Sector Capital Investment Decisions

Top carrier management and finance officers are now more critical as to where capital is to be applied. This has led to increased sophistication of capital project analysis. Detailed technical and financial review is now common practice in many firms.

Capital project analysis is the basic review process now required in most firms before approval is given to acquire assets. It applies to the entire process that ranges from idea conception to eventual replacement analysis. Though it may be informally utilized in some firms, the basic rudiments are usually present in all companies. This process includes: (1) idea generation, (2) prescreening, (3) detailed technical and financial analysis, (4) proposal preparation, (5) reject/accept decision, (6) financing decision, (7) acquisition and implementation, (8) post-audit, and (9) replacement analysis. The critical analytical areas of concern here are the financial analysis and the replacement decision.

■ acquisition analysis

The capital investment decision process involves ascertaining various absolute and relative financial profits of returns to the firm in relation to the total initial cost of the capital asset. The basic process is one of determining which projects promise favorable returns in comparison to other capital applications, as well as providing a basis for selecting the best projects when it is not possible to obtain all of them. Various financial tools have been developed for use in this process. The input information required in these analyses is applicable to all tools.

Initial Investment Cost

The key starting point in capital investment analysis is to determine the total cost of acquiring and implementing a project. Total initial investment cost includes all asset investment-related costs that will be required or charged as a result of the project. These include the capital item purchase price, its installation costs, any related expenses for training employees, the cost of additional maintenance tools as required, and the management costs included in engineering, planning, and bringing the project on-line. If the asset is to replace an existing one, then the net salvage value of the old asset, or the sale price less the cost of dismantling and removing it can then be used to reduce the total initial cost of the new asset. Another factor which can be used to reduce the initial cost is the investment tax credit. The tax credit generally allows the firm to pay less income taxes as a result of investing in a new asset. For example, if the asset costs $1 million and the investment tax credit is 10 percent, then the tax credit will permit the firm to pay $100,000 less income taxes than it normally would. The net effect is to reduce the total acquisition price of the asset to $900,000. Table 19.1 summarizes how total initial investment costs are determined.

■ initial investment cost

Annual Net Benefit

This benefit captures the annual net return or cash spin-off from a capital project. Of concern here is the project net cash experience, not the reported accounting profit. The cash flow, which is of concern to financial and top management personnel, can be significantly different than the accountant's measured profit. Accounting treatment of depreciation, many overhead allocations, and tax planning factors, which are necessary for other reporting purposes, often tend to mask the true cash flows. Table 19.2 illustrates how the annual net cash benefit is determined.

■ cash flow

Table 19.1 Calculation of Total Capital Investment Cost

Fleet cost — purchase price		$1,000,000
Engineering		50,000
Planning		20,000
Management time to bring on-line		10,000
Additional investments:		
Tools		10,000
Site preparation		15,000
Training		5,000
Eliminating old asset:		
Salvage value	(120,000)	
Dismantling cost	10,000	(110,000)
Investment tax credit		(100,000)
Total initial investment cost		$900,000

or $I_0 = \$900,000$

Table 19.2 Computation of Annual Net Benefits

Factor		$
Revenue (freight charge times number of trips per year		$630,000
Less:		
Fuel	($ 60,000)	
Labor	(100,000)	
Maintenance	(25,000)	
Overhead	(25,000)	
Depreciation*	(180,000)	(390,000)
Net before taxes		$240,000
Income taxes (@50%)		(120,000)
Net after taxes		$120,000

Annual Net Benefit = Net After Taxes + Depreciation

$300,000 = $120,000 + $180,000

$$*Depreciation = \frac{Total\ Investment\ Cost}{Number\ of\ Years\ Life} = \frac{\$900,000}{5}$$

Several facets of the annual net benefit concept require elaboration. It is basically constructed in a manner similar to a regular accounting net profit statement. Revenue and natural cost accounts for such things as energy, labor, and income taxes are computed so as to produce a net income-after-tax figure. However, depreciation is added to the net after the tax income is figured. Depreciation is a normal deduction which re-

■ depreciation: noncash expense

duces profit for tax reporting and payment purposes. Since it is a noncash expense, it does not entail a cash outlay in a given year. In fact, it is an accounting expense which acts to shield some of the income. In the example shown in Table 19.2, the firm actually possesses $120,000 + $180,000, or $300,000 in *cash* at the end of the year as a result of the project. This is the key financial indicator of absolute cash return from the project.

Another important factor in the annual net benefit is that it must be calculated each year. Differences in rates, labor costs, energy markets, and volumes will generally cause the annual net benefit figure to vary.

Positive annual net benefits can be determined for a capital asset which produces no revenues. In this instance a new asset might be

■ bottom line

sought to reduce total operating costs. Here, the bottom line total cost of the current asset less the total cost of the more efficient unit becomes *the* annual net benefit of the new proposed asset.

By determining the total initial investment cost as well as the annual net benefit, the carrier manager is now in a position to determine the relative return of this proposed $1,000,000 fleet purchase with a new acquisition cost of $900,000.

Tools of Financial Analysis

Several financial tools are available to analyze the true worth of a proposed investment. In our example, the project will cost $900,000 to acquire ($I_0$, which is the investment cost in Year Zero), and it will return $300,000 per year for five years (NB_1, NB_2, ... NB_5). In total, the firm will receive $1,500,000 for its investment. Four major tools are used to determine whether this $600,000 surplus is desirable or not.

Simple Pay-back. The purpose of this tool is to indicate how long it will take, in terms of time, to gain back the initial investment cost. In the fleet acquisition example, this is computed as follows:

$$\text{Simple Pay-back} = \frac{\text{Initial Investment Cost}}{\text{Annual Net Benefit}}$$

$$= \frac{\$900,000}{\$300,000}$$

$$= 3 \text{ years}$$

If the annual net benefits are different for each year, the simple pay-back can be determined by using the following approach:

Year	Cash Flow	Cumulative Flow	
0	($900,000)	($900,000)	
1	300,000	(600,000)	
2	300,000	(300,000)	
3	300,000	-0-	Simple Pay-back Point
4	300,000	300,000	
5	300,000	600,000	

If the pay-back point is a year and a fraction, the fraction can be interpolated to provide the number of months of the final year.

This tool provides a simple view of project risk. That is, the shorter the pay-back period, the more profitable or safer the project. The longer the pay-back period, the less inherent profitability the acquisition possesses, and the greater the investment risk. If a project does not break even within the project life span, then it will not provide as many dollars as it originally cost to acquire.

■ project safety

Some drawbacks exist with this tool. First, it only indicates a single point in time. No indications are given of total life span dollar return or of where the break-even point is in relation to the life span. Finally, and perhaps most importantly, simple pay-back does not consider the timing of funds flows. It is important to financial personnel to view early funds inflows as more desirable than later inflows. The inflation rate and the opportunity cost of cash make it imperative that a dollar received in year one is considered higher in value than one that will be received in year two. Inflation alone will make the dollar to be received one year from now worth more in purchasing power than the one that will be received two years from now.

■ present value factor

The problems inherent in the simplistic nature of simple pay-back can be overcome through use of an additional component tool called the present value factor (PVF). Table 19.3 is a table of present values. These values are used to discount future cash receipts so that NB_1, NB_2, . . . and NB_5 can all be expressed in terms of their value in relation to today's cash opportunity values or today's purchasing power.

To illustrate this concept, reference to the table shows that if the time value of money is 10 percent, then a dollar in hand is worth $1.00 × 1.000, or $1.00. If the inflation rate is 10 percent, then $1.00 which we will receive one year from now is only worth $1.00 × .9091 or $.909 (90.9¢). That is, the dollar we will receive a year from now will only have a purchasing power of 90.9¢ in today's terms. If it takes two years to receive another dollar, that dollar will only be worth 82.6¢ in today's terms. With this approach we can express all future receipts of all projects into today's terms so that they all have a common denominator.

Table 19.3 Present Value Factors

| | Interest Rate | | | | | | | | | |
YR	1	2	3	4	5	6	7	8	9	10
1	0.9901	0.9804	0.9709	0.9615	0.9524	0.9434	0.9346	0.9259	0.9114	0.9091
2	0.9803	0.9612	0.9426	0.9246	0.9070	0.8900	0.8734	0.8573	0.8417	0.8264
3	0.9706	0.9423	0.9151	0.8890	0.8638	0.8396	0.8163	0.7938	0.7722	0.7513
4	0.9610	0.9238	0.8885	0.8548	0.8227	0.7921	0.7629	0.7350	0.7084	0.6830
5	0.9515	0.9057	0.8626	0.8219	0.7835	0.7473	0.7130	0.6806	0.6499	0.6209
6	0.9420	0.8880	0.8375	0.7903	0.7462	0.7050	0.6663	0.6302	0.5963	0.5645
7	0.9327	0.8706	0.8131	0.7599	0.7107	0.6651	0.6227	0.5835	0.5470	0.5132
8	0.9235	0.8535	0.7894	0.7307	0.6768	0.6274	0.5820	0.5403	0.5019	0.4665
9	0.9143	0.8368	0.7664	0.7026	0.6446	0.5919	0.5439	0.5002	0.4604	0.4241
10	0.9053	0.8203	0.7441	0.6756	0.6139	0.5584	0.5083	0.4632	0.4224	0.3855
11	0.8963	0.8043	0.7224	0.6496	0.5847	0.5268	0.4751	0.4289	0.3875	0.3505
12	0.8874	0.7885	0.7014	0.6246	0.5568	0.4970	0.4440	0.3971	0.3555	0.3186
13	0.8787	0.7730	0.6810	0.6006	0.5303	0.4688	0.4150	0.3677	0.3262	0.2897
14	0.8700	0.7579	0.6611	0.5775	0.5051	0.4423	0.3878	0.3405	0.2992	0.2633
15	0.8613	0.7430	0.6419	0.5553	0.4810	0.4173	0.3624	0.3152	0.2745	0.2394
16	0.8528	0.7284	0.6232	0.5339	0.4581	0.3936	0.3387	0.2919	0.2519	0.2176
17	0.8444	0.7142	0.6050	0.5134	0.4363	0.3714	0.3166	0.2703	0.2311	0.1978
18	0.8360	0.7002	0.5874	0.4936	0.4155	0.3503	0.2959	0.2502	0.2120	0.1799
19	0.8277	0.6864	0.5703	0.4746	0.3957	0.3305	0.2765	0.2317	0.1945	0.1635
20	0.8195	0.6730	0.5537	0.4564	0.3769	0.3118	0.2584	0.2145	0.1784	0.1486
21	0.8114	0.6598	0.5375	0.4388	0.3589	0.2942	0.2415	0.1987	0.1637	0.1351
22	0.8034	0.6468	0.5219	0.4220	0.3418	0.2775	0.2257	0.1839	0.1502	0.1228
23	0.7954	0.6342	0.5067	0.4057	0.3256	0.2618	0.2109	0.1703	0.1378	0.1117
24	0.7876	0.6217	0.4919	0.3901	0.3101	0.2470	0.1971	0.1577	0.1264	0.1015
25	0.7798	0.6095	0.4776	0.3751	0.2953	0.2330	0.1842	0.1460	0.1160	0.0923

Table 19.3 *continued*

					Interest Rate					
YR	11	12	13	14	15	16	17	18	19	20
1	0.9009	0.8929	0.8850	0.8772	0.8696	0.8621	0.8547	0.8475	0.8403	0.8333
2	0.8116	0.7972	0.7831	0.7695	0.7561	0.7432	0.7305	0.7182	0.7062	0.6944
3	0.7312	0.7118	0.6931	0.6750	0.6575	0.6407	0.6244	0.6086	0.5934	0.5787
4	0.6587	0.6355	0.6133	0.5921	0.5718	0.5523	0.5337	0.5158	0.4987	0.4823
5	0.5935	0.5674	0.5428	0.5194	0.4972	0.4761	0.4561	0.4371	0.4190	0.4019
6	0.5346	0.5066	0.4803	0.4556	0.4323	0.4104	0.3898	0.3704	0.3521	0.3349
7	0.4817	0.4523	0.4251	0.3996	0.3759	0.3538	0.3332	0.3139	0.2959	0.2791
8	0.4339	0.4039	0.3762	0.3506	0.3269	0.3050	0.2848	0.2660	0.2487	0.2326
9	0.3909	0.3606	0.3329	0.3075	0.2843	0.2630	0.2434	0.2255	0.2090	0.1938
10	0.3522	0.3220	0.2946	0.2697	0.2472	0.2267	0.2080	0.1911	0.1756	0.1615
11	0.3173	0.2875	0.2607	0.2366	0.2149	0.1954	0.1778	0.1619	0.1476	0.1346
12	0.2858	0.2567	0.2307	0.2076	0.1869	0.1685	0.1520	0.1372	0.1240	0.1122
13	0.2575	0.2292	0.2042	0.1821	0.1625	0.1452	0.1299	0.1163	0.1042	0.0935
14	0.2320	0.2046	0.1807	0.1597	0.1413	0.1252	0.1110	0.0985	0.0876	0.0779
15	0.2090	0.1827	0.1599	0.1401	0.1229	0.1079	0.0949	0.0835	0.0736	0.0649
16	0.1883	0.1631	0.1415	0.1229	0.1069	0.0930	0.0811	0.0708	0.0618	0.0541
17	0.1696	0.1456	0.1252	0.1078	0.0929	0.0802	0.0693	0.0600	0.0520	0.0451
18	0.1528	0.1300	0.1108	0.0946	0.0808	0.0691	0.0592	0.0508	0.0437	0.0376
19	0.1377	0.1161	0.0981	0.0829	0.0703	0.0596	0.0506	0.0431	0.0367	0.0313
20	0.1240	0.1037	0.0868	0.0728	0.0611	0.0514	0.0433	0.0365	0.0308	0.0261
21	0.1117	0.0926	0.0768	0.0638	0.0531	0.0443	0.0370	0.0309	0.0259	0.0217
22	0.1007	0.0826	0.0680	0.0560	0.0462	0.0382	0.0316	0.0262	0.0218	0.0181
23	0.0907	0.0738	0.0601	0.0491	0.0402	0.0329	0.0270	0.0222	0.0183	0.0151
24	0.0817	0.0659	0.0532	0.0431	0.0349	0.0284	0.0231	0.0188	0.0154	0.0126
25	0.0736	0.0588	0.0471	0.0378	0.0304	0.0245	0.0197	0.0160	0.0129	0.0105

For example, if Project A's benefits are $1000 ($NB_1$) and $800 ($NB_2$) and Project B's benefits are $800 ($NB_1$) and $1000 ($NB_2$) and the present value factor selected by the finance personnel in the firm is 10 percent, then the two $1,800 projects compare as follows:

Project A

	Project A
NB_1	$1000 x .909 = $9090
NB_2	800 x .826 = __661__
	$9751

	Project B
NB_1	$ 800 x .909 = $ 727
NB_2	1000 x .826 = __8260__
	$8987

Note, in a simplistic sense, both projects have a total cash return of $1,800. But, this example shows the timing of inflows of Project A to be more beneficial than Project B. The present value factor enables analysis of project cost, return, and the time value of funds.

Table 19.3 *continued*

				Interest Rate				
YR	21	22	23	24	25	26	27	28
1	0.8264	0.8197	0.8130	0.8065	0.8000	0.7937	0.7874	0.7813
2	0.6830	0.6719	0.6610	0.6504	0.6400	0.6299	0.6200	0.6104
3	0.5645	0.5507	0.5374	0.5245	0.5120	0.4999	0.4882	0.4768
4	0.4665	0.4514	0.4369	0.4230	0.4096	0.3968	0.3844	0.3725
5	0.3855	0.3700	0.3552	0.3411	0.3277	0.3149	0.3027	0.2910
6	0.3186	0.3033	0.2888	0.2751	0.2621	0.2499	0.2383	0.2274
7	0.2633	0.2486	0.2348	0.2218	0.2097	0.1983	0.1877	0.1776
8	0.2176	0.2038	0.1909	0.1789	0.1678	0.1574	0.1478	0.1388
9	0.1799	0.1670	0.1552	0.1443	0.1342	0.1249	0.1164	0.1084
10	0.1486	0.1369	0.1262	0.1164	0.1074	0.0992	0.0916	0.0847
11	0.1228	0.1122	0.1026	0.0938	0.0859	0.0787	0.0721	0.0662
12	0.1015	0.0920	0.0834	0.0757	0.0687	0.0625	0.0568	0.0517
13	0.0839	0.0754	0.0678	0.0610	0.0550	0.0496	0.0447	0.0404
14	0.0693	0.0618	0.0551	0.0492	0.0440	0.0393	0.0352	0.0316
15	0.0573	0.0507	0.0448	0.0397	0.0352	0.0312	0.0277	0.0247
16	0.0474	0.0415	0.0364	0.0320	0.0281	0.0248	0.0218	0.0193
17	0.0391	0.0340	0.0296	0.0258	0.0225	0.0197	0.0172	0.0150
18	0.0323	0.0279	0.0241	0.0208	0.0180	0.0156	0.0135	0.0118
19	0.0267	0.0229	0.0196	0.0168	0.0144	0.0124	0.0107	0.0092
20	0.0221	0.0187	0.0159	0.0135	0.0115	0.0098	0.0084	0.0072
21	0.0183	0.0154	0.0129	0.0109	0.0092	0.0078	0.0066	0.0056
22	0.0151	0.0126	0.0105	0.0088	0.0074	0.0062	0.0052	0.0044
23	0.0125	0.0103	0.0086	0.0071	0.0059	0.0049	0.0041	0.0034
24	0.0103	0.0085	0.0070	0.0057	0.0047	0.0039	0.0032	0.0027
25	0.0085	0.0069	0.0057	0.0046	0.0038	0.0031	0.0025	0.0021

Discounted Pay-back. Discounted pay-back provides a measure of how long it will take for a project to pay back its initial investment, but the returning funds are modified to consider the time value of funds. It requires knowledge of the initial investment cost, the annual net benefits, and the appropriate present value factor (or discount rate) as given by corporate finance managers of the firm. In the example here, financial personnel have told us that our funds have a 10 percent opportunity cost associated with them. Discounted pay-back can then be calculated as shown in Table 19.4.

Table 19.4 Computation of Discounted Pay-back

Factor	Flow	10% PVF	Annual Present Value Stream	Cumulative Present Value Stream
I_0	($900,000)	1.000	(900,000)	(900,000)
NB_1	300,000	.909	272,700	(627,300)
NB_2	300,000	.826	247,800	(379,500)
NB_3	300,000	.751	225,300	(154,200)
NB_4	300,000	.683	204,900	50,700
NB_5	300,000	.621	186,300	237,000

The specific discounted pay-back (D.PB) point is 3-plus years. The exact time is computed as follows:

$$\text{DPB} = 3 \text{ years} + \frac{\text{Cumulative Deficit Remaining at End of That Year}}{\text{Total Present Value Stream Available in Next Year}}$$
$$= 3 + 154{,}200/204{,}900$$
$$= 3.75 \text{ years}$$

This tool again gives us a point in time to measure project risk. What is implied is "the project cost $900,000; that was paid back in 3.75 years; that money could have earned 10 percent elsewhere in another project or investment." Like the simple pay-back, this approach only provides a point in time of pay-back. No further measure of like span or total magnitude of dollar return is provided.

Net Present Value. This tool illustrates how many surplus dollars a project will return to the firm after net cash benefits are burdened with the selected company cash opportunity rate. That is, it basically determines that a project will return actual cash inflow benefits, but they will be discounted by the selected present value rate in order to show how much more the firm will earn from the project than it would if it had invested the original cash in an alternative investment earning the selected present value factor interest rate.

The net present value is determined using the same table of computations as the discounted pay-back (Table 19.4). The net present value is the sum of the annual present value stream ($272,700 + $247,800 + ... + 186,300) minus the original investment cost, or $1,137,000 – $900,000 = $237,000.

The same figure can be extracted from Table 19.3 by referring to the last year sum of the cumulative present value stream column. Again, this tool is implicitly saying that if the firm's opportunity or actual cost of funds is 10 percent, it can invest $900,000 into this project and after five years it will be better off in purchasing power by $237,000 than it would have been if it had invested the money in a 10 percent interest bearing security. Or, if the original investment cost was borrowed at 10 percent, the firm can pay that off and have $237,000 in purchasing power left.

The prime advantages of this tool are that it considers the firm's opportunity costs and the timing of funds flows. It also provides a good ranking measure between two or more projects. Discounted pay-back might show two projects as having an equal payback, but net present value shows which one will provide more dollars back to the firm.

■ opportunity cost

One problem with this tool is that it can be difficult to understand until a working familiarity of it is developed. But, once that is done, it is often preferred as a better single indicator of project worth than, perhaps, any other tool.

Internal Rate of Return. The internal rate of return (IRR) provides a percent return of a project, often referred to as discounted cash flow or discounted return. This is usually the most easily understood of all the time value tools because its answer can be related to interest rates or inflation trends.

The IRR is slightly cumbersome to calculate because it must be done on a trial and error basis. In order to find the IRR for a project, we utilize the same table format as that for discounted pay-back and net present value (see Table 19.4). To determine the IRR we must use alternative present value factor (PVF) percents in column 3 (10 percent, 12 percent, etc.) until the use of one will cause the last figure in the cumulative present value stream column (column 5) to become $0. The present value factor percent that accomplishes that is the internal rate of return for the project.

To compute the IRR for our fleet example we see that the key bottom line figure resulting from a 10 percent PVF is $237,000. The following guide rules tell us how we should proceed in various situations:

■ trial and error

Last Figure in "Cumulative Present Value Stream Column"	Action To Take	Result
Negative figure	Use lower PVF	Raises the net benefit discount stream
Positive figure	Use higher PVF	Depresses the net benefit discount stream
Zero, or near zero	None	PVF is the IRR

The above example (Table 19.4) at 10 percent shows us that the figure is a large positive one. We must then try a higher present value factor which provides us with lower discounted present value streams. The following is a trial of a 16 percent PVF.

Factor	Cash Flow	16% PVF	Annual Present Value Stream	Cumulative Present Value Stream
I_0	($900,000)	1.000	(900,000)	(900,000)
NB_1	300,000	.862	258,600	(641,400)
NB_2	300,000	.743	222,900	(418,500)
NB_3	300,000	.641	192,300	(226,200)
NB_4	300,000	.552	165,600	(60,600)
NB_5	300,000	.476	142,800	82,200

The last figure, $82,200, is still too high, so we must again use a higher present value factor. Calculations of other ones result in the following final figure of column 5.

PVF	Final Column 5 Figure
10%	$237,000
16%	82,200
17%	59,790
18%	38,160
19%	17,280
	————1RR
20%	(2,820)

The present value factor that causes the last column figure to be zero, $0, is between 19 percent and 20 percent which is a sufficient answer for this project. A hand-held calculator computes this as 19.85 percent, but this degree of precision is not pertinent for a study involving estimates of cash flows in future periods.

The IRR has a prime advantage in that it is simple to understand. We learn that this project earns slightly under 20 percent. Its main drawback is that it is cumbersome to compute. Small calculators that are available today take the work out of this task.

■ financial tools review

A review of all the financial tools presented here is shown in Table 19.5. Most financial analysts prefer and many top carrier managers seek the results of at least two or more of these tools for each project. In this manner, the decision makers can review each project in terms of pay-back risk, return of time valued dollars, and a percent return. This information is then summarized on proposal forms along with project descriptions and justifications. The financial tools are also often brought into use again after a project has been brought on-line and a post-audit is being made. Post-audits are useful for determining whether or not a project is performing as well as was expected; if not, managers can then alter its use for more profitable performance in alternative ways. Finally, the financial tools are used when capital assets are being considered for discontinuance or replacement.

Transportation Project Planning in the Public Sector

Transportation project planning is the process whereby federal, state, or local groups review the movement needs or demands of a region or population segment, develop transport alternatives, and usually propose or implement one of them. It enables new movement functions to take place or allows an existing one to continue in face of adverse trends or change.

■ public activity

Transportation project planning is a public activity; purely financial returns and other concerns are not the overriding benefits sought. It is a major part of the public activity in the U.S. economy for several reasons. Public transportation processes can open trade or movement where private actions have not or would not have been enticed to do so for financial gain alone. Various cultural and political benefits often come from projects and programs provided publicly. Transportation planning also lowers the cost of living or reduces the social costs of delay or con-

Table 19.5 Review of Financial Evaluation Tools

Tool	Answer	Advantages	Disadvantages
Simple payback	Payback time of original investment; measure of risk	Simple to compute Easy to understand	Does not consider total life flows Does not tell what occurs after the payback point Does not consider time value of funds as well as their timing
Discounted payback	Payback time of original investment; measure of risk while discounting the returning flows	Considers timing and time value of funds Simple to understand	Same as first two points above
Net present value	Surplus dollars returned over and above the return that would have come from investing the funds in another investment at a certain percent return rate	Provides measure of total dollar flow over and above what can be earned elsewhere Considers timing and time value of funds flows	Difficult to understand unless familiar with it
Internal rate of return	The percent return of a project	Simple to understand Considers timing and time value of funds flows	Cumbersome to compute by hand

gestion. Finally, it provides services which are not remunerative but deemed socially necessary or desirable.

Transportation planning is a critical factor in the last quarter of the 20th century. There are many areas of transportation which have experienced withdrawal or abandonment by private firms. Many forms of carriage today are no longer economically profitable or compensatory. Urban bus systems, commuter railroads, rail and urban research and development, and many rail services are examples of transportation forms which would not exist anymore were it not for public sector involvement.

Many forms of transportation require large capital investments which contain cost lumpiness that would normally discourage or basically prohibit private investment. Port dredging and development as well as airport construction are examples of capital items which could not be afforded by the carriers using them. Instead, the ability of a public authority to attract capital enables the asset to be built; cost is recovered through user charges. Public planning of transportation is generally found in situations where environmental or social needs override financial ones. A major argument used in modern subway construction is that although the system might not recover its full costs from the fare box, the city as a whole will gain by increased access to already existing downtown facilities including buildings, offices, stores, and water utility systems. Constructing other facilities in developing suburban areas will not be necessary. Also, existing commuters will save future expenditures because a less costly commuter system, the subway, will eliminate

■ public planning

the need for a second family auto, long driving, excess fuel consumption, need for costly parking in downtown areas, and so on. It is apparent that public planning of transportation involves a different viewpoint and set of objectives than does capital investment analysis in private firms.

An Approach to Public Planning Project Analysis

While the private firm is seeking a financial return to the firm itself, public planning agencies compare the initial costs of a project to the financial, environmental, and measurable social benefits to everyone affected by the project. Thus, it compares total societal cost to total societal benefits whether they be monetary or nonmonetary in nature.

The specific analytical tool typically used in public planning is the benefit-cost ratio (BCR). In essence, it is a measure of total measurable benefits to society divided by the initial capital cost. The formula for it in basic form is as follows:

■ benefit/cost ratio

$$\text{BCR} = \frac{\text{Sum of Yearly Benefits to Society}}{\text{Sum of Costs to Agencies and Those in Society Initially Impacted}}$$

$$= \frac{\text{Sum of Benefits}}{\text{Sum of Initial Costs}} = \frac{\text{Year 1 Benefit} + \text{Year 2 Benefit} + \ldots}{\text{Sum of All Initial Costs}}$$

If the resulting answer is over "1," the project is said to produce a "profit" for society. The figure "1" indicates break-even; less than "1" indicates that the agency will spend more on the project than society will ever reap in long-term benefits.

The major costs of a project include those expenses typically involved in private projects. Planning, engineering, construction, and financing costs are critical. Other costs include delay or congestion measured in terms of dollars per hour and in terms of everyone in society who will be inconvenienced during the construction phase of a transportation project. This is certainly the case in new lock and dam construction with regard to barge operations. Project costs may also include a cost of lost sales to downtown businesses; the stores are more difficult to access during several years of subway construction, for example. The costs of bond financing incurred to construct the system are pertinent also. All costs to everyone are monetarily measured or translated into monetary measures and listed according to the year in which they will occur. Typically, the major expenses arise in the initial years of construction; financing is a major cost carried through the project life.

■ major cost elements

The benefits of a project include any measurable benefit to the agency, other agencies, and the public at large. Benefits include increased employment, decreased prices for products, lowered costs of commuting or freight transfer, reduced maintenance, improved health due to lessened pollution, less travel time due to faster commuting or travel, increased travel, and often a measure for increased recreational benefits. Many

■ social benefits

benefit measures are easily quantified, though others pose analytical difficulties in the form of forecasting volumes and cost relationships in future periods.

Three analytical steps or checks must be undertaken in order to compute the actual benefit cost ratio. First, both costs and benefits must be collected in such a way that *all costs* and *benefits* to both agencies and the general public are included. It is wise to be analytically conservative about costs, assuming they will be incurred by everyone in society and assuming they may be higher than what current estimates show them to be. Similarly, benefits should only be limited to actual benefits that are sound and quantifiable in logical ways. Second, the individual costs and benefits should be summed for each year of occurrence and presented in the respective position of numerator or denominator as shown above. Third, a yearly discount rate should be used against each cost and benefit since most costs and benefits will not be incurred until the future.

■ benefit/cost procedure

The timing and time value of funds is an important part of any capital project analysis. Political controversy exists about the choice of the specific discount rate and its application. Several analytical points can be examined which will shed light on this task. One, the discount rate should reflect the interest cost and impact to the public agency which borrows the initial funds. Second, the rate should become higher in later years so as to reflect increasing risk, inflation, uncertainty, and forecasting difficulties. This is a conservative practice of private project financial managers, and the logic of it can be applied soundly in a public setting. Third, the counting of benefits should cease in some future period even though the project might last longer. This is another practice which is an implicit way of conservatively considering only those benefits within the intermediate term unless a logical case can be made for an extended period of time. These points are made so as to assure that benefit overcounting is minimized, especially for those items such as recreation which are generally not central to the main project need or justification. By including benefits for twenty-five years or more, it is analytically easy to inflate the ratio, or cause it to be above break-even when it would not otherwise be. Conservative risk analysis states that costs should be analytically considered higher and benefits lower than what a first glance measure indicates.

■ time value of funds

An example of benefit cost ratio application to a proposed subway line will show how public planning processes are employed. Costs include those of organization development, design, engineering, initial financing, land purchases, relocation, and disruption to the public. Costs projected into the future include operations, lost property taxes, interest costs, and any other costs directly tied to the project. Benefits to the agencies include lowered operational costs of city buses; alternative application of funds released from the bus operation (reduced street and highway requirements); decreased need to expand highways or downtown parking; increased property, sales, and wage taxes from higher economic activity downtown; avoidance of federal penalties for not reducing city-wide auto emissions; and many others. Benefits to society

■ cost/benefit
subway example

include the income multiplier effect from the initial project investment in the form of employment, reduced unemployment, and general dollar spending and circulation from construction. The general public also gains from savings in direct commuting costs and greater area-wide mobility. The system will improve society in the form of time savings, less pollution, and reduced commuting stress. Since the subway will generally cause the downtown to become more fully utilized, the overall region benefits from the reduced need to expand streets, fire protection, water, electricity, and so on since industry and retail stores might not leave the downtown for the suburbs. In this manner, the unit tax base of the city itself remains low.

As shown above, public planning involves many of the basic concepts inherent in private project planning, but the application is different. The concern of the public agency is costs and benefits to all parties affected by the project. Thus, costs, benefits, and "profits" are measured for society as a whole in tangible and intangible ways.

Conclusion

Financing transportation stands to become more of a critical problem for private and public bodies in the 1980s than in the past. The difficulty of obtaining financing and its high cost will cause more critical analysis of each project or program. This will also affect public agencies where fiscal and financial problems exist; various sunset laws will force more critical analyses to be made. These are laws that require projects, programs, or other laws to be reevaluated and justified periodically or else they are automatically terminated. These factors will no doubt cause the public sector to review its projects and programs more closely and to seek more ways in which users, as well as the public in general, can pay for them.

Study Questions

1. What is capital and what do carriers use it for?

2. What are the relative merits of debt versus equity (stock) financing from the carrier's standpoint?

3. What is a capital project? Cite some examples of capital projects that carriers will often undertake.

4. What is the difference between (a) purchase price and project total initial investment cost; and (b) project profit and annual net benefits?

5. What are the relative merits of (a) simple payback; (b) discounted paybacks; (c) net present value; and (d) internal rate of return?

6. How is the analysis of a public agency project different than a private firm project?

7. Comment upon the following statement: "American transportion is basically privately owned; therefore, there is no public support of this network nor is there any need for such support."

8. Why is there such a strong public commitment to the United States flag merchant marine fleet which is owned by about a dozen private firms?

**Suggested
Readings**

Brealey, Richard, and Myers, Stewart. *Principles of Corporate Finance.* New York: McGraw-Hill Book Co., 1981.

Flood, Kenneth U. *Traffic Management.* 3rd ed. Dubuque, Iowa: William C. Brown, 1975, chap. 2.

Fuller, John W. "Financing State Transit Subsidies." *Annual Proceedings of the Transportation Research Forum,* 1973, pp. 359-70.

Gray, George E., and Noel, Lester A., eds. *Public Transportation: Planning, Operations, and Management.* Englewood Cliffs, N.J.: Prentice-Hall, 1979.

Pegrum, Dudley F. *Transportation: Economics and Public Policy.* Homewood, Ill.: Richard D. Irwin, 1973, chap. 19.

Sampson, Roy J., and Farris, Martin M. *Domestic Transportation: Practice, Theory, and Policy.* 4th ed. Boston: Houghton Mifflin, 1979, chaps. 19, 27.

Taff, Charles A. *Management of Physical Distribution and Transportation.* 6th ed. Homewood, Ill.: Richard D. Irwin, 1978, chap. 8.

Wood, Donald F., and Johnson, James C. *Contempory Transportation.* Tulsa: Petroleum Publishing, 1980, chap. 14.

Case   ## Upstart Trucklines, Inc.

Matt Lawson is owner of Upstart Trucklines, a contract carrier which is based in Atlanta. The firm is four years old and has grown to having a fleet of 30 tractor-trailer combinations which are engaged in continuous, dedicated service to ten contract accounts.

Matt has an opportunity to obtain a new four-year contract with one of the existing accounts. It would involve purchasing another tractor-trailer combination which would cost $60,000. The unit would run 60,000 miles per year and its four-year revenue (excluding future fuel escalations) would be $110,000. Operating expenses, including interest and maintenance, are estimated to be $75,000 in the first year, $79,200 in the second, $84,000 in the third, and $88,800 in the fourth. Matt would depreciate the unit over four years on a sum of the years' depreciation basis which would mean $20,000 in year one, $15,000 in year two, $10,000 in year three, and $5,000 in year four. He is sure he could sell the unit for $10,000 at the end of the contract. His current cost of financing is 15 percent and his income tax rate is 45 percent.

Should Matt invest in the unit and sign the contract?

20 Private Transportation

After reading this chapter you should:

1 Be able to define private transportation.

2 Be able to discuss private transportation in all of the modal types.

3 Understand the nature of private trucking costs.

4 Understand the buy versus lease decision in private transportation.

Private transportation may be construed as "do-it-yourself" rather than "buy it" transportation services. The firm engaged in private transportation is vertically integrated to perform the services provided by for-hire carriers. The private transportation decision is a classic make versus buy decision in which a company must determine if it is cheaper to make (engage in private transportation) or buy transportation (use a for-hire carrier).

■ chapter overview

In this chapter the private transportation issue is examined for all modes, but emphasis is given to private trucking, the most pervasive form of private transportation. Attention will be directed to the decision to enter into private trucking and the operation of a private truck fleet.

What is Private Transportation?

Private transportation is *not* the opposite of public (government) transportation. Private transportation is a legal form of transportation defined as, " . . . any person who transports in interstate or foreign commerce property of which such person is the owner, lessee, or bailee when such transportation is for the purpose of sale, lease, rent or bailment, or in the furtherance of any commercial enterprise."[1]

■ legal definition

The above legal definition may be interpreted as follows: Private transportation is not for-hire transportation of goods owned by the firm that also owns (leases) and operates the transportation equipment for the furtherance of its primary business.

■ working definition

A private carrier does not serve the general public. Rather, the private carrier serves itself by hauling its own raw materials and finished products. The private carrier is technically permitted to haul goods for others (the public) but only if such service is provided free of charge. Of notable exception is the 1980 Motor Carrier Act provision to permit

■ hauling of own goods

private truck fleets to haul the goods, for a fee, of other firms that are 100 percent owned subsidiaries. This will be discussed in more detail below.

The Interstate Commerce Commission (ICC) has strictly enforced the prohibition of private carriers hauling public goods for a fee. This enforcement is an extension of the control over entry for common and contract carriers who must prove public convenience and necessity. However, the 1980 Motor Carrier Act has greatly reduced controls over entry into the common and contract carrier fields, and grants of authority are relatively easy to obtain even for an existing private motor carrier.

Although private trucking is the most common, private transportation is found in other modes as well. A brief analysis of private transportation in rail, air, and water follows.

Private Rail Transportation

■ private rail cars

Private transportation in the railroad industry takes the form of privately owned rail cars moved by a common carrier railroad. Private rail transportation does not exist in the form of a business operating a railroad to transport its goods between cities.

Many businesses have purchased or leased rail cars to assure an adequate supply of equipment during peak demand periods. It is quite common for mining and agricultural firms to own or lease hopper cars which are in short supply (railroad owned) during the harvest season. Recently, increased exports of grains and ores have aggravated the rail hopper car shortage and have caused many firms to acquire or to consider acquiring such equipment to assure a supply of rail cars and continued operation of the company.

■ private siding

Private rail transportation includes the cost of a private siding or spur track connected to a company's plant or warehouse. The rail transportation user desiring service to its door must provide and maintain the rail track on its property.

■ switch engine inside plant

Some large manufacturing firms have built small railroads within the confines of their plants to shuttle rail cars from building to building. Such private railroads may be construed as materials handling systems that move rail cars loaded with goods such as raw materials. The switch engine performs the same function as the fork lift; that is, the switch engine places the rail cars in the proper location to permit loading and unloading. The switch engine of such private railroads does not operate outside the plant limits.

Private rail transportation is not a common form of private carriage as are air, water, and truck. Private rail transportation basically means that the user buys or leases rail cars, provides rail tracks on its property, and, in some limited cases, provides switching within the plant.

Private Air Transportation

Private air transportation, unlike the other modal forms of private carriage, is used extensively, if not exclusively, to transport people. The private airplane fleets are purchased and operated to serve the travel needs of executives. The company plane is normally used by top management, with lower level managers using commercial flights.

■ company personnel carriage

The private airplane fleet is also utilized to transport freight in certain emergency situations. Documents that are needed to consummate an important sale or repair parts that will prevent an assembly line from closing are typical examples of emergency situations in which the corporate jet is called to freight duty. Since the objective of the fleet is to serve the travel needs of management, routine deliveries of freight do not meet the objective of private air fleets.

■ emergency freight

The corporate jet has become somewhat of a status symbol. The private airplane projects an image of success—success both for the company and its managers. Within the organization, the manager who has access to the company plane is viewed by contemporaries as "having made it."

■ image

The cost of flying via a company plane is rather expensive—possibly three, four, or more times greater than commercial flights. Thus, the importance attached to managers using the private plane must be high enough to offset and justify the higher cost. At other times, access to certain communities is rather difficult. This is especially true for smaller communities that have lost many commercial flights as a result of air carrier deregulation. The cost of the manager's time while waiting for commercial flights often can and does justify a private plane expenditure.

■ high cost

Private Water Transportation

The use of company owned or leased ships and barges is quite common in the transportation of bulk, large volume products. The private water carrier transportation of coal, ore, and oil is widely practiced.

■ bulk commodities

. Most private domestic water transportation takes the form of barge operations. Firms lease or buy barges and tow boats to push barges carrying their own bulk product over the internal waterways of the United States. Some firms operate ships that carry ore and coal over the Great Lakes and along the Atlantic, Gulf of Mexico, and Pacific coasts.

■ barge

Private water transportation is most advantageous for the movement of bulk, low value products that move in large volume between limited origins and destinations. As indicated above, coal, ores, and petroleum products are typical products moved by private water carrier fleets. These products are moved regularly and in large volumes from places such as mines and ports of entry, to steel mills, electrical generating plants, refineries, and the like.

. Considerable investment (capital) is required to begin private water carrier operation. This investment includes the capital required for the vehicles (barges, tow boats, ships) and for the dock facilities. It should be noted that the dock facility expenses would be incurred if either private or for-hire water transportation was utilized. The shipper (receiver) is responsible for providing docking facilities to load and unload cargo at the shipper's plant just as the side track is used for rail operations to a shipper's plant. Public ports are available, but the private water carrier would be required to use some form of land transportation (truck or rail) to

■ capital requirements

move the cargo between the public port and the shipper's plant.

The relatively large investment required supports the need for regular, large volume shipments. Also, firms that operate private water fleets tend to have plants located adjacent to waterways. The mining, steel, petroleum, and agriculture industries are significant users of private water transportation.

Private Trucking

■ most pervasive form

Private trucking is the most frequently used and the most pervasive form of transportation in the United States. As indicated in Chapter 8, there are approximately 103,000 firms operating private truck fleets. A recent estimate appearing in Dun's Review places the number of private fleets with five or more power units (trucks) at 285,000.[2]

The exact number of private fleets in operation is very difficult to compile since firms are not required to report private trucking operations to the ICC or other federal regulatory agencies.

Whatever the number of private fleets, private trucking is an integral segment of the transportation system employed by the shipping public. At one time or another, almost every company will study or actually operate a private truck fleet, even if the fleet consists of only one truck. For this reason, an in-depth analysis of private trucking—from the reasons for private trucking to the operation of a fleet—is provided below.

Why Private Trucking?

■ better service

■ lower cost

■ greater control

■ improved customer service

■ moving store

The primary reasons for a firm having a private truck fleet are improved service and lower costs. In either case, the private fleet operator is attempting to improve the marketability and profitability of its products. Through improved levels of service, the firm attempts to differentiate its product (lower transit time) and increase its sales and profits. Reduced costs permit the company to keep prices constant (a price reduction during inflationary times), to lower prices, or to increase profits directly. These private trucking advantages are summarized in Table 20.1

The private truck fleet permits the firm to have greater control and flexibility in its transportation system so it can respond to customer needs, both external (for finished goods) and internal (for raw materials). This increased responsiveness is derived from the direct control that the private carrier has over the dispatching, routing, and delivery schedules of the fleet. Such control means the private carrier can lower transit times to the customer, lower inventory levels, and possibly lower stockouts.

Since the driver is really an employee of the seller, improved customer relations may result from private trucking. The driver now has a vested interest in satisfying customer need and in being courteous. In addition, the private carrier driver would probably exercise greater care in handling freight, and this would reduce the frequency of freight damage.

Some firms utilize the private truck as a moving store, calling on many customers along a route to take orders and to deliver from merchandise in the truck. (The home delivery milk truck, now virtually extinct, is a

Table 20.1 Advantages and Disadvantages of Private Trucking

Advantages	Disadvantages
Improved Service:	**Higher Cost:**
-Convenience	-Transportation cost higher than for-hire
-Flexible operation	-Empty backhaul
-Greater control	-Lack of managerial talent
-Lower transit times	-Added overhead and managerial burden
-Lower inventory levels	-Capital requirements
-Reduced damage	-Cargo damage and theft responsibility
-Driver / salesperson	-Increased paperwork
-Last resort (special needs)	-Breakdowns on the roads
	-Labor union
Lower Cost:	
-Reduced transportation costs / (eliminate carrier profit)	
-Reduced inventory levels	
-Advertising	
-Bargaining power with for-hire carriers	

good example of the moving store.) For such merchandising operations, the for-hire carrier does not permit the firm to exercise the necessary control and direction, and private trucking is the only viable alternative.

The last resort advantage of private trucking emanates from a lack of acceptable for-hire carrier service. Firms that ship products requiring special equipment (for example, cryogenics (liquid gas) require a pressurized tank trailer) have difficulty finding for-hire carriers with such special equipment and are virtually forced into private trucking in order to remain in business. In addition, firms that ship easily damaged products sometimes find it difficult to get for-hire carriers willing to provide service within a reasonable time frame or at a reasonable rate. This last resort turning to private trucking comes from utter frustration with the service levels and the cost of for-hire carriage.

■ last resort

For firms that ship high-valued and, consequently, high-rated traffic, private carriers afford the opportunity of moving goods at a lower cost than for-hire carriers. Private trucking can produce savings in transportation costs since it eliminates the for-hire carrier's profit. This advantage is especially true for private carrier operations that have vehicles loaded in both directions with high value products.

Greater control and flexibility over transportation and the resultant lower lead time enable the private carrier to reduce the inventory levels of the firm and its customers. The cost savings possible are dependent upon the total value of the inventory. For example, if a firm using a private fleet can reduce its inventory level by one day with each day of inventory valued at $1 million, a $1 million savings in inventory level is translated into a cost savings of $200,000 or more a year.[3]

■ inventory saving

A by-product of private trucking is free advertising space. A company trailer is a 40 foot long by 8 foot high moving billboard. The company's name, products, and so on can be exposed to literally millions of poten-

■ advertising

tial customers. Such advertising benefits are more significant for consumer products than for industrial products. The advertisement has a disadvantage also: it informs thieves of the truck's contents.

Finally, private trucking can be a negotiating tool for seeking lower rates from for-hire carriers. The freight that moves via the private fleet is lost revenue to the for-hire carrier. Firms with a private fleet can threaten to divert traffic to the private fleet if the for-hire carrier does not provide a lower rate. Many companies have used this negotiating strategy very effectively to secure favorable for-hire rates.[4]

■ rate negotiating tool

Private trucking is not all positive; it does have disadvantages. As indicated in Table 20.1, the disadvantages of private trucking all result in higher costs of transportation. Probably the most significant cause of higher cost is the empty back-haul. The cost of returning empty must be included in the outbound (inbound) loaded movement. Therefore, the cost of moving freight is really double the cost of the one-way move. For example, if the cost of operating a tractor-trailer is $1 per mile, the cost to move a shipment 1,000 miles and return empty is $2,000 ($1,000 loaded and $1,000 empty).

■ empty back-haul

Newly formed private carriers are hampered with a lack of trucking managerial expertise. The private fleet is really a trucking business that has some unique managerial requirements. Management time of transportation/traffic managers is diverted to private fleet operation. In most cases the existing management does not have the trucking background to effectively operate the fleet. As a result of a lack of in-house talent, the firm must hire outside managers for the specific purpose of managing the fleet. This increases management costs.

■ managerial requirements

Capital availability has been a problem for some firms. The money tied up in such things as truck, trailers, and maintenance facilities is money that is not available for use in the company's primary business. This capital problem can be eliminated by leasing the equipment.

As a private carrier, the firm bears the risk of loss and damage to its freight. To hedge against possible loss, the private carrier can buy cargo insurance or act as a self-insured carrier (merely absorb all losses). Customers receiving damaged goods will contact the seller (private carrier) for reimbursement, and failure (or delay) to pay is a direct indictment against the seller. When a for-hire carrier is used, the seller can "wash its hands" of the claim since the dispute is between the buyer and the carrier, assuming FOB origin terms of sale.

■ claims

For long-distance, multistate operations, the cost of paperwork and maintenance is increased over short-distance or local operations. The clerical costs associated with accounting for mileage driven in various states, gallons of fuel purchased in different states, and vehicle licenses or permits required by different states escalate as the scope of the private carriage operation becomes multistate.

■ paperwork

Breakdowns away from the home terminal or garage requiring emergency road service are more expensive than normal maintenance service. The possibility of such emergency service increases as the operating scope increases. Breakdowns also reduce the service levels and have an impact on customer service and eventually sales and profits.

The final disadvantage of private trucking is the possible addition of another union, the Teamsters, into the company. It is quite common for private fleet drivers to be unionized by the Teamsters, and then the Teamsters attempt to represent the other employees who are not drivers. In some companies the private fleet drivers are members of the union representing the nondriver employees.

Although there are disadvantages to private trucking, the fact that there are so many private truck fleets suggests that the advantages outweigh the disadvantages for many firms. The firm's analysis of costs and benefits of private trucking is very critical at the evaluation stage as well as throughout the operation of the fleet.

Private Trucking Cost Analysis

Efficient and economical private truck operation requires a working knowledge of the actual cost of operating the fleet. The facts affecting the individual cost elements of private trucking must be known in order to permit a manager to make effective decisions that lower costs and improve service. The costs are categorized into fixed and operating (variable) costs and are presented in Table 20.2.

Fixed Costs

■ types

Fixed costs are those that do not vary in the short run. For private trucking, fixed costs can be grouped into four areas: depreciation (lease payments), interest on investment, management, and office and garage. As indicated in Table 20.3, fixed costs are approximately 23.1¢ per mile for fleets of ten tractor-trailers, each operating 131,000 miles per year.

The fixed cost per mile varies inversely with the number of miles operated per year. The greater the number of miles driven, the lower the fixed cost per mile; that is, the total fixed cost is spread over a larger number of miles. Therefore, most private truck fleet managers who refer to the economies associated with increased vehicle utilization are concerned with spreading fixed costs over a larger number of miles.

For example, total fixed cost for the operation described in Table 20.3 is $30,261 (131,000 miles × $0.231). If the vehicle is operated 200,000 miles, approximately 52 percent greater utilization than the 131,000 miles per year, the fixed cost per mile would decrease to 15.1¢ per mile.

■ interest

Interest on vehicles (investment) accounts for 6.4¢ per mile, or approximately 28 percent of total fixed cost per mile in Table 20.3. The recent escalation in the cost of borrowing money—the prime interest rate reached 21 percent in 1980—is a definite contributor to vehicle interest cost being about one-fourth of total fixed costs.

■ management and overhead

In July 1980, management and overhead (office and garage) costs were 5.4¢ per mile or about 23 percent of total fixed costs. It is quite common to find management costs being understated in a private trucking operation. Management time, and, therefore costs, is siphoned from the primary business of the firm to assist in managing the fleet. Rarely is this "free" management talent accounted for in the private fleet cost analysis.

Table 20.2 Private Truck Costs

Fixed Costs	Operating Costs
1. Depreciation (lease)	1. Labor (drivers)
a. trucks	a. wages
b. trailers	b. fringe benefits
c. garage	c. FICA, worker's compensation
d. office	d. layover allowances
2. Interest on investment	2. Vehicle operating costs
a. vehicles	a. fuel
b. garage	b. oil, grease, filters
c. office	c. tires and tubes
d. maintenance equipment	d. maintenance (labor + parts)
	e. road service
3. Management costs	f. tolls
a. salaries	
b. fringe benefits	3. Insurance
c. travel and entertainment	a. liability
d. FICA, worker's compensation	b. collision and comprehensive
	c. cargo
4. Office and garage costs	
a. salaries	4. License and registration fees
b. utilities	
c. rent or property cost	5. Highway use taxes
d. supplies	a. fuel
e. communication	b. ton-mile
	c. federal use tax

■ vehicle depreciation

Vehicle depreciation represented 44 percent of total fixed costs or 10.1¢ per mile. Vehicle costs have increased considerably in recent years and, in all likelihood, will continue to increase. A tandem-axle, diesel tractor will cost approximately $45,000 to $50,000. A forty-foot dry van trailer will cost about $15,000. The cost of a truck depends upon the size, carrying capacity, and engine.

Operating Costs

Operating costs are those costs that vary in the short run. Private trucking operating costs consist of fuel, drivers, maintenance, insurance, license, tires, and user taxes. As indicated in Table 20.3, operating cost in July 1980 was 74¢ per mile.

The total operating cost varies directly with the number of miles operated per year. The greater the number of miles operated, the greater the total operating costs. The operating cost per mile will remain approximately the same.

For example, total operating cost for the example given in Table 20.3 is $96,940 (131,000 miles × $0.74). If the mileage per year is increased to 200,000 miles, total operating cost will increase to about $148,000, with the operating cost per mile at about 74¢. In reality, license, insurance, and certain miscellaneous costs will remain constant per year and then decrease per mile; maintenance costs, however, will increase.

Fuel cost represents about 34 percent, (25.5¢ per mile) of total operation cost. In the last five years, diesel fuel and gasoline prices have risen

■ fuel

drastically and are now about $1.20 per gallon for diesel and $1.30 per gallon for gasoline. A diesel tractor averages about 4.5 to 5.5 miles per gallon and a gasoline tractor averages a little less.

■ fuel efficiency
techniques

Great efforts are undertaken by fleet operators to improve fuel mileage because the savings potential is great. For example, assume the firm depicted in Table 20.3 was able to increase vehicle mileage per gallon by 10 percent, from 5 miles per gallon to 5.5 miles per gallon. The total fuel cost savings for the ten tractor-trailers would amount to $28,590 or 9.1 percent.[5] Such a potential savings is justification for a $200 to $400 expenditure for an air deflector or for radial tires.

■ driver

Driver cost was 28.4¢ per mile or 38 percent of total operating cost as given in Table 20.3. Over-the-road drivers are paid on the basis of the miles driven. City drivers are paid on an hourly basis. Table 20.4 provides an example of a 1981 union contract covering drivers in the Midwest.

■ over-the-road drivers

As indicated in Table 20.4, over-the-road drivers were paid 26.3¢ per mile; this rate of pay was the same whether the tractor-trailer was loaded or empty. The rate was 27.325¢ per mile for driving a tractor pulling double trailers or twins. However, the over-the-road driver was paid by the hour for delays such as breakdowns. If we assume an over-the-road driver drives 115,000 miles per year (2,500 miles per week × 46 weeks) and total fringe benefits cost $11,057 per year, the fringe benefit cost equals 9.6¢ per mile.

Table 20.3 July 1980 Cost of Operating a Tractor-Trailer

Cost Item	¢/Mile	
Fixed Cost		
Depreciation on vehicle	10.1	
Interest on vehicle	6.4	
Depreciation and interest on other items	1.2	
Management and overhead	5.4	
Total fixed		23.1
Operating Costs		
Fuel	25.5	
Drivers	28.4	
Maintenance	9.1	
Insurance	3.3	
License	1.0	
Tires	2.8	
Miscellaneous	3.9	
Total operating		74.0
Total Cost	97.1	

Basis: A ten tractor-trailer fleet, each truck operating one-way trips of 2,500 miles, returning loaded 75 percent of trips, and traveling 131,000 miles per year.

Source: U.S. Department of Agriculture, *Fruit and Vegetable Truck Cost Report*, July 31, 1980.

Table 20.4 1981 Driver Costs

Over-the-Road Driver

26.3¢/mile — 5-axle combination
27.325¢/mile — double trailer
$10.82/hour for delay

City Driver

$11.78/hour: guaranteed 48 hours/week or $612/week

Fringe Benefits	Total Cost	Cost/Hour (2,224 hrs./yr.)[a]
Hospitalization ($39.50/week)	$ 2,054	$ .92
Pension ($46.00/week)	2,392	1.08
Holidays (11 days @ $94.24/day)	1,036	.47
Sick Time (5 days @ $94.24/day)	471	.21
Vacation (3 weeks @ $612/week)	1,837	.83
FICA	1,975	.89
Federal unemployment	42	.02
State unemployment[b]	180	.08
Worker's compensation[b]	1,070	.48
Total fringe cost	$11,057	$4.98

[a]Total hours possible = 52 weeks × 48 hrs./week.   = 2,496 hours
Less Vacation (144 hrs.), Holidays (88 hrs.)
and Sick Time (40 hrs.)   = – 272 hours
                              Hours worked/yr.   = 2,224 hours
[b]Varies by state.

city drivers

The city (pickup and delivery) driver was paid $11.78 per hour. The contract specified that the drivers be guaranteed 48 hours work per week, or $612 per week ($11.78 × 40 hours + $17.67 × 8 hours). With the required time-and-one-half rate beyond 40 hours, the effective hourly rate was $12.75 ($612 ÷ 48 hours).

To this hourly rate for city drivers (and over-the-road drivers) must be added the cost of fringe benefits which amounted to $4.98 per hour. The 1981 total driver costs, then, was $17.73 per hour ($12.75 effective hourly rate plus $4.98 fringe benefits per hour). Fringe benefits represented 28 percent of the total city driver cost.

maintenance

From Table 20.3 we see that maintenance cost (including tire cost) was 11.9¢ per mile or 16.1 percent of total operating cost. Maintenance cost includes the cost of normal preventative maintenance such as oil lubrication and new tires and major and minor repairs. The cost of tires, parts, and labor is included in the 11.9¢ per mile cost, with tire cost representing one-fourth of the maintenance cost.

insurance

The remaining operating costs—insurance, license, and miscellaneous—account for 8.2¢ per mile, or 11.1 percent of total operating cost. Insurance cost includes the cost of vehicle collision and comprehensive protection, public and personal liability, and cargo insurance. The company's rate of accidents determines the insurance premium assessed.

■ licensing

The cost of licensing and registering the vehicle is determined by the size of the vehicle and by the individual state and the number of other states in which the vehicle operates. The license fee for a given truck is not uniform among the states. Most states require a registration fee to use state highways. Thus, the greater the geographic scope of the private truck operation, the greater the license and registration cost.

■ miscellaneous

Miscellaneous costs include such operating items as tolls, overload fines, and driver road expenses (lodging and meals). As a private truck fleet manager, miscellaneous operating costs must be watched closely for miscellaneous costs can "hide" inefficient and uneconomical operations.

A fundamental requirement for an economical private truck fleet is knowing the costs. Once the costs are known and analyzed, an effective decision can be made. In the next section our attention is directed to the major operating decisions in private trucking.

Equipment

The private trucking manager is concerned with two basic equipment questions. What type of equipment should be selected? Should this equipment be purchased or leased? Each of these questions is discussed below.

Selection

The type, size, make, model, type of engine, and so on of the vehicle used in private trucking seems to be an overwhelming problem. However, the equipment used is determined by the firm's transportation requirements. The size of the shipment, product density, length of haul, terrain, city versus intercity operation, and special equipment needs are the equipment determinants to be examined.

■ size

The size of the shipment and product density determine the carrying capacity desired in the vehicle. Shipments averaging 45,000 pounds will require five-axle tractor-trailer combinations. However, a low density commodity such as fiberglass insulation requires a large size carrying capacity, even though the weight of the shipment is low (10,000 pounds of fiberglass insulation can be carried in a trailer 40 feet long).

■ diesel power

Long-distance operations, 300 miles or more one-way and 75,000 or more miles per year, usually indicate the use of diesel-powered equipment. Diesel engines have a longer life and get better mileage than gasoline engines, but diesel engines have a higher initial cost. Some recent developments in diesel engine design have produced an economical short-range, city diesel engine.

■ gasoline power

For intercity operations, the tractor-trailer combination is commonly utilized along with a diesel engine if the distance justifies it. City operations use straight trucks that are gasoline powered. However, some city operations, furniture delivery for example, use small, single-axle trailers with gasoline-powered tractors. The reason for using trailers is to permit loading of one trailer while deliveries are being made with another—service to the customer is improved, and the firm reduces congestion and improves efficiency at the warehouse.

■ terrain

    The terrain over which the vehicle travels affects the selection of certain equipment component parts—the engine and drive train. For mountainous operations, the truck will require a high-powered engine and a low-geared drive train. For level, interstate highway operations, a lower-powered engine with a high-geared drive train is in order. Vehicles designed for mountainous operations are usually restricted to the mountainous regions since it makes sense to use different powered units in different regions.

■ special requirements

    Another transportation factor to be considered is the need for special equipment—refrigeration, power tailgates, high cube capacity, and so on. The nature of the product and customer requirements will dictate the type of special equipment to be considered.

■ sleeper cabs

    A final consideration is the use of sleeper cabs for tractors. The sleeper cab adds a few thousand dollars ($2,000-$4,000) to the initial price of the vehicle and is usually only considered when the trips are over 1,000 miles, one-way. The sleeper permits the use of two drivers, one of whom can accumulate the required off-duty time in the sleeper berth while the other driver continues to drive. The two-driver team produces lower transit time and better service. However, lower transit time can also be accomplished by substituting drivers every ten hours.

    The sleeper cab can also eliminate the cost of lodging for a one-driver operation. Instead of paying for a room, the driver accumulates the required eight hours off-duty in the sleeper berth. It should be noted, however, that there is a fuel cost to run the engine to produce heat or cooling for the driver in the sleeper. This fuel cost for a large diesel engine is 2 to 4 gallons of fuel per hour, or $2.40 to $4.80 per hour (at $1.20 per gallon). The sleeper cost per an eight-hour rest could be $19 to $38, which is somewhat higher than current daily lodging costs.

Purchase Versus Lease

■ capital

One of the disadvantages of private trucking, identified in Table 20.1, is the capital requirement for the equipment. Many firms are finding it difficult to buy money to use in the primary business without buying a fleet of trucks as well. Leasing the equipment for a private truck operation reduces demands on company funds and enables existing capital to be used in the primary business of the company.

    There are two basic types of lease arrangements available: the full service lease and the finance lease. Both types are available with a lease-buy option which gives the lessee the option to buy the equipment, at book value, at the end of the lease.

■ full service lease

    The full service lease includes the leased vehicle plus a variety of operating support services. The full service may require the lessor to provide fuel, license and registration, payment of highway user taxes, insurance, towing, road service, tire repair, washing, substitute vehicles for out-of-service equipment, and normal preventative maintenance. The more services requested by the lessee, the greater the lease fee. The full service leasing fee consists of a weekly or monthly fixed fee per vehicle, plus a mileage fee. In addition, the cost of fuel purchased from the lessor will be charged to the lessee. The full service lease is a popular method of leasing trucks and tractors which require maintenance and other services.

■ finance lease

The finance lease is only a means of financing equipment. Under the finance lease, the lessee pays a monthly fee that covers the purchase cost of the equipment and the lessor's finance charge. No services are provided by the lessor: all maintenance is the responsibility of the lessee. The finance lease is a common method of leasing trailers which require little maintenance.

■ working capital increase

As noted earlier, leasing increases working capital. Existing funds are not drained off into trucking equipment but remain available for use in the primary business. In addition, leasing sometimes does not have an impact on the borrowing limits negotiated with lending institutions.

■ reduced risk

Leasing permits a company to reduce or eliminate much of the risk associated with private trucking. A company can use full service leasing to conduct a trial private trucking operation. The monthly fixed operating costs will be known throughout the lease period; this gives a great deal of certainty to the trial operation. If the trial private trucking is too expensive, the firm can quit operating at the end of the lease or even during the lease term if there is a cancellation clause. (However, there may be a cancellation penalty.) Most companies just starting a private trucking operation would be well-advised to use full service leasing.

■ other leasing advantages

Other advantages of leasing include purchase discounts for equipment, fuel, and parts that the lessee is able to realize through large volume purchases. During the fuel shortages that occurred in 1973 and 1978, major full service leasing companies offered a source of fuel which kept many lessees' private fleets operating. The wide geographic scope of operation of major leasing companies offers full maintenance service throughout the country, which is especially important to private fleets that operate nationwide.

■ cost

Leasing does have its disadvantages. First, leasing may cost more than owning. Further, for large size fleets (thirty or more vehicles), the private fleet operator already has a volume purchase advantage and maintenance expertise. Finally, some companies may have excess funds to employ, and a truck fleet may offer an acceptable return on investment.

The economic test of buying versus leasing is a comparison of the net present cost of buying versus leasing. The net present cost is a discounted cash flow approach that considers the cost and savings of both buying and leasing as well as the tax adjustments.

Fleet Operation and Control

The daily operation of a private fleet is a complex undertaking, and the discussion of daily operations is beyond the scope of this text. However, attention is given to the operational areas of organization, regulation, driver utilization, the empty back-haul, and control mechanisms.

Organizing the Private Fleet

Once the fleet is in operation, many intraorganizational conflicts will arise. These conflicts center on the incompatibility of departmental (user) demands and the private fleet goals.

■ service vs. cost

The private fleet operating goals are usually to provide good service or to lower transportation cost. These goals, together, pose problems for the private fleet manager and open the door for intraorganizational conflict. For example, a division may request the fleet manager to provide fifth day delivery in Houston from New York. To do so would increase transportation costs beyond what was incurred previously by private or for-hire trucks. Although the service is desirable to the customer, it is not cost efficient. The manager is unable to meet both goals.

To combat this conflict, the goal of the fleet is normally a cost constrained service goal. That is, the goal is to provide good service at a given level of cost. Now the fleet manager can provide the best service that a given level of cost will permit.

■ profit center

Another organizational problem is the user's concept that private trucking is free transportation. Many shipments become emergencies that must be made, regardless of the cost, or a customer will be lost. A department may have the idea that the private fleet is already purchased (leased) so it should be used rather than sit idle. As pointed out earlier, operating cost is approximately 75 percent of the total cost or 74¢ per mile; therefore, the truck is not free.

■ free transportation problem

One organizational approach to eliminate the idea of free transportation is to establish the private fleet as a profit center. The income generated by the fleet is a paper or internal budget fee assessed to the using departments. The real costs are subtracted from the paper income to generate a paper profit. The manager's performance is evaluated on this paper profit. To guard against a profit being made at any cost to the user, the departments must be given the option of using the private fleet or for-hire carriers (competition).

■ cost center

Many service-oriented fleets are organized as cost centers. The fleet manager of a cost center usually has difficulty convincing top management and departmental managers of the value of the fleet service to the firm's overall profitability. Where to house the fleet (in which department) is another perplexing question. It is common to see a profit center fleet set up a separate department reporting to the president. Placing the fleet under the control of the marketing, finance, production, or traffic departments tends to give the fleet the bias of the controlling department; for example, marketing tends to want service at any cost.

■ centralized

Finally, many private truck fleets are centralized. Centralized organization permits the fleet manager to provide service to many different departments and divisions, thus increasing the utilization of the fleet.

Controlling the Fleet

A key element to an effective and efficient private truck fleet is control over cost and performances. Table 20.5 contains a list of cost and performance criteria for effective private truck fleet control.

■ functional costs

Costs by function must be collected at the source. Fuel costs (and gallons) should be noted for each vehicle. This notation of functional costs at the cost source permits analysis of individual cost centers for the actual costs incurred. It is very difficult to analyze the fuel efficiency of in-

---

Table 20.5 Private Cost and Performance Control Criteria

Cost	Performance

1. By function
  -fuel (and gallons)
  -driver
  -maintenance
  -interest
  -depreciation
  -tires
  -parts
  -management
  -overhead
  -license & registration
	1. Miles operated
	  -by vehicle
	  -by driver
	
	2. Empty miles
	  -total
	  -by location
	
	3. Man-hours
	  -total
	  -driving
	  -loading and unloading
	  -breakdown

2. Functional cost by
  -vehicle
  -driver
  -plant
  -market
  -warehouse
  -customer
	4. Vehicle operating hours
	  -by vehicle
	
	5. Number of trips
	  -by vehicle/time period
	
	6. Tonnage
	  -by vehicle
	
	7. Number of stops (deliveries)
	  -by driver

---

dividual vehicles in a fleet when fuel costs are aggregated for the entire fleet.

Further, the collection of functional costs by driver, vehicle, plant, and so on will permit analysis of problem areas within the fleet. The use of fleet averages only may conceal inefficient operations at particular markets or plants. However, functional costs by vehicle, plant, and driver can be compared to fleet-wide averages, and a management-by-exception approach can be practiced. That is, if the specific costs (fuel cost/given driver) are within acceptable limits, nothing is done. Management action is taken when the specific costs are out of line with the desired level.

■ performance criteria

The performance criteria to be considered are miles operated (loaded and empty), man-hours expended, number of trips made, tonnage hauled, and the number of stops made. By collecting the above performance data, the fleet manager is able to measure the fleet's utilization and the drivers' productivity. Control measures such as overall cost per mile, per hour, and per trip can be computed and used in determining unacceptable performance areas in the fleet. Such information is also valuable to marketing and purchasing departments that determine the landed cost of goods sold or purchased.

Likewise, performance measures must be collected and identified at the source. Total fleet mileage and total fleet fuel (gallons) consumption will permit determination of overall fleet fuel efficiency. However, collection of fuel consumption and mileage per individual vehicle will provide the information necessary for purchasing fuel-efficient vehicles as replacements or additions to the fleet.

■ productivity measures

The performance criteria enable the fleet manager to analyze the productivity of drivers. The number of miles driven per day, the number of stops (deliveries) made per day, or the number of hours per run or trip are driver productivity measures that can be collected for each driver. From this productivity data, individual drivers who drive fewer miles per day, make fewer stops per day, or take a longer time to make a run than the standards (fleet average for example) are singled out for further investigation and corrective action.

Regulations

■ exempt

As stated earlier, bonafide private trucking is exempt from federal economic regulations. The private carrier need not secure authorization (certificate of public convenience and necessity) to transport the firm's products. Since private coverage is not for-hire service, no tariffs are published.

■ primary business test

To be excluded from these economic regulations, the trucking operation must be truly private carriage. The trucking service must be incidental to and in the furtherance of the primary business of the firm—the primary business test. Thus, the transportation of the firm's raw materials and finished goods in private trucks is bonafide private trucking if the firm takes the normal business risks associated with such products. Normal business risk would include the existence of production facilities, sales outlets, product inventories, and a sales force for the products being transported.

■ subsidary freight hauling

Private fleets are now permitted to haul freight for subsidiaries that are 100 percent owned and to charge a fee for this service. Prior to the Motor Carrier Act of 1980, private fleets were prohibited from transporting subsidiary freight for a fee. For highly diversified companies, this permissible intercorporate hauling means increased fleet utilization, and lower total transportation costs.

■ exempt commodities

A common problem many private fleets face is how to eliminate the empty back-haul and still operate legally. One solution is the transportation of exempt commodities. Exempt commodities may be hauled without ICC authority and other economic regulations. Some examples of exempt commodities are ordinary livestock, agricultural products (grain, fruits, vegetables), horticultural goods (Christmas trees), newspapers, freight incidental-to-air transportation (to and from airports), used shipping containers, and fish.

As of 1978, the private carrier may secure common carrier authority to transport freight over the empty back-haul. This type of ICC authority was granted to the TOTO company, a West Coast firm that sought authority to haul goods for the public, to eliminate empty back-hauls. Until the TOTO decision, the ICC would not grant for-hire authority to private carriers.

Private trucking is subjected to all federal safety requirements in the areas of:

-driver qualifications

-driving practices

■ safety regulations   -vehicle parts and accessories

-accident reporting

-driver hours of service

-vehicle inspection and maintenance

-hazardous materials transportation

These safety regulations are enforced by the U.S. Department of Transportation, Bureau of Motor Carrier Safety.

In addition, the private fleet must comply with the state safety regulations governing speed, weight, and vehicle length, height, and width. Such state regulations fall within the preview of the constitutionally granted police powers that permit states to enact laws to protect the health and welfare of their citizens. Since the safety regulations are not uniform among the states, the fleet management must be aware of specific regulations in each of the states in which the fleet operates.

Before concluding this section on safety regulations, attention must be given to driver hours-of-service regulations. These regulations establish the maximum number of hours (minimum safety level) a driver may operate a vehicle in interstate commerce and consequently they effect the utilization of drivers.

Basically, a driver operating interstate is permitted to drive a maximum of ten hours following eight consecutive hours off-duty. A driver

■ driving time regulations   is prohibited from driving after having been on-duty fifteen hours following eight consecutive hours off-duty. Further, on a weekly basis, no driver can be on duty more than sixty hours in seven consecutive days, or seventy hours in eight consecutive days. Entries of driving activities are recorded on a driver's daily log as shown in Figure 20.1.

The driver's daily log entries must be kept current to the time of the last change of duty, and the driver and carrier (private) can be held liable to legal prosecution for failure to maintain logs.

The logbook is also an excellent source of performance data if the entries are accurate. The driver, vehicle, hours operated, miles driven, and trip origin and destination are found in the log entries. As the fleet management reviews the log to assure driver availability, performance data can be compiled for each driver and vehicle.

Conclusion

Private transportation is found in various forms in all modes of transportation. In air, water, and truck transportation, a firm owns or leases and operates the equipment. For rail, a firm owns or leases the equipment

Figure 20.1 Driver's Daily Log

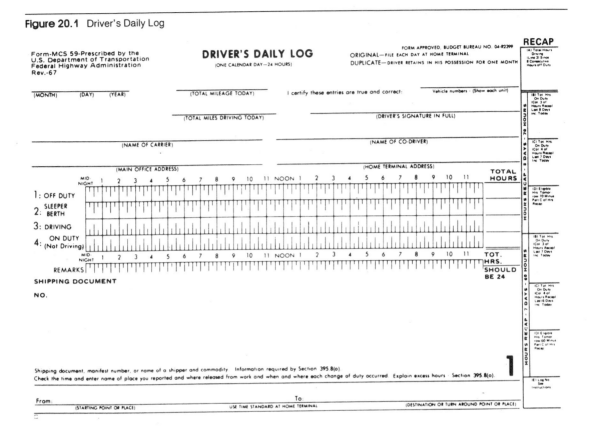

(cars and trucks), but the common carrier railroad actually operates the vehicles. Private trucking is the most pervasive form of private transportation with thousands of companies operating truck fleets.

Study Questions

1. What is private transportation?

2. Why do firms invest in private transportation when it is available on a for-hire basis from carriers?

3. What costs must be considered by management when initiating private carriage?

4. When private operations are in use, what key costs appear and in what form?

5. How are private truck operations different than those of for-hire common carriers? What cost differences are there in each of their "operating ratios?"

6. What economies are gained by using "twins?"

7. What are the pros and cons of leasing and purchasing?

8. Should the private fleet manager charge other departments of the firm for the use of the private fleet?

9. What productivity measures are appropriate in private carriage?

10. How are private fleets regulated as compared to for-hire common carriers?

11. Describe and analyze the basic steps in a lease versus purchase decision.

Notes

1. *The Interstate Commerce Act,* (Washington, D.C.: U.S. Government Printing Office, 1978), Sec. 10524, p. 123.

2. Don Phillips, "Private Trucking: Low-Profile Giant," *Dun's Review* (Oct., 1980): p. 124.

3. Based on an inventory carrying cost of 20% per dollar inventory per year. For a further discussion of inventory costs see Coyle and Bardi, *The Management of Business Logistics,* 2d. ed. (St. Paul: West Publishing, 1980), chaps. 3, 4.

4. Some companies have been too successful in negotiating lower rates. The lower for-hire rates have made the private fleet uneconomical.

5. Assuming fuel costs $1.20/gallon, and each vehicle is operated 131,000 miles per year, fuel cost per truck is $31,440 at 5 mpg. ($1.20/g. $\times$ 131,000 mi./5 mpg.) and $28,581 at 5.5 mpg. ($1.20/g. $\times$ 131,000 mi./5.5 mpg.). The 10 percent increase in mpg. saved $2,859 per truck or $28,590 for ten trucks.

Suggested Readings

Davis, Grant M., and Brown, Stephen W. *Logistics Management.* Lexington, Mass.: D. C. Heath, 1974, chap. 17.

Farris, Martin T., and McElhiney, Paul T. *Modern Transportation: Selected Readings.* 2nd ed. Boston: Houghton Mifflin, (1973).

Flood, Kenneth U. *Traffic Management.* 3rd ed. Dubuque, Iowa: William C. Brown, 1975, chap. 2.

Harper, Donald V. *Transportation in America: Users, Carriers, Government.* Englewood Cliffs, N.J.: Prentice-Hall, 1978, chap. 4.

Langley Jr., C. John, and Wood, Wallace R. "Managerial Perspectives on the Transportation Leasing Decision." *Transportation Journal,* Spring, 1979, pp. 36-48.

Rakowski, James P. "Characteristics of Private Trucking in the United States." *ICC Practitioners' Journal,* July/August, 1974.

Stuessy, Dwight. "Cost Structure of Private and For-Hire Motor Carriage." *Transportation Journal,* Spring, 1976.

Ui, Walter Y., and Hurter Jr., Arthur P. *Economics of Private Truck Transportation.* Dubuque, Iowa: William C. Brown, 1965.

Wagner, William B., and Elam, Rick. "Changing Environment of Truck Leasing." *Transportation Journal.* Summer, 1977, pp. 86-96.

Wood, Donald F. and Johnson, James C. *Contemporary Transportation.* Tulsa: Petroleum Publishing, 1980, chap. 13.

Case

Port Products Inc.

Pete Nolan is the corporate financial officer in distribution for Port Products Inc. (PPI). He is evaluating a truck fleet acquisition proposal that was approved by top management. It is mid-1981 and Pete is now attempting to determine whether to recommend purchasing or leasing the fleet.

The proposed fleet consists of ten tractors that would cost $60,000 each to purchase. Present corporate tax policy requires a six-year depreciation life. The firm, however, would sell the fleet at the end of five years. The private fleet manager estimates that each tractor would net the firm $6,000 each at that time. The company would also incur an overhead expense of $2,000 per year for the fleet if purchased. The present corporate income tax rate is 40 percent.

The best lease of the same make of tractors that Pete and the fleet manager could find is for five years with no overhead expense required. The lease would cost $160,000 per year.

Pete's problem is compounded by the fact that Congress is presently considering a change in the tax laws. The proposed change would allow the firm to depreciate the trucks over a three-year period. The corporate tax rate would also drop to 30 percent.

1. Should Pete lease or purchase the fleet under the present tax laws?

2. Would the new tax law alter the decision?

3. What factors cause Questions 1 and 2 to be different in outcome.

4. What other factors should Pete and the fleet manager consider in this decision?

21   Carrier
         Management I

After reading this chapter you should:

1   Understand various techniques that are useful for efficient carrier management.

2   Appreciate the problems carrier management has in operating its systems effectively.

3   Be able to discuss aids to carrier management in achieving profitable operations.

4   Understand the industry constraints faced by carrier managers.

Transportation firms experience the same laws of economics that production entities experience, but in transport these guiding principles often manifest themselves in different ways. The transportation industry faces and manages its particular set of economic rules in its own way.

Transportation is a service, not a production activity. Except for pure pleasure cruise travel and some auto travel, transportation firms face a derived demand and not a primary demand for their services. Further, transportation is a service that cannot be stored; it is unlike a physical product that can be produced according to certain logistical efficiencies and then held until the market demands it. Transportation managers must seek efficient management approaches through various efficiency techniques or rules of thumb, as well as through responsive management structures.

This chapter presents many of the techniques of transportation efficiency that are inherent to economic principles and that have been used by successful carrier managers. They are in operations, choice of equipment and technology, marketing, and general management techniques. Proper management of transportation also requires a manager to recognize many of the problems found in the field. This chapter also addresses many transportation operations problems.

Techniques of Transportation Efficiency
■ transport goods

The basic goals of efficient transportation firms or organizations include profitability or minimized total cost in light of a public mandate or mission. Individual firms attain their goals through a host of efficiency techniques that appear in operations, equipment technology, overall management of the firm, and the tactical marketing approach taken by the firm.

Operations
■ rule of efficiency

It is most efficient to move in a continuous, straight line whenever possible. This rule describes the most efficient movement for goods and people. It calls for little or no circuity and minimized stopping and restarting. Sporadic movement means energy loss, chances for delay and damage, and an overall increase in costs.

This general rule can be observed in practice in many areas. Rail unit trains are made so that they avoid intermediate classification yards. Truck firms attempt to consolidate long haul loads so that a single through run, with no intermediate handling, is made and the goods can be sorted out for final local delivery at the ultimate destination. The airline industry strives to maximize long haul nonstop flights, because major fuel and engine-wear costs are incurred in take-offs. Further, the costs of maintaining a transportation vehicle in constant motion are small in relation to the energy and effort expended to get a vehicle from rest to a constant cruise speed. This principle can readily be seen in the Environmental Protection Agency's (EPA) automobile fuel consumption ratings in which highway driving is rated as more efficient than city driving.

- general application

Intermediate handlings should be minimized. This rule of thumb bears special attention when different transportation firms meet as part of a through move. Railroads often utilize run-through trains with the engines, the cabooses, and all cars remaining intact in interline moves to minimize interchange time loss. Preblocked cars are another example of this technique in which interlined cars are handled in groups rather than singly. Truck firms interline trailer loads. Freight can be seen moving from interior points in the United States to Europe inside whole containers via rail, truck, and ship without the individual goods being handled.

- minimal handling

The full capacity of the transportation vehicle should be maximized on each run. Transportation costs of trucks, trains, ships, and planes are similar in that the costs of crew, depreciation, licenses, and taxes are relatively fixed costs which are incurred for each run. The variable amount of goods or people in the run will affect fuel costs, some servicing costs, and loading and unloading costs. On the whole, the firm experiences less per unit cost as more passengers or freight are added to a run. Therefore, most transportation managers seek to fill the capacity of the vehicle before dispatching it. In the railroad and trucking industries, managers will often delay runs so that more freight can be accumulated for the long haul. The driver or engine crew is paid the same regardless of the weight in the truck or the cars on the train. Airline marketing and pricing managers utilize low cost excursion fares to entice vacationers to fill what would be normally empty seats in a recessionary market.

- full capacity

Consolidation and break-bulk activities should be utilized for long haul advantages. One means of attaining full equipment use is to utilize a pickup and delivery network to accumulate freight for line-haul efficiency. Truck firms do this with city vehicles which bring different shipments to a terminal for sorting, accumulation, and shipping in bulk to the destination city terminal. This system avoids the prohibitive use of many small trucks and shipments by using large, efficient single units on 400-500 mile runs. Railroads perform this task in much the same way. Many airlines have adopted hub and spoke route strategies around cities

- break-bulk activities

like Atlanta, Memphis, St. Louis, Pittsburgh, and Chicago. Here smaller planes bring passengers from less populated outlying cities to the hub where the larger, more efficient planes can be used for the long haul. At the destination, the process is reversed—goods or people are distributed outwardly from the large destination terminal. This feeder-distributor concept can be seen in Sea-Land's container ship operation where smaller ships perform the pickup and delivery of containers along the U.S. coast to and from Elizabethport, New Jersey, as well as out of various ports in Europe. Large, fast, and fuel-efficient ships move the containers between Elizabethport and a limited number of European cities.

■ empty mileage minimization

Empty mileage should be minimized. Energy is now a major cost in transportation systems. In very few instances can a firm afford one-way loaded movements with empty return hauls. Each mile traveled requires use of energy, and often the payload in freight or passengers represents only a small part of the total energy consumed in the move. That is, the movement of the vehicle itself can often be responsible for a large part of the fuel consumed. For this reason, transportation route strategists, carrier marketing and pricing personnel, and dispatchers strive to arrange two-way or three-way moves with almost all miles bearing revenue payloads. Empty miles represent wasted fuel, labor, capital costs, and lost revenue.

■ effective scheduling

Movements should be scheduled and dispatched so as to fully utilize labor and equipment in line with the market. Transportation service cannot be stored. Since the service must be in place for the market, this rule calls for the optimal equipment to be in place with the required manpower. Neither the equipment nor the required labor should delay the move. In some rail and truck firms, power units accumulate at one end of the system while there is a need for them elsewhere, but there are no crews available to move them back. Likewise, a waste occurs when crews arrive for work and there is no equipment available for the trip or little freight to be handled that day. Some motor carrier firms avoid this problem through use of on-line shipment record systems which indicate to terminal managers how much freight will be arriving inbound during coming shift periods. Thus, crews of optimal size can then be called for particular shifts of work.

Technology and Equipment

■ investment utilization

The more expensive the long haul vehicle, the greater required investment in fast load/unload and other support equipment. Transportation vehicles represent capital investments. The economies of high capital investment call for high utilization of the equipment throughout the day, week, month, or year. Since these expensive investments are only earning revenue when they are running, firms strive to operate with a minimum of downtime or loading and unloading time. This principle can be seen at airports where planes costing $40 million each, arrive and depart within as little as one hour. Mechanized loading equipment is employed for food, luggage, and freight. Instead of hand loading these items, expensive containers are used to load the food and luggage while the plane is enroute. The basic financial principle here is that the cost of ground support equipment is less than the lost revenue which would result from not having the large vehicle itself in operation.

■ size/cost

Generally, the larger the vehicle, or the more freight or passengers that can be moved in it, the less each unit will cost to move. On a daily basis, railroad operating managers generally prefer to operate one long train per day than two shorter trains every twelve hours. With most transportation vehicles, the larger they are, the lower the ton-mile or seat-mile cost will be—for several reasons.[1] One reason is that the manufacturing cost of most forms of propulsion engines makes larger horsepower or thrust engines cost less per horsepower than smaller units. A second reason is that larger planes, trains, trucks, and so on can carry more payload without a proportionate increase in crew requirements. Simply illustrated, both a ten-passenger van and a sixty-passenger bus are operated by one crew member. Tankers capable of carrying 100,000 deadweight tons of oil require forty crew members, whereas older, smaller ships require forty-two to forty-five members. In addition, there are a multitude of other efficiencies (in maintenance, training, and spare parts inventories) in having fewer but larger vehicles in the fleet. Overall, this principle of the larger the vehicle, the less each unit will cost to move is reflected in trucking industry efforts to get larger highway size and weight limits as well as barge industry efforts to get larger locks and dams for larger tows.

The fastest possible speed is not always the most efficient for economical operation. The cost of fuel consumption in relation to speed for most transportation vehicles is shown in Figure 21.1.

■ fuel consumption

As shown, the cost of fast speeds is very high. In the water industry this is often expressed: as the speed of a vehicle doubles, the fuel consumption and horsepower requirements are squared. On the other hand, even with very low speeds, fuel consumption can be costly. For every form of vehicle (including planes and ships), a rough "J" curve fuel consumption exists in which the most fuel-efficient speeds are somewhat less than the vehicle's maximum possible speed.

Figure 21.1 Fuel Consumption in Relation to Speed

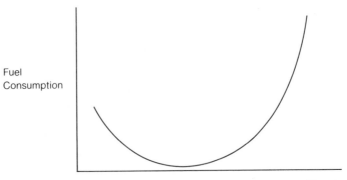

Fuel
Consumption

Speed

Vehicle weight should be minimized in relation to gross weight.
■ vehicle gross weight
Transportation propulsion equipment as well as wings, hulls, rails, and
highway pavements and bridges are designed for certain fixed gross
weights (weight of the vehicle and the payload in freight or passengers).
Therefore, the less the vehicle itself weighs, the more it can carry in the
form of freight or passengers. Similarly, when a BTU of energy is
burned, it is better for it to be spent on revenue-producing weight rather
than on moving the vehicle itself. This is the reason why lighter metals
and plastics are designed for aircraft. Several airlines are changing their
aircraft color schemes to show bare metal on the main body fuselage.
Paint represents several hundred pounds of weight, even on a DC-9, that
can be more effectively utilized for more freight or passenger carriage.

Equipment should be standardized as much as possible. Standardized
equipment simplifies planning, purchasing, crew training, maintenance, and spare parts inventories. When standardization is carried
■ standardized equipment
through with other firms, efficient equipment interchange can then
take place. Standardization came early to the railroad industry in the
form of the standard track width of 4' 8½"; this allowed cars from most
railroads to move over other lines and to avoid rehandling of freight.
Truck trailer hitch systems are now made so that almost total interchange can take place between any two power units and trailers. Even
the airline industry's computerized reservation systems are designed so
that other airlines can key in and make joint reservation and ticketing
arrangements.

Equipment should be adapted to special market and commodity requirements. Many shipping firms require specialized equipment for
economical movement of particular commodities. During the 1960s,
grain shippers desired the larger more economical covered hopper cars
■ equipment adaptability
in place of the traditional smaller box car. Airlines use the smaller DC-9
to serve shorter hop, smaller cities; B727s are used in longer range markets; and jumbo planes are used in transcontinental long hauls. Each
plane is designed for economical operation on certain routes. Transportation managers, however, must take care in adapting equipment. On the
one hand, there is the need to adapt equipment to special markets, and
on the other hand, there is the need to recognize the advantages of standardization. Given the high capital cost and long life of transportation
equipment, only long-range market planning and sound engineering
and financial analysis can provide an optimum balance in this area.

Marketing

■ long-term business

Market commitments should be sought. Transportation service requires
a large financial commitment in routes, terminals, management structure, and equipment. The firm must be assured of long-term business;
this sometimes requires commitments from the firm's users. The rail industry is now using contract rate systems which provide the carrier with
a tangible commitment from customers. This contract often makes it
easier for the carrier to obtain the funds needed for the purchase of required equipment. The airline industry will often seek commitment
from airport authorities in the form of guaranteed terminal space and

long-range airport expansion plans. One of the prime reasons that some contract motor carriage is often economically priced is that the carrier can purchase equipment for specifically defined customer movements. The carrier, then, does not have to build a cost factor into its rates to account for idle equipment.

■ seasonal demand

Marketing, or price techniques, should be implemented to fully utilize equipment during seasonal fluctuations. Since transportation service cannot be stored and must be provided when the market demands it, seasonal markets create a peak and valley situation. If the carrier purchases equipment to handle all demands of the peak period, it then faces costly depreciation, interest charges and opportunity costs with no corresponding incoming revenues on much of the equipment during a slow period. Judicious marketing efforts and pricing approaches can help smooth out the demand experience and allow the firm to maintain less total equipment. Figure 21.2 shows how a smoother seasonal demand can reduce total fleet needs while moving the same amount of tonnage. Carriers can smooth out the peak and valley problems by charging high rates during the high season and lower rates in the off-peak period. This practice is in line with supply and demand economics. It is used in rail grain movements, for example. Further, the airline industry has traditionally charged high trans-Atlantic fares in summer months. Some metropolitan transportation authorities attempt to smooth out rush hour peaks by encouraging staggered work hours in local office organizations, by charging lower fares before 7:00 A.M. and in the evenings, and by offering off-peak shopper or senior citizen fares. In all, the goal is to carry the same or more total freight or passengers on a less seasonal basis with less idle time and less total equipment investment.

Management

■ coordination

Marketing and operations should be coordinated. Many transportation firms operate with a loose coordination between sales and operations. While sales personnel strive to attract more business and revenue, operating personnel strive to reduce total costs, which means minimized runs, trains, and so on. The two departments often come into conflict over daily decisions and long-term planning. A hallmark of successful

Figure 21.2 Seasonal Demand as it Relates to Fleet Needs

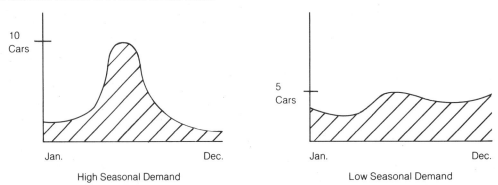

High Seasonal Demand   Low Seasonal Demand

carrier firms is that a close coordination exists between the two departments. A close link assures that marketing efforts are conducted with operational costs in mind and that an operating department does not allow marketing efforts to be wasted on subsequent poor service.

■ profit accountability

Accountability for profit should be placed as low in the firm as possible. It is often difficult for every person in the firm to relate each of their actions to overall profitability. When no accountability system exists, it is difficult to measure good performance. Good accountability systems attempt to measure and present profitability by shipment, traffic lane, terminal, or another responsibility area. A good accountability system should also measure operating performance against selected standards so that minimizing total cost through slow or unreliable service is not always the operating department rule. The accountability system should relate company profit to operating and marketing performance within the realm of the company's market opportunities and needs.

■ reliability

Consistent, reliable service is often more desirable than the fastest possible service. Many surveys of traffic managers and travelers indicate that a later, but reliable, arrival time is generally preferred to a faster time that is less reliable. Many successful carriers set transit time standards that are attainable 95 percent of the time. This system is often preferred by shippers over promises of faster delivery that are only attainable 50 percent of the time. Because both early and late arrival usually incurs cost penalties, shippers will often select carriers that might take a day longer but that are more reliable in deliveries. Discounting the occasional need for fast, emergency shipment service, the cost of reliable but extra time in transit is often perceived as less than that of shorter but unreliable time service. Airlines adapt to normal delays by padding schedules.

■ new approaches

These efficiency approaches have evolved over time and are cited by firms as part of the reason for their corporate success. The list is by no means exhaustive. More guidelines exist in the pricing area. Changes in the business environment, markets, and transportation technology might cause these rules to change as we move farther into the 1980s. The key is that planners and managers should always observe the economies of the firms within which they operate and should steer their companies to the above long-standing approaches or implement new or altered approaches as the conditions change.

Carrier Organization and Management

Transportation companies face some conditions which are not always present in manufacturing firms. These conditions, combined with the available ways in which carriers attempt to work around and with them, mean that there is no *one* ideal form of carrier management.

Problems Affecting Carrier Management

Transportation managers are faced with structural factors that are often somewhat different than those facing executives in other industries. Some of these factors are presented here in a general manner.

Transportation firms are geographically dispersed. By their very nature, carrier operations take place over vast distances. Unlike some manufacturing firms where all operations and management are often under one roof, transportation firms typically operate across oceans, through difficult mountain terrain, and in different countries. This causes carriers to rely upon tight controls, often with decentralized structures and close communications. The dispersion problem is compounded by the fact that the firm's product availability is constantly in motion.

■ dispersal

Carriers present an employee who is relatively low in the organization to the public. Manufacturing firms contact their customers through highly educated and trained sales personnel who are often empowered to make pricing, delivery, and product design decisions. The carrier employee with whom the public comes in contact is most typically a local freight agent, conductor, city dispatcher, reservation agent, stewardess, or truck driver. Though most firms invest large sums in personnel training, the carrier employees in contact with the public, by their very position in the firm, are least likely to affect pricing or service design decisions for their customers. They can cause ill-will in difficult situations if they are not properly trained. This situation is worsened in many firms when management does not permit feedback and ideas to flow from this "front line" group of employees to middle and top management decision makers.

■ employee representative

Transportation operating employees are often minimally supervised. Operating personnel in trucks, trains, barges, and so on are often out of reach of minute-by-minute management supervision. Unlike production crews which are under close supervision, carrier crews often come into contact with their supervisors for only minutes per day and often only by phone or radio. Motor carrier managers know that one of the key productivity problem areas is in local pickup and delivery operations. Without supervision, a driver has the potential opportunity for low performance and little accountability to the terminal managers. This has caused many carriers to implement strong communication and performance measurement systems.

■ minimal supervision

Top management attention is often spent on areas other than marketing and customer relations. Compared to many manufacturing firms, where a large part of top management effort can be spent on productive marketing tasks, carrier firms make their top executives responsible for problems in regulation (state, local, and federal), labor, and finance. Customer- and market-related matters are typically shifted to second place after the legal and financial matters. This will sometimes cause large common carriers to appear to be lax in marketing and customer relations. It might also be the reason that the industry has been criticized at times by nontransportation people for having little marketing sophistication.

■ management attention

The task of efficiently operating the transportation technology of the firm can create "monolithic" management structures. Every mode of transportation operates with vehicles and equipment requiring large investments and numbers of people. Coupled with the problem of geographic dispersion, carrier managements have traditionally attempted to organize along lines of skill specialization. This phenomenon is largely solidified by union labor contract job classifications in this industry. As a result, many carrier structures have evolved into very strong vertical hierarchies consisting of operations, finance, marketing, and many other disciplines. Modern systems management theory shows that vertical management organization is inflexible, resistant to change, a hindrance to cross-communications at low and middle management levels, and often inconsistent with overall corporate goals and missions. This specialization phenomenon is often cited as the reason that larger, mature firms will sometimes tend to be unresponsive to the market and business environment, while smaller growing firms in the same mode display growth and vitality. The rise of regional airlines in the late 1970s is partial evidence of this phenomenon.

■ skill specialization

Single accountability for the transportation service "product" is often minimal. Because of the geographic dispersion factor, carriers often divide the operating department into distinct districts, regions, or divisions. A shipment will often pass through the responsibility sphere of several top operating managers. In interline movements this situation is further complicated since the transportation "production function" is carried out by several carriers between the shipper and consignee. Individual operating personnel, without specific service performance systems measuring their tasks, can lose sight of the need to maintain the company service standard or the assurances made to the customer by the salesperson. In manufacturing settings the production manager can easily be held responsible for the quality of his factory output. Although in transportation service, standards can be established without effective discipline and accountability for service standards, it is difficult to maintain consistent, reliable service.

■ service accountability

It is often very difficult to determine the cost of transportation. Transportation is an activity in which the total cost consists of large amounts of fixed, overhead, and joint costs. These costs, presented in Chapter 12, complicate the task of determining the cost of moving a package of freight or a passenger. Specific production costs can be easily determined in most manufacturing activities. But, in transportation, costs can be affected by season, direction of traffic, volume of other goods in the same movement, the equipment being used, and the relative amounts of business in other parts of the firm.

■ cost determination

All of these factors represent management constraints and conditions in which transportation managers must function. Some of the factors appear to make transportation different from manufacturing, however, the same principles of economics are at play here as in any other business entity. The difference lies in the extent of the constraining factors and how transportation firms function with them.

Transportation Management Approaches to Industry Constraints

In the quest to define "carrier management structure," thought must be given to how firms have reacted in the face of the above problems and constraints. Most carrier managements have evolved from major management approaches.

Methods of Communication

■ communication links

A geographically dispersed organization, especially one in which several spheres of responsibility must be used to produce the total service product, must be linked with communications. Whether it is by teletype, telephone, microwave, or satellite transmission, links must be in place for operating coordination, market and customer needs, and general administration. The quality of communication largely affects whether the firm is centralized or decentralized.

■ decentralized management

A decentralized form of management is usually in place where close local contact is necessary, specific local marketing needs exist, and fast, on-the-spot decision making is necessary. It is also in place when communication is difficult to maintain between a specific area and corporate headquarters. This form of organization generally requires that regional, high level management has supporting staffs at selected dispersed locations. It is a more costly form of organization from a management standpoint. Inherent in this organizational approach is the risk that the entire firm will evolve into many little individual "empires." Problems with this approach include enlarged stores of maintenance parts and equipment. Its primary advantage is that specialized contact exists with local marketing needs and operating conditions.

■ centralized management

A centralized form of organization generally utilizes much line decision making; most staff functions are located at the corporate headquarters, where close communication links are relied upon. Duplication of many management functions is reduced since one larger group at the central point is responsible for each discipline area. A centralized form of management can be more responsive because major trends can be more quickly detected. A major disadvantage of centralized carrier management is that there can be a loss of local contact and knowledge of each area's special needs. The centralized firm must rely upon a high quality, easy to access and use communication system or systems. That is, the advantages of a leaner, centralized management can only be attained at the expense of a good communication system.

The choice of centralization versus decentralization can be total or partial. Successful motor carriers have found that regional maintenance systems are most economical, local sales responsibility is most effective, and central over-the-road dispatching is best.

Methods of Accountability

■ performance systems

Accountability exists when carriers implement and enforce performance measurement systems for middle and lower operating and marketing managers. Without any such system, individual managers would not be made to feel responsible for any particular output or results. Therefore, many carriers have developed systems which attempt to channel managerial behavior in directions congruent with the firm's overall objectives. The two major areas of application are in operations and marketing.

Operating performance measurement systems are difficult to implement because of the problem of establishing what constitutes good operating performance. For one, operating personnel might be instructed to minimize operating costs; cost minimization is a common managerial accounting goal. Under this measurement standard, operating managers will tend to minimize train runs by running fewer, but longer trains on less frequent schedules, or dispatching trucks only when they accumulate full loads. A problem here is that while operating costs are being easily minimized, little or no regard is given to poor customer service and the consequent effects on revenue. Though the accountability approach has significant drawbacks, it prevails in most carrier firms.

■ system problems

Another operating performance system requires the establishment of specific services by top management sanction, for example, a through train every twelve hours between two major terminals, or nightly truck runs regardless of the size of the load. The costs of operating under this given service standard are then established, and the operating personnel are then measured according to favorable budgetary variances from that standard. This system is much better than the pure cost minimization system, but it still does not fully allow for changes due to sound marketing-related service decisions in specific locales or for any changes that require deviation from the standard.

A sound accountability system for marketing performance is also difficult to develop and implement. First, many firms measure sales performance by individual sales efforts that maximize pounds, hundredweight, tons, or carloads of freight that have originated in each sales territory. These measures are easily determined from movement records. However, while a large tonnage might originate in a specific locale, it might not be high revenue producing freight, it might be diverting equipment away from greater revenue producing freight elsewhere in the firm, or it might represent traffic that produces no profit at all. Measuring physical weight or number of loads is not an accurate indication of marketing performance.

■ accountability problems

Another sales reporting system measures revenue produced in each sales territory. This reduces some of the problems in the unit reporting scheme, but it still fails to measure profit.

The most effective accountability systems are designed to measure both operating costs and sales revenues to produce a contribution margin or "profit" for each terminal or district of the company. This approach generally calls for both the sales personnel and operating personnel to be under direct supervision of territorial managers who are responsible not for operations or sales alone but for both in a total area profit context. In this vein, the operating personnel tend to consider the marketing impact of their decisions, and the sales personnel acknowledge the operating cost impact of their sales and revenue efforts. Thus a

■ direct supervision

decision for higher operating costs is not totally avoided when a good new sales opportunity arises. All personnel in the district are in tune with a single performance figure (usually profit).

Market Philosophy

Another factor that affects carrier organization is the marketing orientation adopted by the firm. One major way in which market philosophy affects the shape of the firm is the determination of what traffic segments the firm is to seek. For example, in the motor carrier industry some firms actively choose truckload freight, while others seek the less-than-truckload market. In the truckload setting the firm minimizes its need

■ marketing task

for numerous handling terminals, thus permitting a simple and usually a centralized operating department. On the other hand, those firms seeking a less-than-truckload market require a network of terminals, managers, and so on. In the rail industry some firms organize marketing efforts by major commodity groups. A small number of railroads, however, approach the marketing task from the standpoint of equipment groups. Both approaches produce different organizational structures.

■ combined approach

The other major way in which market or marketing philosophy shapes the organization stems from the combined operating-marketing accountability approach mentioned above. Figure 21.3 illustrates this concept. If a local terminal or regional profit or contribution performance approach is used, then local operating and sales individuals report to a single branch manager and not necessarily to operating and marketing vice-presidents.

Past Corporate Development

One major impact upon management structures that is often overlooked, but nonetheless exists, is past internal political influences and strong individual influences. Business growth from small through medium to large states is such that often departments and functions become the re-

■ past influences

sponsibility of people who have particular strengths, interests, or influences in each area. In the trucking industry, which grew in one or two generations from relatively small family or individually owned firms, the specific form of each function or group of functions in any one firm often evolved from and around certain individuals. Currently the air commuter industry is producing a myriad of management structures. As firms mature from slower growth patterns and as nonfamily or nonfriend management talent is attracted to them, firms will tend to solidify and standardize their management structure so that it is somewhat similar to others in the same mode. This development applies to a degree to the rail and truck air industry as well as to the trucking and air commuter industries.

Conclusion

Transportation firms face conditions that are somewhat peculiar in comparison to those of production firms. The geographic dispersion of carrier firms, the difficulty of direct supervision, and the inability to store transportation services cause management problems that are unique. Modern carriers attempt to overcome these problems and to take advan-

Figure 21.3 Hierarchal versus Profit Center Marketing Approach to Carrier Organizations

Heirarchal Structure

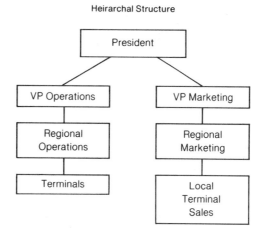

Combined Operations and Marketing Approach

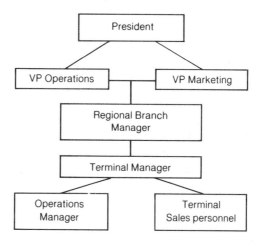

tage of many "laws of transportation efficiency" through various communicational and organizational approaches.

Study Questions

1. Cite the technique of efficiency and the underlying economic principle or principles in the following practices in transportation:
   a. airline standby passenger fares
   b. the charge some railroads assess shippers for movement of the shipper's empty leased car
   c. the proposed 600-passenger Boeing 747 that will replace the 450-passenger version on some dense routes
   d. railroad and motor carrier contract rates.

2. Explain in detail why efficient communication is a necessary requirement in today's transportation firm.

3. Comment upon the statement "top carrier management faces the same challenges as those faced by the corporate managers of a consumer products firm."

4. Why don't some carriers have a line of direct authority between the terminal-based salesperson and the vice-president of marketing?

5. What is the best accountability system for a carrier?

6. Trace the course of either the rail or motor carrier industry from the early part of the century in terms of productivity advancements and the problems and opportunities of management.

7. The question of centralization versus decentralization is an important aspect of a transport firm's (carrier's) managerial philosophy in the areas of both organizational structure and the administration of transactions with customers and suppliers. Why? What advantages or disadvantages relate to this question? (AST&T, Fall 1977, Exam #2).

Notes

1. The automobile deserves special attention with regard to efficiency techniques. The efficiency approach of "the larger, the cheaper" does not appear to apply here. The large auto has traditionally been accused of high fuel consumption. A smaller four- or six-passenger car can operate with less total fuel consumption. Auto "down-sizing" has taken place in efforts to reduce fuel consumption. Producing smaller autos with lighter components is the approach most auto manufacturers have taken in order to bring about legislatively mandated fuel efficiency guidelines.

Suggested Readings

Anderson, Ronald D. et al. "Structure and Analysis of Physical Distribution Goals." *Journal of Business Logistics*, Spring, 1978, pp. 19-30.

Ballou, Ronald H. *Business Logistics Management*. Englewood Cliffs, N.J.: Prentice-Hall, 1973, chap. 12.

Coyle, John J. and Bardi, Edward J. *The Management of Business Logistics*. 2d ed. St. Paul: West Publishing Co., 1980, pt. 4.

England, Wilbur B., and Leenders, Michiel R. *Purchasing and Materials Management*. 6th ed. Homewood, Ill.: Richard D. Irwin, 1975.

Erb, Norman H. "A Note on the Meaning of Physical Distribution Management (PDM)." *Transportation Journal*, Summer, 1975, pp. 56-57.

Harper, Donald V. *Transportation in America: Users, Carriers, Government*. Englewood Cliffs, N.J.: Prentice-Hall, 1971.

Heskett, James L. et al. *Business Logistics*. 2d ed. New York: Ronald Press Co., 1973, chap. 20.

Holloway, Robert J., and Hancock, Robert S. *Marketing in a Changing Environment*. 2d ed., New York: John Wiley and Sons, 1973, chap. 19.

Lancioni, Richard A. "The Decision Process in Physical Distribution Management." *Journal of Business Logistics,* Spring, 1978, pp. 77-94.

Lee, Lamar J., and Dobler, Donald W. *Purchasing and Materials Management: Text and Cases.* New York: McGraw-Hill Book Co., 1977, chaps. 22, 23, 24.

Newman, W. H. et al. *The Process of Management: Concepts, Behavior and Practice.* 3rd ed. Englewood Cliffs, N.J.: Prentice-Hall, 1971.

Case   ## F. C. & E. Railroad Company

The Faber College and Eastern Railroad Company operates throughout Oregon and several states in the Northwest. John Pinto, manager of pricing for the company, is analyzing a request for a special commodity rate from a shipper at Orpoint on the eastern end of the system. The shipper wishes to coordinate shipments from Orpoint to Destcity using the same cars that another division of the firm is using for moves from Destcity to Orpoint.

In the past such round trip rates were unlawful, but regulatory changes now permit them. John sees this as an opportunity to compete for some traffic that he knows is moving from that plant to Destcity by truck. By checking with computer records of car movements, he found that the cars are returning to Destcity empty. Pertinent cost information relating to the cars in question are as follows:

Haul	300 miles each way
One way move cost	$250 empty
	$300 full
Average loss & damage	1% of the value of the product
Car maintenance cost	½¢ per mile
Documents and billing	$22 per move
Value of the goods	$40,000
Switching costs	
origin & destination	$38 each
intermediate	$24
Average car cycle time	
loading	1 day
unloading	1day
in-transit	3 days
Car capital costs	original cost $24,000
(present cars)	fleet is 15 years old
	expected life is 20 years
	interest rate on debt is 5%
New car capital costs	purchase price $42,000
	life 20 years
	interest rate on new debt is 18%

What should John charge for this movement? State a maximum and minimum that should be considered as well. What other factors should be evaluated in this decision?

Carrier
Management II

After reading this chapter you should:

1 Understand, basically, the role the terminal plays in carrier operation.

2 Be able to discuss the functions performed at different types of terminals.

3 Have an overview of the functions involved in managing a transportation company.

4 Understand the specific management functions involved in operating, marketing, and financing a carrier.

■ chapter overview

Carriers, like most industries, have evolved with certain specific management functions and structures. The terminal is the basic organizational unit of carrier firms. This chapter examines carrier terminals and specific carrier activities which are basically common to all forms of carriers.

The Terminal: The Basic Transportation System Component

The physical flow of transportation is linked to the terminals or networks of terminals. They are the local focal point of activity as well as the facilitator of long haul movement. The concept of the terminal will be presented here in the context of motor carriers and railroads, though where applicable, pertinent points will be made with regard to other modes.

Pickup and Delivery Terminals

■ pickup and delivery

The pickup and delivery terminal serves the local area and represents the majority of terminal operations in the motor, rail, and water modes. For pipelines and air travel it is the basic type of terminal used. The local terminal collects and consolidates freight and passengers for efficient long haul movement. It also serves to break down bulk shipments inbound from distant points for final delivery.

Different vehicles are often employed for pickup (PU/D) and delivery than those used for long haul movement. In the motor mode, PU/D operations often utilize 20-foot or 24-foot straight vans that can maneuver in city traffic. These units feed the terminal, which serves to sort all picked up freight into larger groups for long haul movement by 45-foot tractor-trailer units. The process is reversed for inbound movement. In the rail mode, local moves are typically made by a single, relatively low horsepower engine. When a train is made up for outbound long haul movement, it might consist of five or six larger

■ vehicle type

engines designed for higher speed and longer hauls. Thus, the PU/D operations utilize vehicles best suited for that work.

The functions performed at local terminal operations are varied. While there is no one typical terminal, most terminals generally perform certain activities, such as freight sorting or classification, rating and billing, and local dispatching. Sorting is the task of breaking down the freight from local pickup trucks and consolidating it for long haul vehicles, and vice versa. (For railroads, this activity is called classification.) Rating and billing is the activity of determining the proper rate and total charges for each shipment and then billing the paying shipper or consignee. The advantage of local billing is that time is minimized between shipment pickup and bill receipt, and cash flow potential is maximized. Some firms utilize systems in which local terminals input shipment data into electronic transmission terminals, and the rating, billing, and mailing task is performed by a large staff at regional or central points.

Local dispatching is the third activity common to local terminals. It consists of receiving calls for empty car delivery or shipment pickup and arranging for local units to perform that task. Many motor carrier shippers have standing orders for daily pickup. If not, a shipper typically calls the local terminal, asks for the city dispatcher, and requests pickup by stating the pickup firm and location, the commodity being shipped (number of boxes, pallets, etc., and the weight involved), and destination. Instructions are then sent to the pickup truck by radio or held until the driver calls in at one of serveral times during the day.

Functions which are not always performed at specific local terminals, but are found at least regionally, are claims, maintenance, personnel, and sales. Claims is the function of inspecting damaged goods that are the subject of shipper or consignee claims and investigating lost shipments. Some firms have a terminal spot designated as the "OS&D" (over, short, and damaged) dock. This is where lost, damaged, and goods gone astray are consigned for eventual matching up by claims personnel. In some terminals the claims function is performed by full-time claims clerks or supervisors. In others, it is the part-time function of sales personnel.

Maintenance is another task sometimes performed at local terminals. Most firms use local terminals which perform only simple, minimal maintenance tasks. Major maintenance needs are then performed at regional centers where economies in maintenance labor and facilities exist. Firms will then cycle each vehicle through these centers every so often according to a planned maintenance schedule.

Personnel-related work is also done, but only occasionally, at local terminals. The task of hiring, processing, and terminating employment requires much time and effort. Some firms leave this task to the individual terminal manager, whereas others centralize it at regional points. Still others leave the processing of clerical and handling personnel to the local manager, while drivers, train and ship crews, and supervisors are processed at regional points.

■ terminal activities

■ local dispatching

■ regional functions

■ maintenance

■ personnel

■ sales personnel

Sales is another task which is sometimes performed directly under the supervision of the terminal manager. In some firms, the local salesperson reports directly to the marketing department and works from an office at the local terminal or in the same locale. In other firms, the sales personnel are responsible to the terminal manager who has a profit responsibility for that facility.

Long Haul or Break-Bulk Terminals

■ railroad break-bulk terminals

Another basic type of terminal exists in most rail and many motor carriers. Its function is to reclassify and sort freight that is in the middle of long haul movement. These break-bulk or reclassification terminals rarely have contact with the shipping public in the areas of sales, claims, or pickup and delivery operations. Two examples will illustrate this concept. On the Consolidated Rail Corporation's lines, long haul trains are made up daily in Newark, Philadelphia, Allentown, Baltimore, and Potomac Yard in Washington. Each train consists of cars destined to or through St. Louis, Cincinnati, Chicago, Detroit, and Cleveland. No one originating train will contain a sufficient number of cars to make up a complete Baltimore to Detroit train, for example. The company then routes all the trains into Harrisburg or Pittsburgh where the cars are reclassified according to blocks of cars destined for each city. There, complete trains are then made up for a second long haul to St. Louis, Cincinnati, and so on.

■ motor reclassification terminals

In the trucking industry, trailers are shipped out nightly so as to clear each terminal of its freight. Rarely will an Atlanta terminal have enough freight in one trailer to send separate runs to Minneapolis, Milwaukee, and Des Moines. Instead, the single outbound trailer will stop at an intermediate terminal where the freight for each city will be combined with shipments coming from other eastern or southern points so that complete inbound trailers can then be dispatched direct to the appropriate city. Of course, if on any given day a complete load or train can be made up for the distant point, the shipment can then avoid the intermediate handling.

■ hub terminals

A special type of intermediate terminal is found in the air industry. Called hub terminals, they serve as connection points for passengers departing from feeder short and intermediate haul flights from smaller cities and catching outbound spoke flights or long haul jumbo planes. U.S. Air employs this concept at Pittsburgh, American at Dallas, United at Chicago and Memphis, and Delta and Eastern at Atlanta. At these cities a major proportion of enplaning passengers are not originating from the hub city itself. This concept allows economical use of commuter lines and allows company DC-9s and B-727s to feed longer haul L-1011, DC-10, and B-747 jumbos.

Alternative Terminal Strategies

The motor carrier industry is currently moving toward two basic terminal strategies which are: fewer but larger terminals and more but smaller satellite terminals. An example of each is shown in Figure 22.1. The choice of one or the other is largely dependent upon traffic flows and corporate perception.

Figure 22.1 Large versus Small Terminal Trade-offs

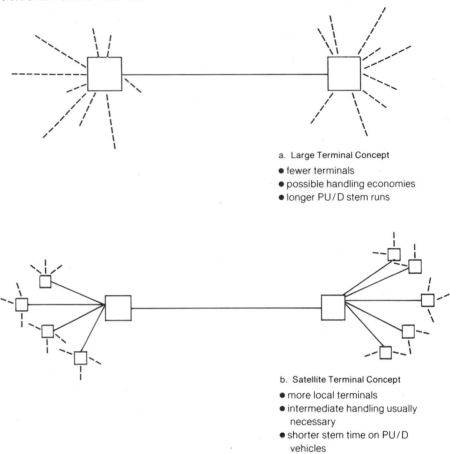

a. Large Terminal Concept
- fewer terminals
- possible handling economies
- longer PU/D stem runs

b. Satellite Terminal Concept
- more local terminals
- intermediate handling usually
  necessary
- shorter stem time on PU/D
  vehicles

The large terminal concept is based upon the notion that larger terminals possess handling economies of scale. This is supported by the fact that since there is more freight consolidated at fewer points, truck runs will generally be more fully loaded throughout the system. A major drawback here is that local pickup and delivery runs cover very large areas, thus stem time on PU/D peddle runs is often high.

The satellite terminal concept requires many more, but smaller feed intermediate break-bulk terminals which then consolidate for long haul. Thus, there is more intermediate handling in this system, but pickup and delivery runs are shortened while long haul and feeder runs to and from the satellites are more fully loaded. A major advantage cited by managers of satellite terminals is that they bring the company operations, sales, and identity to local spots for customer service benefits.

In essence, the debate over the large versus small satellite terminal concept revolves around two key trade-off elements—energy versus la-

■ satellite terminals

■ large terminals

bor. The high cost of energy favors the satellite system, whereas the cost of labor and handling favors the larger terminals.

Specific Carrier Management Functions

■ similar functions

Carriers of all modes have certain basic management functions or disciplines in common. Foremost are operations, marketing, and finance. Other functions of importance to the firm are information systems, labor, claims, and safety, but these are often housed within one of the above functions or grouped in an administrative area. Each one of these functional areas is discussed below in terms of what each one consists of, what their missions typically consist of, what problems they face in the 1980s, and what improvements each can take advantage of for the future.

Operations

■ operating department functions

The operating department generally comprises the largest single cost category of the company revenue dollar. It is responsible for manpower, equipment and terminal facilities, and the normal running of trains, trucks, and so on. Many specific activities are typically performed by operating departments. One activity is to dispatch runs by arranging for the fuel, crews, equipment, and terminal space. In freight operations, dispatching is usually broken down into the arrangement for pickup and delivery runs and the timing of over-the-road or long haul runs. Distribution of equipment to customers for loading is an activity often found in the operating department, if it is not found in marketing. This is an important task because equipment-distributing personnel should be knowledgeable about the types of traffic that are most profitable for the firm to handle. Maintenance is a function often found in operations, but its scale of importance is such that it is presented separately in this chapter. Another operating department function is power distribution. In a railroad or trucking company this entails keeping track of engines and tractors so that a sufficient supply exists. What is to be avoided here is an accumulation of equipment waiting at one point for return loads while a great demand exists for them elsewhere in the firm. Finally, scheduling is often a responsibility of operating personnel. Schedules must take into account the normal traffic demands and flows and the most efficient allocation of company equipment and operating runs.

The objective often imposed upon operating departments by top management is typically cost minimization. The problems associated with this approach have already been discussed; this approach is the reason that operating departments are sometimes measured by their cost performance within an established standard such as a specific number of daily runs or some other desired customer and market-related norm.

Problems facing operating managers in the 1980s are numerous. Foremost is fuel and all forms of energy. This single cost category has been and will no doubt continue to be in the future one of the largest

■ energy supply and cost

supply and price uncertainty problem areas. Cost increases and disruptions in supply constantly require scheduling, power, and equipment adaptations. Operating managers have reacted by attempting to consolidate traffic for fewer vehicle runs.

Energy costs have created a second problem for the 1980s—equipment efficiency. Many modes and firms use equipment that was purchased in previous times when fuel efficiency was not a design and operating consideration. The Boeing 707 and DC-8 airplanes and many ships are examples of this. Firms need the carriage capacity, but fuel costs are such that many times the equipment, even fully loaded, is not economical to operate. Only a passage of time with a new generation of equipment technology will help relieve this problem for operating personnel.

Another problem is productivity. Labor costs have risen sharply in response to labor inflationary pressures. From the 1950s to the early 1970s, motor carriers, railroads, airlines, and other carriers had been able to grant wage increases, yet hold down total company rates because of large technological improvements taking place throughout the industry. Examples of these improvements are the diesel engine, tandem transmission, increased weight and length limitations, the Interstate Highway System, jets, and more productive barge tows. However, during the 1970s there was a slowing of yearly productivity advances and, in fact, fuel costs and environmental requirements may have actually reversed productivity in some areas. This led to a situation where increased labor dollars were no longer cushioned by productivity gains elsewhere in the firm. Now, and possibly into the 1980s, actual negative labor productivity impacts will have to be passed indirectly to the customer through rates and fares.

A related productivity problem is congestion. Past public investments in highways, waterways, and the air system permitted tremendous growth in the motor, barge, and air industries. A slowing of federal and state investment has caused growth demands to push the actual physical limits and maintenance limits of these right-of-way systems. Congestion delays and resulting forced slow operations have led to the use of the same vehicles to produce fewer ton- or passenger-miles per day. Thus, decreased efficiency and the need for more vehicles to handle the same volume occurs.

An increase in noneconomic regulations is another problem confronting operating personnel in the 1980s. The Occupational Safety Hazards Administration (OSHA), Environmental Protection Agency (EPA), the Department of Transportation's (DOT) hazardous materials regulations, and the Resource Conservation and Recovery Act requirements for moving toxic waste products will demand more operating management attention in the 1980s. These system requirements, though positive influences for society as a whole, place financial and manpower demands upon carrier managements in negative ways.

There are some improvements or bright spots on the horizon for operating personnel in the 80s. Computer and efficient communication systems will enable medium and small carriers to adopt systems that will control operations and equipment in increasingly positive ways. Equipment that will be designed for energy efficiency will dominate carrier capital investment activity. Operating personnel will shift from older,

■ equipment efficiency

■ slowing of productivity

■ congestion and delays

■ environmental and safety regulation

■ technology and
equipment improvement

less efficient equipment which has been modified with fuel efficiency devices to equipment with inherent design efficiencies. This will be most noticeable in the new generation of airplanes that have improved engines, wings, and instrument systems. A version of the Lockheed 1011 already has a computerized flight control system that flies the plane with up to 6 percent savings in fuel consumption per flight over a typical pilot flown performance.

Another possible area for improvement is in labor work rules. Railroads have long pointed to restrictive work rules as one of the major sources of poor labor productivity and low profitability. Some progress has been made in this area—carriers have been allowed greater flexibility in available work hours while being allowed to maintain employment or total wage earnings. The regulated motor common carrier industry, which is under competitive pressure from deregulation of that sector, must also seek ways to improve labor productivity. The traditional system of wage-to-rate increases through rate bureaus will not likely permit the present carriers to operate with the current contract labor configuration; some changes will no doubt take place in this area.

■ flexible work rules

Marketing

This is the function of finding, developing, and maintaining profitable business demands for the firm. It typically consists of sales, pricing, market research, equipment planning, route strategy analysis, scheduling (sometimes), and in many instances equipment allocation.

■ maximum total revenue

The marketing department traditionally functions under a rule of maximum total revenue. In sales, this goal is gradually shifting toward a combined marketing revenue and operating cost performance of maximum contribution to the firm. This approach carries over into scheduling, equipment selection, and allocation.

■ new legislation

Problems facing carrier marketing managers in the 1980s will be many. Of primary concern is the fluid nature of carrier pricing caused by the Railroad Revitalization and Regulatory Reform Act of 1976, new Interstate Commerce Commission (ICC) policy on rate bureau activities, the Motor Carrier Act of 1980, and the Staggers Rail Act of 1980.

■ strategy changes

In the past some carriers could enjoy a follow-the-leader approach to pricing and be somewhat assured that other carriers' or a rate bureau's cost analysis would provide a good return for a carrier not having strong internal costing and rate expertise. Also, across-the-board rate increases by all carriers in a region provided some individual protection for many carriers. Now that local rates must all be basically independent in nature, and all-carrier ex parte rate increases are restricted, each individual carrier will have to increase its costing sophistication for sound pricing decision making.

■ pricing decisions

The deregulation movement is also bringing about a long, unsettling period of carrier market and operating changes. It is expected that many carriers will fall in the shake-out period until a new type of carrier marketplace stabilizes. During that period, sound market strategy will be necessary; trouble lies ahead for the firm that merely follows the others or exists largely by reacting to short-term events. Again, increased market sophistication through quality information systems, good costing capabilities, and sound strategic planning will be the key to survival.

A further continuing problem in the 1980s will be fuel. For market managers in the fuel-intensive motor carrier industry, energy will play a major part in the future. Market research will be asked to find niches where motor carriers will maintain a cost or service competitive edge against railroads and private carriage on the one hand and air freight on the other.

■ management information systems

Carrier marketing has benefited from major gains in management information systems. These systems can now provide revenue and operating cost information relatively quickly so that marketing personnel can make profit decisions rather than only revenue-to-tonnage decisions as in the past. These systems measure performance of each salesperson with standards that are sought by the firm as a whole. Some firms' systems even allow sales personnel to test a potential shipment for profitability before the sales call is made upon the shipper. A good marketing information system will also keep track of company traffic flows so as to detect imbalanced opportunities for the profitability of entire traffic lanes and commodity markets. This information provides invaluable input to rate personnel who can then conduct precise analyses in opportunity areas highlighted by these systems.

Finance

■ finance or accounting functions

Finance, or accounting, depending upon the specific title used in each firm, is basically the function of controlling the purely financial resources of the firm. Some specific subfunctions in this area, which can often be separate managerial groups, include the following. Financial accounting is the function of measuring and reporting the financial performance of the firm to management and external interests such as stockholders, taxation agencies, and the Securities Exchange Commission. Managerial accounting is concerned with internal cost information for budgeting and capital investment decisions. Finance personnel are concerned with decisions relating to investments, financing sources, and dividend decisions. Again, all these functions might be found in one distinct department, or they might be spread throughout two or more departments.

■ financial gap

Finance personnel have an active goal or mission, and that is to maximize the financial resources of the firm through profit or company wealth, or both. One criticism that is often made by carrier operating and marketing managers is that some finance departments will tend to invest funds outside the carrier's area of management into new firms or ventures when the carrier itself is in need of capital investments. While this might not appear right from the point of view of the operating firm itself, top management and finance personnel have the charge by stockholders to maximize profits and the value of the stock of the entire firm wherever possible.

Problems facing carrier finance managers in the 1980s appear in the

■ operating costs

costs of operating the firm and in capital. Fuel is a major operating cost. The task of forecasting and planning in a period of fuel price uncertainty makes profit planning very difficult. When a target profit is planned for, then capital investments and monthly cash flow needs can be established.

■ capital cost

Another major problem is capital availability and cost. Transportation is capital intensive. It requires between $2 and $3 of invested capital (in such things as equipment and terminals) to produce $1 of revenue. Capital investments require large cash outlays that must come from internally reported earnings or by bond or stock sales. With external financing the firm competes for funds against other carriers, firms in other industries, and even the government's financing efforts. Capital costs have risen sharply in the past decade. Borrowing interest rates alone are now at percentage levels that were good project rates of return in the 1960s. Combined with the capital cost problem is one of capital shortages or near total unavailability. These problems will no doubt continue during the 1980s and play a major role in carrier finance actions.

■ favorable tax policies

One favorable factor facing carrier finance personnel is that federal tax policies were changed by Congress and that capital investments will be encouraged. Currently, the tax investment credit acts to reduce the effective purchase price of new investments. Accelerated depreciation methods have come into being that will act to further encourage reinvestments in the carrier physical plants.

■ structural reorganization

Another carrier trend that allows for somewhat easier finance sourcing is the move by carriers to structurally reorganize from carriers into conglomerates or holding companies that own the carrier as well as other, often more profitable, firms. In this way the parent company can often raise funds needed by the carrier by selling holding company securities that are strengthened by higher profit earnings from the noncarrier holdings. This trend, however, has been criticized by some as a means of effectively divesting from the transportation business into other more profitable ones. The record of this trend is too spotty to give a clear indication at this point in time. But, many western railroads have benefited from parent company earnings from land, resources, and energy holdings.

Information Systems

■ data systems

Information systems provide management at all levels with data in report formats useful for performance evaluation and decision making. Some specific forms of information handling include the normal billing and payroll functions, but, more importantly, this activity has expanded in the past decade to provide traffic flow data, operating and sales statistics, empty and full load information, shipment tracing ability, equipment distribution information, and contribution margin performance of various sectors of the firm. It is a function often found separate from an accounting department, because the informational needs of low, middle, and top managers are diverse. It is often a group that has physical charge of the computer data handling and communications system of the firm.

The objectives of an information system are to collect and provide users with efficient information that is necessary for carrying out stated managerial responsibilities. This information should be in a format permitting quick analysis by users. The system should also be efficient from a cost standpoint.

In the 1980s, the information system will be called upon, along with other departments, to detect new information needs and formats as the carrier environment and marketplace changes. The system will have to adapt with responsive change in order to be an effective support function. A problem that sometimes occurs is that the computerized information system represents a large technological investment. As such, its managers sometimes tend to require the firm to adapt to it rather than vice versa. This problem can usually be resolved only by top management intervention and by stating explicit missions for the system.

■ responsive information
systems

The future is bright for carrier information systems in that the required processing and transmission technology is rapidly becoming less expensive and simpler to develop and implement for the user. Even medium-size motor carriers can now afford local terminal links with the entire firm.

Maintenance

This function is primarily responsible for the upkeep of moving equipment on motor and water carriers as well as airlines. On railroads, it consists of both equipment and right-of-way. Specific subfunctions include conducting research into improved maintenance equipment, processes, and the optimal timing of special maintenance activities. Another major activity is coordinating purchases with equipment specification development for major equipment acquisitions.

A single managerial goal is difficult to enforce for maintenance. The traditional standard still used in many firms is minimum total cost. This standard will generally tend to encourage the repair of very obvious equipment problems only. Thus, periodic checks, tune-ups, track refinements, and so on are minimized and only broken assets are repaired. Many firms realize today that this is not a cost-effective approach to maintenance. Instead, a specific "downtime" experience standard is established, and the maintenance department is evaluated on the basis of minimum cost within this minimized equipment failure goal.

■ maintenance standards

Problems facing maintenance operations will be in the form of change adaptation. Metric conversion will no doubt be complete by the late 1980s; this conversion will require an investment in entirely new sets of tools. It is estimated that metric conversion will eventually cost the U.S. economy over $3 billion. Though it is a one-time conversion expense that will generally be depreciated by 1990, it does represent a short-term productivity loss in transportation. A second problem facing maintenance managers is employee training associated with equipment change. Though operating managers might desire the latest, most efficient equipment to be purchased each year, these new efficiencies must be analyzed in light of added maintenance department adoption costs. Thus, a major positive trade-off exists between maintenance costs

■ maintenance problems

and fleet simplification strategies. Still another problem exists in the form of top management desiring to reduce the funds tied up in all forms of investments. Spare parts represent high unit costs in the field and no longer does the maintenance manager have a relatively free hand to accumulate spare parts beyond what is felt to be a rational minimum quantity.

■ record keeping analysis

Improvement in this area is occurring in several ways. One improvement is that detailed maintenance record keeping systems are being developed in many firms. Here, analysis can be conducted on each equipment unit and a decision made as to when it should be sold, scrapped, or repaired. Analysis of this type is also conducted to determine optimum points in time or mileages for overhaul. These approaches lead to reducing equipment overmaintenance and undermaintenance.

Another advancement has been made by centralizing the records of repair parts inventories. This reduces accumulations of parts in one terminal unbeknown to another facility in the firm that must purchase the same part on an emergency basis from the outside. This approach also enables the firm to gain some economies through bulk purchasing of many parts.

■ intercompany clearinghouse

Still another maintenance improvement has been the development of intercompany parts clearinghouses. This is an extension of the corporate record system in that firms having surplus parts at specific locations will enter this information into the system so that others experiencing shortages or an emergency need, sometimes in the same city, can obtain the item quickly from another carrier rather than having to order it from a vendor. This is an adaptation of the informal "phone call" system that has long existed between airplane maintenance managers of different carriers at the same terminal.

Purchasing

■ purchasing functions

Purchasing is the function of obtaining supplies, services, and capital assets for the carrier. These purchases range from motive power to stationery and other office supplies, as well as food served to passengers enroute. Specific subfunctions include item research for more effective operation or economy in purchasing, inventory control analysis, the control of financial and legal commitments, and coordination with maintenance, operations, and capital budgeting staffs.

■ set of goals

A single operational goal is difficult to establish for purchasing. Basically, a problem exists because there is a range of price and quality choices available for most purchasable items. If minimized purchase costs was the goal, the firm might experience problems in operations and maintenance with low quality items. Many carriers and firms establish quality standards for major items then evaluate purchasing personnel on the basis of how costs are minimized within that standard while maintaining a high degree of availability of each item. Thus, purchasing is evaluated in terms of optimum quality, lowest total cost to the entire firm, and assurance of item supply. All three individual items converge to provide a set of goals.

■ inflationary pressures

Problems plaguing the purchasing function in the 1980s will primarily be a continuation of those which arose in the mid 1970s. One problem is that inflation in basic commodity prices is causing major cost increases in capital goods. In the early 1970s a large locomotive cost about $200,000, and by 1980 a similar unit cost $750,000. To some degree, the price increases are due to new safety and pollution requirements as well as new fuel efficiency design features. But, the bulk of the price increases are believed to be caused by general inflationary pressures.

■ capital life cycle cost

Another carrier purchasing problem is predicting the operating and maintenance performance of capital equipment in advance. This is a critical analytical point, since the purchase cost is only one cost component in the entire set of total life cycle costs of an asset. Carriers often opt for a higher price asset so as to later enjoy certain operating economies or maintenance efficiencies inherent to the equipment. The problem is compounded when technological advances become available in equipment purchases. Some asset operating performance information is not available in detail until several years of actual working experience have transpired.

■ supply availability

Still another problem facing purchasing managers in the 1980s is the lead time, and in some instances total supply availability, of many company asset requirements. Problems of commodity supply and trends in corporate manufacturing are gradually leading to fewer sources for many complete lines of capital goods. In the rail industry there used to be many suppliers of rail. Today, only one major supplier exists in the United States. Many carriers have had to turn to overseas sources. Purchasing personnel in all modes will choose to maintain close links with supply sources rather than to rely totally upon supplier company sales contacts with them.

■ buyer/vendor coordination

Two significant improvement opportunities are available for carrier purchasing. One that is currently in common use calls for close purchase timing and vendor inventory coordination. When the buying firm commits to a quantity and certain timing of acquisitions during the year, a single vendor can more efficiently produce and store items for release when desired. Here, a commitment by the buyer permits several logistics economies to be attained by the supplier and to be passed on in an improved purchase price. Another potential savings area is in improved purchase-inventory stores control. By better in-house inventory planning, purchasing can procure goods in a manner mentioned above, and the carrier has less investment in spare parts, maintenance items, operating supplies, and even some capital goods. Because of these two coordination items, and the need for greater purchasing department research and input into the capital goods acquisition, this function will gain increased future responsibility and status in the firm.

■ stores control improvement

Claims and Safety

These two functions are in all firms, but they exist in a number of organizational forms and are often housed within other administrative units. In the claims realm, this function includes responsibility for all forms of company liability such as freight, passengers, and employees on the obligation end and vehicles and facilities on the insured end. Safety is often combined in this function because an inverse trade-off exists between attention to safety and costs of incidences, and insurance of liabilities.

■ claim/safety goal

The managerial goal governing the claims and safety area is typically one of minimum total cost of insurance, self insurance, and company safety and handling training systems. Efforts spent on safety training, loss and damage prevention, and security are usually cost-effective in holding down insurance and other liability costs of the firm.

■ cost increase

Problems facing this area stem primarily from inflation. Cost increases from all sources cause insurance claims and the cost of insurance itself to continually increase. Aggravating this situation is the high liability that exists in even small loss and damage units. A lost 100-pound case of mechanical parts bringing a freight bill of, say, $75 can cause a loss and damage claim of over $1,000. Twenty years ago a similar case of parts might have only represented a $200 liability. Employee liability compensation, likewise, has entered the realm of exceedingly high claims.

■ employee selection improvement

Carriers are continually making efforts to control costs in these areas. One major area of attention is employee screening and training. By placing a lot of attention in this area, firms take a prevention approach to claims and safety problems. Another major continuing area of cost improvement, or one which in effect minimizes increases, is the efforts of industry associations. Through the Uniform Freight Classification Committee of the railroads and the National Motor Freight Classification Committee of the motor carriers, strides are often made in improved packaging designs, loading and handling techniques, and employee training. Over the years, suggestions and shipping rules made by these and other groups have gone far toward reducing major loss and damage problems.

Labor and Personnel

This area covers the management of labor relations and personnel at all levels. In specific form, it includes hiring, training, wage and salary administration, labor-management relations in contract labor contexts (negotiations, grievances, etc.), and human resource planning.

■ good management problems minimization

A set of goals is very difficult to define for this area. In one way, the labor-personnel system should supply the skills needed by the firm in the most efficient manner possible. In another, it requires determining and obtaining fair and competitive labor agreements which could then be administered in the most amicable and least cumbersome manner possible. A problem facing labor-personnel managers is that these goals are fairly vague and provide intangible benchmarks against which to strive for. In many instances, managers of this area face criticism when problems arise in wage and salary administration, the availability of required skills, or in contract labor areas. Thus, while these managers attempt to satisfy some positive goals, there is definite attention made to minimizing any negative problem areas. That is, good management of this area is often viewed as that which causes no problems.

■ productivity increase

Inflation and social issues are the root problem areas for this function in the 1980s. In most modes recent labor wage increases have been in excess of the productivity gains made by the carriers. Thus, from an overall standpoint, many carriers have experienced a total decline in productivity in the past few years. The problem is contributed to by the fact that productivity gains in the 1970s have been relatively small, while labor demands for keeping up with the cost of living have often overshadowed, or have been larger, than these gains.

■ social issues

The other major problem area includes labor social problems which range from alcoholism to discrimination and retirement issues. Alcohol is a major human resource problem. Traditional approaches were to terminate employment. Today, firms make concerted efforts to work with and rehabilitate the employee. Discrimination on the basis of race, age, or sex is a human resource planning and management problem that has just come into the corporate setting since the late 1960s. The issue is being resolved by finding, attracting, or keeping persons from these minority backgrounds. The recently legislated retirement age—seventy— is another concern. Because many persons will not be leaving the firm at the traditional retirement ages of sixty-two and sixty-five, this may mean slower employee turnover. Combined with the quest to create upward mobility opportunities for minorities and women, firms will no doubt be faced with special recognition and motivational problems of the traditional white male employee sector in the 1980s and 1990s.

■ work rule flexibility

Some major opportunity areas are emerging in labor and personnel areas. In the organized labor realm, many firms have been seeking work rule flexibility as part of the routine wage negotiation package. Many firms have cited that perhaps inflexible work rules impact more detrimentally upon the firm than do actual wages. An example of how employee flexibility aids the firm can be seen in the labor situation at Delta Airlines. Nearly 90 percent of that firm is not unionized. While the carrier keeps pace with the organized wages throughout the country, a key to its high profitability has been cited as employee utilization. All personnel in the operating segment of the firm (except pilots) can perform their own tasks and can be called upon to fill in on one or two more tasks which are closely related to their jobs.

■ career tracking

Another emerging trend in this area is "career tracking." This consists of developing and following through on specific employee career growth. In the past, an entry level employee who happened to start in operations would tend to remain there. Only the possibility of promotions within operations was offered. Career tracking entails creating logical growth opportunities for managers so that a full range of corporate experiences are available. In this way, the employee's potential might be better reached by exposing him to other areas of the firm, and the firm gains because promoted managers have broader exposure and experience.

Real Estate and Facilities

This department obtains land and facilities for the firm and often is responsible for their maintenance and use. The facilities include offices and terminals, and the acquisition can be made either through lease or outright purchase.

■ function subactivities

Specific subactivities of this function pertinent to each mode are as follows. In the air industry terminals are typically facilities leased from airport agencies of the states or municipalities which own them. The airlines enter into long-term leases with these agencies and then construct leasehold improvements in the form of hangar facilities, gates, lounges, and reservation and ticket spots. In the motor carrier industry, the real estate department searches out terminal sites and is generally responsible for their construction and financing. The rail industry has large investments in land for both rail operations (right-of-way, terminal areas, and offices) as well as resource holdings (coal, timber, and mineral lands). Some railroads have been actively developing idle urban land for nontransportation investment purposes.

The typical managerial objective for real estate is to obtain and maintain the required facilities at a minimum cost. Some firms stress minimum construction cost while others seek the goal of minimum operating and use cost; still others strive for a blend of minimum combined construction and use costs. Problems underlying this function as well as opportunities for the future are situation specific and cannot be discussed in a general manner.

Legal Department

This staff activity is responsible for a range of activities which include adversary matters as well as those involving labor, purchasing, and regulation. Specific subfunctions include rates, operating rights, abandonments, labor relations, contract commitments, and adversary legal proceedings.

A managerial objective for this function is difficult to state, because many legal departments do not perceive their function within the management process. However, law departments basically exist to minimize the liability position of the firm while maximizing the implementation of company plans.

Problems facing the legal area in transportation are two-fold. First, there has been an increase in litigation in most sectors of the economy over the past decade. Transportation has not been immune to this trend, and legal departments have tended to become larger as a result. The other major problem in this area has occurred as a result of the shift from economic regulation to noneconomic regulation. Toxic and waste commodity issues have created managerial problems in which legal departments have also played a role. While the development of these regulations continues to evolve, the legal departments will play a major shaping role.

Conclusion

Modern carriers face external factors and elements inherent to the industry that shape the form and functioning of their managements. Problems of energy and capital shortages have altered many of the long-standing strategies and operational methods. These problems will no doubt persist in the 1980s, and the prudent manager should develop flexible contingency plans for any other possible problem areas.

On the positive side, the introduction of the computer and low cost data transmission systems have gone far in reducing the inherent conflicting tendencies of operation managers who minimize costs, marketing personnel who maximize revenues, and financial personnel who seek to minimize capital investment. Instead of these traditional conflicts being resolved individually through lengthy studies or as a result of internal, political influences, the use of automated profit reporting centers tends to focus the attention of all three parties toward common data and goals. Refinements in data and other communication transmissions will enable carrier managements to be even more responsive and adaptive in the future.

Study Questions

1. How should rail or motor carrier managements cope with continued deregulation?

2. Do you feel it is best for a newly hired person in carrier operations to only be promoted into higher positions in the operating department? Why or why not?

3. Distinguish between a local and a break-bulk terminal.

4. What are the pros and cons of the small satellite terminal concept?

5. Why can't marketing be isolated from operations in the terminal?

6. Why is fleet simplification a sought after goal?

7. What trade-offs exist between purchasing and maintenance?

8. One of the questions often posed in carrier management is whether sales should be: (1) a separate function (reporting from the salesperson to a vice-president of sales and marketing); or (2) a local function (salesperson reporting to a local or regional manager in charge of operations and sales in an area). Discuss the relative pros and cons of each approach in a carrier management context. Distinguish between sales and marketing in a carrier context. (AST&T, Spring 1979, Exam #1).

Suggested Readings

Bowersox, Donald J. et al. *Introduction to Transportation.* New York: Macmillian Publishing, 1981, chap. 16.

Coyle, John J., and Bardi, Edward J. *The Management of Business Logistics.* 2d ed. St. Paul: West Publishing Co., 1980, chap. 2.

Farris, Martin T., and Harding, Forrest E. *Passenger Transportation.* Englewood Cliffs, N.J.: Prentice-Hall, Inc., 1976.

Harper, Donald V. *Transportation in America: Users, Carriers, Government.* Englewood Cliffs, N.J.: Prentice-Hall, 1978.

Lee Jr., Lamar, and Dobler, Donald W. *Purchasing and Materials Management: Text and Cases.* New York: McGraw-Hill Book Co., 1977, chap. 1.

McElhiney, Paul T. *Transportation for Marketing and Business Students.* Totowa, N.J.: Littlefield, Adams, 1975, chap. 2.

Pegrum, Dudley F. *Transportation: Economics and Public Policy.* Homewood, Ill.: Richard D. Irwin, 1973, chap. 22.

Rose, Warren. *Logistics Management.* Dubuque, Iowa: William C. Brown Co., 1979, chap. 1.

Sampson, Roy J., and Farris, Martin T. *Domestic Transportation: Practice, Theory, and Policy.* 4th ed. Boston: Houghton Mifflin Co., 1979, chaps. 8, 18.

Taff, Charles A. *Commercial Motor Transportation.* 5th ed. Cambridge, Md.: Cornell Maritime Press, 1975, chap. 11.

Case   Thruway Transportation Company

The Thruway Transportation Company was in the market for a young and aggressive college graduate to train for its sales department. The company hired John Samason with the intention of making him manager of new accounts. John received his degree in business administration and was exposed to only one course in transportation during his college career. Upon accepting his new position, John decided to review his knowledge of the transportation industry to decide how to organize his sales effort and to decide which points to emphasize in his approach. Remembering the great importance that rates have in the motor carrier industry (that is, they must be adequate to cover variable costs, they must be lawful and legal, and they vary as to structure), John decided that his sales approach would consist of four basic steps:

1. Contact the customers—be sure to have researched the type of business they are in, the types of products they ship, and the origins and destinations of these shipments.

2. Make customers feel that you are really interested in their business—field any questions they pose.

3. Inform customers of the rates that are available to them—try to stress the cheapest rates.

4. Close by restating your desire for their business.

John was sure that, in a competitive industry like trucking, the customer would be interested in the cheapest carrier. However, after making twenty contacts in the first week, John had not yet secured a new account. Being totally frustrated, he contacted his regional vice-president with the information that no potential business existed in his area. The vice-president, however, was aware that the competition in John's area was securing all the new business.

If you were John's regional supervisor, how would you begin to analyze the reasons for his lack of success? How would you attempt to change his sales approach? What characteristics of a motor carrier can make it competitive within a competitive industry? How would you outline a sales approach?

Part VII

Changing Environment of Transportation

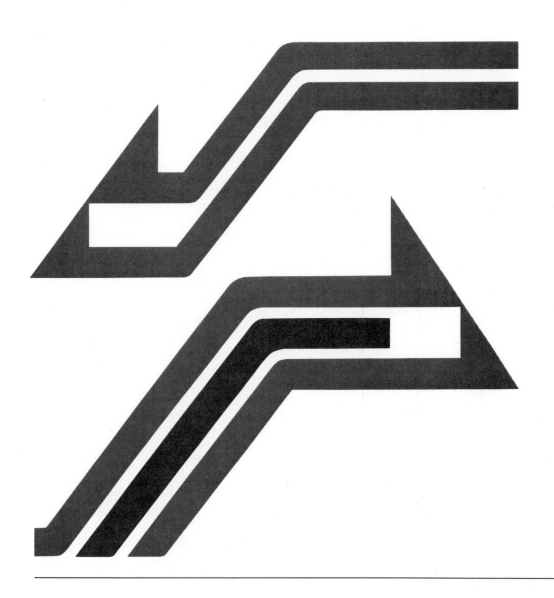

23   The Future of Transportation

After reading this chapter you should:

1   Understand the strategic variables that will affect transportation in the future.
2   Be able to discuss the changes coming in transportation technology.
3   Understand the relationship between technological changes and government regulations.
4   Be able to understand the future problems and opportunities in transportation.

It has frequently been stated in recent years that the decade of the 80s will witness another revolution in transportation comparable to what happened in the middle of the nineteenth century with the development of the railroads or the post-World War I era with the development of alternate sources of transportation service.[1] Whether one agrees with the prognosis of this set of revolutionary changes in the system or not, there is no question that there will be new developments.

The deregulation previously discussed will effectuate change of significant proportions by itself, and deregulation coupled with other factors of an economic and social nature will result in important differences between the system which existed in 1980 and the one that will exist in 1990. It would seem most appropriate to begin by analyzing some of the key variables that will affect transportation and distribution practices in this decade of the 1980s.

■ chapter overview

The discussion of strategic variables will be followed by an analysis of trends in technology which will impact upon the various modes during the 1980s. The final section will deal with the individual modes and how they will be affected by the strategic variables and the changing technology.

Strategic Variables

As stated above, there are a number of strategic variables that should be discussed that will help to shape our transportation system and the distribution environment in general.[2] The major areas to be discussed will include general economic variables, population and demographic variables, energy-related variables, and other general factors.

Economic Variables

Overall, our economy experienced a slower rate of growth during the 1970s as compared to the 1960s. The usual measure of growth is change in gross national product (GNP). During the 1960s, with an adjustment for constant dollars, the rate of change in GNP was approximately 4 percent. In the 1970s the rate of change in GNP was nearer 3 percent, actually about 3.2 percent. During the 1980s the rate of change in GNP is projected to be between that of the 1960s and 1970s, approximately 3.5 percent.

Figure 23.1 shows the projections for GNP as well as for several other related variables. The projections for personal income mirror those for GNP, while the projection for government purchases are projected to increase at a slower rate which implies a decline in their share of GNP.

■ impact on competition

An implication of the slower growth rate is that we will probably not have as rapid a growth in freight ton-miles as was the case in the post-World War II era. This slower growth rate will help to intensify the competition among carriers who will expand by attempting to siphon off each other's business. One should note, of course, that there are many projections of GNP during the 1980s. Some of these projections are higher and others are lower than the 3.5 percent previously indicated. In fact, the 3.5 percent forecast is optimistic compared to many other projections of GNP during the 1980s. Also, the rate of growth in individual sectors such as agriculture and mining will probably vary, and therefore impact differently upon transport segments.

Figure 23.1 also shows another key economic variable for the 1980s, namely, the consumer price index (CPI) which is a measure of the rate of inflation in the economy. During the 1960s, the CPI rose at an annual rate of about 2.7 percent, while in the 1970s, the rate of change each year

Figure 23.1 Projected Growth Rates for Selected Economic Measures, 1977-1990

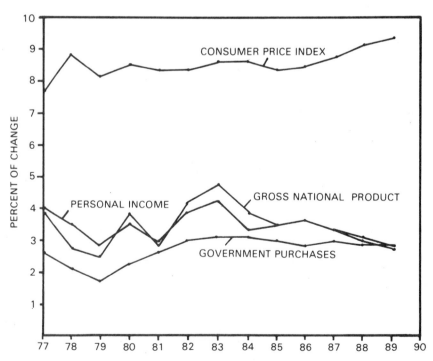

Source: U.S. Department of Transportation, *Profile of the 80s* (Washington, D.C.: U.S. Government Printing Office, 1980) .

■ inflation

was about 7.2 percent indicating a much sharper inflation rate. The CPI projections for 1980 show the same higher level of inflation. Figure 23.1 indicates annual rates during the 1980s of over 8 percent for most of the decade and going over 9 percent near the end of the decade. Once again, there are many projections of CPI for the 1980s, and this one is conservative compared to many. We have witnessed double digit inflation rates several times during short term economic periods, and there are some forecasts which indicate inflation rates as 10 percent or more for the 1980s. A key factor will be what happens to energy prices and some other factors such as productivity rates.

■ cost of doing business

One obvious effect of the high inflation rate is the higher cost of doing business. The inflation rate then, in turn, will probably require transportation companies to increase their rates or prices which may decrease ton-miles carried. The high inflation rate distorts other factors. For example, in recent years many companies have experienced an increase in sales but a decline in profits. It is important to note that the increase in the general inflation rate or price level may only have a nominal impact on some industries. The increases in specific input prices for transportation companies (fuel, for example) are the most important measure of inflation. In fact, this decline in profit rates is another variable worth noting. The decline in profits has affected not only transportation companies but also manufacturing companies. The decline in profits along with some other factors such as high interest rates will make it difficult for transportation companies and private fleet owners to invest in new equipment. General corporate profits during the 1960s were relatively high, while during the 1970s they were markedly lower. The projection for the 1980s is more consistent with that of the 1970s.

■ cost of capital

Another interesting factor is the cost of capital or interest rates. As suggested above, companies usually borrow money for capital investment in new equipment whether for replacement of existing equipment or expansion needs. High interest rates or cost of capital tends to reduce such funding. High cost of capital means shorter pay-back periods are necessary which tends to discourage investment in general. For example, many companies recently have been using pay-back periods of two to three years. This literally means that unless the savings from the investment will pay off the amount invested in two to three years, the investment will not be made. Obviously, there are many potentially viable investments which cannot generate enough savings to pay off the initial investment in two or three years.

The cost of capital has been increasing at an alarming rate, but we sometimes lose sight of just how much change has occurred. For example, in the 1950s the average prime rate of interest for the decade was 2.07 percent while in the 1960s, it was 4.8 percent, and in the 1970s it was approximately 8 percent. In 1980, the average prime rate was over 15 percent, and on several occasions during the early 1980s it rose above 20 percent.

As suggested, high interest rates or cost of capital mean slower asset replacement and less new investment in durable equipment. It is important to keep in mind that historically we have offset rising wage rates with improved productivity that was largely the result of capital investment in equipment.

■ labor cost

Another factor of importance is the labor cost. There are two important aspects of labor cost, namely, wage rates and productivity. Obviously, as long as increased wage rates are offset by increased productivity then such wage increases are not inflationary. In the post-World War II era, productivity from capital expenditures did tend to offset wage rate increases to a large extent which helped to stabilize prices.

■ impact on productivity

As indicated, the capital investment rate will probably be lower at least early in the 1980s, which means productivity gains will have to come from the labor input itself to a large extent and from managerial innovation. There is no question, however, that the productivity gains will be more difficult with the restraint on capital investment. The computer and other factors such as deregulation will force change. It is likely that wage rates will continue to rise given the projected inflation rates. There is a tendency to follow the inflation rate with wage demands which obviously further reinforces the upward trend in prices.

At this point in our discussion, it would appear important to reemphasize something that was pointed out in Chapter 1, namely, the importance of transportation in the economy. As we noted, the estab-

Figure 23.2 Transportation Expenditures as a Percent of GNP

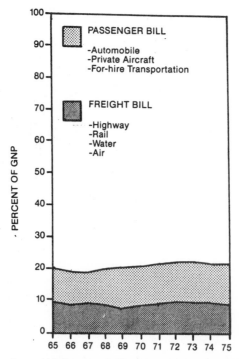

Source: U.S. Department of Transportation, *Profile of the 80s* (Washington, D.C.: U.S. Government Printing Office, 1980).

Figure 23.3 GNP by Major Industry Sector

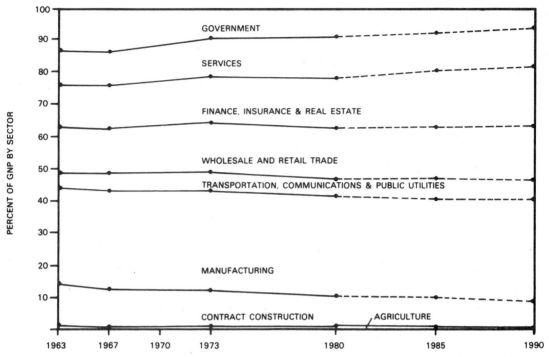

Source: U.S. Department of Transportation, *Profile of the 80s* (Washington, D.C.: U.S. Government Printing Office, 1980).

■ macro effect of transportation

■ industry perspective

■ income

lished definition of industry sectors somewhat conceals the real significance of transportation in our economy. Figure 23.2 indicates that if all expenditures for transportation are added up, they account for about one-fifth of U.S. GNP. The share has remained remarkably stable over time and it seems reasonable to assume or project the same relative share through the 1980s.

A related factor is GNP divided into major industry sectors. Figure 23.3 shows the projected sectorial distribution for GNP which is defined net of imports. As a result, the mining sector does not show up on this chart since imports are expected to outweigh domestic production, that is, it has a negative projection. As Figure 23.3 indicates, there appear to be no surprises in store for the 1980s.

A final economic variable that will be reviewed is income. This will have a direct impact upon travel and travel patterns (usually) and, therefore, is of interest to any transportation discussion. Significant changes in income distribution occurred in the 1960s, but during the 1970s the relative growth of the upper income brackets had slowed down. Since 1975, there has been an increase in the percentage shares of the two higher income categories as shown in Figure 23.4. Changes in lower income brackets were almost negligible. The income distribution

Figure 23.4 Family Income Distribution (in 1978 Dollars)

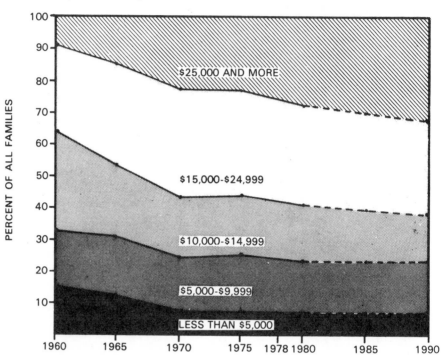

Source: U.S. Department of Transportation, *Profile of the 80s* (Washington, D.C.: U.S. Government Printing Office, 1980).

forecast for the 1980s shows close to 40 percent of U.S. families with incomes less than $15,000 annually. These families are apt to be severely impacted by increases in fuel costs.

■ income distribution

Income distribution by region is projected in Figure 23.5. The South, which is the poorest region, is projected to grow the fastest with an average annual rate of 3.1 percent. The absolute differences projected for the 1990s, however, are relatively small among the four major census areas. But differences tend to be more pronounced among subdivisions within these regions. That is, states in some sections are expected to grow much more rapidly than in others.

■ overview

In general, the economic variables reviewed above suggest that change will be mandated in transportation. The growth in the economy in the post-World War II era along with relatively low interest rates tended to carry the transportation industry along with it and probably concealed the effect of some inefficiencies in the system. During the 1980s and the 1990s transportation companies will require much more managerial skill and higher labor productivity to survive.

■ challenge to transportation

The economic factors will necessitate change, and change will provide opportunity for innovation as well as growth in some companies. There is no question that there are some pessimistic signs for transportation and we have already seen, early in the 1980s, some manifestations of these signs, that is, an increased number of bankrupt transportation companies as well as many financially troubled companies. However, some of this is related to other factors to be discussed at a later point in the chapter.

There are still many opportunities for growth, and more freedom with deregulation to respond to such change. At this stage, we will turn to a discussion of a second factor, namely, population or demographics.

Population and Demographic Change

It is impossible to consider all population and demographic factors in detail, but some attention must be devoted to this area since it has such an obvious effect on transportation. We will primarily concentrate attention upon population change in this section.

Population. Of the three major components of population change (live births, deaths, and net migration), births have been the critical variable in recent years. As Figure 23.6 indicates, the mortality rate (deaths) has been relatively stable over recent decades. There has, however, been a recent downturn in deaths sustained since 1973 that has been largely associated with a reduction in major cardiovascular diseases which reflects improved health care and life-style change. However, overall, the situation has been, and is projected to be, relatively stable as shown in Figure 23.6.

■ major factors

Figure 23.5 Per Capita Income by Region (in 1977 Dollars)

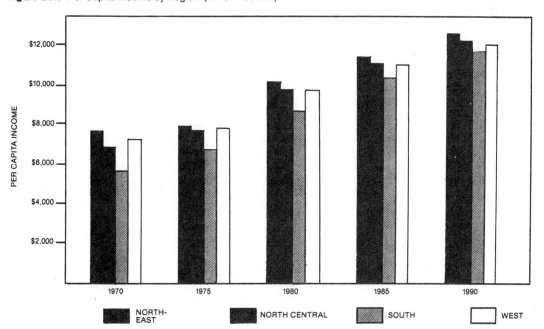

Source: U.S. Department of Transportation, *Profile of the 80s* (Washington, D.C.: U.S. Government Printing Office, 1980).

Figure 23.6 Components of Population Change

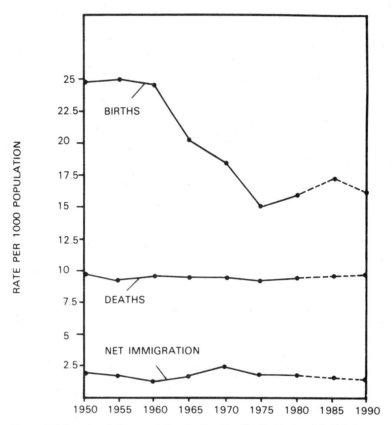

Source: U.S. Department of Transportation, *Profile of the 80s* (Washington, D.C.: U.S. Government Printing Office, 1980).

Net migration rates are largely determined by public policy. There have been more people who want to migrate in recent years than we have allowed to do so. Except for some temporary "blips" such as occurred with Viet Nam immigrants or Cuban immigrants in recent years, the general trend is slightly downward. This same downward trend in migration is forecast for the 1980s as indicated in Figure 23.7.

The key population variable, which has been dropping, is obviously that which is associated with fertility trends, namely, live births. The drop is primarily the result of a decline in fertility rates for women across all age categories. There is a consensus that changing aspirations of women and couples have caused this decline.

Regional differences are important to discuss in any analysis of population in a country as large as the United States. Figure 23.7 shows net migration among census regions for 1975 to 1978. What this clearly shows is that there has been a net migration to the South from other regions. This trend represents a radical reversal of long established trends.

■ downward trend

■ fertility

■ regional difference

■ city concentration

The overwhelming majority of our population lives in metropolitan areas. The 1980s are unlikely to see any significant change in this distribution. The reasons for faster population growth in metropolitan areas are twofold. First, existing areas registered a net migration from nonmetropolitan areas, and second, fast growing areas were frequently reclassified as a standard metropolitan statistical area (SMSA). See Figure 23.8.

Figure 23.9 shows that during the 1980s the number of elderly people will grow substantially both in absolute and relative terms. By 1990, people over sixty-five will account for about 12 percent of the total population. At the same time the proportion of people under eighteen years of age will drop from over 34 percent to under 27 percent. Since dependency and mobility limitations increase with age, these problems will become more critical during the 1980s. In addition, many of the elderly people who survive their spouses may face mobility problems.

■ age trend

Households. One related demographic variable that needs to be considered in the population is the decreasing household size. The largest concentration of single person households is in central cities. However, the household size for other residential areas has also been declining throughout the decade. Table 23.1 and Figure 23.10 summarize this trend and make a projection into the future.

■ single family households

Figure 23.7 Net Migration Among Census Regions (Annual Averages, in 1000)

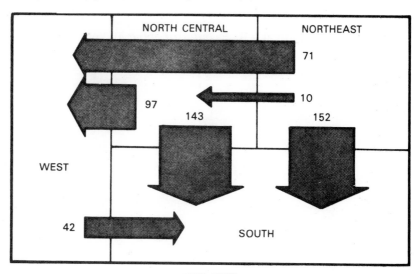

1975-1978

Source: U.S. Department of Transportation, *Profile of the 80s* (Washington, D.C.: U.S. Government Printing Office, 1980).

Figure 23.8 Population in SMSA'S

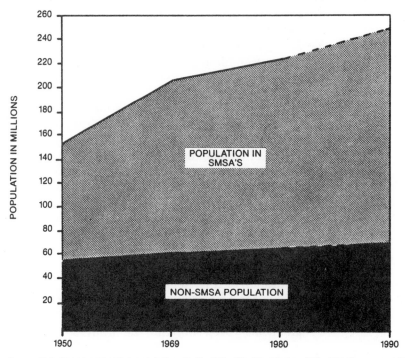

Source: U.S. Department of Transportation, *Profile of the 80s* (Washington, D.C.: U.S. Government Printing Office, 1980).

■ women in work force

Workers. The critical factor in the growth in the labor force has been the increase in participation by women during the last two decades. This trend is expected to increase through the 1980s with the result that women will account for about 40 percent of the total labor force. More women in the labor force will increase the number of part-time workers

Figure 23.9 Age Distribution

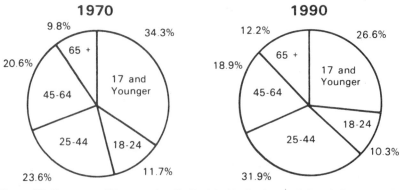

Source: U.S. Department of Transportation, *Profile of the 80s* (Washington, D.C.: U.S. Government Printing Office, 1980).

Table 23.1 Regional Change in Elderly Population

Region	1970		1990	
	People 65 and over (million)	Percent of Population	People 65 and over (million)	Percent of Population
North East	5,176	10.6%	6,718	13.0%
North Central	5,704	10.1%	7,290	11.9%
South	6,018	9.6%	10,391	12.5%
West	3,019	8.7%	5,417	11.7%

Source: U.S. Department of Transportation, *Profile of the 80s* (Washington, D.C.: U.S. Government Printing Office, 1980).

who are employed by their own design. Together with increased use of flexible time concepts by companies, this may help to mitigate peak demand problems for transportation systems. Figure 23.11 summarizes this trend.

The central cities of the largest urban areas have experienced an outflow of jobs, and most of these jobs have moved to smaller urban nonmetropolitan areas. Transportation planning in smaller urban areas will have to account for the increasing share in jobs and total work trips.

Figure 23.10 Average Household Size

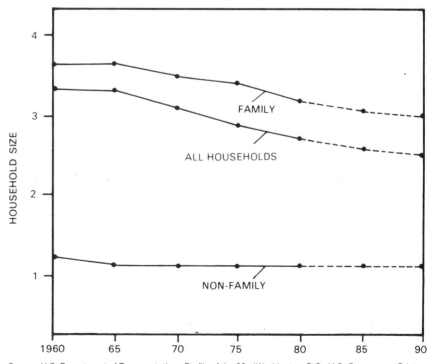

Source: U.S. Department of Transportation, *Profile of the 80s* (Washington, D.C.: U.S. Government Printing Office, 1980).

Figure 23.11 Civilian Labor Force

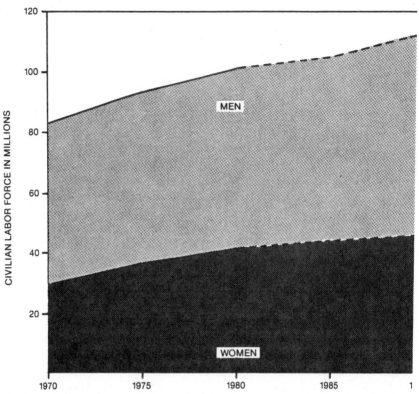

Source: U.S. Department of Transportation, *Profile of the 80s* (Washington, D.C.: U.S. Government Print-ing Office, 1980).

Overview and Impact. In many ways 1990 will resemble 1980 a great deal with respect to population and related demographic data at least as far as trends are concerned. Family households will continue to locate in the suburbs of SMSA's, that is, suburbs will be the location of the largest seg-ment of the population. However, the number of single households will grow with a tendency toward central city location.

■ fuel costs

Most residents of the suburban regions will have to find ways to cope with higher fuel costs. They will be forced to buy smaller cars, arrange carpools, decrease discretionary travel, and use a larger proportion of their income for transportation.

■ adult society

One important difference in our society in the 1980s will be the transi-tion to an adult society, sometimes called "the greying of America." The individuals comprising the postwar "baby boom," will be in the twenty-five to forty-four year age bracket by 1990. Everything points to a lower proportion of households with children which means less concern with school transportation and with the need for movement to child-oriented recreation, and more concern for adult recreation transport needs—such as restaurants and social clubs. Both the time and place utility dimen-sions will be different in this older, childless population.

■ travel growth

It is likely that there will be a growth in travel relative to population growth. This will be caused by an increase in proportion of single occupancy households who have a higher trip rate per person. The increase in multiworker households, as well as the continued trend toward the suburbs, will also affect travel.

It is likely that public transportation use will increase because of these population and demographic factors. Single people and multiworker households can frequently afford the convenience of air travel and will often have a limited time period for travel at one particular time. Elderly people will also tend to use public transportation, air or bus, depending on income, because of age-related problems associated with using the private auto particularly for long trips.

Energy-related Variables

■ oil price increase

Energy could have been considered as one of the economic variables, but its importance to transportation is such that it is being considered separately. Our economy was built to a large extent upon the availability of cheap sources of energy, particularly oil, in the post-World War II era. We have witnessed a rapid escalation in the cost of energy, again, particularly oil, in the post-1973 period. Since 1973, there has been about an 800 percent increase in the cost of oil. There have been varying projections about the cost of oil in the future with many people predicting more increases. In fact, some individuals expect oil to increase up to another 300 percent over the last two decades of this century.

The United States used about 35 percent of all noncommunist oil production in 1980. We doubled our petroleum use between 1960 and 1980 which is almost unbelievable. If we continued at this rate of increase, without an increase in imports, we could deplete our oil reserves by 1990. However, this trend has been changed in a drastic way in the United States in the early 1980s. The high cost of oil has necessitated the types of economies alluded to in the previous section. The percentage of oil imports declined drastically in 1981 to about 25 percent of the total. The significance of this change had a real stabilizing effect on oil prices worldwide.

If the stable oil prices continue, along with more efficient automobiles, the real cost of automobile operation will decrease. This will tend to solidify the demographic trends pointed out previously, for instance, the trend toward suburban living.

In spite of the recent stabilization, there is no question that the higher fuel costs have had and will continue to have an impact upon transportation. Higher fuel costs usually manifest themselves in higher rates. It also makes changes necessary in the less fuel-efficient parts of the transportation system such as air and motor.

Other Factors

Two other factors should be discussed in addition to the economic and demographic type data already covered. First, a brief comment on regulation which was covered in great detail previously. Second, some attention should be given to the political environment.

Regulation. Economic regulation in transportation at the federal level has changed dramatically in recent years. It began with the airlines in 1978 and was followed in the motor carrier and rail segments in 1980. Typically, the changes have been labeled as deregulation. However, there are some individuals who would refer to the changes as reregulation since there are still quite a number of regulatory requirements. There is no question, however, that the acts previously mentioned did allow the carrier much more flexibility and freedom of action.

■ deregulation

The relatively stable environment provided by the regulations previously in existence most certainly protected a number of companies. The change in regulations along with other changes discussed above suggest some important changes in our transportation system to be subsequently discussed.

While economic regulation has been decreasing, the amount of noneconomic regulation has been increasing. The latter includes a regulation regarding hazardous materials, toxic materials, and so on that were previously discussed. These regulations have had, and will continue to have, a major effect upon transportation.

Political Environment. The Republican administration ushered in, in the early 1980s has generally been regarded as being probusiness, and proposals for changes, for example, depreciation rates, have been widely hailed for their positive impact on investment. However, there have been a number of proposals which could have a very negative effect upon particular transportation agencies. These proposals include less funding for public transportation and a decrease or elimination of funding in Conrail and Amtrack. In the final analysis, the changes will obviously have a mixed effect upon various transportation companies.

Summary

This extensive discussion of factors affecting transportation in the 1980s was presented to provide as much perspective as possible into changes likely to come in this period. While the future is difficult to predict and any projection has to be based upon some underlying assumptions, the above analysis will hopefully provide a background for understanding the changes in the future. The next section will take up trends in technology that will affect transportation.

Trends in Technology[3]

Technological innovation will continue to be spurred by traditional motivations and market forces to reduce capital and operating costs, improve customer service, meet consumer demands, and expand markets. But there are new forces of government regulation that will influence change and help determine which innovations emerge. In some cases, government influences are peripheral to traditional transportation goals, and reflect national goals in other fields.

■ overview

There is public concern in such fields as safety, environmental protection, energy conservation, mobility for the elderly and poor, national security, and other matters. In pursuit of varied ends, government influences the nature of technological development in several ways. Traditional market motivations for the transportation industry and its suppliers and motivations produced by government pursuit of various national goals are likely to influence the nature of technological innovations in transportation during the rest of the century. See Figure 23.12.

Automobile Transportation

■ government role

During the 1970s, the federal government became a major force in influencing automobile technology, and is expected to remain a major force to the year 2000. Autos accounted for over 80 percent of total passenger miles traveled in recent years, so it is not surprising that the auto is a prime target for government efforts to conserve petroleum, reduce air pollution, and improve travel safety.

■ legislative impacts

The 1975 Energy Policy and Conservation Act (EPCA) and its amendments set average fuel economy standards weighted by sales for new cars; those standards rise from 18 mpg. in 1978 to 27.5 mpg. in 1985. To meet EPCA objectives, auto industry research can be expected to focus on innovations which increase fuel economy, such as engine modifications or alternative engines, drag reduction, and greater use of lightweight materials in vehicles.

The 1977 Clear Air Act Amendments set strict standards that are to be met in the early 1980s for new car emissions of hydrocarbons, carbon monoxide, and oxides of nitrogen. Future standards may include other classes of emissions. These standards affect the development of both alternative engines and alternative fuels. In the area of safety, pressure from both the government and consumer groups is likely to continue to promote structural changes that improve crashworthiness and further the incorporation of passive and active restraint systems and accident-avoidance systems.

■ profit motive

Aside from government directive, the profit motive continues as an incentive for automobile innovation. Domestic producers, wishing to maintain their competitive positions, will advance innovations which reduce vehicle maintenance, improve reliability, and enhance comfort. A market expansion opportunity which is being watched closely is the small urban auto; the likely candidate is an electric or hybrid vehicle.

Bus Transportation

Traditional market incentives are expected to be important forces for innovation in bus technology. Strategies which increase energy efficiency will not be nearly as significant for buses as for other modes. However, energy conservation technologies developed for autos and trucks may be adapted for buses if cost savings are foreseen.

■ federal role

In the urban market, a recent force behind technological change has been the federal government. For example, the Rehabilitation Act of 1973 has been interpreted as requiring all transit projects receiving federal funds to be accessible to people in wheelchairs. In response to the act, federal design specifications for all new buses purchased with federal aid after September 1979 require low floors and either ramps or lifts for wheelchairs. This interpretation is still being debated.

Figure 23.12 Key Innovations Selected for Analysis

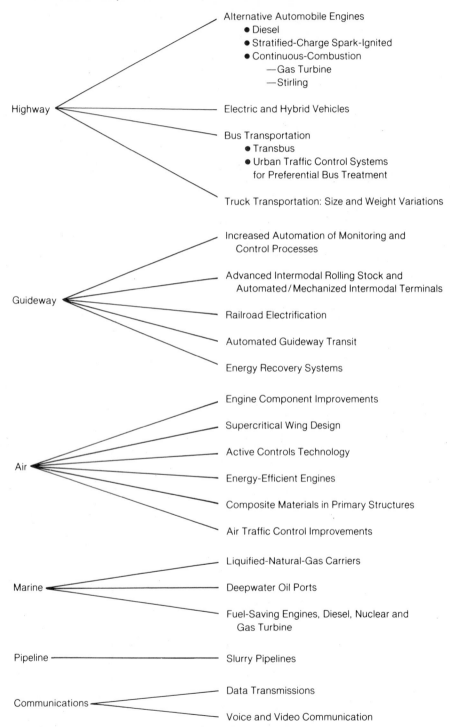

Highway
- Alternative Automobile Engines
  - Diesel
  - Stratified-Charge Spark-Ignited
  - Continuous-Combustion
    - Gas Turbine
    - Stirling
- Electric and Hybrid Vehicles
- Bus Transportation
  - Transbus
  - Urban Traffic Control Systems for Preferential Bus Treatment
- Truck Transportation: Size and Weight Variations

Guideway
- Increased Automation of Monitoring and Control Processes
- Advanced Intermodal Rolling Stock and Automated/Mechanized Intermodal Terminals
- Railroad Electrification
- Automated Guideway Transit
- Energy Recovery Systems

Air
- Engine Component Improvements
- Supercritical Wing Design
- Active Controls Technology
- Energy-Efficient Engines
- Composite Materials in Primary Structures
- Air Traffic Control Improvements

Marine
- Liquified-Natural-Gas Carriers
- Deepwater Oil Ports
- Fuel-Saving Engines, Diesel, Nuclear and Gas Turbine

Pipeline
- Slurry Pipelines

Communications
- Data Transmissions
- Voice and Video Communication

Source: National Transportation Policy Study Commission, *Technological Trends in Transportation and Communications* (Washington, D.C.: U.S. Government Printing Office, 1979).

■ example

New emphasis on traffic engineering techniques that are noncapital-intensive and readily applied to improve existing transportation services has focused attention on applications to urban bus networks. A possible application is an Urban Traffic Control System (UTCS) which can give buses preferential treatment at signalized intersections.

Truck Transportation

■ government role

Technological innovations in trucking are expected to encompass such things as improvements in engines and aerodynamic design, structural weight reduction, and increased use of dieselized engines. Government mandates to improve safety will motivate some change in trucking. Innovation will be sought to improve crashworthiness, and accident-avoidance systems similar to those under development for automobiles may become available for trucks. Increases in vehicle sizes and weights appear to be a major change in the physical characteristics of trucks and truck-tractor combinations which might occur over the next two decades.

Prior to 1956, the individual states had exclusive jurisdiction over the regulation of vehicle size and weight. However, following passage of the 1956 Federal-Aid Highway Act, no federal highway funds could be allocated to states which allowed vehicles to operate on the Interstate System with axle loads, gross-vehicle-weights, and widths exceeding federally imposed limits.

Because vehicles of larger size or heavier weight can carry more cargo, and can often be operated with less energy and at lower cost per ton-mile to the trucker, there is a continuing pressure that restrictions ought to be eliminated or relaxed. Several options are commonly considered for extending these limits.

1. Increase length while maintaining maximum gross weight limits. Such change would benefit the transport of light-density goods. However, significant increases in length pose concern to motorists.

2. Increase gross-vehicle-weight limits, but retain limits on the weight each axle can bear. Dependent on axle spacing (and the use of "bridge formulas") this would encourage the use of multiple axles or (if lengths were also increased) multiple trailers. Such proposals have been criticized on safety grounds and in light of potential negative impacts on structures and competing modes, especially rail.

3. Increase axle load and gross-weight limits. This would encourage heavier loadings. Greater axle loadings are expected to increase some highway maintenance and construction requirements. For this reason and due to safety concerns, such proposals have considerable opposition.

■ impact on other motorists

An important consideration in any move to raise size and weight limits is the impact on other motorists. The question of who would bear the cost of increased maintenance and any additional construction that is required with higher weights, and the potential safety problems with heavier and longer vehicles, are of particular concern to other motorists and to highway agencies. A final concern is a possible increase in motor vehicle freight traffic which might add to highway congestion.

Rail Transportation

overview

Two facets of rail transport—long haul freight movement and urban transit—have potential for technological innovation. In rail freight, the search for profitability in a competitive situation is likely to spur innovations. Better utilization of equipment, more efficient labor utilization, and new equipment (especially in the intermodal area), are targets for technological advances. However, implementing advances that require substantial investment requires overcoming difficulties in raising capital. In urban rail transit, efforts to reduce costs have focused on innovations to decrease labor, energy, and capital construction costs.

rail control systems

Railroads make extensive use of computers and other automatic control systems. Additional use of sensors, detectors and computer hardware to monitor operations and to provide information for management could improve train scheduling, terminal operations, and equipment utilization. The amount of automatic control may increase, but major impediments must be overcome for the implementation of a national system. Expense will be a major barrier, and obtaining uniform data quickly, fears of revealing proprietary information, and difficulties in enticing small but essential lines to join the network will impede the progress of the rail industry toward a full system.

containers

Technological developments are being pursued that will enhance the ability of railroads to move containerized freight. Service improvement is a primary goal of new rolling stock and terminal designs, and it is a factor of importance because rail container transport competes with trucks which by and large offer superior service. Reducing costs by decreasing capital and operating expenses is also a goal. New, more efficient rail cars have been designed to serve specialized regional markets and as prototypes for a standardized car for the entire system.

intermodal terminals

There are several proposals for a variety of intermodal terminals aimed at reducing terminal delay. Less delay would improve service to shippers and cut costs through better equipment use. Some carriers favor expensive, automated terminals that can quickly and efficiently handle existing line-haul equipment with designs that minimize handling.

Market applications for these intermodal concepts will depend on resolution of conflicts about standardization of rolling stock; the level of demand for intermodal transport; the ability of the railroads to raise capital; solving outstanding technical problems; and the modification of existing union work rules.

track electrification

Intercity rail fuel demands may be positively altered by increased track electrification. While net energy savings from the switch may be small, railroad diesel fuel consumption could be reduced if the 20,000 miles of highest-traffic-density routes were electrified. Petroleum equalling 1.5 to 2.0 billion gallons per year could be saved provided all utilities supplying the electric power relied on nonpetroleum energy. Nevertheless, electrification is highly capital-intensive and would require huge levels of investment in return for decreasing fuel and other operating costs.

**Air
Transportation**

From its inception, air transport has been a rapidly changing, high-technology field. Government funding, particularly for defense, fostered many of the technological advances. Innovations in the civilian sector are motivated primarily by economic forces. Changes which increase productivity, reduce operating costs, or enhance customer appeal have been incorporated into each new-generation aircraft. The chief means of improving efficiency has been to increase aircraft speed and capacity. But increasing speed became less cost-effective once jet fuel prices escalated in the mid 1970s. Fuel prices have emerged as a key force for technological innovation, spurring innovations in engines, airframes, and flight control systems. Even though fuel use has become a major concern to aircraft operators and designers, it is not the only factor anticipated to motivate future innovation. Maintenance cost reduction may receive more attention, and safety should continue to be an important design parameter.

- fuel prices

The present commercial jet fleet is powered by a limited number of engine types. These turbofan engines and their variants are expected to be produced for many years and to remain in service well into the twenty-first century. Evolutionary improvements which reduce fuel consumption, maintenance, noise, and emissions are likely to be incorporated into new production versions of these engines. Component improvements to turbofan engines could result in a five percent increase in fuel efficiency alone, a significant savings in view of the large number of these engines to be produced and operated in the future.

- engines

Airfoil technology has improved considerably over the last decade because of rapid advances in computer-aided design techniques. As a result, new wing designs are available today which are superior to those of existing aircraft. The use of a transonic or "supercritical" shape increases the stability of airflow over the wings, reducing drag and thereby saving fuel. The amount of fuel saved depends on cruise speed and distance. The use of supercritical wings on current medium- and long-range, wide-body aircraft could provide fuel savings of approximately 5 percent. Fuel savings for short-range aircraft would be less. Other potential application for this wing shape include general aviation, special-purpose aircraft, and helicopter rotors.

- wing design

The next generation of turbofan engines is not likely to be in service until the 1990s. The approach to that next-generation engine is expected to be through evolutionary improvement of current high-bypass-ratio turbofans and the incorporation of new materials and advanced components. The National Aeronautics and Space Administration is funding much of the initial research leading to a new turbofan through its Energy Efficient Engine Program. Additional benefits of such a new engine include reductions in emissions and noise. Two barriers exist which could delay introduction of the engine: the high capital costs associated with engine development, and the need for major innovations in manufacturing to make engine performance gains affordable.

- engines

Strong, lightweight materials are now being tested in secondary airframe components. These composite materials could permit substantial weight reductions if used in primary aircraft structures such as the

- materials

wings and tail, which would permit a 10 to 15 percent improvement in fuel efficiency over aircraft of conventional structure. Extensive use is not expected until the 1990s because long-term flight experience is required to prove the reliability of composites.

Technological changes may occur in the Air Traffic Control System. Besides striving for improvements in the traditional areas of safety, navigation, and communication, emphasis seems likely to be placed on finding technological means to increase the capacity of existing airports. There has been little construction of new major airports while air traffic has continued to increase. At this time the technological solution with the greatest potential for increasing capacity appears to be reducing the minimum spacing required between aircraft during instrument approach and landing. It is anticipated that current spacing of 4-5 miles between large aircraft could safely be reduced to 2.5 miles, if there were reliable systems to detect and avoid the hazardous wake vortices which trail large aircraft.

Increasing airport capacity by increasing the number of airplanes that can land in a given period has the drawbacks of increased noise, terminal burdens, and reduced runway occupancy time. Airport capacity can probably be increased most efficiently through a combination of operational improvements and new facilities, as well as technological innovation.

Marine Transportation

During the past two decades, technological changes in the marine sector have increased efficiency through greater vessel specialization. Ocean ships grew tremendously in size, especially bulk carriers. Larger vessels cut capital and operating expenses (principally labor and fuel costs) for each unit of cargo moved, but they reduce flexibility. General cargo handling was revolutionized by container and roll-on/roll-off ships, which lowered labor needs and raised productivity, but they increased capital requirements.

■ size increases

In the domestic trades, barge tows on the inland waterways grew to the maximum practical sizes for different reaches of the system. Specially designed coastal barges are now in service. On the Great Lakes, new bulk carriers have expensive automatic cargo handlers, and mammoth vessels confined to the upper four lakes are now in operation. Experimental efforts have been underway to extend the Great Lakes shipping season through technological means.

Efforts to cut costs and improve service should continue to play a key role in creating new marine technology. The developments of equipment tailored to specialized tasks should continue. Ships and equipment that will allow entry into new markets are expected to be developed.

■ oil tankers

The past two decades have witnessed phenomenal growth in the size of oil tankers, because larger tankers can operate at substantially lower costs. However, the east and gulf coasts of the United States contain no port deep enough to accommodate supertankers, so the maximum possible savings has not been achieved. Man-made deep water oil ports could cut the cost of shipping crude oil to the United States. Deep water ports involve sizeable capital outlays, but lower total operating expense compared with current oil importation methods. The net consequences of deep water ports are uncertain, and there is vigorous debate whether regular methods of delivery or deep water ports pose more threat of oil spillage and damage from associated onshore development.

■ diesel engines

Worldwide, diesel engines are the most common marine power plant, but they are not in the U.S. international fleet. Most U.S. ships are powered by steam engines which burn residual fuel, and no U.S. manufacturer currently fabricates large marine diesels. Slow-speed diesel engines consume 20 percent less fuel than comparable steam plants. If the U.S. fleet switched to diesel, a considerable fuel savings would take place, but other matters than fuel economy need to be compared. Diesels are not suitable for every vessel type, and certain undesirable operating characteristics may outweigh potential fuel consumption advantages.

It is unlikely that other engine types will play a major role during this century. Nuclear-powered ships would substitute uranium for petroleum, giving diversification of energy sources. However, construction costs are enormous while economic potential has not been demonstrated, and environmental, regulatory and liability problems may arise.

Marine gas-turbine engines will offer fuel savings if technological improvements occur at the fast pace foreseen by the engine's proponents. They expect that fuel consumption by 2000 will be less than one-half that of present steam turbines. However, achieving that level would require major advances in the use of composite materials. The development of a combined cycle and improved fuel additives—coal as a source of power in certain shipping lines, such as the North Atlantic to Europe line—is another possibility.

Pipeline Transportation: Slurry Pipelines

Technological changes in pipeline transport to the year 2000 are expected to be evolutionary in nature, motivated either by the prospect of operating efficiencies with conventional systems or by the need to meet engineering challenges posed by harsh environments. Examples of future innovations motivated by the former include:

1. greater use of computers to control pressure variations, optimize duty cycles and monitor leak-detection systems;

2. metallurgical improvements to permit higher operating pressures;

3. friction-reducing coatings or additives to reduce friction losses, improve energy utilization and extend capacities of existing systems;

4. heat-engine improvements such as bottoming cycles and gas turbine regenerators to improve energy efficiency through waste heat utilization; and

5. corrosion control improvements to increase safety and reduce maintenance.

Market expansion is a strong motivation for innovative change in the

■ new products

pipeline industry. Traditionally, pipelines have transported liquid and gaseous products almost exclusively. Before the end of the century, however, it is conceivable that solids and slurry pipelines could become important elements of the transportation system, either in competition to or in conjunction with conventional freight transporters. Because of the impact this market expansion could have, slurry pipelines were selected for further review.

■ technology

In order for solids to be transported in slurry form, the material must be finely ground and suspended in a liquid before being pumped through a line. These requirements limit the materials which can be transported to such commodities as coal, ores, minerals, and gravel. Technological feasibility is not in question; slurry pipelines are operating in many countries on a limited scale. Total U.S. slurry pipeline length is less than 400 miles. This total could increase significantly in the 1980s through increased western coal production and the subsequent need to move the coal by rail, barge, and perhaps slurry pipeline.

■ future incentives

In general, transport conditions which favor slurry pipelines over competing modes are long distances, high volumes, no existing rail lines, or inadequate capital to improve poor rail conditions, and high rates of inflation. Aside from feasibility, which can be determined on an origin-destination basis, the future of the coal slurry pipeline is likely to hinge on the ability of organizers to obtain both rights of eminent domain and adequate water supplies.

■ slurry conversion

One intriguing scheme for coal slurry pipeline development is the conversion of underutilized oil and natural gas pipelines to carry slurry. If this change can be made, the flexibility of the entire pipeline system would be enhanced and slurry pipelines would be in operation with far less capital cost. The technical feasibility of conversion hinges on the question of whether the greater abrasiveness of coal will cause excessive wear on the steel used in existing pipelines.

Potential Benefits from Transport Technology Innovation

Table 23.2 summarizes potential effects from implementation of the key transport innovations, investigated by the National Transportation Policy Study Commission (NTPSC). Major effects are divided into eight categories, including traditional concerns such as costs, level of service, safety and accessibility, plus areas of more recent concern, namely, energy and environmental effects. Within each category in the table, a plus indicates a beneficial effect, a minus indicates a potential detrimental effect, and "U" indicates that the potential effect is uncertain. Blanks indicate that no major change is expected. The overall impact on transportation was derived through subjective evaluation by the NTPSC staff of the eight individual categories.

Overview of Future Transportation Systems

With the discussion of strategic variables and trends in technology as background, this section will examine changes forthcoming in each of the modes of transportation. In addition, consideration will be given to the multimodal changes that are likely to occur.

Table 23.2 Potential Benefits to Be Gained from Technological Innovation

	Major Effects on Transportation									Potential Major Barriers						Current Government Role		
	Operating Cost	Capital Cost	Level of Service	Market Expansion	Safety	Mobility/Accessibility	Energy Consumption of Substitution	Environmental	Overall Effect	Technology Feasibility	Capital Formation	Market Acceptance	Industry Characteristics	Government Regulation	Compatability with Support System	Research, Development Demonstration	Finance	Regulation/Mandate
Highway																		
Alternative auto engines:																		
Diesel	+						+	–	u									X
Stratified-charge SI	+						+	+	+									X
Gas turbine and stirling	+	–					+	+	u	X						X	X	X
Electric and hybrid vehicles	u	–	+	u			+	+	+	X		X				X	X	X
TRANSBUS		–	u			+			u								X	X
Urban traffic control systems		+	+				+	+	+							X	X	X
Truck size/weight variation	+	–	u	+	u		u		u	X				X	X			X
Guideway																		
Increased automation of monitoring & control	+		+	+		+			+	X			X			X		
Advanced intermodal rolling stock & Terminals	+	–	+	+	+		+		+	X	X	X	X	X	X			X
Railroad electrification	+	–	+	u			+		u	X						X	X	
Automated guideway transit	+	–	+	+	u	+	+		u							X	X	X
Energy recovery systems	+						+		+							X	X	
Air																		
Engine-component improvement	+						+	+	+							X		
Supercritical wing design	+						+		+							X		
Active controls technology	+						+		+							X		
Energy-efficient engines	+	–					+		u	X	X					X		
Composite materials	+						+		+	X	X					X		
Air traffic control improvements	u	–	+		+		+	+	u	X	X					X	X	X
Marine																		
LNG Carriers				+	u				u	X		X				X		
Deepwater oil ports	+	+	+					u	+							X		X
Fuel saving-engines	u	u		u			+	u	u	X						X	X	X
Pipeline																		
Slurry pipelines	+	u	+	+			u	u	u						X			X

Source: National Transportation Policy Study Commission, *Technological Trends in Transportation and Communications* (Washington, D.C.: U.S. Government Printing Office, 1979).

KEY: + Technology may have beneficial effect   u Effect of technology is uncertain
 – Technology may have detrimental effect   (Blank indicates no major change expected)
 ✕ Factor applicable to implementation of a technology

Railroads

■ mixed outlook

The outlook for rail transportation is mixed. Some individuals feel that the fuel cost situation bodes well for fuel-efficient modes like railroads. Certainly, there are some potential benefits. Many railroads are looking forward, however, to the possibility of increasing many rates with the new rate freedom of the Staggers Rail Act to improve their profit position and to help attract capital. The railroads may improve their situation since their rates may not increase as much compared to other modes, particularly motor carriers. The railroads are faced with cost increases in areas other than fuel that will necessitate rate increases.

■ contract rates

None of the above is meant to imply that railroads will raise all rates. In fact, there is a noticeable trend toward contract rates. In fact, negotiating rates with railroads may be the best approach for shippers to help stabilize rates. The Staggers Rail Act clearly made contract rates more appealing as previously indicated. Obviously such contracts will have to benefit both parties, for example, stable or lower prices for stable or increased volume. Also, railroads with their capital problems will find contract rates more attractive where shippers provide all or a part of the equipment. Railroads for their part will have to improve their service on such contract service.

Motor Carriers

Motor carriers have responded to the fuel increases of the 1980s in a very positive and oftentimes creative manner, for example, "fuel squeezer" diesel engines, wind deflectors, and radial tires. As indicated in the previous section, payload increases through the loosening of state laws constraining weight and physical dimensions of trailers represent an area of significant potential for a technological breakthrough. How soon such changes will come, if at all, is difficult to predict. The increase in rates will favor changing the laws, but at the same time, many states are having trouble financing road repairs and improvements under present circumstances.

■ deregulation important

The Motor Carrier Act of 1980 has the potential of changing the motor carrier segment more than the deregulation acts affecting air and rail. Carriers will be able, of course, to change rates with more freedom and to be more responsive to private trucking threats. Special discount deals on less-than-truckload (LTL) rates were instituted by a number of carriers in the year immediately following the passage of the Motor Carrier Act of 1980. However, given the fuel cost situation and other costs, it is more likely that rates will increase in the 1980s. In fact, it has been forecast that LTL rates will increase in the range of 90 percent by 1985.[4]

■ entry freedom

The newfound freedom of entry in the motor carrier industry will allow the major carriers to fill in their service area gaps. Just as important, the exit freedoms will probably mean poorer service to some areas in spite of the provisions to the contrary in the Motor Carrier Act of 1980. With the increase in service areas, shippers may reduce the number of carriers with which they deal in an effort to overcome the problems associated with the elimination of motor rate bureaus.

■ LTL

It is quite likely that the number of carriers who handle LTL traffic will decrease with higher fuel costs, more competition through deregulation, higher capital cost, and slower growth rates. The comfortable and stable regulated environment of the 1950s and 1960s which protected some inefficient operators will change. The survivors will be fewer in number and more efficient.

■ TL

The truckload (TL) picture is difficult to predict. It is likely that there will be more competition and lower rates in the short run with the freedom of service available to private carriers under the act of 1980. Some common carriers will move to contract carrier status, in effect, and so will private carriers looking for back-hauls to fill those empty trailers. The net result will be more competition with generally lower rates but with more short run fluctuations related to supply and demand. It is likely that there will be additional instability associated with carriers coming and going. Some shippers will forego private carrier service because of the low rates.

It is likely that there will be a shake-out period in the TL business with intramodal and intermodal competition. Over the longer run (1990), it is likely that we will have fewer motor carriers in this segment of the business as well, and the survivors will be lean and efficient.

Air Carriers

■ mixed outlook

The outlook for domestic air carriers is mixed at best. This is particularly true in the air cargo area. Labor, fuel, and capital costs have made it difficult for air carriers. Shippers have been sensitive to high rates and this has made air carriers susceptible in spite of promised trade-off savings in inventory costs.

Rates correspond with fuel, and, consequently, air rates escalated rapidly in 1979 and particularly in 1980. More stable circumstances in fuel costs have improved the air carrier economic and financial situation. However, other costs including labor and capital have continued to squeeze air carriers. Airlines are likely to use trucks to complement their air service and their shorter hauls. Reduced entry restrictions will allow this possibility and will be advantageous to the airlines.

■ large carriers

In the deregulated climate of the 1980s, the larger airlines (scheduled carriers) will closely evaluate marginal business, particularly in the freight end of it. These carriers will have to be particularly innovative in terms of pricing and service combinations to attract traffic.

■ containers

A particular segment to watch is the air cargo container business. The 20-foot box in the all-cargo plane offers some real productivity benefits and has attracted renewed interest for such carriers as Pan American. The carriers are publishing freight-all-kinds (FAK) rates on those containers to help attract business. Ground equipment is a problem, but this should change by 1985 thus allowing efficient handling of 20-foot containers at most airports with scheduled service.

Water Carriers

■ overview

Water carriers have been hit by escalating fuel costs like other carriers, but they have tried to offset those costs with other economies. New propulsion systems are being investigated, as well as new ship designs. However, intense rate competition has made the situation bleak for deep water carriers.

■ inland system

The inland waterway situation will be more stable. The efficiencies of the industry will help it to maintain its competitive position. Railroads will no doubt attempt to garner some of the water carrier business and will be successful to some extent. However, it is unlikely that railroads will make serious inroads in water traffic, unless there are significant technological changes.

Multimodal Service

Intermodal or multimodal transportation has been long hailed as offering significant potential to improve transportation service with lower costs. The potential seen by some individuals has never really been attained. Perhaps this has been attributable to rigid Interstate Commerce Commission policies on intermodalities. Certainly, this situation has changed vastly with the previously discussed deregulation.

■ intermodal traffic

The time would appear ripe for significant growth in intermodal traffic. Railroads, airlines, motor carriers, and water carriers have all shown signs of their service in the intermodal area. Railroads have been developing trailer-on-flat-cars (TOFC) for some time. Sea-Land and others have developed container service, Tiger International is a real intermodal carrier with much-hailed promise. Even motor carriers have the potential at present to expand into the intermodal area. The environment is right for intermodal advances. The advent of more intermodal service is not likely to result in significantly lower rates; fuel and other costs are likely to preclude this. The key to success will rest on service; the carriers will have to provide premium service to attract the business.

Conclusion

Overall, the 1980s and 1990s will see big changes in transportation. All the factors point to change—economic, technological, demographic, and political. A virtual revolution is underway.

Study Questions

1. What key factors will shape the U.S. transportation and distribution network in the 1980s?
2. What impact does high inflation have upon transportation?
3. How does the high cost of money, or interest, impact transportation?
4. How do the demographics of population shape transportation or vice versa?
5. What population shift is taking place geographically in the United States? Might this shift slow down or stop?
6. Cite two technological advances that might come into use in each of the modes.
7. Specifically, what benefits come from advances in transportation technology?
8. What is the outlook for the health of the modes in the 1980s?

Notes
1. S. Ţinghitella, "Transportation Innovation." *Traffic Management* (March 1980): 49.
2. U.S. Department of Transportation, *Profile of the 1980s* (Washington, D.C.: U.S. Government Printing Office, Feb. 1980), pp. 1-25.
3. This section was developed from National Transportation Policy Study Commission, *Technological Trends in Transportation and Communications* (Washington, D.C.: U.S. Government Printing Office, 1979), pp. 93-103.
4. R. C. Heiden, "Trucking Outlook," *Handling and Shipping Management* (January, 1981): pp. 48-51.

Suggested Readings

Bowersox, Donald J. et al. *Introduction to Transportation.* New York: Macmillan Publishing, 1981, chap. 18.

Coyle, John J. and Bardi, Edward J. *The Management of Business Logistics.* 2d ed. St. Paul: West Publishing Co., 1980, chap. 14.

Lieb, Robert C. *Transportation: The Domestic System.* 2d ed. Reston, Va.: Reston Publishing Co., 1981, chap. 20.

Sampson, Roy J. and Farris, Martin T. *Domestic Transportation: Practice, Theory, and Policy.* 4th ed. Boston: Houghton Mifflin Co., 1979, chap. 30.

U.S. Department of Transportation. *National Transportation Trends and Choices to the year 2000.* Washington, D.C.: U.S. Government Printing Office, 1977.

U.S. National Transportation Policy Study Commission. *A Compendium of Federal Transportation Policies and Programs.* Springfield, Va.: National Technical Information Service, 1979.

U.S. National Transportation Policy Study Commission. *National Transportation Policies Through the Year 2000.* Washington, D.C.: U.S. Government Printing Office, 1978.

Vellenga, David B., and Ettlie, John E. "Technology Transfer in Transportation: Problems and Research Questions." *Proceedings: Transportation Research Forum,* 1975, pp. 165-8.

Wood, Donald F., and Johnson, James C. *Contemporary Transportation.* Tulsa: Petroleum Publishing, 1980, chap. 15.

| Case | Advance Trucking |

Bill Fobert is vice-president of marketing for Advance Trucking, a large LTL carrier with nationwide routes. His primary task is to handle national accounts in ways that cannot be covered by local terminal-based sales personnel. Terminal-based sales personnel report to the terminal or regional branch managers and not in direct line to Bill's office. Another function of Bill's office is to coordinate sales programs such as advertising, training, and employee policies with regard to sales personnel.

Bill has been concerned with deregulation. On the other hand, he is enthusiastic about the opportunities it presents for his company. One of the ideas he is getting ready to present to his management is the idea of creating a market research department. This is something very few carriers have within their organizations.

You are being interviewed for a job by Bill. He asks you the following: "What are the basic functions we would have this department perform? What would be needed to set one up? How should we staff it?" How would you answer him?

GLOSSARY

Abandonment The decision of a carrier to give up or to discontinue service over a route. Railroads must seek ICC permission to abandon routes.

Accessibility The ability of a carrier to provide service between an origin and a destination.

Agency Tariff A publication of a rate bureau that contains rates for many carriers.

Air Cargo Freight that is moved by air transportation.

Air Taxi An exempt for-hire air carrier that will fly anywhere on demand; air taxis are restricted to a maximum payload and passenger capacity per plane.

Air Transport Association of America A U.S. airline industry association.

Airport and Airway Trust Fund A federal fund that collects passenger ticket taxes and disburses these funds for airport facilities.

Alaskan Carrier A for-hire air carrier that operates within the state of Alaska.

All-Cargo Carrier An air carrier that only transports cargo.

American Trucking Associations, Inc. A motor carrier industry association that is made up of thirteen subconferences representing various sectors of the motor carrier industry.

American Waterway Operators A domestic water carrier industry association representing barge operators on the inland waterways.

Amtrak The National Railroad Passenger Corporation, a federally created corporation that operates most of the nation's intercity passenger rail service.

Army Corps of Engineers A federal agency responsible for the construction and maintenance of waterways.

Association of American Railroads A railroad industry association that represents the larger U.S. railroads.

Auditing Determining the correct transportation charges due the carrier; auditing involves checking the accuracy of the freight bill for errors, correct rate, and weight.

Average Cost Total cost, fixed plus variable, divided by total output.

Back-haul The return movement of a vehicle from original destination to original origin.

Barge The cargo-carrying vehicle used primarily by inland water carriers. The basic barges have open tops, but there are covered barges for both dry and liquid cargoes.

Basing Point Pricing A pricing system that includes a transportation cost from a particular city or town in a zone or region even though the shipment does not originate at the basing point.

Benefit-Cost Ratio An analytical tool used in public planning; a ratio of total measurable benefits divided by the initial capital cost.

Big Inch A federally constructed pipeline built during World War II that connected Longview, Texas, with the New York-Philadelphia refinery area.

Bill of Lading A transportation document that is the contract of carriage between the shipper and carrier; it provides a receipt for the goods tendered to the carrier and, in some cases, shows certificate of title.

Billing A carrier terminal activity involving the determination of the proper rate and total charges for a shipment and the issuance of a freight bill.

Blanket Rate A rate that does not increase according to the distance the commodity is shipped.

Boxcar An enclosed rail car typically 40 to 50 feet long; used for packaged freight and some bulk commodities.

Bracing Securing a shipment inside a carrier's vehicle to prevent damage.

Break-bulk The separation of a consolidated, bulk load into individual, smaller shipments for delivery to ultimate consignee. The freight may be moved in-tact inside the trailer or it may be interchanged and rehandled to the connecting carriers.

Broker An intermediary between the shipper and the carrier. The broker arranges transportation for shippers and represents carriers.

Business Logistics The physical movement of goods from supply points to final sale to customers, and the associated transfer and holding of such goods at various intermediate storage points, accomplished in such a manner as to contribute to the explicit goals of the organization.

Cabotage A federal law that requires coastal and intercoastal traffic to be carried in U.S. built and registered ships.

Capital The resources, or money, available for investing in assets that produce output.

Carrier Liability A common carrier is liable for all loss, damage, and delay with the exception of act of God, act of a public enemy, act of a public authority, act of the shipper, and the inherent nature of the goods.

Car Supply Charge A railroad charge for a shipper's exclusive use of special equipment.

Certificated Carrier A for-hire air carrier that is subject to economic regulation and that requires an operating certification to provide service.

Certificate of Public Convenience and Necessity The grant of operating authority that is given to common carriers. A carrier must prove that a public need exists and that the carrier is fit, willing, and able to provide the needed service. The certificate may specify the commodities to be hauled, the area to be served, and the routes to be used.

Civil Aeronautics Board A federal regulatory agency that implements economic regulatory controls over air carriers.

Claim A charge made against a carrier for loss, damage, or overcharge.

Class I Carrier A classification of regulated carriers based upon annual operating revenues: motor carriers of property — $\geq$ $5 million; railroads — $\geq$ $50 million; motor carriers of passengers — $\geq$ $3 million.

Class II Carrier A classification of regulated carriers based upon annual operating revenues: motor carriers of property — $1-$5 million; railroads — $10-$50 million; motor carriers of passengers — $\leq$ $3 million.

Class III Carrier A classification of regulated carriers based upon annual operating revenues: motor carriers of property — $\leq$ $1 million; railroads — $\leq$ $10 million.

Classification An alphabetical listing of commodities, the class or rating into which the commodity is placed, and the minimum weight necessary for the rate discount; used in the class rate structure.

Classification Yard A railroad terminal area where rail cars are grouped together to form train units.

Class Rate A rate constructed from a classification and a uniform distance system. A class rate is available for any product between any two points.

Coastal Carriers Water carriers that provide service along coasts serving ports on the Atlantic or Pacific oceans or on the Gulf of Mexico.

Commercial Zone The area surrounding a city or town to which rates quoted for the city or town also apply; the area is defined by the ICC.

Committee of American Steamship Lines An industry association representing subsidized U.S. flag steamship firms.

Commodities Clause A clause that prohibits railroads from hauling commodities which they produced, mined, owned, or had an interest in.

Commodity Rate A rate for a specific commodity and its origin-destination.

Common Carrier A for-hire carrier that holds itself out to serve the general public at reasonable rates and without discrimination. The carrier must secure a certificate of public convenience and necessity to operate.

Common Carrier Duties Common carriers are required to serve, deliver, charge reasonable rates, and not discriminate.

Common Cost A cost that cannot be directly assignable to particular segments of the business but that is incurred for the business as a whole.

Commuter An exempt for-hire air carrier that publishes a time schedule on specific routes; a special type of air taxi.

Comparative Advantage A principle based on the assumption that an area will specialize in the production of goods for which it has the greatest advantage or least comparative disadvantage.

Conrail The Consolidated Rail Corporation established by the Regional Reorganization Act of 1973 to operate the bankrupt Penn Central Railroad and other bankrupt railroads in the Northeast; funding was provided by the 4-R Act of 1976.

Consignee The receiver of a freight shipment, usually the buyer.

Consignor The sender of a freight shipment, usually the seller.

Consolidation The collection of smaller shipments to form a larger quantity in order to realize lower transportation rates.

Container A big box (10 to 40 feet long) into which freight is loaded.

Contract Carrier A for-hire carrier that does not serve the general public, but that serves shippers with whom the carrier has a continuing contract. The contract carrier must secure a permit to operate.

Cooperative Associations Agricultural cooperative associations may haul up to 25 percent of their total interstate tonnage in nonfarm, nonmember goods in movements incidental and necessary to their primary business.

Coordinated Transportation Two or more carriers of different modes transporting a shipment.

Cost Trade-off The interrelationship among system variables indicates that a change in one variable has cost impact upon other variables. A cost reduction in one variable may be at the expense of increased cost for other variables, and vice versa.

Courier Service A fast door-to-door service for high-valued goods and documents; firms usually limit service to shipments of 50 pounds or less.

Demurrage The charge assessed by the railroad for the shipper/receiver holding a car beyond the free time allowed for loading (24 hours) and unloading (48 hours).

Density A physical characteristic of a commodity measuring its mass per unit volume; or pounds per foot^3; an important factor in rate-making since density affects the utilization of a carrier's vehicle.

Density Rate A rate based upon the density and shipment weight.

Deregulation Revisions or complete elimination of economic regulations controlling transportation. The Motor Carrier Act of 1980 and the Staggers Act of 1980 revised the economic controls over motor carriers and railroads, while the Airline Deregulation Act of 1978 will eventually eliminate economic controls over air carriers.

Derived Demand The demand for transportation of a product is derived from the demand for the product at some location.

Detention The charge assessed by the motor carrier when the shipper/receiver holds a truck/trailer beyond the free time allowed for loading and unloading.

Differential A discount offered by a carrier that faces a service time disadvantage over a route.

Dispatching The carrier activities involved with controlling equipment; involves arranging for fuel, drivers, crews, equipment, and terminal space.

Domestic Trunk-line Carriers An air carrier classification for carriers that operate between major population centers. These carriers are now classified as major carriers.

Dormant Route A route over which a carrier failed to provide service 5 days a week for 13 weeks out of a 26-week period.

Double Bottoms A motor carrier operation involving two trailers being pulled by one tractor.

Drayage A motor carrier that operates locally, providing pickup and delivery service.

Driving Time Regulations Rules administered by the U.S. Department of Transportation that limit the maximum time a driver may drive in commerce; both daily and weekly maximums are prescribed.

Dual Operation A motor carrier that has both common and contract carrier operating authority.

Dual Rate System An international water carrier pricing system where a shipper signing an exclusive use agreement with the conference pays a lower rate (10 to 15 percent) than nonsigning shippers for an identical shipment.

Economies of Scale The reduction in long run average cost as the size (scale) of the company increases.

Exception Rate A deviation from the class rate; changes are made to the classification.

Exclusive Patronage Agreements A shipper agrees to use only member liner firms of a conference in return for a 10 to 15 percent rate reduction.

Exclusive Use Carrier vehicles that are assigned to a specific shipper for its exclusive use.

Exempt Carrier A for-hire carrier that is exempt from economic regulations.

Expediting Determining where a shipment is in transit and attempting to speed up its delivery.

Fair Return A level of profit that enables a carrier to realize a rate of return on investment or property value that the regulatory agencies deem acceptable for that level of risk.

Fair Value The value of the carrier's property; the basis of calculation has included original cost minus depreciation, replacement cost, and market value.

Federal Aviation Administration The federal agency charged with administering federal safety regulations governing air transportation.

Federal Maritime Commission A regulatory agency that controls services, practices, and agreements of international water common carriers and noncontiguous domestic water carriers.

Feeder Railroad Development Program Any

financially responsible person (except Class I and Class II carriers) with ICC approval can acquire a rail line having a density of less than 3 million gross ton-miles per year.

Finance Lease An equipment-leasing arrangement that provides the lessee with a means of financing for the leased equipment; a common method for leasing motor carrier trailers.

Financial Responsibility Motor carriers are required to have body injury and property damage (not cargo) insurance of not less than $500,000 per incident per vehicle; higher financial responsibility limits apply for motor carriers transporting oil or hazardous materials.

Fixed Costs A cost which does not fluctuate with the volume of business in the short run.

Flag of Convenience A shipowner registers a ship in a nation that offers conveniences in the areas of taxes, manning, and safety requirements; Liberia and Panama are two nations known for flags of convenience.

Flat Car A rail car without sides; used for hauling machinery.

FOB A term of sale that defines who is to incur transportation charges for the shipment, who is to control the movement of the shipment, or where title to the goods passes to the buyer; originally meant "free on board" ship.

For-hire Carrier A carrier that provides transportation service to the public on a fee basis.

Freight Bill The carrier's invoice for transportation charges applicable to a freight shipment.

Freight Forwarder A carrier that collects small shipments from shippers, consolidates the small shipments, and uses a basic mode to transport these consolidated shipments to a destination where the freight forwarder delivers the shipment to the consignee.

Freight Forwarder's Institute The freight forwarder industry association.

Full Service Leasing An equipment leasing arrangement that includes a variety of services to support the leased equipment; a common method for leasing motor carrier tractors.

Fully Allocated Cost The variable cost associated with a particular unit of output plus an allocation of common cost.

Gathering Lines Oil pipelines that bring oil from the oil well to storage areas.

General Commodities Carrier A common motor carrier that has operating authority to transport general commodities, or all commodities not listed as special commodities.

Going Concern Value The value which a firm has as an entity as opposed to the sum of the values of each of its parts taken separately; particularly important in determining what constitutes a reasonable railroad rate.

Gondola A rail car with a flat platform and sides 3 to 5 feet high; used for top loading of items that are long and heavy.

Grandfather Clause A provision that enabled motor carriers engaged in lawful trucking operations prior to the passage of the Motor Carrier Act of 1935 to secure common carrier authority without proving public convenience and necessity; a similar provision exists for other modes.

Granger Laws State laws passed prior to 1870 in midwestern states to control rail transportation.

Great Lakes Carriers Water carriers that operate on the five Great Lakes.

Grid Technique A quantitative technique to determine the least cost center, given raw material sources and markets, for locating a plant or warehouse.

Gross National Product (GNP) A measure of a nation's output; the total value of all final goods and services produced during a period of time.

Gross Weight The total weight of the

vehicle and the payload of freight or passengers.

Guaranteed Loans The federal government cosigned and guaranteed repayment of loans made to railroads.

Hawaiian Carrier A for-hire air carrier that operates within the state of Hawaii.

Highway Trust Fund Federal highway use tax revenues are paid into this fund and the federal government's share of the highway construction is paid from the fund.

Highway Use Tax Taxes assessed by federal and state governments against users of the highway (the fuel tax is an example). The use tax money is used to pay for the construction, maintenance, and policing of highways.

Hopper Cars Rail cars that permit top loading and bottom unloading of bulk commodities; some hopper cars have permanent tops with hatches to provide protection against the elements.

Hub Airport An airport that serves as the focal point for the origin and termination of long-distance flights; flights from outlying areas are fed into the hub airport for connecting flights.

Igloos Pallets and containers used in air transportation; the igloo shape is designed to fit the internal wall contours of a narrow body airplane.

Incentive Rate A rate designed to induce the shipper to ship heavier volumes per shipment.

Independent Action A carrier that is a member of a rate bureau has the right to publish a rate that differs with the rate published by the rate bureau.

Inherent Advantage The cost and service benefits belonging to the different modes.

Integrated Tow Barge A series of barges that are connected together to operate as one unit.

Interchange Refers to the transfer of cargo and equipment from one carrier to another in a joint freight move.

Intercoastal Carriers Water carriers that transport freight between the east and west coast ports usually by way of the Panama Canal.

Intercorporate Hauling A private carrier hauling the goods of a subsidiary and charging the subsidiary a fee; this is legal if the subsidiary is wholly owned (100 percent) or the private carrier has common carrier authority.

Interline Two or more motor carriers working together to haul the shipment to a destination. Carrier equipment may be interchanged from one carrier to the next, but usually the shipment is rehandled without the equipment.

Internal Water Carriers Water carriers that operate over the internal, navigable rivers such as the Mississippi, Ohio, and Missouri.

International Air Transport Association An international air carrier rate bureau for passengers and freight movements.

International Civil Aeronautics Organization An international agency which is responsible for air safety and standardizing air traffic control, airport design, and safety features worldwide.

Interstate Commerce The transportation of persons or property between states; in the course of the movement, the shipment crosses a state boundary line.

Interstate Commerce Commission An independent regulatory agency that implements federal economic regulations controlling railroads, motor carriers, pipelines, domestic water carriers, domestic surface freight forwarders, and brokers.

Interstate System The National System of Interstate and Defense Highways, 42,000 miles of four-lane limited access roads connecting major population centers.

Intrastate Commerce The transportation of persons or property between points within a state. A shipment between two points within a state may be interstate if the shipment had a prior or subsequent move outside of the state and the intent of the shipper was an interstate shipment at the time of shipment.

Inventory Cost The cost of holding goods; usually expressed as a percentage of the value of the inventory; includes the cost of capital, warehousing, taxes, insurance, depreciation, and obsolescence.

Irregular Route Carrier A motor carrier that is permitted to provide service utilizing any route.

Joint Cost A type of common cost where products are produced in fixed proportions, and the cost incurred to produce one product necessarily entails the production of another; the back-haul is an example.

Joint Rate A rate over a route that involves two or more carriers to transport the shipment.

Lading The cargo carried in a transportation vehicle.

Laid-down Cost The total cost of a product delivered at a given location; the cost of production plus the transportation cost to the customer's location.

Land Bridge The movement of containers by ship-rail-ship; on Japan to Europe moves, ships move containers to U.S. Pacific Coast, rail moves containers to east coast port, and ship delivers containers to Europe.

Land Grants Grants of land given to railroads during their developmental stage to build tracks.

Lash Barges Covered barges that are loaded on board ocean-going ships for movement to foreign destinations.

Lessee A person or firm to whom a lease is granted.

Lessor A person or firm that grants a lease.

Lighter A flat-bottomed boat designed for cross-harbor or inland waterway freight transfer.

Line-haul A shipment that moves between cities and distances over 100 to 150 miles.

Liner Service International water carriers that ply fixed routes on published schedules.

Link The transportation method used to connect the nodes (plants, warehouses) in a logistics system.

Little Inch A federally built pipeline constructed during World War II that connected Corpus Christi and Houston, Texas.

Load Factor A measure of operating efficiency used by air carriers to determine the percentage of a plane's capacity that is utilized, or: number of passengers/ total number of seats.

Localized Raw Material A raw material found in certain locations only.

Local Rate A rate published between two points served by one carrier.

Local Service Carriers An air carrier classification of carriers that operate between areas of lesser and major population centers. These carriers feed passengers into the major cities to connect with trunk (major) carriers. Local service carriers are now classified as national carriers.

Locational Determinant The factors that determine the location of a facility. For industrial facilities, the determinants include logistics costs, operating costs, and employee conditions.

Logbook A daily record of the hours an interstate driver spends driving, off duty, sleeping in the berth, or on duty but not driving.

Long Ton Equals 2240 pounds.

LTL Less-than-truckload, a shipment weighing less than the minimum weight needed to use the lower truckload rate.

Lumping A term applied to a person who assists a motor carrier owner-operator in the loading and unloading of property; quite commonly used in the food industry.

Major Carrier A for-hire certificated air carrier that has annual operating revenues of $1 billion or more; the carrier usually operates between major population centers.

Marginal Cost The cost to produce one additional unit of output; the change in total variable cost resulting from a one-unit change in output.

Marine Insurance Insurance to protect against cargo loss and damage when shipping by water transportation.

Maritime Administration A federal agency that promotes the merchant marine, determines ocean ship routes and services equipment, and awards maritime subsidies.

Market Dominance The absence of effective competition for railroads from other carriers and modes for the traffic to which the rate applies. The Staggers Act stated that market dominance does not exist if the rate is below the revenue to variable cost ratio of 160 percent in 1981 and 170 percent in 1983.

Measurement Ton Equals 40 cubic feet; used in water transportation rate-making.

Merger The combination of two or more carriers into one company for the ownership, management, and operation of the properties previously operated on a separate basis.

Mileage Allowance An allowance based upon distance and given by railroads to shippers using private railcars.

Mileage Rate A rate based upon the number of miles the commodity is shipped.

Minimum Weight The shipment weight specified by the carrier's tariff as the minimum weight required to use the TL or CL rate; the rate discount volume.

Mixed Loads The movement of both regulated and exempt commodities in the same vehicle at the same time.

Modal Split The relative use made of the modes of transportation; the statistics used include ton-miles, passenger-miles, and revenue.

Multiple Car Rate A railroad rate that is lower for shipping more than one carload rather than just one carload at a time.

National Carrier A for-hire certificated air carrier that has annual operating revenues of $75 million to $1 billion; the carrier usually operates between major population centers and areas of lesser population.

National Industrial Traffic League An association representing the interests of shippers and receivers in matters of transportation policy and regulation.

Nationalization Public ownership, financing, and operation of a business entity.

National Motor Bus Operators Organization An industry association representing common and charter bus firms; now known as the American Bus Association.

National Railroad Corporation Also known as Amtrak, the corporation established by the Rail Passenger Service Act of 1970 to operate most of the nation's rail passenger service.

Node A fixed point in a firm's logistics system where goods come to rest; plants, warehouses, supply sources, markets.

Noncertificated Carrier A for-hire air carrier that is exempt from economic regulation.

Nonvessel Owning Carrier A firm that consolidates and disperses international containers that originate at or are bound for inland ports.

Operating Ratio A measure of operating efficiency defined as:

$$\frac{\text{operating expenses}}{\text{operating revenues}} \times 100$$

Out-of-Pocket Cost The cost directly assignable to a particular unit of traffic and which would not have been incurred if the movement had not been performed.

Over-the-Road A motor carrier operation that reflects long distance, intercity moves; the opposite of local operations.

Owner-Operator A trucking operation in which the owner of the truck is also the driver.

Passenger-Mile A measure of output for passenger transportation; it reflects the number of passengers transported and the distance traveled; a multiplication of passengers hauled and distance traveled.

Per Diem The rate of payment for use by one railroad of the cars of another.

Permit A grant of authority to operate as a contract carrier.

Personal Discrimination Charging different rates to shippers with similar transportation characteristics, or vice versa.

Physical Distribution The movement and storage functions associated with finished goods from manufacturing plants to warehouses and to customers.

Physical Supply The movement and storage functions associated with raw materials from supply sources to the manufacturing facility.

Piggyback A rail-truck service. A highway trailer is loaded by a shipper and is driven to a rail terminal where it is loaded on a rail flat car; the trailer-on-flat car is moved to the destination terminal by the railroad where the trailer is off-loaded and delivered to the consignee.

Place Utility A value created in a product by changing its location. Transportation creates place utility.

Police Powers The U.S. constitutionally granted right for the states to establish regulations to protect the health and welfare of its citizens; truck weights, speed, length, and height are examples.

Pooling An agreement among carriers to share the freight to be hauled or to share the profits. Pooling agreements were outlawed in the Interstate Commerce Act, but the Civil Aeronautics Board has approved profit pooling agreements for air carriers during strikes.

Port Authority A state or local government that owns, operates, or otherwise provides wharf, dock, and other terminal investments at ports.

Primary Business Test A test used by the ICC to determine if a trucking operation is bonafide, private transportation; the private trucking operation must be incidental to and in the furtherance of the primary business of the firm.

Primary Highways Highways that connect lesser populated cities with major cities.

Private Carrier A carrier that provides transportation service to the firm which owns or leases the vehicles and does not charge a fee. Private motor carriers may haul at a fee for wholly owned subsidiaries.

Proportional Rate A rate lower than the regular rate for shipments that have prior or subsequent moves; used to overcome competitive disadvantages of combination rates.

Pure Raw Material A raw material that does not lose weight in processing.

Rate Basis Number The distance between two rate basis points.

Rate Basis Point The major shipping point in a local area; all points in the local area are considered to be the rate basis point.

Rate Bureau A group of carriers that get together to establish joint rates, to divide joint revenues and claim liabilities, and to publish tariffs. Rate bureaus have published single line rates which will be prohibited in 1984.

Reasonable Rate A rate that is high enough to cover the carrier's cost but not too high to enable the carrier to realize monopolistic profits.

Recapture Clause A provision of the 1920 Transportation Act that provided for self-help financing for railroads. Railroads that earned more than the prescribed return contributed one-half of the excess to the fund from which the ICC made loans to less profitable railroads. The Recapture Clause was repealed in 1933.

Reed-Bulwinkle Act Legalized joint rate-making by common carriers through rate bureaus; extended antitrust immunity to carriers participating in a rate bureau.

Reefer A term used for refrigerated vehicles.

Regional Carrier A for-hire air carrier, usually certificated, that has annual operating revenues of less than $75 million; the carrier usually operates within a particular region of the country.

Regular Route Carrier A motor carrier that is authorized to provide service over designated routes.

Relay Terminal A motor carrier terminal designed to facilitate the substitution of one driver for another who has driven the maximum hours permitted.

Released Value Rates Rates based upon the value of the shipment; the maximum carrier liability for damage is less than the full value, and in return the carrier offers a lower rate.

Reliability A carrier selection criterion that considers the variation in carrier transit time; the consistency of the transit time provided.

Reparation The ICC could require railroads to repay users the difference between the rate charged and the maximum rate permitted when the ICC found the rate to be unreasonable or too high.

Right of Eminent Domain Permits the purchase of land needed for transportation right-of-way in a court of law; used by railroads and pipelines.

Rule of Eight Prior to the Motor Carrier Act of 1980, contract carriers requesting authority were restricted to eight shippers under contract. The number of shippers has been deleted as a consideration for granting a contract carrier permit.

Rule of Rate-Making A regulatory provision directing the regulatory agencies to consider the earnings necessary for a carrier to provide adequate transportation.

Secondary Highways Highways that serve primarily rural areas.

Separable Cost A cost that can be directly assignable to a particular segment of the business.

Ship Agent A liner company or tramp ship operator representative who facilitates ship arrival, clearance, loading/unloading, and fee payment while at a specific port.

Ship Broker A firm that serves as a go-between for the tramp ship owner and the chartering consignor or consignee.

Shipper's Agent A firm that acts primarily to match up small shipments, especially single traffic piggyback loads to permit use of twin trailer piggyback rates.

Shippers Association A nonprofit, cooperative consolidator and distributor of shipments owned or shipped by member firms; acts in much the same way as for-profit freight forwarders.

Short Haul Discrimination Charging more for a shorter haul than a longer haul over the same route, in the same direction, and for the same commodity.

Short Ton Equals 2000 pounds.

Sleeper Team The use of two drivers to operate a truck equipped with a sleeper berth; while one driver sleeps in the berth to accumulate the mandatory off-duty time, the other driver drives.

Slip Seat Operation A term used to describe a motor carrier relay terminal operation where one driver is substituted for another who has accumulated the maximum driving time hours.

Slurry Dry commodities that are made into a liquid form by the addition of water or other fluids to permit movement by pipeline.

Special Commodities Carrier A common carrier trucking company that has authority to haul a special commodity; there are 16 special commodities, such as household goods, petroleum products, and hazardous materials.

Spur Track A railroad track that connects a company's plant or warehouse with the railroad's track; the cost of the spur track and its maintenance is borne by the user.

Steamship Conferences Collective rate-making bodies for liner water carriers.

Supplemental Carrier A for-hire air carrier subject to economic regulations; the carrier has no time schedule nor designated route; service is provided under a charter or contract per plane per trip.

Surcharge An add-on charge to the applicable charges; motor carriers have a fuel surcharge and railroads can apply a surcharge to any joint rate that does not yield 110 percent of variable cost.

Switch Engine A railroad engine that is used to move rail cars short distances within a terminal and plant.

Switching Company A railroad that moves rail cars short distances; switching companies connect two mainline railroads to facilitate through movement of shipments.

Tandem A truck that has two drive axles or a trailer that has two axles.

Tank Cars Rail cars that are designed to haul bulk liquids or gas commodities.

Tapering Rate A rate that increases with distance but not in direct proportion to the distance the commodity is shipped.

Tare Weight The weight of the vehicle when it is empty.

Tariff A publication that contains a carrier's rates, accessorial charges and rules.

Temporary Authority The ICC may grant a temporary operating authority as a common carrier for up to 270 days.

Time/Service Rate A rail rate that is based upon transit time.

Time Tables A time schedule of departures and arrivals by origin and destination; typically used for passenger transportation by air, bus, and rail.

Time Utility A value created in a product by having the product available at the time desired. Transportation and warehousing create time utility.

TL Truckload, a shipment weighing the minimum weight or more. A rate reduction is given for shipping a TL size shipment.

TOFC Trailer-on-flatcar; also known as piggyback.

Ton-Mile A measure of output for freight transportation; it reflects the weight of the shipment and the distance it is hauled; a multiplication of tons hauled and distance traveled.

Total Cost Analysis A decision-making approach that considers the minimization of total system cost and recognizes the interrelationship among system variables of transportation, warehousing, inventory, customer service, and so on.

Toto Authority A private motor carrier receiving operating authority as a common carrier to haul freight for the public over the private carrier's back-haul; this type of authority was granted to the Toto Company in 1978.

Tracing Determining where a shipment is during the course of a move.

Traffic Management The management of those activities associated with buying and controlling transportation services for a shipper or consignee or both.

Tramp An international water carrier that has no fixed route or published schedule; a tramp ship is chartered for a particular voyage or a given time period.

Transit Privilege A carrier service that permits the shipper to stop the shipment in transit to perform a function that changes the commodity's physical characteristics but to pay the through rate.

Transit Time The total time that elapes from pickup to delivery of a shipment.

Transportation Association of America An association that represents the entire U.S. transportation system, carriers, users, and the public.

Travel Agent A firm that provides passenger travel information, air, rail, and steamship ticketing, and hotel reservations; the travel agent is paid a commission by the carrier and hotel.

Trunk Lines Oil pipelines that are used for

the long distance movement of crude oil, refined oil, or other liquid products.

Ubiquity A raw material that is found at all locations.

Umbrella Rate-Making An ICC rate-making practice that held rates to a particular level to protect the traffic of another mode.

United States Railway Association The planning/funding agency for Conrail; created by the 3-R Act of 1973.

Unit Train An entire, uninterrupted locomotive car and caboose movement between an origin and destination.

Urban Mass Transportation Administration An agency of the U.S. Department of Transportation responsible for developing comprehensive mass transport systems for urban areas and for providing financial aid to transit systems.

Value-of-Service Pricing Pricing according to the value of the product being transported; third degree price discrimination; demand-oriented pricing; charging what the traffic will bear.

Variable Cost A cost that fluctuates with the volume of business.

Von Thunen's Belts A series of concentric rings around a city to identify where agricultural products would be produced according to von Thunen's theory.

Waterway Use Tax A per gallon tax assessed barge carriers for use of the waterways.

Weight Break The shipment volume at which the LTL charges equal the TL charges at the minimum weight.

Weight-Losing Raw Material A raw material that loses weight in processing.

Zone of Rate Flexibility Railroads are permitted to raise rates by a percentage increase in the railroad cost index determined by the ICC; rates may be raised by 6 percent per year through 1984 and 4 percent thereafter.

Zone of Rate Freedom Motor carriers are permitted to raise or lower rates by ±10 percent in one year without ICC interference; if the rate change is within the zone of freedom, the rate is presumed to be reasonable.

Zone of Reasonableness A zone or limit within which air carriers are permitted to change rates without regulatory scrutiny; if the rate change is within the zone, the new rate is presumed to be reasonable.

Zone Price The price of a product is the same at all geographic locations within the zone.

AUTHOR INDEX

SUBJECT INDEX

†